# PINNACLES *and* PLATEAUS
## *- Volume One*

THROUGH THE BOOK OF PSALMS

# PINNACLES *and*
# PLATEAUS
## *- Volume One*

MEDITATIONS WITH THE PSALMIST
*Psalms Chapters 1-30*

# ANDREW C. BESHORE

XULON PRESS

Xulon Press
2301 Lucien Way #415
Maitland, FL 32751
407.339.4217
www.xulonpress.com

**Xulon** PRESS

Paperback ISBN-13: 978-1-6628-3969-6
Ebookr ISBN-13: 978-1-6628-3970-2

# Table of Contents

# Dedication

There are numerous people who have played an influential role in my spiritual upbringing. I certainly would not want to inadvertently leave anyone out. Each of you know who you are. This work and any that follow it is the fruit of the minutes, hours, weeks, and years you have spiritually poured into my life through your instruction, lifestyle, and ministry. You each know who you are.

First and foremost, of course, the risen Lord Jesus Christ - His honor and His glory are the reason why works like this exist. Without Him, I can do nothing. In Him, I live and move and have my being. He upholds me by the Word of His power. In Him, I am complete. He has called me, justified me freely by His grace, is sanctifying me, and will glorify me. This work is part of the fruit of the good work that He has begun in me, is performing in me, and will perfect in me until I behold Him with unveiled face in all His resplendent glory.

Of course, I would be remiss if I omitted the family by marriage which the Lord has blessed me with, namely my precious wife, Melissa, and our children (Camden, Preston, Hayleigh, Anya, Owen, Chloe, Landon, and Braden (did I miss anyone? ☺). You know that a huge reason that this work and any subsequent works exist is because of how important each of you are to me and how much I love each of you. While it can be a fearful and sobering responsibility, it is my joy and privilege serve the Lord to try to be the husband and father to you all.

Next, to my earthly father, Brad Beshore, you know I love you and appreciate how you have provoked me to love and good works over the course of my pilgrimage. Thank you for all you have done for our family over the years. Thank you also to his wife, Margi, for your role in the sanctification of my father.

Next, to my earthly mother, Jackie Beshore, you know I love you and I am forever indebted to you for how you raised me and how you have helped our family meet so many concrete needs.

Next, to my church family. There are too many to name by name. If I leave any of you out, it is not intentional. First, Pastor Michael and his family, including Pastor Miller and his family, and the rest of the Emmanuel family. Even though we no longer worship under the same roof, much of who I am and what I am becoming results from the discipleship I received while under your care. I am grateful for your investment in me more than I can ever express by mere words. I love you and your families and always will. To the Highland family, including Pastors Brock and Underwood, that I currently call my Sunday home. Thank you for your continual support during this stage of my pilgrimage. You have been the hands and feet of Christ to our family during this season and your efforts spent on our family have been tremendous.

Next, to Stephanie H. You have helped me get to where I am, to do the next right thing, and to be present in each passing moment. I love and appreciate you more than I can express. My gratitude for your continued sacrificial investment in me to help me to become the husband and father I need to be after all these years cannot be overstated. JD, Hannah, Josh, and Drew are blessed to have you.

Next, to Brad C. You know who you are. For the years we have known each other, you have helped me grow into the man I am becoming. I appreciate how you have helped me, and, by extension, my family, for the years that we have worshiped and worked together.

Lastly, to the entire incredible team at Xulon Press who helped this first-time author with this entire publishing process. From Lisa W, to Logan M, to Heather K, Jesse K, Mark B, Nina S and whomever else behind the scenes with whom I never had the privilege of corresponding. You patience with me throughout this process has been exemplary. You all are a tremendous blessing to work with and I hope to get the opportunity to collaborate with you on future endeavors.

# Psalms Introduction

*I*n addition to being Israel's songbook, the psalter, the book of Psalms is a great resource for children of the King in any generation. In it, we see many applicable principles about life in any society. In it,

1. We see many glorious pictures if Christ's first coming (e.g., Psalm 22, cf. Matthew 27:46).
2. We also see wondrous pictures of Christ's second coming (e.g., Psalm 2, cf. Revelation 19:11-21, Revelation 20:7-10).
3. We see that believers can expect to experience trouble (e.g., Psalm 3, John 16:33) and that the Lord promises to be with us in the trouble (James 1:2-8, 1 Peter 5:7).
4. In fact, if someone does not experience some form of discipline, whether it be from their own sin or not, they are not participating in Christ's holiness and perhaps have no legitimate claim to the eternal life that He purchased (Hebrews 12:3-11).
5. In the psalms, we see the contrast between the godly and the ungodly (Psalm 1).
6. We see many examples of unjust treatment that the ungodly inflict upon the godly (e.g., Psalm 5:9, Psalm 6:8-10).
7. We see lament over personal sin in the godly (Psalm 6, cf. Matthew 5:4).
8. We see persecution heaped up on the godly (Psalm 7:1-2, cf. Matthew 5:10-12).

9. We see that the expectation of the righteous is that God will vindicate them when they are oppressed for their faith and God will be praised for intervening on behalf of His people. (Psalm 7:6-17, Psalm 17).

10. We see some great prophetic passages that pertain to our Lord and Savior Jesus Christ (Psalm 8:2) and other passages that are quoted in the New Testament (Psalm 8:2-6).

11. We see the ongoing war between the children of the King and the children of the wicked one (Psalm 9:5-8).

12. We see melodies of God's righteous judgments (Psalm 7:11-17, Psalm 9:7, Psalm 9:16-17, Psalm 11:6).

13. We see stark contrasts in the conduct of the wicked versus the conduct of the righteous (Psalm 10:2-11, c.f. Romans 3:10-18).

14. We see the omniscience of God (Psalm 11:4).

15. We see the wicked making life difficult for the righteous (Psalm 12:1-2) and trying to escape God's authority (Psalm 12:4).

16. We see the psalmist in an ungodly environment being reminded to continue to trust the Lord in the face of seemingly impossible difficulty (Psalm 13).

17. We see the foolishness and depravity that results from trusting in anyone or anything other than the Lord (Psalm 14).

18. We see that those who enter the kingdom are an unworthy yet exclusive group that because of their own unrighteous character only enter God's kingdom as a result of God's character and mercy (Psalm 15; cf. Ephesians 2:4, Titus 2:11).

19. We see that the believer can rejoice that they are objects of God's delight (Psalm 16:3) in contrast to the idolaters who hasten after other gods (Psalm 16:4).

20. We see that the Lord Jesus Christ is at the right hand of God and with Him are pleasures forevermore (Psalm 16:11, Psalm 21:8, cf. Hebrews 1:3).

21. We see that the wicked get progressively more aggressive in their actions against the righteous (Psalm 17:9-12).

22. We see the great hope that the righteous have for the future because of their faith in God (Psalm 17:15, cf. Job 19:25, 2 Corinthians 5:8).

23. We see that the Lord is our source of strength (Psalm 18:1, cf. Isaiah 40:31).
24. We see the Lord is our protector in the present and for the future (Psalm 18:2, cf. John 10:27-28, Romans 8:1-2).
25. We see that circumstances in life can be very frightening for the child of God (Psalm 18:4-5).
26. We see David writing about things that would happen to Christ (Psalm 18, Psalm 22).
27. We see the importance of the placement of the Word of God in the life of the believer for daily living (Psalm 19).
28. We see how believers should trust in the Creator over and above anything created (Psalm 20:5-9; cf. Romans 1:18-23).
29. We see how believers, through genuine faith in the one true God, which is the same as having saving faith in the Lord Jesus Christ, will experience ultimate rest and victory (Psalm 21:8-13).
30. We see the tragic picture of Christ on the cross and we get a chance to mourn over our sin that put Him there (Psalm 22, Matthew 5:4, Matthew 26-27).
31. We learn the importance of following the Good Shepherd and how following Him leads to problems, preservation, provision, and permanent residence with Him in eternity (Psalm 23, John 10).
32. We see that God is the Creator (Psalm 24:1-2, cf. Genesis 1-2) and that the Lord Jesus Christ is the Agent through whom creation occurred (John 1:3, Colossians 1:16-17).

What follows is an attempt to glorify God by a layman who at times can identify with the psalmist on many levels. It is my goal that this be the first volume of a multiple volume work through the entire book of Psalms, Lord willing. It is my prayer that as you read this that God can use some part of this and feel His comfort and perhaps be equipped to comfort others (2 Corinthians 1:3-5). Perhaps He can use this to help you abide in Him so He can abide in you (John 15:1-8). The questions for personal reflection are designed to help the reader identify with some of the emotions that the psalmist may have been feeling when his inspired words were penned and to show the reader that the Scriptures are as applicable now as they have ever been. Personal indwelling sin in the lives of believers will be addressed. May this attempt to do the Lord honor by his humble servant bring glory to God!

Blessings in Christ, Andy

# Psalm 1

**1:1. Blessed is the man Who walks not in the counsel of the ungodly, Nor stands in the path of sinners, Nor sits in the seat of the scornful;**

---

From the Beatitudes, given by the Lord Jesus Christ in the Sermon on the Mount (Matt. 5:3-12), we learn that the word 'blessed' means 'happy.' Such a **man** (or woman) is a saved man. This man is one that has his name written in heaven (Lk 10:20). He has eternal life. He is a believer in the gospel of the Lord Jesus Christ (Jn 3:16). This is evident by the way that he lives (Jn 8:12, 1 Jn 1:7).

The **counsel** that this blessed man follows is not ungodly counsel. The blessed man follows godly counsel. Such counsel is based upon God's Word and the principles contained therein (Eph. 5:19). Any other such counsel that seeks to refute God and His Word is ungodly counsel (2 Cor. 10:3-5). Such counsel is false doctrine and should not be followed or spoken (Ti 2:1). Such counsel comes from the Father of Lies, Satan, himself (Jn 8:44).

Rather than **walk in the counsel of the ungodly**, the blessed man reproves such works of darkness and those who teach them by word and deed (Eph. 5:11). A walk refers to a style of life. Rather than walk in darkness, the blessed man walks in the light (1 Jn 1:6-7). The saved sinner may for a time believe and practice unrighteousness, ungodly counsel, but they will never reach a place where they totally reject the Lord finally (Jn 10:28-29). They will return to practicing righteousness and believing righteously since those who have been justified will one day be glorified (Rom. 8:30). After all, the sheep hear the voice of their Shepherd (Ps. 23, Jn 10).

The blessed man, when he came to Christ for salvation, repented from sin and exchanged the sinful lifestyle for the righteous lifestyle (2 Cor. 7:9-11, 1 Thess. 1:9). Yes, saved people do sin every day (Rom. 7:23, 1 Jn 2:1), but saved people who have God's law written on their hearts (Rom. 2:15), who live by God's Spirit (Rom. 8:14), who leads them into all truth (Jn 16:13), will have a constant reminder from the Holy Spirit to not **stand in the path**

**of sinners.** They will not want to run to the same excess of riot as the lost world (1 Pet. 4:4). Their conscience will warn them when they live outside God's will. They will not run into unchecked sin. They will fall into sin because all saved people do so (1 Jn 2:1), and when they do, repentance will follow because the Holy Spirit will reveal the truth about sin to them (Jn 16:8).

Saved sinners will not be able or willing to recognize all sins they commit because the flesh wages war against the Spirit (Gal. 5:17) but those that are recognized can be repented of. Many lost sinners will not be concerned about sins they commit since God is not on their radar (Rom. 1:28). Sinners have chosen to leave the path that God says everyone should follow (Matt. 7:13, Jn 14:6) because they would rather be their own boss than listen to God's will for their lives. They mistakenly think this is better. This is a mistake to think this way since once sinners truly come to God through saving faith in the Lord Jesus Christ, and He reveals Himself to those who abide in Him (Jn 15:4), justified sinners begin in this life to experience the blessedness of communion with the Son of God who loved them and gave Himself for them (Eph. 5:2). The blessed man has humbled himself and God has exalted him (Matt. 23:12).

Rather than **sit in the seat of the scornful,** God has raised him and seated him in heavenly places with Christ (Eph. 2:6). He realizes that he can do no good on his own for there is none good (Rom. 3:10). He understands that any good that proceeds from him only does so because of the Holy Spirit which energizes him because he lives by faith in the Son of God (Gal. 2:20).

Many of the Psalms have verses that could be references to scenes from the life of the Lord Jesus Christ that were written before His incarnation. It is true that Christ perfectly walked in fellowship with his Father (Jn 5:19, Jn 12:49). He did not commit a single sin (1 Pet. 2:22). Christ did not obey ungodly counsel. Rather, Christ rebuked ungodly counsel. Christ corrected ungodly counsel. Christ did not commit the sins that sinners of His day committed. Instead of sinfully scorning sinners, He loved them and spoke to them in efforts to reconcile them to God. He then left His ministry of reconciliation to His disciples (2 Cor. 5:12-21). That ministry continues today and will continue until He returns. This verse focused on what the blessed, godly person should not do. The next verse focuses on what that person should do.

## Questions for self-reflection:

(1) Is the majority counsel that you follow godly or ungodly? Put another way, does the majority of the counsel that you follow find its roots in Scripture or in the philosophies of the world?

(2) Obviously, believers are to associate with unbelievers otherwise nobody would ever get evangelized. Are the majority of your friendships with people who love the Lord or those who do not love the Lord?

(3) How are the characteristics of the blessed man listed in this verse fulfilled by the Lord Jesus Christ?

**1:2. But his delight is in the law of the Lord, And in His law he meditates day and night.**

---

The blessed man has a special **delight in the law of the Lord.** Psalm 119 is dedicated to explaining more about this delight. The blessed man remembers how the law of sin and death (Rom. 8:2) kept him separated from God by sin, kept him alienated from the life of God (Col. 1:21), and kept him on the outside looking in at the Kingdom. The law of sin and death had pronounced judgment against sinful man (Rom. 2:2). He could not escape its curse (Gal. 3:10).

Mankind had an unpayable debt owed to God because of the law of sin and death (Rom. 5:2). By this law came the knowledge of sin (Rom. 3:20). This law exposed sin (Rom. 7:7). This law illustrated unrighteousness that revealed the judgment against ungodliness was reasonable (Rom. 2:3).

But then, when man was dead in trespasses and sins (Eph. 2:1, 2:5, Col. 2:13), alienated and an enemy in his mind by wicked works (Col. 1:21), unrighteous in thought, word, and deed (Gal. 5:19-21), in the fulness of time (Gal. 4:4), Christ, the end of the law for righteousness (Rom. 10:4), came and died for the ungodly (Rom. 5:6). By repentant faith, the lost sinner received redemption's pardon (Eph. 1:7), righteousness (2 Cor. 5:21), and justification (Rom. 5:1). God's love was shed abroad in the sinner's heart (Rom. 5:5). He was adopted into God's family (Rom. 8:15). Instead of being a mere hearer of the Word, he became a doer of the Word (Jas 1:22-25).

Instead of walking in the darkness perpetually (1 Jn 1:6), delighting in the world and the things of the world (1 Jn 2:15-17), his delight became the law of the Lord. His meditation, **day and night,** became that law. That law, he had hidden in his heart, that he might night sin against the One (Ps. 119:11) who loved him and had given himself for him (Eph. 5:2). He delighted in the law after the inward man (Rom. 7:22) because he came to know that his joy could be full (1 Jn 1:4) by abiding in Christ and by Christ abiding in him which would result in his bearing of much fruit (Jn 15:5).

---

Now God's Word, God's Law, instead of being drudgery for the lost sinner, became a treasure for the redeemed sheep. There was nothing more important to the saved sinner than to know the One who bought him. Since this Law was a means through which this benevolent Creator had revealed Himself to His creation which had rejected Him, now this saved saint wanted to know His Lord and treasured the Word that had been graciously been left to man so man could know the One to whom he owed everything.

To **meditate** on it means to think consciously and carefully about it and its implications for our lives. This attitude of high regard for God's Word was definitely held by the Lord Jesus Christ, who frequently corrected the frequent misunderstandings of it held by the people of His day. Followers of the Lord Jesus Christ, Christians, are marked by a similar respect for God as God has revealed Himself to us in His Word.

**Questions for self-reflection:**

(1) Whose thoughts bring you the most pleasure?

(2) If there is someone on this earth that is a role model for you, if you asked that role model what their relationship with the Lord was like, based on how you see them live, what do you think they would say?

(3) Is reading God's Word a mundane chore for you or is it a delight for you?

(4) When you are reading the Bible or in prayer or fellowshipping with other believers, does your mind ever wander to a specific Scripture passage?

**1:3. He shall be like a tree Planted by the rivers of water, That brings forth its fruit in its season, Whose leaf also shall not wither; And whatever he does shall prosper.**

---

The first three verses of this psalm describe a saved man. The following two verses of this psalm describe a lost man.

A hydrated **tree** is a healthy tree. This tree is not nourished by a trickling but is nourished by a free- flowing river. This tree describes a man as a tree that has been planted by the Master Gardener. He did not plant himself. He is planted, translated from Satan's kingdom, and translated into God's kingdom (Matt. 15:13-14, Col. 1:13).

The tree has to stay close to the **rivers of water** in order to **bring forth fruit**, to **not wither**, to **prosper**. Jesus is the Giver of Living Water (Jn 4:14, Jn 7:38). If we are going to be fruitful, productive Kingdom citizens, we, too, need to stay close to the Lord Jesus. We need to abide in Him and meditate on Him and His Word (Jn 15:1-8). If His Word dwells richly in us (Col. 3:16), if we stay renewed (Isa. 40:31, Rom. 12:2), no matter what **season** of life we find ourselves in, we will bear fruit because the Holy Spirit will empower us (Gal. 5:22-25). As we say no to the sinful flesh and say yes to the Holy Spirit (Gal. 5:16), a closeness to the Lord develops that results in sensitivity to the Lord and spiritual growth even in the face of difficulty and persecution. The Father plants the sinners who trust the Lord Jesus Christ into His family, into Christ. They are taught the Word and grow (1 Cor. 3:6, 1 Pet. 2:2).

Growth in private leads to the display of **fruit in its season**. The fruit is unmistakable evidence of the Trinity's working on behalf of the believer (Phil. 2:13). When life gets difficult, the believer does not wither away. They know that nothing can separate them from God's love (Rom. 8:38-39). They know that even if they are the only one who is left standing for truth that God will honor that because God is the lone source of absolute truth, thereby making everyone else a liar (Rom. 3:4).

Because the believers, the trees, stay so close their Lord, no matter how hard life gets due to the varying troubles that come, they will be fruitful, they will prosper, their lights will shine (Matt. 5:16). In addition to this being true about Christians, this is also true of their Shepherd, the Lord Jesus Christ. He stayed close to the Heavenly Father. Everything He did prospered. He did not wither. Even though He died, He triumphantly rose again.

**Questions for self-reflection:**

(1) If a tree has to be well-nourished in order to be healthy, then a believer must be well-nourished to be healthy. What are some things, in addition to the Bible you can use to nourish your soul?

(2) What are some things you can avoid to keep from depriving your soul of the nourishment that it needs to be a fruitful Christian?

(3) If you spend more time feeding the Spirit that lives in you, how do you think that will change your life?

(4) If you spend more time feeding your flesh, how do you think that will change your life?

**1:4. The ungodly are not so, But are like the chaff which the wind drives away.**

Here, a transition takes place between a discussion of the saved, blessed, man, and the lost, **ungodly** man. Shall the ungodly man have access to all the blessings that the godly man has? **Not so!** For all the blessings and benefits that the godly enjoy, the ungodly have the judgment to look forward to (Heb. 10:26-28) as long as they remain in their sins and separated from God (Col. 1:21). Verse two contained more about this.

The ungodly have consciously chosen to reject the truth of God that is intuitive (Romans 1:18-20), that they should know. Instead of bearing righteous fruit (Gal. 5:22-24), the ungodly bear unrighteous fruit (Gal. 5:19-21). Since the type of fruit that is borne illustrates the type of tree (Matt. 7:15-20), the unrighteous fruit illustrates that these people are ungodly. The ungodly are marked by a love for the world (1 Jn 2:15-17) rather than a love for the Word. The ungodly are marked by a lack of reverence for or fear of God. Because the ungodly lack this fear, they do not possess true wisdom. Instead of possessing true wisdom, they despise wisdom and instruction (Prov. 1:7).

Instead of hating evil as the righteous do, the ungodly, love evil. They are fueled by arrogance and the evil way and perverted speech. They are arrogant because they assume that their way is better than God's way. They are the epitome of pride (Prov. 8:13, Jas 4:6). The ungodly do not possess wisdom and understanding because they have missed the foundation of all wisdom and understanding, God Himself (Jb 28:28, Ps 111:10). The ungodly do not have the sure foundation (Matt. 7:24-27) that the blessed man has. The ungodly do not do the whole duty of man which is to fear God and keep His commandments (Eccles. 12:13).

Instead of abiding under the Lord's mercy, the ungodly abide under God's wrath (Lk 1:50, Jn 3:36). Because the ungodly do not abide in God's love, they will not rest satisfied and they will be visited by harm (Prov. 19:23). The ungodly are not the friends of God and God does not make His covenant known to them (Ps. 25:14).

The ungodly have nothing in which to put strong confidence or refuge in which to trust (Prov. 14:26).

Instead of fearing the Lord and possessing power, love, and self-control from above, they have a spirit of fear because this life is all that they have to hold on to (2 Tim. 1:7). The lost have a spirit of slavery to fall back into the fear of judgment and punishment that is the just result that awaits all the ungodly. The justified have the Spirit of adoption and, therefore, as God's adopted child, have nothing to fear (Rom. 8:15).

Rather than remaining planted in the truth, as believers do, unbelievers are tossed to and fro by every wind of doctrine (Eph. 4:14), as by **the wind**, and are blown **away like the chaff**. Since they are not settled in the truth of God, their anchor does not hold. The foundation on which they have built their life will not hold when the storms of life come upon them. Great destruction is in their future if they do not repent and come to the Lord (Matt. 7:24-27, Lk 13:3). Rather than stay with the God that does not change (Mal. 3:6), they change all the time, falling for the latest Satanic scheme (Eph. 4:14). Instead of being reliant upon God and His infinite unchanging wisdom, they are reliant upon their own changing and finite wisdom which amounts to foolishness in God's sight (1 Cor. 1:26-31). Perhaps the wicked one snatches God's truth away from them (Matt. 13:4, 13:19). Perhaps persecution makes them fall away, proving they were never genuine to begin with (Matt. 13:5, 13:20-21). Perhaps they loved the world too much in order to care enough about spiritual things and be fruitful (Matt. 13:7, 22). These have a judgment to endure at the Great White Throne (Revelation 20:11-15) where they will be cast into the Lake of Fire forever with the beast and the false prophet (Rev. 20:10).

**Questions for self-reflection:**

(1) Can it ever be easy to visibly be able to tell the difference between the godly and the ungodly in those that you regularly converse with?

(2) Can it ever be difficult to visibly be able to tell the difference between the godly and the ungodly in those that you regularly converse with?

(3) What might account for the difference between the ungodly that are easy to detect and the ungodly that are not easy to detect?

(4) How can you better detect people from both groups and minister to them?

**1:5. Therefore the ungodly shall not stand in the judgment, Nor sinners in the congregation of the righteous.**

Because **ungodly sinners** have chosen to rely on their own wisdom, wisdom that is earthly, sensual, and demonic (Jas 3:15), because ungodly sinners have chosen to not believe in the Son of God (Jn 3:36), they abide under God's wrathful judgment sentence.

They will **not stand in the judgment** with **the congregation of the righteous**. The congregation of the righteous is reserved for those with a righteousness not their own (Phil. 3:9), the righteousness of the Lord and Savior Jesus Christ. His is an imputed righteousness (Rom. 4:6), given only to those who turn in repentant faith to Him and Him alone for salvation. It is they who receive the free gift of eternal life. The wages of their sin (Rom. 6:23), are paid by Christ for them (1 Pet. 2:24). The righteous are separated from the unrighteous. The sheep are separated from the goats (Matt. 25:31-46). The wheat is separated from the tares (Matt. 13:24-30). The righteous enter into the joy of their Lord and spend eternity with Christ in heaven forever.

The ungodly spend eternity in the lake of fire where there is weeping and gnashing of teeth (Lk 13:28). The ungodly are recipients of the righteous judgment of God. The day is coming that the ungodly will experience in which the Lord Jesus is revealed from heaven with His mighty angels in flaming fire taking vengeance on those who do not know God and on those who do not obey the gospel. They will be punished with everlasting destruction from the Lord's presence (1 Thess. 1:5-9).

The ungodly do not have the grace of the Lord Jesus Christ in which to stand fast. The righteous do. Only the righteous can stand fast in the liberty by which Christ has set them free (Gal. 5:1). God provides them with the grace to be able to stand fast. Only the righteous will be clothed with a wedding garment that will enable them to be in one congregation with the rest of the righteous (Matt. 22:1-14).

There are several New Testament commands for believers to stand fast or stand firm or stand. Such include Romans 11:20,

1 Corinthians 16:13, 2 Corinthians 1:24, Galatians 5:1, Philippians 1:27, Philippians 4:1, 1 Thessalonians 3:8, 2 Thessalonians 2:15, Hebrews 3:6, and Hebrews 4:14.

## Questions for self-reflection:

(1) If someone you love is among the ungodly, how does reading this psalm make you feel toward them?

(2) Since you are among the godly, how does knowing the fate that awaits the ungodly make you think about the salvation that you possess and its benefits that you enjoy?

(3) Thinking about the previous two questions for this verse, what can you do to reach your lost loved ones?

**1:6. For the Lord knows the way of the righteous, But the way of the ungodly shall perish.**

---

There is nothing that **the Lord** does not **know** about anyone or anything in His creation (Jb 37:16, Ps. 147:5, Prov. 5:21, Prov. 15:3, Jer. 1:5, Jn 21:17, Heb. 4:13, 1 Jn 3:20). He has revealed Himself to everyone (Jn 1:18, Rom. 1:19-20, Heb. 1:1-2). In an ultimate sense, the Lord knows the way about everyone. He knows that apart from Him, they can do nothing (Jn 15:1-8). He knows that the only real way to make sense of the world is to see it with eyes of faith.

He has an intimate communion with His **righteous** saints. The Lord approves of the way of life of the righteous. The righteous have a quality of life that is distinct from the quality of life of the unrighteous. The unrighteous walk by sight whereas the righteous walk by faith (2 Cor. 5:7). The Lord and the righteous person communicate with each other. The righteous person abides in Him and He in them. The righteous person seeks the Lord, is found by the Lord, the Lord reveals Himself to them, and they bear fruit (Matt. 11:25-27). The Lord knows the way of the righteous because the Lord has prepared the way for the righteous. Not only that, the Lord IS the way of the righteous (Jn 14:1-6). God loves everyone and loves believers specially (Jn 17:20-26). He knows their way because He has made a new and living way for them (Heb. 10:20). Jesus prepared **the way** (Jn 14:6) for them by living a perfect life in their place (1 Pet. 2:22), dying on the cross as their substitute, and rising again in victory (1 Cor. 15:3-4). The Lord knows the way of the righteous because He walked the way they are supposed to walk (1 Jn 2:6). Those who trust in Him alone for salvation with repentant faith find their way to heaven.

Those who reject Christ and continue to trust in themselves, **the ungodly, shall perish.** The ungodly walks in stark contrast to the righteous. The ungodly walk according to the flesh (Gal. 5:19-21). The ungodly cannot please God (Rom. 8:8). The ungodly live according to the flesh and, therefore, will die (Rom. 8:12-13).

In order to not perish, sinners must believe in Jesus, coming in repentant faith (Luke 13:3). It is the kind of faith that will not fail

---

to produce good works (Acts 2:38, Eph. 2:10). To trust in anyone or anything else will not yield eternal life. Jesus is the only source of true eternal life. God is loving to make that available to sinners who have rejected Him. The ungodly show by their walk that this world is their home. All they have and all they care about is wrapped up in this world which sells them a bill of goods and lies to them when it tells them that happiness comes from what one acquires. The righteous understand that this is a false hope. The righteous understand that true and lasting hope that will not perish, a hope that is living (1 Pet. 1:3), only comes through a true relationship with God through the Lord Jesus Christ.

## Questions for self-reflection:

(1) On what do you base your claim to righteousness?
(2) Do your habitual ways of life demonstrate that the Lord knows you in a saving way?
(3) What is something you can do for someone you know who is among the ungodly who will perish?

# Psalm 2

## 2:1. Why do the nations rage, And the people plot a vain thing?

This psalm is a Messianic prophecy. It is quoted by Peter and John in Acts 4:23-31 after Peter and John had just been let go after having suffered threats at the hands of the chief priests and elders. **The nations rage** against God. Against Messiah. Their willful choice to sin is an illustration of this rage. They choose to reject God's law which is written on their hearts (Rom. 2:15). Every generation is guilty of this (Rom. 3:23). From the time of Adam and Eve (since their deception) the rage has continued (Gen. 6:5, Isa. 53:6).

During Jesus' earthly ministry, this fact was evident on more than one occasion when the Jews attempted to end Jesus' life before His appointed time to die for the sins of the world (e.g., Lk 4:30, Jn 10:39). In the Old Testament, the Jews were God's covenant nation and the nations outside Jerusalem, which were not given the covenants and the promises made up the heathen (Rom. 9:4-5). To put Jesus to death, the Romans and the Jews conspired together or raged. The rage of Jesus' day culminated when the Jews and Romans conspired together to have Jesus unjustly put to death. In every generation since, it is Christianity, not Islam, not Mormonism, not Buddhism that is the most publicly persecuted. It is Christianity and its Christ that is the most notably raged against (2 Tim. 3:12).

They **plot** the **vain thing** of doing things their own way rather than by God's way. They think that by doing so, even if God permits them to be given over to their reprobate minds, that they are somehow beating the system (Rom. 1:28). It was vain for the Jews to have Christ put to death. It did not stop God from fulfilling His plan as they had hoped that snuffing Jesus out would stop His influence. It had the opposite effect. His name is proclaimed all over the globe to this day. They think that just because the sentence is not swiftly carried out, God does not see or God does not care or perhaps God is not even there (Eccles. 8:11).

In the time of the psalmist, Israel vainly imagined that their Messiah would take on a different form than He did. They raged when He came. They rejected Him and sent Him to death on a Roman cross. They vainly supposed they thwarted the plan. In reality, they played right into God's plan. Christ rose, defeating death. Now whoever believes in Him shall not perish but will have everlasting life (John 3:16). It is vain to rage against God. It is better to submit to Him (Jas 4:7).

**Questions for self-reflection:**

(1) Think back to the time before your conversion. In what ways did you act like the heathen nations?
(2) To know that you acted in such ways, how do you feel to know that, despite that, because of the Lord Jesus Christ, you stand in grace (Rom. 5:2)?
(3) Knowing that you stand justified (Rom. 3:24), how does that make you want to live?
(4) Who do you know that, despite your best efforts, continues to rage against God? How can you pray for them? How can you minister to them? Can you be content if they never stop raging against God?

**2:2. The kings of the earth set themselves, And the rulers take counsel together, Against the Lord and against His Anointed, saying,**

---

The earthly rulers that **take counsel together against the Lord** do so against the very One that permitted that they have the authority that they do have (Rom. 13:1). In Jesus' day, the Jewish rulers, namely Annas and Caiphas, along with Pilate from the Romans **set themselves** and took counsel together against the Lord. They worked together, though the Jews were more active than the Romans, to have Christ executed. Since the Lord permits these rulers to rule it is foolish for sthese rulers to come against the One that rules over them and permits them to rule. When the Lord Jesus came the first time, He was opposed by Herod and Pilate, not to mention the Pharisees. So, they took counsel against Him, against the Lord's **Anointed**, as well. They were so opposed to Him that they wanted Him dead and they succeeded, or so they thought.

When the rulers of Jesus' day conspired against Jesus to have Jesus killed, they did not realize that they were conspiring against the One they had been waiting expectantly for. He was their long-awaited Messiah. He was their Mediator. He was their Prophet. He was their Priest. He was their King. He did not meet their expectations. Their willful unbelief led to further blinding, both on their own part, as well as by God.

### Questions for self-reflection:

(1) Everyone is ultimately accountable to the Lord. When people live like this verse describes, who do they demonstrate they are accountable to?

(2) How can you know whether your life demonstrates that you take counsel against the Lord?

---

**2:3. "Let us break Their bonds in pieces And cast away Their cords from us."**

Some of the people in every generation who reject the Lord do so because they think of the Lord's commands as **bonds and cords**. They think that His expectations interfere too much with the freedom that they have supposedly earned or that they think they deserve. They want to have those bonds and cords broken, **cast away**, so they can be free to do what they want.

The truth is that they want to be Lord themselves and do not want anyone or anything else to be Lord of them. Because if there is an absolute Sovereign, that causes conflict with their desire for autonomy. If there is an absolute Sovereign, that means that they would owe Him everything, They don't want to have to owe anyone anything. They want absolute freedom. So, this does not align with who they think God should be. Therefore, they make a god in their own image that suits their idolatrous desire. By doing so, they think that they can break the bonds and cords of the one true God and do what they want. This stems from a lack of reverence for God. How dare He expects that they return to Him a portion of what He has given them!

The gospel calls people to give up their sin and exchange it for righteousness. This results in a change that is demonstrable. The righteousness, in addition to being applied to the invisible account of the sinner, affects their life and is witnessed in the changed behavior of the sinner (1 Jn 2:29). What they fail to understand, due to their carnal minds (Rom. 8:7), is that the freedom that they so desperately want, that they think that they have by rejecting God, actually leads to bondage, bondage to sin (Jn 8:34, Acts 8:23, Rom. 8:19-22, 2 Tim. 2:26, 2 Pet. 2:19) and Satan (2 Cor. 4:4).

True freedom comes when we humble ourselves before God so we can then be free to live for Him (Jn 8:36, Rom. 6:1-11, Gal .4:4-7, Gal. 5:1). In their efforts to try to escape the "bondage" that Christianity imposes on morality, the heathen rage and inflict greater bondage upon themselves. By the rejection of the one true God and the Messiah He sent, they place themselves squarely under the wrath of God (Jn 3:36). Anyone who seeks to live autonomously in every generation unwittingly shows the truth of this very statement by the psalmist. The true believer knows that God's law, which God mercifully wrote on our hearts, is for our protection. They realize that to be set free from the law of sin and death is to be under the law of the spirit of life in Christ Jesus. Any person with any level of conscience has a basic understanding that human law, which has its foundations in God's law, is there for man's good and man's protection. To try to escape its influence is to open oneself up to complete chaos and to subject oneself to great danger.

## Questions for self-reflection:

(1) Who are the earthly authorities in your life?
(2) What is your attitude toward the earthly authorities in your life?
(3) Do you want the Lord to be Lord of your life more than you want to be Lord of your own life?
(4) Regarding your answer to number three above, would the people who know you best agree with your answer?

**2:4. He who sits in the heavens shall laugh; The Lord shall hold them in derision.**

---

Rather than being upset or scared by the plots of the heathen, rather than be worried about the attempts to overthrow His rule over them, God, **He who sits in the heavens, laughs.** The people who rage and plot vain rebellion do so against the One who has given them life (Gen. 2:7, Deut. 32:39, 1 Sam. 2:6, 2 Kgs 5:7, Neh. 9:6, Jb 10:12, Jb 33:4, Jn 1:3, Acts 17:25, 1 Tim. 6:13, Rev. 11:11) and the authority that they enjoy (Dan. 2:21, Dan. 4:17, Jn 19:11, Rom. 13:1). They will have to answer to Him for what they did with the gifts He has benevolently lavished upon them. It is the height of insanity to treat the benevolence of God with such contempt!

As peoples and nations try desperately to shut out gospel influence, God sits in the heavens and laughs. As children rebel against the authority of their parents and insist upon their own freedom (Ephesians 6:1-3, Colossians 3:20), He who sits in the heavens laughs. As parents abuse the authority entrusted to them by God, He who sits in the heavens laughs (Eph. 6:4, Col. 3:21). As citizens look for ways to shirk the government that God has given to be a terror against evildoers, while they find ways to go undetected by the government, He who sits in the heavens laughs (Rom. 13:2). While wives who insist upon unbiblical "equality" with their husbands which really amounts to female headship, which perverts the earthly picture that God left for the church to employ of the relationship between the church and her Lord, He who sits in the heavens laughs (Eph. 5:22-33). While husbands take headship of their families to abusive extremes in the name of God, He who sits in the heavens laughs (Eph. 5:22-33). While employers unjustly take advantage of employees for their own benefit, He who sits in the heavens laughs (Eph. 6:9, Col. 4:1). While employees work dishonestly, stealing from employers and fail to get held accountable, He who sits in the heavens laughs (Eph. 6:5-8, Col. 3:22-25). As corruption runs rampant in locations where people have been

---

entrusted with the responsibility of upholding the law, while the citizens in those cities suffer, He who sits in the heavens laughs.

The fact that anyone thinks that they can rebel against God's authority blatantly as these in this passage and others do, and not reap what they sow, is laughable (Gal. 6:7-8). The fact that the heathen are permitted to rebel and God appears to do nothing about it immediately underscores God's compassion, mercy, patience, and love for everyone, even those in opposition to Him. They fail to appreciate that as much as they enjoy the freedom of their willful sin now, a day is coming where their enjoyment will be stripped away and will be replaced with just and fair suffering that will last for all eternity. One has to ask themselves, is it better to suffer now and avoid suffering for all eternity or is it better to avoid suffering now and have to suffer for all eternity? Those who have received God's compassion and mercy and are in a relationship with Him as a result of it can from time to time forget just how compassionate God is (Jon. 4:11). For **the Lord** to **hold them in derision** for plotting against Him, is another way of expressing the Lord's amusement at the heathen's vain plots against Him.

## Questions for self-reflection:

(1) Is God worried about our rebellion against His authority?
(2) How does God's reaction to others' rebellion to His authority make you feel about the sin in others' lives?
(3) How does God's reaction to your rebellion to His authority make you feel about the sin in your own life?
(4) Does knowing that God feels the same about your rebellion that He feels about rebellion in other people help you be more compassionate with other people?
(5) For people that you know and love who have willingly decided against following God, what can you do to show them that following God is actually a more desirable thing?

**2:5. Then He shall speak to them in His wrath, And distress them in His deep displeasure:**

---

Because the nations rage, because the people plot a vain thing, because the people, especially rulers that God has promoted to their positions of authority, try to get out from under God's authority, because they try to live autonomously, God has **wrath and deep displeasure** aimed toward people who do this.

He has created them. Whether they realize it or not, by virtue of God's creation of them, He has ownership of them. Since they do not return their allegiance to Him, He is upset, and rightfully so. The people who rebel against God perhaps reap the natural consequences of their sin and the result is the feelings of **distress**.

Perhaps God enforces forced consequences against people who make light of His Word or His rulers. Perhaps, God allows famines or pestilences, or one of the other things in the list in Matthew 24. Whatever consequence God decides is appropriate for anyone who is in opposition to His claim on their lives is completely just and appropriate for God to enforce.

In response to sin, after a time of patience and grace to allow for repentance, unrepentant sinners should expect God to come to them in His wrath. If He did not come to hold sinners accountable for their high treason against His Law, He would be unjust. He would not honor His Word.

For God to distress sinners who need to repent is actually a kind thing for God to do. He brings about consequences, some natural and some forced, against human sin. If sinners will see the consequences which God allows as merciful means to elicit repentant responses from sinners and restore relationships between man and God and between man and man, fruitful living can resume and God's wrath against the sinner can subside. If sinners refuse to humble themselves and repent, they should expect God's wrath to come against them in the forms of God's choosing. Perhaps it will be in the form of confusion (Gen. 11). Perhaps it will be in the increase of falsehood to drown out the dearth of truth (2 Tim. 4:3-4). Perhaps His deep displeasure and wrath against humanity will be evident in their rebellion against His authority which will take shape in their lifestyles.

Rather than putting others before themselves, they will put themselves before others evidencing that their love for themselves supersedes their love for others (2 Tim. 3:2). Rather than being willing to help others with the means that God in His kindness has permitted them to enjoy, they will heap up for themselves treasures on earth that will be destroyed that they will be unable to take with them into eternity (Matt. 6:19-21, 1 Tim. 6:6, 2 Tim. 3:2). Rather than being the humble people that God receives, they are the prideful people that God resists (2 Tim. 3:2, Jas 4:6). Rather than reverencing God and His great name, they blaspheme it, showing the contempt with which they hold their Creator (Exod. 20:7, 2 Tim. 3:2). Rather than honoring the parents that bore them, that raised them up, that provide for their every need, they disobey and dishonor their first earthly authority, crumbling the foundation on which they will view all authority throughout their lives (Exod. 20:12, Eph. 6:1-3, Col. 3:20, 2 Tim. 3:2). Rather than realizing that everything they enjoy in this life is from the loving hand of a benevolent Creator (Jas 1:17), they think they achieve and acquire everything solely by their own efforts (2 Tim. 3:2). Rather than bring their consciences into subjection with the revealed will of God, they chase the latest fads and are tossed to and fro by every wind of doctrine (Eph. 4:14, 2 Tim. 3:2). Rather than putting on love, the supreme Christian ethic, rather than loving others more than they love themselves, they step on others at their expense to elevate themselves (Phil. 2:3, 2 Tim. 3:3). Rather than remembering that God's forgiveness reaches as far as the east is from the west, and using that as fuel to prompt them to forgive others, they built up bitterness and refuse to forgive others (Matt. 18:21-35, Eph. 4:32, 2 Tim. 3:3).

Slanderers make it their practice to speak things about Christians which are not true in an effort to see Christians harmed or silenced (Matt. 5:10-12, 2 Tim. 3:3). These people, against whom God's wrath (Rom. 1:18) is revealed, also lack self-control (2 Tim. 3:3). They live in unrestrained lust. These people who have rejected God's authority will be brutal. They will be unduly harmful to others to bring pleasure to themselves (2 Tim. 3:3). God defines what is good and the people who hate Him will despise what God has called good and will run after what God has called evil (2 Tim. 3:3). Because they are double-minded (Jas 1:8), despisers of God will be traitors in that they will turn against what God calls good and turn to what God calls evil (2 Tim. 3:4). Despisers of God will trust what they perceive, even if it opposes what God has said, over what God has said. In becoming self-willed and obstinate, they will trust their faulty reasoning above His perfect wisdom. This is the epitome of pride (2 Tim. 3:4). Even if ceasing to practice what God calls evil interrupts what they think to bring them pleasure, they will ignore God's clear instruction and exert their own autonomy rather than live under God's authority, showing that love for their own pleasure was more important than any love for God they may have at one time professed (2 Tim. 3:4).

### Questions for self-reflection:

(1) What difficult circumstances are you experiencing currently?
(2) Could those difficult circumstances be happening as a result of any personal sin in you?
(3) Are you relieved that you belong to God or do you wish to be free from that relationship with Him?
(4) Would you want God to be perfectly just or would you want God to be fickle like you and me?
(5) What is your most prized earthly possession and would you be able to give it up if God asked you to?

## 2:6. "Yet I have set My King On My holy hill of Zion."

While the nations rage and the people imagine a vain thing, while people experience God's wrath and deep displeasure as a result of their sins against Him, while they are dead in trespasses and sins (Eph. 2:1), God sent His Son into the world at the perfect time in history (Gal. 4:4). He came to Jerusalem, the city on a hill. By His death, burial, and resurrection, people are saved, and the church flourishes. Christ, the King of Kings and Lord of Lords, has become the exalted One to whom every knee will bow (Phil. 2:12). Christ is **King** over what was once ruled by David (Lk 1:32). After Christ rose, He ascended back to heaven and awaits the time for His return. When He does return, the New Jerusalem will come down and we will be in the eternal state (Rev. 21:9-27).

Today, Christ is over all things pertaining to the church (Eph. 1:22). The church is the God-ordained recipient of all heavenly blessings (Eph. 1:3-14). The church is on earth to glorify God and reach the world with the gospel message that sinful men can be reconciled to the God they have offended by their sins through faith in Christ (2 Cor. 5:20).

Today, Christ is seated at the right hand of His Father (Heb. 1:3). When Christ came the first time, He came to the **holy hill of Zion** to His own but they did not receive Him (Jn 1:11). When He humbled Himself (Phil. 2:8), He was despised and rejected (Isa 53:3). After being lifted up for the sins of the world (Jn 3:14, Jn 8:28), He rose from the dead (1 Cor. 15:4) and ascended back to the right hand of the Majesty on high (Heb. 1:3). From there, Christ rules at the right hand of the Father and is the king on the throne of the lives of the saints. He ever lives to intercede for them as their Prophet, Priest, and King (Jn 6:14, Heb. 4:15, Heb. 7:25).

The saints live as His subjects in His kingdom that He rules from heaven in their hearts now that He will one day reign from the earth (Lk 17:20-21, Rev. 21:1-8). Believers willingly became His subjects, bowing the knee to His sovereign rule. Unbelievers will be forced to bow and will be one of those under His feet (1 Cor. 15:27, Phil. 2:10).

Christ is equal with God the Father (Jn 14:7-11, Col. 1:15-18, Col. 2:9) and is, therefore, the King of God the Father's choosing to rule and reign. Christ is the Mediator between God and man (1 Tim. 2:5) and is the Mediator of a better covenant (Heb. 8:6). God in eternity past planned to send Christ at the perfect time in history to redeem a people to Himself (Gal. 4:4-5) and to purify a people that would be zealous for good works (Ti 2:14). They are His workmanship created in Christ Jesus for good works that God has ordained that they should walk in (Eph. 2:10).

Christ is the King of kings and is the King of all the saints. He rules over all rulers, even those that refuse to acknowledge His rightful rule (Eph. 1:21). The only reason pagan earthly rulers are able to continue in their rebellion against Him is because He permits them to take their next breath (Dan. 2:21).

## Questions for self-reflection:

(1) Who rules your heart and life? Would you loved ones agree?
(2) God has ordained that His people walk in good works? How have you demonstrated that recently?
(3) How does your submission to the Lord look? Does it look voluntary or forced?

**2:7. "I will declare the decree: The Lord has said to Me, 'You are My Son, Today I have begotten You.**

Kings make decrees. God the Son makes a **decree** based on what His Father has told Him. The Father decreed that He would send the Son to be the Savior of the world (1 Jn 2:2). The Father decreed that Christ would come when He came (Gal. 4:4-5) to the people to whom He came (Jn 1:11) for the purpose He came to them (Jn 1:29).

The purpose for which Christ came into the world was decreed by God from eternity past that He would substitute for sinners (Rom. 5:9, 2 Cor. 5:21). The Son did everything the Father asked of Him. Christ is not a created being, as some heresies teach. Rather, He is co-eternal with the Father and Holy Spirit (Gen. 1:26, Gen. 11:6, Jn 1:14, Jn 8:58, 1 Tim. 3:16, 1 Jn 5:7). He showed Himself to be God at His baptism (Lk 3:22) by having all members of the Trinity present. Christ has been Prophet (Mk 6:4), Priest (Heb. 4:14-16), and King (Rev. 19:16) from all eternity. He was declared to be to Son of God with power by His resurrection from the dead (Rom. 1:4). It was plainer to see His deity to those who saw the events of His life that revealed His supernatural power. Jesus is revealed as Messiah to those to whom the Son wills to reveal it (Matt. 11:27).

If the Father is speaking these words from eternity and if God's Word, in one sense, in the infinite mind of God, has been completed from eternity past, then there is no difficulty with Christ being **begotten**. He is God the Son in that He took on humanity without divesting Himself of deity. He performed His office Mediator of a better covenant as a human (Heb. 8:6). He could not substitute for human sinners if He were not human Himself. He likewise could not satisfy God's justice if He relinquished any of His deity. He maintained both full humanity and full deity while becoming the final offering for sin (Heb. 10:10).

At any rate, if it refers to His kenosis, His taking on humanity in order to be the human propitiation for sin (1 Jn 2:2), His time on earth does have a beginning. If eternity is one long, unending day, then '**Today**,' could refer to eternity past.

**Questions for self-reflection:**

(1) Instead of reading this devotional commentary, what would you be doing right now if the Son had not become your Substitute and begotten you?

(2) How did the Son first reveal Himself to you? What precipitated you first seeking Him?

(3) Are you okay with God leaving some mysteries, such as how Christ could be fully God and fully Man?

**2:8. Ask of Me, and I will give You The nations for Your inheritance, And the ends of the earth for Your possession.**

Whether God the Father is speaking to Christ the Son or whether Christ the Son is speaking, the truth of the verse is still the same. The Lord Jesus Christ is the heir of all things (Heb. 1:2-3). The Father and Son have intimate, perfect communion because there is no sin that interrupts that communion. There is no dis-agreement between any Member of the Trinity. Christ could ask anything of His Father and the Father would grant it because they are equal deity and the Son always did that which pleased the Father (Jn 8:29, Jn 14:10-14). When Christ asked the Father to let the cup pass from Him (Matt. 26:39), He asked for that to pass from Him only if it was the Father's will for it to pass from Him. Since it was the Father's will for the Son to die as a substitute for sinners who were otherwise without hope (Ps. 69:9, Isa. 53:4-6, Mk 10:45, Jn 10:11, Jn 11:50, Jn 15:13, Rom. 5:6, 2 Cor. 5:14-15, Gal. 2:20, Gal. 3:13, 1 Thess. 5:10, Heb. 2:9, Heb. 9:28, 1 Pet. 2:21, 1 Pet. 2:24, 1 Pet. 3:18, 1 Jn 3:16), the Son still had to die. The Son did the same works as the Father (Jn 9:3). Since they did the same things as one another and since they shared the same divine essence (Jn 10:30, Phil. 2:6), Christ could accurately say, "If you have seen Me you have seen the Father" (Jn 14:7-11).

It is good that nothing that the Son asked for from the Father was withheld from Him because it could have been that all the spiritual blessings (Eph. 1:3-14) that pertain to the adopted (Rom. 8:15) sheep would have been withheld but they are not. So, the Son can ask whatever He wills of the Father and the wills of the Father and the Son are in perfect step with each other. The **nations** are the **inheritance** of the Trinity since all who believe in the Son have been given to the Father as a love offering from the Son to the Father (Eph. 5:2). This refers to the people in the nations who have embraced the Son by faith. "Nations" refers to the non-Jews since the Jews were the original recipients of the Messiah's first Advent (Rom. 1:16). The sheep from the four cor-ners, **the ends of the earth**, become a part of God's **possession**,

His peculiar people (1 Pet. 2:9), His bride (Eph. 5:23), the church when they come to Christ by faith.

## Questions for self-reflection:

(1) In an ultimate sense, what on this earth do we own?

(2) In an ultimate sense, what on this earth does God own?

(3) If our families had perfect sinless patterns of relation to one another like the Son and Father enjoy, how would that change things?

(4) If we were truly resigned to fulfilling God's will as He wanted it rather than imposing our own wills on situations, how would that change things?

(5) If the Trinity members were not in perfect union with one another, how would that affect our ability to trust God?

## 2:9. You shall break them with a rod of iron; You shall dash them to pieces like a potter's vessel

The rebels from the nations reject the loving, generous provision of the Trinity. Those that reject God can expect to be rejected by God. Rather than let the God to whom they owe everything rule them, because of their hard and impenitent hearts, they insist on ruling themselves (Romans 2:5). They abide under His wrath now (Jn 3:36, Rom. 1:18-32) and will abide under His wrath for all eternity after their time in this life comes to an end (Rom. 5:9, Rev. 19:15). Those who reject the Son can, regardless of which nation from which they hail, if not in this life, then surely in the next life, expect to be broken into **pieces** under their weight of God's judgment (Matt. 21:44, Matt. 25:41-46).

As it is true that there will be people from every tribe, tongue, and nation that will worship the Lord (Rev. 5:9, Rev. 7:9), it must likewise true that there will be people from every tribe, tongue, and nation that will reject the knowledge of the one true God that was providentially made available to them. Those who reject such merciful knowledge, a knowledge that could lead to their forgiveness if they would turn to Him in repentant faith, will instead lead to their judgment as everyone will be held accountable to what they do know (2 Cor. 5:10). All are without excuse (Rom. 1:20). These will succumb to the fierceness of the winepress of the wrath of God (Rev. 14:17-20, Rev. 19:15). These will have their part in the lake which burns with fire and brimstone (Rev. 20:15, Rev. 21:8). This is the fate of them that obey not the gospel of the Lord Jesus Christ (2 Thess. 1:8). It was a savor of death unto death for them (2 Cor. 2:16). They are vessels of wrath fit for destruction (Rom. 9:22). The works of the flesh were the pattern of their life (Gal. 5:19-21). Since they were not led by the Light of the World, they stumbled because they could not see where they were going (Jn 8:12, Jn 9:4, Jn 11:9). The darkness that blinded them in this life will lead to darkness and blackness forever for all eternity (Matt. 8:12, Matt. 22:13, 2 Pt 2:4, 2 Pt 2:17). Instead of loving Him who first loved them (1 Jn 4:19), they instead loved their sin and would not turn from it and embrace the One who loved them and gave Himself for them (Eph. 5:2). The time for God's mercy will by now have passed since they went their whole lives rejecting the evidence for His existence. They rejected the provision He made for their souls at Calvary. Christ demanded too much of them. They thought they had more freedom to live for themselves rather than to live for the Lord. How wrong they were! As they get **dashed to pieces like a potter's vessel,** they wish they could have another chance. But their time has passed. After the Jews rejected their Messiah by sending Him the cross, in 70 A.D., Rome dashed them when Rome came and overthrew the Jews.

## Questions for self-reflection:

(1) Before you came to Christ for salvation, what was the biggest thing that kept you from coming to Him?

(2) When did you first realize that God was offended by your sin?

(3) Are you more concerned with dealing with your own sins or are you more concerned about dealing with the sins of those closest to you?

(4) Since you cannot make someone who is blind able to see again, what can you do to keep your sanity as you try to interact with those who persist in willful blindness to the things of God?

(5) When you think of the eternal fate of the willfully blind, are you more likely to stay angry at them or more likely to be compassionate with them?

**2:10. Now, therefore, be wise, O kings; Be instructed, you judges of the earth.**

---

This psalm begins with the nations raging against the Lord (Ps. 2:1-3). This verse is a patient, merciful, loving call by the Lord to the nations to repent of their rebellion and turn (or return) to Him and be spared of fearful judgment that awaits should they stay in their sins (Heb. 10:31). Those who set themselves up against the Lord are given yet another opportunity to humble themselves and avert judgment (Isa. 66:2, Jas 4:10). Rulers provide the example for living for the people over which they rule (Rom. 13:1-7). If their subjects see haughty, prideful rulers, the laypeople can be expected to be haughty and prideful themselves as well (Matt. 10:25). If the subjects see humble, righteous rulers who treat them as they would want to be treated, the subjects will more likely be humble and righteous as well (Lk 6:31, Rom. 12:17-21). Counsel taken against the Lord cannot be ultimately successful, even it appears to be temporarily successful (Eccles. 8:11).

The kings of the earth will never be wise in a godly, biblical sense until they humble themselves under the mighty hand of God that He might exalt them in due time (1 Pet. 5:6). God gives them grace because they have humbled themselves before Him (Jas 4:6). When God's grace appeared before all men (Ti 2:11), these wise kings, embraced what they knew to be true of the God of the universe. Currently, at the outset of this psalm, the heathen rages against God and His authority. In that ongoing state of rage, they are not wise. Those in authority set the tone for those under them. The layperson is under the rule of the king. The patterns set by those in authority will be picked up by those under their rule (for the better or for the worse). While kings or people in authority may be blessed with physical wealth or earthly knowledge that aids them in the execution of their offices as kings, it amounts to foolishness and poverty in comparison to the infinitely wise and bountiful God (1 Cor. 1:25, 1 Cor. 3:18-20).

If the earthly kings rage against the God who permits them to rule (Dan. 2:21, Rom. 13:1), that is tantamount to foolishness as one day they will be brought low whether it is in this life or it is in the next life. Some, like Nebuchadnezzar, are fortunate to learn that lesson before it is too late (Dan. 4). The wisdom that earthly **kings** have does not amount to true wisdom if it is not based upon the fear of the Lord (Prov. 1:7). Rather than trust in their own wisdom or riches or earthly aids, they would **be wise** to trust the Lord will all their hearts, not lean on their own understanding, and acknowledge the Lord in all their ways so that He would direct their paths (Prov. 3:5-6).

The judges of the earth are under the authority of the kings. The kings appoint the **judges**. When God comes to correct them because of their sinful ways, they would be well instructed to turn from their own sinful ways and turn to the Lord who allowed them to be in the position of influence which they currently enjoy.

The position that rulers are allowed by God to enjoy is a stewardship for which they will be held accountable (Matt. 25:14-30). It is a sobering responsibility to think of it that way. Kings, judges and anyone with responsibility for or authority over anyone or anything on this earth would do well to **be instructed** and to take that thought captive to the obedience of Christ (2 Cor. 10:5).

### Questions for self-reflection:

(1) There is a time when all of us, not just the rulers on the earth rage against the Lord. What does it say about God's character that He gives people who actively rage against Him an opportunity to 'be wise?'

(2) If rulers are prideful and those being ruled often follow suit, what personal changes does that make you think about making so that others do not follow a poor example that you may be leaving behind?

(3) If you are in a position of authority, what are some practical steps that you can take to show that it is the Lord that is ordering your steps?

(4) If you are in a position of authority and if the Lord called you home today, when you gave an account for the stewardship that the Lord had entrusted to your care, what would He find?

**2:11. Serve the Lord with fear, And rejoice with trembling.**

---

The nations, should not rage (Ps. 2:1). The people should not imagine a vain thing (Ps. 2:1). The Lord is an exclusive deity (Deut. 6:13, Lk 4:8). He does not condone worship that is meant to be directed to only Him to be shared among multiple deities (Exod. 20:3-6, Exod. 23:13, Lev. 19:4, Lev. 26:1, Deut. 7:26, Ps. 16:4, Isa. 45:20, Isa. 46:7, Jer. 1:16, Jer. 11:12, Hos 11:2, Mic. 5:13, Hab. 2:18, Acts 17:16, Acts 17:29, Rom. 1:23, 1 Cor. 6:9, 1 Cor. 10:7, 1 Cor. 10:14, 1 Cor. 10:19, Gal. 4:8, Gal. 5:20, 1 Thess. 1:9, 1 Jn 5:21, Rev. 9:20). He is the only God that is worthy of true worship (Exod. 20:3, Exod. 34:14, Deut. 5:7, Deut. 6:13-14, 2 Kgs 17:35-36, 1 Chron. 16:25, Ps. 29:1-2, Ps. 96:4-5, Ps. 148:1-2, Rev. 4:8-9).

Men will worship anything created to pacify their consciences and to meet their need for purpose in life (Rom. 1:21-23). We know this is true because they do it so rampantly. Unless they arrive at the conclusion that the one true God, the God of Scripture, the Lord of heaven and earth (Gen. 14:22, 2 Kgs. 19:15, 1 Chron. 29:11, 2 Chron. 2:12, Ezr 5:11, Ps. 115:15, Ps. 121:2, Ps. 124:8, Ps. 134:3, Ps. 146:5-6, Isa. 37:16, Matt. 11:25, Lk 10:21, Acts 14:15, Acts 17:24), is the only appropriate object of worship, they will have missed the objective.

All of life, apart from the worship of the one true God is utterly meaningless. Apart from Him, we can do nothing (Jn 15:5). In Him, we live, move, and have our being (Acts 17:28). Life only makes sense when all aspects of life are interpreted through the lens of the reality of this one true God. Sinful man who wants to remove His influence from their lives, wants to quiet his conscience and enjoy himself rather than to think that one day he will wake up and will have to answer to this God for how he lived his life (Eccles. 12:14, Matt. 7:21-23, Matt. 16:27, Jn 5:22, Acts 17:31, Rom. 2:1-3, Rom. 2:6-11, Rom. 2:16, Rom. 14:10, Rom. 14:12, 1 Cor. 3:11-15, 1 Cor. 11:31, 2 Cor. 5:10, 1 Tim. 5:24, 2 Tim. 4:1, 2 Tim. 4:8, Heb. 9:27, Heb. 10:30, Heb. 13:4, Jas 4:12, 1 Pet. 1:17, 1 Pet. 4:5, Rev. 2:23, Rev. 11:18, Rev. 20:11-15).

---

Because God is the Creator (Gen. 1:1), He is the supreme authority over all of creation, including every person. This is why He has the right to demand our allegiance to Him. This is why it is sin that warrants death and judgment to any and all who do not worship God. Kings and rulers should not plot against the Lord. They should take heed to the aforementioned warning of judgment that awaits the enemies of the Lord. Rather than resist Him, if they submit to Him, they can avoid much affliction. But they can also take heed, because even those who enjoy a covenant relationship with Him can be subject to divine chastisement (Heb. 12:3-11).

Most people will serve everything but Him. They will make a god in their own image who bows to them so they do not have to bow to Him. This could be especially true of those with earthly power. They can tend to become self-sufficient. Such people fail to remember that it is the Lord to sovereignly allows people to rule on His schedule, not their schedule (Dan. 2:21). They must remember that they must give an account for the stewardship that God entrusted to them. Those with earthly power should know the principles of morality and justice recorded in God's Word and strive to build their earthly kingdoms in ways that will please the Heavenly King.

Earthly rulers are serving the Lord in one sense anyway. Their kingdoms are subservient to His overarching kingdom. They will have to answer for their handling of the kingdom entrusted to them (Matt. 25:14-30). They can rejoice for the time being for the power and influence that they enjoy at the present, but if they mishandle it, it will not be long before they find themselves trembling before the Ruler of rulers. It is right to serve the Lord with fear over and above any created thing. After all, He gave rise to them. He is supreme over them.

While we will at one time or another be accountable to someone on this earth as our earthly relationships play out (Ephesians 6:1-9), everyone will have to be accountable to the Lord. Everyone will stand before Him and either be welcomed into His eternal presence with joy and banished from heaven and cast into the Lake of Fire (Rev. 21:1-8) forever where there will be weeping and gnashing of teeth (Matt. 8:12, Matt. 22:13, Matt. 24:51, Matt. 25:30, Lk 13:28).

The nations, in the beginning of this psalm, were called on the carpet for rebelling against God's sovereign claim on their lives and for conspiring to overthrow Him. They thought He was oppressive. God laughed at them because of their pride and the futility of their efforts. He would mete out justice at the appropriate time. The Lord Jesus would come at the fulness of time (Gal. 4:4-5) to redeem a people to Himself to purify a people zealous for good works (Ti 2:14). The rest would be separated, as sheep from goats (Matt. 25:32), where they will be judged and punished eternally (Matt. 25:46).

God calls these pagan kings to humble themselves before Him, to be spared this wrath. They have been mercifully given the chance to repent and believe the gospel, to obey the revelation that had been exposed to them at the time. For the rest of us, we have the complete picture. We know how the story ends. We know that Christ is the conquering King who will put all His enemies under His feet (1 Cor. 15:27). We know that until that day, He graciously gives rebellious men from all walks of life from all levels of social strata gracious opportunities to repent and believe the gospel. Then they will serve the Lord with fear. They will respect Him and not do anything to knowingly earn His disapproval and warrant potential chastisement.

It is very possible for most people to stay in their current employment and serve the Lord in that employment. The psalmist called the kings of the day to do just that. When the kings of the earth, humble themselves and **serve the Lord with fear, to rejoice with trembling** will naturally follow. They will be able to rejoice because they will have a righteousness that has been imputed to them that is not their own (Phil. 3:9), but was procured for them by the Lord Jesus Christ through His sinless life, sacrificial atoning substitutionary death on their behalf, and His triumphant resurrection (1 Cor. 15:3-8). They will have to rejoice with trembling because they will not want to be knowingly live in such ways so as to invite divine chastisement and disapproval of their conduct (Heb. 12:3-11).

## Questions for self-reflection:

(1) What are some ways we can be prone to give the worship that should be reserved for God alone to other people or things?

(2) If we know that we are supposed to set our minds on heavenly things, what makes us so prone to set our minds on earthly things at such an alarmingly unhealthy rate?

(3) If we were to allow the Holy Spirit to more fully control our consciences and lead our decision making, how might our lives look different? What would be some things that we would remove from our lives? What would be added to our lives?

**2:12. Kiss the Son, lest He be angry, And you perish in the way, When His wrath is kindled but a little. Blessed are all those who put their trust in Him.**

---

It is fairly plain from the context of this psalm that the **Son**, is the Son of God, the Lord Jesus Christ. It is likewise apparent that a **kiss** is a sign of affection. This is not the kiss of Judas Iscariot (Lk 22:48). No. This is the kiss of heartfelt devotion. This is a kiss of love without reservation that the bride saves for her husband, the Bridegroom (Song of Sol. 1:2). This verse is a call for the nations, which were earlier said to be raging in opposition to Him, to embrace the Son, to embrace the gospel, to have their sins forgiven (Col. 1:14), to receive pardon (Isa. 55:7), to obtain justification by faith (Gal. 2:16).

If sinners don't kiss the Son, if they don't turn from their sins and come in repentant faith to the Lord Jesus Christ, God will deal with them by His **wrath** and displeasure. They will be broken by God's justice, and ruled with His rod of iron (Ps. 2:9, Rev. 2:26-27). They will be the vessel that is broken into pieces by His just wrath. They will be crushed under the fierceness of the winepress of the wrath of God (Rev. 14:17-20).

To be saved from anything, the thing to be saved from must be an unpleasant thing that one normally tries to avoid. The thing which sinners need to be saved from is God and/or God's wrath (Rom. 5:9). While God is a God of love and commended His love toward those He created in His image (Gen. 1:27) in that while we were sinners Christ died for us (Rom. 5:8), outside of Christ, because sinners choose to sin, sinners abide under God's just wrath (Jn 3:36). He mercifully allows man the gracious opportunity to repent and believe the gospel (Eph. 2:3-4).

They have been given enough knowledge to be able to do that and they are without excuse (Rom. 1:20). Those who do humble themselves (Jas 4:6, 1 Pet. 5:6) and come to God through faith in Christ, receive mercy and abundant pardon. Those who refuse to do so, those who refuse to submit to the knowledge that they do have, will experience God's wrath. These will show that, due to their willful, unrighteous suppression of the truth (Rom. 1:18), that this is what they have earned (Rom. 2:4, Rom. 6:23). Those who receive Christ by faith do not have to receive God's wrath because Christ received it in their stead (Romans 5:9). Those who refuse to bow before Christ in this life will bow before Him in the next life when every knee will bow and every tongue will confess that Jesus Christ is Lord to the glory of God the Father (Phil. 2:9-11).

There are two ways of life: the narrow way that leads to life and the broad way that leads to destruction (Matt. 7:13-14). There is no middle ground between these two ways (Lk 11:23). All who are for Christ are eternally Christ's and will enjoy heaven with Him forever. All those who are against Christ are eternally Satan's and will be expelled from Christ's heaven to the place of outer darkness where there is weeping and gnashing of teeth (Lk 13:28) where they will **perish in the way**.

His wrath, which had been abiding upon them because of the unbelief (Jn 3:36) will be **kindled** against those who have chosen to reject Him and have died in that rejection. It is not that if they had known they would have turned to Him. They loved their sin too much, like the Pharisees of Jesus' day, like the people of the days of the prophets, to see the need to humble themselves and forsake sin and receive forgiveness from God. He is merciful to extend the warnings to them, to warn them before He comes in justice. He is loving to extend the invitation for the nations to serve Him with fear and to rejoice with trembling before Him. He is not unfair to judge and be **angry** at those who reject Him. He has given them life and breath. Everything they enjoy is a gift of His common grace and generosity. Those who reject Him should be held accountable for dismissing the provision He has made for them. It is reasonable for them to perish. They have kindled His wrath by their willful rejection of Him.

The saved can look at the punishment suffered by those that reject Him and can rejoice that they are safe since they have placed **their trust in Him who lives forever** and not in anything or anyone that perishes. However, they must remember that it is He who has saved them and not they themselves. The kings of the earth and the subjects under those earthly kings who have misplaced affections which are not directed at the Lord who made them, but are instead directed at various things in this world, have kindled God's wrath against them. The saved avoid that wrath and are blessed by their relationship with Him.

**Questions for self-reflection:**

(1) If you are married, if you have children, if you are in a relationship with a significant other belonging to the opposite sex, do you only kiss them one time ever or do you repeatedly kiss them or show your love for them repeatedly?

(2) Would you kiss a stranger in the ways that you kiss your spouse or children (not that you kiss your children like you kiss your spouse ;))?

(3) How does your life demonstrate that you continue to kiss the Son rather than giving Him just a one-time kiss?

(4) Do you have family members or people in your regular sphere of influence who need to kiss the Son? If so, does the picture of the Son that you convey to them make the idea of kissing the Son attractive?

(5) If we say we truly love our neighbor as ourself, and if our neighbor has not come to Christ, since where they will spend eternity is more important than anything else, what are we doing to help our neighbor see their need to kiss the Son?

# Psalm 3

**3:1. Lord, how they have increased who trouble me! Many are they who rise up against me.**

---

The psalmist is righteous. He publicly follows the **Lord**. If he did not follow the Lord, or if he followed the Lord in more of a hidden manner, he might face less opposition. The psalm title says David wrote this when he fled from his son, Absalom. Absalom had tried to take his father's kingdom away (2 Sam. 15).

David writes many things that are pertinent to Christ. This is one of those things. Many rose up against Christ. David's son, Absalom, rose up against David. This psalm could also be applied to Christ as if He were saying these things Himself during His ministry. Jesus' disciple, Judas Iscariot rose up against Jesus (Lk 22:1-6). David's enemies **trouble**d him. Christ's enemies troubled Him, whether they be the Jewish religious leaders of Christ's day (Matt. 12:14), whether they be Christ's disciples who forsook Him and fled (Mk 14:50), or whether he be Judas Iscariot who betrayed Him (Lk 22:48). When Christ was arrested, the beating (Lk 22:63), scourging (Mk 15:15), spitting (Matt. 26:67), mocking (Lk 22:63), and crucifixion was not done by friends but by enemies.

This psalm can be a comfort to contemporary followers of Christ who experience trouble from God's enemies. This trouble that will **rise up against** them comes in many forms. People oppose Christ and His followers and have done so since the first Avent. This opposition will continue until the end of time. Such opposition finds its source in the prince of the power of the air, Satan himself, and works itself out in the lives of the sons of disobedience (Eph. 2:2). Christ said to His disciples that in this world they should expect to have trouble (Jn 16:33). Christ said that it is to be expected to be persecuted for the faith of Him who died and rose again (Matt. 10:23). Jesus, by the power of the Holy Spirit, inspired the apostles to write similarly (2 Tim. 3:12, 1 Pet. 1:6-9, Rev. 2:8-11).

It is not surprising that this happens given that the message of the cross is an offensive message because it calls men sinners. Men disagree with that because they think they are normally good (Prov. 20:6). They mistakenly think that the God of the Bible should be just like them (Ps. 50:21). They think that they are basically good and that there is not enough bad in them that would warrant such hostility from the 'God of love' that they have sinned against. They have a liberal view of the cross, that it is one of several successful ways to God whereas Christ Himself said He is the only way to the Father (Jn 14:6). Maybe their view of the cross does not have to do with the punishment of sin. Scripture is clear that our sins irreparably damaged our relationship with God beyond repair (Isa. 64:6, Jer. 17:9, Jn 3:36, Rom. 3:9-23, Eph. 2:1-10). God had to intervene and did so by sending Christ (Gal. 4:4-5) to reconcile us to Himself (2 Cor. 5:12-21).

The gospel calls people to abandon self-worth and self-ability and implores people to confess their unworthiness (Jas 4:6-8). It shows us that we are unworthy (Isa. 64:6) and that Christ is worthy (Rev. 5:8-14). Most people have too high a view of themselves to see their need to do that. Satan fuels this opposition to the truth. He was behind the first opposition to God's Word and God's authority (Gen. 3:1ff). He is behind all present opposition to God's authority. He will be behind all future opposition to God's authority. People who reject the one true God, who reject the God of the Bible, **have increased** with each generation and they have always caused trouble to the genuinely righteous (Matt. 24:3-28), to those who realize they have no righteousness of their own (Phil. 3:9) but are entirely dependent upon the Lord for His imputed righteousness, which is freely given to those who place repentant faith in the Lord Jesus Christ alone for salvation.

It is not necessary for Christ's disciples to go out of their way to find persecution. It just finds them because the world hates them because the world hates Him (Matt. 10:22).

### Questions for self-reflection:

(1) If you are a parent, how would you feel if one of your children tried to have you killed like Absalom tried to have his father David killed?

(2) Have you ever experienced trouble in the form of persecution because you are a follower of Christ? How did that make you feel?

(3) How can experiencing persecution be a blessing and a comfort?

(4) In the Bible, did Jesus or the disciples or the prophets before them have to look for persecution or did it find them?

**3:2. Many are they who say of me, "There is no help for him in God." Selah**

For David to hear that God was not there to **help** him, whatever their reason for saying that to him, must have been incredibly disheartening for David to hear. After all that the Lord had seen David through, David knew that **God** had to have been the One to sustain him (Ps. 54:4). If David's enemies believed that God was there, they did not believe that God cared enough about David's plight in order to intervene on David's behalf. Christ's enemies said something strikingly similar to Him when He was on the cross (Matt. 27:43).

Satan tempted people then and actively tempts people today (1 Pet. 5:8) to believe the same lie, that God is not there, or that if he is there, He does not care enough to intervene on their behalf. Those who listen to such lies listen to the father of lies (Jn 8:44), Satan, himself. Satan fills the hearts of people who fail to properly trust God with lies (Acts 5:3). God was the source of deliverance for the psalmist prior to the time that this was penned. He is the Savior of His people throughout all ages (1 Tim. 4:10). When His enemies see His people suffer, they often mistakenly think that God really does not care enough to intervene on behalf of His people. This is a gross miscalculation on the part of His enemies. When Christ hung on the cross for our sins, the mockers said something similar when they mockingly implored God to intervene on behalf of His Son to let Him down from the cross.

In the immediate context, as the previous verse revealed, Absalom, David's son, was after David (2 Sam. 15). Those who had joined the cause of Absalom in the fight against David no doubt echoed a similar sentiment to what is expressed in this verse. David's enemies did not anticipate that David's God would come through for him to rescue him.

Satan has used and continues to use the same tactics against saints today. He plants doubts in the minds of the saints. Even if Satan cannot separate the true believer from God's love (Rom. 8:38-39), Satan can influence the believer to the point where the believer becomes less fruitful because the flesh is winning the battle with the Spirit (Gal. 5:16-18). If the believer gets overtaken in a trespass, they may become so discouraged so as to doubt that forgiveness really is available to them. They might doubt God's love and provision for them, wrought by Christ on the cross, really is sufficient to cover their multitude of sins (1 Pet. 4:8).

The believer must meditate on God's Word (Jb 23:12, Ps 1:2) and think about how God has come through for them in times past and has shown Himself to be faithful on numerous occasions (Rom. 8:28, 2 Cor. 1:10). They must remind themselves that this life is but a vapor (Jas 4:14) and that these afflictions are but for a moment and they are light in comparison to the reward that awaits them in eternity (2 Cor. 4:17). They must remember that the grace for today is sufficient for the trouble that today contains (Matt. 6:34, 1 Cor. 10:13, Phil. 4:19). They must remember that God has worked and continues to work everything for the good of those who love Him and who are called according to His purpose (Rom. 8:28).

Since God does not change (Num. 23:19, Ps. 102:25-27, Isa. 40:8, Mal. 3:6, Heb. 13:8), what was true for saints of old can help saints of today and tomorrow. When persecution arises, when affliction increases, God can be trusted to supply the grace and the wisdom to do the next right thing, to overcome the next temptation and the next. When sin overtakes the believer, they can go to their Advocate, Jesus Christ the righteous, who lives to intercede for them (Heb. 7:25, 1 Jn 2:1-2). Since the Father is well pleased with Him (Matthew 3:17), they do not have to worry about being cast out (Jn 6:37). While they are not worthy, He is infinitely worthy. He will keep His sheep until the end (Jn 10:27-28). It is incumbent on the saints to have their minds renewed with the truth of God so that they can access it when they are tempted by the enemy to doubt His promises (Rom. 12:2).

**Questions for self-reflection:**

(1) Have you ever been criticized or mocked or ridiculed for following God?

(2) Read 1 Corinthians 11:1. How do our lives look like Paul and Christ? Does our Christianity align with the world or confront the world?

(3) How can we know we are believing God's truth or the devil's lies?

(4) Have you ever felt God's comfort in the midst of suffering? What was that like?

(5) Have you ever experienced what amounts to a Satanic attack from an unbeliever or a circumstance? What was it like?

(6) If nothing can separate us from God's love, what is the point of Satan trying to attack us since He cannot take us from belonging to God?

(7) What are you doing to protect yourself against Satanic attacks?

**3:3. But You, O Lord, are a shield for me, My glory and the One who lifts up my head.**

---

Even though everyone seemed to be against the psalmist, even though everyone seemed to be against the **Lord** Jesus Christ, including His own disciples when He was arrested (Matt. 26:56), even though many times it can feel as though it is the sheep against the world (Jn 15:18), the Lord is **a shield for** His own. By the imputed righteousness of the Lord Jesus Christ (Rom. 4:5), the sheep are shielded from God's wrath which abides upon the unbelieving (Jn 3:36, Rom. 5:9).

God equips the saints, who are clothed in the righteousness of Christ with the shield of faith among the other parts of the armor of God. Attacks come from Satan in all different directions at the believer. God permits Satan to attack believers as He did with Job. But Satan must work under the sovereign permission of God.

God the Father was a shield for Jesus during Jesus' earthly life. There were times that God the Father was a shield to Jesus. Baby Jesus was shielded from wicked King Herod who sought to have Him killed (Matt. 2:1-23). Jesus was protected from premature death and arrest (Jn 10:39). There were times during Jesus' earthly ministry when Jesus would have died before His appointed time if it were not for the Father's supernatural intervention (Lk 4:30). Even in Jesus' death, the Father helped Him (Jn 5:19).

When our head is down, He is the **One who lifts up my head**. After Christ died, His disciples' heads were down because they thought they would never see Jesus again. They had forgotten that He had told them that He would rise again. Due to their forgetful hearing, their heads were down (Mk 16:14). Seeing Christ risen from the dead no doubt lifted up their heads. Their faith had become sight.

Believers in any generation can be confident (not prideful) that God will be with them and protect them and equip them to face anything. Satan will tempt them to sin. Satan will tempt them to doubt (1 Cor. 10:13). Jesus, our faithful High Priest was tempted in every way like us, yet without sin (Heb. 4:15). If our hope is in Him, the wrath that is supposed to be reserved for us is taken by Christ and we receive the helmet of salvation, the breastplate of righteousness, the shield of faith, the belt of truth, and shoes for gospel communication (Eph. 6:10-20). The helmet protects the believer from a fatal death blow that would cause the forfeiture of salvation. In other words, in Christ, salvation is secure. Nobody can pluck the sheep from the protective hand of the Good Shepherd (Jn 10:27-28). A shield protects a soldier when an enemy fires upon them. Paul wrote to the Ephesians about the shield of faith (Eph. 6:16), which protects believers from Satan's attacks. That shield was there for David. That same shield is there for believers of every generation. God's protection is around all believers to protect them from their faith becoming shipwreck. God protects them against temptation by calling to mind what they have learned in the Word so that it can be used to overcome the Wicked One (Ps. 119:11, 1 Jn 2:13). The truth of God's Word forms the basis of this protection.

The Lord Jesus Christ pleads on behalf of believers to keep them from suffering God's just wrath against their sin (Heb. 7:25). Jesus took the punishment that they deserve in their place in His suffering death on the cross on their behalf (Rom. 5:9, 1 Jn 2:2). Even though David suffered greatly, even though the Lord Jesus Christ suffered incomparably, the sufferings did not compare to the weight of **glory**, eternal heaven with the Trinity, that awaits all those that believe the gospel (Rom. 8:18).

When we are down, it is God who works to lift up our heads. The Father lifted up Jesus' head when Jesus rose from the dead (Rom. 10:9). The same power that raised Jesus from the dead quickens believers to strengthen them to walk by faith (Rom. 6:4). Even though David received some earthly glory while he was an earthly king, David knew that it was ultimately the sovereign purpose of God that permitted David to ascend to the throne. Any earthly glory that David received from others during his time in authority was received as a result of God's permission and God's work in His life. The Lord Jesus came to give glory to the Father and did so perfectly in His life, death, and resurrection (Jn

17:4-5). God lifted up the head of the psalmist when David came to authority over all Israel. God lifted up Jesus' head when He raised Jesus from the dead. God lifts up the heads of the saints He has reconciled. He raises them to seat them in heavenly places (Eph. 2:6). He raises them from spiritual death to spiritual resurrection. He raises them from sorrow in circumstances to trust in Himself even in normally sorrowful circumstances. Even though believers will suffer the death penalty as wages for their sin (Rom. 6:23), believers do have a resurrection to look forward to in which they will join the Lord and reign with Him (2 Tim. 2:12).

## Questions for self-reflection:

(1) If we more consistently reminded ourselves that, in Christ, we are shielded from God's wrath, how might that help us better handle our trials when our trials come?

(2) You already have the armor of God at your disposal if you are a believer. What can you do to make sure that it is working at its fullest potential for you?

(3) How does meditating on the glory of heaven help us face difficult circumstances?

**3:4. I cried to the Lord with my voice, And He heard me from His holy hill. Selah**

---

The psalmist was afflicted by some source. It was definitely some sort of thorn in the flesh (2 Cor. 12:7-10). Perhaps it was a physical enemy army. Perhaps it was a physical disease. Perhaps it was a spiritual enemy that persuaded others to collectively oppose the psalmist because of his faith in God. No matter who or what the enemy of the psalmist was, the psalmist went to the most appropriate place for help against his enemies. The psalmist went to the Lord.

The psalmist knew of the truths that had yet to be canonized when this psalm was written. He knew that effectual fervent prayers availed much (Jas 5:16). He knew that if he did not regard iniquity in his heart that the Lord would hear him (Ps. 66:18). He knew that today had sufficient trouble (Matt. 6:34). He knew that worrying about his future would not add anything to his life (Matt. 6:27). He knew that God would supply the grace that he would need to respond in a way so as to not harm his testimony before his enemies (Phil. 4:19). He was beginning to see that it was to be expected for God's people to suffer for following Him (Matt. 10:16-26, 2 Tim. 3:12, Jas 1:2-8, 1 Pet. 1:6-9).

Perhaps the only evidence for God that the enemies of the psalmist would ever see is the demonstration of patient trust by the psalmist in the face of adversity. He knew that when there was no earthly source on which to count for help with his adversity, the Lord would be there, as He is even when there is earthly help. After all, the earthly help is a means which is made accessible by the Lord's mercy (Heb. 4:16). The urgency of the psalmist's prayer is amplified by taking note of the fact that the psalmist **cried to the Lord**. He knew that the Lord had saved him spiritually. He knew that he had a righteousness that was not his own which had been imputed to his account, not because of anything good in him but solely because of the Lord's mercy (Phil. 3:9). He knew that God could answer his prayer in the way that he expected the Lord to if it pleased the Lord to do so. Even if the Lord did not answer the psalmist in the manner in which he wanted, the psalmist could trust in the omniscience of God that God knows what we need before we ask Him (Matt. 6:8) and that He will never leave or forsake His own (Deut. 31:6, Heb. 13:5).

Today, now that we have the complete revelation from God, first in the person of the Lord Jesus Christ (Heb. 1:2) and in the written record of the Scriptures (2 Tim. 3:16), we can trust God to provide what we need to face anything we face (Phil. 4:19). Because David approached the Lord with a believing heart and from a righteous life, David knew that the Lord **heard** him **from His holy hill.** Even though the Canon was not yet complete, David knew that His God was rich in mercy (Eph. 2:4). David knew that God would answer his prayers even if he did not always understand what the answer was. The Lord Jesus Christ had an even more intimate fellowship with the heavenly Father. Whereas David and you and I have sin that impedes our access to the throne of grace from time to time, since there was no sin in Christ (1 Pet. 2:22), He had perfect access and fellowship to the Father until the moment when the sins of humanity were placed on Him on the cross (Ps. 22:1, Matt. 27:46, Mk 15:34). God listens to His people's cries for mercy and help and He will come through for them in their time of need.

### Questions for self-reflection:

(1) What health problem do you have or does a loved one have that you can cry out to the Lord about?
(2) Who do you know that needs to come to the cross for salvation that you can cry to the Lord about?
(3) Is there anything in your life that might keep the Lord from hearing your prayers?

**3:5. I lay down and slept; I awoke, for the Lord sustained me.**

---

The psalmist was in trouble from every side. This is not uncommon for New Testament believers. David had been fighting against Absalom, his traitorous son (2 Cor. 4:8). Absalom was trying to kill David, his father. It is interesting to consider that the psalmist, despite the fierce trouble from his own son who sought his life (2 Sam. 15), David had enough peace in his soul such that he was able to sleep. After spending so much time fleeing from danger and wondering if he ever would find a place of safety with which to take comfort, the psalmist knew that he could not handle his trouble without help from the Lord.

The psalmist's own strength was woefully insufficient. He knew that the strength of the Lord was greatly sufficient. He knew the length of his life was sovereignly determined by the Lord and that worrying would not help his situation (Jb 14:5). Worrying would only hurt his situation (Phil. 4:6-7). He had to fully trust the God that he claimed had brought him to this point. At the end of the day, when the striving had ceased, and when it was time to **lay down and** sleep, the only way he would awake the next day, is if **the Lord sustained** him. David **awoke** because the Lord protected him in the face of his struggle. Even though David slept, he knew that the Lord never sleeps nor gets weary (Ps. 121:3-4).

The only way any of us can face what we have to face is because the Lord sustains us. The only way we can patiently face whatever adversity we face is if the Lord sustains us. When David awoke, he realized he was the recipient of divine mercy. God protected him the night before. God had granted him his next heartbeat, his next breath, and protection from his enemies.

If this pictures Christ, when Christ died on the cross for the sins of the world, He lay down and slept. He awoke when He rose from the dead. He rose from the dead because the Lord, His Father, sustained Him (1 Cor. 6:14).

For Christ's followers, we too have enemies. Some enemies are people. Some enemies are our own personal sins. Some enemies are the allurements of the world. All such enemies take us away from devotion to Christ. When we realize this, the Lord in restoring grace, reveals Himself to us again and the sweet fellowship can continue. Sometimes the earthly trial for the believer is so severe that the only thing that keeps them going is the sweet and sustaining presence of the Lord who promises to provide grace to handle everything that He allows to come into the life of His saints. Sometimes only the peace that passes understanding that Christ provides is all that the believer has to keep them enduring (Phil. 4:6-7). Sometimes, the believer is very much aware that their trial is so severe that the only reason they came out on the other side of the trial is that the Lord sustained them. The Lord uses His Word, His Holy Spirit, His ministering spirits to sustain His own.

**Questions for self-reflection:**

(1) Are you trying to handle your trouble on your own or are you experiencing help from the Lord?

(2) If you are experiencing help from the Lord, how is He helping you?

(3) When you wake up each day, do you thank the Lord for sustaining you?

(4) If you are not careful, what specifically do you encounter that has been known to reduce your sensitivity to the Lord?

**3:6. I will not be afraid of ten thousands of people Who have set themselves against me all around.**

---

Because the Lord sustained David, David knew that there was nothing for him to fear (Ps. 27:1). Even as perilous as David's surroundings became at times, whether it be Goliath threatening him (1 Sam. 17:31-58), or whether it be Absalom and his traitorous mob (2 Sam. 15), David knew that, no matter what, if God was for David, none could be against him (Rom. 8:31). Nothing could separate David from God's love (Rom. 8:38-39).

David had plenty of heroic episodes told in his biography, whether it was killing a lion, killing a bear, killing a giant, or fighting against his own son (1 Sam 17:34-36, 1 Sam. 17:31-58, 2 Sam. 18:1-8). All of these were distressing in their own ways. He could faithfully face these or any other such obstacle because David knew that the Lord would be there for him.

This could be a foretaste of when Judas and the many soldiers came to arrest Christ (John 18). At that moment, it was Christ who was **not afraid** of the multitudes who had **set themselves against** Him. In fact, the soldiers fell to the ground as if it was them who were afraid (Jn 18:6) David and Jesus could both say they were not afraid because of their trust in the Lord. They would survive for as long as the Lord willed for them to survive.

David was a type of the Lord Jesus Christ. Like David, Christ also escaped death because it was not yet His sovereignly determined time to die (Lk 4:30). When the time appointed by the Father arrived, the mob of Romans and Jews was successful at arresting Jesus (Jn 18:12), falsely accusing Jesus (Jn 18:30), holding a mock trial of Jesus (Jn 18-19), and crucifying Jesus (Jn 19:17-27). Christ had perfect trust of His Father's plan for His life, as His prayer life reveals (Jn 17) along with His obedience to His Father.

Christ had many people who had set themselves against Him all around. They cried out for His blood at His mock trial before Pilate (Matt. 27:22). Believers of every generation can also experience harsh persecutions from the enemies of the gospel (2 Tim. 3:12).

It can be tempting for a believer to take matters of vengeance into their own hands (Rom. 12:17-21). It can be difficult to wait for the Lord for Him to save (Prov. 20:22). It can be tempting to fret rather than trust. It can be trying to humble oneself to remember that but for the grace of God, they would not be able to see the truth for what it is and they would be in the group of those that now persecute them. Believers must be ready for the answer of the hope that is within them (1 Pet. 3:15), but if they get called upon to give that answer they better give it with humility and reverence for the Lord who gives them the words to say in moments of persecution (Matt. 10:19-20).

## Questions for self-reflection:

(1) Can we ever become so caught up in this life that we forget that if God is for us that we have nothing to truly fear?
(2) David knew the Lord would be there for him as he faced his obstacles. How does remembering that God is with us help us to face our obstacles?
(3) If you were to be treated harshly for the sake of the gospel, how would you prevent yourself from repaying evil for evil?

**3:7. Arise, O Lord; Save me, O my God! For You have struck all my enemies on the cheekbone; You have broken the teeth of the ungodly.**

---

The psalmist asks the **Lord** to **arise** because the action or lack of action (perceived by the psalmist) makes it seem to the psalmist as though the Lord was not around or perhaps even asleep. The truth is that God never gets weary or sleeps (Ps. 121:3-4). The psalmist thought that the Lord should have intervened to act on his behalf by now but was confused as to why He had not.

During His earthly ministry, Christ went to the Father frequently in times of prayer. Some of those times in prayer with the Father are recorded in the gospels (e.g., Mk 1:35, Lk 5:16). Christ is our example as New Testament believers (1 Pet. 2:21). As such, we know that He has given us access to grace (Rom. 5:2) and to the Father (Eph. 2:18) through His death on the cross for our sins (Jn 14:6, Eph. 3:12, Heb. 7:25, Heb. 10:19). When we cry out to God to save us from our sins and give us the free gift of everlasting life through Jesus Christ the Lord, He becomes our Father (Rom. 6:23, Matt. 6:9). Even when we sin against God, the blood of Christ cleanses us from sin (1 Jn 1:9) and allows us to continue to come boldly before the throne of grace (Heb. 4:16).

When we as His people sense that He could act in some way that we feel would be most beneficial to us and He does not act according to how we would like Him to act, it can feel to us at moments like those that God is slumbering somewhere and leaving us to fend for ourselves. We feel like He should **save** us and in moments such as these, we feel as if he is not going to save us.

David knew that God was his source of deliverance from his enemies. So, he knew that he needed to ask God for help. David knew that the Lord could help him overcome all his enemies like the saints from every generation know. David knew there had been times in the past, in the history of God's people, and even in David's own history when God had intervened on behalf of His people with decisive blows that enabled the cause of God to

---

continue to go forth (e.g., Exodus). In such times God had **struck** His **enemies** such that it was clear who He fought for (Exod. 14:25).

When the **ungodly** had their teeth broken by the Lord, it was as if their **teeth** were then unable to bite and devour their prey. It was tantamount to saying that God had rendered the enemies of His people ineffective. He had incapacitated them. In a sense, at the cross, Christ has broken the teeth of Satan and all his minions (Jn 16:11, Rom. 16:20, Gal. 1:4, Heb. 2:14-15, 1 Jn 2:13-14, 1 Jn 3:8). He has forever defeated death. The righteous will never be condemned (Rom. 8:1). Nothing can separate them from the love of God (Rom. 8:38-39).

## Questions for self-reflection:

(1) Have how you seen the Lord arise and save you in difficult circumstances in your life?
(2) If God were to ask you if you thought you came before His throne of grace for mercy and help in your time of need enough, how would you answer? Do you go to Him enough?
(3) Is it possible to go to God for anything too much?
(4) Have you ever felt like God was slumbering?
(5) How have you seen God demonstrate in your life that He is fighting for you?

**3:8. Salvation belongs to the Lord. Your blessing is upon Your people. Selah**

---

There is one **Lord** and God (Deut. 6:4). It is God who justifies (Rom. 8:33). Eternal salvation is God's work. Even though man does turn to God in repentant saving faith, man does not save himself. God saves repentant sinners. God is the God of **salvation** (Rev. 7:10). God is the author of salvation (Hebrews 5:9). The Lord Jesus Christ is the Author and Finisher of our faith (Heb. 12:2).

The Trinity planned for all the parts of redemption in eternity past. God the Father chose us before the foundation of the world (Eph. 1:4). God the Father and God the Son made a covenant to save sinful humanity. God the Father sent God the Son to earth to redeem humanity (Gal. 4:4). God the Son (1 Tim. 3:16) lived a perfect life (1 Pet. 2:22), died as humanity's sinless substitute (Isa. 53:5-6, 1 Pet. 2:24), was buried, and rose again (1 Cor. 15:4). Now, the Son ever lives to intercede for His own (Heb. 7:25). After the Son returned to His Father's right hand, He sent a Helper, the Holy Spirit, God the Spirit, to live inside all believers (Ezek. 36:27, Jn 14:16-18, Jn 16:13-14, Rom. 8:9, 11, 14, 1 Cor. 3:16, 1 Cor. 6:19, Gal. 4:6, 2 Tim. 1:14). The Spirit leads believers (Gal. 5:18, 1 Jn 2:27). It is His **blessing** to His **people**. The Holy Spirit comforts His people. The Holy Spirit reminds His people of His truth, the truth they have come to believe, that empowers their living.

When sinners are justified, when they receive saving faith, they are endowed with every spiritual blessing (Eph. 1:3). Those blessings will follow the saved throughout their lives, even when they find themselves in adverse circumstances. Those blessings will go with them into eternity.

**Questions for self-reflection:**

(1) Did you save yourself or did the Lord save you?

(2) If the Lord saved you, do you keep yourself saved or does the Lord keep you saved?

(3) If God's performance on our behalf saves us and keeps us saved, does that help us live with more or less anxiety?

(4) If our performance saves us and keeps us saved, does that help us live with more or less anxiety?

# Psalm 4

**4:1. Hear me when I call, O God of my righteousness! You have relieved me in my distress; Have mercy on me, and hear my prayer.**

The psalmist knew that, as a sinner, he had no **righteousness** of his own that he could hearken to in order to commend himself to **God**. Like the psalmist, we have no righteousness that we can cling to in order to get ourselves into heaven (Phil. 3:9, Ti 3:5). Our sin has stripped us of any supposed merit (Isaiah 64:6). We need the merits of another. We need the righteousness of another.

On the other hand, the God of the psalmist, the one and only true God, is the only perfectly righteous Being that has ever been or ever will be (Exod. 9:27, Deut. 32:4, 2 Chron. 12:6, Ezr 9:15, Neh. 9:8, Ps. 7:9, Ps. 11:7, Ps. 19:9, Ps. 35:24, Ps. 40:10, Ps. 48:10, Ps. 50:6, Ps. 71:19, Ps. 96:13, Ps. 97:2, Ps. 97:6, Ps. 99:4, Ps. 111:3, Ps. 116:5, Ps. 119:7, Ps. 119:142, Ps. 119:137, Ps. 129:4, Isa. 5:16, Isa. 41:10, Isa. 45:21, Isa. 46:13, Isa. 51:8, Jer. 9:23-24, Lam. 1:18, Dan. 9:14, Dan. 9:16, Mic. 6:5, Mic. 7:9, Zeph. 3:5, Zech. 8:8, Rom. 3:5, 2 Tim. 4:8). God alone is without darkness of any kind (1 Jn 1:5). He is the God of our righteousness. So, the righteousness received by Him is the only righteousness that will ever do.

Praise God for Jesus Christ the Righteous, the propitiation for our sins (1 Jn 2:1). By faith in Him, His righteousness is imputed to our account (Rom. 4:5) and our sin is imputed to His account (2 Cor. 5:21). We are set free (Rom. 5:1-2).

Jesus experienced **distress** in the form of persecution by the Jews and Romans, persecution that ultimately culminated in His death on the cross for our sins. Jesus experienced distress over His erring disciples as their weak faith was a frequent source of frustration for Him (e.g., Lk 9:54-55). As our perfect High Priest (Heb. 4:14-16), He was perfectly patient. He perfectly endured the shame that His trials, suffering, and death led to (Heb. 12:2). Jesus conquered that distress. His patient endurance through all of it is our example.

Saints experience distress when personal conviction over sin takes place. When saints feel the weight of their sins and how that separates them from God and from others it can lead to feelings of distress. Circumstances in life can cause **distress** for sinners. While we all prefer to have lives of ease, it oftentimes is the crucible of trials that promotes spiritual growth (Jas 1:2-8). It is when the earthly comforts have been stripped away from believers that oftentimes they reach the place where they realize that God is their only recourse. Then they remember that He is there for them and they experience fresh doses of mercies (Lam. 3:22-23).

There is no way for sinners to experience the relief they seek from the distress caused by sin unless sinners confess and forsake sin (Prov. 28:13). When sinners realize that God's wrath abides upon them as a result of their willful, sinful unbelief (Jn 3:36) and well as their sinful actions (Rom. 1:18-32), they realize that they are in need of God's mercy. This feeling of alienation from God (Col. 1:21), when it impresses the sinner, can lead to distress.

Fortunately, the same God that is angry at the wicked (Ps. 7:11) is the same God that is rich in **mercy** (Eph. 2:4) and He will **hear** the **prayer** of those who humbly **call** out to Him (Jas 5:16). When they do so, they can be **relieved** by Him. Fortunately, as ungodly as we are, Christ died for the ungodly (Rom. 5:6) to justify the ungodly (Rom. 4:5). He relieves us from the burden of our sins. For the sinning believer, only through confessing and forsaking sin can they alleviate the distress that sin causes (Prov. 28:13, 1 Jn 1:9).

It is apparent from the verses that follow in this psalm that the psalmist was acquainted with his personal sin. It is apparent that he understood that he could not claim inherent goodness. If the psalmist was going to be relieved in any way shape or form, the relief was going to be the agent of God's merciful care for him and not something he deserved. Because we are sinners by nature and by choice, children of wrath (Ephesians 2:3), as it were, any good we experience is a result of God's mercy and love.

Even the common grace that the wicked enjoys is an effort on God's behalf to get the wicked to consider the One to whom they owe everything. It is the mercy of God that ensures that sinners are not consumed immediately upon sinning (Lam. 3:22-23). It is the because of the mercy of God that sinners get to enjoy the blessings of this earthly life (Matt. 5:45). It is the mercy of God to reveal Himself to sinners who have rejected Him (Matt. 11:27-30, Gal. 4:4-5). It is merciful of God to make a way of salvation for sinners (Eph. 2:4). God could have let us sin our way into eternal hell. We would have had nobody to blame but ourselves. But God did not do that. He intervened so that we would not have to experience that fate. Since we cannot save ourselves, if we cry out to God to save us by putting repentant faith in the Lord Jesus Christ who lived a perfect life and died on the cross for our sins (Lk 13:3, Acts 2:38, Heb. 11:6), we receive the forgiveness that we so desperately need (Eph. 1:7) as well as all the heavenly blessings (Eph. 1:3-14).

**Questions for self-reflection:**

(1) What righteousness or merit of your own do you possess that you can ask God to consider?
(2) Have you received God's righteousness as a free gift of God through faith in the Lord Jesus Christ?
(3) Has your personal sin ever distressed you?
(4) Have the actions of others ever distressed you?
(5) In what ways have you experienced God's grace today?

**4:2. How long, O you sons of men, Will you turn my glory to shame? How long will you love worthlessness And seek falsehood? Selah**

---

The psalmist, David, came against those who oppressed him. That group was led by David's son, Absalom (2 Sam. 15:12). In Christ's time, the religious leaders of His day oppressed Him and came against Him (Matt. 12:9-14, Matt. 22:15-22, Matt. 22:34-46, Mk 8:11-12, Mk 10:2-9, Mk 12:13-17, Mk 12:28-34, Lk 7:39-40, Lk 20:20-26, Jn 8:3-11). In every generation since Christ's first coming, ungodly worldly leaders have oppressed and persecuted God's people (Matt. 5:10-12, Acts 4, Acts 5, Acts 7, Acts 9, Acts 12, Acts 13, Acts 14:7, Acts 18:8-22, Acts 16, Acts 17:1-12, Acts 17:13-34, Acts 18, Acts 19, Acts 21-23, 2 Tim. 3:12). They will continue to do so and it will get worse up until Christ returns (Matt. 24:9-12).

The psalmist was ridiculed for following the Lord. The Lord was David's **glory**. David's oppressors made God, David's glory, seem like **shame**. They ridiculed David for placing his faith in a God they could not see. Since David was allowed to suffer, it appeared to David's enemies that God did not care about David or that God was not really there for David. Since David endured such hardship in return for following God, David's enemies took that to mean that God must not be that great if He were to allow His supporters to suffer so much. Not only that, Absalom's supporters came against David to set up Absalom in David's place.

In Christ's time, the Jews set out to overthrow Christ's influence with the people as it was He who was threatening their control and influence (Jn 11:48). Since Christ returned to heaven (Acts 1:9-11), Satan's minions have sought to snuff out Christianity in every generation. They despise God's authority (2 Pet. 2:10) and want nothing of the easy yoke and light burden that comes with being a child of God (Matt. 11:27-30). An easy yoke is too much for them. A light burden is too oppressive to them. Following anyone or anything other than the one true God is **worthlessness**, so spending one's time on such pursuits is a worthless waste of time.

Instead of seeking truth in the God of truth, such oppressors sought falsehood then and **seek falsehood** now by having something other than the one true God in which to put confidence. False doctrine entered into the world in the Garden of Eden when Satan twisted God's Word, lied to Eve, and Adam and Eve sinned (Genesis 3). Since then, everyone has followed in their footsteps (Romans 3:9). The problem with the strategy of making something other than God more important than God is that the God of the universe is jealous (Exod. 20:5, Exod. 34:14, Deut. 4:24, Deut. 5:9, Deut. 6:15, Deut. 32:16, Deut. 32:21, Josh. 24:19, Ezek. 36:5-6, Ezek. 39:25, Nah. 1:2, 2 Cor. 11:2) and will not permit people to obtain righteousness from anyone or anything else. His enemies, who try to dethrone Him and His people (Psalm 2), while they may appear to succeed temporarily in appearing to mitigate the spreading Kingdom of God, will ultimately be judged (1 Cor. 15:26-27). Today, people seek all sorts of alternative ways for eternal bliss to their own detriment. People are led astray into false doctrine and practices (2 Tim. 4:3). Their end will be a sad one (2 Pet. 2).

**Questions for self-reflection:**

(1) If someone very close to you turned their back on you and came against you, whether it was because of your faith in God or some other reason, how would you feel?

(2) Look up a story of persecutions or martyrdoms of Christians in some place other than where you live. How do you think those Christians endure that?

(3) If you had to endure such persecution or threats to your personal safety, how would you handle that?

(4) If others were to look at your life, would others surmise that you have submitted yourself to God's authority? Why or why not?

(5) If someone were to look at how you spend the bulk of your recreational time, would they surmise that God is your supreme desire? Why or why not?

**4:3. But know that the Lord has set apart for Himself him who is godly; The Lord will hear when I call to Him.**

---

The psalmist writes to those that oppress him. Believers in any generation can trust the truth of what follows. God **set apart** David **for Himself** to rule Israel. God set apart David for a position of prominence. God set apart the Lord Jesus Christ to be the Messiah (Jn 17:19).

God has **set apart** all believers from every generation to live separately from the unbelieving world and to inherit eternal life and the Kingdom (Heb. 10:10). He has set apart the godly from the people of the world who oppose God. He has set apart the godly to bear fruit (Jn 15:1-8), to suffer persecution (2 Tim. 3:12), to be illuminated by the Holy Spirit (1 Cor. 2:12), to have renewed minds (Rom. 12:2), to walk humbly before Him (Mic. 6:8), to walk in the light (Jn 8:12, 1 Jn 1:7), to be holy (Exod. 19:6, Exod. 22:31, Lev. 11:44-45, Lev. 19:2, Lev. 20:26) to predestination (Rom. 8:29, Eph. 1:5), to adoption (Eph. 1:5), to acceptance in the beloved (Eph. 1:6), to peace with God (Rom. 5:1, Eph. 2:14), to redemption (Eph. 1:7, Col. 1:14), to the riches of His grace (Eph. 1:7), to wisdom (Eph. 1:8), to prudence (Eph. 1:8), to the knowledge of the mystery of His will (Eph. 1:9), to an inheritance (Eph. 1:11, Eph. 1:14, 1 Pet. 1:4), and to a place prepared for them (Jn 14:2-3).

Believers have been set apart, or sanctified, to this and did nothing to earn this. It is all of grace. People who are set apart like this are not set apart because they are somehow better than unbelievers. No. Both unbelievers and believers are sinful (Rom. 3:9). Believers have responded with saving faith to God's grace which has appeared to everyone (Ti 2:11), whereas unbelievers have not responded with saving faith to the same grace. The god of this age has blinded them (Matt. 13:4, Matt. 13:19, 2 Cor. 4:4) and has stolen the Word from them.

All those who have been set apart by God for a relationship with Him, those who are godly, will be with Him in eternity (Jn 3:16). Such redeemed saints can be confident that because they call upon the Lord with faith that He will hear when they **call to Him** (1 Jn 5:14). He will act on their behalf.

## Questions for self-reflection:

(1) When you think about all the ways in which you have been set apart by God, how does that make you react?

(2) What did you do to earn your set apart status?

(3) When you think about your set apart status, how does that make you feel when you think about unbelievers?

**4:4. Be angry, and do not sin. Meditate within your heart on your bed, and be still. Selah**

---

Anger without a righteous reason behind it is sinful anger. Anger that arises in saints should be for righteous, not selfish reasons. Anger that is frequently practiced and is infrequently interrupted is sinful anger. Anger that arises out of honor for God and is properly expressed toward those in opposition to Him with self-control is anger that gives God glory and is **not sin**. Righteous anger gets **angry** at the same things that God gets angry at. Selfish anger does not. Such righteous anger is directed at the honor and glory of God that is neglected in the commission of sinful acts.

Selfish anger is more concerned with self than with others. Selfish anger results when we get angry when the actions or inactions of others inconvenience us in some way. When the anger that we experience has more to do with the action or inaction of the person and less to do with the God that is angry at sin, then the anger is unrighteous anger. It is sinful to get angry without a cause, as Jesus taught (Matt. 5:22).

It is possible to have anger well up in the soul and have it stay in the soul and not come out in sinful acts implemented on others. When this anger is felt, when it does not lead to outbursts of wrath (Gal. 5:20), when it does not lead to fleshly responses (Rom. 8:1-13), that is not sinful anger.

When we have quiet, at such a time when we can **meditate**, be it in **bed** or elsewhere, where we can **be still**, we can think about the day's thoughts and actions and see what sins need confessing so that we can make sure we have done our part to ensure that we have done all we know to do to make whatever wrongs we have committed against the Lord and/or others right once again (Rom. 12:18, Jas 5:16, 1 Jn 1:9), as it is paramount to live peaceably as much as we can.

We might become angry at the inactions or actions of others. Rather than rashly react, we can take our time, meditate on our beds, and make sure that our responses to the parties that have led to us getting angry are done in a controlled, God-honoring manner. Outbursts of wrath do not commend God's righteousness to a generation that so badly needs it (Jas 1:20). See Ephesians 4:26 where Paul quotes this verse.

Part of taking every thought captive to the obedience of Christ (2 Cor. 10:5) is ensuring that, regardless of the actions or inactions of others, our responses to those actions or inactions are not millstones that inhibit others from accepting the truth of the gospel (Matt. 18:6). Let the message of Christ's death the cross for sinners be the stumbling block to sinners (1 Cor. 1:23) and not the fleshly actions committed by His sheep.

## Questions for self-reflection:

(1) What is the difference between righteous and unrighteous anger?
(2) How often is our anger really and truly what God would consider righteous anger?
(3) How can you be angry and not sin?
(4) When you react to something that makes you angry, are you helping someone see Christ, or keeping someone from seeing Christ?

**4:5. Offer the sacrifices of righteousness, And put your trust in the Lord.**

---

The only **sacrifices** that are valid are those done by God's prescribed methods. The sacrifices that Israel was required to offer were recorded in the Law. A key feature was that they were to be without blemish (Lev. 1:3, Lev. 1:10, Lev. 3:1, Lev. 3:6, Lev. 4:3, Lev. 4:28, Lev. 4:32, Lev. 5:18, Lev. 6:6). They were to be offered with faith, with a full confidence that God would accept their faithfulness. If they were not fully trusting in the Lord for honoring their attempt to do what He had asked, there would be no basis for which they could hope that God would receive what they offered to Him.

The New Testament believer must come before God through faith in the Lord Jesus Christ. Any supposed sacrifice, including those for giving or worship, if not done with hearts full of faith and devotion to the Lord, are sinfully brought and should be avoided. In the Old Testament, there were plenty of examples of people offering improper sacrifices. God came against people who sacrificed like this and He came against them harshly. Old Testament sacrifices had to be without blemish because they were pictures of the final sacrifice of the Lord Jesus Christ, the spotless Lamb of God (Jn 1:29, Heb. 10:14).

Sacrifices were brought improperly if there was not appropriate faith in the hearts of those who brought the sacrifices (Heb. 11:6). God abhorred such sacrifices in which people honored Him with their lips but their hearts were far from Him (Isa. 29:13, Matt. 15:8). God also wants sacrifices of a broken and a contrite heart (Ps. 51:17). He wants people who have proper attitudes toward Him, toward their own sin as well as the sin in the world in which we live. He wants us to be wholly devoted to Him. The believer has Christ's **righteousness** imputed to His account (Rom. 3:21-22, Rom. 4:5, 2 Cor. 5:21). So, any sacrifice of true worship, for the New Testament believer, is a sacrifice of righteousness.

For our eternal well-being, **trust** must be **in the Lord**. Trust must not be in the government, friends or family, not even in religion. It can be tempting to put trust in ourselves, belonging to a church or in organized religion or in family or in friends. People have improperly trusted all sorts of people or things since the Garden of Eden. As important as some of those things can be, as much as some of those things can be used by God as a means of grace in the life of a believer, they are not to be trusted in for salvation (Ps. 146:3). Only Christ is sufficient for salvation (Heb. 11:6).

## Questions for self-reflection:

(1) Are your 'sacrifices' of worship offered from a heart full of faith?
(2) If we had to offer sacrifices repeatedly like they did in the Old Testament, how stressed would you be having to look for just the right one?
(3) How relieved are you to know that bringing our own sacrifices into God's presence now is no longer necessary thanks to the finished work of Christ on our behalf? Are you truly resting in His finished work?
(4) When was the last time you were broken and contrite over your sins?

**4:6. There are many who say, "Who will show us any good?" Lord, lift up the light of Your countenance upon us.**

---

Because David was being sought by his own son, Absalom, there was a shortage of people he could readily turn to for earthly help. For us, **many** fellow humans with a sinful nature like we have will likewise let us down just like we will let them down. They are sinful like we are sinful. The things we put our hope in from this world that the Lord, in His kindness towards us, permits us to enjoy, will either break or will become mundane as we get bored of them. The more we put our hope in the people or the things of this world, the more disappointed we will become. None of those things is perfect. Each of those things is subject to corruption (Rom. 8:20-21).

In response to his adversity, David beseeches the **Lord** to look on him. He asks for God's gracious presence to make an obvious appearance. He asks to be reminded of the truth of who God is and how He has come through for David (and others) up to this point (Rom. 15:4). David could look back if he could look through the forest of his circumstances to see the trees that God planted in his life (Gen. 50:20, Rom. 8:28). God's love, favor, and grace had been shown in the past and were being exhibited presently.

Whenever we go through unpleasant circumstances, it can be easy to focus on the bad things that happen to us. God would rather that we focus on who He is and the inheritance (Eph. 1:11, 1 Pet. 1:4) that He has prepared for those whose hope is in Him. If our hope is in Him, His **countenance** is **upon us**. When we realize that and are intentional about seeking His countenance, He shines it on us with His light. When we see life through the lens of His countenance upon us, we will know that it will be the Lord **who will show us any good.**

When the Lord Jesus Christ came, there were few that showed Him any good. It appeared that many only wanted Him for His miracles (Jn 6:26-27). They did not want to worship Him for who He is. It was evident that the countenance of the Father was on Christ as Christ was able to finish the mission He came to do (Jn 17:4).

As believers in any generation are strengthened with His might in the inner man (Eph. 3:16), they too can accomplish anything that is God's will for them to accomplish (Phil. 4:13). When the riches of God's grace rest on a believer, the light of His countenance will be evident for others to see as that believer's life will be one of good works and fruits of the Spirit (Matt. 5:16, Gal. 5:22-24, Eph. 2:10). When His countenance is on His people, they can better commend the beauty of the gospel to the lost and dying world that desperately needs to see it.

**Questions for self-reflection:**

(1) Have you ever needed help but didn't know who to ask for help?

(2) Have you ever had something of yours that you cared deeply about get broken?

(3) Does God ever break His promises?

(4) If the things we care deeply about can easily break, and God cares deeply enough about us to save us, how can we show God that He is more important to us than our things?

(5) How can you experience more of the Lord's countenance upon you?

(6) Do you value your relationship with the Lord more because of what He can do for you or because of who He is?

(7) How does your life demonstrate that God's countenance is upon you?

**4:7. You have put gladness in my heart, More than in the season that their grain and wine increased.**

When the Lord has heard our cry to Him for the righteousness that He must mercifully impute to us because we could never earn it on our own (4:1), He **puts gladness in** our **hearts** because He has forgiven us (Eph. 1:7, Col. 1:14). The punishment that had been reserved for us has instead been applied to the account of Christ in a vicarious atonement (Isa. 53:4-7, 1 Pet. 2:24). When might in the inner man (Eph. 3:16), they too can accomplish have caused and has granted us pardon, this puts gladness in our hearts (4:1). When the Lord who is rich in mercy (Eph. 2:4) shows us the great mercy that has been given to them who were undeserving of such mercy, He puts gladness in our hearts (4:1). When we come before the throne of grace for mercy and help in time of need (Heb. 4:16), when we call upon the Lord in distress, and the Lord answers us (Psalm 18:6), hears our prayers (4:1), and puts us in a high place, He puts gladness in our hearts.

When the Lord executes righteous retribution against those who love worthlessness and seek falsehood (4:2) and comes to the rescue of His spiritual offspring, it puts gladness in our hearts. When the righteous understand that the Lord has set them apart to inherit all the heavenly blessings (4:3), it puts gladness in the hearts of the saints. When believers offer their bodies as living sacrifices (Rom. 12:2) as sacrifices of righteousness to the One who freely gave them a righteousness that is not their own when they put their trust in the Lord (4:5), it puts gladness in their hearts.

When the Lord lets His countenance shine upon us, when the Lord shows us His goodness, when we are sensitive to the Lord's presence, no matter what circumstances we find ourselves in, we can find gladness in our hearts because we have made the Lord our hope (4:6). Our hope, when placed correctly in the Lord who loved us and gave Himself for us (Eph. 5:2), can bring us more joy than the happiness our enemies experience in their material prosperity. God wants us to hope in Him, not in what He has allowed us to enjoy.

Those who have their hope directed someplace other than in the Lord, tend to get discouraged and frustrated without remedy when they do not get their way because they look to the world to provide lasting peace and contentment when only God can provide that. That is the sin of idolatry whenever we substitute anything and ask that the thing provide what only God can provide (Rom. 1:25). Unfortunately, we also often get misplaced priorities. We are prone focus on the gift rather than the Giver of every good and perfect gift (Jas 1:17).

When believers think about the permanence of their spiritual condition rather than the passing of their circumstances (Rom. 8:30, Phil. 1:6), that can put gladness in our hearts as well. Even if our enemies prosper while we suffer (Jer. 12:1), we can trust that God will right all wrongs and will avenge us in His timing. As the emissaries of Satan seemingly have their way alongside the righteous who suffer, believers like the psalmist know that the worst that can happen to them is that they take their final breath here on earth and are immediately in the Lord's presence (2 Cor. 5:8).

**Questions for self-reflection:**

(1)  In what ways has the Lord put gladness in your heart?

(2)  In what or in whom is your hope placed?

**4:8. I will both lie down in peace, and sleep; For You alone, O Lord, make me dwell in safety.**

The psalmist, despite his unpleasant circumstances, could rest easy because he knew that, no matter what happened to him in life on this earth, nothing could take away the eternal inheritance that awaited him in the next life in heaven (Rom. 8:38-39). He knew that as long as the Lord watched over him, nothing would befall him that was outside of God's permission (Matt. 10:29). God's presence and power sustained him (Acts 17:28). God allowed his next breath. God permitted his enemies failure or success. God was His protector. There was nothing to be afraid of because his future was ultimately secure by the Lord. He could **lie down and sleep in peace**. He could **dwell in safety** for as long as the Lord permitted him to do so (Ps. 56:11, Ps. 118:6, Prov. 29:25, Matt. 10:28, Heb. 13:6).

**Question for self-reflection:**

(1) Can the people who see you the most who know you the best tell by watching how you live that the Lord makes you dwell in safety?

# Psalm 5

**5:1. Give ear to my words, O Lord, Consider my meditation.**

The psalmist, David, called out to the Lord. David wanted the Lord to hear him, to **give** His holy **ear to** his **words**, specifically when he prayed. When David was thinking about the Lord, David wanted the Lord to be thinking about him. Prayers to God should not be mere rehearsed words (Matt. 6:7), but should flow out of an earnest seeking of the Lord. Someone who prays to God should not look to others to emulate what they do. They are responsible for their own unique prayers as incense to the throne room. The Holy Spirit who leads believers into all truth (Jn 16:13) should be trusted to lead the prayers of believers as they seek God's intervention and as they extol God for who He is (Rom. 8:26-27). The psalmist wanted God to hear him as the psalmist hears those who talk to him. He knew that God was higher than him and God would need to humble Himself in order to hear anyone's prayers. David's **meditation** came before his prayer. The psalmist had to think it before it came out of his mouth. As every thought is to be taken captive to the obedience of Christ, every thought uttered in prayer should likewise be taken into the same captivity (2 Cor. 10:5).

**Questions for self-reflection:**

(1) How have you sought the Lord today?
(2) As you have drawn near to God, have you sensed God draw near to you?
(3) Have you ever prayed the Scripture back to God? How might that change your prayers if you did?

**5:2. Give heed to the voice of my cry, My King and my God, For to You I will pray.**

---

David knew that the Lord was there for Him. He had shown Himself to be reliable in the past. David asks the Lord to continue to be there for Him. In order to receive the benefits one receives from entering the Lord's presence, the psalmist knew that he had to avail himself to the resources of the Lord repeatedly, which are received when we go to Him in prayer. He knew that the Lord hears when we call out to Him in faith (Ps. 34:17). Like the Lord Jesus Christ, David had enemies that caused living for the Lord to be more challenging.

David was king in Israel. Christ The Lord is **King** of Kings (Rev. 17:14, Rev. 19:16). David ruled over the kingdom that God had entrusted to his care (1 Sam. 16). Christ rules over everyone and everything (Heb. 2:8). This is why Christ is King of kings and Lord of lords. The Lord of lords became Lord to David when David humbled himself and put saving faith into the Lord. It was then that God became King to David.

Christ will always be Lord to everyone. However, Jesus becomes Lord to individual sinners in the sinner's awareness when sinners turn from sin and trust Christ alone to save them (Heb. 11:6). Christ becomes the covenant God to the sinner when the sinner embraces Him as Savior and Lord even though, in the ultimate sense, they are already accountable to Him even if they have not yet bowed the knee to Him (Phil. 2:10).

Christ went to the Father in prayer regularly (Matt. 11:25-27, Matt. 26:36-46, Mk 14:32-42, Lk 3:21, Lk 6:12, Lk 22:39-46, Jn 11:41, Jn 17). Even as He hung on the cross, He interceded before those who killed Him (Matt. 27:46, Lk 23:34). Christ knew that His Father would heed His cry because they sought the glory of each other (Jn 17:1-5). Believers in any generation can trust the promise that if we ask anything of God with hearts of authentic faith, the Lord will also give heed to the voice of our cries as well (1 Jn 5:14). The fact that God hears our prayers is one benefit (there are many benefits) in believing that God does not change (Num. 23:19, Mal.

3:6, Jas 1:17), that Jesus Christ is the same now as He always has been (Heb. 13:8).

If God came through for people who came before us, we can trust Him to come through for us now in our present circumstances (Rom. 15:4, 1 Cor. 10:1-11). The Lord reigns over all those who reign (Dan. 2:21). Heaven is His throne. Earth is His footstool (Isa. 66:1). As king, David knew that he was ultimately accountable to the Lord. David knew that the Lord ultimately ruled his life. He acknowledged that divine authority under which he lived in his prayer. David knew that God had lavished His grace upon him. As a recipient of that grace, David knew that he owed **God** everything, including his very life. The Lord was the only One worth praying to. Everyone and everything else were in subservience to the Lord. David acknowledged that.

## Questions for self-reflection:

(1) Is Christ your true King?

(2) Can others tell Christ is your true King?

(3) Christ has allowed you to have a sphere of influence. How have you handled that stewardship?

(4) In what ways do you still sense your accountability to God?

**5:3. My voice You shall hear in the morning, O Lord; In the morning I will direct it to You, And I will look up.**

---

The **morning** is an appropriate time to seek the Lord. After a night's sleep, it is suitable to thank God for His protection from the night before (Ps. 32:7). It is correct to thank the Lord for giving life and breath and allowing the body to function to keep His people alive (Ps. 119:116). It is proper to thank the Lord for providing all that will be needed for the upcoming day's events (2 Pet 1:3). It is good to remember that the Lord upholds us by the Word of His power, so if we can endure to the end of the day, that owes to the Lord's sustaining grace upon us (Heb. 1:3). All these are a few good reasons to **direct to** the Lord our thoughts and **look up** to Him who condescends to look down upon us (Ps. 53:2).

An appropriate time to consider God's sovereignty over these areas of our life is the morning, as it is in the morning when we first open our eyes that we notice that the Lord protected us, so we survived the night (Ps. 3:5). When we arise in the shelter where we slumbered the previous night, we recognize that the Lord protected us (Isa. 4:6). When we notice that the things that we protect in our homes are still intact even after we slumbered, we appreciate that the Lord protected us from those who might otherwise cause us harm (Jb 1:10, Lk 11:21).

In addition to considering how God protected us during the night, the morning is also an appropriate time to consider how God can work on our behalf in the upcoming day (Num. 14:14, Ps. 42:8, Ps. 78:14). He can permit us to travel safely to our destination, whether at school, work, or both. He can allow or cause us to cross paths with others with whom we need to be prepared to interact. He can allow or cause our endeavors to be successful today. We must trust Him fully. We need to go to the Lord to remember that our presence may be the only Christian presence someone may see today or ever, so we should walk worthy of our callings and represent our Lord well (Eph. 4:1). We should remember that no matter what we face during the day's events, the Lord provides sufficient grace to meet our every need (Phil.

4:19). The psalmist has such strong faith that it causes him to look up, expecting a timely answer to his prayers. He anticipates that God knows his needs before he asks (Matt. 6:8). He trusts that God will answer Him because he has not regarded iniquity in his heart (Ps. 66:18). The answer to all prayers must come from the throne of grace, located up in heaven (Heb. 4:16). In heaven, angels and saints who have gone before us see God face to face. They know His perfections in ways we do not because we are still packaged in the sinful flesh that still wars with the Spirit (Gal. 5:17). In heaven, no such war exists. Those in heaven see God as He is (1 Jn 3:2) and know more certainly how He works on behalf of His people (Matt. 5:8, Rom. 8:28-30).

**Questions for self-reflection:**

(1) In the morning, when you wake up, how often do you think to thank God for preserving you the previous night?
(2) Other than at mealtimes, when do you stop throughout your day, even if it is just for a few seconds, and direct your thoughts to God?
(3) How often do you thank God for providing even the most mundane things for life?
(4) Before the busyness of the day ensues, do we pray for God to go before us and prepare the way for us?
(5) If you knew that yours was the only gospel presence someone would see today, how would that change how you acted toward them?
(6) How often do you think about heaven?
(7) Since, as a believer, heaven is your final destination, do you think you can prepare better now for the day when it is your turn to go there finally? If so, how?

**5:4. For You are not a God who takes pleasure in wickedness, Nor shall evil dwell with You.**

---

**God** is holy (Rev. 4:8). We are unholy (2 Tim. 3:2). His holy nature and our unholy nature are like oil and water; they do not mix. Because God is holy, He cannot have our unholy sin in His presence (Hab. 1:13). **Evil, our evil, cannot dwell with** Him. Sin is the transgression of His law (1 Jn 3:4). That is why when we come before Him in prayer in this life, we must confess our sins (1 Jn 1:9) because He will not hear us if we regard iniquity in our hearts (Ps. 66:18).

God permits people to sin. He would be just and right to kill a sinner upon the commission of any of their multitude of sins. However, since God is rich in mercy (Eph. 2:4) and does not wish for any to perish but for all to come to repentance (2 Pet. 3:9), He allows man to make his choice and either submit to God or submit to the devil (Jas 4:6-8). If a sinner rejects God, they accept the devil. If a sinner resists the devil, they submit to God. There is no middle ground.

God does not **take pleasure in wickedness**. Since God sustains us and gives us our next breath such that we can continue living and committing sin, one can argue that, while God does not take pleasure in the wickedness of our sin, He does permit it to continue to happen by continuing to let us live despite our many sins (Rom. 2:4). Divine permission of sin could be a way that God demonstrates the volume of His grace. When he justifies the ungodly (Rom. 4:5) and gives them eternal life, despite their sins, they receive the gift of God instead of the wages their sin earned (Rom. 6:23).

Our sin is wickedness and separates us from Him (Isa. 64:6). It is an affront to Him. It keeps the lost, those who reject God's mercy, out of heaven. God's reaction to the sin of the lost does not bother the lost while they are on earth. They do not like to retain God in their knowledge (Rom. 1:28). Since they reject God by their willful continuation in sin (Heb. 10:26-31), God rejects them and lets them pursue their sinfulness. The lost person should not presume on God's grace and assume He can just overlook their sins because God is patient and loving. God cannot do that. There must be a reckoning (Acts 17:30-31, Rom. 2:6, 2 Thess 1:7-9). For the Christian, Christ became their substitute (1 Pet. 2:24). Non-Christians assume their own penalty. Even Christians who sin affect their relationship with God. Sin expelled Adam and Eve from the Garden (Gen. 3). Sin led to the first murder (Gen. 4). Sin led to God destroying most of all humanity except for Noah and his family in a global flood (Gen. 7).

God does not enjoy anyone's death (Ezek. 18:23, Ezek. 18:32). Since we are so sinful and evil, God had to deal with our sin somehow since He loves us so much (Rom. 5:8). So, to deal with the evil of our sin and to show us His love for us, God sent Jesus to die as our substitute to satisfy His just wrath against our sin and show us His love (Rom. 5:9, Eph. 2:3, Rom. 5:8, Jn 3:16). For all repentant sinners, God looks on His sinless Son and passes over our sin. So, He can judge our sin by judging Christ instead of us. He is able, then, to permit us to enter heaven because of His love for us and not compromise His justice.

## Questions for self-reflection:

(1) Have you thanked God for His mercy today?
(2) Does your lifestyle demonstrate that you have submitted to God or to the devil?
(3) Does your lifestyle convey the gratitude to God that should be fitting for a believer?
(4) When you witness the lost who do not like to retain God in their knowledge, does your heart break for them, or are you angry because of how their sin affects you?
(5) When you contemplate how God commended His love toward you, does that motivate you to be more evangelistic?

**5:5. The boastful shall not stand in Your sight; You hate all workers of iniquity.**

---

Because they are lost, the **boastful** are prideful. Therefore, God resists them (Jas 4:6). Rather than humble themselves before God's mighty hand that He might exalt them (1 Pet. 5:6), they exalt themselves. As long as they continue to exalt themselves, the Lord will never accept them. These are wicked. They oppose God with their thoughts, words, and actions. Even if they seem morally upright on the outside, such people fail to do all that they do to glorify God (1 Cor. 10:31, Col. 3:17). This makes them boastful.

Not until the boastful humble themselves will they be accepted by the Lord (1 Pet. 5:6). Not until they see themselves as men or women with unclean lips (Isa. 6:5) will they see the need to turn from sin and turn to God for the righteousness they so desperately need (Rom. 4:5, 1 Cor. 6:9). Instead, they lean on their own fallible understanding because they are too prideful to trust in the infallible Lord (Prov. 3:5-6). They think more of themselves than they should (Phil. 2:3-4). They think they know better than those who know the Lord and alienate themselves from others not as wise as they think they are (1 Cor. 1:20-31).

God rejects such prideful people. God resists the proud but gives grace to the humble (Jas 4:6). On the day of judgment, the prideful will be consumed in God's righteous judgments. These cannot expect to receive God's blessings because they have not submitted themselves to Him (Rom. 10:3). Because of their supposed wisdom or other worldly achievements, they might ignorantly suppose that God (if He were even real) would gain much by adding them to His 'team.' This is selfish foolishness. Instead of arguing against Him and suppressing the truth in an unrighteous manner (Rom. 1:18), they need to become humble and contrite (Ps. 51:17). They need to humble themselves so God can exalt them rather than exalting themselves for God to humble them (Matt. 23:12).

Without the requisite humility and brokenness over sin, these will not stand in the sight of the Lord (Ps. 1:5). Instead, they will abide under His wrath and be cast into the lake which burns with fire and brimstone (Rev. 21:8). Those who habitually **work iniquity**, who commit it without regard for God's commands against it, those not restrained by the Holy Spirit's influence against it are those who are objects of God's wrath (Matt. 7:21-23). There may be some inside the church like this. There will be several outside the church who are like this. God hates them because they **hate** Him. He has a continued aversion toward them because they sin against Him. He can love the same people in the sense that Christ died for them since Christ died for all (2 Cor. 5:14-15). However, as long as they do not embrace Christ, His wrath will abide upon them (Jn 3:36). God exhibits hatred toward such workers of iniquity because they fail to accept the provision God has made for their souls.

Everyone is a worker of iniquity. Apart from divine influence, men will love their sin and not pursue righteousness imputed to those with faith in Christ and flee from the wrath to come. Workers of iniquity become slaves to sin rather than slaves to righteousness (Rom. 6:11-14). There is no struggle between the Spirit and the flesh because the Spirit is not present in them to wage war with the flesh (Gal. 5:17).

Perhaps most frightening of all is not that there are such workers of iniquity found in the world outside of the corporate assembly, but there are also such workers of iniquity in local congregations. They creep in unawares and lead the undiscerning astray from the truth (Jude 4). These workers of iniquity abide under the wrath of God due to their unbelief. Barring repentance and belief in the gospel, they will spend all eternity in the lake which burns with fire and brimstone under the wrath of God.

**Questions for self-reflection:**

(1) Does your life resemble a boastful person or a humble person more?

(2) In conversing with people who cross your path, even if they do not mention God or Jesus, could you tell the difference between the boastful and prideful and the humble? How?

(3) As a believer, how do you react internally to them when you converse with a boastful person? Do you find their evident pride to be bothersome?

(4) How can you cultivate more humility in your own life?

(5) How does it make you feel to know that God can hate anyone?

(6) Do you know anyone who has overtly rejected the gospel? While God loves them, He is also angry at them and expresses His hatred for them in verses like this. Can you pray for those outside of the gospel of grace so they may become objects of His love? Can you share the gospel with them?

**5:6. You shall destroy those who speak falsehood; The Lord abhors the bloodthirsty and deceitful man.**

---

Those who speak against true religion are **those who speak falsehood** in this passage. There are two types of religion. One is the worship of the true God, the God of the Bible (Matt. 7:14). The other religion consists of everything else (Matt. 7:13). It comes in all shapes and sizes. Some of it attaches itself to Christianity. Some of it does not. Anything lacking sufficient biblical support falls under the category of false religion.

Religion involves belief. Even belief in no deity is a form of religion. It is a form of religion because it is a system of beliefs that inform actions. Compared to biblical Christianity, any religious system that is not biblical Christianity is a falsehood because biblical Christianity has Christ as its source (Matt. 16:17-18, 1 Cor. 3:11, Eph. 2:20). All other systems have Satan as its source because everything else is lies, and Satan is the father of lies (Jn 8:44).

Biblical Christianity submits to the authority of Scripture because Scripture is the direct revelation by God through the pen of man (2 Tim. 3:16, 2 Pet. 1:20). Everything else has humanity for its final authority. Anything with humanity serving as its authority is plagued by sin because humanity consists of men and women who, at their cores, are sinners by nature and by choice. Since there is no sin in God (1 Jn 1:5), true religion found in God's Word will lead to imputed righteousness (Rom. 4:5) that is lived out in a lifestyle of practical righteousness (1 Jn 2:29). Such true religion places itself under the truth of God revealed in the Person of the Lord Jesus Christ and the Scriptures (John 1:18). This absolute truth overthrows everything else which amounts to falsehood. Adherents to the falsehood of these other religions will be destroyed for their sin, including but not limited to rejection of the one true God.

This falsehood has its roots in the Garden of Eden when Satan, the Father of lies, told the first lie to the first woman, Eve, and then she told her husband, and together they plunged humanity into sinfulness that will not be corrected until Christ returns

---

(Gen. 3). Biblical Christianity affirms the deity (Phil.2:6), sonship (Rom. 1:4), and Messiahship of the Lord Jesus Christ (Jn 4:25-26). Anything that denies that is something that speaks falsehood (2 Jn 1:9). Adherents to this falsehood follow the devil, even if they do not acknowledge that he exists (Gal. 1:8). All those who speak falsehood will have their part in the lake which burns with fire and brimstone (Rev. 21:8).

Cain was the first **bloodthirsty and deceitful man** (Gen. 4). Those who lead others down the path of false religion also are bloodthirsty and deceitful (Jude 1:16-19). **The Lord abhors** them as well. David knew that even if he did not witness their destruction himself, their destruction was a sure thing because of the character of his God (2 Thess. 1:6-10).

**Questions for self-reflection:**

(1) When you witness or hear others speak falsehood against the truth of who God is, do you react with complacency or godly anger?

(2) When you think about the destruction that awaits those who speak falsehood, do you rejoice that they will be destroyed, or does your heart break for them?

(3) Does God sit on the throne of the religion you purport to follow or do you? How can you be sure?

(4) Since you have named the name of Christ and identified yourself as a Christian, would others say that a noticeable change has happened with you?

**5:7. But as for me, I will come into Your house in the multitude of Your mercy; In fear of You I will worship toward Your holy temple.**

David spoke of the privilege of corporate worship. When David was prohibited from the public worship of God this brought sadness. After the time of prohibition had passed, the opportunity to worship presented itself again. He was well aware that the only reason he was able to come into the Lord's **house** was because of his merciful God. God is rich in **mercy** (Eph. 2:4). The fact that God would save anyone and bestow upon them all the spiritual blessings that belong to all those who are in Christ illustrates this mercy (Eph. 1:3). Our sins against Him and Him alone have earned us all death (Rom. 6:23). Our iniquities have carried us away (Isa. 64:6). They have separated us from Him like death separates the spirit from the body (Eph. 2:1). God condescending to become Man and dwell among us (Jn 1:14) in order to reconcile man to Himself (2 Cor. 5:18) to provide man with salvation that man could not provide for himself illustrates this mercy. In gratitude for what God has done for them, the redeemed will want to know what God expects of them in return and will find out that He expects them to **worship** Him (Matt. 4:10, Rom. 12:2).

In addition to worship, those whose hearts have been changed by the truth will serve others. Because the saints begin to realize the magnitude of the mercy that has been shown to them in the person of Christ, they will want to show others that same mercy so others can become citizens of heaven as well (Matt. 5:16). Serving others is one form of worship. God's people are a people that are zealous for good works (Ti 2:14).

Those who begin to grasp how rich God is in mercy want to be in God's house with God's people to offer **worship toward** His **holy temple** whenever possible. They will not forsake the assembling such as is the manner of some (Heb. 10:25). They know that because two or more are gathered in His name to share in the worship experience of lifting up the voice in song and sitting under the preaching that God is in their midst when God is worshiped in Spirit and in truth (Matt. 18:20, Jn 4:24).

Believers in every generation since Christ's ascension realize what the angels realize (Heb. 1:6): that the Lord Jesus Christ is our object of worship (Rev. 4:9, Rev. 5:14). He is the cornerstone of the temple (Ps. 118:22-23, Isa. 28:16, Matt. 21:42-44, Acts 4:11, Eph. 2:19-22, 1 Pet. 2:6-8). We are the temple, the church, His body (1 Cor. 3:16-17, Eph. 2:19-22, Eph. 5:23, 1 Pet. 2:5). The body supports the building. Believers support each other. Even though the gates of hell will not prevail against the church of God (Matt. 16:18), one of the reasons that is true is because faithful believers faithfully serve and meet needs that are well-suited for their unique Holy Spirit gifts. Because of the opportunities to make a positive impact in the lives of others who need to be ministered to when the corporate gathering takes place, believers cannot forsake the assembling (Heb. 10:25) and they can do so with a spirit of expectation that the hours that they gather are hours where God's grace gets a unique opportunity to touch the lives of people who need it most. Believers know firsthand the edification they receive just being in the same building with fellow believers. They know the encouragement they have received from believers. They know the encouragement they can give believers (1 Thess. 5:11). They know to obey those that rule over them because they watch for their souls (Heb. 13:7, Heb. 13:17). They know that in the worship service, two or more are gathered in His name, therefore He is there with them (Matt. 18:20). They know that God's Word, which goes forth during the corporate worship service, will not return void but will accomplish its intended mission (Isa. 55:11). They know that God is so amazing and kind toward them for saving them, even though they committed high treason against Him, that He deserves their worship. They will want to offer God whatever feeble worship they can with reverence and fear (1 Pet. 3:15). They know it is right for God to be worshiped.

## Questions for self-reflection:

(1) For David, corporate worship was a privilege. Do you "have" to go to church, or do you "get" to go to church?

(2) When you go to church, are you more excited about what you share in common with those there with you, or are you more annoyed with your differences?

(3) For those who you wish were more like you, how can you serve them better and model your beliefs for them?

(4) In the corporate gathering, how can you be a blessing to others?

**5:8. Lead me, O Lord, in Your righteousness because of my enemies; Make Your way straight before my face.**

---

We need the **Lord** to **lead** us in His **righteousness** (Ps. 23:3) because we have no righteousness on our own (Phil. 3:9) that we can point to that is worth following (Rom. 3:9-23). Jesus Christ is the righteousness of God (1 Cor. 1:30). He possesses the only righteousness that gets sinners to the Father (Jn 14:6). We become the righteousness of God in Him (2 Cor. 5:21). God is just to punish sin and can justify us (the ungodly) when we place saving, repentant faith in the Lord Jesus Christ alone for salvation (Rom. 3:25-26). That saving faith grants sinners the everlasting imputed righteousness which is required for entrance into heaven that is impossible to obtain through the law (Rom. 3:20). Sinners receive that righteousness when they exercise initial saving faith. That righteousness sustains them throughout their earthly pilgrimages. That righteousness gains them entrance into heaven, where they will hear, "well done good and faithful servant" (Matt. 25:21). It is not a righteousness that they can earn because any sin destroys it. Since Jesus committed no sin (1 Pet. 2:22), He is the only One qualified to give it to others. He takes our sin upon Himself. He gives us His righteous, perfect life (2 Cor. 5:21). That is the great exchange of the gospel. That is how the gospel reveals the righteousness of God (Rom. 1:16-17).

Once God saves us, His Spirit renews our spirit as we renew our minds in His truth (Rom. 12:2). As we expose ourselves to more of His truth, we see more of what practical righteousness looks like in the lives of His people (1 Jn 2:29). Righteous sinners who avail themselves to the means God supplies for them to employ so that they will grow in grace (2 Pet. 3:18) will display more practical righteousness as the overflow of their inwardly righteous lives. We could never lead ourselves in the way of this righteousness apart from the Holy Spirit's aid because our indwelling sin would cause those efforts to be unfruitful. Jesus Christ in us, the hope of glory (Col. 1:27), God working in us as we work out our salvation in fear and trembling makes this possible (Phil. 2:12-13).

---

We have **enemies** all around us. Some of them are physical enemies (Matt. 5:43). Some of them are spiritual enemies (Eph. 6:12). Sometimes we are an enemy to ourselves because of our own choices to sin. All these enemies have the common goal of leading us away from God's ways and into Satan's ways. Therefore, we need the Lord to lead us against those enemies of ours (Ps. 23:3) so that we can overcome them because we are not sufficient in ourselves to overcome temptation without divine assistance (1 Cor. 10:13).

When we follow the Lord, He **makes** our **way straight**. If we renew our minds in God's truth consistently (Rom. 12:2), we know what He expects of us in each situation because He supplies all we need for every situation (Phil. 4:19). His will is perfect (Rom. 12:2). He will never lead us astray. His Word is perfect (Ps. 19:7). His Word gives us sufficient instruction for anything we might face (2 Tim. 3:16). If we abide in Christ, Christ abides in us (Jn 15:1-8), and He leads us by the Spirit into all truth (Jn 16:13).

When the Lord leads us, He leads us in the ways of His **righteousness**. When we let the Word of Christ dwell in us (Col. 3:16), the Holy Spirit brings it to our mind so we can properly respond to temptations when they come like Christ did (Matt. 4). When the Word is an intimate part of us, it instructs us in anything we face.

## Questions for self-reflection:

(1) What enemies are you up against?
(2) How are you trusting the Lord to lead you?
(3) Is your life an evident example to others that God has changed your life?
(4) What physical enemy is most prevalent in your life?
(5) What spiritual enemy is most prevalent in your life?
(6) How can you be your own worst enemy?

**5:9. For there is no faithfulness in their mouth; Their inward part is destruction; Their throat is an open tomb; They flatter with their tongue.**

The psalmist's enemies have **no faithfulness in their mouth** because the God of the psalmist does not lead their mouths. Since God does not lead them, what does lead them changes in form frequently, but its source is Satan. Since God does not lead them, their mouths speak death (Rom. 3:13-14). The rottenness of the grave comes out of their mouth. What comes out of their windpipe is like snake poison. Instead of being known for honesty and integrity, they are known for deceit. Instead of using their mouths to praise the One that has given them life, they blaspheme the One who allows them to continue in sin. Their mouth, which lacks faithfulness, produces equally unfaithful actions. Therefore, they cannot be trusted (Rom. 1:31).

The God of the psalmist is faithful (1 Cor. 1:9). The psalmist trusts in the faithfulness of his God. Since the psalmist's enemies have not made the one true God their hope as the psalmist has, they cannot speak with the same hope or faithfulness that the psalmist can speak with. God speaks truth (Rom. 1:25, Rom. 3:7, 2 Cor. 6:7, 1 Tim. 3:15, 2 Tim. 2:15, Ti 1:1). The disciples of the one true God will also speak the truth because a disciple is like his Master (Matt. 10:25).

Unbelievers cannot be trusted to speak the truth because the foundation from which they operate is one based on falsehood. Nobody who does not follow the true God can speak with **faithfulness** because the foundation from which they speak is an unfaithful foundation that has its origins with the father of lies (Matt. 7:28-29, Jn 8:44). Only the one true God is perfectly faithful all the time because there is no darkness in Him (1 Jn 1:5).

Rather than **their inward part** being one of edification like those who follow the true God (Eph. 4:29), the inward part of the enemies of the gospel is one of **destruction** (Rom. 3:16). Their inward part is destruction because their foundation is wicked. It is wicked because it comes from the Wicked One, Satan himself

(1 Jn 5:19). Christ's enemies are wicked to the core. They often plot against Christ's ambassadors (Acts 23:11-22). They devise evil continually, especially against the godly (Gen. 8:21). The **throat** of the enemies of the psalmist was **an open tomb** (Rom. 3:13). Death was in it and came out of it instead of the words of life that come forth out of those with the gospel on their lips (Jn 6:68).

False teachers have mouths that are like open tombs. They speak flattering words that make people who are destitute of discernment want to follow their lies (Prov. 7:5, Rom. 16:18). **Their tongue** is the instrument which they use to **flatter** others, including God. God repeatedly condemns flattery (Ps. 5:9, Ps. 12:2-3, Ps.55:20-21, Ps. 62:4, Prov. 26:28, Prov. 27:6, Prov. 28:23, Prov.29:5, Jer. 9:8, Rom.16:17-18, 1 Thess. 2:5-6). They think God will receive their flattery, but He will not because He seeks those who worship in Spirit and in truth (Jn 4:24). The fountain of their mouths is a polluted spring that cannot be stopped apart from the Spirit of God. They may pretend to follow God, but they will follow their own devices instead. They tell others what they want to hear so the others will follow them instead of God (Matt. 7:15-20, 2 Pet. 2).

## Questions for self-reflection:

(1) When you see people with no faithfulness in their mouths, does that make you sad?
(2) Do you have an easy time trusting people? Why or why not?
(3) Can the people you relate to most frequently trust you to be truthful all the time?
(4) Do your actions habitually demonstrate that your inward part is edification or destruction?
(5) Are your words life-giving or death-inducing?

**5:10. Pronounce them guilty, O God! Let them fall by their own counsels; Cast them out in the multitude of their transgressions, For they have rebelled against You.**

---

God's enemies (Col. 1:21) already stand **guilty** before Him because of their sins (Rom. 3:19). The psalmist asks God to make the reality of their guilt plain to them and others (Jn 3:18). Ideally, such a realization would lead God's enemies to be humbled to such a degree that they will humble themselves (1 Pet. 5:6), stop persecuting the psalmist, and come to the one true God. If the enemies of God and of the psalmist see themselves as God sees them, unclean and undone before Him (Isa. 6:5), perhaps the guilt and the punishment that awaits them should they die in their sins (Jn 3:36, Rom. 5:9) will be incentive enough for them to humble themselves and repent before the holy God that they have offended (Matt. 4:17).

If they fail to humble themselves in such a way, the psalmist asks that his enemies be allowed to reap what they have sown (Gal. 6:7-8). The psalmist asks that his enemies not be spared from any part of God's just judgment against them (Ps. 78:50, Isa. 47:3, Jer. 21:7, Lam. 2:17, Lam. 2:21, Lam. 3:43, Ezek. 5:11, Ezek. 7:4, Ezek. 7:9, Ezek. 8:18, Ezek. 9:5, Ezek. 9:10, Rom. 11:21, 2 Pet. 2:4-5). Such judgment is reasonable in light of humankind's sin against a holy God (Rom. 2:2). The fact that a sinner is not killed immediately upon committing that first sin is illustrative of a merciful God extending mercy toward those that abide under His wrath due to their unbelief (Jn 3:36). These sinners have already proven themselves to be guilty because their sinful nature has shown itself repeatedly in the sinful choices they have made (Rom. 3:9-23).

The psalmist prays that the **counsels** that God's enemies have adopted, counsels that are plainly opposed to godly counsel from God's counselors, begin to fail such that those that practice such things will recognize that God's judgment is against them. He asks that their unrighteous plans be rendered unsuccessful. If the plans and counsels of the ungodly are not allowed to succeed, perhaps that will be a means that shows God's enemies that fighting against God is futile.

The psalmist asks God to come against the wicked and **cast them out** and remove them from the earth and the presence of the psalmist. Ultimately, all those who oppose Christ and His ambassadors will be cast out and have their part in the lake that burns with fire and brimstone (Matt.8:12, Matt. 19:21, Matt. 22:13, Matt. 25:30, Lk 18:28-30, Rev. 21:8). This judgment will be their end because **of their transgressions** and will happen to them because **they have rebelled** against God by their own choice to sin against Him. Each choice we make to sin against God is rebellion. It is a choice that says that man's way is more important than God's way. It attempts to cast God off of His throne and take a seat there ourselves. Rebellion is as the sin of witchcraft (1 Sam. 15:23), and it is within God's righteous character to judge the unrighteous (Matt. 16:27, Rom. 2:6, Rev. 22:12) just as much as it is within God's righteous character to reward the righteous (Ps. 58:11, Isa. 62:11, Matt. 10:41-42, Matt. 19:29, Mk 10:29-30, Col. 3:23-24, 2 Tim. 4:7-8, Heb.10:35, Rev. 2:10).

### Questions for self-reflection:

(1) When was the last time you thought about how obstinate you were to God's rule over your life before He opened your eyes to the truth?

(2) When you came to Christ, did you come to have a better life, or did you come to have your guilt before God removed?

(3) What were some of the specific ways in which God's goodness led you to repentance?

(4) Is there anyone you know whose life is an apparent example that God's judgment is against them? How can you pray for them and minister to them in the hopes that they may see your good works and glorify the Father in heaven?

**5:11. But let all those rejoice who put their trust in You; Let them ever shout for joy, because You defend them; Let those also who love Your name Be joyful in You.**

---

Someone thinking rightly about themselves knows that nothing good is in them (Rom. 7:18). If there is nothing good in us, at least not when we are in the flesh (Rom. 8:8), then any good that comes from us must ultimately be the result of God who has given us His goodness via the Holy Spirit (Rom.15:14). Someone who has been filled with the Holy Spirit, any Christian, can **rejoice** because they have **put their trust in** the Lord. These put no confidence in the flesh (Phil. 3:3). These rejoice not because of the gifts they have received, but they rejoice in the Giver of the gifts (1 Cor. 12:4-6, Jas 1:17). These rejoice because this world is not their home (Jn 15:19, Jn 17:16, Phil 3:20), but a place has been prepared for them (Jn 14:2-3). The Lord has given such people eternal life (Jn 3:16). There is no more fabulous treasure than that (Mk 8:36).

As a result of their standing with God, they can **ever shout for joy** because they have the God that will **defend them** from attacks that come from Satan and from those that do Satan's bidding (Eph. 6:10-20). The God who has made them right with Himself through the shed blood of Christ is the source of their joy (Phil. 3:1, Phil. 4:4). Those that love God's name are true believers. They love God because God loved them first (1 Jn 4:19). They love God not only because of all the blessings that are theirs because they are in a relationship with Him, but also because of who He is.

True believers can be joyful in God because they know that no matter what happens to them in this life, nothing can separate them from God's love (Rom. 8:38-39). God will preserve them (Ps. 31:23). They know that, because of Christ, God has a place prepared for them (Jn 14:2-3). Their names are written in heaven (Lk 10:20). If God has begun the good work in them, it is guaranteed that He will perform it since His Word will not fail (Phil. 1:6, Isa. 55:11).

True believers love God for who He is and what He has done in, through, and around them. True believers love God's revelation to them, the Lord Jesus Christ, the Holy Spirit who leads them into all truth, and God's finished Word because it contains everything they need to know about who God is and what He expects of them. True believers love other believers because the same Lord bought them and waits for them to join Him in their home (1 Jn 4:11). As believers understand more of all that is theirs in Christ, it is understandable that they would **love** His **name** and **be joyful in** Him.

## Questions for self-reflection:

(1) In whom is your trust? Would others who know you best agree with how you answered the previous question?

(2) How have you witnessed God defend you or others?

(3) Do you ever think about eternity?

(4) Does thinking about eternity affect how you live your life in the present?

**5:12. For You, O Lord, will bless the righteous; With favor, You will surround him as with a shield.**

---

The saved, **the righteous**, are **surround**ed by many **bless**ings they have received from the hand of the **Lord** (Eph. 1:3). He has chosen them (Eph. 1:4). He has adopted them into His family (Eph. 1:5). He has accepted them into His family (Eph. 1:6). He has redeemed them (Eph. 1:7). He has forgiven them (Eph. 1:7). He has given them wisdom (Eph.1:8). He has revealed His will to them (Eph. 1:9). He has given them an inheritance (Eph.1:11). He has brought them to spiritual life when they were spiritually dead (Eph. 2:1-5). He has imputed righteousness to their account and removed sin from their account (2 Cor. 5:21). He has raised them to new life (Eph.2:6). He has seated them in heavenly places in Christ (Eph. 2:6). He has saved them from wrath (Rom. 5:9). He has torn down the wall created by sin that had separated them from God (Eph. 2:14). He has reconciled them (Eph. 2:16). He has given them peace with God (Rom. 5:1). He has given them access to the Father (Eph.2:18). He has given them everything they need to serve Him in this life (2 Pet. 1:3). He has done everything required for them to join Him in the next life (Rom. 5:8).

For these reasons and others, the righteous have God's **favor** all around them. God has given believers armor (Eph. 6:10-20) to fight the good fight of faith, including the **shield** of faith (Eph. 6:16). They have been shown kindness while they were not deserving of such kindness (Ti 3:3-7). They were blessed with godly wisdom when they were foolish (Ti 3:3). They were blessed with grace for obedience when they were disobedient (Ti 3:3). They were blessed with the truth when they were deceived (Ti 3:3). They were blessed with the capacity and abilities to serve others when they formerly served their own various lusts and pleasures (Eph. 2:10, Ti 3:3). They were blessed with peacefulness (Matt.5:9, Rom. 12:18) when they were previously malicious (Ti 3:3). They were blessed with contentment (Phil. 4:11) when they were previously envious (Ti 3:3). Believers need to educate themselves about what God has blessed them with so they will be better able to utilize all the blessings that are already theirs through Christ. Some of these are just the blessings of this life. There are also the blessings that come with eternal life and are not experienced until eternity. They will be with God forever and will get to see the face of the One that purchased them. The aforementioned shield protects the believer from Satan's fiery darts (Eph. 6:16). Since the shield's protection surrounds them, the protection must be necessary to fend off the attacks that come from all sides. Satan must look for any unprotected portion and try to wield his attacks at parts that he notices that are more vulnerable than others. So, the believer has a responsibility to avail himself of the spiritual armor and grow in grace to be fully equipped to handle the attacks when they come. Believers did not do anything to earn these blessings. They are gracious gifts from their heavenly Father.

**Questions for self-reflection:**

(1) If you stopped and intentionally took time to thank God for all the physical blessings you enjoy in this life, how long do you think it would take?
(2) The earthly blessings that we enjoy can only be enjoyed temporarily. How long can the spiritual blessings that are ours in Christ be enjoyed?
(3) When you look at Christ for the first time in eternity, how do you think you will react? How would you want to react?

# Psalm 6

**6:1. O Lord, do not rebuke me in Your anger, Nor chasten me in Your hot displeasure.**

---

The psalmist knew that the Lord **rebuke**s those who choose to stay in their sin rather than turn to Him in humility. The Lord rebukes by His Word, the Holy writ; the inspired Canon, when the sheep renew their minds in it (Rom. 12:2, 2 Tim. 3:16). The Lord rebukes via the preached Word (2 Tim. 4:2). In the regular church meeting, where the Word of God is preached, rebukes from the Lord's Word mixed with the Holy Spirit can bring life-giving rebukes to dull hearers. Sometimes, the Lord rebukes people by allowing them to reap when they sow (Gal. 6:7-9). Sometimes circumstances can be so harsh that they can seem like rebukes of divine chastening from God above done by the God of love (Heb. 12:3 ff.). Sometimes the rebukes of the Lord's anger that believers feel are the pricks of a guilty conscience when the conscience is awakened by the Law (Rom. 3:20).

People in a covenant relationship with the Lord need not fear the Lord's **anger** in the same way as those who willfully reject the Lord Jesus Christ (Heb. 12:7). Those who are not in a relationship with God through the Lord Jesus Christ abide under the wrath of God (Jn 3:36). These need to be saved from wrath through Christ (Rom. 5:9).

Those in that relationship with Him receive **chasten**ing in a way that is for their benefit (Heb. 12:10). It is to teach them something about God's character or something about their sin. The end result of such divine chastening is for the spiritual good of the sheep (Heb. 12:11). The chastening is done **in hot displeasure** because of God's holiness and humanity's sinfulness. It is reasonable for God to experience hot displeasure with His justified children when God does rebuke a wayward sheep. God's **rebukes are** always done from a place of love because God seeks to purify His child and not to harm His child through the instruction of discipline. Earthly parents mirror this in the discipline of their earthly children (Eph. 6:4). Parents serve as earthly proxies for the Heavenly Father and can wisely use such unpleasant opportunities as a chance to do the most significant spiritual building in the lives of their children (Prov. 22:6).

**Questions for self-reflection:**

(1) Is there anything in your life that would make the Lord want to rebuke you in His anger or chasten you in His hot displeasure?

(2) What resources are you availing yourself of to help you experience that rebuke and chastening that can benefit your soul?

(3) When you read His Word, do you ever feel that conviction?

(4) Do you ask God to purify you? What if the ways He needed to purify you were unpleasant for you to experience? Would you be willing to be purified in God's prescribed way?

**6:2. Have mercy on me, O Lord, for I am weak; O Lord, heal me, for my bones are troubled.**

---

Like every true believer, the psalmist knows that he is a sinner in need of God's **mercy** (Ps. 51:1, Matt. 5:7, Acts 7:59-8:1, Heb. 4:16). Unlike God, man's supposed power amounts to weakness (1 Cor. 1:25). For God to supply man with strength, God who possesses infinite strength must supply finite man who lacks strength (Exod. 15:2, Ps. 18:2, Ps. 27:1, Ps. 27:14, Ps. 28:7, Ps. 68:34-35, Ps. 81:1, Ps. 119:28, Prov. 10:29, Isa. 41:10, Isa. 40:29-31, Hab. 3:19).

The psalmist, like the rest of us, is a sinner by nature and by choice. Human sinfulness is the source of human weakness. Because Adam and Eve sinned in the Garden (Gen. 3), they were limited in their strength. We, as their offspring, are limited in our strength. The godly man knows that he is insufficient in his own strength. Man is **weak** in comparison to God. God's 'weakness' is stronger than man at his strongest (1 Cor. 1:25). God's 'foolishness' is infinitely stronger than man's supposed wisdom. Man would not have any wisdom if it were not for God creating man in His image (Gen. 1:27) and endowing man with wisdom that no other creature is blessed with (Exod. 28:3, Jb 11:6, Ps. 51:6, Prov. 2:6, Eccles. 2:26, Isa. 33:6, Dan. 2:21, Dan. 2:23, Lk 21:15, Acts 7:10, Col. 1:9, Jas 1:5, 2 Pet. 3:15).

Instead of this exalted position leading man to humble himself and seek God for mercy and relationship, man exalts himself (Matt. 23:12, Lk 14:11) against the God who has given him life (Gen. 2:7, Deut. 32:39, 1 Sam. 2:6, 2 Kgs 5:7, Neh. 9:6, Jb 33:4, Ezek. 16:6, Jn 1:3-4, Acts 17:25, 1 Tim. 6:13). It is the height of insanity for man to exalt himself against God. God opens the eyes of some to see their misery. He helps them see the utter lostness in which they operate (Lk15:17-19, Lk 19:10). Man who has humbled himself and who has been humbled before God understands this and knows that he is but dust (Ps. 103:14). He was created from dust and will return to dust (Gen. 3:19).

The good news for man is that while in that hopeless condition, when man could not save himself, Christ died for the ungodly

(Rom. 5:6) so that God could be just and punish man's sins and justify the ungodly when the ungodly place repentant faith in the **Lord** Jesus Christ (Rom. 3:16). God reconciled man to Himself through the death, burial, and resurrection of the Lord Jesus Christ (Col. 1:21). Through faith in the finished work of Christ on man's behalf, man is raised from his alienation and restored to a position of reconciliation (2 Cor. 5:18-19).

The psalmist's sin has caught up with him and resulted in some sort of a discipline situation that the psalmist recognizes as coming directly from the Lord (Heb. 12:3-11). He knows that the Lord has sustained him to this point, and he knows that the Lord will need to continue supporting him if he is going to get to the other side of this trial (Jas 1:2-8). He asks for **heal**ing. Sometimes the healing that the Lord brings is not necessarily a change to the physical situation we find ourselves in. Sometimes it is divinely imparted grace and faith that helps us endure harsh circum-stances and maintain the trust and a good testimony in front of others who need to see it.

When we are at our weakest in, and of ourselves, when we reach the limits of what we can accomplish on our own, we are forced to go beyond our limit and trust God to do in us what we could never do ourselves. Perhaps the psalmist is troubled by his sinfulness or his circumstances. Only the Lord can bring sufficient healing to our physical condition and our mind and soul when we are in that state.

### Questions for self-reflection:

(1) What can you do best? Does knowing that your best cannot begin to approach the weakness of God humble you?
(2) Does your salvation in Christ make you humble or prideful?

**6:3. My soul also is greatly troubled; But You, O Lord—how long?**

According to the context of the previous verses in this chapter, the psalmist is **greatly troubled** by his own indwelling sin. To be troubled about one's own sin is a New Testament virtue (Matt. 5:4, Rom. 6:12-19, Rom. 7:21-25). The psalmist does not want to have to wait too **long** for the **Lord** to remove, or at least ease, his burden about his own indwelling sin.

**Questions for self-reflection:**

(1) Does your own indwelling sin ever trouble you enough to want to make the necessary changes?
(2) What have you done to ease your own burden?

**6:4. Return, O Lord, deliver me! Oh, save me for Your mercies' sake!**

Because of his indwelling sin, the psalmist senses his weakness, insufficiency, and dependence on the Lord's intervention in his life. The Lord does not seem as close to the psalmist as He once did. He wants the **Lord** to **return** to him. The psalmist feels as if his sin has created this separation between himself and the Lord. He desires for that separation to go away so he can feel the intimacy that he once felt.

The Lord is omnipresent. He really doesn't go anywhere. But our sin can create a sense of separation. As in our human relationships, sin can destroy intimacy. Sin and its corruption destroy our intimacy with God and causes humankind's sense of their proximity to God to diminish. It is that for which Jesus had to die so that man's intimacy with God could be restored (Eph. 2:14). This is not because God changes, for He does not (Mal. 3:6). If an adverse change occurs to harm man's relationship with God, it is attributable to man.

The psalmist's enemies and his indwelling sin were troubling him greatly (Ps. 32:3-4, Ps. 51:3-4). If allowed to dominate our thoughts, our circumstances can cause us to lose the sense of God's presence because we will think about them when we should think about Him (Phil. 4:8). We can lose the sense of His love and tenderness with us if He is not dominant in our thoughts.

If we have come to saving faith in the Lord Jesus Christ, nothing can separate us from God's love (Rom. 8:38-39). If we have been adjudged as righteous in God's court based on the finished work of the Lord Jesus Christ, there is no more condemnation for us (Rom. 8:1). If we have drawn near to God and submitted to Him (Jas 4:7-8), the Lord will remain near to us. If we abide in Him, He will abide in us (Jn 15:1-8).

The psalmist felt great stress from his circumstances. He trusted that the Lord could **deliver** him from his afflictions. The Lord may allow us to experience unpleasant circumstances in this life to purify us and cleanse us from sin (2 Cor. 12:7-10, Jas 1:2-8). Because the righteous can even call out to the Lord to deliver them, it is evident that the Lord is merciful. It should be most apparent that the Lord is merciful to the righteous, those who have Christ's righteousness imputed to them. Because the Lord has saved them from eternal punishment, it is plain that He can affect their temporal circumstances as well. Deliverance may look different depending on the occasion. Deliverance may be a complete removal from a trying situation. Deliverance may be a proper attitude in a difficult situation that must continue. Either way, the problem could always be worse than it currently is. His mercies can deliver us from anything, depending on how we look at it.

## Questions for self-reflection:

(1) Have you ever felt distant from the Lord like the psalmist did?
(2) Have you ever seen the destructive effects of sin in your human relationships?
(3) If sin negatively affects our human relationships, how much more must sin affect our relationship with the Lord?
(4) Have you ever experienced the Lord's purifying effects from the furnace of affliction?
(5) How has the Lord delivered you from difficult circumstances in the past?

**6:5. For in death there is no remembrance of You; In the grave who will give You thanks?**

---

The psalmist wants to continue to live so that he can remember and thank the Lord (Ps. 7:17, Ps. 9:1, Ps. 28:7, Ps. 69:30, Ps. 95:1-3, Ps. 100:4-5, Ps. 107:1, Ps. 118:29, Ps. 136:1-5, 2 Cor. 9:15, Eph. 5:20, Phil. 4:6, Col. 2:7, Col. 3:15, Col. 4:2, 1 Thess. 5:18, Heb. 10:28-29, Rev. 7:12, Rev. 11:17). Those **in the grave**, those who have already experienced death, cannot remember the Lord–at least not in the same way as when they were alive. Someone who has died and left earth and has gone on into eternity cannot tell others on the earth of the Lord anymore. They have left the presence of humanity and have entered into the presence of God (if they are believers) for all eternity (2 Cor. 5:8).

While the redeemed are on earth, since they do not know how many days God has appointed for them (Jb 4:5, Ps. 139:16, Heb. 9:27), they should redeem the time since the days are evil (Eph. 5:15-16). They should seek the kingdom of God (Matt. 6:33) and desire to win souls because that is a wise thing to do (Prov. 11:30). From eternity, since their eternity is fixed based on what they did with the Lord while on earth, there will be a **remembrance** of Him. One group will spend all eternity praising Him for so great a salvation. This group will remember fondly the works performed by the Lord on their behalf (Ps. 9:1, Ps. 105:1-2). One group will spend all eternity weeping and gnashing their teeth, hoping for some relief that will never come (Lk 13:28). From the grave, the saints will not be able to remember the Lord or **give thanks** to the Lord for others on earth to see. Fellow saints before the throne of heaven will be able to praise the Lord with each other for all eternity. The lost will wish they had done so but will have nobody to blame but themselves for their rejection of the Lord.

### Questions for self-reflection:

---

(1) Would you rather die to be with the Lord forever, or would you rather live and continue to thank Him with your life? Why?

---

(2) Have you ever felt envious of those who have been delivered from this body of death so they could go to be with the Lord forever?

(3) Would people who know you best say that you live predominantly for this life or for the next life?

**6:6. I am weary with my groaning; All night I make my bed swim; I drench my couch with my tears.**

---

The affliction endured by the psalmist had left the psalmist feeling rebuked, chastened, troubled, **groaning**, weak, **weary**, teary, and cast off. Hardship had likewise had left the psalmist asking for mercy, healing, divine intervention, and deliverance. Perhaps he felt the weight of his sin and his struggle against it (Ps. 32, Ps. 51, Rom. 7:13-25, Gal. 5:16-17). Perhaps his sin led him to believe that his adversity was a consequence of personal sin. This, of course, is a possibility.

Another possibility is that God is testing him behind the scenes to prove his character as He did with Job. There will always be something for the righteous to groan about because the sinful world we all live in is a constant reminder of that with all its imperfections (Rom. 8:22).

An additional possibility is that the physical health of the psalmist was not at its peak. Less than ideal physical health can make normal function much more difficult. It can cause our reactions to adverse circumstances to be led by the flesh rather than the Spirit (Rom. 8:5-8).

The psalmist is doing the right thing by crying out to God for assistance in his affliction. God helps His sheep in their furnace of affliction by meeting them at the place where they need it most and providing them with the grace to endure their trial (Phil. 4:19). Rather than get discouraged by all this testing that leads to **groaning** (Rom. 8:22-23), the righteous can rejoice that the Lord works behind the scenes in the lives of His people. He uses various means to accomplish His will in their lives (Rom. 8:28). This process can be less than pleasant for the sheep to endure. But the sheep can know that the pruning process that the Lord employs, while unpleasant at times to endure, results in more fruitfulness (Jn 15:1-2).

Crying so many tears that the **bed swim**s and the **couch** is covered **with tears** are obvious hyperbolic statements meant to illustrate the excessive sorrow felt by the psalmist about his personal sin. The psalmist's melancholy may also relate to the suffering that he was appointed to endure (Phil. 1:29). That the tears flowed **all night** indicates that sorrow was so disturbing to the psalmist that it prevented him from being able to sleep. He was up all night, overtaken by the stress of his circumstances. Lives full of sorrowful seasons are often the lot of the godliest saints. The things that bring the most sorrow in life can upset the normal sleep rhythms of the saints. Even though the godliest saints know that the Lord permits or causes everything they endure, they still do not have to enjoy the unpleasant seasons of life even though, deep down, they know that its appointed end is more fruitfulness. Nothing the psalmist did could bring relief.

There is no justifying act that a lost sinner can perform. The only justifying act that will do has already been done. The Lord Jesus Christ lived a perfect life, died on the cross as a payment for human sin, and rose again to prove that His sacrifice satisfied the holy demands of His righteous Father. Only faith in the Lord Jesus Christ can appease the wrath of this holy God (Romans 5:9). Perhaps this passage is prophetic of Christ when he was weary from praying all night and crying tears of anguish just before suffering the wrath of God against human sin (Matt. 26:36-46, Mk 14:32-42, Lk 22:39-46).

**Questions for self-reflection:**

(1) Can you identify with the psalmist's feelings in this verse? If so, why could you identify with the psalmist's feelings? What happened in your life to cause you to be able to identify with the psalmist's feelings?

(2) While you felt this way, or while you feel this way (If you still do), what happened when you cast your cares upon the Lord?

(3) Do you get as bothered about your sins as the psalmist got in this verse?

**6:7. My eye wastes away because of grief; It grows old because of all my enemies.**

---

Circumstances had caused the psalmist much **grief**. Personal sin may have caused his misery. His enemies may have been the source of his suffering. Sins committed by others may have caused him distress. Ungodly professors of religion loosely associated with the one true God, Who is the God of the psalmist. These ungodly professors claimed godliness. However, they did not possess the Holy Spirit that actually produces godliness (2 Tim. 3:5), which may have caused the psalmist grief. He does mention **enemies.**

Those opposed to the God of believers are enemies of that God and, by extension, the people who follow the one true God. Sometimes the enemies who have made it inside the church, wolves disguised as sheep (Acts 20:29-30, Jude 1:4), are more difficult to endure than those who want nothing to do with any form of religion. Sometimes these people cause more grief because what we thought they once were and convinced others they once were turned out to be one big lie. It can be a significant source of sorrow to know that some of those that we love and care about most have deceived themselves into thinking they belonged to the Lord. Those who at one time appeared to have followed the Lord actually have followed the father of lies (Jn 8:44) all along.

While the enemies to God and God's people can seem tremendous and insurmountable at times to the godly, it can be reassuring for the saints to remember that God in them is greater than Satan and his minions (1 Jn 4:4). It can be grief-inducing to know that, barring a divine miracle, there is nothing that will keep them from being cast into outer darkness where there is weeping and gnashing of teeth (Matt. 22:13). Sadly, this is the final end for all unbelievers. They are God's enemies and, by extension, also the enemies of the sheep. Even though unbelievers are enemies to the sheep, believers still have the responsibility to love them as that is a command by our Lord (Matt. 5:43-48). After all, the Lord

---

loved us when we were His enemies and died so that we would instead be His friends (Col. 1:21).

In addition to people, an oft-forgotten enemy is indwelling sin (Rom. 7:21-25). The results of acts of sin committed can be devastating (Gal. 6:7-10). Those with the Holy Spirit have more sensitivity to sin than do people without the Holy Spirit. Holy Spirit conviction can cause much grief to a devout Christian. Satan is also an enemy of believers (1 Pet. 5:8). Finally, the world is the enemy of believers (Jas 4:4). These enemies can cause excessive tears that fall in such volumes that it can feel as if the **eye wastes away because of grief.**

## Questions for self-reflection:

(1) What are you going through that is a constant source of grief for you?
(2) Could viewing unsaved people who treat you poorly as enemies of God who need salvation from God help you treat them better?
(3) How can we keep ourselves from becoming deceived about our salvation?
(4) What can you begin to do today to love your enemies better?

**6:8. Depart from me, all you workers of iniquity; For the Lord has heard the voice of my weeping.**

---

The psalmist knew that his Lord was stronger than all the taunts of the **workers of iniquity** combined (Exod. 15:13, Jb 9:4, Jb 9:19, Jb 12:16, Jb 26:14, Jb 37:5, Jb 37:13, Ps. 21:1, Ps. 21:13, Ps. 24:8, Ps. 29:1, Ps. 62:11, Ps. 65:6, Ps. 68:28, Ps. 68:34, Ps.93:1, Ps. 96:6-7, Ps. 147:3-5, Isa. 45:5-7, Jer. 32:27, Jer. 50:34, Matt. 19:26, 1 Cor. 1:25, 1 Cor. 10:22, Eph. 6:10, Rev. 5:12, Rev. 18:8). He knew that the Lord **heard the voice of his weeping.** He knew his cries were heard. He knew his tears were felt in the throne room of heaven (Ps. 34:15, Prov. 15:29, Mk 11:24, Jn 9:31, Jn 14:13-14, Jn 15:7, 1 Cor. 14:15, Phil. 4:6-7, Phil. 4:13, Col. 4:2, Heb. 4:16, Heb. 11:6, Jas 1:5-7, Jas 5:16-18, 1 Pet. 3:12, 1 Jn 3:22, 1 Jn 5:14-15). He knew that the Lord saw what the wicked people on the earth did to harm the psalmist and the rest of God's people. There is nothing that the Lord misses (1 Sam. 16:7, 1 Chron. 28:9, 2 Chron. 16:9, Jb 28:24, Jb 34:21, Ps. 11:4, Ps. 33:13, Ps. 53:2, Ps. 90:8, Ps. 139:2, Ps. 139:3-4, Ps. 139:7-12, Prov. 5:21, Prov. 15:3, Isa. 40:28, Jer. 16:17, Jer. 23:23-24, Lam. 3:50, Acts 1:24, Heb. 4:13, 1 Jn 3:20). He is intimately involved in every detail of the lives of His people and supplies them with the grace that they need to follow the Spirit and not the flesh such that they can overcome any temptation (Rom. 8:28, Phil. 4:19).

In every generation, workers of iniquity will surround believers (Ezek. 3:18, Matt. 5:45, Lk 19:10, Jn 17:13-19, 2 Cor. 5:20, 2 Pet. 3:9). Workers of iniquity will oppose the godly and seek to stamp the righteous out (Jn 16:2). The voices of the iniquity workers will often be louder than those of the righteous (2 Tim. 3:12, 1 Jn 5:19). The wicked always oppose the righteous and are one of the many means God employs to test the faith of the righteous (Gen. 22:1-2, Exod. 16:4, Exod. 20:20, Deut. 8:2-3, Deut. 8:16, Deut. 13:3-4, Judges 7:4-7, 2 Chron. 32:31, Jb 23:10, Ps. 11:5, Ps. 17:3, Ps. 26:2, Ps. 139:23, Isa. 1:25, Zech. 13:9, Mal. 3:3, Mal. 3:10, Jn 6:5-6, 1 Cor. 3:12-15, Jas 1:2-8, Jas 1:12, 1 Pet. 1:7). Since after a sinner gets saved, he commonly stays in the world, it becomes evident that it is God's will to leave the saints here to show the perishing world the difference between the righteous and the unrighteous (Matt. 5:16, Matt. 7:15-20). God provides sufficient grace to the righteous to endure the threatenings levied against them by the unrighteous (Phil. 4:19).

The godly should not form alliances with the ungodly as God and Satan should not be on the same team (2 Cor. 6:14-18). Unfortunately, in this fallen world, that is inevitable from time to time. When it does happen, God gives sufficient grace and wisdom to the righteous to know how to handle such adversity. They can ask God for understanding to endure those trials, and they can trust that He will provide them with that wisdom (Jas 1:2-8). The righteous should not join the unrighteous in their sinful practices but rather reprove them (Eph. 5:7-14). The fruit that the righteous bear will be demonstrably different from the fruit that the unrighteous will bear. The Lord will separate the sheep from the goats on judgment day (Matt. 25:31-46). The psalmist knew that ultimately the Lord was on his side and therefore, he need not fear; there was nothing that man could do to him (Ps. 118:6).

Since everyone is a sinner by nature and choice and since not all sinners turn to the Savior to receive forgiveness, it is normal and expected that sinners and saints dwell under the same heaven on the same earth until they meet their Maker. The psalmist knew that he could come boldly before the throne of grace for help in his time of need (Heb. 4:16). He knew of a personal Advocate even though He had not come yet (1 Jn 2:1). He knew that Advocate interceded on his behalf (Heb. 7:25). He knew that his Lord heard the voice of his weeping and would answer in the best time and in the best way.

**Questions for self-reflection:**

(1) How does it make you feel to know that when you are down and when you take your burdens to the Lord that He hears you?

(2) When you see the wickedness that pervades the society in which you live seemingly have total freedom and

righteousness get minimized by those opposed to God, does that upset you?

(3) Our Lord promised that persecution and affliction would be a normal part of life for His people. Have you experienced persecution and affliction?

(4) Before the Lord saved you, did you ever persecute Christians, even subtly? If so, how do you feel about that now?

(5) If you have ever been on the receiving end of persecution, when you think about the Day of judgment when the Lord will separate the sheep from the goats, does that make you happy for your sake, sad for their sake, or perhaps a little bit of both?

**6:9. The Lord has heard my supplication; The Lord will receive my prayer.**

---

The psalmist knew that **the Lord** hears all those that belong to Him. He knew that his **supplication**, like the supplications of all the righteous, would make it all the way to heaven. He knew the throne of grace was available to him as it is to all believers (Heb. 4:15-16). At the beginning of this chapter, he had asked the Lord not to rebuke and chasten him (Ps. 6:1). He knew that he was a sinner and deserved God's wrath, but he also knew that as one in a covenant relationship with God, he could also count on God's sustaining presence to be with him. He also could depend on God's forgiveness. He knew that as a sinner, he needed daily mercy from the Lord. Everyone on this side of the Garden of Eden is a sinner and requires mercy (Ps. 6:2). Fortunately, God is rich in mercy (Eph. 2:4). It is the Lord's mercy that keeps us from being consumed (Lam. 3:22-23). It is our sin that keeps us weak and keeps us, whether we realize it or not, dependent upon the Lord's mercy. Our sin can make us physically suffer for fear of reaping what we have sown (Gal. 6:7-10). In that state, it is only the Lord that can bring healing to us.

While we call out to the Lord during our time of suffering and while He appears to be silent, we can be prone to doubt that He cares for us or that He is really there (Ps. 10:1, Ps. 13:1, Ps. 22:1, Ps. 35:22, Ps. 71:12). It becomes normal to ask God how long He plans to let the wicked prosper or how long He plans to let His enemies appear to have their way (Ps. 6:3, Ps. 94:3). He knew that ultimately his enemies stood no chance against the Lord of heaven and earth, who was on the side of the psalmist (Ps. 118:6, 1 Cor. 15:26-27). He asked the Lord to be merciful to him and to act against his oppressors (Ps. 6:10). He was confident that the Lord would do as he asked because he knew the character of God (Exodus 34:6, Ps. 25:6, Ps. 103:8, Ps. 119:77, Dan. 2:18, Amos 5:15). The Lord Jesus Christ mediates between God and man (1 Tim. 2:5). The psalmist was confident that God was the ultimate Judge (Gen. 16:6, Gen. 19:24-25, Josh. 6:24, Josh. 7:24-25, Judg. 2:11-15, Judg.

---

11:27, 1 Sam. 3:12-13, 1 Sam. 24:15, 1 Chron. 28:9, 2 Chron. 26:16-21, Ps. 7:8-9, Ps. 7:11, Ps. 9:8, Ps. 9:19-20, Ps. 50:6, Ps. 58:11, Ps. 75:7, Ps. 82:8, Ps. 94:2, Ps. 96:13, Ps. 98:9, Ps. 110:6, Isai. 2:4, Isa. 3:13, Isai. 33:22, Isa. 66:16, Jer. 1:16, Jer. 11:20, Jer. 17:10, Ezek. 33:20, Dan. 4:3-33, Dan. 5:22-30, Dan. 7:9-10, Mic. 4:3, Zeph. 3:8, Acts 5:3-10, Acts 12:22-23, Rom. 2:16, 1 Cor. 4:5, 2 Tim. 4:8, Heb. 4:13, Heb. 9:27, Heb. 10:30, Heb. 12:23, Jas 4:12, Jas 5:9, 1 Pet. 4:17, Rev. 20:11-15) and would act with His best interests in mind, even if that meant that the psalmist did not get what he asked for.

Paul and the Lord Jesus Christ experienced this themselves (2 Cor. 12:8; Matt. 26:39). Since Christ has satisfied God's wrath against believing sinners (Rom. 5:9), and since Christ has given believers access to the Father (Rom. 5:2), believers can know that the Lord will receive their prayers (Ps. 4:3, Ps. 34:17). They can understand that God can use their prayers as means to accomplish His will (Jas 5:16). They can know that there is nothing that the Lord cannot handle, and so there is nothing that they have to fear (Phil. 4:6-7).

### Questions for self-reflection:

(1) Does being reminded that the Lord hears you if you belong to Him make you want to go to Him even more than you already do?

(2) Can we ever go to the throne of grace too much?

(3) How have you received the Lord's mercy today?

(4) Looking back at your days as a lost person, can you now see with eyes of faith how you have reaped what you have sown? How has the reaping and sowing that has happened in your life changed since the Lord saved you?

(5) Have you seen your prayers get answered recently?

**6:10. Let all my enemies be ashamed and greatly troubled; Let them turn back and be ashamed suddenly.**

---

The psalmist knew that the Lord had the power to change the circumstances that the psalmist found himself in if it was the Lord's will to do so. The rebukes and chastening that the psalmist felt could be removed from the psalmist and levied against his enemies instead - if that was the Lord's will. The Lord could restore strength to the psalmist if that were the Lord's will. The Lord could heal the psalmist physically from what ailed him if that was the Lord's will. The Lord could change what the psalmist hoped He would change if that were the Lord's plan for the psalmist's life.

Even if the Lord did not permit the circumstances for the psalmist to change, that did not change the fact that the Lord is merciful. The psalmist was still alive. The psalmist could still lift his voice to the Lord. He could still bear witness to the Lord while being sorrowful about his circumstances. Sin and its consequences are sad, and it can be okay to display the sadness. However, the sadness from the circumstances should not overwhelm the deep-seated joy that the believer has because of the Lord. The believer knows that God hears His people when they come to His presence in faith.

The psalmist asks God to act in a way that is so obviously demonstrative of His righteousness that the psalmist's **enemies** would have no other option but to conclude that God worked on behalf of the psalmist (Exod. 14:25). He wanted them brought to a place of such suffering that they would have nowhere to look but up to the God who would save them if they would look to Him (Isa. 45:22, Heb. 12:2).

The psalmist wanted his enemies to **be ashamed and troubled** like he had been so they would turn to the Lord, who would receive them and pardon them (Jn 1:12). The psalmist wanted his enemies forced to turn back from pursuing him and to be reconciled to God (2 Cor. 5:20) and the psalmist so they could live at peace with each other (Rom. 12:18). The psalmist wanted his oppressors to be ashamed for persecuting him so severely. He longed to see his enemies brought by God to a place of such turmoil that they would conclude that the psalmist's God fought against them. It could also be that the psalmist wished for his enemies to perish in like manner to how the Egyptians perished when they pursued Israel in the Exodus account – suddenly (Exod. 14).

## Questions for self-reflection:

(1) Do you believe that the Lord can change your most challenging trial if He chooses to do so?
(2) Do you pray that those who oppose you for your faith are allowed by God to see what their sin does to you?
(3) If the Lord decides it is best not to take away your thorn in the flesh, how can you say with confidence that the continuation of the trial is illustrative of God's mercy?
(4) How have you seen the Lord fight for you?

# Psalm 7

**7:1. O Lord my God, in You I put my trust; Save me from all those who persecute me; And deliver me,**

The psalmist knew that the **Lord** was **trust**worthy. He knew that of all the supposed 'gods' there were, between the Lord and the gods of the heathen, the Lord was the only one that was real and the only one that was worth trusting (1 Chron. 16:25, Ps. 95:3, Ps. 96:4, Ps. 97:9, Ps. 135:5). The Lord was with David (1 Sam. 18:14). The Lord had revealed Himself to the psalmist directly (e.g., 1 Sam. 23:2, 1 Sam. 23:4, 1 Sam. 23:11, 1 Sam. 23:12, 2 Sam. 2:1, 2 Sam. 5:19, 2 Sam. 5:23-24, 2 Sam. 21:1). When the psalmist exercised personal faith in the Lord, the Lord and the psalmist began their relationship in a temporal sense. The psalmist and God were in a covenant relationship with one another. The psalmist came to acknowledge that the Lord is his **God** and was worthy of his trust. The psalmist could place complete confidence in the Lord and could know that nothing was too hard for the Lord (Gen. 18:14, Jb 42:2, Isa. 59:1, Jer. 32:17, Jer. 32:27, Matt. 19:26, Mk 10:27, Lk 1:37, Lk 18:27, Eph. 3:20-21) and that the Lord fought for His people, including the psalmist (Exod. 14:14, Exod. 14:25, Deut. 1:30, Deut. 3:22, Deut. 20:4, Josh. 23:3, Josh. 23:10, Ps. 23:4, Ps. 144:1, Isa. 54:17).

As it was with the psalmist, so it is with believers in any generation. Since God does not change (Num. 23:19, 1 Sam. 15:29, Ps. 33:11, Ps. 89:34, Ps. 102:27, Ps. 119:89, Isa. 40:8, Isa. 46:10, Mal. 3:6, Lk 21:33, Heb. 7:24, Heb. 13:8), the Lord is worthy of trust at all times in every generation. The Lord reveals Himself to people by Creation (Rom. 1:20), by His Son (Heb. 1:2), and by the Word which tells about the Son (Jn 5:39). When believers place saving faith in Christ alone for salvation, they become members of God's family (Eph. 1:5). However, when the psalmist and the rest of the family of believers trust the Lord, this is not a one-time event. Putting one's trust in the Lord is something that needs to occur in the lives of genuine believers repeatedly. During times of peace and prosperity, the Lord should be trusted.

During times of strife and want, the Lord should be trusted. Attacks from the Wicked One will tempt them to doubt and forsake the truth they have known (Matt. 13:4, Matt. 13:19). Some people can have a spurious faith with no depth that will not stand when the heat of trouble bears upon it (Matt. 13:5-6, Matt. 13:20-21). The cares of this life can choke out the fruitfulness that the Lord exacts upon a person's life (Matt. 13:7, Matt. 13:22). The psalmist was like a good ground hearer (Matt. 13:8, Matt. 13:23). His soul could rest quietly in the Lord no matter what went on around him since the Lord was faithful to His promises (Ps. 145:13), and since he was a recipient of eternal life by faith in the Lord (Genesis 15:6, Rom. 4:5, Rom. 5:1).

The psalmist had his fair share of people after him. They came after him to **persecute** him. Paul wrote to Timothy and reminded him that it is normal for believers to expect persecution (2 Tim. 3:12). Believers of every age can expect it. Our Lord, our example (1 Pet. 2:21), was persecuted as well, even to the death. His followers, during his earthly ministry, faced persecution (Matt. 10:16-26). The psalmist knew that the Lord is worthy of our trust no matter what season of life we find ourselves. The psalmist trusted that the Lord could **deliver** him from whatever circumstance he faced if God willed for that deliverance to happen. David wrote this psalm when Saul was after him (1 Sam. 24).

**Questions for self-reflection:**

(1) Would the people who know you best conclude that the Lord is also worthy of their trust?

(2) If nothing is too hard for the Lord, how does that change your attitude toward your most difficult present adverse circumstance?

**7:2. Lest they tear me like a lion, Rending me in pieces, while there is none to deliver.**

---

The psalmist knew that his persecutors could commit great evil and inflict severe harm on him - and even kill him. **Lion**s are fierce and powerful, so the psalmist evoked that imagery here (2 Tim. 4:17, 1 Pet. 5:8). He compared those who opposed him and opposed his God to a lion. A lion is a creature that is supreme in power to any other human. It will devour its prey with its carnivorous teeth, rending it in pieces. This imagery evokes the complete destruction of its target. The psalmist knew that his enemies wanted to utterly destroy him because they could not stand the God who fought on the psalmist's behalf.

A lion evokes fear in the boldest of creatures. A lion that rends its prey **in pieces** will completely consume that prey, killing it, rendering it useless to others, and using the prey to satisfy itself. The world, the devil, and the devil's workforce share that goal with the lion. The devil and the world, which lies under his sway (1 Jn 5:19), seek to destroy sinners and bring them to hell with them. The devil seeks to make believers unfruitful (Lk 22:31).

It is incumbent upon the believer to walk in the Spirit and not fulfill the lusts of the flesh (Gal. 5:16). The believer must remember that they have been made soldiers in the Lord's army (2 Tim. 2:3-4). The Lord has equipped them with all the weapons they will need to engage this formidable foe (2 Cor. 10:4-5, Eph. 6:10-20).

The psalmist knew that whether or not he could escape from his enemies was ultimately up to the Lord. There could be **none to deliver** the psalmist if it were not for the Lord allowing deliverance to happen. Persecutors would have their way with the psalmist and all other believers because believers will always be the minority. Therefore, believers must be wise as serpents and gentle as doves (Matt. 10:16) while trusting the Lord for protection for as long as they are on the earth.

The psalmist would have to keep his divine appointment (Acts 17:30-31), so the deliverance would have to be within the bounds of what God allowed for the psalmist. Hence, the only One who is mighty to save from the devouring lion and rapacious world is the one true God.

## Questions for self-reflection:

(1) How have you seen the people of the world treat the people of the Lord like the lion that tears its prey in pieces?
(2) How has your life invited persecution?
(3) If your life has not invited persecution, would you invite persecution if persecution were to happen?
(4) What if that persecution were to come from people you thought you could trust?

**7:3. O Lord my God, if I have done this: If there is iniquity in my hands,**

---

If there was some sin that the psalmist had done that provoked his enemies to come after him, David wanted to know if he had done something to provoke such hostility from Saul. David had multiple opportunities to take Saul's life while Saul persecuted David, but David chose to repay evil with good. Choosing to repay evil with good is one thing that sets believers apart from unbelievers (Matt. 5:38-48).

## Questions for self-reflection:

---

(1) Does there always have to be iniquity in our hands for our lives to invite persecution from our enemies?
(2) How can we use persecution to love our enemies better?
(3) What if by loving our enemies, our enemies never change? Will we still think it is worth it to trust the Lord?

**7:4. If I have repaid evil to him who was at peace with me, Or have plundered my enemy without cause,**

---

While Saul was at peace with David, David had not **repaid evil to him who was at peace with** him. While Saul conspired against David to harm David (1 Sam. 18, 1 Sam. 19, 1 Sam. 21, 1 Sam. 22, 1 Sam. 23), David did not conspire to harm Saul (1 Sam. 24).

When persecuted by evildoers, Christ did not repay evil to them either (Matt. 9:11, Matt. 9:34, Matt. 12:14, Matt. 12:24, 1 Pet. 2:23). As much as He could, He lived peaceably with them (Rom. 12:17). Saul had no good reason to persecute David. Saul was David's **enemy without cause** (Ps. 35:19, Ps. 109:3). David had multiple opportunities, while Saul was trying to exterminate him, to kill Saul instead. Still, David chose not to kill Saul because the Lord had prohibited David from doing so (1 Sam. 24:6, 1 Sam. 26:10-11).

The Jewish leaders of the day were Christ's enemy without cause (Ps. 69:4, Jn 15:25). So likewise, Christians today have enemies in the world who hate their Lord and Savior and who hate the practically righteous life that exudes from them as it is a source of conviction for the lost. Today, Christians are called to live in such a way to not bring reproach on the name of Christ, the One they say they represent. Instead, Christians emulate their Master when they love their enemies and repay evil with good (Matt. 5:44, Rom. 12:21).

### Questions for self-reflection:

---

(1) When people are unkind to you or treat you poorly, is your first instinct to lash out at them, think mean thoughts about them, or bless them?
(2) Are you doing everything you can to live at peace with those around you?
(3) If you are in conflict with someone, have you done everything possible to restore with them?

(4) If you do everything to restore with them, but they are not ready to repair with you, can you trust the Lord for them to repair with you when they are ready, or will you get anxious?

**7:5.** Let the enemy pursue me and overtake me; Yes, let him trample my life to the earth, And lay my honor in the dust. Selah

---

If the psalmist was guilty of the things listed in the preceding verses of the psalm, then it was reasonable for **the enemy** to **pursue** him, **overtake** him, **trample** his **life to the earth** and **lay** his **honor in the dust.** It was reasonable for the psalmist to be persecuted to the point of death in retribution for his ill-treatment of his enemy – if he had genuinely mistreated his enemy. But the psalmist had not mistreated his enemy. He was proclaiming his innocence. That for which he had been accused had no merit. David's primary objective was to honor his Lord. If he was guilty of dishonor of his Lord, he recognized that he deserved death.

In fact, everyone is guilty of such dishonor of the Lord (Rom. 3:9-23). Because everyone is a breaker of the law of God (Jas 2:10), everyone deserves to have the enemy of death pursue and overtake them. It will happen to everyone if they do not first see the rapture (1 Thess. 4:13-18).

**Questions for self-reflection:**

---

(1) Are we really ready to receive God's discipline for our indwelling sin like the psalmist seemed to ask for in this verse?
(2) When we receive mistreatment for our faith, are we despondent or encouraged because Jesus said to expect it?
(3) Is your primary objective to honor the Lord or to escape trouble?
(4) Are you prepared to meet the Lord when you die? How do you know?

**7:6. Arise, O Lord, in Your anger; Lift Yourself up because of the rage of my enemies; Rise up for me to the judgment You have commanded!**

---

The psalmist had waited patiently for the Lord's intervention in his circumstances. As yet, the Lord had not yet intervened, or at least not to the liking of the psalmist. The psalmist knew that the Lord knows everything that humankind does on the earth. He sees the good and the evil that is performed (1 Chron. 28:9, Jb 28:24, Jb 34:21, Ps. 14:2, Ps. 33:13, Ps. 53:2, Ps. 139:3-4, Ps. 139:7-12, Prov. 5:21, Prov. 15:3, Jer. 16:17, Jer. 23:23-24, Acts 1:24, Heb. 4:13, 1 Jn 3:20). The psalmist knew that the Lord must have **anger** toward those who oppose him (Ps. 7:11) since to oppose the psalmist is tantamount to opposing the God of the psalmist (Matt. 12:30). The Lord Jesus echoed this when He indicated that those who persecute His people persecute the Lord Himself (Jn 15:20, Acts 9:4).

It looked to the psalmist as if God did not care enough about the plight of the psalmist. When adverse circumstances perpetuate, it can look like wickedness is winning while righteousness is losing. The psalmist knew that could not be true about the God he served, so he called out to God. He knew that because the Lord had to be angry about what was going on, there must be something that the Lord could do to make His displeasure about what was happening manifest. The Lord could **arise** on behalf of the psalmist and vindicate the faith of the psalmist.

It would not be wrong for the Lord to come in vengeance against His enemies. The psalmist knew this. He knew that the Lord could **lift up** Himself **because of the rage of** the **enemies** of His people. These enemies make up the heathen, and we met them in Psalm 2 (2:1). For believers who see injustice go on all around them because of the rage of their enemies, it is easy to get impatient to wait for God to make right all that sin has made wrong. For the psalmist, it looked like the psalmist's enemies were the most powerful ones in the situation with the psalmist.

---

For God's people in every generation, the number of ungodly people compared to the amount in the godly remnant can make it seem like the enemy is raging around them. The psalmist knew that this was not true and asked the Lord to show Himself. Since the Lord had not yet intervened for the psalmist, it was as if the Lord was asleep and needed to **rise up** from sleep. "Wake up and help me," cried the psalmist. While the Lord never sleeps (Ps. 121:4), it can seem like He does sometimes when we think He should act in a way that we deem would be righteous, but for reasons known only to Him, He does not act in the ways that we think that He should.

## Questions for self-reflection:

(1) How long are you willing to wait for the Lord to intervene in your most challenging circumstance?

(2) How do you know that the Lord is or is not intervening?

(3) Would you be willing to wait until eternity for your circumstances to change if that was the Lord's will?

(4) If you were to ask the Lord to change you rather than your circumstances, how might that change your attitude about your circumstances?

**7:7. So the congregation of the peoples shall surround You; For their sakes, therefore, return on high.**

The psalmist knew that his enemies were God's enemies. He knew that what he was insufficient to do himself, God could sufficiently intervene to accomplish. David knew that God's faithful **congregation of the peoples** would **surround** God with worship and advocate for God's true servants, like the psalmist. In every generation, believers can come boldly before the throne of grace (Heb. 4:14-16), make their requests known to God (Phil. 4:6-7), and trust their great High Priest to intercede for them (Heb.7:25) continually.

**For** the **sake** of the rest of His special treasure (Exod. 19:5), the psalmist wanted the Lord to **return on high** and work on behalf of the people that He had redeemed from Egyptian bondage. David calls on God to return on high and come against his enemies so that all would know that there is one true God and He is on David's side (Ps. 118:6)! David wanted him and the rest of God's people to be able to worship God freely. The congregations of the peoples would be seeking the Lord, hoping to get a glimpse of His presence and glory to have something to remind them of their object of trust. If the Lord returned on high, there would be a concrete image forever etched in their minds of when God met them and made Himself known.

God is always worthy of our trust whether we sense His proximity or not. Even if God does not deliver us from our troubles in this life, there is always the next life where we will forever be in His presence in heaven, forever separated from sin and adversity. Perhaps the psalmist received a divinely inspired foretaste of what it may be like when the Lord Jesus returns to establish His Millennial Kingdom. When he asked the Lord to **return on high**, this could refer to when the Lord returns since the Mount of Olives is the high place that the Lord will return to (Acts 1:9-12).

The Lord Jesus Christ redeemed Christians from the bondage to sin and Satan and brought them to Himself (Col. 1:13-14). He will return to usher them with Him to heaven to the eternal state after the Millennium (1 Thess. 4:17, Rev. 21:1-3).

## Questions for self-reflection:

(1) Since your salvation, how have you seen the Lord help you with what you were unable to handle yourself?

(2) Since you know that the Lord is on your side, how does that help you face adversity more confidently?

(3) When you contemplate heaven and the absence of sin and suffering that will be the lot of all believers in eternity, does that make you rejoice? If so, do you rejoice more because your circumstances will change or more because of what God has done for you to make it possible?

**7:8. The Lord shall judge the peoples; Judge me, O Lord, according to my righteousness, And according to my integrity within me.**

The psalmist comforts himself with the truth of God's inevitable judgment against all those that oppose Him and His people (Gen. 18:25, Gen. 19:24-25, Josh. 6:24, Josh. 7:24-25, Judg. 2:11-15, 1 Sam. 3:12-13, Ps. 110:6, Jer. 1:16, Jer. 11:11, Jer. 25:17-27, Dan. 5:22-30, Amos 9:1-4, Matt. 25:41, Acts 12:22-23, 2 Pet. 2:4-11, Rev. 6:15-17, Rev. 20:11-15). Saul opposed David without a cause (1 Sam. 19:5), and David wanted God to vindicate him. Even though God's enemies and the psalmist's enemies seemed like legitimate threats to God's people and God's work, trust in God is always better than fear of the unknown. Even though the danger faced by the psalmist was authentic, the psalmist knew that God was ultimately in control and would be glorified even in the judgment of His enemies.

The psalmist could die at the hands of his persecutors. Even if he did, he knew his death would be precious to the Lord (Ps. 116:15). He knew that the Lord would ultimately vindicate Himself and, by extension, those that have previously died for the causes of the Lord (Rev. 6:10). Since the psalmist had searched his own heart and had been established as righteous before God (by faith and not works – Eph. 2:8-9), he could trust that God would vindicate him either in this life or in the next. God has appointed a day in which He will judge the world in **righteousness** (Acts 17:30-31). If the Lord's anger against He and His people's enemies did not arise in the psalmist's lifetime, there was safety in trusting the Lord.

The Lord had commanded the judgment of His enemies. It happens on a small scale every day as people are allowed to reap with wickedness that they have sown (Gal. 6:7-10). It occurs on a small scale when the wages of sin are collected from those who die (Rom. 6:23). It happens on a small scale when the Lord's patience runs out, and an account is demanded (Lk 12:20). The Lord will one day return to gather His people to Himself and remove the sheep from the generation of the ungodly (1 Thess. 4:13-18). From what is allowed to happen in the world, it is not always easily discernible to everyone, especially not to God's people, that God is at work behind the scenes. But He is. He is working it all out (Rom. 8:28, Eph. 1:11).

The psalmist asks the **Lord** to **judge** him. He knows that judgment starts with God's people (1 Pet. 4:17). He knows that he must be purifying himself to one day be in the presence of One infinitely pure (Heb. 12:14, 1 Jn 3:3). He must know that he possesses no everlasting righteousness on his own but that he must trust fully in the righteousness of another, namely God Himself, a righteousness that is received today by faith in the Lord Jesus Christ (Phil. 3:9). So, the righteousness of which David speaks here must relate to the fact that he committed no act deserving of such treatment by Saul. Saul had no justifiable reason to be pursuing David with such aggression. David wanted God to vindicate him in the court of Saul. So, even those living in moral uprightness, with personal **integrity**, can experience unjust persecution (2 Tim. 3:12).

### Questions for self-reflection:

(1) If the Lord were truly to judge you according to your righteousness, what would He find?

(2) When was the last time that you considered that God gets the glory for saving sinners AND for judging sinners? Does that truth affect your attitude toward serving God?

(3) If you are suffering for your faith, are you willing to wait until the next life for the Lord to vindicate you?

(4) Do you look forward to your day of judgment? Why or why not?

(5) In what subtle ways have you seen God at work in the details of your life and your society?

**7:9. Oh, let the wickedness of the wicked come to an end, But establish the just; For the righteous God tests the hearts and minds.**

---

Sometimes when **the wicked** are allowed to prosper (Ps. 94:3), it can seem to **the just** that the Lord is not there or that the Lord does not care enough to intervene in the cause of **the righteous.** Sometimes God allows the wicked time to sow their **wickedness.** Wickedness will abound because evil people are allowed to live on the earth. God, in His patience, graciously allows the wicked to seek Him and find Him. Most do not. While they live, their wickedness persists in the world and gets progressively worse. Corruption will not cease while we live on an earth that has been cursed by sin (Rom. 8:22). The wicked will remain on the planet until the eschatological end of everything. It is at this time that the wicked are all cast into the Lake of Fire forever. The New Heavens and New earth will consist of only the righteous.

For now, however, both the righteous and the wicked are required to share the same planet. God has reasons for not immediately taking the justified out of the world once they have come to saving faith. Perhaps the righteous are not immediately removed from the earth so that the watching world can easily distinguish between the righteous and the wicked that His saints may glorify the Lord. The Scriptures, especially the Proverbs, are full of principles that illustrate that it is plain that there will be demonstrable differences between the righteous and the unrighteous (Ps. 37:21, Prov. 10:11, Prov. 12:5), Prov. 13:5, Prov. 15:28, etc.).

The psalmist asks for the Lord to remove the wicked that most greatly afflict him. Even if the psalmist does not see his request granted during his lifetime, it is a promise that it will eventually happen since heaven will be a sinless place, and the eternal state for the believer will be devoid of corruption (Rev. 21-22). Perhaps the darkness of the wicked can **come to an end** by the death of the wicked or the removal of the reprobate from society. The absolute best resolution to this conundrum is for the lost to come to saving faith and no longer live for their wickedness but instead live for righteousness. That would be a much preferable way for the wickedness of the wicked to come to an end. When the wicked become part of God's family, they no longer must be considered wicked but may be regarded as righteous before God instead. When the vilest and most wicked sinner humbly turns in repentant faith to the Lord Jesus Christ for reconciliation, justification, pardon, forgiveness, and eternal life, that justified sinner has been saved by grace through faith, by God's gracious gift. They are rooted and grounded in love (Eph. 3:17) as God, by the Spirit, works to **establish the just.**

Christ's imputed righteousness to the account of the repentant believer forms a firm foundation from which nobody can be eternally removed (1 Cor. 3:11). They remain in a permanently fixed position. God's love abides upon them. As they abide in Christ, He will abide in them and lead them by the Spirit into all truth (Jn 15:1-8, Jn 16:13). The justified sinner purposes to grow in grace (2 Pet. 3:18) by trusting in the Lord (Isaiah 26:4), renewing their minds in His Word consistently (Rom. 12:2), coming into His presence regularly in bold, persistent, expectant prayer (Heb. 4:16, Jas 5:16) and surrounding themselves with a community of godly believers to edify them and hold them accountable (Prov. 27:17, 1 Thess. 5:11, Heb. 10:25).

**God tests the hearts and minds** of everyone so it will be demonstrable to themselves and to others whether or not they belong to him. What is in their hearts fills their minds and comes out through their words and actions (Ps. 1:1-2, Lk 6:45, Jas 1:12-15). The testing that the Lord put believers through purifies them from things in this world that take away from the devotion that belongs to Him (2 Tim. 2:19, Ti 2:14, Jas 4:8, 1 Pet. 1:22-25).

## Questions for self-reflection:

(1)  When you see wickedness around you go on unchecked, how do you react internally?

(2) Does your internal frustration with living in sinful situations around you, wherever they may be, ever come out in sinful angry outbursts?

(3) Are there people you pray for to come to saving faith that have not come to saving faith? If so, how can you minister specifically to them today?

(4) Do you ever wish you could be in heaven now?

(5) Is there someone that is lost that you especially don't get along with? How would you react if that person got saved?

**7:10. My defense is of God, Who saves the upright in heart.**

The psalmist receives attacks as all the saved do from time to time. Such attacks against the righteous have their source in Satan, the ultimate arch-enemy of God. God and Satan have waged war over humanity since the beginning (Gen. 3, Jb 1, Jb 2), and that war will rage on until the very end (Rev. 20:10). Satan recruits people, all of which oppose God, and those who oppose God oppose those who belong to God.

The enemy's attacks against the godly can be attacks against their physical condition (Jb 2). Additionally, the attacks can be on their mental state (Acts 26:24). Finally, the attacks can be from the spiritual realm where Satan accuses the brethren (Rev. 12:10).

No matter what attacks came upon the psalmist, no matter where the attacks on the psalmist came from, the psalmist knew that as a saved sinner, **God** had saved him (Rom. 8:38-39). Therefore, the God of the psalmist **saves** sinners because He is a saving God (Isa. 45:21-22). The Lord is a merciful (Eph. 2:4), kind (Ti 3:4), benevolent (Jas 1:17) Savior. The Father makes sinners **upright in heart** (Prov. 14:2).

The uprightness of the heart does not save the saint. Instead, because the saint has a new life principle, uprightness of heart will be an expected result (Rom. 6:4). Consequently, growth in the grace and knowledge of the Lord Jesus Christ will take place (2 Pet. 3:18). Moreover, once saved, the redeemed have access by one Spirit to the Father of mercies (2 Cor. 1:3, Eph. 2:18).

The child of the King has on the spiritual armor to face any situation (Eph. 6:10-18). That armor is more for **defense** than for offense. There is a helmet to protect justified sinners from attacks on the head that would lead to a fatal death blow (Eph. 6:17). There is a shield to protect against impacts to the body (Eph. 6:16). There are shoes (Eph. 6:16) that allow the one running the race for a prize to run well to win the prize (1 Cor. 9:24-27).

Once saved, sinners have One who ever lives to intercede for them (Heb. 7:25). The same saved sinners have an advocate to plead their case before the Father and the Judge of all (1 Jn 2:1).

When the Judge of the living and the dead opens the books (Rev. 20:11-13), those who have embraced the Lion of the Tribe of Judah (Rev. 5:5) will avoid the lake of fire (Rev. 21:8). The Lord Jesus is our defense against Satan. He forever defeated him and made a public spectacle of the prince of the power of the air (Eph. 2:2) by rising from the dead (Col. 2:15). The Lord Jesus is our Advocate against sin (1 Jn 2:1). He leads us by the Spirit into all truth and reveals God's will to us (Jn 16:13).

## Questions for self-reflection:

(1) If you experience hardship for your faith from people, how does it make you feel about those people knowing that Satan is behind their persecution directed at you?
(2) Since you initially professed faith in Christ, how have you become more upright in your daily conduct?
(3) How have you seen Jesus fight for you?

**7:11. God is a just judge, And God is angry with the wicked every day.**

---

**God** has many attributes. Some are communicable. That means that all humans, those created in His image (Gen. 1:27), can practice some of those attributes themselves because God gave them an ability, less perfect than God's ability, to practice them. When humans practice anything God has communicated to them, human sinfulness always taints it (Rom. 5:12). That is why humans practice things less perfectly than God does. God is not affected by sin (1 Jn 1:5).

God created humans with a sense of right and wrong because God put that in them in the form of their conscience (Rom. 2:15). Sadly, most people are more concerned with the evils of others than they are with their own. (Rom. 2:21-23). Most people think they are basically good (Pro. 20:6). They deceive themselves into thinking their sin is not as bad as it truly is (Matt. 7:1-5, Rom. 7:13). All human sin is first against God (1 Jn 3:4) and second against others (e.g., Exod. 20:12-17).

Since God is the source of every blessing that we enjoy, both physical (Jas 1:17) and spiritual (Eph. 1:3), He is right to be **angry** at the unrighteous wicked because they respond to His blessing with daily sin in its various forms. Understandably, He is wrathful at those who have rejected Him and His goodness **every day.** Rejection of God and His goodness is sin. That aforementioned goodness is there to lead them to repentance, and they despise it (Rom. 2:4). Many people incorrectly think that God should be all love and mercy and not simultaneously justly angry at human sin. God can practice more than one attribute at a time. Because He is also loving and merciful at the same time as He is angry, He can let us live while we continue to sin against Him because He loves us and wants us to come to Him (Isa. 65:2). God's wrath is revealed against humanity as they demonstrate that they are His enemies by their sinful lifestyles (Rom. 1:18-32). God can still be merciful to not kill them immediately with each sin they commit against Him (Lamentations 3:22, Ephesians 2:4).

---

Even though we survive it for a time, our sin against Him makes Him angry, and, as **a just Judge**, He must punish our sin because sin is rebellion against His authority over us. Because He loves us, if we look to Him, He can forgive and make us just before Him because of Christ (Isaiah 45:22). He poured out His wrath upon Christ so we could go free (Romans 5:9). If we don't turn to Christ, we suffer His anger for all eternity in the fierceness of the winepress of the wrath of God (Revelation 19:15). If we turn to Christ, Christ takes the punishment we deserve, and we are declared righteous, not because we are righteous, but because Christ's righteousness is imputed to our account (Romans 3:22).

## Questions for self-reflection:

(1) Why are we less willing to look at our own sins and more willing to confront others about their sins?
(2) What are some ways in which the lost spurn God's goodness?
(3) In what ways do saved people still spurn God's goodness?
(4) Since Christ, who did not deserve our punishment, received the punishment that was reserved for us so that we can go free, does that make you want to worship the Lord?

**7:12. If he does not turn back, He will sharpen His sword; He bends His bow and makes it ready.**

---

**If** a lost man **does not turn** from his sins **back** in repentant faith to God, the One who has provided everything a man needs in this life (2 Pet. 1:3-4) and who has provided the way for man to have eternal life (Gal. 4:4), if a man does not turn back to God and start to live for the Lord as opposed to living for himself (Rom. 14:8), if a man does not repent and believe the gospel (Lk 13:3), if a man is not born again (Jn 3:3-7) and changed by God's grace, if a man has not passed from death to life (1 Jn 3:14), if God has not made man alive (Eph. 2:1), if a man has not had his sins blotted out by God (Acts 3:19), then that man continues to be at war with God.

Man, apart from Christ, is still in his sin and is at war with God. Christ's sacrifice on man's behalf makes it possible for the conflict between man and God to come to a merciful end (Jn 3:16). God has done all He can do from His end to stop the war and usher in peace (Eph. 2:15, Rom. 5:1-2). Man, who rejects the gospel and continues in his sin, continues the war. Man must humble himself so that God can exalt him (1 Pet. 5:6). Man must repent of his sin and turn to Christ in repentant faith (Matt. 4:17, Heb. 11:6). Man must come to God for pardon, redemption, forgiveness (Eph. 1:7), and everlasting life (Jn 3:16). If man will not turn from sin and turn to Christ, man continues to live in opposition to God. Man does not realize that God is at war with His enemies (Rev. 19:11).

God, when a man chooses to reject Him willfully, **sharpens His sword** and **bends His bow**. Even though He is **ready** to do so, God does not strike man immediately upon man's first sin because God is merciful (Eph. 2:4). God does not desire anyone to perish but wants all to come to repentance (2 Pet. 3:9). God loves humanity so much and wants us to be with Him forever. That is why He sent Christ to take the punishment we deserve, to be the propitiation for our sins (1 Jn 2:2), to become sin for us (2 Cor. 5:21) so that we could become the righteousness of God in Him.

---

**Questions for self-reflection:**

(1) Is a sharp sword and a bent bow ready to strike its object?

(2) If a sharp sword and a bent bow picture instruments of God's judgment against the wicked, does it sound like God is pleased with the wicked?

(3) As a Christian, to know that you were once lost and, in this condition, does this help you become more grateful for God's gracious salvation? Does this help you want to become more evangelistic?

(4) Is man more likely to humble himself and come to God for the salvation that he so desperately needs by only hearing about God's love for him, or does a lost man need to hear the bad news about sin, so he better understands the good news about the gospel?

**7:13. He also prepares for Himself instruments of death; He makes His arrows into fiery shafts.**

God can step into time and **prepare** things or people to harm those in opposition to Him. This harm can be a merciful, non-lethal circumstance that leads the caught sinner to a place of repentance (Jn 5:14). Injury or illness in such instances serves as God's merciful providence. While painful at the time, it proved to be for the greater spiritual good for the lost sheep that the Shepherd employed so that the sheep would enter into the flock of God. Things like diseases, natural disasters, or other calamities are various means that God uses to get people's attention to show them that He is there and that eternal destruction awaits them if they do not repent (2 Thess. 1:8-10). Some of the aforementioned instruments are deadly to some but not fatal to all.

Some readers may object that for God to afflict or kill anyone with unannounced calamities is unloving, unwarranted, and makes God into a moral monster. Jesus answered this very objection in Luke 13:1-5, where He implied that such disasters could happen to people in the natural course of living in a fallen world. Because something catastrophic happens to some people but not to other people, Jesus taught, does not necessarily mean that those on the receiving end of the judgment of the catastrophe were worse sinners than those who did not receive such demonstrable justice. All are condemned already for failure to believe in the Son (Jn 3:18). All are under sin (Rom. 3:9). All are under the sway of the wicked one (1 Jn 5:19). All are children of wrath (Eph. 2:3). For those who have not come to saving faith, it is not as if they would have come to their senses and believed the gospel if God had just let them avoid the disaster and live a little longer. God would not allow a sinner perish that He knew would come to saving faith if only that sinner would be able to hear the gospel.

God from eternity knows who are His before they even become His in time (Jer. 1:5, 2 Tim. 2:19). Since God requires repentance and faith to obtain justification (Gal. 2:16), those whom God knows will become sheep will graciously be given the opportunity to hear the gospel, respond to the gospel with repentant saving faith, and pass from death unto life (Jn 5:24).

While it is true that the Lord knows the godly, it is equally true that the Lord knows the ungodly. He knows the true from the false even while some do not realize it themselves because Satan has deceived them (Rev. 12:9). God even uses the choices made by the spirit employed by the ungodly to accomplish His purposes (Eph. 2:2). God even allows the god of this age to blind others who will not believe anyway (2 Cor. 4:4).

God knows the future from the present from the past. There is nothing that takes God by surprise (Ps. 139:1-6). So, if these **instruments of death** catch humanity by surprise and some perish who have yet to hear the gospel at the time that they perished, God knew their status before Him. God, from eternity, knew they never would respond to Him in time, so had they lived longer, it would not have made a difference. They would not have lived longer because, since God knows that past from the present from the future, since He sees it all together, He knew when the calamity was coming, and He knew who would be affected by the catastrophe. He knows the divine appointment of everyone (Heb. 9:27). The **fiery shafts** that inflict this harm can be those **arrows** (people) that persecute His people since it is expected that God's people will be persecuted for following Him (2 Tim. 3:12).

## Questions for self-reflection:

(1) If you are reading this and you have discovered that you are not right with God, will you turn to Him today and be spared this wrath?

(2) If you are saved, looking back to your life before you were a Christian, what instruments of death were prepared for you that were God's means to bring you to a place of repentance?

(3) How would you act differently if you knew that you were the means by which one of God's children would hear the gospel and be saved?

**7:14. Behold, the wicked brings forth iniquity; Yes, he conceives trouble and brings forth falsehood.**

---

**The wicked** are synonymous with the lost. The **iniquity** that the unrighteous **bring** forth marks their lifestyles (Rom. 3:9). God reveals His wrath against their unrighteous iniquity (Rom. 1:18). They are full of iniquity (Jb 15:16). It will manifest itself in different forms in different people of different ages. But the sinful nature with which humanity is born thanks to Adam and Eve's sin in the Garden will inevitably produce sin (Rom. 3:23). Even the good deeds that the unrighteous do, because those deeds are done devoid of faith in the God that has given them life, amount to nothing more than filthy rags (Isa. 64:6). God weighs not only the actions but also the attitudes and the thoughts of those He has created in His image (Gen. 6:5, 1 Sam. 16:7, 1 Kgs 8:39, 1 Chron. 28:9, Ps. 19:14, Ps. 24:4, Ps. 26:2, Prov. 16:2, Prov. 21:2, Prov. 27:19, Jer. 12:3, Jer. 17:9-10, Hos 6:6, Matt. 12:34, Matt. 15:19, Mk 7:21, Lk 6:45, Lk 16:15, Acts 1:24, 1 Cor. 4:5, 1 Thess. 2:4, 2 Tim. 2:22, Heb. 4:12-13, Heb. 10:22, Jas 4:8, 1 Pet. 3:3-4, Rev. 2:23).

For the unrighteous, God's law, though impressed upon their conscience (Rom. 2:15), is not the deterrent from sin that it is for the righteous (Rom. 8:7). For many, God and His law are mocked (2 Chron. 32:17, Ps. 14:1-2, Ps. 74:8-12, Ps. 74:17-23, Jer. 17:15-16, 2 Pet. 3:3-6, Jude 1:17-20). Such people fail to realize, even as they mock and scoff, that, ultimately, God is not mocked (Gal. 6:7-8). They will reap what they sow. While they busy themselves and **conceive trouble and bring forth falsehood** against God and God's children, the saints must wait patiently to not give place to the devil (Eph. 4:27) and let God repay with His vengeance in His timing (Rom. 12:19), trusting that God will make every wrong right.

While the wicked conceives trouble, planning his next iniquitous choice, he does so with the brain that he has received from God as a gracious gift. While his hands and feet are swift to shed blood (Rom. 3:15), he shed that blood using the extremities that God has created him with and expected that he would glorify Him with (1 Cor. 6:18-20). This is why sin is such an affront to a holy

God. We can only commit the sins we commit because God gives us the next breath with which to practice them (Dan. 5:23). God allows our brains to function such that they conceive of the iniquity that we commit with our body parts. God, and our neighbor, whom we should love as we love ourselves (Mk 12:31), receive our wicked plots. The duo that we are to love we instead treat with contempt because we lust and do not have (Jas 4:2). We commit many of these sins with little regard to man's reaction to them. We give little regard to what God says about the sins we plot. Yet, God patiently, mercifully, lovingly restrains judgment for the perfect time because God's justice, unlike man's justice, is always executed perfectly and at the perfect time (Jb 34:12, Ps. 9:7-8, Rom. 12:19).

The righteous must remember that while they were unsaved, God was very patient with them (Gen. 18:32, Exod. 34:6, Num. 14:18, Num. 14:27, Neh. 9:16-17, Neh. 9:30-31, Ps. 78:38, Ps. 86:15, Ps. 103:8, Ps. 145:8, Isa. 7:13, Isa. 42:14, Isa. 48:9, Jer. 15:15, Ezek.20:17, Jon. 4:2, Mic. 7:19, Joel 2:13, Nah. 1:3, Acts 13:18, Rom. 2:4, Rom. 9:22-24, 1 Pet. 3:20, 2 Pet. 3:9). If the righteous can remember that fact, that can help them be more patient with others as they wait for God to right all the wrongs that the wicked have perpetuated (Ps. 103:8, Prov. 20:22).

Sometimes the unrighteous think wrong things about God, and these improper thoughts are a stumbling block that prevents them from coming to Him for salvation. One of the many offensive thoughts that the wicked have about God is that it is wrong for the Lord to be so holy and just to punish anyone for anything. They cannot reconcile how the God who they have heard is loving and merciful would punish anyone. What such misinformed people fail to consider is that the love (Jn 3:16), mercy (Eph. 2:4), grace (Titus 2:11), and patience is being extended to them as it is extended to everyone else while they blaspheme His holy name and live selfishly for themselves instead of living for Him as they should. While they mock Him for His retribution, He patiently endures it giving them time to seek Him so they can find Him (Jer. 29:13). If they do not seek Him and find Him, it is not His fault. It is their own fault. They have brought forth iniquity (Ps. 51:5), conceived trouble (Ps. 58:3), and brought forth falsehood as they made a god in their image in their likeness rather than worshipping the one true God who made them in His image (Rom. 1:23).

## Questions for self-reflection:

(1) How has your life changed with respect to your attitude toward and practice of iniquity since your salvation?
(2) When you think of your loved ones who remain outside of the faith, how are their lives different from yours?
(3) If God were to put your thoughts up on a screen for everyone to see today, would you be embarrassed?
(4) Are God's commands a burden to you that you wish you did not have to bear, or is it your pleasure to strive (albeit imperfectly) to follow God?
(5) Do you wish that God would treat others more harshly because of their sins? Do you wish that God would treat you more harshly because of your sins?

**7:15. He made a pit and dug it out, And has fallen into the ditch which he made.**

---

The wicked set traps for the righteous, thinking themselves to be so clever. The Jews did so to Christ in Luke 20. In addition, the Jews did so to the apostle Paul in Acts 23.

The wicked often think themselves to be so much wiser than the righteous (Rom. 1:22). They believe that the righteous are so foolish to live in such a dedicated way to a 'blind faith.' They think that since there is more evidence for godlessness rather than deductively concluding that the available evidence suitably points to the reality of God, they would be better off to live for themselves. So, they try to set traps for the righteous to get the righteous to stumble in their faith. They do not realize that by doing so, they become the millstone that Christ talked about that deserves strict judgment (Matt. 18:6). In doing so, the wicked have unwittingly **made a pit and dug it out** for themselves. They have, unbeknownst to themselves, made a trap for themselves to fall directly into God's hand (Heb. 10:31).

While they live in this unrighteous way, they have no fear of reaping what they have sown (Eccles.8:11). They are a law unto themselves (Rom. 2:14) and are not subject to God's law (Rom. 8:7). Such people are in the flesh, and those in the flesh cannot please God (Rom. 8:8). When they stray for so long that they are given over to reprobation (Rom. 1:28), or when they meet God in judgment (2 Cor. 5:10), it will be evident that they will have their part in the lake which burns with fire and brimstone (Rev. 21:8). It will be apparent that the **ditch** they had hoped to catch the righteous in will instead be reserved for them. The story of Esther illustrates the principle here, where the wicked Haman was himself hanged on the gallows (Est 7:1-10) that he had hoped to snare Mordecai with (Est 5:9-14).

**Questions for self-reflection:**

(1) Before the Lord saved you, what traps did you set for the righteous by your unrighteous lifestyle?

(2) Are you humbler since your justification, or were you humbler before you received Christ's righteousness?

(3) Did you feel more secure in your lifestyle living for yourself when you were lost, or do you feel more confident in your lifestyle living for God now as a child of the King?

**7:16. His trouble shall return upon his own head, And his violent dealing shall come down on his own crown.**

---

That which the doer of evil planned to do against others will be done to that doer of evil themselves. The judgment that the doer of evil hoped to see come upon others to whom it is not suited will instead **return upon** themselves. **His violent dealing** will **come down on his own crown.** The **trouble** they hoped to set up for another will ensnare them instead. See the notes on the previous verse.

Esther is an apt illustration of the principle just described. It also happed somewhat like this for Judas Iscariot. Iscariot wanted to get rid of Jesus, and he liked money. The jealous Jews used that to their advantage and bribed Judas to deliver Jesus to them so Jesus could be crucified (Matt. 26:14-16). After Judas did what the Jews wanted Judas to do, Judas felt the sting of guilt that he should have felt all along (Matt. 27:3-5). But by then, it was too late. Jesus would soon die for sin and sinners. Judas could not do anything to stop the foreordained result. However, rather than go to God in repentance and for reconciliation, Judas was overcome with guilt and ungodly sorrow (contrast with the godly sorrow Paul defines in 2 Corinthians 7) that led to him taking his own life (Matt. 27:3-5).

It is common for the wicked to plot against the righteous and try to undermine the righteous in one way or another. Scripture records that happening to Paul (Acts 9:23, Acts 23:12-35). In this life, the righteous will sometimes be allowed to continue for God with virtually no resistance from the ungodly (1 Chron. 22:9). Other times in this life, the persecution will be very heavy against the righteous (2 Tim. 3:12).

Whether the righteous suffer from a little persecution or a lot of persecution, the righteous still should respond with trust in the sovereignty of the Lord. If the persecution from the unrighteous is heavy, the righteous can live according to Scripture. They cannot repay evil for evil (Rom. 12:17). They can follow Christ's example, who was reviled and did not revile in return but trusted

His Father to avenge Him in due time (1 Pet. 2:23). They can repay evil with good and make the unrighteous feel guilty for their unjust mistreatment (Rom. 12:19-20). If the unrighteous experience a season of reaping for the sowing they have done in this life, perhaps the Lord can use that to bring the unrighteous to a place of repentance. Maybe the reaping will create a response of brokenness over sin and of humility that will result in the unrighteous humbling themselves under the mighty hand of God that He might exalt them in due time (1 Pet. 5:6). Perhaps they will humble themselves so God can exalt them (Matt. 23:12).

## Questions for self-reflection:

(1) When you were lost, if you knew that God said that the wickedness you plotted would return in measure to you, would that have changed the way you planned to do evil?
(2) In times of persecution, do you wish to be living back in seasons without persecution?
(3) If you live without persecution, are you grateful to God for your relative peace?
(4) If you suffer for the faith, if someone who had persecuted you came to saving faith, how would you respond to that person?

**7:17. I will praise the Lord according to His righteousness, And will sing praise to the name of the Lord Most High.**

One of the ways the Lord demonstrates His righteousness is by vindicating the righteous. God shows this sometimes by letting the wicked get caught in their own schemes. He shows this by judging the wicked in various tangible ways. He shows this by rewarding the righteous in specific ways. When the psalmist recognized judgment from reaping and sowing had occurred, it showed evidence to the psalmist that the Lord was working behind the scenes in the minutia of life. The Lord had always worked everything together for the good of the psalmist (Rom. 8:28).

All the saved can **praise the Lord according to His righteousness.** The saved have the righteousness of the Lord imputed to their account. When they were dead in trespasses and sins (Eph. 2:1), He raised them and seated them in heavenly places (Eph. 2:6). He made them alive, giving them His righteousness, and taking their sin so He could forgive them. Thus, the justified saints begin to be sanctified and one day will be glorified (Rom. 8:29-30).

The Lord has been vindicating His righteousness in His people in every generation since the beginning. Genesis records this when Cain slew Abel (Gen. 4) in that Cain had a consequence after he killed his brother. Scripture demonstrates this in the Flood account when Noah, a preacher of righteousness (2 Pet. 2:5), predicted God's righteous flooding of the earth when he repeatedly warned those who perished in the floodwaters by the preaching that came before the rains. The Lord vindicated His righteousness in the life of Joseph when He elevated Joseph to a place of prominence in Egypt (Gen. 41) after Joseph's brothers thought to do Joseph harm (Gen. 37). Also, the Lord vindicated His righteousness when Moses delivered Israel from Egyptian bondage through various signs and wonders and drowned Pharaoh and the Egyptians in the Red Sea (Exod.). The Lord vindicated His righteousness by having godly kings like David and Solomon sit on the throne in righteous authority over God's people.

Most importantly for the entire human race, the Lord vindicated His righteousness in the sending of the Lord Jesus Christ at the fullness of time to live a perfect life and die a substitutionary death (Gal. 4:4-5). He is fully God (1 Tim. 2:5, 1 Tim. 3:16), so He satisfied God's demand for perfection. He is fully man, so He fully satisfied man's need to keep the Law (Matt. 5:17). Through faith in Christ, the unrighteous receive the righteousness of Christ and eternal life (1 Cor 6:9-11). The just, whose faith is in the risen Lord Jesus Christ, **sing praise to the name of the Lord Most High** for the redemption that He caused on their behalf.

### Questions for self-reflection:

(1) When has the Lord vindicated you for your righteous life?
(2) Are there other ways that you can see God working all things together for your good?
(3) Are there people you have shared the gospel with who have not responded to the gospel with saving faith? How does their lack of saving response make you feel? How do you think Noah felt when the preacher of righteousness did not get a single convert to his preaching? How do you think Noah felt when the Lord vindicated Noah by sending the flood?

# Psalm 8

**8:1. O Lord, our Lord, How excellent is Your name in all the earth, Who have set Your glory above the heavens!**

---

The psalmist affirms that the **Lord**, His Lord, is the only true Lord that there is (Jas 2:19) **in all the earth**. People want to run from the accountability that God demands of them. They want to be their own boss. They do not want anyone telling them what to do. Christians understand that they are bought with a price and are not their own (1 Cor. 6:19-20).

Since He is the only Lord, His **name is excellent**. No other name can compare to the name above all names (Ps. 148:13, Phil. 2:9-10). Since Jesus Christ is Lord, every knee will bow to Him either in this life or in the next life (Phil. 2:9-11). The psalmist has met the Lord personally, like others before him who have tasted and seen that the Lord is good (Ps. 34:8). He knows this, in part, because the Lord supernaturally revealed Himself to the psalmist and other inspired writers before him to write what he (and they) recorded in the inspired Word (2 Tim. 3:16). God's name refers to the totality of Who He is, how He has revealed Himself to humanity, and how He has graciously reconciled them unto Himself through Christ and the gospel (2 Cor. 5:18). It truly is an excellent thing that man, as sinful as he is, can be brought into a place of fellowship with the One whom he has so egregiously offended by willfully choosing to sin. When a sinner properly understands his miserable, wretched condition (Rev. 3:17) before a holy and righteous God, he also understands that for him even to have an opportunity to be reconciled to that God is a very loving thing for that God to provide (Rom. 5:8).

It is excellent for such a transcendent Being to create everything and make man a little lower than the angels (Ps. 8:5, Heb. 2:7). He then equips man, because He created man in His own image (Gen. 1:27), with the ability to create and discover that He is there so that He can be the object of man's worship. Man can scarcely comprehend how a holy God would condescend to bring sinful humanity into a relationship with Him. After all, God owes wicked man nothing, and when sinful humankind comprehends that he owes his Creator everything, God's reconciling grace makes God so glorious that man can scarcely comprehend it.

That **glory**, from man's perspective, God's glory, is **above the heavens**. Man's only appropriate response is humble submission and worship to the One who so graciously gave man life and everything he needs for life and godliness (2 Pet. 1:3-4). God's glory was made visible through the perfections of Christ. His glory came down and tabernacled among men on the earth for a time. He perfectly displayed all of God's attributes and showed mankind the Father. After His humiliation, the Father exalted Christ the Son to the His right hand, where His glory remains above the heavens.

**Questions for self-reflection:**

(1) When you were lost and lived as though you were accountable to nobody, was your life easier or harder?
(2) What ways is the Lord is superior to all other names, gods or otherwise?
(3) In what ways have you tasted and seen that the Lord is good?
(4) If God did not have to create us and equip us so that we could search for and find Him, why would He do that?
(5) How are you demonstrating God's glory through the gospel of Christ to others?

**8:2. Out of the mouth of babes and nursing infants, You have ordained strength, Because of Your enemies, That You may silence the enemy and the avenger.**

---

Psalm 8:2 is quoted in Matthew 21:16 when Jesus rebuked the Pharisees when the Pharisees criticized Jesus for having children come to Him and for recognizing Him as the Messiah, while the Pharisees refused to acknowledge Jesus rightly as Messiah. In one sense, the miracle of life, uniquely appreciated and celebrated by the human race, is so miraculous that humans can recognize it as somewhat miraculous. However, they cannot fully describe it.

Many months of divine miracles have to take place from conception to birth so that the mother can produce milk and the baby can cry for that milk. The whole thing is quite miraculous. Parents should glorify God in that alone. Natural processes could never be sufficient to explain such a miracle. It is doubtful that the animal kingdom would even begin to contemplate these realities.

There is a figurative sense in which these words from the psalmist can be interpreted. The apostles and early church were the first to take the gospel message from Jerusalem after Christ's ascension and into the whole world. The message was so new, like a newborn mother's milk, that those who brought the news were new converts, and what came out of their mouth was analogous to what came **out of the mouth of babes and nursing infants.**

The message that they delivered had God's **strength** and Spirit behind it and was and is mightily used to save souls. The gospel brings spiritual power to those affected by it. It is how the Holy Spirit fills hearts and gives strength to believers. The **enemies** of the gospel display their enmity by their reaction to the message and in their treatment of the ambassadors of Christ. God has **silence**d His enemies by giving sheep testimonies that the lost cannot argue with so that the power behind the disciples is most obviously God's power (2 Cor. 4:7). The saved praise the God who bought them (Eph. 1:6). Their Lord and His followers strengthen the believers of the gospel. When the kingdom grows, this silences the enemy and avenger, Satan and his followers.

---

## Questions for self-reflection:

(1) What miracles have you experienced that you have taken for granted?

(2) As a saved person, what is your reputation among the unbelieving community?

(3) How can you silence Satan and his followers by your way of life?

**8:3. When I consider Your heavens, the work of Your fingers, The moon and the stars, which You have ordained,**

God created and dwells in **heaven** (Gen. 1:1). God made the **moon and the stars** (Gen. 1:14-19) when He spoke them into existence. They are **the work of** His **fingers**. He causes them to shine (Jb 38:7). The Lord formed the constellations (Jb 38:31). We can see the sky and some of the stars ourselves without the aid of a telescope. The human eye can look at the moon and the stars, while the human eye cannot look at the sun due to its brightness. God **ordained** these heavenly bodies as part of His glorious creation so that we would look to it and reasonably conclude that such beauty and order must necessitate a Creator that made and upholds it all (Heb. 1:2-3).

## Questions for self-reflection:

(1) When you consider the order with which everything was created and exists, how could people possibly believe that it all came about by random chance rather than by intelligent design?

(2) When you think about your loved ones who do not know the Lord, are you angry that they have rejected Him, or do you melt with compassion for them?

(3) How can you demonstrate the love of God to someone you know who is an unbeliever today?

**8:4. What is man that You are mindful of him, And the son of man that You visit him?**

---

Hebrews 2:6 quotes this verse. When the psalmist considered the splendor of creation, he understandably felt comparatively minute and insignificant. Compared to God in His greatness, **man** is frail, weak, and sick. For God to condescend to the level that He would seek a relationship with fallen man is remarkable. The **Son of Man** is a common title for Christ in His humanity (Matt. 12:32, Lk 19:10, Jn 1:51). Christ, in addition to being fully man, was also full deity (Col. 2:9). Christ assumed human nature in His incarnation but did not possess the sinful nature that the rest of us have (Phil. 2:5-11). That is why He could be tempted like we are and yet be without sin (Heb. 4:15). The title Son of Man is most frequently used by Christ to describe Himself.

God the Father **visit**ed God the Son with His presence to equip the Son to faithfully execute His divine mission of making purification for His people (Heb. 1:3). It is nothing short of miraculous that God the Father would be so **mindful** of the human race that had so devastated their standing with their Maker to sin His favor away. Miraculously, God took such great pains to reconcile the human race back to Himself after making such ruin of themselves. It is to the great benefit of mankind that God would **visit** them in the person of Christ to provide that propitiation once and for all so that man could approach God and have his sins removed. God the Father visited Christ in such a way to give Christ all the power and enablement He needed to be our perfect substitute.

### Questions for self-reflection:

---

(1) When you consider the splendor of creation, do you react like the psalmist, with humility and worship, or does it not affect you much?
(2) When you think about how God would condescend to have a relationship with you, does that make you want to draw even closer to Him, or would you instead keep God at arm's length?
(3) Who can you tell today about God's great love for them?

---

**8:5. For You have made him a little lower than the angels, And You have crowned him with glory and honor.**

Hebrews 2:7 quotes this verse. God's made Christ's human nature to be **a little lower than the angels.** Christ's union with the Father was so intimate that the two had the same essence (Heb. 1:3). God the Father had to be highly mindful of the close ties He would have with God the Son since they would work together on a plan to redeem sinful humanity.

Christ became lower than the angels when He took on human flesh and condescended to the earth to be our Substitute. God the Father **crowned** Christ the Son **with glory and honor** since God the Son completed the work He had set out to do (Jn 17:4, Heb. 1:3). He had asked His Father to glorify Him (Jn 17:1), and His Father obliged (Jn 12:28). God the Son was equal with God the Father in nature but took on humanity and became a servant for sinful humanity (Phil. 2:6-8). He endured rejection and humiliation, unlike any angels. He had an ordinary upbringing (Isa. 53:2). There was nothing that made Him stand out to others. Though He had a miraculous conception, He had a normal birth. The lack of much of a record of His childhood before the inauguration of His earthly ministry leads one to conclude that His life to that point was ordinary.

Despite all this, His Father paid exacting attention to every detail. He made the world, upheld all things by His Word (Col. 1:16-17), and yet had no place to sleep (Lk 9:58). God's glory radiated through Him (Matthew 17:1-12), yet He was reviled (1 Pet. 2:23). He had to learn obedience from what He suffered (Heb. 5:8), yet He was perfectly obedient (Phil. 2:8). He experienced sorrow, grief, and pain, each resulting from human fallenness, yet without possessing a fallen nature of His own.

God the Father did not need a human nature. God the Son needed human nature to be the Substitute for sinful humanity (2 Cor. 5:21). Christ taught obedience to earthly authorities (Mk 12:17) and was subject to them while on earth. Christ put on human nature. Angels did not put on human nature. In that way,

Christ was a little lower than angels. Christ, as fully human, was subject to sickness and suffering to which angels are not subject. Angels are not subject to sorrow. Christ was subject to sorrows. Christ lived under God's Law (Matt. 5:17, Gal. 4:4-5). Angels did not live under God's Law.

After Christ paid for sin, God the Father raised God the Son from the dead (Acts 13:30) and elevated Christ to the Father's own right hand (Eph. 1:20). He gave Him the name above all names so that every knee will bow to Him. Man who achieves the highest level of authority cannot expect every knee on heaven and earth to bow to him (Phil. 2:9-10). All judgment has been given to the Son (Jn 5:27). Finite man cannot say that. Finite man can hope to achieve an earthly position and judge a portion of humanity from that office.

Man cannot rightly require worship of fellow man. God can require worship from all His creation, including man. Sinful man is not crowned with glory. His sin prevents that in this life. The God-Man, the Lord Jesus Christ, however, was crowned with glory and honor. When God raised Him from the dead, He made a spectacle of the devil (Col. 2:15). He became the Judge of the living and the dead (2 Tim. 4:1). He was crowned with a crown of thorns so He could receive a crown of glory and honor. Now, from the right hand of the Father, He ever lives to intercede for the saints (Heb. 7:25), who have come to the Father by faith in the Son.

### Questions for self-reflection:

(1) Do you ever think about what it must have been like for Christ to have such intimate fellowswhip with the Father in heaven before His incarnation?

(2) Do you ever think about what Christ may have felt like He lost with respect to His proximity to the Father in the time that He came to earth to save His people?

(3) Do you ever think about how frustrated Christ must have been with the contrast of sinless heaven to the sinful world into which He entered?

(4) Do you ever think about how frustrated Christ must have been with the human ignorance that the society into which He entered willingly lived in?

(5) Are you glad the Christ humbled Himself for you so that you could be exalted to heaven with Him?

**8:6. You have made him to have dominion over the works of Your hands; You have put all things under his feet,**

---

Hebrews 2:7-8 quotes this passage. The translators seem to have switched the subjects as the lowercase 'him' could refer to the rest of humanity instead of the Lord Jesus Christ. **The works of Your hands,** referring to works made by God's hands, must be created. The sense may be that God has put humanity in charge of God's creation. It all ultimately belongs to God (Ps. 24:1). God entrusts it to man as stewardship for man to utilize for God's glory (1 Cor. 4:2), and in the creation account, God told man to take dominion over what He had created (Gen. 1:27-30).

Suppose the 'him' refers to the Lord Jesus Christ. In that case, this could also be saying that God the Father gave God the Son **dominion**, or rule, or charge, over all the works of God's hands after His resurrection. This historical event proved Christ's lordship when God exalted Him and gave Him the title above every other (Matt. 28:18, Phil. 2:9-11). There is biblical support for that point, as the New Testament tells us that Christ created everything and holds everything together (Col. 1:16-17). Christ, Himself said, after His resurrection, that He had been given all authority (Matt. 28:18). So, since Christ has all power and authority, everything over which Christ has absolute authority is **under His** proverbial **feet** (1 Cor. 15:26-27). This includes **all things**. Everything depends upon Christ for existence. Christ even permits wicked forces to exist, and they will bow to Him. Demons were cast out by His Word during His first advent (e.g., Matt. 8:28-34). All evil will be cast into the Lake of Fire one day (Rev. 20:7-15).

Christ is the Head of the church (Eph. 5:23). The church is subject to Christ (Eph. 5:24). Christ has given the church work to do (Matt. 28:18-20). He has given them dominion over the works of His hands. The primary work that Christ has employed the church to do is the preaching of the gospel. Once someone receives Christ by faith and joins the church, they edify one another (Rom. 14:19, Rom. 15:2, 1 Cor. 8:1, Eph. 4:11-12, Eph. 4:15-16, 1 Thess. 5:11), provoke one another to love and good works (Hebrews 10:24),

---

follow God in their families between Sundays, and serve God in their various callings between Sundays. The goal of all this is for those who belong to the church to be a light that commends the glorious gospel to the dark world that so desperately needs to see and hear it.

## Questions for self-reflection:

(1) Is there anything that does not ultimately belong to God?
(2) Would God be pleased with how you are handling what He has entrusted into your care?
(3) Since everything depends on Christ for its existence, then even your enemies depend on Christ for their existence. Knowing this, how will you treat your enemies differently?
(4) Knowing that wicked people who oppose you will one day bow to Him, does that help you treat them better now?

**8:7.** **All sheep and oxen—Even the beasts of the field,**

Referring to the previous verse, if the Lord Jesus Christ is the subject as opposed to the rest of humanity, which is a distinct possibility, then this verse teaches that God is sovereign over all **the beasts of the field,** including but not limited to **all sheep and oxen.** This is a true statement.

God can use animals to accomplish His purposes. He used birds to tell Noah and his family that it was safe to come off the Ark (Gen. 8:6-12). God placed an animal, a ram, at the right time in the right place so that Abraham would not kill his son, Isaac (Gen. 22). God used animals to bring plagues upon the Egyptians (Exod. 8 Frogs, Exod. 8 Lice, Exod. 8 Flies, Exod. 9 Livestock, Exod. 10 Locusts). Likewise true is that God gave man authority over God's creation. Animals can be used for food and clothing.

**Question for self-reflection:**

(1) How has God used the animal kingdom to provide for you?

**8:8. The birds of the air, And the fish of the sea That pass through the paths of the seas.**

---

God can use **the birds of the air** to accomplish His purposes. God used birds to tell Noah and his family that it was safe to come off the Ark (Gen. 8:6-12). God used quails, a bird from the air, to feed his unthankful people (Exod.16). God used ravens to feed His prophet, Elijah (1 Kgs 17). Jesus spoke about how since God takes care of birds not made in God's image, how much more can we, those created in God's image, trust God to take care of us (Matt. 6:26). The psalmist spoke of how the birds sing to their Creator, showing us that we need to as well (Ps. 104:12). The psalmist said that God knows every bird (Ps. 50:11). The Lord Jesus used birds to illustrate those who do not respond to the gospel (Matt. 13:4). Jesus said that no bird dies apart from Divine knowledge or permission (Matt. 10:29). God said that people die to be food for birds (Jer. 7:33). All creation, including birds, are ultimately under God's sovereign rule (Ezek. 38:20).

God likewise uses **the fish of the sea** for His purposes. First, he created them to show that He is there (Gen. 1:21). Second, God brought a great fish to swallow a disobedient prophet (Jon. 1:17). Third, God used that same fish as a location for that same prophet to seek and find the Lord in humble repentance (Jon. 2:1-10). Fourth, Jesus used just a couple of fish to show His deity by multiplying them (Matt. 14:14-21). Jesus either created fish out of nothing or brought fish to where the disciples could catch them to feed and provide for the disciples after His resurrection and prove to the disciples that Jesus had raised from the dead as He said He would (Jn 21:1-14). God uses all His creation to proclaim His glory. Because of Christ, man has the freedom to use the creation to provide for himself responsibly.

**Questions for self-reflection:**

(1) Is there anything that God created that God cannot use to accomplish His purposes?

(2) How can God use you to accomplish His purposes?

(3) How is God presently using you to accomplish His purposes?

**8:9. O Lord, our Lord, How excellent is Your name in all the earth!**

See 8:1, as this same phrase is repeated there.

# Psalm 9

**9:1. I will praise You, O Lord, with my whole heart; I will tell of all Your marvelous works.**

---

The psalmist was ready to sing in joyful **praise** to the **Lord**. It was going to be public vocal singing, not just quietly singing in the head. His heart was joining his head in this song. This was not a case of honoring the Lord with the lips while the heart was far from Him (Matt. 15:8). If the setting is in a public place of worship with a congregation, this is a good reminder that worship is not just the time when music is playing. Instead, worship is the entire time.

Beyond that, worship should not merely be a Sunday morning activity. Worship should be an everyday lifestyle that springs from the **whole heart** of the redeemed (Ps. 1:2, Rom. 12:2, 2 Cor. 10:5, 1 Pet. 3:15). It is not something to check into on Sunday morning and check out of on Sunday afternoon. It is to be engaged in from sunrise to sundown consistently and practiced from the opening of the eyes to the shutting of the eyes repetitively. Singing, listening intently to what the Lord is saying through His preached Word from the pulpit, and listening for His voice when reading the Word during private devotions can all be worshipful activities. Believers can worship when we think of all He has done for us or when we pray to Him.

Our problem is that our whole hearts are often not adequately prepared to properly praise the Lord because we have divided affections too often. When we worship the Lord corporately, we cannot do so in the intended, prescribed manner if there exists a tension in our hearts between the things of the Lord and the cares of the world (Matt. 13:22). If we direct the meditations of our hearts toward heaven, if we have set our affections on things above rather than on things of the earth (Col. 3:1-3), it will be more feasible for the saint to praise the Lord with the whole heart. The cares of the world should be left at the door when entering the Lord's house.

The psalmist must understand, we must realize, that our human limitations affect our ability to praise the Lord with our whole hearts. Our most pious acts of devotion are still affected by the Fall, by our indwelling sin. If that were not true, then all the New Testament commands to put off sin would be pointless if there was no sin to put off. When we think about how lost and undone we were before God redeemed us, this can result in praising the Lord with our whole hearts. When we think about how our sinful natures lived for sin and self and how when we were lost, and without strength, Christ died for the ungodly (Rom. 5:6), this can result in praise lifted to the Lord. It can be overwhelming when we think that it was not just us who was in this desperate condition, but it was the entirety of the human race who shared in our desperation. Yet there will be people from every tribe, tongue, and nation in heaven (Rev. 7:9) worshiping the Lord in heaven before the throne. Therefore, the justified saint should unashamedly praise the Lord. As much as we can, as much as our sinful condition permits, by utilizing divine grace, we should worship the Lord with hearts that have been consecrated to Him.

All of God's **works** are **marvelous**. He created the heavens and earth out of nothing by speaking it into existence (Gen. 1). He created the human race out of the dust of the ground in His own image (Gen. 1:26-28, Gen. 2:7). He upholds everything by a Word (Col. 1:16-17, Heb. 1:2). He provides for the birds of the air (Matt. 6:26), the fish of the sea, and the human race (Matt. 6:33). He worked the salvation of members of the human race by enacting a plan in eternity past to condescend and become fully human while remaining fully divine and becoming a curse for sinful man so that lost man, undone and depraved, could be set free from sin's bondage (Gal. 3:13, Gal. 4:4-5). He prepared a place for them that where He is, there we may also be (Jn 14:2-3). One of the most marvelous works performed by God, perhaps the most marvelous work, is regenerating a lost sinner. He raises them from spiritual death and makes them alive (Eph. 2:1-5). He gives their spiritually blind eyes new spiritual sight. He unstops their spiritually deaf ears allowing them to hear spiritual things with understanding. He invigorates their spiritual paralysis. He makes them a new creation (2 Cor. 5:17).

One day, He will judge all the living and the dead (2 Tim. 4:1). One day, the roaring lion (1 Pet. 5:8) will have no one left to devour because he will be cast forever into the lake of fire (Rev. 20:10). One day, the cohorts of the roaring lion will be lumped into all the enemies, which will all end up under His feet (1 Cor. 15:26-27). One day, all the dead in Christ will rise (1 Thess. 4:16). One day, He will set up His eternal kingdom. All God's works are marvelous.

## Questions for self-reflection:

(1) Do you worship God throughout the week or only on church mornings?

(2) How can you be more mindful of God's presence throughout the entire day?

(3) What is your attitude to the teaching you hear? Do you want to understand it to apply it, or do you look for exceptions?

(4) Do you hunger for God's Word daily?

(5) Like Jesus, do you live by every Word that proceeds from God?

(6) How can you separate from the world more completely and separate unto God more fully?

(7) Aside from general creation, what marvelous works has God done in your life to make you into the person you have become?

**9:2. I will be glad and rejoice in You; I will sing praise to Your name, O Most High.**

---

The psalmist knows that it is futile for him to boast about his accomplishments. He knows that it is futile to boast in his strength (1 Cor. 1:26). He knows that salvation is by grace through faith and not of works (Eph.2:8-9). He knows that any deliverance he has experienced is ultimately not due to his strength but because the Lord got the victory. As a child of God, he knows that he has received many kingdom benefits that the lost do not understand and will never enjoy (Eph. 1:3). He is aware that the righteousness he possesses has nothing to do with anything in himself but has everything to do with the Lord and His imputed righteousness (Phil. 3:9). He knows that any good that comes out of him only does so because the Lord works in him to will and to do His good pleasure (Phil. 2:12-13). He knows that he is forgiven because the Lord is merciful to forgive him despite his sins (Eph. 2:4). He knows that there are many reasons for a child of the King to **rejoice**.

For all the salvation benefits enjoyed by the righteous, there are many reasons to **sing praise to His name**, the name of the **Most High** God. The things of this world that bring pleasure, which are ultimately good and perfect from the Father of lights (Jas 1:17), are objects that sinful humanity far too often treasures and adores to sinful extremes. In doing so, they bless the gifts and not the Giver of the gifts. These are improper affections. These are affections that have been set on the earth. According to the apostle Paul, the proper affections are to be placed above, towards heaven (Col. 3:1-3). The regenerated heart sees this. Christ becomes the ultimate object of joy and worship because He communicates every spiritual blessing to the sheep (Eph. 1:3-14).

No wonder He is the One in whom we are to rejoice. No matter what circumstances befall the child of God, they can always sing praise to His name because the worst that can happen to them in this life is the killing of the body (Matt. 10:28). At that time, they will immediately be with the Lord, where sorrows will cease (2 Cor. 5:8).

## Questions for self-reflection:

(1) What reasons do you have to rejoice in God? Write a list.
(2) When you have trouble and trials, if you were to refer to the list you wrote above, would that help you endure the hardship?
(3) Have you ever felt joy because of the salvation you enjoy in Christ?

**9:3. When my enemies turn back, They shall fall and perish at Your presence.**

---

In Exodus, when Egypt pursued Israel after initially letting Israel go, they perished in the presence of the Lord as He used Moses to cause the Red Sea to drown them (Exod. 14). When the plot of wicked Haman was discovered, he perished in the king's presence, which was a type of how God's enemies will perish before Him (see Est). David had his share of enemies **turn back** and perish at God's presence. The Philistines turned back when Goliath was killed (1 Sam. 17). Joshua's enemies turned back and fell at the presence of God's army all through the book of Joshua.

When Jesus confronted and cast out demons, the demons had no choice but to turn back and be cast out (Matt. 8:28-34). When Jesus identified Himself at His arrest, those who were out to get Him fell at His presence (Jn 18:5-6). When the Lord returns to take back everything for Himself and correct everything that man has corrupted, He will come in such a way that His enemies will **fall and perish at** His **presence** (2 Thess. 1:6-9). Ultimately, all God's enemies will perish in His presence forevermore. There is good reason for God's people to be glad and rejoice in the Lord, for them to sing praise to His name because He avenges His justice when His **enemies** perpetuate violence against His people. God will make all wrongs right. His people need to have the patience to wait for God to do so in His timing.

### Questions for self-reflection:

---

(1) Even if it appears that your enemies have free reign now and are not close to turning back, how does it help you endure to know that they will one day turn back?
(2) What can you do to become more patient and help you endure the hardships that come your way?

**9:4. For You have maintained my right and my cause; You sat on the throne judging in righteousness.**

---

Since their covenant relationship began, the psalmist knew that God was for him and not against him (Rom. 8:31). Likewise, he knew that since God was for him, none could be against him (Ps. 27:1, Ps. 56:9, Ps. 118:6, Heb. 13:6). None could separate the psalmist from God's love (Rom. 8:38-39). Even though there would be times of adversity (Jas 1:2), the psalmist knew that God would be with him and supply him with sufficient resources to do God's will (Phil. 4:19). God helped the psalmist overcome his enemies. The psalmist and His God shared a common **cause**. Since the psalmist and God fought for each other and not against each other, the psalmist could count on God to support him. God allowed the psalmist to succeed in this instance because that best vindicated God in this specific circumstance. God's ideal does not always win out. God's ideal is seldom the most popular choice among the heathen.

God's always judges with **righteousness**. God's people can always count on God to make perfect rulings even if His directives do not appear to be the path of least resistance for the righteous. God has appointed a day to judge the world in righteousness (Acts 17:30-31). On that day, He will acquit the just and will by no means clear the guilty (Exod. 34:7). The saved will inherit eternal life and a kingdom (Matt. 25:23). He provides them with grace from His **throne** of grace (Heb. 4:16). The lost will have their part in the lake of fire (Rev. 21:8). God's judgment is always the proper judgment because there is no darkness in God to pollute His judgment (1 Jn 1:5). While the wicked prospers, it may not appear to the righteous that God's judgment is succeeding (Jer. 12:1).

Perhaps His people should remember that God is also concerned about performing the invisible work inside his people during the adversity He allows in their lives (Phil. 1:6). His people already know that He fights for them and is powerful enough to change their circumstances if the change in circumstances is in His sovereign plan. Therefore, the righteous should continue to patiently endure their momentarily light affliction and trust that they have a great reward awaiting them after they take their final breath (Jas 1:12, Matt. 5:11-12).

## Questions for self-reflection:

(1) Do your circumstances ever cause you to doubt the reality that God is really for you and not against you?

(2) How have you seen God provide resources for you to endure temptation?

(3) Are you relieved to know that a day is coming when God will make all wrongs right?

(4) How has God used the adversity He has allowed you to experience to promote spiritual growth in you?

**9:5. You have rebuked the nations, You have destroyed the wicked; You have blotted out their name forever and ever.**

---

The psalmist could sing praise to the Lord with his whole heart (Ps. 9:1). He could be glad and rejoice in the Lord (Ps. 9:2). The Lord had done marvelous works (Ps. 9:2) that the psalmist benefited from when the Lord turned the enemies of the psalmist back (Ps. 9:3). The Lord's providence had overrun these wicked heathen **nations** that oppressed the Lord's people. The Lord **rebuked** the nations that came against the His people by divinely stopping their persecution. God killed the heathen people and **destroyed** them from among the land of the living. He **blotted out forever**. They would no longer afflict the psalmist or any other godly people.

In our day, Christians are persecuted by the unrighteous (2 Tim. 3:12). The unrighteous will not inherit God's kingdom (1 Cor. 6:9). When a sinner trusts Christ for salvation, that is a rebuke to the enemies of the cross (1 Cor. 1:18). The gospel rebukes the pagan philosophies of the present age (Col. 2:1-10). The doctrines of the day elevate secularism and attempt to reduce the influence of godliness. They try to overrun historic Christianity and induce conformity to the world (Rom. 12:2). The biblically literate Christian recognizes this and is not surprised by this (1 Tim. 4:1-5, 2 Tim. 2:14-26, 2 Tim. 3:1-9, 2 Tim. 4:3-4, Ti 1:10-16, Ti 3:9-11, Jude 1:5-19). The biblically literate Christian realizes that in every generation, there will be a segment of the population that Satan influences that attempts to lead people away from the truth of God. The gospel is a solid rebuke to these false teachers. The gospel is the power of God unto salvation to those who are being saved. The gospel is foolishness to those who are perishing (1 Cor. 1:18). It is a rebuke to the heathen nations since they reject it so strongly. They would not be willing to trade their sin and selfishness for the sacrifice and service that the gospel demands.

When oppressors to the truth reap what they sow and eventually die, they meet God in judgment on their appointed day (Heb. 9:27) and are destroyed (Rev. 21:8). It is as if the wicked

---

want to perish. While they would never admit that to the righteous, their response to the offer of reconciliation seems to indicate otherwise.

One day, the righteous will be able to rejoice because those who oppress them will meet their ignominious end and will have **their name blotted out forever**. Thus, while on the one hand, it will be sad that the unrighteous will meet their appointed end, it will be joyous because the God of righteousness will have vindicated His name and His people when He metes out judgment on the wicked.

**Questions for self-reflection:**

(1) How have you seen the Lord put a stop to wicked agendas?
(2) Does your life rebuke the pagan philosophies of the day?
(3) How are you protecting yourself from being led away from the truth?
(4) When you hear the gospel preached as one who has claimed to have responded to it with saving faith, is it music to your ears, or does it make you uncomfortable?

**9:6. O enemy, destructions are finished forever! And you have destroyed cities; Even their memory has perished.**

The psalmist had a particular **enemy** that God had forever removed from the earth. In every generation, the righteous have enemies that oppress them (Matt. 5:11-12). In the end, the Antichrist will be the ultimate enemy (2 Thess. 2:8). Satan now is the enemy of the church and, therefore, of individual Christians (Jn 14:30, Jn 16:11, Eph. 6:11, 1 Jn 3:7, Rev. 12:7, Rev. 20:2, Rev. 20:10).

There will come a future day when Satan and all his minions will be cast into the Lake of Fire forever and ever. (Rev. 20:10). This will keep the new heaven and new earth free from his influence. Thus, there will be perfect peace on the earth.

Before this time, however, Antichrist and those who follow his evil lead will wreak havoc on the earth. Prophetic passages in Daniel (Dan. 7) and Revelation (among others) foretell of the time when they will exert their influence and then will be forever vanquished when the Lord returns (Rev. 11:2, Rev. 19:20).

God will **destroy** what the unrighteous have built, and the unrighteous will no longer influence the world. When they perish, righteousness will so consume everything that even the memory of the activity of the unrighteous will be no more. It will have **perished.** The righteous will rule with their King on the earth from Jerusalem. See Revelation 21-22. All the enemies of the Lord Jesus Christ will be under His feet (1 Cor. 15:26-27).

### Questions for self-reflection:

(1) Have you seen the church experience opposition?
(2) Have you ever publicly opposed the church?
(3) Now that you are in the church, what is your attitude towards those who oppose the church?
(4) Are you happy that the enemies of God will end up in the lake of fire, or do you want to see them rescued through the gospel?

(5) When you think about the time on earth when there will be no more sin, and there will only be righteousness, what kind of emotions do you have?

**9:7. But the Lord shall endure forever; He has prepared His throne for judgment.**

---

In contrast to the unrighteous who will all perish, the righteous **Lord shall endure forever**. The eternal God has no beginning or end (Ps. 90:2, Jude 1:25, Rev. 1:8). Even while the influence of Satan perpetuates on this earth now (Ps. 2:1, 1 Jn 5:19), a day is coming when it will end (1 Cor. 15:26-27, Rev. 20:10-15). His enemies, one by one, are ending up under His feet, and one day they will all be under His feet. He sits in heaven and laughs as they rage against Him (Ps. 2:4). While Satan's people think they are winning, that concept is almost humorous to the Lord because He knows that He is working His plan according to the counsel of His will (Eph. 1:11) for the good of His people (Rom. 8:28).

The Lord has always been the ultimate eternal Judge of all humanity. Even as the world schemes to overthrow His influence, He waits patiently for their divine appointment when they will face Him (Acts 17:30-31. Heb. 7:27). When they do, He opens the books and renders His eternal verdict (Rev. 20:12). The question is the same for everyone: What did you do with my Son? Those who received Christ enter into the eternal bliss and perfect peace of everlasting life. Those who rejected Christ enter into eternal torment reserved for those who led ungodly lives (Ps. 112:10, Matt. 8:12, Matt. 22:13, Matt. 25:30, Lk 13:28, Jn 3:36, Rev. 21:8). He reserves His righteous **judgment** for them (2 Pet 2:9).

Sometimes the Lord intervenes in history for righteous judgment against His enemies in the lives of His people. There are times when the Lord waits for the appointed day of death to judge. Either way, nobody can escape the judgment **throne** of God (2 Cor. 5:10). People go to great lengths to try to live longer and cheat death. There is no escaping it. The unrighteous cannot escape their fate. The righteous have nothing to fear because the Lord has saved them from the wrath to come through the atoning death of the Lord Jesus Christ.

---

**Questions for self-reflection:**

(1) What emotions do you have when you think about the end of Satan's influence?

(2) When you think about the judgment of condemnation that you will avoid because of your faith in Christ, what emotions does that cause you to have about those who are still in their sins?

(3) What Bible stories come to mind when you think about God stepping into history to judge sin for the benefit of His people?

(4) What are some things that you have heard that people will do to try and live longer?

(5) If some of the people in #4 above were told about how to obtain eternal life through faith in Christ and live that way forever, what would most of them say?

**9:8. He shall judge the world in righteousness, And He shall administer judgment for the peoples in uprightness.**

---

See Acts 17:31. Jesus Christ is the Man by which all **the world** will be universally **judged in righteousness.** The verdict of the common judgment depends upon what one does with Christ. Christ **administers judgment in uprightness** to all the peoples on the earth. Nobody can escape this judgment. God created everyone with the knowledge that He is there and that they are accountable to Him. If they deny that, it is because they suppress the truth in unrighteousness. For their unrighteous suppression, they must answer (John 3:36, Romans 1:18).

If they refused to receive Christ, they are Satan's, and Satan is theirs (1 Jn 5:19). Such people inherit everlasting punishment in the lake, which burns with fire and brimstone (Rev. 20:14). If they received Christ, they are Christ's, and Christ is theirs. Such people inherit eternal life and an eternal kingdom (Jn 3:16, Matt. 25:34). They will be judged fairly. Even the righteous have sins that they commit after their justification that need to be regularly confessed and forsaken (1 Jn 1:9-2:2). God righteously deals with those sins as well as iniquity gets applied to Christ's account, and Christ applies His righteousness to the account of the saints (2 Cor. 5:21). He ever lives to intercede for them (Heb. 7:25).

The righteous receive an imperishable crown (1 Cor. 9:24-25, a crown of rejoicing (1 Thess. 2:19), a crown of righteousness (2 Tim. 4:8), a crown of glory (1 Pet. 5:4), and a crown of life (Rev. 2:10). These might all be the same crown. On the other hand, these might all be different crowns. Either way, the saints have something to look forward to and be excited about. On the other hand, the unrighteous have something to be afraid of, namely God Himself. It is a fearful thing to fall into His hands in judgment (Heb. 10:31). While it is true that He will repay in His vengeance (Deut. 32:35, Rom. 12:19), it is equally as true that He is very patient (2 Pet. 3:9) to give mankind the opportunity to humble himself so that he can be exalted (Matt. 23:12) and can be spared this judgment.

---

**Questions for self-reflection:**

(1) Before your conversion, when you understood the weight of your sins and the judgment that awaited you outside of Christ, what emotions did that elicit in you?

(2) When you go through life now as a saved person, what are some of the ways you see the world around you suppressing the truth of God in unrighteousness?

(3) Do you think it is fair for God to judge His creation in the manner that He does?

(4) As a saved person, have you ever imagined what the crown that awaits your arrival in heaven looks like?

(5) Have you ever thanked God for His patience with you?

**9:9. The Lord also will be a refuge for the oppressed, A refuge in times of trouble.**

---

In a physical sense, those with no strength or resources to provide for themselves make up the oppressed. Such people are commonly taken advantage of by the unrighteous. The unrighteous' greatest goal is to satisfy themselves, to get as much of this earth's wealth or prestige, even if it comes at the expense of the righteous.

In a spiritual sense, the sheep, the saved, the redeemed are frequently oppressed by the ungodly. Often it is the righteous that the unrighteous specifically target in their acts of oppression. It is the Christians whose court cases governments won't hear because lawmakers are against Christian principles. Christian business owners turn away business from 'customers' who only visit their establishment in the hopes of exploiting them and shutting them down.

For believers who find themselves in these straits, the Lord is still their **refuge** in times of trouble. The Lord is the One they can turn to for mercy and help in time of need (Heb. 4:14-16).

For the lost, who feel **oppressed** by the weight of their sin, sinners who have separated themselves from God can turn to the God they have offended in humble repentance. God then becomes their refuge for the rest of their pilgrimage on earth. Nothing can separate them from His love (Romans 8:38-39). He is their Anchor. He is their Advocate (1 John 2:1). He is their peace (Eph. 2:14). He is their hiding place (Ps. 32:7). He is their shield (Ps. 3:3). They hope in His Word (Ps. 119:114). They know He is a God who has fulfilled His promises. They know He is a God who is fulfilling His promises. They know He is a God who will fulfill His promises (Ezek. 12:28). We can trust Him.

Noah and his family were in a time of trouble when the Floodwaters were on the earth (Genesis 8). For them, the Ark was their refuge in their time of trouble. The Ark pictures Christ. He is our **refuge in** our **times of trouble.** He protects our eternal security from utter ruin when the storms of this life come crashing and pouring against us.

## Questions for self-reflection:

(1) Have you ever been oppressed? Do you know anyone who has been oppressed?
(2) As a believer, is it difficult to bear if you have endured faith-related oppression?
(3) As a believer, if you hear in the news of stories of Christian business owners suffering for their decision to stand on faith, are you surprised that it happens in our society? Do you think the rate at which it currently happens will stay the same in your life, or will it get worse?
(4) How has God shown Himself to be a refuge for you in times of trouble?

**9:10. And those who know Your name will put their trust in You; For You, Lord, have not forsaken those who seek You.**

---

**Those who know** God's **name** know His name because they have turned to Him in repentant faith. They have **put their trust in** Him. They have tasted and seen that the Lord is good (Ps. 34:8). They have believed on the Lord Jesus Christ in order to become saved (Acts 16:31). Salvation has come to their house (Lk 19:9). They have been justified (Rom. 3:24). They have received eternal righteousness (Rom. 4:5). Their sin has been put as far as the east is from the west (Ps. 103:12). The God who is rich in mercy has visited them (Eph. 2:4). They have been born again (Jn 3:3). God's love has been shed abroad in their hearts (Rom. 5:5). They have passed from death unto life (1 Jn 3:14). They are complete in Him (Col. 2:10). They were dead and have now been made alive (Eph. 2:5). They have been washed by the blood of the Lamb (Rev. 7:14). The Lamb of God has taken away their sins (Jn 1:29). They are one of the sheep who has heard His voice. He knows them. They follow Him. He has given them eternal life. They will never perish. None will pluck them out of His hand (Jn 10:27-29). They have this treasure in earthen vessels. The power is God's and not theirs. They are hard-pressed on every side. They are not crushed. They are perplexed but not in despair. They are persecuted but **not forsaken**. They are struck down but not destroyed. They are carrying about the dying of the Lord Jesus in their body that they might manifest in themselves the life of Jesus (2 Cor. 4:7-10). For them, to live is Christ and to die is gain (Phil. 1:21). Whether they live or die, they are the Lord's (Rom. 14:8). When the storms of life overtake them, because they seek Him, He does not forsake them (Matt. 7:7-8). He is their Anchor that holds within the veil (Heb. 6:19). The more they **seek** Him, the more He will reveal Himself to them. The more they abide in Him, the more He abides in them (Jn 15:1-8). The more they walk in the light, they enjoy fellowship with Him and He with them (1 Jn 1:7).

Those who know the name of the Lord put their trust in Him because they know He will take care of them because they have seen Him take care of them in the past. They can trust that He will take care of them in the present and the future. From the pages of Scripture, they know that God has taken care of those who belong to Him in every generation. Since He has done so, He is worthy to be trusted by the current generation and subsequent generations until He returns (Rom. 8:28). The righteous seek the Lord and are found by the Lord to be saved. After justification, a life of continually seeking the Lord ensues. They lift their requests to the throne room (Phil. 4:6-7), trusting God to meet them where they need Him most.

**Questions for self-reflection:**

(1) Read Matthew 7:21-23. Does the Lord know you?
(2) Provided that the Lord knows you, how has your life changed since the Lord has known you?
(3) Does it comfort you to know that the Lord will not forsake you?
(4) Has the Lord revealed Himself to you in tangible ways?
(5) How has the Lord demonstrated to you that He is worthy of your trust and worship?

**9:11. Sing praises to the Lord, who dwells in Zion! Declare His deeds among the people.**

---

The psalmist knows that the only One suitable to **sing praises to** is **the Lord** (1 Chron. 16:25, Ps. 96:4). There was a whole history from which the psalmist could draw for recorded reasons for why it was proper for him and everyone else to praise the Lord.

**His deeds** done **among the people** are numerous. He could start in Genesis with creation (Gen. 1). He could recount how the Lord created everything out of nothing by merely speaking it into existence. He could think about how humanity, the crown of His creation, was put on earth (Gen. 2). He could think about how, even in judgment, He had preserved a remnant with which to start over, from which eventually a Savior would come (Gen. 6-8). Praises can rise to the Lord because even though the earth is all His (Ps. 24:1), one day a new heaven and new earth are coming which will be free from the plague of original sin (Revelation 21). Praises can go up to the abode of the Lord because He has given us physical life (Acts 17:25). Praises can rise to the Lord because He has given us spiritual and eternal life because of Christ (Jn 1:12). Praises can go up to the Lord because of His mercies which are new every morning and are evident to the saved (Lam. 3:22-23). Praises can go up to the Lord because He has sent forth His Spirit into our hearts so that we can cry out Abba Father (Rom. 8:15). Praises can go forth to the Lord because the Spirit leads us into all truth (Jn 16:13).

Praises can go forth to the Lord because He has formed the church (Matt. 16:18, Acts 2, 1 Timothy 3:15), groups of people from every tribe, tongue, and nation (Rev. 7:9) who with one voice can cast their crowns at His feet (Rev. 4:9-11) and worship His holy Name. His people can praise His name for who He is. They can be grateful that He is rich in mercy (Ephesians 2:4), that He is compassionate (2 Kgs, 13:22-23, Ps. 103:8, Ps. 103:13-14, Ps. 116:5, Isa. 30:18, Isa. 49:13, Isa. 49:15-16, Lam. 3:22, Hosea 1:7, Joel 2:13, and more). They can worship Him because, even if it seems like the devil is winning now, there is coming a day when the Lord's side will ultimately be victorious while Satan's side is vanquished (Rev. 20:10). We can rightfully praise the Lord for what He has done, what He is doing, and what He will do. The saints can make a joyful noise to the Lord because the grace of God has appeared to them and taught them to deny ungodliness (Ti 2:11).

Believers can magnify the Lord because they can come boldly before the throne of grace for mercy and help in times of need (Heb. 4:16). Believers can praise the Lord because they are His temple (1 Cor. 3:16). They can worship Him right where they are. Everything that has breath can praise the Lord because the whole earth is full of His glory (Ps. 150:6, Isa. 6:3). The deeds of God's grace, goodness, and faithfulness in the lives of the saints can be told all over the world so that others may hear and believe.

**Questions for self-reflection:**

(1) What are some of the deeds that the Lord has done in your life that are worth recounting to others?
(2) What are some of the attributes of God for which you can praise Him for who He is?
(3) How has the Lord shown you His grace, goodness, and faithfulness? Take time to praise Him for each of these.

**9:12. When He avenges blood, He remembers them; He does not forget the cry of the humble.**

---

When the wicked perpetuate their wickedness, the righteous have to wait patiently for the Lord to **avenge** them (Ps. 27:14). Eventually, their God will avenge them. When He does, it will be evident that the Lord fights for His people and against His enemies, who are also the enemies of His people (Exod. 14:25, Ps. 68:21, Ps. 110:1). When God's people cry to God, God hears their **cry**, and His people can take comfort knowing that vengeance is His (Deut. 32:35, Rom. 12:19). He will repay.

In the generations since Christ's first coming, His servants have shed their **blood** in defense of Him (Rev. 17:6). As with Abel, their blood cries out, and the Lord will **avenge** them on His timetable (Gen. 4:10). If '**He remembers them**' refers to the righteous, God remembers their cry and will avenge them in His timing (Gen. 9:5). If 'He remembers them' refers to the unrighteous, He remembers their sin and will repay it by pouring out His wrath (Ps. 7:16, 2 Thess. 1:6-10).

The **humble** are the saved that God receives (Jas 4:6, 1 Pet. 5:6). God listens to those whose hearts are right with Him. **He does not forget** those who **cry** out with hearts of faith to the One who upholds all things by the Word of His power (Prov. 15:29, Heb. 1:3). For the righteous, even though they can be burdened by their sin (Matt. 5:4), by the sin of the world (Prov. 24:1), by the path the wicked One has the world on (1 Jn 5:19), and various trials (1 Pet. 1:6), the righteous can trust that God is working all things together for their good (Rom. 8:28) and will make all wrongs right one day in His timing (Gal. 6:7-8, Is. 30:26).

#### Questions for self-reflection:

(1) As the wicked continue to perpetuate their wickedness in the world with reckless abandon, how is remembering that the Lord does not forget the cry of the humble a help?

---

(2) What are some past stories of God's faithfulness to His promises to His people found in the Bible that are most encouraging to you and why?

**9:13. Have mercy on me, O Lord! Consider my trouble from those who hate me, You who lift me up from the gates of death,**

The psalmist wants deliverance from his earthly enemies, **those who hate** him. These enemies cause a lot of **trouble** for the psalmist. If the rescue comes, credit can go to the **Lord**'s **mercy**. The Lord's mercy is sufficient for deliverance from physical enemies as well as spiritual enemies. The Lord's mercy is likewise sufficient for deliverance from ourselves, as we can be an enemy to ourselves when we keep giving in to temptation.

The saved person obtains mercy from the Lord when they receive redemption through the blood of Christ via belief in the gospel (Eph. 1:7). The justified sinner can continue to come to the Lord for mercy (Heb. 4:16). When the saints come to the Lord with their needs and wants, they can receive an abundance of mercy because God is rich in mercy (Eph. 2:4). The sheep realize their constant need for **mercy** and how blessed they are to be able to return to the Lord repeatedly for that mercy (Lam. 3:22-23). Sinners receive mercy from the Lord when they begin their relationship with Him. Afterward, their need for daily mercy from the Lord continues for the rest of their lives. The justified saint still has a daily struggle with sin that continues until death. The need for the Lord's mercy to sustain them and supply them with the grace that is theirs for them to wage successful war by the Spirit against the flesh will never stop on this side of the grave (Gal. 5:17). Those who fight the battle in their flesh apart from God's help will lose as the flesh will overpower the Spirit.

The psalmist knows that the Lord is sufficient to deliver him from anyone or anything. His deliverance is a result of His compassion that He exercises on everyone. However, the saved also get the Lord's deliverance in ways that the unsaved do not.

The psalmist asks the Lord to avenge him against those who **trouble** him, who have him close to **the gates of death**. The psalmist has physical and spiritual enemies that originate with Satan. He needs protection from these enemies. He knows that the Lord helps those who are His, and he petitions the Lord for more of that help. The psalmist knows that the Lord is compassionate. The Lord is there to help His own with their struggles. Each person has a divine appointment with death that only God knows (Heb. 9:27). The person can ask God to intervene on their behalf and keep them from perishing. They can refer back to when the Lord brought them from the kingdom of darkness and brought them to Himself (Col. 1:13-14). Based on gospel deliverance having happened to them in the past, in the present, they can go to God knowing that deliverance in the present is possible if the Lord wills it. And even if He doesn't deliver them in their prescribed way, saints can trust the Lord to know what is best. Perhaps deliverance is not a change in circumstances. Perhaps deliverance is a change in attitude toward circumstances. Only the Lord truly knows. We should trust Him regardless.

## Questions for self-reflection:

(1) Does the faith you profess to have cause the enemies to your faith to come out of the woodworks to persecute you, or are you able to mix in with everyone else easily?

(2) How have you experienced the Lord's deliverance from people who are not supportive of your faith?

(3) How have you come to appreciate the daily mercy and grace that the Lord provides for you?

(4) How have you grown in your ability to wage successful spiritual war against the flesh and Satan?

**9:14. That I may tell of all Your praise In the gates of the daughter of Zion. I will rejoice in Your salvation.**

All the acts of the Lord's intervention in the psalmist's life are memories that the psalmist can call upon to **tell** others of the Lord's working on his behalf. The believer can **praise** God for this working of the Lord all the days of their lives. Believers are responsible for sharing the Lord's mercies with others (Mk 16:15, 2 Cor. 5:20, 1 Pet. 3:15). He wanted to be able to tell others about the Lord of his life. If the Lord did not deliver him from his enemies, he would not have the opportunity to do so.

When believers are in the straits of trouble, because the trouble can seem overwhelming, they can become too distracted by the harsh circumstances. When challenging circumstances crowd out the awareness of the Lord's mercy in life, the saint is less likely to think about and tell others about how the Lord is worthy of praise. Even though in all circumstances, the Lord is worthy of praise, for some believers, it may be more difficult for them to give the Lord the glory that is due to His name if their suffering is too severe. When God delivers believers from temporal circumstances, they can rejoice in salvation from those circumstances.

Even if the Lord denies deliverance from difficult temporal circumstances, believers still can rejoice for the permanent salvation that Christ wrought for them. If the Lord delivered the psalmist, the psalmist could publicly praise the Lord in front of others by going to the city **gates** (Matt. 10:32). He also could worship the Lord publicly with other believers.

The psalmist could rejoice for the temporal salvation of the Lord in deliverance from his earthly enemies. So likewise, all believers can rejoice for the eternal **salvation** that is theirs in Christ. They have been delivered from every spiritual enemy in the ultimate sense since Christ has defeated them all (1 Cor. 15:26-27, Col. 1:13-14, Col. 2:15). So now, while they work out their salvation (Phil. 2:12-13), the saints can **rejoice** at the gracious opportunity bestowed upon them to show forth the praise of the Lord that bought them (Matt. 5:16).

## Questions for self-reflection:

(1) What has the Lord done for you about which you can tell others?
(2) What keeps you from telling others about what the Lord has done for you?
(3) If you have been saved from God by faith in Christ, what do you have to fear?
(4) How can you show forth the praise of the Lord that bought you?

**9:15. The nations have sunk down in the pit which they made; In the net which they hid, their own foot is caught.**

---

The psalmist continues with the theme developed in this psalm's preceding verses. God had defeated the psalmist's enemies and had delivered the psalmist. Early in the history of Israel. God delivered Israel from Egypt in the story of the Exodus. The Lord delivered David from enemies that sought him. The enemies tried to trap people like the psalmist in various ways **in the pit which they made.** It turned out that the enemies had been trapped themselves by their very own trap, not unlike Haman being hanged on the gallows he had made to ensnare Mordecai (Est 7).

Israel, God's redeemed people, are those who are on God's side (Exod. 19:5-6). Everyone else makes up **the nations.** The nations tried to trap God's people and to overthrow God's influence. But, in the end, it will backfire on them. They will get caught in **the net in which they hid,** and **their own foot** will be **caught** because God fights for His people (Exod. 14:25, Deut. 1:30, Deut. 3:22, Josh. 23:3, Josh. 23:10, 1 Sam. 17:47, 2 Kgs 19:35, 2 Chron. 20:15, 2 Chron. 32:8, Neh. 4:20). In every generation since Christ's first Advent, Christ's enemies, led by the Wicked One (Jn 8:44, 1 Jn 5:19), Satan himself, have come against Christ's people and, by extension, Christ Himself (Jn 15:20, Acts 9:4). In the end, they will perish in the Lake of Fire forever (Rev. 20:14-15). In trying to bring Christ's people to an end, they will bring themselves to an end.

### Questions for self-reflection:

(1) How can Scripture's recounting of historical victories God wrought in the lives of His people be an encouragement in your life as you go up against God's enemies?

(2) Can the way that God's enemies are trapped by the very traps that they have set for God's people encourage God's people today? How?

(3) If Christ has overcome all your enemies by His death on the cross, how can you walk in that victory?

**9:16. The Lord is known by the judgment He executes; The wicked is snared in the work of his own hands. Meditation. Selah**

---

God makes Himself known in a variety of ways. One of the various ways in which God makes Himself known is **by the judgment He executes**. From the beginning, God has been a God of judgment. When Adam and Eve sinned, God rendered judgment in killing an animal to cover them (Gen. 3:21). When Cain killed his brother Abel in the next chapter, The Lord responded with a verdict and a consequence (Gen. 4:11-12). When wickedness got worse (Gen. 6:5), God, after a period of grace during which Noah built the Ark (Gen. 6:13-22), responded with the flood judgment, killing everyone who was outside of the Ark (Gen. 7:1-24). God's greatest act of judgment against sin was when His own Son, the Lord Jesus Christ, the propitiation for our sins (1 Jn 2:2), died as our substitute as the once for all sacrifice for sins (1 Pet. 3:18).

God will return one day to finally render judgment that will last for all eternity against the ungodly when He returns in flaming fire to take vengeance on those who do not obey the gospel (2 Thess. 1:7-10, Rev. 20:10-15). He will also bring all the sheep to be with Him forever in eternal heaven (Matt. 13:30, Jn 14:2-3). **The wicked is snared in the work of his own hands** when the wicked plots his wickedness, and the wickedness comes back against him on the day of judgment (2 Pet. 3:7). The wicked one himself will be snared in his plots and will be eternally judged in the lake of fire (Rev. 20:10). The wicked may even be caught in this life when he is allowed to reap what he sows by receiving consequences for his own sins (Gal. 6:7). The wicked, those who did not bow in allegiance to Christ, will also suffer eternal judgment (Rev. 20:11-15). The Antichrist will be ultimately judged (Rev. 20:7-10). God executes judgment to show who He is.

**Questions for self-reflection:**

(1) Are there other Bible stories not mentioned above that remind you of God's judgment?

(2) Refamiliarize yourself with the story of Esther. How was the Lord made known by the judgment He executed in that story? How was wicked Haman snared in the work of his own hands?

(3) Have you seen this principle play out in society in your lifetime? How so?

**9:17. The wicked shall be turned into hell, And all the nations that forget God.**

Regardless of whether they are righteous or unrighteous, everyone dies because everyone sins (Ezek. 18:4, Rom. 6:23). The **wicked**, all those outside of Christ, including **all the nations that forget God**, end up in **hell** (Matt. 8:12, Matt. 22:13, Matt. 25:30, Rev. 19:20, Rev. 20:10, Rev. 20:15, Rev. 21:8). Hell is traditionally believed to be the place of conscious, eternal torment (Lk 16:23) for all those who reject God's love to follow their own way (Isa. 53:6). When the sinner that has not been redeemed meets their divine appointment (Heb. 9:27), the soul of that sinner goes immediately to hell, where it awaits the final judgment. When judgment is over, the unjust sinner goes into the lake of fire where they will be tormented forever and ever (Rev. 20:11-15).

The gospel is beautiful because everyone is wicked and, therefore, everyone deserves this fate. But the gospel commends God's love (Rom 5:8) and God's rich mercy (Eph 2:4) to unworthy sinners in that all those who place humble (1 Pet. 5:6), repentant (Matt. 4:17) faith (Heb. 11:6) in the Lord Jesus Christ alone. Such justified sinners receive forgiveness (Eph. 1:7) and everlasting life (Jn 3:16) from the God that they have offended by their sins (Col. 1:21). Instead of being consigned to this eternal hell, they can be admitted into glorious heaven as a gift of God's grace, through their faith in their Substitute, the Lord Jesus Christ (Rom. 3:21-26, Eph. 2:8-9).

All the nations who forget God are those who reject the gospel. Apart from hearing and believing the gospel, this makes up sinners from all over the globe. Just as people from every tribe, tongue, and nation will believe the gospel and enter heaven (Rev. 5:9), so too, people from every tribe, tongue, and nation will reject the good news and spend eternity abiding under the wrath of God for their unbelief (Jn 3:36) because they forgot God and loved their sin too much. The gospel demanded too much from them. It called them to give up their life of self-seeking and demanded that they die to themselves (Matt. 10:38, Lk 9:23, Rom. 6:6-7, Rom.

8:12-13, Gal. 2:20, Gal. 5:24, Gal. 6:14, Eph. 4:22-24) and live for One greater than they.

Some might object that God is unloving to send anyone to hell. The doctrine of hell does not make God unloving. The reality is that God loves them enough to grant them physical life (Gen. 2:7, Deut. 32:39, 1 Sam. 2:6, 2 Kgs 5:7, Neh. 9:6, Job 10:12, Job 33:4, Jn 1:3, Acts 17:25, 1 Tim. 6:13, Rev. 11:11). God loves everyone enough to let the rain fall on the just and the unjust (Matt. 5:45). God gives both the lost and the saved many things to enjoy (Neh. 8:10, Ps. 118:24, Eccles. 2:24, Eccles. 3:12-13, Eccles. 5:18, Eccles. 8:15, 1 Tim. 6:17). Each of the reasons above and more gives everyone enough evidence to show them that God is there, that He loves them, and that He did everything required for their salvation. The sad reality for such sinners is that they have no excuse (Rom. 7:7, Gal. 3:24) because they refuse to humble themselves. They have access to enough information to admit that there is Something and Someone greater than they to whom they are accountable. They have intuition and common sense to utilize to show them that creation screams that there must be a Creator (Rom. 1:20). To admit that the innate knowledge of right and wrong that all of us have (Rom. 2:15) points to an absolute standard of right and wrong which they have rejected has left them without excuse (Rom. 7:7, Gal. 3:24). Had they accepted the little light they had, God would have revealed more light to them until they had sufficient light to find Him and be saved. But since they rejected what they had been given, more revelation was mercifully withheld (Matt. 13:12).

## Questions for self-reflection:

(1) Who do you know and love who would end up in hell if they died today?

(2) If you love them, what can you do for them to show them the love of God through Christ so they might repent, believe the gospel, and avoid hell?

(3) How can you keep from worrying that you did not do enough to show your neighbor their need for the Lord?

(4) Is it loving for a parent to discipline a child with temporary unpleasant methods if the temporary unpleasant methods will likely lead to the child avoiding the more extreme unpleasant permanent punishment? If so, how is that different than God disciplining His people so they will avoid hell?

(5) If you are saved, does that make you better than the unsaved? Why do you believe and others do not?

**9:18. For the needy shall not always be forgotten; The expectation of the poor shall not perish forever.**

---

**The needy** and **poor** could be two different ways to refer to the same people. It is undoubtedly true that in heaven, there will be people who on earth had many earthly riches. It is also true that in hell, there will be people who had minimal worldly possessions. Frequently, however, those who have an abundance of resources are not as prone to see their need for God because they think they can provide for themselves and have no need for God (Matt. 19:23-24). On the other hand, commonly, those with a dearth of resources are more prone to see their need for God as they know that God is the provider of everything they need (Prov. 10:3, Matt. 6:33, Matt. 7:11, Phil. 4:19, Jas 1:17, Jas 2:5). Thus, the latter group is more likely to see their need for dependence upon the Lord.

Those who realize their need for God's grace, those identified as the poor in spirit (Matt. 5:3), are those who will **not be forgotten** by God and **shall not perish forever**. These are they who know to avail themselves of the throne of grace for an abundant supply of God's grace for their need (Heb. 4:16). While the faithful among the poor and needy may feel that God has forgotten them at times, as their destitution or other adverse circumstance continues or worsens, the reality is that God has not forgotten them. He has given them access to Him through Christ (Eph. 2:18, Eph. 3:12, Heb. 10:19). When the saved avail themselves of all the spiritual blessings at their disposal (Eph. 1:3), the saved will know themselves not to be forgotten. The saved will know that their incorruptible inheritance (1 Pet. 1:4) will **not perish**.

The hard part for the justified saint is to wait to receive the imperishable crown and the incorruptible inheritance. We too often want heaven on earth, and we get impatient when things on earth fail to fulfill us as only God can. God does not want the world to satisfy us. If it did, we would not long for a better place like heaven where we will be with Him and see Him as He is forever (Heb. 13:14).

---

In heaven, believers will have entirely renewed minds. The minds they had worked so hard to renew (Rom. 12:2) in their spiritual warfare with the flesh (Gal.5:17) will no longer have a flesh with which to contend in eternity. Their minds will be perfected. The poor of this world who have been chosen to be rich in faith (Jas 2:5) will have their expectation of an eternal city finally realized and fulfilled in eternity where they will gaze with unveiled face at the glory of their great King (2 Cor. 3:18). They will return to reign with Him before the eternal state (Rev 19:14), and all their enemies will be under the feet (1 Cor. 15:26-27) of the One who bought them with his own blood (Acts 20:28).

## Questions for self-reflection:

(1) In the culture in which you live, do you live among the class considered poor, middle-class, or wealthy?

(2) How does it make you feel to know that God will not forget you? Does that fact make you want to go to Him more than you already do with your requests?

(3) In a moment of great spiritual need, have you ever felt the comforting touch of God on your soul? What was that like?

(4) What will be the best part of heaven for you?

**9:19. Arise, O Lord, Do not let man prevail; Let the nations be judged in Your sight.**

---

The psalmist knew that if the **Lord** graciously intervened on his behalf as He had done previously (Ps. 9:5-6), that he would see ultimate success against those who oppressed him. Even if the enemy experienced temporary success against him by creating hardships and making his life otherwise more difficult than normal, the psalmist could still trust the Lord that He would make all wrongs right in His timing.

**The nations**, those that oppose God and God's people, are constantly trying to undermine God and God's people through various means. They will not finally **prevail**.

The psalmist beseeches the Lord to cause His plan to succeed. He asks the Lord to execute the judgment He has promised and has foreshadowed throughout His Word (Gen. 3:15, Rev. 20:10). In every generation, a battle rages between God's forces and Satan's forces. This battle will persist until the Lord returns. Wicked man and the Wicked One that leads all wicked men will seem at times that they prevail against God and believers in the One True God (i.e., Christians).

While the wicked seem to have their way and the Christians seem to be able to do nothing about it, Christians who fail to remember that God allows all things for His purposes (Rom. 8:28) might be tempted to lose hope. But they must not lose hope. The same God who created all things (Gen. 1:1, Gen. 2:4, Exod. 20:11, 2 Kgs 19:15, Jb 38:4, Ps. 24:1-2, Ps. 33:6, Ps. 104:24, Ps. 121:2, Prov. 16:4, Isa. 64:8, Jer. 32:17, Jn 1:3, Rom. 1:20, 1 Cor. 8:6, Col. 1:16, 1 Tim. 4:4, Heb. 1:2) and upholds all things by the Word of His power (Heb. 1:3), works everything after the counsel of His own will (Eph. 1:11) and will once day bring about the consummation of all of history such that all His enemies are judged and under His feet (1 Cor. 15:26-27).

The righteous have the responsibility, while they wait for that faithful day, to do their duties which God has appointed for them, to not avenge themselves (Rom. 12:19), to not give place to the devil (Eph. 4:27), to live peaceably with everyone as much as they can (Rom. 12:18).

## Questions for self-reflection:

(1) In what ways does it appear that man (God's enemies) prevails over God's people now?

(2) Does knowing that the Lord gains ultimate victory over His enemies bring you comfort?

(3) When God's enemies stand at the Great White Throne of judgment, what do you envision that will be like?

(4) When you see the Lord, and He tells you to enter into the joy of the Lord, what do you think that will be like?

**9:20. Put them in fear, O Lord, That the nations may know themselves to be but men. Selah**

---

The psalmist concludes this psalm by asking God to judge those who have not submitted to the Lord. The righteous remnant felt pressure which the rebels created. The saints wanted to experience some relief. In an ultimate sense, the final earthly kingdom will be destroyed forever (Rev. 18:10, Rev. 20:10).

While the righteous patiently wait now, they can ask the Lord for help. It is within the realm of possibility that the Lord could bring adversity in various shapes and sizes against the unrighteous in the hopes that they would properly identify it as coming from the Lord. Once the wicked correctly identify the negative results of their experience as coming from God, they could hopefully make the wise decision to turn from their sins and turn to the Lord for deliverance.

The **fear** of the **Lord**, even fear initially caused by fear of retribution, rather than the fear akin to worship, is an excellent motivator to depart from sin (Prov. 16:6, Acts 5:11, Heb. 10:27, Heb. 10:31). When the **nations** recognize that, as men, they are feeble, finite, fragile, and frail, they may know themselves to be utterly dependent upon the Lord for everything, including their next breath. Since the nations are **but men**, though they rage against God (Ps. 2:1), it will all be futile. If the Lord brings us to that place of spiritual poverty and we submit to Him, our lives will be blessed by Him (1 Pet. 5:6). While this blessing may not come in the form of an easy life filled with material prosperity and relative ease, it will come in the form of a blessed relationship with the Lord Jesus Christ with whom we will share in eternal bliss.

**Questions for self-reflection:**

---

(1) What would have to happen to the nations for them to realize that they are but men and humble themselves before God?

---

(2) How can the righteous remnant band together to support one another as the war between God's forces and Satan's forces rages on?

# Psalm 10

## 10:1. Why do You stand afar off, O Lord? Why do You hide in times of trouble?

Due to the persecution received by the psalmist (10:2), the psalmist felt as if the **Lord** was **afar off**. Perhaps he felt as if his God was truly near that he should not experience trouble in this life. Maybe he thought that the trial he experienced was not necessary for someone as faithful as he felt himself to be. God uses afflictions in the lives of His people to purify them (Jb 23:10, Prov. 17:3, Isai. 48:10, Dan. 12:10, Zech. 13:8-9, Rom. 5:3-4, Jas 1:12, 1 Pet. 1:7).

The source of the trial is not the issue in the first portion of the verse. The overwhelming sense of the circumstance left the psalmist feeling as if there was a disturbance in the psalmist's proximity to the Lord. For the psalmist and for all those that belong to the Lord, the reality is that the Lord is never afar off. Sometimes, even for the believer, it can feel when the circumstances of this life get overwhelming that He has withdrawn His gracious presence from us. Sometimes God waits to assist us. When He waits to help us, while we wait for Him, it can feel like He is not there or unaware of how our circumstances make us feel. We want His help so we can be relieved from our pain, but often, we forget at the moment that sometimes it is the pain that keeps us close to Him.

Regardless of whether or not He allows the pain of the trial to continue, staying close to Him is most important. It is more vital for us to be close to Him than it is for us to be happy about the circumstances in our life. Having difficult circumstances with which to deal in this life can make it easier for us, as His weak fleshly creatures, to remember that we must be utterly dependent upon Him to persevere through our difficulty. Becoming intimately aware of this reality can greatly comfort believers who suffer from various trials (Jas 1:2-8, 1 Pet. 1:6-9). God never truly hides from those that are His since He never removes His saving presence from those that are His (Jn 6:37). However, he can hide our sense of His presence, especially when we, as His people, are disobedient to Him. In times of persecution or other **times of trouble**, God can also seem to **hide** from His people. God may seem to hide to elicit more earnest cries from the sheep to the Shepherd since as they seek Him, they will find Him (Matt. 7:7-8, Lk 18:1-8).

## Questions for self-reflection:

(1) Have you ever, since your conversion, felt far from the Lord?
(2) In an effort to help that unpleasant feeling, what have you done to help you feel not as far from the Lord?
(3) Could God ever pull back from us to get us to pull back closer to Him?
(4) If it feels as if God is not as close to you as you think He should be, is there anything in your life that could be contributing to that?

**10:2. The wicked in his pride persecutes the poor; Let them be caught in the plots which they have devised.**

---

The devil and those who do his bidding make up **the wicked**. God's people make up **the poor**. Because of his pride, the devil fell from heaven (Ezek. 28:11-19 – devil = 'king of Tyre'). All **persecut**ion directed towards God's people ultimately originates with the devil since God and His 'team' are at war with Satan and his 'team,' including the Antichrist.

God's people are described as being poor in spirit (Matt. 5:3), and the devil will seek to attack them. God's people are described as being poor of this world (Jas 2:5). They can expect to receive persecution (2 Tim. 3:12). The psalmist knows that God can intervene in his situation such that the wicked can be caught in the very plots they have devised against the righteous, namely the psalmist himself. He knows that his enemies can succumb to the same **plots they have devised** so tirelessly to execute against the psalmist. So, the psalmist prays that the wicked have their plans return upon their own head. He asks that the wicked die the same way that they hope to see the righteous die.

There is great irony here, as was the case with Haman and Mordecai, where Haman was hanged on the very gallows he had constructed for the hanging of Mordecai (Esther 7:10). As his own plot caught Haman, so can the wicked from every generation be snared by their own plots against the righteous.

**Questions for self-reflection:**

---

(1) Looking back now on your life before your conversion, can you think of any instances when your pride surfaced and prevented you from seeing yourself as you truly were before God?

(2) Since your conversion, how have you had to continue to battle to keep your pride at bay?

(3) What did it take for you to become sufficiently humble to the point where you were ready to admit your guilt before God and receive the forgiveness that Christ offers?

(4) Have you ever been in a situation where praying this prayer would be appropriate for you to do?

**10:3. For the wicked boasts of his heart's desire; He blesses the greedy and renounces the Lord.**

**The Lord** should be the object of our boasting. The righteous are righteous because the Lord is their predominant **heart's desire**. They want, more than anything, to live in such a way that brings honor and glory (brings attention) to Him.

In contrast, the wicked, those outside of a saving relationship with the Lord Jesus Christ, want to bring attention to themselves. Therefore, they will **boast** in anything and everything except the Lord. They will especially boast in themselves as if anything 'good' comes out of them because of them. But, in reality, anything good that comes out of them comes out despite them.

Those led by Satan and his minions, **the wicked**, find things about themselves that they can boast about relatively simply. These things do not have to be sinful activities necessarily. In that case, they merely fail to ascribe the good that comes from them to God. Other times, the wicked boast in wicked acts that they perpetuate. The wicked also boasts in the sinful acts committed by others. The viler the action, the more the occasion to brag about it. The wicked blesses those opposed to the Lord, those whom the Lord opposes (Jas 4:6). The wicked ascribes to human diligence rather than the Lord's gracious providence any increase that comes to himself or others.

The wicked see the **greedy**, who ascribe their monetary gains to their own wisdom and strength rather than attributing any good and perfect gift as coming from the Father of lights (Jas 1:17), and **blesses** them. They do not acknowledge that the Lord is the Giver of every good and perfect gift. Perhaps the wicked does not employ lawful means in acquiring wealth. Instead, they **renounce the Lord**. They think they are the source of their increase. This could be what Paul had in mind when he called covetous people idolaters (Col. 3:5).

## Questions for self-reflection:

(1) What things in your life compete with the Lord for the title of 'my heart's desire'?

(2) When something good happens to you, or when you do something good that others recognize as good, do you first think of yourself or the Lord?

**10:4. The wicked in his proud countenance does not seek God; God is in none of his thoughts.**

---

**The wicked in his proud countenance** is too prideful and self-sufficient to see their need to **seek God** for anything. Their pride prevents them from even thinking about God (Rom. 3:11). The wicked do not see the need for God because he can do it all without any help. He has taught himself all he needs to know, and if there is something else to know, he can teach that to himself because he, not God, is the source of all knowledge. Therefore, there is no need for divine assistance for the wicked.

The sense of right and wrong that the lost person lives by is perverted and subjective, frequently altering based upon the latest 'knowledge' they have acquired. There is no room for an absolute source of right and wrong in the minds of the wicked. Instead of experiencing life through the final authority of God, the definitive rule for the wicked is their limited, ever-changing, human experience. Instead of seeking to know what God calls right through His Word, the wicked are known for doing what is right in their own eyes (Judg. 21:25, Prov. 21:2).

The godly realize that such knowledge, which fuels the pride of the wicked, will be their downfall (Prov. 16:18). The pride of the wicked undergirds everything in their life. Since God receives the humble, the prideful will be rejected on judgment day, barring a miracle of divine proportions (Jas 4:6). The fact that God is angry with the wicked every day (Ps. 7:11), including them, because of decisions such as theirs to reject Him (Rom. 1:28), does not concern them because they are concerned only with themselves.

**God is in none of his thoughts** because the thoughts of the wicked are too self-centered to have any room in them that can include God. Therefore, the god conceived of in the mind of the wicked is not the true God. If the wicked even believes that a god exists, rather than the one true God, the God of Scripture, the god that the wicked makes is a god of their own making. It is a god that kowtows to man's ever-changing whims. It is a god that is as fickle as is man. It is a god that has no concern for right or wrong

---

or no zeal for his own honor. It is a god that will not hold anyone accountable for how they live. It is a god that will punish nobody and will reward everybody, regardless of how wicked they are. The wicked ignores the warnings of the conscience until they stop altogether (1 Tim. 4:2). He thinks that this life is all that there is. He thinks that his entire purpose is to make the most of this life on earth now for himself because there is nothing to look forward to after this life ends (Isa. 22:13, 1 Cor. 15:32).

The just, on the other hand, know that this life is not all that there is. God is prevalent in the thoughts of the righteous. They seek Him daily (Jer. 29:13). They make Him their Rock (2 Sam. 22:47), their Redeemer (Isa. 54:5), their Portion (Ps. 16:5). They find righteousness (2 Cor. 5:21), peace (Eph. 2:14), forgiveness in Him (Eph. 1:7).

## Questions for self-reflection:

(1) Before your conversion, did you ever fall into the trap of thinking that your ability was only a product of your ingenuity or wisdom and had nothing to do with God?

(2) Since your conversion, have you ever forgotten to give God credit for good things you have been able to accomplish?

(3) If your conscience is subject to the ever-changing knowledge that humankind acquires for himself, on what objective basis can any moral statement be made?

(4) Since the prideful are opposed to God and His truth, chances are they will not respond to His truth if you were to share it with them. If that is the case, how can you show Christ to them?

(5) If this life is all that there is, does life have any real meaning?

(6) If this life is not all that there is and there really is a judgment after death, what then is the meaning of life?

**10:5. His ways are always prospering; Your judgments are far above, out of his sight; As for all his enemies, he sneers at them.**

To the righteous, it can frequently appear that the **ways** of the wicked are **always prospering**. The righteous need to remember that God lets His rain fall on the just and the unjust (Matt. 5:45). He does good to all men, especially to the household of faith (Gal. 6:10). He hopes that His goodness will lead people to repentance (Rom. 2:4).

The wicked have a conscience that has been seared with a hot iron (1 Tim. 4:2). Since the conscience of the wicked is not affected by, is not subject to, God's law (Rom. 8:7), the wicked will do whatever is necessary to prosper continually. The ways of the wicked are also monstrous, shocking, and disturbing. Their thinking is so warped that it can be appalling to some with the Spirit.

God's **judgments** are too high for the wicked. They are **out of** the line of **sight** of the wicked. The mind of the wicked is set on earthly rather than on heavenly things (Rom. 8:7, Col. 3:1-3). They are so earthly-minded that they are no heavenly good. Though written on the hearts of the wicked, God's law does not influence them (Rom. 2:15, Rom. 8:7). Since there is no fear of God before their eyes (Rom.3:18), they are too interested in doing what is right in their own eyes (Judg. 21:25, Prov. 21:2). They are too interested in pouring forth foolishness out of their mouths (Prov. 15:2). Destruction and misery are in their ways (Romans 3:16). The poison of asps is under their lips (Rom. 3:13).

When they hear of the punishment afflicted on evildoers like them, whether that punishment was inflicted by God directly or by God's agents of justice indirectly, the judgments are not taken seriously. They think the Lord is slack concerning judgment. They do not care that the Day of the Lord will come as a thief in the night (2 Pet. 3:9-10). The story of how Egypt drowned in the Red Sea due to God's miraculous intervention is thought to be a mere fairy tale instead of being taken heed unto (Exod. 14). The wicked **sneers at his enemies**, made up of the righteous, because he sees his relative ease compared to the adversity of the righteous and thinks himself, wrongly so, to be superior to the righteous.

**Questions for self-reflection:**

(1) Have you ever become envious of the wicked when you have seen the ways of the wicked prospering while your ways appeared to you to not prosper in the same way?

(2) If you were to witness the ways of the wicked prospering and your ways not prospering, how might your attitude toward that situation change if you were to ask God to lead the wicked to repentance?

(3) The only reason you see the world as you do as a saved person is because God's grace extended towards you became apparent to you. Since this goodness you experience came from God, could remembering that help you keep a proper perspective when relating to the wicked?

**10:6. He has said in his heart, "I shall not be moved; I shall never be in adversity."**

---

It is the wicked who **has said in his heart, 'I shall not be moved; I shall never be in adversity.'** He says this to himself. He is happy with where his life is and would not want to do anything to change that. Everything in this world is as he would like it to be, and he would like to do whatever it takes to keep it that way. He is so self-sufficient that he does not expect anything adverse to come his way. He is so sinlessly perfect (so he erroneously thinks) that he has attained a level of perfection that nobody else has reached. He is more like the antichrist than he is like God. He acts as if he thinks he could teach God Himself a thing or two. He considers himself so wise to believe that he can learn from nobody other than himself. Nobody is more powerful than he (so he foolishly thinks). He thinks he is so intelligent that nothing terrible will ever happen to him because he can outsmart the adversity before the adversity has time to affect him. These are they who do not like to retain God in their knowledge (Romans 1:28). These are they that God gives over to a reprobate mind (Rom. 1:28).

### Questions for self-reflection:

---

(1) How would we ever know if we were too content with where we are and not open to the Lord making significant changes in our lives?
(2) Have we ever been so prideful as to think that life would always be easy for us?
(3) Have we ever been too prideful to receive correction?
(4) Have we ever acted as though we know better than God and could teach God a thing or two about how to govern the universe better?

**10:7. His mouth is full of cursing and deceit and oppression; Under his tongue is trouble and iniquity.**

---

Perhaps the apostle Paul had this verse in mind in Romans 3:14. The wicked have **mouths** that are anti-God. Their mouths are **full of cursing**. Rather than blessing the God who is the Giver of every good and perfect gift (Jas 1:17), the God who supplies ALL our needs according to His riches (Phil. 4:19), they attribute the goodness of God that should lead them to repentance (Rom. 2:4), to some other unsuitable cause. They may make false statements full of **deceit** to achieve their own goals rather than submit to God's will for their lives (Jas 4:7). Such deception has its origins with the Wicked One, Satan, the Father of Lies (Jn 8:44), rather than with the Father of Lights (Jas 1:17). Satan and those who do his work want to impose difficulty upon believers through **oppression**. Believers need to remember to submit to God and not take matters into their own hands.

The human heart is located under his tongue. Words come out of **his mouth** from **under his tongue**. What comes off the tongue must first come from the heart (Matt. 12:34, Matt. 15:19). Trouble and iniquity come from a heart that is controlled by the flesh. Such a heart does not submit to God. It is a heart that that is marked by **trouble and iniquity** of all forms.

### Questions for self-reflection:

(1) What is your reaction when you hear a stranger to God curse God and blaspheme His name?
(2) What is your reaction when people attribute good that happens to them to something other than God?
(3) What is your reaction to the dishonesty of others?
(4) Are you as hard on yourself as you are on others?

**10:8. He sits in the lurking places of the villages; In the secret places he murders the innocent; His eyes are secretly fixed on the helpless.**

---

The wicked always look for clever ways to overtake the unassuming. They try to influence the powerful so that their influence can advance by piggybacking on the efforts of the powerful. This appears to have been the motivation of Judas Iscariot, at least from a human perspective. Such wicked people try to influence the righteous and capsize their faith, like their father, the devil (Jn 8:44), who aims to steal, kill, and destroy (John 10:10). They come **in secret** to **the innocent** (Jude 1:4), those that can be easily persuaded by their cunning, as Eve was in the Garden (Gen. 3) and lead them to believe all sorts of lies and make it difficult, if not impossible, to come to saving faith.

The innocent are not innocent in their standing before God. They, too, have sinned like everyone else (Rom. 3:23). These are innocent, figuratively speaking in the sense that they have not deliberately attempted to undermine the truth as the wicked have. Those who are not as aware of the devil's schemes and those under his sway (1 Jn 5:19), those without biblical discernment, and those disillusioned with pure and undefiled religion (Jas 1:27) of some hardships become easy targets.

The wicked **secretly fix** their **eyes on the helpless**, those that feel the weight of their sin (Ps. 51, Matt. 5:4, Jas 4:8-10), and feel the effects that sin has had on the world to curse the world. Satan sits back and attempts to attack church members to render their permanent faith useless so they can no longer be effective tools in the hands of the mighty God who bought them. The helpless are also gullible in ways such as with their resources. Because they are people of means, the helpless may be too eager to 'help' and give to the cause of a false prophet (1 Tim. 6:3-5, 2 Pet. 2:3). The false prophet knows who these are, and they prey heavily upon them.

It is incumbent on the faithful Christian to be as wise as a serpent and gentle as a dove (Matt. 10:16). The true Christian must take every thought captive to the obedience of Christ (2 Cor.

10:3-5). It is wise for the Christian to put on the whole armor of God so that they will be able to withstand the devil's attacks when they come because they will come (Eph. 6:10-20). If the Christian has their armor on and is ready to engage the active enemy, the adversary (1 Pet. 5:8), the accuser of the brethren (Rev. 12:10), they will be better able to wage victorious warfare.

**Questions for self-reflection:**

(1) Have you ever seen wickedness permeate society in governmental laws?

(2) Have you ever seen wickedness pervade families?

(3) How can you protect yourself from assuming practices and beliefs that God calls wicked?

(4) What can you do if you cannot protect others from assuming practices and beliefs that God calls wicked?

(5) How can you protect yourself from false teaching?

**10:9. He lies in wait secretly, as a lion in his den; He lies in wait to catch the poor; He catches the poor when he draws him into his net.**

---

The devil is referred to as a roaring lion in Scripture (1 Pet. 5:8). The devil employs false teachers. Many false teachers do not even realize they belong to the devil. Some false teachers think they belong to God. Such false teachers are sadly and dangerously deceived. The false teachers who intentionally mislead the minds of the simple for their own benefit **secretly wait** to capture their unsuspecting prey, like **a lion in his den**. They prey on the spiritually weak, hoping **to catch the poor**, who are not firmly planted in the solid foundation of the truth of God's enduring Word, the sole source of absolute truth. The false teachers, and by extension, Satan and those under his control, draw the spiritually immature into the net when they least expect it (2 Tim. 4:3). The false teachers make the house of God into a den of thieves (Matt. 21:13). They steal them away by their allurements (Jn 10:10).

The culmination of the false teachers is found in Revelation 17. Babylon the Great is referred to as the Mother of Harlots (Rev. 17:5). Many saints die for the truth while Babylon the Great perpetuates lies that a sad many believe (Rev. 17:6). Those poor in discernment easily fall for their schemes and are those that the wicked one **draws into his net**. Satan will use anything he can to lead people away from the truth of who God is and into his realm of lies.

Believers need to be on their guard and watchful that they resist the temptation to quit following Christ when life gets tough. They need to remember that the glory that awaits them in the next life is far greater than any suffering God may allow them to suffer in this life (2 Cor. 4:17). They need to be working on purifying themselves from worldly influences that would take away from the worship of the true God (1 Jn 3:3).

**Questions for self-reflection:**

(1) How can you protect yourself from Satanic lies?
(2) If your loved ones refuse to defend themselves from Satanic lies, what can you do?
(3) How are you presently purifying yourself from worldly influences?

**10:10. So he crouches, he lies low, That the helpless may fall by his strength.**

---

Before a predator animal pounces on its prey, it **crouches low** to go undetected to project safety when in reality, grave danger is imminent. The false teacher is like that predator. **The helpless** are the spiritually weak who are prone to give in to the enemy's lies (Gal. 1:6-9). The enemy, symbolized by the lion in the previous verse, has much **strength** with which he can lead people away from the truth and into lies and anything that exalts itself against God (2 Cor. 10:5).

The helpless have a low resistance to the error of the lion. The cares of this life make the vulnerable more susceptible to Satan's schemes. The love for the world that characterizes the helpless is the fuel they need to abandon religion altogether and abandon the knowledge of the one true God they once honored with their lips. They prove that their heart has been far from Him (Matt. 15:8). They show that their life has been a sham. They show that they never took heed to the warnings of the Lord. Though they thought they stood on the Lord because their house was built on the sand of the world, when the storms of life came that caused them to doubt the reality of God and His truth, great was their fall (Matt. 7:24-27). The lion looks for those going through trouble. Those can be more prone to believe the lies of the lion.

### Questions for self-reflection:

---

(1) How can we build up our resistance to the lies of the enemy and prevent ourselves from being counted among the helpless?

(2) Read Matthew 10:26. Read Philippians 1:6. If someone professes to know Christ but then forsakes Him completely and denies Him for one of the world's many philosophies, is this happening an indication of someone who once possessed salvation and lost it? Or is this happening indicative of someone who deceived themselves into thinking they possessed salvation but who never truly did possess salvation?

(3) Read 2 Corinthians 13:5. When was the last time you examined yourself to see whether or not you were truly in the faith?

---

**10:11. He has said in his heart, "God has forgotten; He hides His face; He will never see."**

---

When the wicked runs from God, he has a deficient view of his sin, thinking it to be not very significant. When his sins are not immediately addressed in obvious ways by the unseen God, the wicked wrongly concludes that God does not see, or God does not care, or God does not even exist (Eccles. 8:11). He concludes that God is not watching when he sees others sin recklessly and get no apparent demonstrable retribution. He mistakes God's patience and common grace for lack of existence (Rom. 2:5). He does not realize that God will hold them accountable for every deed (Rom. 2:6, Rom. 2:8), idle word (Matt. 12:36), and thought (Rom. 2:16). The wicked try to plant lies in the minds of the faithful or anyone (Gen. 3:4). This is true of the devil himself as well as those who do the devil's work.

The devil tells lies such as those quoted in this verse. When the devil says, **"God has forgotten,"** this contradicts the truth about God that an omniscient God forgets nothing. God knows everything. God works everything, both the bad and the good, together for the good of those that love Him (Rom. 8:28). When the Bible speaks of God "remembering our sins no more" (Heb. 8:12), that is best understood not in the sense of literal forgetting as we might think of forgetting something. Instead, it is best understood that when sins were committed, they were not held against us (because of the forgiveness found only in Christ).

When the wicked insinuate the lie that God **"hides His face,"** he lies by saying that God will not be there when the righteous seek His face, that God will not respond in some manner. While it is true that sometimes when we seek God, we will not get the answer that we expect, it is never true that God does not hear us if we cleanse our hearts from any known sin before entering His presence (Jn 9:31). The wicked one tells lies to try to plant lies into the minds of God's people, telling them that God does not see the affliction of His people. This is false. Sometimes, God allows His people to endure afflictions to purify them, grow their faith, and make them more like Christ (Jas 1:2-8). When going through some of these things, it can sometimes seem like God is not there or does not care, but in reality, God is never against His children (Rom. 8:31). Even when he allows things that are less than pleasant to enter our lives, or something other than what we would pick for ourselves, we can respond to these things righteously. Afflictions can be an excellent means to purify ourselves, to reduce our amount of conformity to this world (Rom. 12:2), to grow in the grace and knowledge of the Lord (2 Pet. 3:18). He wants us to endure suffering to refine us and makes us more like Christ.

## Questions for self-reflection:

(1) What is your reaction as you see sin run rampant in your society all around you with no apparent godly intervention?
(2) As a believer, does the thought that God will hold you accountable to every thought, word, and deed, thrill you or scare you? A little bit of both?
(3) How has your life changed since God 'forgot' your sins?
(4) Are there habits you can develop to help you respond to life's trials in a more God-honoring way?

**10:12. Arise, O Lord! O God, lift up Your hand! Do not forget the humble.**

---

For **'Arise, O Lord!,'** see note on Psalm 3:7.

The psalmist knows that the Lord's **hand** is the symbolic instrument He uses to exert His power, not a literal hand. He is asking the Lord to intervene on his behalf and rescue him. In Exodus, when Moses raised his hands against God's enemies, God's people won against God's enemies. In the same story, when Moses' hands were not raised against God's enemies, God's enemies won against God's people (Exod. 17:11). Earlier in Exodus, the Lord said His hand would be against the Egyptians when the Egyptians suffered from the plagues (Exod. 7:5). The Egyptian magicians recognized that God's finger was against Egypt (Exod. 8:19). The writer of Hebrews would later assert that it is a fearful thing to fall into God's hands (Heb. 10:31). So, God's hand is an instrument of judgment as well. The psalmist here asks the Lord to intervene on his behalf by judging his enemies. God's enemies do not want to fall into God's hands (Heb. 10:31). The humble have submitted themselves to God the Father through the Lord Jesus Christ (Jas 4:6-8, 1 Pet. 5:6). God will exalt such people (Matt. 23:12) and seat them in heaven with Christ (Eph. 2:6).

God will **not forget the humble**. The humble receive God's grace (Jas 4:6). When a sinner comes to God through faith in Christ for conversion, everlasting life, and justification, they are humbled so that Christ can be exalted in and through them (Matt. 23:12). No matter what they go through, no matter what earthly travail they face, no matter what the earthly enemy, the Lord is with them (Rom. 8:35-39). While to the humble believer, it may at times feel as though God has forgotten them, the reality is that God has not and never will forget them and will always be with them (Joshua 1:9). Rather than forget them, the believer is the recipient of every good and perfect gift (Jas 1:17), the recipient of mercy and help in time of need (Heb. 4:16), and the recipient of every spiritual blessing (Eph. 1:3-14). The humble are often called to suffer for His sake silently. Silent sufferers like the psalmist may have no other recourse other than to go to the Lord for His intervention on their behalf. There may be no change to their circumstances. They may need to rely on God's power to sustain them in the affliction rather than hoping for God to remove the discomfort.

## Questions for self-reflection:

(1) How have you seen God deliver you from trouble in the past?
(2) How has your life been an example of exalting the risen Christ for others to see?
(3) If you are going through a trial that seems to have no end in sight if God's power were to sustain you in the affliction, what would that look like?

**10:13. Why do the wicked renounce God? He has said in his heart, "You will not require an account."**

---

**The wicked renounce God** when they say that He is not real (Ps. 14:1) or when the wicked assert that Scripture says untrue things about God (Ps. 19:7-11, Prov. 30:5, Matt. 5:17-20). The wicked renounce God when they live apart from His standard (Rom. 3:19-20). The wicked reject God when they ignore the conscience that God has given them and knowingly break the Law He has written on their hearts (Rom. 2:15). The wicked deny God when they consider Christ's blood an unclean thing (Heb. 10:29). The wicked abandon God when they consider the preaching of the cross to be foolishness rather than consider it to be the power and wisdom of God unto salvation (Rom. 1:16, 1 Cor. 1:18). The wicked renounce God when they attack His nature and attributes. The wicked forsake God when they criticize the way He has acted in history or in the way He works presently. When the wicked look into God's law and deem it unfair rather than full of wondrous things, they renounce God (Ps. 119:18). The wicked renounce God in more ways than this.

The wicked **has said in his heart** that God **will not require an account** for sin. They scoff when they are confronted with the prospect of impending judgment. To them, it is comical that a 'God of love' would possess any holiness with which to **require an account** for, much less judge and punish anyone for sin. The wicked renounce God when they refuse to walk in God's law (Ps. 119:1). The wicked renounce God when they refuse to keep His testimonies and only seek Him when convenient for them to do so (Ps. 119:2). The wicked renounce God when they drink iniquity like water (Jb 15:16) rather than doing no evil (Ps. 119:3). Rather than hiding God's Word in their hearts that they might not sin against Him (Ps. 119:11), the wicked rail against God's Word and sear their consciences against it (2 Tim. 4:2). The wicked renounce God when they put God on trial and ask God to defend Himself against how He has chosen to act on behalf of His people and against His enemies throughout history. The wicked renounce

God when they assume that all the martyrs who have shed their blood for the cause of Christ throughout all the ages did so in vain. They will be shocked to find that their railings against the One who could save them will be turned to rubbish when they have to bow to Him (Phil. 2:9-11).

## Questions for self-reflection:

(1) How have you seen the wicked renounce God?

(2) Was there a time when you were among the wicked who renounced God?

(3) If there was a time when you were among the wicked who renounced God, what changed? How did you change from a renouncer to an embracer?

(4) When you run into someone who renounces God today, do you feel sad for them? Or do you go about your business and leave them alone as long as they leave you alone?

**10:14. But You have seen, for You observe trouble and grief, To repay it by Your hand. The helpless commits himself to You; You are the helper of the fatherless.**

As the wicked continue to renounce God, as the wicked continue to think God does not see, as the wicked wrongly surmise that God is not there, is not involved, does not care, or does not even exist, as the wicked insists on being self-sufficient, God sees. God sees everyone and everything (Heb. 4:13). God sees the **trouble and grief** endured by the righteous at the hands of the wicked. He sees even the hidden thoughts and motives of all people, both the just and the unjust (1 Sam. 16:7, Ps. 94:11, Ps. 139:2, Ps. 139:4, Ps. 139:23-24, Isa. 66:18, Matt. 5:28, Matt. 12:25, Mk 2:8, Lk 9:47, Lk 11:17, Jn 2:25). There is nothing hidden from His sight. He sees into the hearts of His creatures, namely humankind, and sees all the way through.

When the wicked appear to prosper, the righteous do not need to fret because the God of the righteous sees and will render to each man according to his works (Rom. 2:6). God will remember the persecution, martyrdom, and oppression His people endure at the hand of the people of Satan (Rev. 6:9-11). Vengeance belongs to the Lord, and He will **repay** in His timing (Rom. 12:19). Those who do not have ample resources to provide for themselves realize that they are more helpless than those who do have resources. Therefore, such vulnerable people are more likely to seek the help they need from the One who will supply all our needs according to His riches (Phil. 4:19). These might be physical needs, emotional needs, or spiritual needs. Whatever the need, because **the helpless commits himself to** the Lord, the Lord is there to help the helpless. God will not leave His people since He is their Father. He becomes the Father to **the fatherless**. He becomes their **helper**. He helps them with whatever they need in the physical realm as well as in the spiritual realm.

**Questions for self-reflection:**

(1) When you think back to your life before you became a Christian, when you consider some of your most despicable sinful choices when you consider that God saw every bit of it, how does that make you feel? Is there a mix of shame for what you did along with gratitude for His grace and forgiveness?

(2) How does the knowledge that He sees affect how you live now? Does it motivate you to take every thought captive to the obedience of Christ?

(3) When you have committed yourself to the Lord, how have you seen the Lord come through and meet physical and spiritual needs in your life?

**10:15. Break the arm of the wicked and the evil man; Seek out his wickedness until You find none.**

The psalmist asks God to intervene against the enemies of the psalmist, who are also God's enemies. **The arm** symbolizes a source of power (Isa. 53:1). So, this is a request to take the limited power of the wicked and evil man away and make it bow to the limitless power of God. The psalmist wants the persecution, oppression, and whatever hardship he endures at the hands of his enemies to cease. When Christ was crucified, He made a spectacle of His enemies, which is already partially fulfilled (Col. 2:15). Also, in the future, Satan and all those who have followed him will be cast into the Lake of Fire forever (Rev. 20:10, Rev. 20:15). There will be a time when all the enemies of Christ will be under His feet (1 Cor. 15:26-27).

The psalmist asks God to remove the **wicked and evil man** from the post that he currently occupies from which he can persecute the psalmist. The psalmist asks the Lord to fully avenge him by overtaking the source of the persecution such that his enemies are no longer able to practice their denial of the God of the psalmist and the persecution of the psalmist.

### Questions for self-reflection:

(1) Do you look forward to the time when you will no longer have to endure the wickedness in the world caused by unbelievers?

(2) Do you look forward to the Day of judgment so that you can hear "Well done good and faithful servant" and so your enemies, Christ's enemies, will be put under His feet?

(3) If your life had fewer trials, would you recognize your dependence upon the Lord more, or would you realize your reliance upon the Lord less?

(4) If your life had more trials, would you recognize your dependence upon the Lord more, or would you recognize your reliance upon the Lord less?

**10:16. The Lord is King forever and ever; The nations have perished out of His land.**

---

Jesus Christ is **the Lord** (Matt. 7:21-22, Lk 6:46, Jn 13:13, Phil 2:11). He is the promised **King** and has been King from all eternity from before creation. Before He came the first time, He was prophesied as a King. He admitted that He was King Himself to people who were unwilling to see Him for who He is (Lk 23:1-3). People tried to make Him a King but for the wrong reasons (Jn 6:15). In His First Advent, however, He was not received as King (Jn 1:11). Instead, He was punished as a criminal (Lk 23:32-33). He told Pilate that His kingdom was not of this world (Jn 18:36). When He rose from the dead, He proved that what He said was true. He was seen by many after His resurrection (1 Cor. 15:5-8) before He ascended back His Father's right hand (Acts 1:9-11, Heb. 1:3) and sat down at the right hand of God (Hebrews 1:3).

He will return to judge the world on the appointed day (Acts 17:30-31). He will set up His earthly kingdom (Revelation 21) before it transitions to His heavenly kingdom. Christ rules in the hearts of His people now (Lk 17:20-21). When all Christ's enemies are under His feet (1 Cor. 15:26-27), when all the ungodly have been cast into the lake of fire forever (Rev. 20:10, Rev. 20:15), then **the nations will have perished out of His land.** Then, His Kingdom will have no end (Lk 1:33). The nations that will perish out of His land when His Kingdom has no end are made up of all of God's enemies.

### Questions for self-reflection:

---

(1) If you met Christ as King on earth today, knowing what you know now, how would you respond to Him?
(2) If you knew that tomorrow you would pass away and be ushered into eternity where you would face Christ the King before the Judgment seat of Christ, what would you do today?
(3) Have you ever imagined what the earthly kingdom would be like? What does it look like?

**10:17.** **Lord, You have heard the desire of the humble; You will prepare their heart; You will cause Your ear to hear,**

---

**The humble** person has removed all that impedes his communication with God. The humble person is the one that God receives, whereas the proud person is the one that God resists (Jas 4:6). The prideful person is the one that lifts themselves up only for God to knock them down (Matt. 23:12). The humble person is the one that knocks themselves down only for God to lift them up (1 Pet. 5:6). The humble person has dealt with his sin, first at the cross (1 Jn 2:2) and second by consistent sin confession (1 Jn 1:9). The kingdom of God belongs to the humble person (Matt. 5:3). The humble know that they can enter the Lord's presence whenever they want (Heb. 4:16, 1 Pet. 5:7). Sometimes the humble do not know what to pray for. In such instances, the Spirit leads them (Rom. 8:26). God fills the humble **heart** with a sense of His glory to **prepare** the redeemed sinner to enter His presence. God helps the mind be appropriately set on things above (Col. 3:1-3), to have a proper meditation (Ps. 1:2), and to be adequately shepherded (Ps. 23). When the Spirit directs the believer to pray according to the Spirit, in alignment with God's truth, the Spirit of the humble person bears witness with God's Spirit (Rom. 8:16).

Humble hearts are in tune with God's will and pray according to God's will. Humble hearts expect God to answer their prayers according to His will and His time (1 Jn 5:14). The humble and weary believer can trust knowing that God will hear them when they come before Him in humility once they have first dealt with their sin (Ps. 66:18). The humble believer needs to be resigned to the fact that the answer that comes back from God to their request may not be according to their will but will be according to His will. The humble believer recognizes that when God does answer their prayers, it may not necessarily be according to how they would prefer that He answer. But the divine answer will always be what is best (Matt. 7:9-11). The believer does not doubt in God's power to answer the requests brought toward the throne of grace (Heb. 4:14-16). God fills the heart of the humble believer with the expectation that He will answer their prayers according to His will (1 Jn 5:14). Since the humble person **desires** to see God's will be done on the earth as it is in heaven (Matthew 6:10), they know that when they pray with pure hearts that the Lord has **heard** them.

## Questions for self-reflection:

(1) What can you do or not do to ensure that God hears you?

(2) If you had to live a life full of suffering for many decades, would you do it knowing that you had eternity with Christ in heaven to look forward to?

(3) Why do the humble who can enter the Lord's presence whenever they want not take advantage of that privilege as often as they could?

(4) Does your spirit bear witness with God's Spirit that you belong to Him?

(5) How often do you experience God answering your prayers?

**10:18. To do justice to the fatherless and the oppressed, That the man of the earth may oppress no more.**

---

**The fatherless** have nobody noteworthy to aid them and help them. They are more sensitive to their lack of personal physical protection. They are utterly dependent on help from another. They are more prone to sense the presence of the loving God who meets their needs (Phil. 4:19, Jas 1:27). He pleads their cause since they need extra help since they cannot help themselves.

**The oppressed** feels as if they have nobody to take up their cause. They are fighting the majority with seemingly none to support them.

The lost sinner is the same way. They cannot save themselves. Once they become aware that they have no spiritual resources with which to protect themselves (Matt. 5:3), the eternal God miraculously illuminates His justice and love before them. He shows them that His love and His justice kissed at the cross where Jesus took their punishment so they could be set free (2 Cor. 5:21, 1 Pet. 2:24). Once justified (Rom. 3:24), no matter what the saved sinner endures, nothing can separate them from God's love (Rom. 8:38-39). Between Christ's First Advent and His Second Advent, many forms of external persecution come upon Christ's sheep that come from **the man of the earth** that have them feeling oppressed and forsaken (2 Tim. 3:12). Persecution comes seemingly from all sides, even sometimes from those they would least expect to give it.

The devil is the leader of all those that are the enemies of the Cross of Christ. Satan is the father of lies (Jn 8:44) and has deceived an entire army into thinking that the world is better without Christians. They are misled into being duped by any world philosophy that puts itself against the God of Scripture. The ruler of this world (Jn 12:31) has the power to influence for now and is taking full advantage of it. The devil is busy running through a barrage of tactics designed to **oppress** God's people. Believers who experience such persecution should take heart, knowing that their Master Himself was also persecuted (Lk 6:40, Jn 15:20).

The saints should trust God patiently, reminding themselves that Christ will avenge all wickedness, even if it does not occur in their lifetimes (2 Thess. 1:8). One day, the persecutor will end up with the rest of God's enemies, in the lake of fire where his persecution and oppression will be rewarded with everlasting destruction (Rev. 20:10).

## Questions for self-reflection:

(1) Who do you know that would qualify as "fatherless"?
(2) What can you do to be God's hands and feet to help them?
(3) Was there ever a time in your life when you recognized your spiritual poverty before God?
(4) Have you experienced the love of the Lord from the crucible of affliction?
(5) Have you ever experienced persecution or oppression for your faith? If you have, how have you responded? If you have not, how do you think you would react if you ever did?

# Psalm 11

**11:1. In the Lord I put my trust; How can you say to my soul, "Flee as a bird to your mountain"?**

---

The unrighteous are prone to trust in themselves (Ps. 118:9, Isa. 31:1, Isa. 31:3, Jer. 17:5, Gal. 6:3). As a result, they will be brought low (Prov. 16:18-19, Prov. 29:23). They are a disgrace (Prov. 11:2). They are an abomination to the Lord (Prov. 16:5). They think they know better than everyone else about everything. Therefore, nobody else is worthy of entrusting themselves to. If they acknowledge that God even exists, He is not worth trusting, as He does not govern affairs perfectly or to their liking, so they would just as well continue to choose their own finite, sinful strength over His infinite light any day.

In addition to putting too much trust in their sinful selves, the unrighteous can also put too much faith in their fallible fellow man (Ps. 118:8, Ps. 146:3, Mic. 7:5). They also trust in the things they possess rather than the One who allows them to have those things (Prov. 11:28, Matt. 6:19, Lk 8:14, 1 Tim. 6:9, 1 Tim. 6:17, Ti 2:11-13, 1 Jn 2:15-17). These are all examples of misplaced objects of trust. None of these things or people should be objects of saving trust or security.

Since this world is not our home (Mk 8:36, Jn 15:19, Rom. 12:2, 2 Cor. 5:2, Phil. 3:20, Heb. 13:14, Jas 1:27, Jas 4:4, 1 Jn 2:15-17), believers should be setting their minds on things above (Col. 3:1-3), replacing trust in things and people in this world with confidence in the sovereign King of kings. Even when life does not go the way we want, this does not mean that God is not worth trusting.

While God's providence can seem mysterious, at times, for reasons unknown to us, He allows us to experience various forms of trials. Trials help us to persevere (Jas 1:12). Trials help us to do good when we do not feel like it (Gal. 6:9). Trials help us trust God even when we do not understand what is happening (see Job, Prov. 3:5-6). Trials can come in response to our own sin (Prov. 19:2-3). Trials can help make us humbler (2 Corinthians 12:7). Trials can be a form of correction for sin (Prov. 3:11-13). Trials can come so we can become more like Christ in His suffering (1 Pet. 4:12-16).

---

Trials can help us grow in Christlikeness (1 Corinthians 11:1). Trials develop our character (Rom. 5:3-6). Finally, trials increase our faith in the Lord (Jas 1:2-6).

Successfully living through trials in ways that honor the Lord gives God glory (Ps. 40:4-5, Ps. 71:14-17). When we experience these difficulties, they do not mean that God has missed something or made some mistake. A self-righteous man thinks himself to be worth trusting. Not the psalmist. Not the rest of the just. The just know that they cannot trust in themselves, their things, and other people because sin, even sin they cannot recognize within themselves, prevents them from seeing themselves as they ought–with brokenness and humility (Ps. 51:17). The just also know that they cannot trust the wisdom of others when that supposed wisdom has not been sufficiently checked by God's wisdom (Prov. 1:7).

The only Being capable of not misusing our complete trust in Him is the Lord who made everyone and everything. We can trust Him in the best of times. We can trust Him in the worst of times. We can trust Him in times of leanness. We can trust Him in times of abundance.

Others were telling the psalmist to **flee to** a **mountain.** The acquaintances of the psalmist evidently were overtaken by fear of the circumstances that were affecting them. Or his acquaintances were trying to intimidate him into fearing and fleeing for himself. The psalmist would have none of that. The psalmist further explains why he has been told to flee to the mountain in the verses that follow.

## Questions for self-reflection:

(1) Do you ever catch yourself behaving as one who trusts in themselves rather than one who trusts in the Lord?
(2) What do you think you could do better than God can do it?
(3) Have you ever put too much faith in fellow man at the expense of faith in God?

(4) How have you demonstrated trust in physical elements of the world to the neglect of faith in God?

(5) Looking back on your life, how have you seen evidence of the trials which God has permitted you to endure causing you to persevere better?

(6) What specifically in your life prevents you from seeing yourself with a proper sense of humility?

**11:2. For look! The wicked bend their bow, They make ready their arrow on the string, That they may shoot secretly at the upright in heart.**

---

**The wicked** came in the direction of the psalmist. Those the psalmist knew saw the wicked coming before the psalmist did. The psalmist's acquaintances encouraged the psalmist to follow them in fleeing the apparent danger. The trust of the psalmist had to be in the Lord. Only the Lord could reliably protect the psalmist in the face of such insurmountable odds. The wicked, about to carry out their evil plan, readied their **arrow**s to **shoot at the upright** psalmist and his companions.

As it was with the psalmist, so it is for every generation of believers. Satan and his minions come after Christ and His flock (Jn 13:2, Acts 5:3, 1 Cor. 7:5, 2 Cor. 11:3, 2 Cor. 11:14, 1 Thess. 3:5). Even though Christ has won the battle already (Rom 7:25, Rom 8:37, 1 Cor. 15:57, Heb 2:14), and despite the unchangeable truth that Satan will ultimately be unsuccessful in his futile attempts to overthrow the King of Kings and Lord of Lords (Matt. 16:18), Satan will still try (Rev. 12:9). He will at least try to preoccupy the saints with as much as he can before he enters the Lake of Fire forever and ever (Rev. 20:10). Until then, Satan will use those who have come against God's people to disrupt God's Work, but, ultimately, God's Work will not be defeated.

In every generation, this is an issue. Martyrs give their lives for the faith (Acts 7:54-60, Rev. 6:10). Oppressive governments make living out honest Christian convictions to be a criminal offense (Matt. 10:17). They aim to stamp out the influence of God and His people to the point where His people have to go into hiding. Some **secretly** hash out attempts to harm or kill the righteous. Others are more public. This does not catch the righteous remnant off guard because they know to expect this.

Holy writ predicts the wicked world's hostility enacted upon the righteous (2 Tim. 3:12). When believers get persecuted for their faith, they are blessed (Matt. 5:10-12). Believers should expect corrupt governments to fight against them (Matt. 10:18).

---

Believers should expect even the religious to treat them poorly (Matt. 10:17). It is not uncommon for the very families of believers to turn against them (Matt. 10:21). When these things happen, as difficult as they are to endure, believers who trust the veracity of what God has said in the Bible can take comfort that God is fulfilling His Word in their lives. When believers see Scripture fulfilled in their lives, it can increase their faith and give them boldness to keep the faith.

## Questions for self-reflection:

(1) If you were the psalmist and the wicked had bent their bow in your direction, how would you respond?

(2) If you have not experienced persecution, do you think that the fact that Scripture predicts that it will happen to God's people would make it easier for God's people to endure it when it comes?

(3) Have you ever had a family member turn on you because of your faith?

(4) If persecution has not impacted your life yet, what can you do now so that you will be better prepared to endure it when it does happen to you?

**11:3. If the foundations are destroyed, What can the righteous do?**

---

**If the foundations are destroyed**, it will look to the righteous like the world is falling apart. God is the foundation of all morality. The first law ever to be given to man was given to man by God in the Garden of Eden (Gen. 2:15-17). From that point on, the foundation for good morality, a foundation predicated on obedience to God's expectations, has been under attack. God has always tried to help man come back to Him by giving man a law and writing that law upon man's heart (Rom. 2:15), but man's heart, since Genesis 3, has been set on rebellion against God (Rom. 3:9-23). This has been fleshed out in society as well as in the home. This has been carried out in governments. True religion is the object of persecution. Immorality is championed. The wicked entrap the righteous. It will look to **the righteous** perhaps that they **can do** nothing to stop it. It will seem as if all good and right in the world is overtaken by Satanic wickedness (1 Jn 5:19). It may seem like the government is doing the bidding of the devil rather than doing the job God gave it to do (Rom. 13:1-7). Freedom of religion in some places gets threatened by oppressive radicals who persecute the truth to try to replace it by intimidation.

When the righteous seem to drop like flies, and the raging wicked seem to set themselves up against the righteous (Ps. 2:1), the righteous can remember the Lord of the Word who said that He can see everything that the wicked perpetuate on the earth (Prov. 15:3). The righteous can trust the Lord to execute His wrath on a lost world in His timing (2 Thess. 1:7-8). The righteous can trust that the Lord will avenge His people when He determines (or has determined) that the time is right. If the wicked majority attacks the truth, the righteous can go boldly before the throne of grace and ask God to intervene on their behalf (Heb. 4:16) and trust God for the results. If the change does not come when the righteous think it should come, then they must change what they ask. Instead of asking God to bring the change they want to see, perhaps the righteous should ask for God to help them become the change they want to see. Maybe the change that is needed is less from without and more from within. The righteous can enter into the Lord's presence by the veil, through the flesh of Christ, and come boldly to the throne of grace for mercy and help (Heb. 4:14-16). They can receive help to react to injustice in ways that are pleasing to God. They can plead with God to bring an end to wickedness and the exalt righteousness.

## Questions for self-reflection:

(1) Since you became a believer and have seen in Scripture that the world is in opposition to true believers, in what ways have you seen the foundations get destroyed in the society in which you live?

(2) How have you seen immorality get promoted by the world?

(3) In what ways has the government abdicated its responsibility to protect believers?

(4) In a wicked world such as this one, how is it comforting to know that the Lord sees what is going on?

**11:4. The Lord is in His holy temple, The Lord's throne is in heaven; His eyes behold, His eyelids test the sons of men.**

The **holy temple** of **the Lord**, God's dwelling place, originates in heaven (Deut. 26:15, 1 Chron. 21:26, 2 Chron. 30:27, Jb 22:12, Ps. 2:4, Ps. 20:6, Ps. 33:13, Ps. 102:19, Ps. 103:19, Ps. 123:1, Eccles. 5:2, Isa. 63:15, Isa. 66:1, Lam. 3:41, 50, Dan. 5:23, Matt. 6:9, Matt. 10:32-33, Matt. 12:50, Matt. 16:17, Mk 11:25-26). When Jesus condescended to redeem sinful humanity, believers became the Temple (1 Cor. 6:19). There will be a new temple in eternity, once identified as God Himself (Rev. 21:22). The **throne**, from which the Lord rules, **is in heaven**. He judges from there (Acts 17:30-31). Since He is far above His creatures since He created everything, including every human that ever was, is, and will be, His children can trust that He will rule well, that He will do a better job of ruling their lives better than they ever could.

God's **eyes behold** everything everyone does. He sees when the wicked act wickedly. He sees when the righteous act righteously. When the wicked think about God's knowledge of them, they often consider themselves better than they genuinely are (Prov. 20:6). When the righteous think about God's knowledge of them, they are more likely than the wicked to give an honest assessment of themselves (Ps. 51:3-4).

God will allow things to happen to people to **test** them. He does not tempt anyone (Jas 1:13) but will test them to enable them to grow spiritually (Jas 1:2-8). He will test them to see for themselves if their character needs to grow in particular areas. The testing may involve discipline that is not pleasant but is often necessary for growth in godliness (Heb. 12:3-11). He can test them to see the place His Word has in their lives as it is the discerner of the thoughts and intents of the heart (Heb. 4:12).

**Questions for self-reflection:**

(1) How do you feel to know that Christ has given you access to the Lord in His holy temple?
(2) How has the testing of the Lord in your life resulted in your spiritual growth?

**11:5. The Lord tests the righteous, But the wicked and the one who loves violence His soul hates.**

---

**The righteous** are only righteous because they have looked to the Son (Isa. 45:22) by faith (Rom. 4:5, Rom 5:1, Gal. 2:16, Eph. 2:8, Heb. 11:6), and God imputed the righteousness of Jesus Christ to their account (Rom. 4:24). Their righteousness has nothing to do with themselves (Phil. 3:9). For those who belong to the Lord, the Lord works on them to make them more like Jesus (Rom. 8:29).

Sometimes, when the Lord works on His people, the work takes the form of various **tests**. While the Lord knows everything to know about everyone He has created in His image (Gen. 1:27), including those He has created again for good works (Eph. 2:10), He wants the righteous to demonstrate the righteousness that they say they possess by external righteousness. (1 Jn 2:29). He wants the testing to result in fruit-bearing in the lives of those who abide in Him (1 Jn 15:1-8). The fruit will be visible, albeit in varying degrees, in each of His sheep (Matt. 13:8, Mk 4:20, Lk 8:8), but the fruit will, without fail, be visible (Matt. 7:16) and lasting (Jn 15:16). Even when the Lord disciplines and chastises His own, He does so out of love for their good (Heb. 12:3-11).

**The wicked and the one who loves violence** do not possess eternal life. The wrath of God abides upon them (Jn 3:36). They are alienated from God by their wicked works (Col. 1:21). They are dead in trespasses and sins (Eph. 2:1, 5). They suppress the truth about who God is in unrighteousness (Rom. 1:18). They live in foolishness, disobedience, deceit, consumed with lust and pleasure, malice, envy, hatred toward others (Ti 3:3). Perhaps this wicked one has found his way into the church. Maybe he has acquired for himself a form of godliness (2 Tim. 3:5) but has missed out on the power of God unto salvation (Rom. 1:16). Obviously, people who do not care about following Christ can bring harm to true believers. What's more, those around the church that lack the true righteousness of those in the church inflict significant damage upon God's bride.

---

Because of this, Jesus, who intercedes on behalf of His own (Heb. 7:25), protects His sheep. God the Father is angry at the wicked for this and the plethora of other atrocities that the wicked perpetuate (Ps. 7:11). Such oppressors, those who love violence, will be storing up wrath for the day of wrath (Rom. 2:5). While they do so, they do the bidding of the wicked one, Satan himself.

God's soul hates the violence they perpetuate as well as the soul themselves. God can do things that those created in His image (Gen. 1:27) cannot do. For instance, God can hate someone at the very same time He loves the same person. God **hates** the workers of iniquity (Ps. 5:5), and, in this verse, that includes the one who loves violence. Such a person lives in unchecked sin. In their sins, they hurt themselves and others by their words and actions (Rom. 3:13-18) and their lack of action (Jas 4:17). God shows His aversion to those who unashamedly sin against Him by letting them go on (Rom. 1:24, Rom. 1:26, Rom. 1:28), unrestrained in their sins, in this life as they await eternal condemnation (Jn 3:19) in the next life. While they do not feel the need to see the heinous nature of their sins against God in this life, they will bear their guilt in the flames of everlasting fire in the next life (Rev. 21:8).

## Questions for self-reflection:

(1) How have you sensed the Lord working on you to conform you to the image of Christ?
(2) How have others seen that the internal righteousness you say you have is authentic?
(3) How do you live in the tension of knowing that you received salvation by grace through faith and not of works (Ephesians 2:8-9) and that sheep demonstrate genuine salvation by producing fruitful works (Ephesians 2:10)?
(4) How has the Lord disciplined you in ways that were unpleasant to bear?

(5) Can you now see how the discipline ended up being good for you to experience?

(6) Are you glad that God has been patient with you while you loved violence?

**11:6. Upon the wicked He will rain coals; Fire and brimstone and a burning wind Shall be the portion of their cup.**

---

**The wicked** are all led by Satan and those who work for him. Therefore, eternal punishment awaits all those who do not worship the one true God, the God of the Bible, God the Father, Jesus, God the Son, and God the Holy Spirit, the Holy Trinity. This fate awaits the majority of the world since Jesus said the way of the righteous is narrow and the way of the wicked is broad (Matt. 7:13-14).

**Fire and brimstone** were the instruments of judgment employed by the Lord against the wickedness found in Sodom and Gomorrah (Gen. 19). That was a type for the eternal fire that awaits the wicked as described by Jesus during His earthly ministry (e.g., Lk 13:28) and within Revelation (Rev. 20:11-15, Rev. 21:8). The consequence described here by the psalmist will by no means be pleasant to endure for the wicked. Those who reject the Son and willingly choose to follow their own sinful paths will endure this horrific eternal fate. It will come upon them when they do not expect it (Lk 12:20). They will be desperate for relief that will never come (Lk 16:24).

**Burning wind** will accentuate the agony. That will be their **portion**. They chose that portion for themselves. Jesus taught that there would be degrees of punishment in hell (Matt. 10:15).

Jesus described God the Father pouring out His wrath upon Him as a **cup** (Jn 18:11). So likewise, here, the wrath is also described as a cup. The instruments fire and brimstone are in the cup of God's wrath that He will pour out upon the unbelieving since they chose their sin instead of choosing to follow the Lord.

**Questions for self-reflection:**

---

(1) Since God took you off the broad road that leads to destruction and put you on the narrow road that leads to life, how has your attitude towards those on the wide road changed?

---

(2) Does the consequence that awaits the wicked should they continue to persist in their rebellion toward the God that loves them concern you enough to do something to try to win them to the Lord?

**11:7. For the Lord is righteous, He loves righteousness; His countenance beholds the upright.**

Because **the Lord is righteous** (Deut. 32:4), He always does what is right. Even if what He does seems wrong to us from time to time, because He is perfect, the fault is with us, and not with Him (1 Jn 1:5). Because **He loves righteousness**, therefore He practices righteousness.

One way that He perfectly practices righteousness is to punish the wicked (2 Thess. 1:5-10). He is not wrong to do this. The wicked have chosen the path of wickedness for themselves (Eccles. 8:11). God has not forced them to choose evil. They decided according to their nature. As they rejected more knowledge that was there to point them back to the God (Rom. 1:28), they had alienated themselves from God by their wicked works (Col. 1:21), and their wickedness increased (Gen. 6:5, Gen. 8:21).

Those who belong to Him who have His nature also practice righteousness (1 Jn 2:29). God practices righteousness perfectly. God's followers practice righteousness imperfectly because people have a sinful nature (Rom. 7:21). God does not have a sinful nature (1 Jn 1:5). God cannot sin.

Because God is righteous and the people made in His image are unrighteous (Rom. 3:10), the only way unrighteous humanity can be with God in heaven eternally is to have the righteousness God requires (Matt. 5:20). Since people are sinful, they need the righteousness of Another, Jesus Christ, the righteous, fully God and fully man who took their place (2 Cor. 5:21). Those whose faith is in Christ alone have Christ's righteousness imputed to them, have their sins forgiven, and possess eternal life (Rom. 4:5). The Father loves the Son, and when sinners place repentant faith in the sinless Son, instead of being children of wrath (Ephesians 2:3), the love of God is shed in their hearts (Rom. 5:5), and they walk in His love (Eph. 5:2). Actions done by the righteous by faith in the Son of God are approved because God looks at the Son and sees His righteousness (Eph. 2:10). The righteous walk by faith and not by sight (2 Cor. 5:7). The **upright** are the saved, and God looks at the saved with **His countenance** and blesses them with all spiritual blessings (Eph. 1:3).

## Questions for self-reflection:

(1) If others who do not know you were to look at your life, would the snapshot that they see make them curious as to know what makes you different from everyone else?
(2) Was the Lord wrong to flood the whole earth? Why or why not?
(3) How has the Lord shown you His love for you?
(4) Would the people who know you best say that you walk by faith or by sight?

# Psalm 12

**12:1. Help, Lord, for the godly man ceases! For the faithful disappear from among the sons of men.**

---

The psalmist is experiencing evident persecution from without. He looks around for another **godly man** like himself who could comfort him and support him but cannot find one. He wants to find another person who, like himself, is in a covenant relationship with the Lord of heaven and earth. He wants to find someone who has received grace, mercy, and adoption. He wants to find someone who has a holy lifestyle like his. He wants to find someone who knows the Lord as he does. The psalmist feels all alone. He feels like he is the only one he knows who knows the One True God. He feels like he is the only one who knows what it is like to be in a covenant relationship with the One True God. Nobody shares the faith of the psalmist. Nobody that the psalmist encounters has noticed the God of the psalmist working behind the scenes like the psalmist has seen God working behind the scenes. Nobody the psalmist knows sets aside time to seek the Lord until the Lord is found (Isa. 55:6). Nobody the psalmist is acquainted with strives for personal holiness as the psalmist does (Lev. 20:26, Heb. 12:14). Nobody the psalmist knows is known for doing good to others, like the psalmist is known for doing good (Eph. 2:10, Ti 2:14). Nobody the psalmist knows is characterized by sanctifying the Lord in their hearts (1 Pet. 3:15). Only the psalmist has concerned himself with walking in the light (Jn 12:35, 1 Jn 1:7). The psalmist felt alone because there was nobody he shared spiritual fellowship with (2 Cor. 13:14).

When the psalmist experienced trouble, he knew to go to the only permanent refuge. He went to the Lord for his aid. Nobody else seemed to think to do that. After **faithful** people **disappear**ed from around the psalmist's side, all that seemed to be left were the worst of the worst. Those that remained seemed to walk in the flesh, not in the Spirit (Rom. 8:1) and seemed to walk in a way that was not pleasing to the Lord (Rom. 8:8). Those that remained shared the same fleshly, ungodly tendencies. They were the opposite in disposition to the psalmist. Where the psalmist was godly, the remaining were ungodly. Where the psalmist was spiritual, the remaining were carnal. Where the psalmist was regenerate, the remaining were unregenerate. Where the psalmist was godly, the remaining were ungodly. Where the psalmist was faithful, the remaining were unfaithful. Where the psalmist had belief in the One True God, the remaining lacked such belief. It seemed as if they all conspired against David. When the Lord Jesus came, He came unto His own, but they did not receive Him (Jn 1:11). In every generation since Christ came, most of those who have lived have been ungodly in disposition. Most have rejected the grace and revelation they have received to go their own way. Rather than living for the Lord, they live for themselves. Rather than acknowledge the One True God, they are a god unto themselves (Exod. 32:31) with a law unto themselves (Rom. 2:14). They do this to their ruin.

## Questions for self-reflection:

(1) Have you ever felt like the only godly person in your immediate circle of influence?

(2) If you suddenly lost all your believing family and friends to some tragic accident and you were the only one left, how would you find solace?

(3) If you noticed that everyone else that you know that had at one time or another named the name of the Lord had lost all interest in the things of God or had stopped bothering to cultivate personal holiness in their own lives, how would you respond?

**12:2. They speak idly everyone with his neighbor; With flattering lips and a double heart they speak.**

---

The godly people have ceased and no longer surround the psalmist. Instead of building up the holy people, such as the psalmist, with their words, the ungodly people make up the majority and **speak idly with** others. They make up lies about godly people such as the psalmist to increase the opposition to the psalmist. Instead of righteous, edifying speech coming off the lips of the justified, ungodly destructive speech harms the godly (Ep. 4:29). The people surrounding the psalmist were known for this corrupt speech. The people of every age who do not know the Lord Jesus Christ are likewise known for such sinful speech (Matt. 15:19, Rom. 3:13, Jas 1:26, Jas 3:1-12).

Corrupt speech has marked false teachers from every age, beginning with Satan in the Garden to Eve (Gen. 3:4-5). Such false teachers are known for **flattering lips** that gullible, non-discerning people fall prey to (Matt. 7:15-23, 2 Pet. 2:1-22). They are double-minded (Jas 1:8) in that they might speak positively about the godly to their face or when convenient. Still, they turn on the saints with their words whenever the opportunity arises for them to stay with the popular majority. They will put up a front in the presence of one group and change their disposition when in the company of another group to remain popular with both groups. Isaiah prophesied about this (Isa. 29:13).

The Lord recognized this about the people of His day (Matt. 15:8-9). Such people exist in every generation. They profess godliness for a time, but their lives lack the power to demonstrate godliness consistently (2 Tim. 3:5). They **speak with a double heart** because rather than meaning what they say and saying what they mean, they frequently say one thing and mean another. The undiscerning will trust them and be led astray, while the wise will have biblical discernment and will not fall prey to their lies.

**Questions for self-reflection:**

(1) Have you ever been ridiculed for following Christ?

(2) Have you overheard people who did not know you were a Christian speaking poorly about Christ or other Christians? How did that make you feel?

(3) Have you ever seen anyone treat someone nice to that person's face and then, when they were away from that person, talk badly about them behind their backs?

(4) Since the God of the universe knows everything, including the things we hide from others, how do you think He feels about it when His people are poorly spoken of and otherwise badly treated in hidden ways?

(5) Have you ever said one thing and did the opposite? Does that sort of thing lend credibility to your faith or take credibility away from your faith?

**12:3. May the Lord cut off all flattering lips, And the tongue that speaks proud things,**

---

The psalmist asks **the Lord** to intervene and stop those who lie with their **flattering lips**. In the previous verse, the psalmist asks for the Lord to stop the false teachers who were hurting him. The psalmist did not take matters into his own hands. He asked the Lord to do the work for him. The Lord could allow or cause some event that would lead to the cessation of the lips of the flatterers. The flatterers could perish or be otherwise providentially hindered in some other way. If the flatterers die, they will have to answer their Maker according to their deeds (Rom. 2:6), which will be a fearful thing (Heb. 10:31). If the flatterers do not repent, they will join the rest of the ungodly from every previous generation in the lake of fire (Rev. 21:8).

In every generation of human history, God has had a people for himself (Rom. 11:5). In each generation, God's people have been opposed (2 Tim. 3:12). The people who oppose God's people often flatter with their lips or some other type of dishonest speech (Matt. 5:10-12). The psalmist asks the Lord to come to his aid by putting an end to such flattery with the lips. The psalmist knows that he can trust that if the Lord does not end the flattering lips in this life through some tangible means, then it is guaranteed that such flatterers will succumb in the judgment under the Lord's feet in the next life (1 Cor. 15:26-27). The psalmist asks the Lord for relief from the lies by killing and sentencing such false teachers so that righteousness can advance unhindered. The psalmist goes on to ask the Lord to **cut off the tongue that speaks proud things**. This amounts to anything that exalts itself against God and hearkens forward to Paul's words to the Corinthians when Paul asks the Corinthians to bring every thought captive to the obedience of Christ (2 Cor. 10:3-5). Christ's people can count on the Lord to avenge His and their enemies (Rev. 19:15). The psalmist knows that ultimately God will not receive the proud; He only will receive the humble (Jas 4:6). All those that speak such proud things will be rejected by God and sentenced to eternal fire (Rev. 21:8). The psalmist knows that God will finally avenge him in this way. Still, while he waits for the glorious day when he is vindicated, while his suffering continues, he struggles to respond to his adversity appropriately. He knows he must continue to trust the Lord to work in him, through him, and around him for the glory of God.

## Questions for self-reflection:

(1) Have you ever heard lies being told about other Christians?

(2) How do you think Jesus and Paul felt when others lied about them in the stories that we read in Scripture?

(3) Do you think it would be easier to take matters into your own hands and force flatterers and the prideful to stop flattering and proud speech, or would it be easier to wait for the Lord to intervene in His way and His time?

(4) If you were to intervene to attempt to stop flatterers and proud speech, how would you know that the Lord wanted you to intervene and not wait for Him to do it another way?

(5) Does the judgment that awaits flatterers and proud speech excite you in that you rejoice that they will get the judgment that they are earning for themselves, or does their impending judgment make you sad because you wish they would not perish? Or is it a little of both?

**12:4. Who have said, "With our tongue we will prevail; Our lips are our own; Who is lord over us?"**

The enemies were more concerned with cleverly framing their words than they were with the truth of what they were saying (Eph. 4:14, 2 Tim. 4:3-4). They wanted to do what they could to paint the psalmist in as bad a light possible so the psalmist would have to suffer while they prospered (Jer. 12:1). They felt as if nobody should rule over them (2 Pet.2:10).

The psalmist knew that God ruled over him and, ultimately, also his enemies, even though they refused to acknowledge that fact. The Lord of the psalmist was the Lord of heaven and earth (Acts 17:24), even if they did not like to retain God in their knowledge (Rom. 1:28). The wicked spoke more loudly than the righteous. The unjust seemed to prosper at the expense of the just. Despite this, the psalmist, as well as the rest of the righteous, knew their duty was to patiently persevere by trusting the Lord and not looking to take vengeance into their own hands; God would repay (Rom. 12:19). The ungodly thought they could get away with saying and doing whatever they wanted against the godly privately and civilly, and no harm would come upon them (Eccles. 8:11). They fail to acknowledge that even ungodly rulers are put into positions of authority by the Lord (Dan. 7:25). They thought they could live as if the **Lord** was not there, that there was ultimately no lord over them (2 Pet. 3:1-10). They were their own final authority. They were a law unto themselves (Romans 2:14). In living this way, they and Satan, the one for whom they do their bidding, exalt themselves against all that is called God (2 Cor. 10:3-5, 2 Thess. 2:4). Everyone who willfully rejects Christ does this when they choose to sin as, in choosing to sin, they set themselves up as **lord** instead of putting the one true Lord in His rightful place on the throne of their lives. They fail to realize that after death comes judgment (Heb. 9:27), and every knee will bow, and every tongue will confess that Christ is Lord (Phi. 2:11).

**Questions for self-reflection:**

(1) Are you more concerned about being articulate or about being truthful?

(2) If you are your own authority, if there is no higher authority than you, how would you ever know you are wrong if you trust nobody but yourself?

(3) How can Christians persevere in the faith and show the love of Christ in the face of hostile opposition?

(4) How can Christians know when to share the truth in love with unbelievers and when to keep it to themselves?

(5) If someone fails to be convinced by the words that you say of the truth of who God is, what else can you do to show them the reality of God?

**12:5.** "For the oppression of the poor, for the sighing of the needy, Now I will arise," says the Lord; "I will set him in the safety for which he yearns."

---

**The poor** and **needy** are the saved, the justified, the redeemed, the sheep. The unsaved frequently target the poor in spirit (Matt. 5:3). These same victims of **oppression** are often poor in this world as they frequently do not have access to the same earthly resources as the ungodly do (Jas 2:5) (with exceptions, of course).

The troubles that befall a Christian can cause a lot of uncomfortable **sighing** on the part of believers. It can be frightening not to get along with the people of the world who lie under the sway of the wicked one (1 Jn 5:19). It can seem like the father of lies (Jn 8:44) is out to end the work done for the truth. Since the prince of the power of the air (Eph. 2:2) controls most of the world (Eph. 2:2), and since the minority is under the control of the Holy Spirit (Matt. 7:13-14), it can seem to the righteous that there is no hope. Sighing in the believing remnant can occur when believers do not always get the same opportunities financially as do unbelievers because of their faith. This can be another form of persecution that the lost world uses against the believing remnant.

The saved should use such oppressions as opportunities to cry out to the Lord for grace and help (Heb. 4:14-16). That is an excellent time to remember that this world cannot be our hope (Rom. 8:18, Heb. 13:14). God who rules the world is our sufficient hope. Some people who are persecuted for their faith (Matt. 5:10-12, 2 Tim. 3:12) may groan for relief from their seemingly insurmountable burden. They could lose their families or their goods (Matt. 10:21-23). God's people call out to God for relief, and according to His rich mercy (Eph. 2:4), He will **arise** and answer them (Ps. 18:6, Ps. 118:5). He will not do it until it is His time to do it. The Lord arises at the perfect time according to His plan. He may not arise in the way or at the time that His people think that He should. But we do not always understand His timing and His reasons as well as He does.

---

So, His people better not get impatient as they wait for Him to intervene on their behalf. They should trust that nothing takes God by surprise, and He is worthy to be trusted and praised for the 'good' as well as the 'bad' that happens to us (Rom. 8:28, Phil. 4:19). The Lord here, in 12:5, answers the cry of the psalmist from 12:1. The righteous have ultimate **safety** from all their enemies. Nothing can harm them eternally to the point where they would lose their salvation (Rom. 8:38-39, Rom. 8:1, Phil. 1:6). Christ protects them from spiritual harm, and in Him, they are secure. Even if trouble befalls the sheep in this life, after this earthly life ends, when they are with Him and see Him as He is (1 Jn 3:2), the safety they **yearn**ed for will finally be theirs.

## Questions for self-reflection:

(1) Are there times in your life to which you can point as evidence that God has come to your aid in various circumstances and settings?
(2) Has your faith ever elicited opposition from those who do not share it?
(3) When you cried to the Lord when your faith was opposed, how did the Lord come through to aid you?
(4) Does having to wait to receive an answer to your prayers increase or decrease your faith? Does it depend on the circumstance?

**12:6. The words of the Lord are pure words, Like silver tried in a furnace of earth, Purified seven times.**

---

In the immediate context, **the words of the Lord** help the oppressed know that the Lord fights on their behalf. The people of the Lord know that their Lord will arise for them when it is fit for Him to do so (Josh. 1:7). Often it may feel like the Lord waits to emerge until the righteous have exhausted all efforts of their own to better their predicament. But the Lord knows what He is doing even if His people do not understand. The Lord will make His people safe. The enemies of the Lord who speak doublespeak with flattering lips, as described earlier in this psalm, are in grave danger because the Lord uses the effectual, fervent prayers of the righteous to accomplish His purposes (Jas 5:16).

Since God is light (1 Jn 1:5) since there is no unrighteousness in God (Rom. 9:14), we can be sure that God's words **are pure** (Prov. 30:5). They are contrasted here to the words of the psalmist's oppressors. The words of the wicked are marked by impurity (Ps. 5:6, Ps. 38:12, Ps. 58:3, Ps. 59:12, Prov. 13:5, Prov. 16:27, Prov. 16:29, Isa. 59:4, Isa. 59:7, Rom. 1:29, Romans 3:13, 2 Tim. 3:2, 2 Tim. 3:3, 2 Tim. 3:6, Ti 1:10, Ti 3:3). Since God's words are pure, there is nothing unholy mixed in them. They are the perfect, unadulterated truth. They are pure milk (1 Pet. 2:2).

The Lord said in the previous verse that He would arise on behalf of His people and save them from their oppressors. In this verse, the psalmist made the statement to reassure the psalmist and the reader that the psalmist's words are true. The saved man knows that it is not wrong to live by every Word that proceeds out of God's mouth (Deut. 8:3, Matt. 4:4, Lk 4:4). Man can put his hope in what God has said because Christ has fulfilled many of the prophecies in the Scriptures, and others await fulfillment at His Second Advent. God's words, recorded for humanity in the Holy Scriptures, are perfect in the original autographs (Prov. 30:5, 2 Tim. 3:16). They contain the pure mind of God perfectly preserved by imperfect man.

---

The Lord Jesus Christ is the Word that became flesh (Jn 1:14). He was tried more extensively than anyone of His servants (Heb. 4:15). Christ endured temptation further than anyone else ever will because He never gave into temptation and committed sin. The rest of us cross the line from temptation to sin at various times in our pilgrimage (1 Jn 1:8, 1:10). In Scripture, the number seven often refers to perfection or completion.

So, for the Lord's words to be **purified seven times** refers to the Lord's Words standing up to scrutiny, having the dross melted off as **in a furnace of earth**. The Lord's words are exceedingly pure. In Him are all the treasures of wisdom and knowledge (Col. 2:3). When believers trust Christ and His words, they become vessels of mercy (Rom. 9:23). While the Lord, Satan, and the world will try them many times, they will come forth as pure gold (Jb 23:10, 1 Pet. 1:7).

## Questions for self-reflection:

(1) How has the Word of God brought you comfort in difficult circumstances?
(2) Could it be intentional that God does not want us to understand everything about the world and about how He works so that we will put faith in Him?
(3) Are your words ever like the words of the wicked? How does that make you feel when they are?
(4) How does God giving us a perfectly pure Word so that we can know Him demonstrate that God loves us?

**12:7. You shall keep them, O Lord, You shall preserve them from this generation for ever.**

If **'them'** refers back to verse five, them is identified as the poor and needy. As verse six states, God's Word is so sure that the reader can be sure that God will **keep** the poor and needy. God receives the poor and humble, those who recognize their utter dependence upon Him. God will **preserve** the poor and needy from being consumed by the present wicked **generation** that seeks to take advantage of them.

God's power through the gospel keeps the poor and needy (1 Pet. 1:5). The gospel is the power of God unto salvation (Rom. 1:16). The Lord Jesus Christ's finished work on their behalf keeps the poor and needy. Those who come to Christ are kept and not cast out (Jn 6:37). God keeps His own from stumbling (Jude 1:24). The saved are never plucked out of God's hands (Jn 10:27-28). The roaring lion will not be able to devour them (1 Pet. 5:8). God has chosen the poor of this world to be rich in faith (Jas 2:5). God provides for those who realize they are insufficient in and of themselves (Matt. 11:28-30). If 'them' refers to the Lord's words, that the Lord's words are tried, purified words, then the Lord's words will be preserved. The finished Canon of Scripture records the Lord's preserved words (Ps. 12:6-7, Isa. 40:8, Matt. 5:18, Mk 13:31, 2 Tim. 3:16, 1 Pet. 1:24-25).

Since the Lord's Word is sure (Ps. 19:7), the instruction contained in them are the very words of God. Therefore, we can trust the Lord's words. God's wisdom is more consistent and reliable than man's wisdom (1 Cor. 1:18-25). Man's word frequently changes. God's Word never changes because God does not change (Mal. 3:6, Heb. 13:8). Man is double-minded (Jas 1:8). God is not double-minded. Sin pollutes man's word. Sin does not defile God's Word. God's Word is reliable, whereas man's word is not.

**Questions for self-reflection:**

(1) Does seeing that God preserves His own give you more confidence you face the trials that exist in your life?

(2) Since God will preserve you, how can you look at your trials differently?

**12:8. The wicked prowl on every side, When vileness is exalted among the sons of men.**

---

**The wicked** surround the righteous (2 Cor. 4:8-9). Specifically, in context, the wicked **prowl on every side** of the righteous. The wicked are more numerous than the righteous (Matt. 7:13-14). The attacks of the wicked against the righteous seem relentless at times. The wicked seem to have the whole world with them taking up their cause against all that the righteous care about (1 Jn 5:19). The wicked seek to persecute and oppress the righteous from every side (2 Tim. 3:12). The devil seems to be hard at work employing the wicked to harass the righteous as much as possible. The wicked appear to want to harm the righteous to stamp out their cause, silence them, and take away the righteous' livelihood. As a result of this oppression and persecution, the righteous constantly need supernatural preservation and protection from the wicked. Fortunately for the righteous, their God is their shield and protector (Ps. 18:2). They need divine protection to sustain them from the onslaughts of the enemy army. Nothing reaches the righteous apart from Divine permission (Matt. 10:29, Rom. 8:28). The prayers of the righteous are a means that God uses to protect His people from the devil and the devil's people (Jas 5:16).

**Vileness is exalted among the sons of men** frequently when the cause of the vile is prioritized over the cause of the righteous. The wicked often yell louder and get more attention than the righteous. The unrighteous have a larger troop than do the just. Their influence is more voluminous. Consequently, their agenda gets further with the majority than does the righteous agenda. The righteous frequently need to be very cautious to avoid harm from the wicked when possible. The righteous should not lose hope when this happens. The Scriptures are clear that this is expected among God's people in a lost and dying world that stands in stark contrast to godly principles. The godly are dependent upon the Lord for preservation as the vileness of the wicked seeks to harm the righteous.

---

**Questions for self-reflection:**

(1) Does it feel like the righteous make up the majority in your society?

(2) In what ways do the wicked attack the righteous in your society?

(3) How have you heard through the news or perhaps personally witnessed the Lord preserve the righteous in the face of persecution?

(4) What are some examples of how vileness is exalted above righteousness?

(5) How can knowing that God predicts this in His Word be a comfort?

# Psalm 13

**13:1. How long, O Lord? Will You forget me forever? How long will You hide Your face from me?**

---

It is thought that David wrote this psalm when he fled from Absalom. When the psalmist's life was in danger, he naturally feared he would not survive. He thought the Lord had forgotten him since the **Lord** allowed him to be in such a predicament since he was being allowed to suffer for what felt to him like a **long** time.

We are too prone to mistake a lack of removal of adverse circumstances for lack of divine intervention. As a result, God often allows us to go through various forms of suffering to teach us things. These things do not always seem pleasant to us while we go through them (Heb. 12:3-11, Jas 1:2-8). Some can think of the different things that God allows us to endure for our spiritual growth as our enemies. However, when the believer considers that all things work together for their good, then even the troubles we endure are good for us (Romans 8:28).

It is not always God's will to immediately deliver His people from their affliction. When God's people do not sense God's love and grace as sensitively and powerfully as they once did, they incorrectly surmise that He has forgotten them. God truly does not **forget** His people, even if it feels that way to them from time to time. When life does not go the way God's people wish that it would, it can feel like God has forgotten us or cast us off. It may feel like He is not even there as His enemies are allowed to triumph for a season.

As the psalmist continued to experience this adversity, whatever it was, the psalmist felt as if God hid His **face from** him. He had lost the sense of God's loving presence. He no longer felt as if God approved of him. Perhaps he felt this way because he did not receive the deliverance that he thought he should. When the adversity of the circumstances is more prevalent in our thinking than the God of our circumstances, we are more prone to forget about His love which has been shed in our hearts (Rom. 5:5).

In those seasons of difficulty, when we do not get our way, it is sadly too common to forget that God's grace appeared to teach us to deny ungodliness (Ti 2:14). God's grace appeared to teach us to not live by bread alone but by God's Word (Matthew 4:4). Instead of trusting that God's grace is sufficient in us and that His power is made great in our weakness (2 Cor. 12:7-10), we become too much like Israel and lust after evil things instead of learning from their example (1 Cor. 10:1-6). It is not necessarily because of displeasure or discipline on God's end that He removes His influence from His people. Sometimes God's people are allowed to go through various trials to grow their spiritual character. As believers, no matter what they go through on this side of eternity, nothing can change the fact that they, as objects of His love, will inherit all the precious promises that await the saints in glory (Rom. 8:31-39). God cannot forget His people (Ps. 94:14, Isa. 49:14-15).

## Questions for self-reflection:

(1) What is one example of a circumstance you have endured, or possibly currently find yourself in, that makes you feel like the Lord has forgotten you?

(2) How have you seen past troubles that you have endured work for your spiritual good? How has adversity in your life led to spiritual growth in your life?

(3) What would it take for you to ask God to teach you through the affliction instead of asking God to remove the affliction from you?

**13:2. How long shall I take counsel in my soul, Having sorrow in my heart daily? How long will my enemy be exalted over me?**

When the psalmist took **counsel in** his **soul,** it resulted in daily sorrow in his heart. Because of the curse of indwelling sin, our hearts can often make us feel worse than we should as sons and daughters of the King (1 Jn 3:20). Even our well-meaning friends can lead us to despair with their counsel if their counsel opposes what God says is true (Phil. 4:8). This happened to Job. God is a wonderful counselor (Isa. 9:6). His counsel is wonderful to His children because when they follow it in humble obedience, the result is a closer walk with Him and greater sensitivity to His abiding presence (Jn 15:1-8, Jn 16:13).

When a person relies upon himself instead of relying upon the Lord, the result can be **sorrow.** The way of God is the way of peace (Ps. 119:165). The psalmist felt as though God was hiding from him. Feeling as though God was afar off left the psalmist feeling daily sorrow in his heart. He longed for the sensitivity to God's presence to return. The psalmist felt like God was hiding from him.

Consequently, he could not take counsel in God. He had to take counsel on someone other than God. That partially included himself. Indwelling sin makes it such that God's people are unable to hear His voice. Missing God like the psalmist did lead him to put too much negative attention on his circumstances rather than positive attention on God. This negativity led to sorrow in the heart for the psalmist.

The psalmist had temporal enemies that had **exalted** themselves **over** him. When the psalmist thought of his enemies, he understandably felt fearful and sorrowful. For the believing child of God, even if there is no physical enemy to flee, there will always be spiritual enemies such as Satan and sin. When the consequences of sin beat believers down, it can feel like sin engulfs them. It can feel like Satan is out to get them, and he is (Lk 22:31). When believers feel the attacks from the world, Satan, and unbelievers, it can feel like the world, which is not the believer's home (Heb. 13:14), is an exalted enemy. When unbelievers and believers have conflict, and the unbelievers' unrighteous agenda seems to prevail, it can feel like people are exalted enemies. When the attacks come against the believer (and they will), God's people must remember that they belong to the One that is in them. He that is in them is greater than he that is in this world (1 Jn 4:4).

## Questions for self-reflection:

(1) When you find yourself sorrowing over your own trials, do you find that you are taking counsel in your own soul, or are you taking counsel with God?

(2) Have you ever received bad spiritual counsel from a trusted source? What did you do when you realized that the counsel you received was bad?

(3) Has your sensitivity to God's presence and will for you increased since you have professed to know Him?

(4) Have you ever felt like God had hidden from you? If so, what did you do to change that?

**13:3. Consider and hear me, O Lord my God; Enlighten my eyes, Lest I sleep the sleep of death;**

---

The psalmist thought he was close to death, at least if **God** failed to intervene on his behalf. Circumstances for the psalmist seemed so dire that he felt that his next breath could have been his last (Jb 27:3, Isa. 42:5, Isa. 57:16, Dan. 5:23, Acts 17:25). The psalmist seemed willing to acknowledge that his life was fleeting compared to eternity (Jas 4:14).

The psalmist calls out to his God. He knew he was in a relationship with the One who could deliver him. The psalmist knew that as bad as life on this earth had gotten for him, that God would preserve him if that were according to God's plan for his life (Jb 14:5). He knew that his enemies seemed insurmountable at times. However, he also knew that God had protected him from his enemies in the past. Because of this, the psalmist could trust the Lord to do so again. If God were compassionate, He would preserve the psalmist.

If God was to **consider and hear** the psalmist, the psalmist could continue to serve the Lord for a while longer. As long as the Lord considered that a fitting thing for him to do, the psalmist would continue to honor his King. The circumstances that troubled the psalmist could have made him feel down or disturbed or discouraged. He knew that the Lord could help him to rise above that. So, the psalmist asked the Lord to **enlighten** his **eyes**. He could have been physically suffering. He could have been mentally suffering. He could have been emotionally suffering. He could have been spiritually suffering. No matter the need, no matter the source of suffering, the Lord, the God of the psalmist, could help him. If God could help the psalmist set his affections on things above rather than on things of the earth (Col. 3:1-3), then the psalmist could experience the refreshing from the Lord and be invigorated to continue serving the Lord. If the psalmist could once again see the world through the lens of God-centeredness rather than man-centeredness, then the psalmist could be a productive servant of the Lord. He could remember that the Lord was his light and his salvation (Ps. 27:1). He could remember that his enemies didn't stand a chance against his God. **Death** is called by the name '**sleep**' in the Scriptures (1 Kgs 11:43, Lk 8:52-53, Jn 11:11, 1 Cor. 15:6, 1 Cor. 15:20). The psalmist wanted the Lord to strengthen him to continue to serve the Lord rather than die.

## Questions for self-reflection:

(1) Have you ever felt like if God did not do something that you would die?
(2) Do you honestly believe that there is nothing that God cannot do (except sin) for you?
(3) How has the Lord helped you succeed in trials or suffering?
(4) How has the Lord's presence comforted you when difficult circumstances did not change to your preference?
(5) How do you know whether you view the world with a God-centered lens or a man-centered lens?

**13:4. Lest my enemy say, "I have prevailed against him"; Lest those who trouble me rejoice when I am moved.**

---

The psalmist wants the Lord to intervene on his behalf amid his difficult circumstances. When He does, the enemies of the psalmist will not think that they have gotten the better of the psalmist or the God of the psalmist just because they are causing the psalmist **trouble**. The psalmist wants God to make Himself known so it will be evident to all those who know the psalmist that there is nobody or nothing stronger than the God of the psalmist. The psalmist thinks that if things don't turn out well for him, it will look to God's enemies like God is hiding from the psalmist. It will look like God has forgotten the psalmist. It will look like this God that the psalmist claims is worth trusting is not as wonderful as the psalmist says He is if the enemies of the psalmist are allowed to **prevail** over the psalmist.

So, for God's reputation, the psalmist asks God to deliver him. The psalmist wants to be able to **rejoice** in his God. He does not want to allow his enemies to rejoice in their oppression of the psalmist. If God does not deliver the psalmist, if God does not rescue the psalmist, then the enemies of the psalmist might rejoice that they have overtaken the psalmist. Therefore, the psalmist did not want to allow his enemies to rejoice over his misfortune.

First and foremost, the primary enemy of the psalmist and all believers from every age is Satan himself (1 Pet. 5:8). Next, the world is the enemy of the believer. (Jn 16:33). Third, those who have trusted in anyone or anything else other than the one true God trouble the psalmist. Each of them keeps the psalmist from living as devoted to the Lord as he should. Sin in all its forms can also be an enemy to the believer because sin interrupts the believer's fellowship with God and keeps the believer from being as fruitful as possible (Eph. 4:18, Col. 1:21). Because the psalmist spent much time on the run fleeing his enemies, he spent much time away from his family. He had earthly treasure, but he would have rather had peace with his God, even if that meant that he had to endure earthly suffering (2 Cor. 4:17). Fortunately for the righteous, the enemy will never ultimately be victorious against God's elect permanently (Rom. 8:33).

**Questions for self-reflection:**

(1) Have you ever seen God's enemies get smug because of the hardship that God's people experience that His enemies seem to avoid?
(2) Have you ever seen God's enemies criticize God's people because of the 'foolish' beliefs of God's people?
(3) Have you ever seen God's enemies rejoice over the apparent misfortune of God's people?
(4) What keeps you from living as devoted to the Lord as you could?

**13:5. But I have trusted in Your mercy; My heart shall rejoice in Your salvation.**

---

The psalmist was familiar with God's promises. He was divinely inspired to write about some of them, and he was mentally and experientially acquainted with them as well. He knew from his past experiences and what God had directly revealed to the psalmist about Himself that God was merciful (Matt. 5:7, Mat. 9:13, Lk 6:36, Eph. 2:4, Heb. 4:16, 1 Pet. 1:3). The fact that the psalmist was able to write about God's **mercy** when the psalmist was a sinner was a testimony to the mercy of God.

The psalmist had prayed to God before and had seen God answer his prayers, so he had past examples of God's exercising mercy in his life to which he could recall. He **trusted** God for his present and his future. He vacillates between complaints about God forgetting him, his enemy succeeding against him, and him being on the verge of death. Despite these adverse circumstances, the psalmist knows deep down that his God is mightier than anyone or anything else. Past stories of God's intervention in the life of His people perhaps instilled faith in the psalmist that could counteract the doubt that is so sadly typical from such finite creatures as himself.

He leaves the doubt that he had previously expressed and returns to confident trust. He did not trust in himself. He knew there was nothing good in him. No. The psalmist directed his trust toward God because God had delivered him and could deliver him for as long as His will was to do so. His God was so merciful that He could do anything that the psalmist asked Him to do (Eph. 3:20-21). And even if God did not do what the psalmist asked Him to do, God was still merciful to allow the psalmist and other sinners like the psalmist to take their next breath.

The psalmist had experienced temporal **salvation** in the past from adverse circumstances. He had also experienced eternal salvation from his sins and from God's wrath, which abides over alienated sinners (Jn 3:36, Col. 1:21). For the New Covenant Christian, God is rich in mercy (Eph. 2:4) and has provided eternal redemption through the blood of Jesus Christ for the salvation of their souls (Eph. 1:7). The heart of the psalmist, the heart of every believer, can **rejoice** in the salvation God provided at Calvary. When the Lord Jesus Christ, the Word, became flesh (Jn 1:14), became sin for us (2 Cor. 5:21), bore our sins in His own body on the tree that we might live righteous lives to the glory of God (1 Pet. 2:24), He provided our reason to rejoice.

## Questions for self-reflection:

(1) What causes people to be deceived into thinking they are trusting in the Lord's mercy when they are actually trusting in something else improperly?
(2) How have the biblical stories of God working on behalf of His people been a comfort to you?
(3) What reasons has God given you to rejoice in His salvation?

**13:6. I will sing to the Lord, Because He has dealt bountifully with me.**

Regardless of his circumstances, the psalmist can sing to the Lord because he knows that the Lord has been merciful to him. The Lord has delivered him from past physical enemies. The Lord has delivered Him from the power and penalty of his own sins. Even if there have been times when the Lord has felt far off from the psalmist, the unchanging reality based on God's unchanging character and revelation is that God is always there for His people. Therefore, his people must avail themselves to His presence and His help. Belief in God's promises results in the joy that comes from mouths that **sing to the Lord**. Believers have this joy because when they think of who they were before God's rich mercy came to them, it is undeniable that God **dealt bountifully with** them. Now all spiritual blessings are theirs (Eph.1:3). This is reason to sing to the Lord.

## Questions for self-reflection:

(1) In what ways has the Lord dealt with you that have been bountiful?
(2) What enemies have you been delivered from by the Lord?
(3) What causes believers to forget their bountiful deliverance?
(4) How can you keep from forgetting the Lord's bountiful deliverance in your life?

# Psalm 14

**14:1. The fool has said in his heart, "There is no God." They are corrupt, They have done abominable works, There is none who does good.**

---

Psalm 53 essentially repeats Psalm 14. Paul quotes this in Romans 3. Though the Old Testament was written primarily to Israel, this verse contains universally applicable truth across all cultures (2 Tim. 3:16). There are plenty of people of various religious persuasions who play the part of a **fool** by rejecting the revelation of the one true God. This God has revealed Himself to humanity in the form of creation (Rom. 1:20), by way of conscience (Rom. 2:14-14), and in these last days by His Son (Jn 1:18, Heb.1:1-2).

People who say **"there is no God"** show themselves to be foolish. Some people who make this brash declaration may declare it blatantly by uttering the foolish words that declare that there is no God. Others may claim that He does exist but then live in such a manner to undermine such a verbal profession (2 Tim. 3:5). Such people who make such ignorant declarations are not fools in the sense that they lack cerebral intelligence. Instead, they are fools based on the morality they have chosen for themselves. Their moral choices are not based on an unchanging standard (found in God) but instead find their basis in the latest information they have. This information on which they base their morality and worldview is frequently changing. The foundation on which to base the philosophy of one's life should be based upon a standard that does not change. Basing one's philosophy for how to live life on a standard that changes as frequently as the weather is not reliable (Matt. 7:24-27).

The fool described in this verse does not understand the things of God (Rom. 8:7). They are blind to spiritual truth (2 Cor. 4:4). They are deaf to spiritual truth. They are without spiritual life (Eph. 2:1, 5). They are on the road to apostasy as they have consciously and repeatedly rejected God's revelation (Rom. 1:18-32). Many of Christ's miracles were done partly to show the physical types of this spiritual reality. These fools have no practical righteousness, despite their claims to the contrary with which they can boast in themselves (Eph. 2:9, 1 Jn 2:29). Since the fool says in his heart, "There is no God," he at least has enough discernment to keep such a repulsive thought (that there is no God) to himself. If they can convince themselves that there is no God, then they can live as they wish without fear of retribution (so they think). There can be no accountability to a non-existent deity. They then have the freedom to be their own final authority. What is right and wrong changes for them, as do the seasons. If there is no omniscient Being who knows all their wicked thoughts and actions, they can think and do what they please with no concern for what might happen to them as a result of it. If there is no God, there is no God to mock, and there is no need to be concerned with the concept of reaping and sowing (Gal. 6:7-8). If there is no God, one does not have to fear falling into His hands (Heb. 10:31). If there is no God, there is no day of judgment to prepare for (Heb. 9:27, 2 Pet. 2:9). If there is no God, there is no point to living righteously now, zealous for good works, because there is no treasure to prepare to receive (Matt. 6:19-21, Ti 2:14).

Such people who make this philosophy the basis for how they live their lives **are corrupt**. Such people are putrid before the Lord. They have taken the great gift of physical life bestowed upon them by the gracious God and allowed it to spoil. They are like the smell of a decaying corpse, dead in trespasses and sins (Eph. 2:1). They defile themselves by sin. This misjudgment of this reality taints everything they do. They are wise to do evil and foolish not to do good (Jer. 4:22, Rom. 16:19). They take God's straight way and pervert it. The aforementioned corruption comes out of their mouths and, in their works, comes out of the abundance of their hearts (Matt. 12:33-34). They are the millstone that drags others with themselves into the fiery pit that awaits all reprobates (Lk 17:2). Their **works** are **abominable** because, like their words, their works are extensions of their hearts, which are likewise abominable since the fruit that a tree produces indicates the type of tree (Matt. 12:33).

The spiritually righteous, those who possess righteousness in Christ alone for salvation, do not do anything to earn that righteousness. Instead, it is imputed to them by faith alone in Christ alone (Rom. 4:5). The Spirit of Christ, working in them to will and to do for His good pleasure, produces such fruit in the lives of believers (Phil. 2:13). But believers are not passive in this exercise (Phil. 2:12). Good works done from anything other than a heart of faith in the Living God are sinful (Rom. 14:23). Among such workers of iniquity, there is **none who does good**.

**Questions for self-reflection:**

(1) Do you know anyone who says there is no God?
(2) How has the Lord revealed Himself to mankind through creation?
(3) How has the Lord revealed Himself to mankind through conscience?
(4) How can you keep from forgetting the Lord's bountiful deliverance in your life?
(5) How has the Lord revealed Himself to us by His Son?
(6) How can the lives of Christians proclaim the veracity of God?
(7) How can the lives of non-Christians proclaim the veracity of God?
(8) Does your morality frequently change based upon new information, or does it remain the same?
(9) If proper morality can only be based on the most recent information, how could anyone in any previous generation have known that they had the proper morality?

**14:2. The Lord looks down from heaven upon the children of men, To see if there are any who understand, who seek God.**

Paul established in Romans 3:11 that, "There is none who seeks after God." The sovereign Lord can see everything done by all His creation as He **looks down from heaven.** The **children of men,** made in God's image (Gen. 1:27), will have to give an account to Him for everything they do and say (Eccles. 12:14, Matt. 12:37, Jas 3:1). The fact that when the Lord looks down from heaven and sees the children of men denotes that the Lord sees everything they do and speak. This speaks of the Lord's omniscience (Ps. 147:5, Jn 21:17, 1 Jn 3:20, Heb. 4:13). When God reset the human race after the Flood with Noah and his family, it became clear that the moral decay continued with Noah and his family (Gen. 6:5, Gen. 8:21). The Lord looked down as men wickedly constructed the Tower of Babel as they tried to get to God in their own way rather than by faith, the prescribed way (Gen. 11). He looks from His throne and sees everything everyone does. All the good. All the evil. His knowledge of it all is absolutely perfect.

When God looks **to see if there are any who understand,** He wants to see if there are any who understand spiritual things. From the way that humanity chooses to live, it becomes quickly apparent that none understand, that none **seek God.** Sinful humanity, as lost and dead in sins as they are (Eph. 2:1), cannot see God or understand just how far they have alienated themselves from Him (Col. 1:21). It is a vicious cycle. They alienate themselves from Him. He alienates Himself from them. There is a mutual enmity. If sensitive mankind objects to this position, one must merely consider a human parent of children.

The parent can continue to love and provide for the child. But as long as the child refuses to submit to the parent's authority, there will be inescapable alienation between parent and child. If a parent repeatedly provokes their child to wrath, no matter how obedient the child is, there will be an adversely affected relationship. God is a perfect parent. Our sins alienate us from Him. In the human state of alienation from God, separated humanity cannot see God for who He is and is also unable to see himself for who he is before God. Instead, man makes a god in his own image and bows down to it to his own ruin. The natural man does not understand or submit to God (Rom. 8:7).

It is the gospel and only the gracious, merciful, kind, and loving gospel of God in the finished work of Christ on the cross on behalf of sinful humanity that can reverse the curse in which humankind has found itself. It is only through the grace of God that has appeared to all man that man can recognize his great need (Ti 2:11). Christ is the only escape from everlasting condemnation. For any person to seek God so that they might find Him, sinful humanity would have to deny themselves, take up their cross, and follow Christ (Matt. 16:24). Instead, most will choose to ignore their consciences as well as the evidence that God has placed all around them in the animal and plant kingdoms to show us that He is there and will inevitably conclude that God is not there so they can do as they please. Thus, man will not seek the assembling but will rather forsake it until God's grace intervenes (Heb. 10:25), and the Holy Spirit directs.

## Questions for self-reflection:

(1) Is there anyone who can avoid having to give an account to God?
(2) Has general morality improved or gotten worse as time has gone on?
(3) Why is there such a lack of proper understanding of spiritual things?
(4) What are some ways in which mankind makes idols in contemporary society?

**14:3. They have all turned aside, They have together become corrupt; There is none who does good, No, not one.**

---

Quoted by Paul in Romans 3:12, the theme of the universal sinfulness of mankind continues with this verse. There is nothing humanity can do to commend himself to holy God. The debt incurred by his own choice to sin is too immense. Everyone has **turned aside** from God's way to follow their own sinful way. God will exact the debt from everyone. Either man pays it himself with eternity in hell, or man trusts Christ to pay it for him. That is the crux of the matter. There has been a time in the life of all the living when they reach the age where they can obey or disobey moral instruction. Some refer to this as the 'age of accountability.'

At some point, everyone ignores the conscience that God gave them and disobeys the law written on their hearts (Rom. 2:15). Then, more willful rebellion ensues as they get older and understand more of the difference between right and wrong. God's way is straight and narrow (Matt. 7:13). Man makes God's way crooked and wide (Matt. 7:14). Isaiah the prophet tells of something similar (Isa. 53:6). Instead of walking in the light, they walk in darkness (Jn 8:12). Instead of following the way (Jn 14:6), Christ's way, they have turned aside to follow their own way, the way that is opposite to the way of peace (Rom. 3:17).

They are like decaying corpses; **they have become corrupt.** As decaying corpses get progressively worse as time elapses, so does the depraved sinner. As they get older, the ways of manifesting that depravity continue to assert themselves. Corrupt leftovers are not fit to be used but are only fit for discarding. The corrupt sinner is likewise not suited for use by God, not until they have come to Christ for salvation and pardon. The alienated sinner is like a farm animal that rolled around in a mud puddle. Their sinfulness completely covers them. Their sinfulness overshadows any possible positive quality about them. The sinner's mind and body are so affected by the Fall that it is evident to the discerning. To emphasize that wickedness universally overtakes man and that nobody can escape this indictment, God inspired the psalmist to repeat the phrase used at the end of verse one: **'there is none who does good.'**

## Questions for self-reflection:

(1) How have you turned aside from God's ways to follow your own ways?
(2) What would you be doing now if God had not changed your story?
(3) What can you think of in the world that is corrupt?
(4) When lost people react in manners like this verse describes, knowing that there is a sense in which they cannot help themselves, can that help you treat them with more compassion?

**14:4. Have all the workers of iniquity no knowledge, Who eat up my people as they eat bread, And do not call on the Lord?**

It is mind-boggling to the psalmist how **all the workers of iniquity** can live in this world as though there is no God, how they can act so selfishly, how they can see all the order and design screaming at them and conclude that there is no God. It is puzzling to the psalmist that anyone can live as though God will not one day punish the wicked while finally rewarding the righteous. God personally revealed Himself to the psalmist to record much of that revelation for others after him to read. It is befuddling to the psalmist that anyone can conclude anything other than that the heavens declare the glory of God (Ps. 19:1). It is a mystery to the psalmist how people can commit such atrocious acts of sin all around him. It is understanding for the psalmist to see how sinners deserving of God's judgment can mete out judgment against others for similarly disturbing acts. It is confusing for the psalmist that these same sinners cannot discern that they should be accountable themselves. There must be a God of Justice behind the innate sense of justice humanity has within them. Fallen man wants justice meted out on the acts committed against himself. That same fallen man hypocritically does not wish to receive the justice he so rightly deserves for the sinful acts he commits (Rom. 2:1).

Justice demands accountability. Courts and correctional facilities have been created in societies to illustrate this. Surely there must be an underlying principle for this. God is that principle. **Knowledge** of God is unmistakable. Since a building requires a builder, since a painting mandates that there must be a painter, it does not take a sizeable leap of faith to logically deduce that creation necessitates that there must be a Creator (Ps. 19:1). Those created in His image (Gen. 1:27), whether they acknowledge it or not, are accountable to Him (Matt. 12:36, Acts 17:30-31, Heb. 9:27). What is even more unimaginable to the psalmist is how Israel, those to whom this psalter was written, could come to this conclusion when they are the very ones to whom the revelation of

God had been given (Rom. 3:1-2). God had made them His peculiar people (Exod. 19:5), had redeemed them, and had made a nation out of them (Gen. 12:1-3, Exod. 12), and He had given them a law (Exod. 20-22).

The Messiah to the whole world, revealed to them in their Scriptures before He even came (1 Cor. 15:3-4), would come from them (Acts 22:3). The Temple system, set up by the ordinance of God for the people to remind them of their sinfulness, was a recurring reminder that sin, their sin, had to be dealt with (Hebrews 10:1-4). How could all these frequent reminders have been for naught? God's people need not be forgetful hearers of the Word (Jas 1:22-25). God's people need to be faithful to rehearse God's truth to those under their care for whom they bear responsibility (Rom. 15:4, Eph. 6:4). Those who reject God treat those who believe in God poorly. They **eat** them **up as they eat bread**. In every generation in parts of the world, the righteous minority suffers persecution at the hands of the godless (Matt. 5:10-12, 2 Tim. 3:12). They **do not call on the Lord** and mock those who do call on the Lord. These wicked people who treat God and God's people with such contempt do so with the knowledge that He is there and they care not that they have to answer to Him.

### Questions for self-reflection:

(1) Does it ever surprise you how the lost can reject God so flippantly and arrogantly?
(2) Do the choices that lost people make concerning laws they want governments to enforce ever cause your outrage?
(3) Does the prospect of the judgment that awaits the lost that you have mercifully avoided only because of the kindness and love of our God and Savior the Lord Jesus Christ ever cause your sadness over the state of the lost?
(4) Do the people you know see that you live your life as though you are accountable to Someone or something greater than yourself?
(5) How have you seen the ungodly treat the godly with contempt?

## 14:5. There they are in great fear, For God is with the generation of the righteous.

The people who live as though God does not exist **are in great fear**. Even though they professed that God was not real, the way that they lived certain aspects of their lives illustrated that guilt for wrongdoing was inherent to the human race. Accountability for evildoers was still something that they found reasonable. They eventually realized that they too committed evil acts and were therefore also evildoers. Even if atheists believe that God will not punish lawbreakers, atheists will still obey many civil laws because they understand that broken laws deserve punishment. Governments and police forces exist for this reason (Rom. 13:1-7). Evildoers could sense that their rebellious lifestyles warrant judgment (Rom. 2:1-2). If God was not real, who would oversee this judgment they felt was inescapable (Rom. 2:3)? If God was real, they knew their actions deserved judgment. They could sense that the law written on their hearts had been violated (Rom. 2:15). They could tell that if **God** did exist, He would surely vindicate his people, **the righteous**. The wicked still were prudent to lock their doors and protect themselves against evildoers (Rom. 12:18). It is inescapable that there is a God. Even the unrighteous who suppress the truth in unrighteousness (Rom. 1:18) will one day come to that realization. They worked so incredibly hard to silence their divine warning system, their conscience, so they could live as they wanted (1 Tim. 4:2) rather than to live with any accountability to the One who created them in His image (Gen. 1:27, 2 Cor. 5:10).

The righteous know that **God is with** their **generation**. They know that God will reward each man according to his works (Rom. 2:6). God sustains His people with His presence. He goes before them and gives them wisdom. He helps them with their circumstances that are affected by enemies of various types, shapes, and sizes. God gives His people supernatural strength to overcome their enemies, including indwelling sin. His people know that they have ultimate victory. Therefore, the righteous have no reason to fear, whereas the wicked do (Lk 12:5, Heb. 10:31). Since God is with His people, none can be against them (Rom. 8:31). Even if the wicked plague the righteous, because the righteous know that God is with them, they know that God equips them with everything they will need to face the afflictions that are a part of the fallen human condition.

## Questions for self-reflection:

(1) Ideally, why do parents give children rules? Because they want to be overbearing or to protect them from danger?

(2) Why does everyone, even the godless, know that universally some things are wrong?

(3) Why do evildoers have an innate sense of justice so that most of them want to see others who commit atrocious acts reap what they have sown?

(4) Does the idea that God will reward everyone according to their works excite you or cause you to fear? Why?

**14:6. You shame the counsel of the poor, But the Lord is his refuge.**

The fools among the children of men have all turned aside. They have become workers of iniquity that **shame the counsel of the poor**. Unbelievers shame the counsel of the believers. Believers trust in the Lord and believe what He has said about Himself in His Word. Trusting in the Lord is challenging for believers to do when everyone around them refuses to trust the Lord. Unbelievers think believers are foolish to put their trust in a God they have not seen. Unbelievers would rather trust in someone or something they can see, touch, or experience.

Believers trust **the Lord** to be their **refuge** even in the face of opposition from unbelievers. The saints know that it is normal to be rejected by those who have made this world their home. Fortunately, the sheep know that this world is not their home (Heb. 13:14) because the Lord Jesus has prepared a place for them (Jn 14:2-3) and preserves them by the power of His Word (Heb. 1:3, 1 Pet. 1:5) until it is time for them to join Him in eternity forever.

### Questions for self-reflection:

(1) In what ways do unbelievers shame the counsel of believers?
(2) Can you see gravity?
(3) If you cannot see gravity, how do you know that it exists?
(4) If everything you know and love that is on this earth suddenly was stripped from you, would you persevere in the faith? How do you know?

**14:7. Oh, that the salvation of Israel would come out of Zion! When the Lord brings back the captivity of His people, Let Jacob rejoice and Israel be glad.**

---

Jesus Christ is not only the **salvation of Israel**, but He is the Savior of the whole world (Jn 3:16, 1 Jn 2:2). He is the Author and Finisher of our faith (Heb. 12:2) and the Captain of our salvation (Heb. 2:10). He is the only name by which anyone can be saved (Acts 4:12). There will be people from every tribe, tongue, and nation before the throne in heaven (Rev. 7:9).

Israel wasted the privilege of having their Messiah come to them first (Rom. 9:3-4, Rom. 10:1-3). He came to Zion, to Israel, though Israel did not receive Him (Jn 1:11). The people known and loved by the psalmist and by the psalmist's God had sent themselves into spiritual **captivity**. They had sinned away their blessings and had rejected their only hope, the One True God. Satan had taken them captive by his relentless devices. They were in bondage to Satan, the law, and sin. The god of the age had blinded their minds (2 Cor. 4:4). They were alienated from God by their wicked works (Col. 1:21). They were dead in trespasses and sins (Eph. 2:1, 2:5). They had willingly entered into bondage from a cruel taskmaster.

But, in the fulness of time, when they needed it most, Christ came, made of a woman, made under the law, to redeem those who were under the law by becoming the substitute for sinful humanity (Gal. 4:4-5). He set the captives free (Luke 4:18). He became sin for wicked sinners because of His great love for us (2 Cor. 5:21, Eph. 2:4). He satisfied God's righteous requirement for perfection and commended God's love (Rom. 5:8) for the people created in His image (Gen. 1:27) who had all gone astray like sheep and turned to their own ways (Isa. 53:6). God the Father laid on Christ the iniquity of us all (Isaiah 53:6). Now, to those whose faith is in Christ, the captivity has been brought **back,** the death sentence has been commuted, the people of God can **rejoice and be glad**. God did for them through Christ what they could not do for themselves. He has redeemed them (Eph. 1:7), pardoned them

(Isa. 55:7), and forgiven them (Col. 1:14). All the spiritual blessings in heavenly places belong to them (Eph. 1:3-14). All the sinner can do is bask in the glory of God's great love for them and give their lives to Him in worshipful service (Rom. 12:1).

## Questions for self-reflection:

(1) How did Jesus demonstrate that He is the salvation to Israel and to the rest of the world?

(2) How do you know that you merely struggle with sin and are not in complete captivity to sin?

(3) When you read the gospel and how your sin separated you from God, how you deserved judgment for that, and how God delivered you from that judgment by the finished work of Christ on your behalf, does your spirit well up with gratitude toward God for doing that for someone as sinful as you, or has it become commonplace?

(4) Does hearing the gospel make you want to sit back, enjoy life, and wait for eternity, or does it make you want to serve the Lord and find ways to bring as many as who will come with you to heaven?

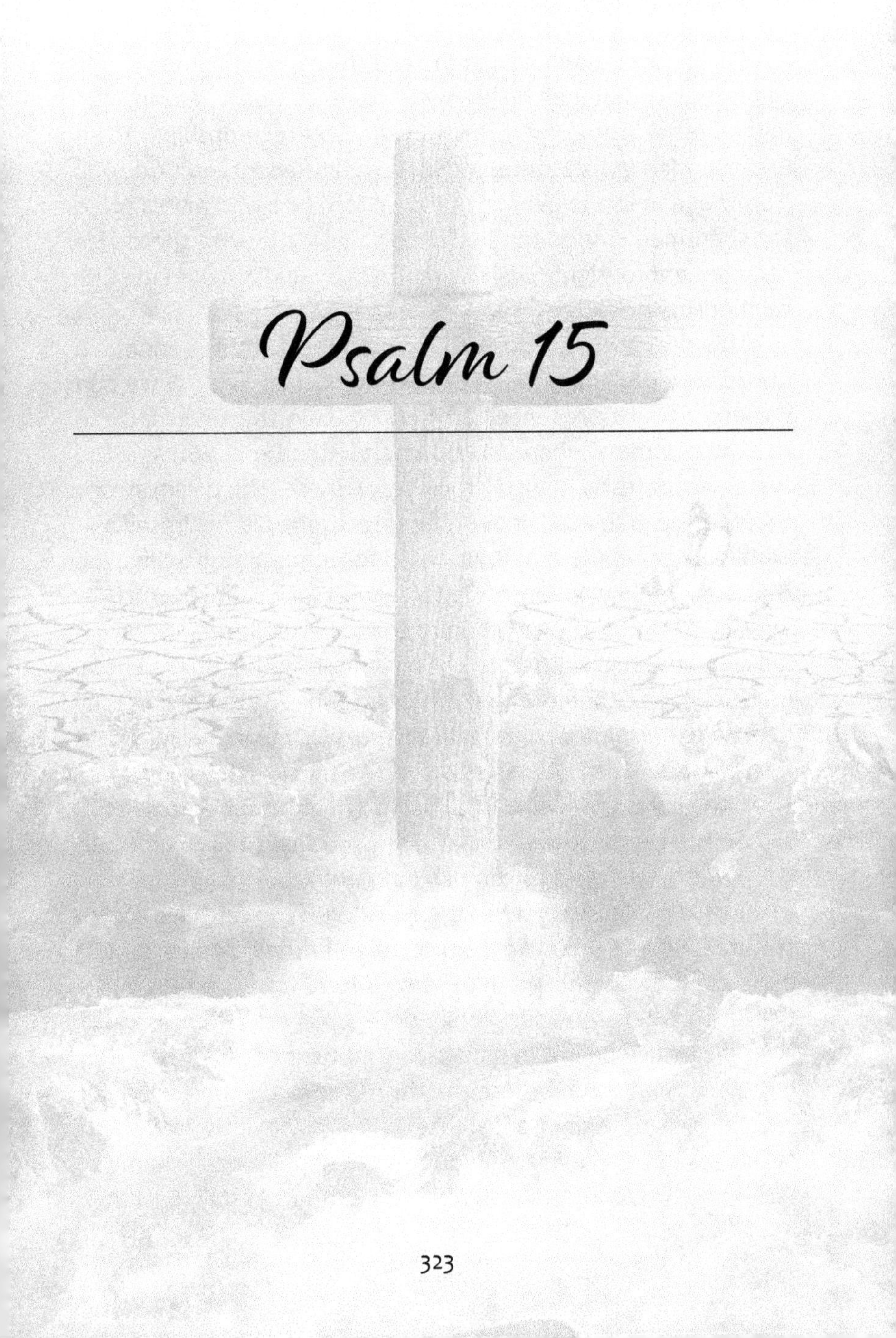

# Psalm 15

## 15:1. Lord, who may abide in Your tabernacle? Who may dwell in Your holy hill?

Psalm fourteen mourned the sad state of lost humanity and made it plain that man on his own is unfit for God's heaven. Man in the flesh is in no condition for an amicable relationship with his Creator. Man in that state needed a great Reconciler. God, who became man in the person of Christ to take sinful man's place, satisfied man's need for perfection while meeting the divine requirement for righteousness set forth by His Father, made that relationship possible.

This psalm has to do with saved people, their benefits in Christ, and the characteristics that mark their lives. Once constructed, God's presence came to dwell in the **tabernacle** in the old economy when sin was dealt with (Exod. 26:1-37). Old Testament priestly ministry took place there. The psalmist saw that there was so much indwelling sin present within himself and within other people that it was hard for the psalmist to imagine that God would want anything to do with such sinful people.

God graciously gives His Spirit to indwell believers. Believers make up the church. The church convenes together on the Lord's Day. Believers continue to enjoy access to the Lord as long as they deal with their sin by confessing sin and walking in the light (1 Jn 1:7-9). The Lord Jesus Christ is called the **Tabernacle** of God (Rev. 21:3). The parts that went into constructing the Tabernacle have symbolism that points to Christ. The Lord Jesus tells us that He will **abide** in us if we abide in Him (Jn 15:1-8).

So, the psalmist here asks the question, 'Who can have access to God?' People who allow sin to reign in their bodies cannot expect a holy God to permit them to have access to His clean presence when they sin wholly pollutes them (Rom. 6:12-14). However, once believers have cleansed their consciences (Heb. 9:14), they can come before the throne of grace for mercy and help in their time of need (Hebrews 4:16). They can avail themselves of Christ's cleansing blood to continually wash them (Jn 13:8, 1 Cor. 6:11, Eph. 5:26, 1 Jn 1:7). They can successfully cast their cares upon Him with thankful hearts, knowing that He cares for them (1 Pet. 5:7). The same people who can dwell in His **holy hill** can abide in His Tabernacle. The rest of the psalm will answer who meets the qualifications.

## Questions for self-reflection:

(1) How did man mess up his relationship with God such that man cannot abide in the Lord's tabernacle?
(2) How did God fix His relationship with mankind such that man can abide once again in the Lord's tabernacle?
(3) How can you keep your indwelling sin at bay so that your relationship with God can be as fruitful as possible?
(4) As time has gone by, as you have identified as a Christian, have you sensed an increasing awareness of the Lord's presence and conviction in your life?
(5) What can cause your sensitivity to God to decrease?
(6) What can cause your sensitivity to God to increase?

**15:2. He who walks uprightly, And works righteousness, And speaks the truth in his heart;**

---

The one who **walks uprightly, works righteousness, and speaks the truth in his heart** has had an encounter with the Lord Jesus Christ. He has been forgiven, justified, sanctified, and will be glorified (Rom. 8:30). Christ has begun a good work in them and will perform it (Phil. 1:6). As a result of being changed by God's grace, this saved sinner, justified freely by grace (Rom. 3:24), begins taking baby steps to walk worthy of the calling with which they have been called (Eph. 4:1). They will not be without sin (1 Jn 1:8), but the trajectory of their life will be a noticeable growth in holiness (Heb. 12:14), a growth in conformity to Christlikeness (Rom. 8:29). There will be no unbroken pattern of sin that will mar their overall testimony. While works do not save them, it will be evident that grace has saved them (Eph. 2:8-9). The truth of the gospel will have noticeably wrought a work of grace within them that can only be attributable to the power of God (Rom. 1:16). When they receive Christ Jesus the Lord, they will so walk in Him (Col. 2:6). Such a person will practice righteousness (1 Jn 2:29). They receive the righteousness they possess by faith in Christ. They demonstrate the righteousness they possess by doing good to all, especially the household of faith (Galatian 6:10). Their contagious zeal for good works will become contagious (Ti 2:14). God has ordained that this be true of believers, that they walk in good works (Eph. 2:10). They will let their righteous light shine before the outside lost world such that some may see it and glorify their Father who is in heaven (Matt. 5:16). In addition to letting their good works serve as testimony to those outside the church, it will also be true that the believer will work righteousness to fellow believers.

All of this upright walking and working of righteousness, in addition to **truth-speak**ing, must take place at the same time as the war that must still be waged against the sinful flesh (Gal. 5:17), so there is not a level that we should be looking to reach to where we will feel assured of our salvation. Our works could never save

---

us (Ti 3:5). No amount of good works could ever be sufficient to effectively cover what only Christ's perfect sacrifice could perfectly cover. Therefore, we must never base our assurance upon our performance. Our sin is too great but, praise God, His mercy and grace are greater (Rom. 5:20).

The point is if someone is going to name the name of Christ, if they are going to call Him theirs, if they are going to say that they are His sheep, that He is their Shepherd, if they are going to claim to not walk in darkness but to walk in the light instead, there must be some level of demonstrable change. If there is not the slightest difference in conduct from before they professed Christ to the present, then the chances are that they may never truly have encountered Christ, despite their words to the contrary. Since the gospel is a gospel of truth, since Jesus is the truth of God (Jn 14:6), since lying is a sin that has always been seriously handled on the pages of Scripture, truthfulness will mark God's people (Col. 3:9). There will not regularly be an underlying attempt to deceive others with language. They will mean what they say and say what they mean (Matt. 5:37). Since they now serve the God of truth, they will be known for being people who tell the truth.

## Questions for self-reflection:

(1) Would those who know you best tell others that you walk uprightly, work righteousness, and speak the truth?
(2) If it is true that you are known for these character qualities, are you more likely to take the credit for these qualities, or are you more likely to praise God for His work in you?
(3) In what ways do you do good to others, especially other believers?
(4) Do you ever feel the sinful flesh trying to fight the Holy Spirit for control of your life?
(5) Would others who knew you before you named the name of Christ, when they see you now, notice that you live like a different person?

**15:3. He who does not backbite with his tongue, Nor does evil to his neighbor, Nor does he take up a reproach against his friend;**

To **backbite** is to say mean or spiteful things about a person, especially when the person to whom the backbiting speech is directed is not present. One who backbites is too cowardly to say mean and hurtful things to the face of others (which they should not do anyway), so they say those things behind the backs of others instead. Such backbiting can have devastating effects on those to whom it is directed. Backbiters go around saying destructive things about people when they should edify them instead (Eph. 4:29).

Backbiting is a behavior that should be avoided, especially by those who name the Name of Christ. It is no better to backbite because what can be hidden from man cannot be hidden from God (Heb. 4:13). Man can go to elaborate lengths to conceal his thoughts and actions from others who may retaliate, but nothing can be hidden from God, not even our thoughts. So, as creatures created in God's image (Gen. 1:27), it is imperative that we take every thought captive to the obedience of Christ (2 Cor. 10:5) and not give God an excuse to chastise us for our sins (Heb. 12:3-11). If one is tempted to backbite against his fellow man, that one should consider that someone else, or perhaps even their victim, could find things to spread about them as well. Reputations and relationships can be ruined by backbiting. To answer the question posed in the original verse in this psalm, the one who does not backbite is the one who may come into God's presence.

The one who **does** not do **evil to his neighbor** is the one who may come into God's presence. When their neighbor does evil to them, they remember that the Spirit calls them to repay evil with good (Rom. 12:17-21). When someone hits them on one side of the face, rather than strike back in revenge, they can remember that vengeance belongs to the Lord and give them the other cheek instead (Matt. 5:39, Lk 6:29). When unbelievers act as unbelievers do, the righteous can respond with righteousness and display the transformation that Christ has done in them by the Spirit in a way that will be evident to those watching (Matt. 5:16).

In addition, the one who may come into God's presence **does not take up a reproach against his friend.** He does not intentionally do things to hurt the reputation of his friend. If a mutual acquaintance brings a damaging report against that friend, the one who comes into God's presence will have none of it because they do not want to do anything to harm their relationship with God or with their fellow man. The righteous person will do what he can to preserve the reputation of others even if that means his own reputation takes unjust damage. After all, Christ had inaccurate reports and unfair accusations brought against Him. He did not revile back when He was reviled (Matt. 7:12, 1 Pet. 2:23).

### Questions for self-reflection:

(1) When your enemies are not around, do you speak kindly about them, or do you look forward to receiving opportunities to bad-mouth others since you know that nothing will happen to you for doing so?

(2) Have you ever found out that you have been on the receiving end of backbiting? How did you react to hearing that?

(3) What extreme measures have you implemented to ensure that someone did not find out about something mean you did or said about them?

(4) How can we better take every thought captive to the obedience of Christ?

(5) Do you know of anyone whose reputation was unfairly harmed by backbiting?

(6) When someone evilly treats you, is your first reaction getting them back or doing good to them?

**15:4. In whose eyes a vile person is despised, But he honors those who fear the Lord; He who swears to his own hurt and does not change;**

---

The one who comes into God's presence does so walking worthy of the calling with which he has been called (Eph. 4:1), as a tree that is bearing good fruit (Matt. 7:15-20), and as a doer of God's will (Matt. 7:21-23). The previous two verses showed some examples of this.

**A vile person** is an ungodly person who has rejected the one true God for an immoral lifestyle. The one who can come into God's presence loves the ungodly enough to try to reach them with the gospel but not at the expense of their own testimony (Eph. 5:11). The godly person does not **despise** the vile person to where they do not try to reach them. But they hate their lifestyle enough to not join them in it. The rest of the ungodly world will run to the same excess of riot (1 Pet. 4:4) as the ungodly, but the justified will rise against the pull of the world and reprove the deeds of darkness rather than participate in them.

Godly people fear the Lord enough to have a strong reverence for the Lord and not make it their habit to intentionally violate God's Law or make light of His expectations for His people. **Those who fear the Lord**, while they do so with imperfection due to the war waged between the Spirit and the flesh (Gal. 5:17), still understand that the Lord expects conduct befitting of a child of the King (Eph. 4:17). They know that there should be such a difference between their lifestyles and the lifestyles of the lost such that the lost world should have the urge to ask them for the reason of the hope that is within them (1 Pet. 3:15).

Fellow believers demonstrate **honor** to **those who fear the Lord** by loving them with sacrificial service. When they serve each other, they also serve the Lord.

**He who swears to his own hurt and does not change** fears the Lord to such a degree that he will do whatever is necessary to maintain his relationship with the Lord and whatever is needed not to compromise his testimony in front of people.

---

## Questions for self-reflection:

(1) Is your lifestyle different enough from the lifestyle of ungodly people around you to the point that people who know you best would say that you despise the lifestyle of the ungodly?

(2) Do you make excuses for your sin, or does it cause you to experience personal brokenness?

(3) Would people who know you best tell others that you fear the Lord when you were not watching?

(4) When was the last time that you showed sacrificial love to a fellow believer?

(5) When was the last time that you showed sacrificial love to an unbeliever?

**15:5. He who does not put out his money at usury, Nor does he take a bribe against the innocent. He who does these things shall never be moved.**

The one who comes into God's presence handles the increase that the Lord has graciously given him appropriately (1 Tim. 6:10). He does not take advantage of other less fortunate people to try to get rich himself. He treats the poor fairly and tries to benefit them whenever he can instead of taking advantage of them for his selfish benefit. He does not use the resources of others to hamper **the innocent**. He does not lie about the innocent to elevate himself. He does not intentionally see that the innocent come down on the wrong side of the law since they are, after all, innocent. Instead, he treats him justly, as he would want to be treated (Matt. 7:12).

The child of God that walks worthy of their calling (Eph. 4:1), that walks in the light (1 Jn 1:7), and that is a doer of good (Gal. 6:10), **shall never be moved** from his permanent spot in God's kingdom. He may slip into sin as all believers do from time to time (1 Jn 1:9). However, the trajectory of his life is one of increasing holiness. He shall never be moved from the narrow way that believers find themselves on (Matt.7:13). He shall never be moved from a direction of moving in conformity to the image of Christ (Rom. 8:29). Since he is not moved from Christ-likeness, he shares common interests with fellow believers and does not move from sweet fellowship with them and with their common King (1 Jn 1:7). Since God has begun a good work in them, the believer knows that He will perfect it and perform it until they see Christ face to face (Phil. 1:6).

## Questions for self-reflection:

(1) Is it more common for you to take advantage of other people for your benefit, or is it more common for you to benefit others at your own expense?

(2) Are you growing in love for the things of God while at the same time growing in discomfort at the sinful lifestyle of those whose home is this world?

# Psalm 16

**16:1. Preserve me, O God, for in You I put my trust.**

The death and resurrection of Christ are commonly thought to be the subject of this psalm. Therefore, if Christ is speaking, He is coming before **God**, His Father, in prayer (Matt. 14:23, Mk 1:35, Lk 3:21, Lk 5:16, Lk 6:12, Lk 9:28). Christ regularly entered into prayer with His heavenly Father.

Shortly after His birth, wicked King Herod felt threatened and tried to have Baby Jesus killed because once Herod heard that Jesus was King of the Jews since the people recognized Herod at the time as King of the Jews, Herod viewed Jesus as a threat to his throne. From this threat, Jesus needed preservation. Herod thought if he killed Jesus, He would no longer pose a threat to Herod's kingdom (Matt. 2:16-18).

When Satan tempted Jesus in the wilderness (Matt. 4:1-11), He was protected from harm at the hands of Satan as well as by creation during a forty-day fast (Matt. 4:2). During his ministry, there were multiple times when His enemies would have killed Him if they could have, but His Father intervened to **preserve** Him until the appropriate time (e.g., Lk 4:30). Christ repeatedly said He entirely submitted to doing His Father's will (Matt. 26:39, Matt. 26:42, Jn 6:38). He came to do His Father's work (Jn 4:34). He only did what His Father told Him to do (Jn 8:28-29).

Unlike the rest of us who followed after Adam, no sinful nature plagued Christ (1 Jn 3:5). But, unfortunately, times of sinful unbelief mix with our trust in God (1 Jn 2:1). And even our strongest moments of faith are still affected by sin, as is everything we do, think, and speak. For this reason, the New Testament is full of commands to believers to put off sins and put on righteous acts to replace them (e.g., Eph. 4:25-30).

Such was not the case with Christ. Christ did not have a sinful nature that needed putting off. His trust in His Father for everything He said, did, and thought was entirely without sin of any kind (Heb. 4:15). Christ's trust in the plan His Father had for His life was not interrupted by sinful worry. He knew His life was totally up to the control of His Father. Even as He hung on the cross, He cried out to the Father as He knew nothing that happened to Him was by accident (Mk 15:34, Lk 23:34, Lk 23:46, Jn 19:26-27, Jn 19:28-30). Even between His death and His resurrection, His **trust** in His Father's plan was steadfast, and it needed to be as His resurrection was the proof that He is who He said He is (Romans 1:4). Even now, Christ puts His trust in His Father that as He intercedes for us (Heb. 7:25), His Father will hear those intercessions, and the sheep will be preserved (Jn 10:27-28).

## Questions for self-reflection:

(1) If God the Son thought it was a good idea to put His trust in His Father, why are those created in God's image (you and me) so reluctant and inconsistent at putting out trust in God?

(2) God preserved Christ on multiple occasions before his appointment with death. How has God preserved you from death or trouble in the past?

(3) Do you read of the holiness of Christ and want your life to emulate that with greater consistency?

(4) In what ways can you exhibit greater trust in God?

**16:2. O my soul, you have said to the Lord, "You are my Lord, My goodness is nothing apart from You."**

Up until the quote, this verse could begin with David speaking to the church. Another possibility is that God the Father is talking to God the Son. **"You are my Lord"** refers to Christ in His humanity, referring to God the Father as Christ's Lord. Christ is fully equal with the Father (Phil. 2:6). Though fully equal with the Father, Christ still became a servant to the Father (Jn 6:38). He was made under the law in the fulness of time (Gal. 4:4), came to perfectly execute the Father's will for His life, fully submitted to His Father, and, therefore, showed God the Father to be His Lord. God the Father was Lord to the Son while the Son walked on the earth.

When Christ here said, His **goodness is nothing apart from** God, He referred to His special goodness and its effect on the church. First, His goodness builds the church and makes the church more like Him (Rom.8:29-30). Second, His goodness lavishes every spiritual blessing on every church member (Eph. 1:3-14). Third, his goodness commends God's love toward sinners so they can be saved from God's wrath, which abides upon them because of their sin (Rom. 5:8-9). Fourth, his goodness causes God's grace to appear to everyone that they would deny ungodliness (Ti 2:11-12). Fifth, His goodness shows the fulness of deity in Christ (Colossians 2:9) so that His perfect life, substitutionary death, and resurrection provide everything needed for sinners to be justified freely by His grace (Rom. 3:24). Sixth, His goodness gives us a righteousness that we could never achieve on our own (Phil. 3:9). Seventh, His goodness gives us forgiveness of sins (Eph. 1:7). Eighth, His goodness gives us peace with God such that we are no longer God's enemies, but instead, we are at peace with God (Rom. 5:1), having been reconciled to Him by the blood of the cross (2 Cor. 5:12-17). Ninth, His goodness gives us redemption, having repurchased us to God from slavery to sin and Satan (Col. 1:14). His goodness does not give us the wages that our sin deserves; instead, His goodness gives us the free gift of eternal life through Jesus Christ our Lord (Rom. 6:23).

## Questions for self-reflection:

(1) Does the fact that God the Son would humble Himself so that you could be exalted to heaven with Him cause you to react with humble gratitude?

(2) How does your life demonstrate that you have experienced God's goodness?

**16:3. As for the saints who are on the earth, "They are the excellent ones, in whom is all my delight."**

All **the saints who are on the earth** have partaken of the goodness described in the previous verse. God's goodness led them to repentance (Rom. 2:4). They have become a part of Christ's believing body, the church (Eph. 5:30), and are growing to become more like Him (Rom. 8:29). They have received all of the spiritual blessings (Eph. 1:3-14) and spend their lives learning about those blessings (Eph. 4:11-16, 2 Pet. 3:18). They have received God's love (Rom. 5:5) and have been saved from God's wrath (Rom. 5:9), which now no longer abides upon them (Jn 3:36). They have seen God's grace and have been taught by God's grace to deny ungodliness (Ti 2:11-12). They have been taught by God's grace to see Christ for who He is and have come to Him for justification (Rom. 3:24, Rom. 5:1). They have received Christ's righteousness after realizing their own righteousness amounted to nothing but filthy rags before God (Isa. 64:6). They have received forgiveness (Eph 1:7). They have received peace with God (Eph. 2:14). They have been reconciled to God after previously being God's enemy by wicked works (Col. 1:21). They have become slaves of Christ instead of being slaves to sin (Rom. 6:16-23). They have received the free gift of God, eternal life, instead of receiving the wages their sin has incurred, death (Rom. 6:23). They have been chosen in Christ before the foundation of the world so they would be holy and blameless before Him (Eph. 1:4). The observable quality of holiness that marks their lives makes them distinct from the lost world around them that ensures that they will see the Lord (Heb. 12:14). They walk in newness of life (Rom. 6:4). They have a quality to their lives that displays that their affections are set on things above (Col. 3:1-3). The goodness that fills them and comes out of them does not come from their own doing. Instead, the righteousness of Christ is the spring out of which that goodness flows (Rom. 15:14). The kindness of God has so affected their hearts that kind service now exudes from them toward others (Gal. 5:22). These positive traits, wrought by the indwelling Holy Spirit that lives within the saints, are juxtaposed against the sinful flesh. The flesh and Spirit war against one another until the saint is called home to glory (Gal. 5:17).

Christ, the Speaker in this verse, recognizes His sheep as **excellent ones**. They are not excellent because of anything about themselves. Rather, they are His workmanship (Eph. 2:10). Being His workmanship makes them excellent. He has seated them with Himself in heavenly places (Eph. 2:6). He has chosen them out of the world (Jn 15:19) to be rich in faith (Jas 2:5). Believers are the objects of Christ's **delight**. Because Christ delights in believers, He works on them to conform them into His image.

## Questions for self-reflection:

(1) How does your life demonstrate that God delights in you? Do you only say that He is your Lord, or do you also demonstrate that He is your Lord?
(2) Has God's grace taught you to deny ungodliness?
(3) Has God's grace freely justified you?
(4) Before you received God's righteousness through Christ, in what were you trusting?
(5) How has God shown Himself to be powerful to you?

**16:4. Their sorrows shall be multiplied who hasten after another god; Their drink offerings of blood I will not offer, Nor take up their names on my lips.**

---

The psalmist changes directions in this verse, switching subjects from the saved to the lost. He no longer directs his words to those under grace. He now aims his words to those under the law. These know not the Lord Jesus Christ. They have not come to Him for pardon. Instead, God's wrath remains upon them (Jn 3:36). Rather than walk in the light, these walk in the darkness (1 Jn 1:6-7). Instead of being of God the Father, their father is the devil (Jn 8:44).

We know this because they **hasten after another god**. To hasten oneself after any god other than the God of the Bible, the God that has revealed Himself to mankind through the Son Jesus Christ (Heb. 1:2), is to set oneself up with **multiplied sorrows** in the next life for sure and in this life perhaps. The multiplied sorrows that come by hastening after another god come as a consequence of sowing and reaping. As long as they sow their idolatry, they have the lake of fire to reap with the cowardly, unbelieving, abominable, murderers, sexually immoral, sorcerers, and liars (Rev. 21:8). Instead of taking the evidence of creation (Rom. 1:20) and of conscience (Rom. 2:15), these exchange the truth of God for a lie and worship something created rather than exalting the One who made everything (Rom. 1:23, 1:25). Instead of following the Christ of the Bible as He has revealed Himself to be on its pages, they follow a savior of their own making, an idol.

To offer **their drink offerings of blood** or **take up their names on** His **lips** would be to accept their vain worship. To accept such worship would be tantamount to allowing them to fake their worship. Tolerating such obeisance would be to accept them drawing near to Him with their mouths while staying far away from Him with their hearts (Matt. 15:8). God is not okay with this. He will not accept this. The form without the reality will not be accepted into His presence. He wants hearts that are full of Him as well as actions that are devoted to Him. He will not accept half-hearted devotion.

Those who think they worship God but do so with mixed affections do not offer true worship. God does not accept that. If we are not entirely for Him, we are against Him (Matt. 12:30). People who reject the true God and worship a form, a god of their making, are not on the lips of Christ the Intercessor as He pleads for the saints (Heb. 7:25). Christ says that He prays for believers, not for unbelievers, at least not in the same way (Jn 17:9). He has given unbelievers over to judgment (2 Pet. 2:9).

## Questions for self-reflection:

(1) What sorts of things do people hasten after that the Scriptures liken to gods?
(2) How could someone who hastens after other gods reach a place of such sorrow that they would want to turn from their other gods to the one true God, the God of Scripture?
(3) In what ways can genuine believers still engage in vain worship?

**16:5. O Lord, You are the portion of my inheritance and my cup; You maintain my lot.**

---

Like the Levitical priests in Numbers 18, David said that the **Lord** Himself was his **inheritance**. The Lord upholds all things by the Word of His power, and so the Lord maintains David's lot (Heb. 1:3). The Lord kept David going (Ps. 3:5). The Lord preserved David from his enemies (Ps. 31:23) and kept David alive for as long as He appointed that David remains alive (Heb. 9:27).

Christ's singular goal in life was to fulfill His Father's will perfectly. For the Lord Jesus Christ, doing the will of God the Father was so much more important to Him than anyone or anything else (Jn 4:34) that, for Christ, the church, given to Christ by the Father, was His inheritance (Eph. 1:22). The love that God the Son had for God the Father will never be matched. Christ had perfect enjoyment of His Father's presence because sin never interrupted it. He was never out of fellowship with His Father until that fateful moment on the cross that the psalmist prophesied about (Ps. 22:1, Matt. 27:46). When he completed His mission, He would be crowned with glory and honor and would get to return to His heavenly abode (Heb. 2:9). God will **maintain** the **lot** of Christ by keeping the church preserved (Prov. 2:8, Matt. 16:18, 2 Thess. 3:3, Rom. 8:29-30, Phil. 1:6) for salvation to be received by Christ as His inheritance.

## Questions for self-reflection:

---

(1) Since you have been saved, have you ever thought about the fact that the Lord kept you alive even in your rebellion against Him so that you could experience His grace and salvation?

(2) Is it any wonder how, for the people who have tasted and seen that the Lord is good, that they would willingly give the Lord everything they could and put forth maximum effort in service to Him a la Romans 12:1?

(3) Why are we so quick to want to trade the eternal crown of righteousness that awaits the saints in heaven for the passing pleasures of this world?

**16:6. The lines have fallen to me in pleasant places; Yes, I have a good inheritance.**

---

The **pleasant** and **good inheritance** of the Lord Jesus Christ is the church. The Lord Jesus Christ will present the church, His inheritance, to the Father (2 Cor. 4:14). The inheritance of the church is eternal life and eternity spent in heaven. The church is pleasant to the Trinity, and They have worked eternally to choose them, sacrifice for them, and keep them throughout the ages. God endows the church with wedding garments (Matt. 22:1-14). They have a righteousness that is not their own. Another, namely Christ Jesus, has supplied this righteousness. For the church, wherever Christ has them go for Him is pleasant as long as they go there in service to Him. The church has the Holy Spirit, the earnest of the inheritance (Eph. 1:14) that awaits them in eternity. The Holy Spirit leads believers into pleasant places according to God's unchanging truth (Jn 16:13). The Spirit applies the truth of God to the hearts of believers so that believers will know and believe the truth about who God is. The Spirit of Truth conveys what He has done according to how He has revealed Himself to us in His Word, and through the world He created (Jn 15:26, Jn 16:14).

### Questions for self-reflection:

(1) When you consider your saved standing before God, does it humble you to know that God would save such a sinner as you, or do you feel like God is lucky to have you?

(2) Have you considered that all three parts of the Trinity are just as deserving of worship?

(3) What do you imagine heaven to be like?

(4) Since your conversion, is there an increasing awareness of God's truth in your life?

(5) Since your conversion, do you experience an increasing frustration at the sin and willful blindness that the world exhibits to the things of God?

**16:7. I will bless the Lord who has given me counsel; My heart also instructs me in the night seasons.**

---

As the psalm began, it was posited that Christ was speaking. Christ fully trusted His Father. Humanly speaking, as a mere man, the psalmist had to fully trust God, as do believers in every generation. God is the source of goodness. Identified as distinct from the wicked by their imputed righteousness and holy living, the saints on the earth are the objects of God's delight. Those who hasten after another God, those opposed to God and His people, will not be received by God if they do not turn to God in repentant faith. The ungodly will exert their influence upon the world. In this fallen world, people like the psalmist who believe in the one true God know that no matter what befalls them in this life, they can still trust the Lord to get them all the way home to heaven.

So, in this verse, the truth (**counsel**) about God and who He is causes the psalmist to **bless the Lord** in worshipful praise. Believers praise the Lord for Who He is and for what He has done. If the subject of this psalm is the Lord Jesus Christ Himself, then Christ blesses His Father for giving Him counsel to be able to be our perfect Savior up until the cross. After the cross and after His ascension, He and the Father continue to have perfect fellowship. They both continue to work on behalf of believers. When the people of God meditate on who God is and on what He has done for them (Ps. 1:2, Eph. 1:3-14), that can be a helpful tool in getting one's mind off of the problems that come with living in a sinful world.

The Lord Jesus Christ is the Wonderful Counselor about whom Isaiah prophesied (Isaiah 9:6). We can cast our cares on Him because He cares for us (1 Pet. 5:7). His grace is sufficient for us (2 Corinthians 12:9). The peace that He provides can guard our hearts and minds (Phil. 4:7). The heart of the Lord Jesus Christ was so in tune with His Father (Jn 4:34, Jn 6:38, Jn 8:29, Jn 10:30) that He quickly and readily was instructed by the Father. He readily **instructs** His sheep now by the Spirit (Jn 16:13). The counsel the sheep receive from their Shepherd is perfect counsel that originates in the Trinity.

Before Christ's betrayal, He prayed in the Garden of Gethsemane at **night**. His Father instructed Him to His **heart** before His arrest and ultimate atonement for His people (Matt. 26:36-46). Then, when the powers of darkness, led by Satan, appeared to be having their way, Jesus' heart was instructed to perfectly obey the Father's will so that He could be tempted in every way that we are and not commit sin (Heb. 4:15).

If the psalm is not interpreted through the lens of Christ being the speaker, it may instead be interpreted through the lens of believers in subsequent generations. In that instance, it is still true that believers can still receive counsel from the Lord, explicitly from the Holy Spirit, and the sheep can be a means by which they can bless those around them with fruits that come as a result of the Lord's counsel. They can go to the Lord in prayer (Heb. 4:16) because the Lord Jesus Christ has given them access by one Spirit to the Father (Eph. 2:18).

**Questions for self-reflection:**

(1) What about the way you live makes you different from those who do not name the name of Christ?
(2) What truths about who God is and what He has done have caused you to bless the Lord?
(3) How has the Lord's counsel helped you live for Him in this world that is radically opposed to Him?
(4) When the difficulties of life overtake you, how is it evident that the Lord's counsel instructs your heart to live for Him?

**16:8. I have set the Lord always before me; Because He is at my right hand I shall not be moved.**

---

The psalmist always had the Lord on his mind. Like the blessed man in Psalm 1, this psalmist always thought about the Lord's expectations of him in this life (Ps. 1:2). He thought about what the Lord had said and how it affected how he was to live in this world.

For the New Testament believer, **the Lord** Jesus Christ is **always set before** us (1 Pet. 2:21). If Christ becomes the object of our affections (Col. 3:1-3), the pursuit of our life (Phil. 3:14), growth happens (Jn 15:5, 2 Pet. 3:18). When the Lord is at our right hand, He is close to us. When He is close to us, we can hear His instruction to us. We can feel His help to us. We can quickly take refuge in Him. We can effectively protect ourselves from attacks when they come. We can avail ourselves of the defensive armor He provides (Eph. 6:10-18).

If we rest in Christ and His finished work on our behalf, we **shall not be moved** from steadfast devotion to Him. **Because He is at** our **right hand**, we can continue to serve Him dutifully and serve the people He has placed in our lives, knowing that whatever happens is meant for our good (Rom. 8:28), and nothing can separate us from His love (Rom. 8:38-39).

If Christ is the subject of this verse, it fits nicely as God the Father was always before God the Son as it was the privilege and duty of God the Son to fulfill the will of God the Father faithfully. Everything Christ did He did for the glory of His Father to point people to His Father to show people His Father (Jn 17:4). He could accurately say, "If you have seen Me, you have seen the Father" (Jn 14:9). Since Christ is at the Father's right hand (Heb. 1:3), the Son is very close in proximity to the Father in heaven. They are quickly able to work with the Holy Spirit to aid believers. Christ was not discouraged from nor moved from His function as Prophet, Priest, and King.

## Questions for self-reflection:

(1) How often is God in your thoughts? Do you only think about what God can do for you, or do you also think about who He is?

(2) How do your thoughts about God affect how you relate to others, including those closest to you?

(3) Do you feel secure in God knowing that Christ sits at the Father's right hand, interceding for you?

**16:9. Therefore my heart is glad, and my glory rejoices; My flesh also will rest in hope.**

---

The **heart** of the psalmist **is glad** because the Lord is always set before him (16:8). His future is secure (Rom. 8:38-39). The psalmist's heart is glad because the psalmist regularly receives counsel from the Lord and the psalmist's heart regularly instructs him (16:7). The meditation of the heart of the psalmist is on the future inheritance that awaits him (16:6), the Lord Himself. On the Lord, the psalmist has staked his life (16:5) because the psalmist knows that the Lord takes up his cause. The psalmist has great hope that causes his flesh to rest because the enemies of the psalmist, those that hasten after another God, will not receive the same glorious end that the psalmist will receive (16:4). While the psalmist will experience ultimate joy because he embraced the God of the universe, the enemies of the psalmist will have multiplied sorrows due to their rejection of the God of the psalmist (16:4). The psalmist and the remainder of those who place their hope in God the Father, the Lord Jesus Christ, and the Holy Spirit can **rejoice** because they are the delight of the Trinity (16:3).

Not only have they avoided eternal wrath and condemnation, but this triune God also blesses them with every spiritual blessing (Deut. 28:1-14, Eph. 1:3-14). Even when the **flesh** of the psalmist **will rest in hope** in the grave at the end of his earthly pilgrimage, when he takes his final breath, he only sleeps (Acts 7:60). The psalmist can patiently wait with the rest of every believer from every generation for the day when all the dead in Christ will rise first (1 Thess. 4:16). He can rejoice now, knowing that to be absent from the body is to be present with the Lord (2 Cor. 5:8). God the Son could rest in hope in the grave because heaven knew that He would rise again. He had foretold His resurrection. Whenever we put our faith in God instead of ourselves, no matter what we are allowed to endure this life, we can view it in a positive sense.

God the Son had a glad heart and could rejoice. After He had completed His earthly mission to die as the Substitute for sinful humanity, He would return to the right hand of His Father where

He would remain, ever-living to intercede for the saints (Heb. 7:25). He would be our Advocate (1 Jn 2:2). The psalmist could not say that he had glory while he walked on the earth. Only God the Son has such **glory.** He even displayed it to a few privileged disciples (Matt. 17:1-13), and His purpose while on earth was to demonstrate the glory that was His before the world began (Jn 17:5) to the rest of the world that did not receive Him (Jn 1:12).

**Questions for self-reflection:**

(1) If your hope is in the Lord, your heart should be glad. List as many reasons as you can think of off the top of your head why your heart should be glad as a child of God?

(2) How does it make you feel that, if you are a believer, you are a delight of the Trinity? What do you think about when you meditate on the truth that you are the delight of the Godhead?

(3) Because Jesus advocates for and intercedes for you, your future is secure. Knowing that He does that for you, does that make you want to take your sin flippantly or seriously? Why?

**16:10. For You will not leave my soul in Sheol, Nor will You allow Your Holy One to see corruption.**

---

Peter quotes this verse in Acts 2:27 as referring to the resurrection of Christ. This could only refer to Christ since everyone who has gone to the grave has stayed in the grave. Even if they were temporarily removed from the grave by a divine miracle (e.g., Lazarus in John 11), they all returned to the grave, except for Christ. He ascended back to the Father, never to return to the grave (Acts 1:9-11). Christ did not continue to be dead. He proved He is God by His resurrection from the dead (Rom. 1:4).

Nobody since Adam, except for Christ, can be described as holy in any sense since everyone except for Christ is polluted by sin and their inheriting Adam's sinful nature (Rom. 5:12-21). Therefore, only Christ can be designated as a **Holy One** since the sin nature bypassed Him because He is fully God and God has no darkness (1 Pet. 2:22, 1 Jn 1:5).

In this verse, '**Sheol**' refers to where invisible souls separated from the body reside. It is the place of the dead. Christ's soul and body did not stay put. On the third day after Christ's death (1 Cor. 15:3-4), Christ's **soul** returned to His body, and many people saw Him alive bodily in a miracle of divine proportions (1 Cor. 15:5-8). Christ's body did not remain separated from His soul long enough **to see corruption**. His body did not decay as everyone else's has. Since He is morally free from corruption (Heb. 7:26), physically, He was free from corruption. His glorious resurrection prevented that from happening. God raised Him from the dead (Rom. 10:9).

Christ is the Holy One because Christ's is the only human nature not corrupted by sin (2 Cor. 5:21). All who have ever descended from Adam and Eve experience that corruption (Rom. 5:12-21). So, those who embrace the Son by faith have imputed to their account Christ's righteousness, and their sin is imputed to Christ's account so that they can experience justification based on the merits of Christ rather than condemnation based on their own merits (Rom. 4:5-6).

---

**Questions for self-reflection:**

(1) What Messianic title in this verse alludes to Christ that means that it could refer to nobody else?

(2) Who else since Christ has died a historical death and had eyewitnesses to their resurrection?

(3) Who else has not had a sin nature with which to contend?

(4) Is there anyone else besides Christ to which this could refer?

**16:11. You will show me the path of life; In Your presence is fullness of joy; At Your right hand are pleasures forevermore.**

In context, if this verse is taken with the previous verse, this would be Christ speaking. If the previous verse refers to Christ's resurrection, then this verse also refers to Christ and His resurrection. When God the Father **show**ed Christ **the path of life**, the Father showed the Son that the path of life includes the resurrection (Matt. 16:21, Matt. 17:22-23, Matt. 20:17-19, Mk 8:31, Mk 9:7-10, Mk 9:31-32, Mk 10:33-34, Mk 16:9-11, Lk 9:21-22, Lk 18:31-33, Jn 7:33-34, Jn 10:14-18, Jn 14:1-4, Jn 14:18-20, Jn 14:27-31, Jn 16:3-10, Jn 16:19-20). The dead in Christ rise first unto eternal life (1 Cor. 15:22, 1 Thess. 4:16, Rev. 20:6). When Christ rose from the dead, He illustrated this truth as the first fruits (1 Cor. 15:23). The difference between Christ and those who rose from the dead before Christ rose again is that when Christ rose, He did so, never to die again. Those who were risen in the Old Testament ultimately died again. When Christ rose from the dead, after He completed His post-resurrection appearances and works, He ascended back to His Father's right hand (Ps. 110:1, Matt. 26:64, Mk 12:36, Mk 14:62, Mk 16:19, Lk 22:69, Acts 1:9-11, Acts 2:33-34, Acts 5:31, Acts 7:55-56, Rom. 8:34, Eph. 1:20, Col. 3:1, Heb. 1:3, Heb. 8:1, Heb. 10:12, Heb. 12:2, 1 Pet. 3:22)

Christ is the path that gets sinners to everlasting life with the Father. He is the way (Jn 14:6). There, **in** His Father's **presence, is fullness of joy**. He left that proximity in His humiliation (Phil. 2:5-8). In His exaltation, the Father glorified Him (Jn 17:5, Phil. 2:9-11). He had finished His work. Sorrow had lasted through the night. It was morning. Joy had come because full fellowship with His Father had resumed. The Father had answered His prayer to have His joy restored and to glorify His name again (Jn 12:28, Jn 17:13). Those who place their repentant hope and faith in this risen Lord are allowed to enjoy a measure of this fellowship (1 Jn 1:3).

The saints have the earnest of the inheritance in the Person of the Holy Spirit (Eph. 1:14). By that Spirit, all believers, no matter how 'weak' or how 'strong,' enjoy access by one Spirit to the

Father (Eph. 2:18). Believers can come boldly before the throne of grace for mercy and help in their time of need (Heb. 4:16). They can enter into the presence of the Holy One and experience joy for themselves, knowing that no matter what they endure in this life, nothing can separate them from the love of God (Rom. 8:38-39).

Since Christ sits at the **right hand** of the Majesty on high (Heb. 1:3), by faith in His finished work on their behalf, people from every tribe, tongue, and nation (Rev. 7:9) now can cast their crowns at His feet (Rev. 4:10). They can trust that one day they too will join Him in eternal heaven and enjoy all the **pleasures** that God's glorious redemption provided **forevermore**. In heaven, for the believer, when sorrow, sadness, and sickness have been eliminated forevermore (Rev. 21:3-4), the believer will then experience complete joy for themselves, knowing that all the pain and toil and sacrifices they made during their earthly pilgrimage were worth it.

## Questions for self-reflection:

(1) What was the path of life that led to our redemption for Christ? How did He become our Savior?
(2) What did Christ do that the dead in Christ also get to do?
(3) If everyone got to go to heaven, do you think that the people who spent their lives living for themselves instead of living for God would have fullness of joy by being in God's presence?
(4) Is there anything or anyone on this earth that can give the redeemed more joy than Christ Himself?
(5) Do you expect that there will be something that you can do on earth that you cannot do in heaven that you would wish you could do in heaven?

# Psalm 17

**17:1. Hear a just cause, O Lord, Attend to my cry; Give ear to my prayer which is not from deceitful lips.**

The psalmist called out to the **Lord** to avenge him in his conflicts with his adversaries. The psalmist trusted that the Lord is a righteous Judge who always does the right thing - even if it appears that the wicked are having their way and the righteous are not having their way (Jer. 12:1). Because the psalmist is a just (righteous) person, he knows that the Lord judges on behalf of His people and will always support His people against their enemies. Sometimes that means that the support provided by the Lord comes in the form of temporal endurance rather than permanent removal (Ps. 3:3, Ps. 4:3, Ps. 5:12). The believer knows that at Calvary, Christ triumphed over the enemy, making a public spectacle of them (Col. 2:15), such that no matter what believers endure in this life, nothing can separate them from God's love (Rom. 8:38-39). So, believers look unto Jesus, the Author and Finisher of the faith, who endured the cross on their behalf so that they could endure any momentary light afflictions by considering His example (2 Cor. 4:17, Heb. 12:2, 1 Pet. 2:21, 1 Pet. 2:23).

The believer knows that Christ intercedes for them (Heb. 7:25). They know that when they cry out to Him, He will **attend to** the **cry** of the humble. The Lord cares for those who humbly cast their cares upon Him (1 Pet. 5:7). If believers do not regard iniquity in their hearts, He hears them (Ps. 66:18). Since believers can trust that God hears them because the Son intercedes before the Father on their behalf, the believer has the sure privilege that they can come boldly before the throne of grace before the throne of heaven and trust that God will answer them (Heb. 4:16).

The psalmist knows that his **lips** are not **deceitful** as unbelievers' lips are. Instead, the psalmist is a genuine believer. As such, as long as he does not regard iniquity in his heart, the psalmist knows that the Lord will **give ear to** and hear his prayers and will answer them in the way that the Lord sees fit to do so. That the psalmist's prayer in this passage was a cry and was from his lips indicates that this prayer was more likely audible rather than mental. The psalmist's prayer was not like the prayers of the Pharisees, who often prayed for others to hear them. The Pharisees wanted to be noticed by others in their praying (Matt. 23:14). They did not care about true communion with their heavenly Father. Because of that, it was evident God was not truly their Father. No. They were of their father, the devil (John 8:44). Christ had uninterrupted, genuine communication with His Father, up until that moment on the cross where He asked God why He forsook Him (Matt. 27:46, Mk 15:34). If believers confess known sin, they also maintain their fellowship with God and one another (1 Jn 1:9). The psalmist felt the weight of the presence of his enemies, as the psalm will reveal in the following verses.

The psalmist asked the Lord to sustain him when all around him was collapsing. Believers in any generation can go to the same Lord for the same sustaining grace because God does not change and because Jesus Christ is the same mighty High Priest for us today as He was during His First Advent (Heb. 10:4, Heb. 10:10, Heb. 10:12, Heb. 10:14, Heb. 10:19-21, Heb. 13:8). He has given us everything we need to humbly serve Him in life (2 Pet. 1:3). We have the grace at our disposal to tap into all of it.

### Questions for self-reflection:

(1) How can the Lord avenge you in your trials with people or with circumstances without you sinfully taking matters into your own hands?

(2) How can you keep an eternal perspective knowing that Christ triumphed over your enemies long ago while you still have to face your enemies in this life, and in this life, your enemies will seem to be winning the battle?

(3) If you cry out to the Lord for help with your enemies and trials, how will the Lord attending to your cry look like in your specific context? Could the Lord attending to your cry also

refer to His grace strengthening you to survive trials without doing something to damage His reputation?

(4) Do you want to have an honest relationship with God and with your sin?

**17:2. Let my vindication come from Your presence; Let Your eyes look on the things that are upright.**

The psalmist entered into the **presence** of the Lord, proclaimed his innocence, and asked God to vindicate him before those with whom he had a conflict. Those he fought with had accused him of **things** of which he knew he was ultimately not guilty. He also knew that God knew that he was not guilty of those things. Even if he could not persuade his enemies of his innocence, the psalmist had to take solace in knowing that the God who gave him his next breath (Jb 27:3), who ordered all his steps (Ps. 37:23), had declared him not guilty of the things of which he had been accused.

The psalmist knew that the Lord's **eyes** looked to and fro all over the place and could see everything (1 Sam. 16:7, 2 Chron. 16:9, Jb 28:24, Jb 34:21, Ps. 33:13, Ps. 139:3-4, Prov. 5:21, Prov. 15:3, Jer. 16:17, Jer. 23:23-24, Acts 1:24, Heb. 4:13, 1 Jn 3:20). The psalmist asked God to intervene on his behalf such that those who accused him would have irrefutable proof that the psalmist was innocent. The psalmist wanted God to work out the situation to make it apparent to those familiar with the situation that the psalmist was not in the wrong. Rather, the psalmist was among the **upright.** The God of the universe was on the side of the psalmist.

The psalmist trusted that the Lord could look on the things happening to him and orchestrate results and events such that the psalmist would experience ultimate vindication. However, the psalmist had to be willing to trust that ultimate final vindication may not be in the Lord's plans for him in this life. Instead, he might need to rely on the Lord's justifying grace to see him through until he made it to eternity and was accepted into heaven to be with the Lord and the rest of the saints for eternity.

Like the psalmist, our Lord and Savior, Jesus Christ, was falsely accused by those who ultimately had Him put to death on a cruel Roman cross (Matt. 12:22-32, Lk 22:2-3). Christ entrusted Himself to the will of His Father (1 Pet. 2:23), knowing full well that His Father meant everything for His (and our) good (Rom. 8:28).

Christ experienced ultimate **vindication** at His resurrection when He triumphed over His enemies (Col. 2:15), proving He was who He had said He was all along. The enemies who had Christ put to death thought they were winning that day. But Christ's absolute trust in His Father yielded a victorious outcome for which all the saints in every generation can rejoice, knowing that, because of Christ, there is now no condemnation for them (Rom. 8:1). They are more than conquerors (Romans 8:37). Their names are written in heaven (Lk 10:20). They have peace with God (Rom. 5:1). They are reconciled to God (2 Cor. 5:18). They have been entrusted with the ministry of reconciliation (2 Cor. 5:19).

## Questions for self-reflection:

(1) What have you done to make yourself innocent before God? Does this realization make you prideful or humble?

(2) Have you ever been accused of something from which you knew you were innocent, but there was no convincing anyone of your innocence?

(3) If you are currently going through an oppression situation, how would God vindicating you look?

(4) Has anything ever happened to you that demonstrated that God was on your side?

(5) If you were to entrust yourself to the Father, how would you live differently?

**17:3. You have tested my heart; You have visited me in the night; You have tried me and have found nothing; I have purposed that my mouth shall not transgress.**

---

God **tested** the **heart** of the psalmist. God tests the hearts of everyone (Jer. 17:10). God does not tempt anyone (Jas 1:13). God tests His people to see where their allegiance lies. When His people pass the test, spiritual growth occurs (Jas 1:3-4). Even though God knows what is in our hearts (Acts 15:8), He allows us to go through things so that we will see what He already knows about our hearts.

When it was **night**, personal sin overtook David. In that state, God **visited** David in His amazing grace, overcame David's sinfulness, and David came to saving faith when he turned to the Lord. All God's people have unique versions of when the Lord visited them in their seasons of night and the light of the glorious gospel shined in their hearts (2 Cor. 4:1-6). Once saved, God's people each have stories from different seasons in their pilgrimages when they endure a particularly dark time. In those times, God visits them to remind them that even when the world around them seems like it is collapsing, God is still on the throne and still working all things together for the good of those that love Him (Rom. 8:28).

God's people can view trials and afflictions as a gracious tool in the hand of the Master disciplinarian. God disciplines those He loves (Heb. 12:3-11). While that discipline is not pleasant to endure, if rightly endured, it can be a valuable tool in teaching us about our own sinfulness, frailty, weakness, and desperate need for His sustaining grace. When we endure trials, that is when God has **tried** us and found nothing to correct at that moment.

It cannot be true that God did not find sin in the psalmist since all those who descended from Adam have sin natures that lead to the commission of sins (Rom. 3:9-23). So, if this verse refers to the psalmist, this must be limited to a specific trial the psalmist endured in which he overcame a particular temptation. The psalmist regularly had to confess his sins to God (1 Jn 1:9) and even laments his own sins in other passages (Ps. 51).

If this refers to the Lord Jesus Christ, then it is certainly true about our Lord that there is no sin in Christ (2 Cor. 5:21). That had to be so for Him to be our faithful High Priest (Heb. 4:15). Christ, as fully God, has no darkness in Him (1 Jn 1:5). He endured any temptation imaginable to a fuller extent than we ever could and never gave in to the temptation and committed sin. No taint of sin was ever found in Christ, the Second Adam. Even when people tried to convict Christ of sin, they could not honestly do so because He could not and did not sin (Jn 19:4). They had to lie about Him to convict Him of anything (Mk 14:56-58).

The psalmist had to shut his mouth to **not transgress** with his **mouth**. At times, when circumstances get especially difficult, it can be tempting to speak our minds. When we are quick to do that, it can sometimes be a foolish thing to do because sin often comes out of our mouths when we don't think about what we say before we say it. Sometimes it is best to stay quiet and be angry but not sin (Eph. 4:26, Jas 1:19-20). During the trials of Christ's life, there were times when He kept quiet because saying something at the moment was not going to be beneficial (Matt. 27:14). It would have amounted to casting pearls before swine (Matt. 7:6).

Christ patiently endured everything the Father allowed Him to experience. Everything we endure is something that God has allowed us to experience. Since Christ is our example that we should walk in His steps (1 Pet. 2:21), we should endure knowing that these momentary light afflictions prepare us for a greater weight of glory ahead (2 Cor. 4:17). When the people of the day reviled Christ, He did not revile in return (1 Pet. 2:23). We should patiently endure when people revile as well.

**Questions for self-reflection:**

(1) In what ways has God tested your heart?
(2) When you have been tested, how did you pass the tests?
(3) Think back to your conversion story. Do you have an account that God can use to show that He still visits people in the night and changes their lives?

(4) As you have come through adversity, can you look back and
    see how God has worked things together for your good?
(5) How has God's disciplining process helped you grow?
(6) Does your heart rejoice when you overcome temptation?

**17:4. Concerning the works of men, By the word of Your lips, I have kept away from the paths of the destroyer.**

---

Ungodly **men** in opposition to the psalmist try to undermine the psalmist by wicked **works** (Col. 1:21). When they attempt to interrupt the psalmist's fruitfulness, the psalmist takes refuge in God's **Word**, the Word that came from the **lips** of God, that perfect inspired instruction (2 Tim. 3:16). It has kept the psalmist away from the paths of the wicked men who rebel against God and who are in conflict with the psalmist.

Such wicked men are in **the paths of the destroyer**, the roaring lion (1 Pet. 5:8), who comes to seek, kill and destroy (Jn 10:10). Satan is a brutal enemy, but the believer can trust the truth that Christ has overcome Satan such that Satan cannot pluck believers out of God's family once they have become a part of God's family (Col. 2:13-15, 1 Jn 2:13). Even if Satan can cause problems, nothing will separate God's children from receiving eternal life once they have received God's gracious gift (Phil. 1:6). What Satan can do for the believer is make them unfruitful. So, believers need to follow Jesus' example and take daily heed to God's instructions so that they can use it to effectively overcome temptation when it comes (1 Cor. 10:13, Jas 1:22).

God's instruction has reminded the psalmist of what God expects of him. God's completed Word has done the same for each of His children in each generation since the cannon was completed (2 Tim. 3:16).

## Questions for self-reflection:

(1) Has anyone tried to undermine your Christian testimony? How did you react to that?
(2) In such situations, has God blessed you with His comfort stemming from your obedience to His Word?
(3) When you face trials of various kinds, can you honestly count it all joy?
(4) If you were to suffer for being a believer, do you think you would count yourself privileged to suffer for Christ?

---

**17:5. Uphold my steps in Your paths, That my footsteps may not slip.**

David knew that he was insufficient to stay in God's **paths** if God did not intervene to help him. He knew he was sinful and, as such, would be prone to **slip** off God's paths and go his own way if he had to live his life without the benefit of Divine assistance. The need for Divine aid does not mean that David is not responsible for his actions (Phil. 2:12-13). All of humanity, created in God's image, is responsible for choosing who they will serve (Josh. 24:15). Mankind has been endowed with a conscience to know right from wrong (Rom. 2:15). God wrote His Law on their hearts. Man can choose to heed the divine warnings and have their **steps** upheld by Omnipotent God. Or, humanity can ignore the warnings and fall prey to sin (Jas 1:12-15). Believers can avail themselves to the power of the Holy Spirit and receive Divine enablement to serve the Lord in every area of their lives (Phil. 4:19). With the Spirit's help, believers possess the capability to overcome any temptation (1 Cor. 10:13). When believers succumb to temptation, God is not to blame for their failings. They have only themselves to blame if their **footsteps** slip (Jas 1:13). When God's people trust in the Lord, they can do anything God asks of them because God provides the grace to accomplish all that He asks us to accomplish (Heb. 13:20-21).

**Questions for self-reflection:**

(1) Are you sufficient to stay on God's path in your own strength? Why or why not?
(2) How has God shown you from the lives of others who have not walked in God's paths what evil can happen when we go our own way rather than in God's ways?

**17:6. I have called upon You, for You will hear me, O God; Incline Your ear to me, and hear my speech.**

---

The psalmist had come into the Lord's presence before His throne of grace because there were many times when he needed the help that only God could provide (Heb. 4:16). He had plenty of experience on which he could draw to remind him that when he **called** out to God that the Lord would **hear** him. Based on those past experiences when the psalmist knew that the God of the universe had heard him, now the psalmist came back to the Lord expectantly trusting God to listen to him again, as long as he came with clean hands and a pure heart (Ps. 24:4). Likewise, the psalmist knew that if he prayed according to the Lord's will, that he could trust the Lord to accomplish His will - even if the Lord's plan was not what he thought it should be or if it was not particularly pleasant to endure.

## Questions for self-reflection:

(1) Have you experienced the divine help that only God can provide in a difficult situation? In your experience, how did that look?
(2) How has God shown you that He hears you when you call upon Him?
(3) How can you know whether or not your prayers are according to His will?

**17:7. Show Your marvelous lovingkindness by Your right hand, O You who save those who trust in You From those who rise up against them.**

God specially directs His **lovingkindness** to the redeemed (Rom. 5:5), those who have come to Christ in saving faith. Christ sits at the Father's **right hand** (Heb. 1:3). So, that lovingkindness proceeds from Him, from Christ, from the right hand of God, at the direction of His Father. (Jn 12:49). The Trinity has accomplished the work of salvation. The sheep, who hear and **trust in** the Son's voice (Jn 10:27), possess and are led by the Holy Spirit (Rom. 8:14). They have the fruits of the Spirit in their repertoire, including love and kindness (Gal. 5:22). God has chosen to save the sheep because of His rich mercy (Eph. 2:4). So, lovingkindness is a gift dispensed by a loving God to the objects of His love. The full extent of the lovingkindness of God shared with His children is not something to be fully understood in this life as the depth and breadth of the love of God can only be understood to a certain point by hearts that still are affected by sin (Rom. 11:33).

The Trinity made a covenant to save humanity from the power and penalty of sin (Gen. 12:1-3). The plan has been in place since eternity past. The Godhead continues to work together to accomplish it currently. The Father chose sinners for salvation (Eph. 1:4). The Son exercised the plan of salvation by living a perfect life, dying on the cross for sin, and rising again for the justification of many (Gal. 4:4-5). The Holy Spirit comes to live inside believers and leads them into all truth (Jn 16:13). The right hand of the Father is the location where Christ sat after His ascension. The right hand is also identified as the place of power of God (Ps. 118:16). So, Christ is the power of God.

Man is foolish to trust in his own power or wisdom (1 Cor. 1:20, 1 Cor. 1:25). Man would be wise to embrace Christ and partake in the lovingkindness of God. Man is nothing apart from God's power and wisdom. Even those who do not give God the credit that God deserves do so ignorantly. The brain with which they think ungodly thoughts is a gracious gift given to them by the God that they deny. God rewards those who diligently seek Him (Heb. 11:6). God directs the paths of those who trust in Him rather than in themselves (Prov. 3:5-6).

When the enemies of God and the enemies of God's people **rise up against them**, whether those enemies be actual literal people, or whether they be the spiritual enemies such as those doing Satan's bidding or the indwelling sin the believer wars against for their entire earthly pilgrimage, God's people can trust that God will never leave or forsake them (Deut. 31:6). They are more than conquerors (Rom. 8:37). If God has justified them, God will glorify them (Rom. 8:30). God will ultimately **save those who trust in** Him.

### Questions for self-reflection:

(1) How have you benefited from the marvelous lovingkindness that proceeded from the right hand of God?
(2) How have you responded to the marvelous lovingkindness that proceeded from the right hand of God?
(3) Would those who know you best say that you have been a different person since you became a Christian?
(4) Since you became a Christian, has your understanding of God improved? How could you understand God better than you currently do?

**17:8. Keep me as the apple of Your eye; Hide me under the shadow of Your wings,**

---

**The apple of** the **eye** is a weak part of the eye. Humanity is weak compared to God because society is inherently weak and sinful while omnipotent God is not. The apple of the eye is very sensitive. Man will work very hard to ensure that his eyes are protected. If harm were to come to his eyes such that he could no longer enjoy God's creation through the eyes any longer, this would be very disappointing for someone accustomed to being able to use the eyes. God protects His people very closely. He ensures that, while temporal hardships may come to them in this life, nothing they encounter will come upon them apart from Divine permission. Everything that happens to them is for their ultimate good (Rom. 8:28). **The shadow of** God's **wings** is a name for God's presence. The psalmist asks God to protect him by keeping the psalmist close to God. The closer the sheep stay to God through prayer, through meditating on the Word (Ps. 1:2), through walking in the light (1 Jn 1:7), the more fruitful their lives become (Jn 15:1-8).

**Questions for self-reflection:**

(1) When you think about your weakness compared to the strength of God, does it make you glad to know that you have an all-powerful God that can accomplish amazing things for you?

(2) When you think about humanity's weakness compared to God, does your heart break toward those who reject God knowing that the all-powerful Creator is against them? Does it break your heart enough for you to try to reach the lost with the gospel?

(3) Since your life is hidden with Christ in God, nothing can separate you from God's love. How should this truth change the way we live?

(4) What can you do today to begin to become more fruitful?

---

**17:9. From the wicked who oppress me, From my deadly enemies who surround me.**

---

As all believers in every generation understand, the psalmist had enemies - **wicked** people who sought to do the psalmist physical, mental, and spiritual harm. The wicked like to oppose God's truth as well as the people who proclaim it (Matt. 7:15-20, Acts 20:29-30, Gal. 1:8, 2 Thess. 2:1-12, 2 Tim. 3:12, 2 Tim. 4:3-4, Jude 1:4-19). They like to make the path for God's truth to go forward as challenging to travel as possible. They ultimately will not prevail against God and God's kingdom, but they can cause harm to those who follow God (Matt. 16:18).

Since the **psalmist's enemies** were **deadly**, the psalmist knew that if they could catch him, they would want to kill him. However, the psalmist also knew that nothing would happen to him apart from God's permission (Heb. 9:27). But the longer God protected the psalmist and kept the oppressors from harming or even killing the psalmist, the more the difference the psalmist could make for God's kingdom.

In every generation, among the people who oppose God and God's people, some are so determined to rid the earth of God's influence that they will even go to lengths so extreme that they will be involved in killing God's people. Little do the persecutors know, sometimes when someone dies for their faith, rather than the death slowing down the influence of God and God's message, it can often make the attention God gets even more potent. It actually can have the opposite effect that the persecutors want. That is like what happened with Christ in the first century. The Jews hoped that by killing Jesus that they would be rid of Him forever. Instead, He rose from the dead. He ever lives to intercede for the saints (Heb. 7:25). Now His message gets preached and spread all over the globe. The **wicked** may **surround** the righteous in their attempts to stamp out the influence of the righteous, but, ultimately, nothing can prevent God's work from being accomplished. God uses man's free choices to achieve His ultimate purposes, which always have His glory and the good of His people in mind.

## Questions for self-reflection:

(1) Who in your society oppresses you for your beliefs? If you do not receive oppression for your beliefs, are you sure you engage your culture enough?
(2) Is living your Christianity in a society that is post-Christian easy? Should it be as easy as it is?
(3) If you were to be persecuted for your faith, what is the worst that could happen to you?
(4) If you knew that more people would come to saving faith due to your death, would that change the way you live?

**17:10. They have closed up their fat hearts; With their mouths they speak proudly.**

---

Lost people have **closed, 'fat hearts'** that are so full of what has made their hearts fat that they do not possess spiritual discernment or awareness of their surroundings. They do not regard God in their days at all, much less take every thought captive to the obedience of Christ (Rom. 3:18, 2 Cor. 10:5). They are too focused on their own talents and abilities that they fail to see the need to glorify God for those talents and abilities. Their hearts have become so full of the world that they are dull to spiritual things (Eph. 4:19). Rather than look at everything they enjoy as a gracious gift from God above (Jas 1:17) instead, **they speak proudly** as though they accomplished everything by their own skill and ability (e.g., Rev. 3:16). They glorify themselves rather than glorifying God as they should do. They are the epitome of self-centeredness. They are the proud people God resists instead of being the humble people God receives (Jas 4:6).

The psalmist had enemies that were after him. Perhaps these enemies of the psalmist were religious people who gave lipservice to the God of the psalmist (Jn 16:2). Maybe, though, they put too much emphasis on what they know or on their performance, and perhaps they failed to have a personal relationship with God like the psalmist had. If that were the case, that would be a lot like the Pharisees of Jesus' time. They knew a lot. They did a lot. Perhaps they thought they were serving God while doing all that. However, Christ uncovered the truth that because they did not sincerely devote their hearts to Him, all the trappings of religion were useless (Matt. 23:1-36).

So, it is with us. If we are not careful, our hearts can get fat with the gifts that came from the Giver when they should be growing in love for and devotion to the Giver Himself. We can be guilty of speaking proudly about our abilities or knowledge with our **mouths** when instead we should glorify God for giving us the knowledge and letting us use it for His glory and not our own glory.

---

**Questions for self-reflection:**

(1) What are some of the things that can make our hearts fat?

(2) What can we do to make sure we are growing in biblical discernment?

(3) What happened such that you changed from being one that did not regard God to one who did regard God?

(4) How do you react now to selfish people who have no concern about God and live as though there is no God?

(5) What are some things that can make us prideful if we are not careful?

**17:11. They have now surrounded us in our steps; They have set their eyes, crouching down to the earth,**

---

The wicked had **surrounded** the psalmist everywhere the psalmist looked. The psalmist could not take any **steps** without being made very aware of the presence of his enemies. Being surrounded by enemies requires the servant of the Lord to be very aware of the Lord's sustaining grace. Perhaps it is more likely that the servant of the Lord is mindful of the Lord's presence with them when they are in situations where it is noticeable that they have lost the ability to protect themselves. David certainly had been surrounded by his fair share of enemies throughout his life. Likewise, Judas and the soldiers surrounded Christ at Christ's arrest (Matt. 26:47-56). When Jesus had His trials, wicked men set on having Him killed smothered His steps. Likewise, followers of Christ in every age are acutely aware that troubles are on their every side (2 Cor. 4:8). Persecutions come from without (2 Tim. 3:12). Indwelling sin starts from within (Rom. 7:17). Satan's attacks at times seem relentless (Eph. 6:16). Even though the steps of the just are led by the Spirit into all truth (Jn 16:13), they are also in a war with the flesh that will not stop until they take their final breath (Gal. 5:17). The wicked **have set their eyes** and are **crouching down to the earth** in the sense that they look like they do not pose a threat to the righteous when in fact, they most certainly do. Judas Iscariot did this in one sense when he came with the Romans soldiers to arrest Christ in that he kissed Christ to feign friendship (Matt. 26:48-49). Likewise, wolves in sheep's clothing that infiltrate the church do so looking innocent enough (Matt 7:15-20, 1 Tim. 4:1, Jude 1:4). They make themselves attractive enough so their devilish schemes can deceive church members who lack discernment. The child of God needs to have incredible discernment and be ever watchful while ensuring that they are always on guard against attacks from the devil, which can come at times from the most unlikely of sources (2 Tim. 2:15).

---

## Questions for self-reflection:

(1) What happens in your life that makes you more sensitive to your surrounding spiritual enemies?

(2) When things happen to make you more aware of your spiritual enemies, are you likewise more aware of the Lord's sustaining grace?

(3) Do you think that God would rather have us realize that we have resources to protect ourselves, or would God rather we have no resource other than to go to Him?

(4) What are some ways in which the wicked threaten the influence of the righteous?

(5) How can you better protect yourself and your family from attacks from the devil?

**17:12. As a lion is eager to tear his prey, And like a young lion lurking in secret places.**

**As a lion eager to tear his prey and like a young lion lurking in secret places,** the wicked plot to overtake the righteous. Satan and his minions plot to make the believer unproductive or to take them out entirely. They plan surprise attacks on unprepared saints to try to throw them off as if eliminating one saint can stop God from accomplishing His will. Nothing can stop God's will (Isa. 14:27). If one saint stops being productive or dies, God can easily raise someone who will take His banner. The believer must not get impatient while he waits for the Lord to intervene in his situation against his enemies (Jas 1:3).

**Question for self-reflection:**

(1) What are some ways that Satan and his minions can make believers unproductive?

### 17:13. Arise, O Lord, Confront him, cast him down; Deliver my life from the wicked with Your sword,

The psalmist seems uneasy because his enemies, the wicked, appear to advance their objective. Perhaps the psalmist fears that if the Lord does not jump into action, the righteous influence led by the psalmist will be counteracted too strongly by the opposing unrighteous effect. On the other hand, if the Lord were to **arise, confront** the psalmist's enemies, and save the psalmist from his enemies, the psalmist could continue to serve the Lord. The psalmist wants the **Lord** to prevent his enemies from succeeding in carrying out their plot against him. The psalmist would not object if the Lord arose to stop them altogether. If the Lord were to stop this evil influence from coming against His servant, the psalmist, not only would the psalmist continue to be able to serve the Lord, but others privy to the psalmist's situation could become convinced of God's power.

God raises up people to be instruments of His wrath on the earth. Since the earth contains both righteous and unrighteous people simultaneously, the saints have to endure some trials in this life that come upon them due to the sins of others. The psalmist wants righteousness to have a clear path and wants wickedness to have no path. Assisting the progress of the Lord's plan is a noble goal for all believers. However, often it seems like an uphill battle since the world lies under the sway of the wicked one (1 Jn 5:19). The psalmist knew that God was entirely capable of using some means to **deliver** his **life from the wicked** with some tangible instrument (i.e., a sword). The psalmist knew that God is a God of justice and that he could trust God to mete out justice in His perfect time in His perfect way and bring retributive justice against His enemies.

**Questions for self-reflection:**

(1) Other than at church, are there any other places in your travels where the righteous influence seems to outweigh the unrighteous impact?

(2) What are some ways in your life that you have seen the Lord overcome spiritual enemies of yours, confront them, and cast them down?

(3) Are there any spiritual enemies in your life now that you would like to see the Lord cast down?

(4) If there are spiritual enemies of yours that the Lord in His providence has deemed fit not to cut down as yet, what can you do to remain faithful while the trial persists?

**17:14. With Your hand from men, O Lord, From men of the world who have their portion in this life, And whose belly You fill with Your hidden treasure. They are satisfied with children, And leave the rest of their possession for their babes.**

The psalmist continues his thought from the previous verse. He asks the Lord to deliver his life **from men of the world who have their portion in this life**. Their god is the god of this age who has blinded the minds of the unbelieving (2 Cor. 4:4). The devil's influence is working behind the scenes in the lives of these men who oppose the psalmist. Those who oppose God and who oppose the psalmist are making life more troublesome for the psalmist.

The psalmist trusts that the **Lord** can stop the evil influence that comes against him whenever it aligns with God's will for the psalmist. As fast as God permits the wicked to exert their influence, just as quickly can God cause their power to cease. After all, it is God who is in control of the length of our lives and who determines when we take our final breaths (Jb 14:5, Ps. 39:4, Ps. 139:16, Heb 9:27). Men of the world have not been called out of the world like believers have (Jn 15:19). Men of the world are men who lie under the sway of the wicked one (1 Jn 5:19). Men of the world have nothing in this life to look forward to other than what this life can offer them. Therefore, all they can enjoy in this world and this life is what consumes them. While they gain this whole world, they will lose their souls in the end (Mk 8:36). This world and this life are what they enjoy more than anything else, and their enjoyment of it will keep them shut out of heaven (Jas 4:4, 1 Jn 2:15-17).

God has saved the sheep out of this world (Jn 15:19), and their hope is not in this world because they understand that their home is not in this world (Matt. 16:26, Rom. 12:2, Phil. 3:20, Heb. 13:14, Jas 4:4, 1 Jn 2:15-17). Because the people who belong to Satan **fill** their **belly** with **treasure** God hides for them to find, when they do find it, since they have no interest in the Lord who is the Giver of every good thing (Jas 1:17), they have no interest in selling it for the pearl of great price, namely Him (Matt. 13:45-46). They find their fulfillment in things in this world (Matt. 13:22). They lay up treasures on this earth (Matt. 6:19), so much so that they leave much to their **children**. They enjoy the gift, the children, more than or rather than the Giver of good gifts (Jas 1:17). Because they were so focused on consuming all that they could while here on earth (Lk 12:13-21), rather than using their affluence to make the world a better place, they failed to use the talents and resources God had supplied them with for God's purposes and glory. Therefore, they show themselves to be the wicked servant of the parable of the talents (Matt. 24:25-28).

**Questions for self-reflection:**

(1) How have you seen the devil's influence work behind the scenes in your society?
(2) How have you seen the devil's influence work behind the scenes in your family?
(3) Have you seen the Lord providentially put a stop to an evil influence that threatened your family?
(4) Many people fill their lives with lusts and passions instead of being consumed by everlasting pleasure in the pursuit of God. Why?
(5) Is your life right now more like the wicked servant or a faithful servant of the parable of the talents?

**17:15. As for me, I will see Your face in righteousness; I shall be satisfied when I awake in Your likeness.**

---

The psalmist's enemies seemed to have an easier time than did the psalmist because the enemies of the psalmist were not on the run. They were not in constant danger. They did not constantly have to look over their shoulders. They were too busy being satisfied in themselves and in how much they could consume. They were too busy being dominated by the world system that they took no thought about what awaited them after this life. It mattered not to them that after this life comes death, the wages of sin (Rom. 6:23), and then judgment (Heb. 9:27). It did not dawn on them that people like the psalmist were praying for God to intervene against them and their sinister plots.

The psalmist had decided long ago that it was better for him to keep his soul even if that meant giving up on the notion of profiting in this world (Matt. 16:26). He knew this world was not his home (Heb. 13:14). He knew that when he closed his eyes in death, he would open them and be in the presence of the Lord (2 Cor. 5:8). He knew that while he was in this world, he could pursue God, and God would reveal Himself to him (Jer. 29:13, Matt. 7:7). The more he abided in God, the more God would abide in him, the more fruit he would bear (Jn 15:1-8). The more fruit he did bear, the more it would be undeniable to those who opposed him that there was a force behind what the psalmist did. Whatever that force was, it was greater than the psalmist (1 Jn 4:4). Even his enemies would have to admit as much.

He knew the longer he remained on this earth, that meant the closer he got to **see**ing the **face** of God **in** perfect **righteousness**. He knew he would be like God and would see Him as He is when we did **awake in** the **likeness** of God in heaven (1 Jn 3:2). Until he saw God in eternity, however, he still had to be faithful where God had him. He had to behold God by faith by using the means that God had made available to him.

Believers today have the completed Scripture to go along with the indwelling Holy Spirit. For the psalmist, setting his mind

---

on things above like those mentioned above (Col 3:1-3) helped put trials of this life into perspective. He knew that at that point, there would be nothing left to pursue in this life. That would mean that he had finished his work. That would mean that he finally could enter into the joy of his Lord (Matt 25:23). Once there, perfect uninterrupted fellowship and worship would occur throughout eternity (2 Cor. 3:18). Finally, he would **be satisfied**.

There will come a day when the dead in Christ will rise and will go to be with the Lord in heaven (1 Thess. 4:16-17). They will put off mortality and put on immortality (1 Cor. 15:53). Corruption will put on incorruption (1 Cor. 15:54). Body and soul and perfect knowledge all in one place - heaven! In heaven, we see Christ in all His perfect holiness.

## Questions for self-reflection:

(1) Is there more apparent danger for Christians or the irreligious in your society?
(2) What is your reaction toward people with an apparent lack of concern for spiritual things or the afterlife? If those who know you were to ask the irreligious, would the irreligious say that you showed more love and compassion to them or that you showed more impatience with them?
(3) What are you doing consistently to demonstrate for those that know you that this world is not your home?
(4) How can you cultivate more fruit in your life?
(5) When you think of the opportunity to see God's face after death, is it more accurate for you to say that you are excited about it or that you are ambivalent about it?

# Psalm 18

**18:1. I will love You, O Lord, my strength.**

Here, David declares his **love** for the **Lord**. In addition, these words could undoubtedly apply as being uttered from within the Trinity from Christ the Son to God the Father. Christ the Son knew that He had come to the earth to do the will of His Father. He knew that His Father was the source of His **strength**. The two members of the Godhead had intimate fellowship with each other. In addition, all believers can love the Lord who gives those created in His image strength.

The psalmist, David, knew that God gave him the strength to carry out his tasks. He knew that his days were numbered (Ps. 90:12). He knew what Paul knew: in the Lord, we live, move, and have our being (Acts 17:28). All believers know what David here knew: that the Lord is the source of our strength. For that, believers know that it is their duty and their joy and honor to love and serve the God who has given them life and every good thing (Jas 1:17).

We can love God for what He has made for us to experience and enjoy (Rom. 1:19-20). We can worship God for the things He has made for us to discover that we have yet even to discover.

Of course, the most excellent reason to worship and love God is for the love that He commended toward us in that while we were sinners, Christ died for us (Rom. 5:8). We can love God the Father because He chose us in Christ before the foundation of the world (Eph. 1:4). We can love Christ because He took our place and saved us from wrath (Rom. 5:9). When we were dead in sins, Christ made us alive (Ephesians 2:5). When we were enemies in our minds by wicked works, Christ reconciled us (Col. 1:21). We can love the Holy Spirit because He washes us and renews our minds (Ti 3:4-7). The Holy Spirit assures us that we are believers (Rom. 8:16). The Holy Spirit helps us to understand the Scriptures (1 Cor.2:10-16). The Holy Spirit convicts of sin (John 16:5-11). The Holy Spirit helps us to know how to pray (Rom. 8:26-27). The Holy Spirit reminds us heaven awaits us (Eph. 1:14).

Not only does God save us (Ti 2:13), sanctify us (Heb. 10:14), pardon us (Matt. 9:6), redeem us (Eph. 1:7), and justify us (Rom.

3:24), He gives us the privilege of serving Him. He lets us offer our bodies as living sacrifices (Rom. 12:1). He lets us set our affections on things above rather than on things of the earth (Col. 3:2). He allows us to experience anxiety about the cares of this life and the problems that our sins have caused us so that we will cast our cares on Him (1 Pet. 5:7) and realize that He is the peace that passes understanding (Phil. 4:7). He lets us feel the separation and enmity that our sins caused between the Trinity and us only to experience having the weight removed when He nailed the ordinances that were against us to the cross (Col. 2:14). He allows us to experience trouble in this world and then gently reminds us that it was He who overcame the world for us (Jn 16:33). He permits us to experience the alienation of an orphan (Col. 1:21) so that we will come to Him for adoption (Eph. 1:5).

So that we will not be sheep without a Shepherd, The Good Shepherd (Jn 10:11) sends us the Comforter (Jn 14:16) to lead us into all truth (Jn 16:13) and away from the lies of the wicked one. He allows that Spirit to bear witness with our spirits that we are the children of God (Rom. 8:16). He gives us glimpses through the earnest of the inheritance, the Holy Spirit (Ephesians 1:14), of what will be our permanent inheritance one day (1 Pe. 1:4). He allows us to be merciful to others so that we will remember how He has been merciful to us (Matt. 5:7) because He is rich in mercy (Eph. 2:4). He allows us to hunger and thirst for righteousness so that He can fill us with Himself, the source of that righteousness (Matt. 5:6). He allows us to mourn over our sinful state so He can comfort us with His pardon (Matt. 5:4). He mercifully allows us to live in our pride to understand later that becoming poor (in spirit) can make us spiritually rich (Matt. 5:3, Jas 2:5). As we, His bride, continue to go to Him, the Bridegroom, for washing in the Word (Eph. 5:26), He makes our hearts purer so that we will see more of Him (Matt. 5:8). As we live in this world that is very clearly in opposition to Him, He allows us to go into it and make peace with those who are His enemies (Matt. 5:9).

He allows us to be ministers of reconciliation to tell others how they can be mercifully, lovingly, compassionately, graciously, kindly reconciled to the God they have so grievously offended by their sin (2 Cor. 5:18). He allows some of His sheep to experience persecution for righteousness' sake (Matt. 5:10) to appreciate all He did and continues to do for us all the more. He allows us to experience weakness to remember that He is strong in us (2 Cor. 12:10). Finally, he calls us to remember that nothing can separate us from His love (Rom. 8:38-39), to remember that if He has justified us, that He will glorify us (Rom. 8:30). When we remember all these things, it should not be difficult to love the One who loves us so much.

## Questions for self-reflection:

(1) If someone asked those closest to you what or who do you love more than anyone or anything else, What would they say?
(2) What do you imagine it would be like to have perfect fellowship and relationship with God the Father?
(3) How does God give you the ability to do what you can do well?
(4) What is one aspect of creation that causes you to wonder at God?
(5) What aspects of your secure salvation cause you to wonder at God?
(6) What are some ways since you trusted in Christ for salvation that you have experienced God's rich mercy?
(7) From when you first believed until now, how have you seen and understood more about God and how His world works?

**18:2. The Lord is my rock and my fortress and my deliverer; My God, my strength, in whom I will trust; My shield and the horn of my salvation, my stronghold.**

---

See 2 Samuel 22:2-3. In the first verse of this psalm, the psalmist professed his love for **the Lord** and said that the Lord gave him strength. He is the same as He has always been, so He strengthens His people today as well. In this verse, the psalmist explains more specifically using symbols how the Lord did that for him.

A large **rock** provides shelter for those who need safety from the elements. So, the Lord keeps the sheep secure under His covering. He is the sure foundation upon which one can build the house of a life of faith so that it will not come crashing down when the storms of life crash up against it (Matt. 7:24-27). So likewise, the Lord provides shelter for His people from their physical or spiritual enemies.

The Lord is the **fortress** protecting His people from the attacks originating from Satan and Satan's forces. He has an army of angels at His disposal, which He can enlist at any time to support the saints (Matt. 26:53). Even if the Lord allows some of Satan's attacks to reach us, as He did with Job (Jb 1:12), the Lord will not allow us to experience temptation beyond what we can endure (1 Cor. 10:13). If believers remember to put on the Armor of God, then when the attacks come, they will be prepared (Eph. 6:10-20). To deliver is 'to rescue from bondage or danger.' Sinners are in bondage to sin (Jn 8:34, Rom. 6:18) and in danger of eternal punishment (Jn 3:16, Rom. 5:9).

The Lord is the **deliverer** of His people from all their enemies, some of which are temporal in nature. Through the finished work of the Lord Jesus Christ, God especially has delivered us from more persistent enemies such as death (2 Cor. 1:10), the power of darkness (Col. 1:13), this present evil age (Gal. 1:4), and sin. The psalmist does not acknowledge God simply as a God, as one of many gods. No. He gives God the glory that is due to His name. He is the One true God (Exod. 20:3). He demands complete allegiance from His people. He becomes their greatest ally for all the days of their earthly pilgrimage once they bow to Him in this life. To those who harden their necks and reject Him, He becomes their adversary.

For those who **trust** in Him, God is their **strength**. He enables them to face anything, even death, with faith to know that the worst that can happen to them is physical death. Yet, even that is not disheartening to a believer because, at death, they are immediately ushered into the Lord's presence to spend eternity with Him (2 Cor. 5:8). Then, their faith will have finally become sight. They will have finally received their incorruptible inheritance (1 Pet. 1:4).

Through faith, God becomes the **shield** of those who entrust themselves to Him. He protects them from the fiery darts that come from Satan and those who do Satan's work (Eph. 6:16). Since the Lord has provided in the past, we can trust Him now and in the future. If we take Him at His Word, we know that nothing can separate us from His love (Rom. 8:38-39). We understand that the worst that can happen to us is physical death (Matt. 10:28). We know that Christ has already defeated Satan (Col. 2:15). There is nothing to fear. God, who is powerful enough to speak the whole universe into existence (Gen. 1), is likewise powerful enough to preserve His own until the divine appointment with Him (Heb. 9:27). It is best to understand the **horn** as a symbol of power. God is the power behind eternal **salvation**. To demonstrate this, God the Father sent Christ the Son forth at the fulness of time (Gal. 4:4) to live a perfect life (2 Cor. 5:21), die a substitutionary death (1 Pet. 2:24), and rise again for our justification (Rom. 4:25). All who come to Him in repentant faith will not perish but have everlasting life (Jn 3:16).

Christ is the **stronghold,** or place of security, for His people. His people have ultimate security because of all He has accomplished on their behalf. None can pluck them out of His omnipotent hand (Jn 10:28).

## Questions for self-reflection:

(1) In what ways has the Lord been a shelter for you? From what does He shelter you?

(2) In what ways has the Lord been a fortress for you? From what has He protected you?

(3) From what has God delivered you? Lookup New Testament usages if you need to.

(4) In what ways is God your strength?

(5) In what ways is God your shield? What does He protect you from?

**18:3. I will call upon the Lord, who is worthy to be praised; So shall I be saved from my enemies.**

---

See 2 Samuel 22:4. The psalmist has already professed his love for **the Lord,** who has come through for him in the past. The Lord has been the source of recurring strength for the psalmist. The Lord has proven Himself to be a worthy object of the psalmist's trust. The Lord has been a suitable source of protection for the psalmist. Since the Lord has previously delivered the psalmist, it is little wonder why the psalmist would **call upon** the Lord to be **saved from** his **enemies.** The psalmist knew that the mercies of the Lord were new every morning (Lam. 3:22-23). The psalmist had personally met the Lord in various circumstances, and in those circumstances, the Lord had proven Himself. No wonder the psalmist was eager to call upon the Lord. The Lord had revealed Himself to the psalmist previously. The psalmist was ready for the Lord to reveal Himself now. The Lord had dispensed grace to the psalmist previously. The psalmist knew he needed more grace now. He knew that the Lord was the source of the grace that he so desperately needed, and he knew that the Lord would provide it. Since the psalmist was in a relationship with the Lord, he knew that he could call upon the Lord, and the Lord would meet him in his need (1 Jn 5:14). He knew that if the Lord did not take away his problem, at least the Lord would provide the grace needed to endure his trial (2 Cor. 12:7-10). For this limitless supply of grace (Heb. 4:14-16), the Lord was worthy to be praised by the psalmist and still is worthy to be praised by all those created in His image (Gen. 1:27).

Sadly, most created in His image choose to praise themselves, or some object or objects of the creation rather than the Creator who is blessed forever amen (Rom. 1:25). The New Testament Christian can call upon the Lord at any time (1 Thess. 5:17) because the Lord Jesus Christ had given us access by one Spirit to the Father. (Eph. 2:18). Christ has made a new and living way into God's presence (Heb. 10:19-20). When believers think back to their condition before coming to Christ, it should make them realize

---

that the Lord is worthy to be praised. They were dead in trespasses and sins (Eph. 2:1, 2:5, Col. 2:13), were alienated from God in their minds by wicked works (Col. 1:21), without strength (Rom. 5:6), deaf and blind to spiritual things (2 Cor. 4:4), polluted in their own blood (Ezek. 16) with stony hearts (Ezek. 11:19, Ezek. 36:26). But, in that state, the God who is rich in mercy, (Eph. 2:4), who was so grievously offended by their treason, humbled Himself (Phil. 2:8), put on humanity (Phil. 2:7), lived a sinless life (1 Pet. 2:22), died on a Roman cross (Rom. 5:6), and rose again (1 Cor. 15:4) to reconcile lost humanity to the God who was so offended (Rom. 5:10, 2 Cor. 5:18).

No wonder **the Lord is worthy to be praised**! The Lord Jesus Christ, by grace through faith, becomes ours. We, too, shall be saved from our enemies by faith in Him, namely sin, death, and hell.

## Questions for self-reflection:

(1) Should the Lord be called upon only for eternal salvation, or should the Lord be repeatedly called upon during the lifetime?
(2) How does your life demonstrate that you are one that consistently calls upon the Lord?
(3) In what ways has the Lord demonstrated to you that He is worthy to be praised?
(4) What enemies does the Lord save His people from today?

**18:4. The pangs of death surrounded me, And the floods of ungodliness made me afraid.**

See 2 Samuel 22:5. God the Father saved Jesus the Son from His enemies (18:3) when **the pangs of death surrounded** Him. David was the frequent target of attacks from his physical enemies, especially Saul (1 Sam. 18:10-11, 1 Sam. 19, 1 Sam.20:33, 1 Sam. 23:9, 1 Sam. 24, 1 Sam. 26) and Absalom (2 Sam. 16). There were times when David fled his enemies when he felt like the pangs of death surrounded him. When David fled for his life, certainly the floods of ungodliness **made** him **afraid**. He felt like his next breath could have been his last.

Jesus, likewise, escaped near-death experiences until His time had come (Lk 4:30). Christ's life, especially when we read about in His earthly ministry, was filled with sorrow (Isa. 53:3). When it was time for Christ to suffer and die for our sins, He could no longer escape as the time for Him to fulfill God the Father's purpose for His life had arrived. He sweated drops of blood when He contemplated bearing God's wrath against sinners, becoming a curse for humanity (Lk 22:44, Gal. 3:13).

**The floods of ungodliness** that had come upon our Lord throughout His earthly ministry were coming to a head. He would suffer and die for wicked sinners, many of which were directly involved in what He endured. All these years later, we were indirectly involved in what He suffered as it was our sins as well for which Christ died (1 Cor. 15:3). It was our ungodliness that He knew about even before we ever lived that made Him afraid. It made Him afraid because He knew that all that sin made His Father angry and would need avenging. He knew that He needed to take God's perfectly just wrath against our ungodliness. He knew His Father was holy (Lev. 11:44) and angry at the wicked every day (Ps. 7:11). He knew His Father's anger was not unwarranted. No. He perfectly executed it at the perfect time against our perfect Substitute. He experienced the insults (Heb. 12:3) and beatings of wicked men patiently (Lk 22:63-64). He experienced alienation from His own disciples (Matt. 26:56). He endured the forsaking of His Father (Ps. 22:1, Matt. 27:46).

He felt the lack of acceptance from the people He so graciously came to save. As He ministered with the love and grace of His Father, supporting Him by the power of the Holy Spirit, the spiritual apathy grew. The hearts grew colder. The pomp of religion choked out actual heart devotion. No wonder when He confronted the hypocrites who were experts at going through the motions without a trace of reality, they got defensive. No wonder they hated Him. He had the truth. They didn't want the truth. They wanted their prestige. They didn't care about eternity. They were too caught up in themselves to consider that their rejection of the One who came to save them would cause them to miss out on the eternal blessing they mistakenly thought was there because of their heritage.

## Questions for self-reflection:

(1) In what ways did the pangs of death surround the Lord Jesus Christ?
(2) In what ways did the pangs of death surround David?
(3) Have floods of ungodliness ever made you afraid?

**18:5. The sorrows of Sheol surrounded me; The snares of death confronted me.**

---

See 2 Samuel 22:6. This was true of the psalmist. This was also true of our Lord. The truth is that for everyone born of Adam, death is an unavoidable reality (Ezek. 18:20, Heb. 9:27). As was established in the previous verse, David, the psalmist, frequently fled for his life from pursuers who wanted him dead. Scholars commonly regard **Sheol** as the deceased's place or the grave (Gen. 37:35, Num. 16:33, 1 Kgs 2:9, Jb 7:9, Jon. 2:2). David had **sorrow** when he thought that death was imminent.

When our Lord contemplated His own death, as has been previously established, it brought Him displeasure. But, unlike David, unlike the rest of the human race, the Lord Jesus Christ rose again (Matt.28) and ascended to heaven (Acts 1:9-11). The rest of humanity awaits the day when the dead in Christ rise first (1 Thess. 4:16), meet the Lord in the air (1 Thess. 4:17), and will forever be with the Lord. Thus, we have a great hope. Since death could not hold our Lord, the believer can know that we too will rise after Christ, the Firstfruits (1 Cor. 15:20).

When Judas Iscariot came after our Lord in the Garden of Gethsemane with the soldiers and their weapons (Matt. 26:46, Mk 14:43, Lk 22:47, Jn 18:3), He knew that the **snares of death confronted** Him. He knew the time had arrived. He had prepared His disciples for it (Matt. 16:21). Sadly, they did not understand until much later. Fortunately for them and the rest of us, the Lord is patient with us, even when we are too dull to understand things that should be very understandable.

The Jews had been plotting how they would have our Lord killed for some time now (Jn 11:45-57). Finally, the moment had arrived. They would win, or so they thought. Satan had had his way. Christ would be out of the way. So, Satan and Jesus' other opponents thought. Christ made a spectacle of His enemies (Col. 2:15).

One day, our Lord will cast all His enemies into the lake of fire (Rev. 20:10, Rev. 20:15, Rev. 21:8). Until then, the godly remnant can trust that the Captain of their salvation (Heb. 2:10) surrounded Himself with Sheol's sorrows and ensnared Himself with the death we have all earned ourselves because of our sin (Rom. 6:23) so that we will not have to. If we take the ministry of reconciliation to those in desperate need of reconciliation, Christ can be their sin-bearer as He is our sin-bearer (1 Pet. 2:24).

**Questions for self-reflection:**

(1) From whom did David have to flee to save his life?
(2) How was Jesus, before His death, surrounded by the sorrows of the grave and the snares of death?
(3) How was the apostle Paul put close to death?
(4) In the world today, are there locations where Christians are close to death? Where?

**18:6. In my distress I called upon the Lord, And cried out to my God; He heard my voice from His temple, And my cry came before Him, even to His ears.**

---

See 2 Samuel 22:7. The psalmist experienced **distress** for reasons that have been well established in the previous verses of this psalm. The Lord Jesus also experienced distress, as was described in the earlier verses. Jesus knew that His Father heard Him when **He cried out to** Him (Jn 11:42). The Father and Son enjoyed perfect fellowship until the cross. In the distress of the cross, our sinless Savior called upon the Lord, called upon His Father. Even though the Father had forsaken His Son while His Son bore the sins of humanity, the Father still heard the voice of the Son from His temple because God knows everything.

The psalmist knew that the Lord was capable of answering him and saving him. As the psalmist reaped what his enemies had sown and fled for his life, he felt distressed. Likewise, Christ in His humanity, as the religious leaders sought to end His influence (Jn 5:18), as His own disciples' weakness came through (Lk 9:37-42), as one of His own disciples would betray Him (Lk 22:21-23), must have felt distressed. Additionally, today, Christ's followers can expect to experience much the same treatment as their Lord did, as a servant is not above his Master (Jn 13:16). If they persecuted the Shepherd, the sheep should expect the same treatment (Jn 15:20). When the Shepherd got smote, the sheep scattered (Matt. 26:31, Mk 14:27).

This life, lived on the earth that humanity's sin has plagued, will be filled with many forms of trouble that cause distress. It is when the sheep think of the hardships that await them in this world that they would do well to remember their Lord's words, "In the world, you will have tribulation; but be of good cheer I have overcome the world" (Jn 16:33). Because Jesus overcame the world, the saints are more than conquerors in Christ (Rom. 8:37). The sheep are overcomers (1 Jn 2:14). Like Jesus called out to His **God** and Father when He was in distress, the sheep can call out to the Lord, to the Father, to whom they now enjoy access because of Christ's finished work on their behalf, when they are in distress (Eph. 2:18). There is no problem that the sheep will ever face that could ever be too difficult for the Creator to handle.

When believers cry out to God in faith, **He hears their voices from His temple**, heaven, if they don't regard iniquity in their hearts (Ps. 66:18). The throne of grace is always accessible to the saints (Heb. 4:16). They have a most sufficient Advocate to plead their cause (1 Jn 2:1). Because they are justified, they will be glorified (Romans 8:30). Anything that they endure in this life is for their ultimate good (Rom. 8:28). When believers seek the Lord while He may be found (Isa. 55:6), they can be confident that He hears them and that he rejoices over them to do them good (Deut. 28:63). God wants His sheep to come to Him with hearts full of faith. He is pleased when they do, and He uses their effectual fervent prayers to avail much in the lives of the saints (Jas 5:16). The saints whose hearts are full of love and worship of the One who saved them can know with confident assurance that when they cry out to Him, their cries will make it to the God of heaven, **even to His ears.**

## Questions for self-reflection:

(1) In what ways has the Lord answered you when you were in distress?

(2) How can the Lord use those experiences in your life so that you can be an encouragement to others?

(3) Besides persecution, what are some other situations God's people can find themselves in that lead to distress?

(4) What problem that the sheep face that is too difficult for the Lord to handle?

(5) What is something that would prevent the Lord from hearing His people when they call to Him?

**18:7. Then the earth shook and trembled; The foundations of the hills also quaked and were shaken, Because He was angry.**

---

See 2 Samuel 22:8. When Christ was on the cross, He called out to His Father (Matt. 27:46, Lk 23:34). The Heavenly Father heard His Son. When Christ gave up the ghost and breathed His last (Mk 15:37), **then the earth shook and trembled** (Matt 27:51). At the same time, **the foundations of the hills also quaked and were shaken.** When these things happened, they were supernatural acts done to show those present that God the Father was present at the death of God the Son.

These things happened partially to show that God the Father **was angry** at what was allowed to happen to His Son (Ps. 7:11), even though it needed to happen so that there would be a payment for sin (1 Jn 2:2). God the Father had to look away from the Lord Jesus Christ when He was on the cross (Ps. 22:1). God was angry at human sin, which put His Son on the cross and would send everyone else since sin entered the Garden of Eden to the grave (Rom. 6:23, 1 Cor. 15:3-4). God was angry that humanity was so sinful that they could not even keep the one law that impinged upon their freedom God had so graciously given (Gen. 2:15-17) to those He created in His image (Gen. 1:27).

God was angry that the Jews, His covenant people, to whom He sent the prophets and with whom He made all the promises, spurned Him so wickedly. He was angry that the Jews of Jesus' day took the love that God commended toward them so flippantly that they had Him executed.

If things were written as an example for us (1 Cor. 10:11), we should learn not to take any sin lightly, especially our treatment of His Son, the love offering for our sins. God is rich in mercy (Eph. 2:4) toward us to make way for our forgiveness. For us to respond to that mercy with anything but love and worshipful obedience is wicked. When we sin, He could kill us on the spot, but He does not because He is slow to anger (Ps. 103:8), patient (2 Pet. 3:9), and compassionate. We should respond to these attributes of the Holy One with awe, love, and obedience. When we do not, we

---

show that we do not understand how bad our sin is, nor do we know how gracious the God we continually sin against is.

**Questions for self-reflection:**

(1) How did God the Father show that He was present at the death of God the Son?
(2) Why did the earth shake and tremble, and why did the foundations of the hills quake and shake? Why was God angry?
(3) If human sin required the slaughter of animals and if it required the death of God the Son, the Son of Man, what should be our attitude toward our own sin?

### 18:8. Smoke went up from His nostrils, And devouring fire from His mouth; Coals were kindled by it.

---

See 2 Samuel 22:9. After Christ breathed His last (Mk 15:37), God's wrath dramatically appeared at Golgotha. God's righteous anger at the sin which put Christ on the cross unveiled in the earthquake (Matt. 27:51-54, Mk 15:38). So many generations removed from that frightful scene, it can be difficult for Christ's disciples to put themselves there and mentally bring themselves to appreciate that it was not only the Romans' sin, not only the Jews' sin, but their own sin, our own sin, my own sin, that put the Lamb of God (Jn 1:32) on the cross to give Himself for the sins of the world (1 Jn 2:2).

When the Old Testament sacrifices were appropriate for their time, God showed by a miraculous sign that they were satisfactory (1 Kgs 18:20-40). God's anger at sin was on full display for those present. Perhaps it was not adequately understood by most on hand at the foot of the cross. Most likely, it is not properly understood, even if it is more completely understood now since the Canon has been completed to more fully instruct the saints. Nevertheless, the spotless Lamb was consumed in the fury of the wrath of the Father against human sin even though the Lamb Himself did not sin (1 Pet. 2:22).

When Christ proclaimed it was finished, the Father gave His approval (Jn 19:30). The **smoke went up from** the Father's proverbial **nostrils**. The **devouring fire** went forth **from** the Father's anthropomorphic **mouth**. The **coals** had properly **kindled** the Son. His death on our behalf sufficiently atoned for every sin committed by everyone in every generation for all time. The God-rejectors now are as the kindled coals. Whether they realize it or not, they await the day (if they do not repent and turn to Christ) for God's wrath to come upon them for all eternity (Jn 3:36).

Thankfully for everyone, the same God who is angry with the wicked every day (Ps. 7:11), angry with those who spurn His goodness for their own way (Rom. 2:4) is also rich in mercy (Eph. 2:4), is full of compassion (Ps. 145:8), and is abounding in lovingkindness

(Ps. 36:7). He made a way for lawbreakers like us to be forgiven. He commended His love toward us in that while we were sinners, Christ died for us (Rom. 5:8). Saints worldwide can rejoice that Christ has reconciled them to the Father (2 Cor. 5:18).

## Questions for self-reflection:

(1) How was your sin also responsible for Jesus' death on the cross?
(2) Was Jesus deserving of His death for your sins?
(3) Is there any sin of yours, past, present, or future, that the blood of Christ is not sufficient to cover?

**18:9. He bowed the heavens also, and came down With darkness under His feet.**

---

See 2 Samuel 22:10. The wrath and vengeance of God came on Sinai at the giving of the Ten Commandments (Exod. 19). God called to Moses from the mountain (Exod. 19:3). The Lord humbled Himself and condescended and brought Himself to man's level during that time so that His people would know the Law and know what their God expected from them. The Lord gave the people a glimpse of His holiness. (Exod. 19:16).

Similarly, the wrath and vengeance of God came down on Golgotha came down when Christ breathed His last during His First Advent (Matt. 27:50, Mk 15:37, Lk 23:46, Jn 19:30). God **bowed the heavens** when the wrath of God the Father against humanity for the sin of humanity **came down** and entirely poured out on Christ, the Sinless Son. Every drop, even to the dregs, had been used. The earth, **under His** (God's) **feet** (Isa. 66:1), was filled **with** total **darkness** because humanity had chosen, instead of embracing His Son, to reject and crucify His Son (Matt. 27:45). The Lamb of God consumed the Father's wrath so that He might take away the sins of the world (Jn 1:29). So that He could extend love (Jn 3:16, Rom. 5:8), grace (Ti 2:14), and mercy (Eph. 2:4) to sinners, God the Father inflicted His wrath (Rom.5:9) and justice (Rom. 3:26) upon God the Son, the sinless Substitute for sinners of the worst kind (Isa. 53:4-6), of which I am one, of which we all are (Rom. 3:9-23).

The earth is God's footstool (Isa. 66:1). Sin's penalty against transgressions committed in every generation was dealt a fatal blow with by the cry from the cross. "It is finished" (Jn 19:30). Darkness would give way to light, however, as God the Son, just a short time later, would rise from the grave, defeating death, proving that He was who He said He was (1 Cor. 15:4). He had humbled Himself (Phil. 2:8). Now, God had exalted Him (Phil. 2:9). One day every knee will bow, and every tongue will confess that Jesus Christ is Lord to the glory of God the Father (Phil. 2:10-11). Since God bowed the heavens, since darkness was under God's feet when the death of Christ atoned for sin on our behalf, we should have a strong motivation to serve others for the Lord's sake and partake in the ministry of reconciliation (2 Cor. 5:18)

## Questions for self-reflection:

(1) How did God bow the heavens?
(2) When Christ died, was there any of God's wrath that was not used up?
(3) Now that Jesus has been exalted, are you ready to meet Him?

**18:10. And He rode upon a cherub, and flew; He flew upon the wings of the wind.**

See 2 Samuel 22:11. Regardless of who the specific cherub is, God utilized the cherub to see what happens on the earth beneath. Perhaps God keeps the cherub close by so that He can instruct it in the ways it is to carry out God's work on the earth below (Acts 12:23). Angels have been shown in Scripture to be agents that carry out God's work (Matt. 28:2). This cherub can be thought of similarly. The wind blows quickly in whichever direction it is going (Jn 3:8). Wings enable creatures who have them to perform their designated tasks rapidly. This verse could speak to the quick help that God, who **rode upon a cherub**, provided to the Son, as he faced opposition during His earthly ministry (Matt. 4:11) and as His time on the earth wound down even up to the scene at Golgotha.

Perhaps the **wings of the wind** provided quick, timely aid to the Son in those times when the Lord Jesus sought His Father in prayer. As a result, the Son had immediate access to His Father. The beauty of the gospel is that the Son has given us this same access, by one Spirit, to the Father (Eph. 2:18). It is this amazing grace bountifully provided to every believer in which they stand and by which they receive everything they need for life and godliness (2 Pet. 1:3). It is one of the many blessings with which believers have been blessed in the heavenly places (Eph. 1:3) that God has legions of angels at His disposal (Matt. 26:53) that can help anyone at any time as they did Christ our Lord. It is a blessing that the enemies of God can only affect believers as much as God lets them (Jb 1:12, Jb 2:6). Believers would be wise to trust in an omniscient God that anything He allows to touch them, He has designed for their good to make them more like His Son (Rom. 8:28-29).

**Questions for self-reflection:**

(1) What purpose do cherubs serve?
(2) When you think that Jesus has given us the same access that He has to the Father, what is your reaction?
(3) Is there anything that you legitimately need that the Trinity cannot provide?
(4) If there is something difficult you have had to endure, is it something God cannot handle?

**18:11. He made darkness His secret place; His canopy around Him was dark waters And thick clouds of the skies.**

See 2 Samuel 22:12. When people reject the light that they have been given and exchange the truth of God for any of the deceitful lies this world has to offer (Rom. 1:25), God, in judgment, can remove His restraining influences and let mankind pursue what his sinful heart wants (Rom. 1:24, Rom. 1:26, Rom. 1:28). This is an act of judgment performed by God against sinners that have willfully chosen to reject His advances (Rom. 1:21). God can do no more than to save sinners than what He has already graciously done. He has given Christ, the spotless Lamb of God (Jn 1:29), to be the propitiation of the sins of the world (1 Jn 2:2). If man does not take God on His terms now, he should not expect to have God on man's own terms later.

When man rejects the light of the glorious gospel (2 Cor. 4:4), man should expect that the light that was once present before the sinner's eyes can be replaced with further **darkness**, as God gives them over to their own sinful desires. Their minds become reprobate (Rom. 1:28). God gives them over to that reprobate mind so that their reprobation will become increasingly evident with time. This happened to the Jews when they rejected Christ in the first century. This continues to happen to those who have rejected the gospel since then. The **thick clouds of the skies** of the fog that engulfs the sinner who has rejected God works to further and further obscure the truth from them to where they reach the point that they are past feeling (Eph. 4:19). The only remedy is to seek the Lord while He may be found (Isa. 55:6) because now is the accepted time for salvation (2 Cor. 6:2).

**Questions for self-reflection:**

(1) How would you know if you had interactions with someone from whom God had removed divine restraints?
(2) What can you do more of to make sure that you remain appropriately sensitive to God's direction in your life?

(3) What can you do less of to make sure that you remain appropriately sensitive to God's direction in your life?
(4) Do you think you are above being given over to a reprobate mind? How can you keep your humility?
(5) Who do you know who lives as though they have been given over to a reprobate mind? What can you do to help them see the truth?

**18:12. From the brightness before Him, His thick clouds passed with hailstones and coals of fire.**

See 2 Samuel 22:13. Suppose Christ is **the brightness before Him** (before the Father). In that case, this could refer to the judgment that awaits those who reject Him (Jn 3:36). People of the first century who saw Christ during His First Advent rejected Christ. Since Christ first came to the earth, people in every generation reject the knowledge given to them via creation (Rom. 1:20), conscience (Rom. 2:15), and Scripture. This knowledge informs them that God is there, that He holds everyone accountable (2 Cor. 5:10), and that He loves them enough to offer salvation to them even after they have sinned so grievously against Him (Col. 1:21).

Before Christ came, **thick clouds** were over the people preventing them from seeing what God was really like (2 Cor. 4:3, 2 Cor. 2:16). When Jesus came, He was the exact representation of God's nature (Heb. 1:3). In Christ, the fulness of the Godhead bodily dwelt (Col. 2:9). He was greater than Abraham (Jn 8:56). He was greater than Jonah (Matt. 12:41). They were men. He is God (Jn 8:58). When He was transfigured on the Mount, His brightness shone forth for a few of the privileged disciples to see (Matt. 17:1-18). When the Light of the World (Jn 8:12) came into the world to His own, as glorious as it was, it was also tragic because His own did not receive Him (Jn 1:11). Christ was a savor of life unto life for one group and a savor of death unto death for another group (2 Cor. 2:16).

Those that rejected Him were irritated and wounded, albeit not in a productive, saving way, by Christ's ministry of reconciliation that He came with and that He left with the disciples (2 Cor. 5:18). Instead, He was rejected swiftly by people who were too wise to humble themselves before Him (1 Pet. 5:6). When we are too wise in our own eyes, that can prevent us from seeing ourselves as we really are (Jas 4:6). It prevents us from seeing our own need for God's grace because we get more focused on getting others to see their need for God's grace that we refuse to look at ourselves and our own need for forgiveness (Matt. 7:1-6). If sinners don't recognize their own blindness to the point where they submit to God and resist the devil (Jas 4:7), they subject themselves to the **hailstones and coals of fire** that await those who are under God's judgment.

## Questions for self-reflection:

(1) Assuming you are in Christ, have you thought about the judgment that awaited you before you came to Christ? Have you thought about the judgment that awaits those you know who have not come to Christ? Does this knowledge motivate you to share the gospel with people so that they can avoid the judgment you will?

(2) What are some things that prevent people today from seeing Jesus for who He is?

(3) How can we prevent ourselves from being wise in our own eyes? How can we ensure we have a properly balanced perception of ourselves, balancing the humbling indwelling sin with the exuberant hope of what Christ has accomplished for us?

**18:13. The Lord thundered from heaven, And the Most High uttered His voice, Hailstones and coals of fire.**

---

See 2 Samuel 22:14. When the Lord's Word goes forth, **the Lord** thunders from heaven, as He did when He first gave the Law on Mount Sinai (Exod. 19:16). When His Word goes forth, He expects those who hear it to respond to it and be hearers and doers of the Word, not hearers only, deceiving themselves into thinking because they are religious that they must be righteous before Him (Jas 1:22, Jas 1:26). God has had people taking His message into the world from the time of Adam, who had to communicate God's message to his wife (Gen. 2:15-17, Gen. 3:2). After Adam, according to the Scriptures, Noah was a preacher of righteousness (2 Pet. 2:5), meaning that Noah preached God's message to those that perished outside of the Ark. It got so bad that when those people ignored the warnings and refused to enter God's merciful Ark, that the time for patience ran out. Then the Flood came (Gen. 7). Every time He gave the inspired revelation, gracious God demonstrated mercy by showing the blessings that come from obedience and the curses that come from disobedience (Deut. 28).

Finally, the fullness of time came (Gal. 4:4-5). Because God is rich in mercy (Eph. 2:4), despite all the unrelenting sins of His covenant people, on top of the evils from people who were not His covenant people, God showed mercy. He corrected any misconceptions that people may have had about Him not being loving, not being patient, not being kind, not being merciful, about Him failing to live up to His part of the covenants (See 1 Cor. 13:4-7). He sent Christ to be the propitiation of the sins of the whole world (1 Jn 2:2). He showed His love for the world that He gave His only Son that whoever believes in Him receives everlasting life (Jn 3:16).

Today, God's Word goes forth when His people read it (Jb 23:12, Rom. 12:2) and when it is preached from His pulpits or in the streets as if it is **thundered from heaven**. Today, God uses His mouthpieces. On behalf of **the Most High** God, the faithful

---

have **uttered His voice,** and He will recognize them as His faithful servants in the next life. Those who reject Him now will face the great Judge on His white throne (Rev. 20:11-15), where it will be like **hailstones and coals of fire** raining down on them should they scoff at God's gracious offer of reconciliation through the Son.

## Questions for self-reflection:

(1) Have you ever thought about listening to the preaching of the Word in church as a way in which the Lord thunders from heaven?

(2) If we are not careful, how can we be prone to fall into the trap of being religious without being genuinely righteous before God?

(3) How is the story of Noah and the Ark an illustration of God's patience?

(4) Is there anyone you know who is in great danger of experiencing the hailstones and coals of fire if they do not repent? What are you willing to do about that?

**18:14. He sent out His arrows and scattered the foe, Lightnings in abundance, and He vanquished them.**

---

See 2 Samuel 22:15. God sent prophets into the world and sent the Messiah into the world to separate the sheep from the goats (Matt. 25:31-46), to gather the wheat and **scatter** the tares (Matt. 13:24-30). He sent plagues against His enemies that His people did not suffer from (Exod. 9:3-4, 6; Exod. 9:22-23, 26; Exod. 10:21-23; Exod. 11:4-7). He parted seas to **vanquish** the enemies of His people while letting His people cross on the dry ground so that the difference between His people and the enemies to His people would be made plain (Exod. 14).

In the New Covenant, the sheep, those who have responded to the gospel with saving faith, have been called out (Jn 10:3), separated from the world (Lev. 20:26, Jn 15:19, Jn 17:16, Rom. 12:2, 2 Cor. 6:17, Eph. 5:11, Jas 4:4, Rev. 18:4), separated unto the Lord. The sheep's lives should bear such stark contrast to the perishing world that it is evident that **lightnings in abundance**, symbolic of judgment and God's righteousness (Exod. 19:16, Exod. 20:18, Rev. 4:5, Rev. 8:5, Rev. 11:19, Rev. 16:18, Rev. 20:9), surround those who have rejected God's merciful provision. This difference, easily spotted by the saints, should cause their hearts to break for the condition of the lost.

Rather than get upset with them for being blind (2 Cor. 4:4, Eph. 4:18), something they are powerless to change, the saved person should take his blind friend by the hand and lead him to the Great Physician until He applies the healing touch of gospel grace such that the blind man can see. When the **arrows** and lightnings of the gospel message go forth, the righteous should remember that they too were once dull to the things of God before God met them (1 Cor. 6:11, Eph. 2:1). They would do well to remember that if it were not for God intervening in their story (Gal. 4:4-5, Eph. 2:4), they would be the ones scattering and perishing. God's grace opened their eyes to their desperate condition. They responded. God gets the glory.

---

So, for those who oppose God and God's people, we should be patient, compassionate, loving, and merciful, just as God is with us before we come to Him and after we come to Him through faith in the Lord Jesus Christ. Not everyone will respond to the affliction that sin brings with repentant faith. Some will respond with further hardness. Those tasked with the Great Commission are to present the truth and trust God with the results.

## Questions for self-reflection:

(1) In what ways does Scripture show that God sent arrows to scatter the foe?
(2) What Bible stories record God vanquishing His enemies?
(3) In light of Luke 13:3, Romans 15:4, and 1 Corinthians 10:6, how can Old Testament stories be examples for us? How do the stories act as arrows and lightnings?
(4) How can we make sure that we are living in such a way that we point people to the truth and not away from it?
(5) How can you take a spiritually blind person by the hand and help them see the truth?

**18:15. Then the channels of the sea were seen, The foundations of the world were uncovered At Your rebuke, O Lord, At the blast of the breath of Your nostrils.**

---

This verse is almost a verbatim quote of 2 Samuel 22:16. When Israel crossed the Red Sea in Exodus 14, **then the channels of the sea were seen. The foundations of the world** that were laid immediately under what became the Red Sea **were uncovered at** the **rebuke** of the **Lord** against the Egyptians. When Moses lifted his rod, **at the blast of the breath of** the **nostrils** of the Lord, the waters went back, and Israel crossed on dry ground while Egypt drowned.

Going back to the previous verse, when God's Word goes forth, as the seas part and separate, the Word separates the sheep and the goats, as the sheep are known for an obedient response to God's Word while the goats are known for a disobedient response to God's Word (Matt. 25:31-33, Jn 10:27). When God's people feel the struggle that comes with living as a light in such a dark world, the righteous can trust in the Lord and know that He will fight for them, as He has fought for His people all along (Exod. 14:14, Exod. 14:25, Deut. 1:30, Deut. 2:34, Deut. 3:22, Deut. 20:4, Joshua 10:42, Josh. 23:3, Josh. 23:10, Isa. 54:17, 2 Cor. 10:3-5, Eph. 6:10-20). He will rebuke the enemies of His people and allow His people to stand out as the shining lights that they are (Phil. 2:15).

The Lord has historically fought for His people against His enemies. The pages of Scripture and saints from every generation testify to this fact. If the Lord fights for His people, then the Lord fights against the enemies of His people. Since the Lord does not change (Mal. 3:6, Heb 13:8), He continues to fight for His people against their enemies. This is true in every generation before these inspired words were penned and in every generation since these inspired words were penned. Now, the Lord arms people with spiritual weapons to face any enemy and promises that His people will be with Him in eternity forever. With these promises supporting believers, there is no reason to fear anything that this world, which is under the sway of the wicked one (1 Jn 5:19), can throw at them.

**Questions for self-reflection:**

(1) Are there any afflictions in your life that are like the Red Sea crossing for which you need to trust God to work in ways in which you are incapable of working?
(2) How have you seen God's Word separate sheep from goats? Does their lack of response to God make you angry or sad when you think of the goats? Or both?
(3) How have you seen God fight for you against your enemies?

**18:16. He sent from above, He took me; He drew me out of many waters.**

---

This verse is almost a verbatim quote of 2 Samuel 22:17. When the Lord's people go through trials in this life, God sends help in the form of angels or providence or gentle nudges from the Holy Spirit to remind the sheep of what their Shepherd expects of them by leading them into all truth (Jn 16:13).

Before that was possible, before the sheep could be sons of God led by the Spirit of God (Rom. 8:14), Christ came down, being **sent from above** by His heavenly Father (Jn 20:21). He tabernacled among men (Rev. 21:3). He was tempted in every way as we are yet without sin (Heb. 4:15). He died on our behalf (Rom. 5:8). But that was not the end! Death could not hold Him (Acts 2:24). He rose from the grave, defeating death, becoming the firstfruits of those who will rise from the dead (1 Cor. 15:20).

He experienced trials and suffered on this earth (1 Peter 2:23). His Father **drew** Him **out of many waters**. Since He experienced forms of what we experience in our trials, He can sympathize with our weaknesses (Heb. 4:15). He can be our faithful High Priest because, unlike us, He did not sin in response to His trials as we are so prone to do (Heb. 4:15). When Satan tempted Christ in the Wilderness, at the end of the temptation, God the Father sent from above angels to minister to Him and drew Him out of the many waters of Satanic temptation (Matt. 4:11, Mk 1:13). When Christ rose from the dead, God the Father sent from above an angel to roll the stone away from the tomb (Matt. 28:2, Mk 16:4-5, Lk 24:4, Jn 20:1). Many times, Christ had upset the people of His day to the point that He was near death. On those times when Christ miraculously escaped because 'His time had not yet come' (Jn 7:30), perhaps the Father took Him and miraculously protected Him until the moment when it was time for Christ to die as our sacrificial Lamb. It could be that after Christ had finished with all His post-resurrection appearances when it was time for Him to sit down at the right hand of the Majesty on high (Heb. 1:3) ever to live to intercede for the saints (Heb. 7:25), that God similarly took

Him like He took Elijah (2 Kgs 2). God the Father took Christ, drew Christ out of many waters, out of many troubles in His earthly life. Choices made by sinful humanity caused each of these. When God the Father raised Christ from the dead (Acts 13:30, Rom. 10:9, 1 Cor. 6:14) to prove that Christ was who He said He was, He exalted Christ to the right hand of the Father. The Father gave Christ the name above all names (Phil. 2:9) and a seat close to Him (Rom. 8:34). God opened the floodgates of divine access for all the saints (Eph. 2:18). We now have a great privilege of humbly, reverently approaching the throne of grace for help in our time of need (Heb. 4:16). When we face trials in this life, we know that God can send angels to help us if that is His will. As Christ went through hardships, we will go through different difficulties of our own (Jas 1:2-8). If we keep our eyes on Christ and off our problems (Heb. 12:1-2), God's grace will strengthen us to persevere in ways that would not have been possible in our own strength. Sometimes, God's sending to us from above, taking us out, drawing us out from many waters, is not as much removing our hardships from our lives as much as it is coming near to us while we are in the crucible as it heats us so that when it gets uncomfortable, we will look on Him and not the flames so that He can sustain us (Dan. 3:19-25).

## Questions for self-reflection:

(1) How has the fact that Christ is a sympathetic High Priest to you been a help to you in your Christian pilgrimage? Think of just a couple of ways.
(2) Thinking back to the previous question, is there anyone you know who does not know the Lord that could benefit from hearing your answer to number one?
(3) Has God ever intervened in a circumstance in your life in such a way that it reminded you of how He sent angels to others?

**18:17. He delivered me from my strong enemy, From those who hated me, For they were too strong for me.**

---

This verse is almost a verbatim quote of 2 Samuel 22:18. If David Is the writer, and if David is writing of himself, note that David had no shortage of those that could qualify as a **strong enemy.** God was on David's side and **delivered** him from his enemies. It could refer to Saul. It could refer to Goliath. Either way, God was with David and was David's deliverer.

Jesus Christ is the Son of David. Several of the statements in the psalms are prophetic and picture the Lord Jesus Christ. Therefore, this statement could refer to Christ. In His humanity, there were times when His Father miraculously spared him from death before His appointed time (Jn 10:22-39). In those instances, God the Father delivered Christ from those enemies who were out to destroy Him (Jn 5:18).

For David and Christ, Satan led those enemies who **hated** them. Satan hates Christ and those on Christ's side. Satan filled the Pharisees with their hatred of the Lord when the Lord came against their religion and asked them to forsake it for Him and His ways. He asked them to stop clinging to their external righteousness and exchange it for internal righteousness that only Christ can supply (Phil 3:9). God the Father did deliver Christ from the Pharisees early on until it was time for Him to be our Substitute. For this, the Jews hated Christ. Satan also hates Christ because Christ keeps people from joining Satan in hell.

The enemies of God's people are always **too strong for** them to take on in their own strength. David could not have defeated his enemies had not God been on David's side. Likewise, if the Lord Jesus Christ had not been fully God, if He had been only fully man, He would not have been able to overcome the assaults levied at Him by the Jews and Romans. He would have stayed in the grave because they were too strong for Him.

The good news for David, the good news for Jesus, and the good news for all of Jesus' disciples is that when we are weak, then we are strong (2 Cor. 12:7-10) because His power is made great in our weakness. It is good news that Christ energizes us even when we are at our weakest points to submit to God and resist the devil (Jas 4:7). It is good news that we do not have to live this life alone (Gal. 2:20), but with Christ in us, we can overcome temptation (1 Cor. 10:13). Temptations are too strong to overcome for many of us in the flesh, but by the Spirit, we can do all things through Christ who strengthens us (Phil. 4:13). Since Christ disarmed all principalities and powers (Col. 2:15), we must walk in the Spirit and not the flesh (Gal. 5:16). Because Christ overcame the world (Jn 16:33), because believers are already in one sense seated in the heavenly places (Eph. 2:6), they have the spiritual resources at their disposal now also to overcome the wicked one (1 Jn 2:13).

While the wicked one may have the whole world lying under his sway (1 Jn 5:19), Christ has called the sheep out of the world that they might be light-bearers who expose the spiritual darkness that is inherent to the world system (Col. 1:13). They do this by taking every thought captive to the obedience of Christ (2 Cor 10:5). Believers then, by the power of Christ, can likewise be delivered from their enemies, which are too strong for them.

## Questions for self-reflection:

(1) Who are the strong enemies from which God has delivered you?
(2) How can the stories of David's and Jesus' rescue from their enemies encourage you in your battles against your spiritual enemies?
(3) When you are going through a time of spiritual weakness, how can you tap into God's strength to help you overcome your weakness?
(4) Christ has defeated all the enemies that pose a threat to His people. Now His people never have to be afraid of condemnation. How can we walk in that victory without succumbing to the fleshly desire to worry?

**18:18. They confronted me in the day of my calamity, But the Lord was my support.**

---

This verse is almost a verbatim quote of 2 Samuel 22:19. If the verse refers to the Lord Jesus Christ, **they** who **confronted** Him must refer to the Jews and the Romans who were immediately involved with his crucifixion. Christ's death was the ultimate **day of calamity** since it was the day when He suffered and paid for the sins of the world and became the Savior to those who place repentant faith in Him and Him alone. As He was throughout His earthly life from birth to ascension, God the Father was the support of God the Son the Lord Jesus Christ, even when His time to substitute for us had arrived. Christ's meat and drink were to do the will of the Father (Jn 4:34). The Son always did those things that pleased the Father (Jn 8:29). Christ filled His life with frequent times of solitude before His Father (Lk 5:16). Sin never interrupted the constant fellowship between the Heavenly Father and the Son. The Father perfectly supported the Son in whatever He needed. Since sin in the saints breaks fellowship with the Godhead (Ps. 66:18), since there was no sin in the Son (Heb 4:15), there was nothing to break the perfect union between the Father and Son until the Son hung on the cross, until the wrath of God was spent on the sinless Son (Rom. 5:9) as He took our place (Isa. 53:4-6, Mk 10:45, Jn 10:11, Jn 15:13, Rom. 5:6, Rom. 5:8, Rom. 14:15, 2 Cor. 5:15, 2 Cor. 5:21, Gal. 2:20, 1 Thess. 5:10, 1 Tim. 2:6, Ti 2:14, Heb. 2:9, Heb. 9:28, 1 Pet. 2:21-25, 1 Pet. 3:18, 1 Jn 3:16) and the Father forsook the Son (Ps. 22:1, Mat. 27:46). Except for that moment, the **Lord** Father was the perfect constant **support** for the Son. The Son relied, leaned, and depended upon His Father.

Today, the saints have access by one Spirit to the same Father (Eph. 2:18). For the saints in every generation, the Lord is our support. If we come to the Father by Jesus the Son, we receive that support, mercy, and help in our time of need (Heb. 4:16). God knows we need that mercy, for our sins have separated us from Him (Isa. 59:2, Eph. 2:12). Our sins have caused our own personal calamity between ourselves and God. Fortunately for us, the

God whose wrath was upon us because of our sin (Jn 3:36, Eph. 2:3) humbled Himself (Phil. 2:8) in the fulness of time (Gal. 4:4), became human, and became our sinless substitute, our propitiation (1 Jn 2:2), our sin-bearer, and appeased the wrath of the Father for us (Rom. 5:9). The Lord Jesus Christ has made a new and living way (Heb. 10:20) for us to boldly approach the throne of grace (Heb. 4:16). We can come for cleansing (1 Jn 1:9), pardon (Ps. 82:1), forgiveness (Eph. 1:7), redemption (Col. 1:14), counsel (Isa. 9:6-7), and any support we need because the Lord Jesus Christ is sufficient for anything we face (2 Pe. 1:3).

**Questions for self-reflection:**

(1) How have you seen that the Lord has been your support when you have faced different calamities during your pilgrimage?
(2) Do you have examples of how the Lord has supported you in your trials such that you could share your examples of the Lord's support and be an encouragement to someone who may need encouragement?
(3) Does it bring your comfort to know that Christ gave you access to His Father and His Father is your Father?
(4) Where do people who do not know the Lord go for support for their troubles? Why are those sources of relief insufficient compared to the Lord?

**18:19. He also brought me out into a broad place; He delivered me because He delighted in me.**

---

This verse is almost a verbatim quote of 2 Samuel 22:20. Heaven is a place with many rooms (Jn 14:2) and is the dwelling place of God. Jesus, God the Son, and God the Father shared the same real estate before the incarnation and after the ascension. Heaven is the place to which the psalmist refers when he refers to the **broad place**. To save sinners, Christ left heaven, and after finishing the work He was sent to do, He returned to heaven, having prepared a place for us (Jn 14:2). The place is narrow enough to only have room for all those who have placed personal repentant faith in the Lord Jesus Christ (Matt. 7:13). But it is broad enough to fit a whole multitude who have washed their robes in the blood of the Lamb (Rev. 22:14). All those who have ever died as believers continue to reside there now. They will return with their Lord at the end of the age (Rev. 19:14).

God **delivered** David because David made God the source of his trust (Acts 13:22). The Lord Jesus Christ made the Father His **delight** as well and said He came to do the Father's will (Jn 4:34), only those things that please Him (Jn 8:29). The church, those who have come to God by faith in Christ, are likewise objects of God's delight. He proved this by sending Christ to die for and deliver everyone who is saved (Rom. 5:8). Now the Trinity works on behalf of every believer (Eph. 1:4, Jn 3:16, Jn 16:13, Rom. 8:2).

In return, believers can delight themselves in the Lord and can know that the Lord will give them the desires of their hearts (Ps. 37:4). When believers delight themselves in the Lord, it is the Lord that becomes the supreme desire of their hearts. As believers abide more in the Lord, the Lord abides more in them (Jn 15:1-8). They then enjoy a rich relationship based upon the finished work of the Lord Jesus Christ, who died to make the relationship possible.

---

**Questions for self-reflection:**

(1) When you think about what had to happen for you to receive access to heaven, do you respond with worship, or have you heard it so much that it has become commonplace for you?

(2) Are you heavenly-minded enough to be content if this was your last day on earth, or do you think that you would be sad if you had to leave someone or something behind?

(3) As a believer, God delights in you. Does that excite you? Does that make you want to live more robustly for Him? Does the fact that God delights in you cause you to think any differently about your life now? Do you want to show Him that you delight in Him?

(4) Would the people who know you best say that you delight yourself in the Lord?

**18:20. The Lord rewarded me according to my righteousness; According to the cleanness of my hands He has recompensed me.**

---

This verse is almost a verbatim quote of 2 Samuel 22:21. David had no personal **righteousness** of his own that **the Lord** would recognize as worth rewarding (Rom. 3:20, Ti 3:5). Even man's most noble works are mixed with sin. Sin mars fellowship with God. Man wrecks his righteousness with his conscious choice to sin (Jas 2:10). Man's sin ensures that man's righteousness amounts to nothing more than filthy rags (Isa. 64:6). Man's sin makes him unholy. Since God is holy (Isa. 6:3), since man is unholy, unholy man cannot see the holy Lord without God's help (Heb. 12:14). Sin must be atoned for so man can access God. The only righteousness that garners God's approval is the imputed righteousness of the Lord Jesus Christ (Rom. 3:22). Those who place repentant faith in the Lord Jesus Christ alone for salvation are **rewarded** with pardon (Isa. 55:7), forgiveness (Eph. 1:7), redemption (Col. 1:14), and obtain the righteousness of Christ imputed to their account (Rom. 4:5) that enables them to enter into God's presence. The righteousness that the Lord rewarded in David had to be imputed righteousness that, before Christ came the first time, looked forward to the coming One and since Christ came, looks back to His finished work.

Man's righteousness could never be meritorious for man's salvation because all of man's works are affected by his fallen nature due to man's sinfulness (Isa. 64:6). David's **hands** had no actual inherent **cleanness**. Therefore, the righteousness for which David was **recompensed** had to be innocence before his enemies in the sense that David's enemies wanted to harm him even though David had done them no wrong. This is much like Christ Himself, who was the object of hatred by the religious rulers of His day even though the Sinless One had perpetrated no wrong against them (Jn 8:40. Jn 10:32).

Saul pursued David. David had not wronged Saul in a way that warranted Saul's seeking to kill David. God rewarded David's gentle treatment of Saul despite Saul's vengeful treatment of

David by prospering David's kingdom (1 Sam. 18:14, Matt. 5:9, Matt. 5:44, Rom. 12:14, Rom. 12:17-18). Christ was the best possible picture of such treatment. Where David did have a sinful nature and did commit sin (e.g., 2 Sam. 11) mixed with all his righteous deeds, Christ did not commit sin (1 Pet. 2:22) because, as God, He did not have a sin nature with which to commit sin, even though He could be tempted like us (Heb. 4:15).

While David did prosper because of his kindness toward Saul and others, the ultimate rewards David received could be given by God based on God reckoning David righteous by faith (Gen. 15:6). David's hands were in no way clean. He was such a bloody man that God would not let David build the temple (1 Chron. 17, 1 Chron. 28:3). Nevertheless, David was faithful to what God had called him to do. His offspring, Solomon, would be the one who would get to build God a house. The two of them would look forward to the perfect One, the Lord Jesus Christ, who would make the everlasting temple of God (1 Cor. 6:19) when He would die on the cross for the sins of the world so that all who place repentant faith in Him would become part of that temple. Nothing in us is worth trusting in to receive righteousness from God. We must fully, wholly trust in Christ's finished work on our behalf since our hands are not clean.

## Questions for self-reflection:

(1) What personal righteousness do you possess that the Lord would deem to be worthy of rewarding?
(2) Are you looking at Christ's finished work to save you, or are you looking at someone or something else?
(3) Do you know anyone who is trusting in someone or something other than Christ alone for salvation? What can you do to point them to the Savior?

**18:21. For I have kept the ways of the Lord, And have not wickedly departed from my God.**

---

This verse is almost a verbatim quote of 2 Samuel 22:22. Obedience to God's revealed will marked the psalmist's life. God's Word permanently records the Lord's ways for us. Obedience to God's Word is a distinguishing characteristic of genuine believers (Matt. 7:21-23, Jn 14:15, Jn 14:21, Jn 14:23-24, Jn 15:10, Jas 1:22, 1 Jn 2:3-5, 1 Jn 2:29, 1 Jn 3:7, 1 Jn 3:24, 1 John 5:3). The believer's obedience is always an imperfect obedience because, even for believers, there will always be a war between the flesh and the Spirit (Gal. 5:17). Lies from the enemy (Jn 8:44, 2 Cor. 11:3, Rev. 12:9) will try to enter that the Spirit will need to actively rebuke (Jas 4:7). Sinful believers have to daily go to the throne of grace for mercy (Heb. 4:16). The Lord Jesus Christ, the spotless Lamb of God (Jn 1:29, 1 Pet. 1:19), became sin for us and knew no sin (2 Cor. 5:21). He bore our sins in His body on the tree to bring us to God (1 Pet. 2:24). Jesus humbled Himself (Phil. 2:8) by coming down from heaven to show us the way (Jn 14:6) since we had chosen all sorts of ways of perversion. When Jesus had finished purging our sins (Heb. 1:3), He sat down at the right hand of the Majesty on high, and now ever lives to intercede for us (Heb. 7:25).

Christ perfectly **kept the ways of the Lord and never wickedly departed from God** as we all do. We all wickedly depart from God. We fail to believe what God has said. We fail to do as God has said. We are fraught with iniquity. Even unintentional or ignorant sins separate from God. Unlike us, who often live to please ourselves, the Lord Jesus Christ always did what pleased His Father (Jn 8:29). Only He can be our merciful High Priest (Heb. 2:17). He satisfied God's requirement for perfection (Jn 17:4), being fully God Himself (Phil. 2:6), and perfectly substituted for mankind (2 Cor. 5:21) who needed perfection of holiness to see God (Heb. 12:14). The psalmist could not truthfully say that he never wickedly departed from God. Like all born since Adam except for Christ, the psalmist had a sinful nature and committed plenty of sins worthy of death and judgment (Rom. 3:9-23). The psalmist had to look forward, by faith, to the sacrifice of God's promised Messiah.

Instead of looking to ourselves, the writer and the reader must look back to the promised Messiah (Hebrews 12:2). His sinlessly perfect life, which we could never live, and His death in our place, commended in love toward us (Rom. 5:8), are the only sufficient means to cover our multitude of sins (1 Pet. 4:8). To look at anyone or anything else is to miss Christ altogether. Christ never sinfully departed from His service to His Father. Presently, He continues to be our Advocate (1 Jn 2:1) and Intercessor. Therefore, since we are more like the psalmist than the Son, the sinless Son is worthy of our complete trust.

## Questions for self-reflection:

(1) Would the people who know you best agree that you strive, albeit imperfectly, to keep the ways of the Lord?
(2) Why do you associate with the Lord? Is it only to avoid eternal judgment? Is it because He is worthy of your worship? Another reason?
(3) In what ways have you wickedly departed from God today? This week? Last week?
(4) Since we keep wickedly departing from the Lord, are we better off trusting in Christ?

**18:22. For all His judgments were before me, And I did not put away His statutes from me.**

---

This verse is almost a verbatim quote of 2 Samuel 22:23. As king, David became intimately familiar with God's law (2 Sam. 23:3, 2 Chron. 19:6, Ps. 2:10, Prov. 16:12, Prov. 20:28, Prov. 29:14) because he needed to be able to faithfully apply it in the lives of the people over which he ruled (Jas 1:25). For Solomon, David's son, this became a recurring theme in his inspired writings (Prov. 19:8, Eccles. 2:13). David delighted after God's Law (Ps. 19:7-11), as did Jesus (e.g., Matt. 4:4, Matt. 4:7, Matt. 4:10), as did the New Testament writers (Rom. 7:12). These writers knew there was no higher standard because God's Word came directly from God Himself by inspiration (2 Tim. 3:16). There is no higher authority than God since God appoints all earthly authorities (Dan. 2:21, Rom. 13:1). God's Word should be the highest form of authority in the lives of everyone. But since not everyone believes, God's Word, at the very least, should be the highest form of authority in the lives of all believers. Since the Word comes from God, and God gives the Holy Spirit to all believers at the time of salvation, the believer's Holy Spirit leads them into all truth (Jn 16:13), the truth that is consistent with the teaching of Scripture.

As believers consistently renew their minds in God's Word, believers become more sensitive to God's will for their lives and become transformed into Christ's image (Rom. 12:2). The disciple becomes more like his Master the more time he spends with his Master (Lk 6:40). Christians spend time with Christ in prayer and in the Word. It begins to dwell in them richly. They speak it to themselves. They speak it to others (Col. 3:16). They even sing it. It becomes a part of their being. They live it out. Living out the Word is a mark of godly wisdom, wisdom from above (Jas 1:5, Jas 1:22). Christ is the example for believers to follow (1 Pet. 1:21). Believers will never live up to the perfect standard that Christ set. Since Christ continually intercedes for them (Heb. 7:25), they do not have to be perfect. Christ was perfect for them. All the

---

condemnation that would be theirs for their unbelief (Jn 3:19), Christ took for them (Rom. 8:1).

God's perfect **judgments** were ever **before** Christ. Christ did everything that the Father sent Him to do (Jn 17:4). God's Law, His **statutes**, were perfectly carried out by Christ since the believer could never perfectly fulfill them (Matt. 5:17-18). Christ perfectly accomplished taking the death that everyone deserves because of their sin when He, the spotless Lamb of God (Jn 1:32), became sin for us (2 Cor. 5:21) because of the great love with which He loves us (Eph. 2:4). He executed everything necessary for our salvation. Christ perfectly kept the law that nobody can keep.

David kept the law as much as was possible for him to do. However, David's obedience still had its moments where it mixed with his indwelling sinfulness. This inconsistency happened since David was fully human, though not divine, and, therefore, had a sinful nature. Christ, on the other hand, while fully human, like David, and like the rest of us, unlike David, Christ is fully divine (Philippians 2:6). As God, Christ had no sinful nature. That is why as our merciful High Priest, He could experience temptation as we do yet without sin (Hebrews 4:15). That is why Christ can substitute for us (Heb. 9:28). As fully human, Christ perfectly took the place of sinful humanity and lived the perfect life for us that we could never live (1 Pet. 2:22, Rom. 3:23). As fully God, Christ perfectly satisfied God's requirement for perfection.

By faith in Christ's perfect sacrifice on their behalf, all believers in the person and work of the Lord Jesus Christ receive Christ's righteousness imputed to their accounts, and Christ gets their sin imputed to His account (Rom. 4:5). They become partakers of the divine nature (2 Pet. 1:4) and inherit every spiritual blessing (Eph. 1:3). By faith, God puts His Spirit within them (Ezek. 36:26). The law written on their hearts (Rom. 2:15) is lived out in them as they love their neighbor as themselves (Mk 12:31). Christ destroyed the penalty that lawbreaking warrants so that the end of this life is not the end for all believers. Because of Christ, believers have eternity to look forward to in the presence of God.

**Questions for self-reflection:**

(1) Are the Lord's judgments before you such that you make a concerted effort to order your life after them?

(2) Is it apparent to those who know you best that your primary desire is to live in such a manner as to be pleasing to the Lord?

(3) How can believers know that they are being led by God's Spirit and God's Law rather than by man's?

(4) As a Christian, what is your attitude toward the Lord's judgments and statutes as found in the Bible? Do you think that the Lord would find your attitude toward Him and His Word to be generally pleasing?

**18:23. I was also blameless before Him, And I kept myself from my iniquity.**

---

This verse is almost a verbatim quote of 2 Samuel 22:24. David lived in such a way that he **was blameless before** the Lord for all practical purposes. David was not wholly free from sin at any point during his life (e.g., 2 Sam. 11). Scripture is clear that the war between the flesh and the Spirit continues until the final breath (Gal. 5:17). However, David had lived in such a way that there was no heinous act that would disqualify him from his divine appointment after the incident with Bathsheba.

While all believers should not make sinless perfection their goal (it is impossible), they should strive to be growing closer to their Lord (2 Pet. 3:18). One way in which growing closer to the Lord happens is by renouncing known sin when it makes its entrance (Col. 3:8-10). As believers take whatever measures necessary to be cleansed from sin (Matt. 5:29-30), they will grow spiritually into the type of person that God calls them to be. Others might not like them, especially unbelievers, when they confront sin in their own lives that the vast majority condones and embraces (Matt. 5:10-12). However, being a disciple of Christ is not a means to win a popularity contest. Instead, it is a daily call to deny oneself and take up one's own cross (Lk 9:23). It is a call to separation from the world and its lusts and separation unto Christ (1 Jn 2:15-17). It is a call to personal holiness (Heb. 12:14) and a life of growth into being a servant (Jn 13:12-17, Eph. 5:25, Phil. 2:7) who becomes more and more like his Master as time elapses.

As the believer's walk takes on more of this 'blameless' characteristic, as the believer takes measures to be **kept from iniquity**, the more they become like Christ. Having applied the text to the fully human David, there is also an application to God the Son, the Lord Jesus Christ. The Lord Jesus, since He had no sin nature, was blameless before the Father (1 Pet. 2:22), Him who sent the Son into the world (Gal. 4:4-5) to be the propitiation for our sins (1 Jn 2:2). While Christ was tempted in every way like we are, yet He kept Himself from iniquity (Heb. 4:15). David tried to separate from sin, from his iniquity. David was imperfect at doing so. Christ, on the other hand, our perfect Substitute, was perfect at keeping Himself from iniquity. He is the only adequate provision for covering our sins. He is completely righteous.

## Questions for self-reflection:

(1) If believers are to strive to grow closer to the Lord, what are the best ways to do that?

(2) If believers consistently deny themselves and separate from the world, should they expect the world to appreciate believers doing that, or should believers expect the world to mock and persecute them?

**18:24. Therefore the Lord has recompensed me according to my righteousness, According to the cleanness of my hands in His sight.**

---

This verse is almost a verbatim quote of 2 Samuel 22:25. Even though the psalmist did not contain any **righteousness** of his own that he could bring to **the Lord** to earn himself favor with God (Gal. 2:16), the psalmist was righteous by faith (Rom. 4:5). The psalmist had the righteousness that makes people acceptable before God imputed to his account. Now, instead of having his past, present, and future sins held against him, God now showed mercy to the psalmist and accepted him in the beloved. He had received forgiveness, redemption, adoption, pardon, and the myriad other benefits that belong to all those who trust in Christ alone for salvation (Eph. 1:3-14).

Even though we look back to the cross to receive these benefits while the psalmist looked forward to the cross to receive these benefits, all who believe receive the benefits because the righteousness is obtained by faith and not works (Gal. 2:16). With such righteousness imputed to sinners' accounts, even though our **hands** are not truly **clean** in God's sight when God the Father looks at us, God the Father sees Christ's perfect righteousness, not our sin. Christ's righteousness allows God to **recompense** sinners with eternal life rather than punish them with eternal condemnation.

## Questions for self-reflection:

(1) What righteousness did the psalmist possess that could earn him favor with God?
(2) Apart from Christ, what does our righteousness get us? What can we earn ourselves apart from Christ?
(3) As a believer, now that God has recompensed you with His righteousness through your faith in Christ, does that make you want to sit back and wait for when God brings you to eternity

or does it make you want to live in such a manner to show others that this righteousness is available to them as well?

(4) Would you be concerned about someone who said that God had justified them and that after their supposed justification, they just sat back and lived a life that was just as immoral as before they claimed justification?

**18:25. With the merciful You will show Yourself merciful; With a blameless man You will show Yourself blameless;**

---

This verse is almost a verbatim quote of 2 Samuel 22:26. The **merciful** person is merciful to others primarily because they realize that the God of the universe has shown them immeasurable and undeserved mercy. They have offended this God due to their sin (Matt. 5:7, Rom. 3:9-23). The merciful person realizes their unholy condition and that without holiness, they cannot expect to see the Lord (Heb. 12:14). They recognize that one of the pieces of evidence showing that God has forgiven them is that they extend that forgiveness to others since what others do to wrong them pales in comparison to how they wronged God by their own sin (Matt. 6:14-15, Matt. 18:21-35). The merciful person realizes that God has been immeasurably gracious and forgiving with them and that, as a result, the least they can do is be gracious and forgiving to others.

The longer one is in a relationship with God, the more aware they become of the grace that God has shown them. They begin to take less and less for granted. They see God's hand at work more and more in what happens around them and to them. They appreciate that even the 'bad' that happens to them is still a tool that a gracious heavenly Father has in His toolbox to help His sheep see things from a more proper perspective (2 Cor. 12, Heb. 12:3-11, Jas 1:2-8). Since God has been infinitely merciful to us to send Christ at the fulness of time (Gal. 4:4-5) so that we can share in the grace that saves, extending a form of that grace to others by being merciful and forgiving to them should be a natural outflow from the life of a believer.

Christ's ministry was a constant visual reminder of God's mercy. All those Christ healed, raised from the dead, fed, and ministered to all received extensions of God's mercy. Christ was a constant doer of good because His Father is a doer of good. God's goodness leads men to repentance (Rom. 2:5). Christ came forth into the world because God is a God of mercy. God didn't want anyone to perish but wanted all to come to repentance

(2 Pet. 3:9). God sent Christ to the earth when we were dead in trespasses and sins to raise us from spiritual death and give us spiritual life (Eph. 2:1-5). The mercy that we do not deserve was poured out abundantly on us when God poured His wrath out abundantly upon Christ. Instead of getting the wrath that our sins deserve, Christ took the wrath in our place so that we could receive mercy instead of wrath (Rom. 5:9).

Nobody, not even saved people, is **blameless** in the word's plainest sense (1 Jn 1:8-10). Everyone sins; even saved people sin after their salvation. Saved people, generally speaking, are more sensitive to their sin and more readily go to the merciful High Priest to make right what sin has made wrong (Heb. 4:14-16). When the blameless person walks in the Spirit and not in the flesh (Gal. 5:16), they show the power of God in their lives such that all attempts at explaining their changed lives in natural, non-spiritual terms are woefully inadequate. The most logical explanation for the new nature (2 Cor. 5:17) is the amazing grace of the merciful Father who loved him so much that He gave His only begotten Son for him (Jn 3:16). By their changed lives, saved people display that God powerfully keeps His own by the power of His Word (1 Pet. 1:3-5). When the saved live like they should (Matt. 5:16, Ti 2:14), they commend the gospel to the lost, and perhaps, God's grace can shine and open the eyes of the blind so the dead in trespasses and sins can sense God's rich mercy, and they will turn to the Lord who can abundantly pardon (Isa. 55:7).

## Questions for self-reflection:

(1) How has God shown Himself merciful to you today?
(2) How can you show someone who does not know God that God is merciful?
(3) How has your understanding of God's mercy changed and improved since you first believed?
(4) How could you become more sensitive to your sins?
(5) How is your life a demonstration of God's power?

**18:26. With the pure You will show Yourself pure; And with the devious You will show Yourself shrewd.**

---

This verse is almost a verbatim quote of 2 Samuel 22:27. Before coming to Christ, everyone is in a state of pollution before God (Isa. 64:4, Rom. 3:23). Nobody starts pure before God. By the early exercise of their sinful nature, they show the cleansing blood of Christ has not purified them (Heb. 9:14, 1 Jn 1:7). Sin still pollutes their thoughts, words, and actions (Isa. 6:5, Isa. 64:6, Matt. 15:19-20).

Once a sinner humbly turns from sin and self to the only Savior, the Lord Jesus Christ, for pardon (Eph. 1:7), for reconciliation with God (2 Cor. 5:18), for redemption (Col. 1:14), and for forgiveness (Eph. 1:7), they are **pure** before God (Jas 4:8). The blood of the Lamb washes such repentant sinners (1 Cor. 6:11, Rev. 7:14). While they are not pure in the sense of sinless perfection, they are pure at least positionally before God as God, because of Christ, has declared them to be not guilty (Rom. 3:24). Christ has become their sin-bearer (1 Pet. 2:24). They have become justified freely by Christ's grace.

These sinners that have been justified by grace live by the Spirit (Rom. 8:14) and walk in the newness of life (Rom. 6:4). They lean on God's ways. God shows Himself to be pure to them as He abides in them as they abide in Him (Jn 15:1-8). God becomes the object of their worship and devotion. His commands are not burdensome to the saved like they are burdensome to the lost (1 Jn 5:3). Instead, God's commands become a treasure to the saved (Ps. 19:10-11, Ps. 119:72, Ps. 119:127, Ps. 119:162).

While the saved realize that their works do not save them (Ephesians 2:8-9), they understand that their spiritual strength to withstand anything that comes their way is related to their level of obedience to God's revealed will. God fills people who pursue Him with His presence (Eph. 2:10). As God fills believers with more and more of His presence, the more that they pursue Him, the more they will love what He loves and hate what He hates (1 Jn 1:7). As a result, the lifestyles of the saved will become more like

Him; they will become purer (Rom. 8:29). Jesus said that the pure in heart would see God (Matt. 5:8). They will begin to live more like He calls them to live as they pursue His will for their lives. When God imputes His righteousness by faith to the repentant sinner (Phil. 3:9, Heb. 11:7), the sinner begins a lifetime of being conformed to the image of Christ.

Those who are **devious** in the sense that they are against God, in contrast to the pure, will find that God is opposed to them (Jas 4:6). The devious look for ways to deviously undermine God and His people to their own advantage. God's people, even before Christ, and also since Christ, have been on the receiving end of opposition that sometimes took on violent forms and even death in some circumstances (2 Tim. 3:12). As the lifestyles of the righteous actively confront the sin of the culture in which they live, it is reasonable that the righteous receive harsh treatment at the hands of those who oppose Christ. The devious will exhibit that, as much as they are against God, God is also against them. The more they live like He does not matter to them, the more God will abandon them to their sinful choices, and the day of grace will pass (Rom. 1:18-32). When lost people encounter righteous people during their course of business, a marked difference between the children of the devil and the children of the God of heaven will pervade. One group walks in the light while the other group walks in darkness. Even if members from both groups name the name of Christ, the lifestyles will show who is authentic and who is counterfeit. When sin comes to the surface (and it will in both groups), the way that sin is handled will be different, depending on which group to which the sinner belongs. If the sinner belongs to the Savior, they will deal with their sin to bring peace between God and man, whereas if the sinner does not belong to the Savior, they will be more focused on self-preservation rather than peace with God and man.

**Questions for self-reflection:**

(1) How has God shown Himself pure to you today?
(2) In what ways were you impure before God before your justification?
(3) Today, in what ways have you demonstrated that many of your ways continue to be impure before God?
(4) Are God's commands burdensome to you?
(5) Is your lifestyle becoming purer?
(6) When you see the lifestyle of the devious, do you long for the freedom to join the devious in their lifestyle but feel like you cannot because you have named the name of Christ?
(7) How do you decide if indwelling sin is merely a "struggle" or if it controls you? Would God choose the same way as you have?

**18:27. For You will save the humble people, But will bring down haughty looks.**

---

This verse is almost a verbatim quote of 2 Samuel 22:28. Commonly, Scripture refers to the saved as **the humble**, while Scripture refers to the lost as prideful or haughty. The humble, the saved, are often afflicted by various issues in their life. Some of it is their own indwelling sin (1 Jn 1:8-10). Some of it is persecution from unbelievers (2 Tim. 3:12). Some of it is trials of various kinds that do not have to do with religion. Some of them are health, work-related matters, or family-related matters. Almost anything can fall into the category of a trial.

No matter what it is, the believer is responsible for handling it with joy and patience (Jas 1:2-8). Even if the adverse circumstances never end in this life, the excellent news for the saved, for the humble, is that one day they will be with their Lord (2 Cor. 5:8). Those who endure receive the crown of life (Matt. 24:13, Jas 1:12). They can trust that God will ultimately **save** them from all their distresses because, even if they never get deliverance in this life, since they belong to God through Christ, they will one day be in heaven where there will be no more sorrow or tears (Rev. 21:3-4). Trials and afflictions bring sorrow and tears even to the strongest in the faith. God does not promise to remove the trial from the saved. God promises to be with the saved in the trial like God was with the men in the fiery furnace (Dan. 3). His grace is sufficient for them (2 Cor. 12:9). The prideful, the **haughty** who resist God will experience the day when God will **bring down** their rebellion to the grave and the judgment after that (Heb. 9:27). God did not force the haughty to pick their rebellion. They chose their rebellion themselves. They showed they loved the world more than they loved the Lord who made them (Jas 4:4), making themselves an enemy of God. Before the day of death (nobody knows when their day is), humankind must humble themselves to escape God's judgment so that God will lift them up and they can then avoid the judgment that awaits the ungodly (1 Pet. 5:6).

---

## Questions for self-reflection:

(1) Are people that you regularly associate with generally humble?

(2) If people are not humble, could the entertainment people choose to entertain themselves with affect that? How so?

(3) Would a stranger conclude that you love the world in an ungodly way?

(4) How do you demonstrate humility to others? (5) When you think about how Christ humbled Himself for your justification, does that motivate you to walk humbly before your God?

**18:28. For You will light my lamp; The Lord my God will enlighten my darkness.**

---

This verse is almost a verbatim quote of 2 Samuel 22:29. The Lord Jesus Christ enlightens His disciples by grace (Jn 8:12). The **light** of the glorious gospel shines in their hearts (2 Cor. 4:4). It provides light to every aspect of their lives. The gospel brings every thought captive to the obedience of Christ. The Word lights their path (Ps. 119:105). Christ's followers hide His law in their hearts that they might not sin against Him (Ps. 119:11). The Holy Spirit is the continuous oil/light that leads believers into all truth (Matt. 25:1-13, Jn 16:13) that enables believers to be doers of God's will (Matt. 7:21). The Lord Jesus Christ, when he hung on the cross and died, was in **darkness**. When he rose from the dead, God **enlighten**ed the darkness of His death. Now, all those who come to faith in Him have the light of life (Jn 8:12). They are translated from the kingdom of darkness into the kingdom of the Son (Col. 1:13). Specifically for the psalmist, David, God prospered his kingdom. God blessed David spiritually with His presence.

**Questions for self-reflection:**

---

(1) If you are justified before the Lord, if He has saved you, He has lit your lamp. What has changed for you since He has lit your lamp?

(2) How have you learned about the darkness that was in your own heart prior to the Lord shedding the light of the glorious gospel on your heart?

(3) Does the light that was not previously in you but is currently in you motivate you to show others the light so that they too may experience it for themselves?

**18:29. For by You I can run against a troop, By my God I can leap over a wall.**

---

This verse is almost a verbatim quote of 2 Samuel 22:30. With God's help, David overcame his enemies, such as Saul (1 Sam. 24) and the Amalekites (1 Sam. 30). With help from the same God that helped David, the Lord Jesus Christ was able to triumph over death (Acts 2:24) and the evil forces led by Satan (i.e., the Pharisees) when He fulfilled the Father's plan in dying as our substitute and rising again. In doing so, He made a public spectacle of the principalities and powers of the demonic realm (Col. 2:15).

David knew that with God's help, he could **leap over a wall** to defeat any obstacle that stood in his way. He knew that God would protect him for as long as it was God's will to preserve him. The Lord Jesus Christ broke down the wall that the law and our sin created between us and God the Father when He died on the cross to pay the penalty for our sins (Eph. 2:14). By the power of the Holy Spirit, all believers have access to the Father (Eph. 2:18). Believers can overcome any spiritual obstacle by tapping into the spiritual power that is theirs through faith in Christ.

### Questions for self-reflection:

(1) Since your conversion, practically speaking, how has Christ helped you overcome your enemies?

(2) Do you look forward to being freed from the sinful flesh that wars against the Spirit or do you want to stay here as long as you can so you can enjoy as much as you can?

(3) In Christ, now you can leap over the wall that your sins built, and you can run for the prize of godliness. Do you have any interest in doing that? What would that look like if you were to do that?

**18:30. As for God, His way is perfect; The word of the Lord is proven; He is a shield to all who trust in Him.**

---

This verse is almost a verbatim quote of 2 Samuel 22:31. God's **way is perfect** because His being is without sin (1 Jn 1:5). When **God** causes or allows things to happen in the lives of the wicked, whatever God does allow to happen to them, it is right for God to allow it. Likewise, when God causes or allows things to happen in the lives of the righteous, whatever God does allow to happen to them, it is right for God to allow it (Rom. 8:28). There is nothing wrong with what God chooses to do or not do. Just because sinful man fails to understand all that God does, why God does it, and when God does it, it never means that God is wrong to do what He does. Everything that God causes or permits to happen is in some way reflective of His attributes. Nothing that God allows or causes to happen contrasts Who He is. God can only act in ways that are consistent with His nature.

God has chosen to reveal Himself to people, those created in His image, through creation (Rom. 1:20), conscience (Rom. 2:15), and Christ (Heb. 1:2). We learn about each of those through His Word. His Word is proven to be true. As humanity discovers more about how the world works, the Bible, though not exhaustively yet sufficiently, sheds light on much that the world has discovered and will discover. As science discovers new things, some of those things are in the Bible, showing that **the word of the Lord is proven**. If human philosophy contradicts what Scripture plainly teaches, philosophy, not Scripture, must be rejected. Christ came to fulfill that Word, those things that foretold of His first coming (Matt. 5:17). Christ will come again to accomplish the things that tell of His second coming. Between the first coming and the second coming, His people are responsible for obeying Him (2 Cor. 10:5). Christ overcame the world and the wicked one when He died as man's substitute. He protects and preserves the sheep until their final breath when eternal life for them begins. As the fiery darts come on the sheep, the Son is the shield that protects them from fatal blows. Satan and man have the power to kill the body (Matt. 10:28, Jn 10:10). God preserves the soul of the saints (Ps. 97:10) and ensures that none perish (Jn 10:28). The saints must **trust** the Lord that He will keep them until the end (1 Pet. 1:5). As believers entrust themselves to Him, the Lord protects them from Satan and the means that the wicked one employs (Eph. 6:16).

## Questions for self-reflection:

(1) When you go through difficult trials, do you doubt that God's way is perfect?
(2) How has the Lord proven His Word to you?
(3) How has the Lord rewarded you for trusting Him?
(4) How can we interpret the world through the lens of Scripture and not the lens of man's philosophy?

## 18:31. For who is God, except the Lord? And who is a rock, except our God?

This verse is almost a verbatim quote of 2 Samuel 22:32. There is but one God (Deut. 6:4). There are plenty of imitations, but none of the representations is the real thing. People from the beginning have tried unsuccessfully to fill their lives with temporal things that can never permanently satisfy the hungry soul. The things of the world that come in various shapes and sizes are woefully inadequate. The gods that the heathen have attempted to make since the beginning fail to bring lasting peace. The gods that man in contemporary society tries to make fail to supply permanent comfort. The sad reality is that whenever we worship anything created, we make that thing into a god. Sometimes we don't even realize we do this. We do this with our jobs, our spouses, our children, our possessions. All of these are good things. But none of these good things should replace the Giver of every good and perfect gift (Jas 1:17). Only He is worthy of our worship. Unfortunately, we often mistake the gifts for the Giver of the gifts.

**God is** the immovable **rock** (1 Cor. 10:4). He does not change (Mal. 3:6). He is the shelter from the storm (Isa. 25:4). He is the protection from the wrath to come (Matt. 3:7). All false gods are not immovable like the one true God. All three persons share the exact attributes. What is true of the Father is true of the Son is true of the Spirit because they are all the same one God (Deut. 6:4). No other gods can be trusted for temporary life, provision for this life, or eternal life. God, who commands all to repent because He has appointed a day in which He will judge the world in righteousness (Acts 17:30-31), has provided His Son, the Lord Jesus Christ, as how alienated man (Col. 1:21) can have access by one Spirit to the Father (Eph. 2:18). Christ is worthy of our praise and worship.

**Questions for self-reflection:**

(1) When you think of biblical stories related to God being like a rock, what comes to mind?

(2) When you think of the characteristics of a literal, actual physical rock, what comes to mind? How is God like that?

(3) How has God shown Himself to be a rock for you? How has He been with you in the storms of life? How has He manifested Himself to you in the storms of life?

**18:32. It is God who arms me with strength, And makes my way perfect.**

---

This verse is almost a verbatim quote of 2 Samuel 22:33. God provides His people with physical **strength** and mental and spiritual strength to face anything that comes their way. He **arms** them with the armor to fight any spiritual foe (Eph. 6:10-20). Many earthly enemies also have mindsets that also make them spiritual foes. God the Father provided Christ, God the Son, with the strength to carry out God's will (Jn 14:31). God, the Holy Spirit, gives power to Christians to be doers of the Word (Eph. 3:7, Eph. 3:16).

God the Father made the **way** of Christ **perfect**. Christ did not sin (1 Pet. 2:22). He perfectly executed everything the Father asked of Him (Jn 17:4). Whatever He did prospered. Every obstacle that Christ encountered, He overcame in His perfect way. He won a perfect victory over His enemies, sin, death, Satan, and hell, on the cross, where He also made a public spectacle of His enemies (Col. 2:15).

David, the psalmist, could not say that his way was at any point in time perfect since David was like the rest of us in that he had a sinful nature that frequently got the better of his spirit (Gal. 5:17). In the inner man, David may have wanted to serve the law of God, but there were plenty of times where David served the law of sin and death (Rom. 7:21-23). The struggle with sin is real for any Christian. For all believers, God arms each of them with strength (Col. 1:11). He equips them with the armor of God (Eph. 6:10-20). He gives them the power to overcome any temptation with the way of escape that he has provided (1 Cor. 10:13).

While their way will be polluted by sin from time to time, ultimately, their way will be perfect because the Lord Jesus Christ, the Good Shepherd (John 10:14), has gone before them in perfection (Heb. 6:20). The Lord Jesus Christ's perfect life is the ideal substitute for sinful man. By faith in Him, the sinner's way is made perfect because the righteous Father looks at them and sees that the Son has made their way perfect (Rom. 12:2). They could never make their own ways perfect (Isa. 64:6, Rom. 3:23). Therefore, sinners must depend upon the Lord Jesus Christ to have His perfection imputed unto them (Rom. 5:1).

## Questions for self-reflection:

(1) For the believer, from where does the strength of God come?
(2) Can you name all the parts of the spiritual armor from Ephesians 6?
(3) Are you putting on the Ephesians 6 armor every day?
(4) How can you tell whether or not a philosophy is for God or against God?
(5) When you recognize you have been serving the law of sin and death rather than the law of Christ, how do you resume serving the law of Christ?
(6) When you are tempted to sin, how does God show you the way of escape from the temptation?

**18:33. He makes my feet like the feet of deer, And sets me on my high places.**

---

This verse is almost a verbatim quote of 2 Samuel 22:34. God specially designed **the feet of deer** to dash to or from a destination. Deer feet allow them to exit from danger as quickly as they enter it. The psalmist here praises the Lord because the Lord allows him to run from danger to safety. God allows His spiritual offspring to remind themselves of His ways as revealed by His Word, as they hide His Word in their hearts that they might not sin against Him (Ps. 119:11). He enables them to practice the fear of the Lord, to demonstrate wisdom. They show this by successfully applying the Word to the life (Prov. 1:7, Matt. 7:21-23, Jas 1:5, Jas 1:22).

Christ did what the Father asked Him, only what pleased the Father (Jn 8:29, Jn 17:4). Since He perfectly pleased the Father, He is an adequate Shepherd (Jn 10:11) to help the sheep be doers of the Word and not hearers only (Jas 1:22). He can help them do the will of God.

God **sets** His people in safety from their enemies according to His will. He protects them physically as long that is His will. Even if it does not end up being His will for physical protection, the Lord does preserve His saints (Prov 2:8) such that none that genuinely believe will perish (Jn 10:28-29), but all genuine believers will enjoy eternal life.

In Christ, genuine believers are seated in heavenly places (Eph. 2:6). Their eternal life, in one sense, is already fixed. He who began the good work will complete it (Phil. 1:6). But, from their born-again date until their final breath, they are responsible for working out their own salvation, trusting that God works in them (Phil. 2:12-13). Christ was able to quickly get away from danger when it was God's will for Him to be able to do so (Jn 10:39).

When it was time for Christ to die, after Christ's humiliation, Christ was exalted to the Father's right hand (Phi. 2:8-9). He remains there on the **high places** of heaven ever living to intercede for the saints (Heb. 7:25). Christ now has the name above

---

all principalities and powers, above every name (Eph. 1:21), Lord, to the glory of God the Father (Phil. 2:11). Our responsibility is to praise Him for who He is and submit to His Lordship in light of who He is and what He has done for us.

## Questions for self-reflection:

(1) Do deer run sloppily or skillfully?
(2) Do deer run slowly or quickly?
(3) How are you at recognizing danger before it is too late?
(4) If you could be better at recognizing danger before it is too late, how would you become better at doing so?
(5) Is it enough to just be better at recognizing potentially sinful situations, or must we also be able to react to them?

**18:34. He teaches my hands to make war, So that my arms can bend a bow of bronze.**

---

This verse is almost a verbatim quote of 2 Samuel 22:35. Christ teaches the sheep to use their **hands to make war** by putting on the whole armor of God (Eph. 6:10-20). Even when believers are up against physical foes, they need to put their spiritual resources to good use. The gospel is good news to those who apply it to their lives. It is not good news to those who know it in their heads but fail to apply it to their hearts. The primary war that entangles Christians is spiritual (Rom. 7:13-25, 2 Cor. 10:4-5, Gal. 5:17, 2 Tim. 2:3-4, 1 Pet. 5:8-9). Their spirit wars against their flesh (Gal. 5:17). When they take the armor that is theirs, they can fight off any enemy that comes in any form that it comes (1 Cor. 10:13). When believers arm themselves with God's wisdom, they can respond to any situation in a God-honoring way (Jas 3:17-18).

Christ made perfect war against enemy forces, all of which are led by Satan. When Christ faced temptation in the wilderness (Matt. 4:1-11, Lk 4:1-13), He used God's perfect Word to overcome each assault on His person and work. Additionally, he used God's perfect Word to correct misconceptions of His time about God's Word. Believers can use the same Word to counteract enemy philosophies and should do so to cast down any imaginations that exalt themselves against Christ (2 Cor. 10:3-5). When Christians put on the armor of God, they equip themselves with God's arsenal with which they have so much spiritual strength. It is as if they **can bend a bow of bronze** (figuratively speaking).

A Spirit-filled Christian experiences spiritual victory that gives them confidence in any situation. They can have such confidence because they know that no matter the obstacle, since the God of the universe is on their side, they have nothing to fear (Ps. 118:6). They know that they do not go into battle alone. Though they cannot see Him, the Angel of the Lord goes with them against their enemies (Exod. 23:20-23). Christ is the example that we should follow His steps (1 Pet. 2:21). When Christ was tempted in the wilderness, He used the sword of the Spirit (Eph. 6:17) to overcome Satan's temptations (Matt. 4:1-11). The serpent's head was bruised (Gen. 3:15) at Calvary, where Christ defeated sin, death, and hell forever. Believers can walk in that victory now (Rom. 6). They will experience ultimate triumph on the other side of the grave (1 Cor. 15:20-28, 1 Cor. 15:50-57).

## Questions for self-reflection:

(1) In what war are believers involved? Who is the believer's enemy? Who is the believer's general?
(2) How did Christ overcome the devil's temptation? Has that tactic been helpful to you?
(3) How does it feel, realizing that the God of the entire universe is on your side no matter what you face?

**18:35. You have also given me the shield of Your salvation; Your right hand has held me up, Your gentleness has made me great.**

---

This verse is almost a verbatim quote of 2 Samuel 22:36. A **shield** protects a soldier when a soldier is in a war against a formidable foe. The shield protects the soldier from whatever the enemy is shooting at them. It is a means of defense. The psalmist could have been in a literal war against a physical foe. The Lord could have intervened on his behalf with physical deliverance from a near-death experience, as was the case with David and Goliath. So, likewise, was the case for Israel when they were bitten and had to look at the serpent for deliverance (Num. 21:4-9, cf. Jn 3:14). The serpent was the means the Lord used to deliver the people.

The contemporary believer is involved in a spiritual war with the forces of darkness (Eph. 6:12) headed up by that serpent of old (Rev. 12:9), the roaring lion (1 Pet. 5:8), the father of lies (Jn 8:44), the accuser of the brethren (Rev. 12:10), Satan. Satan is the invisible force behind everything that is against God. To counteract such enemy forces, believers in the risen Lord, who have had Christ's righteousness imputed to their account, have spiritual armor that has to be constantly worn (Eph. 6:11).

One of the pieces of spiritual armor is the shield of faith (Eph. 6:16). **Salvation**, apart from faith, is non-existent (Eph. 2:8). Without faith, it is impossible to please God (Heb. 11:6). Active faith at work in justified saints is God's means to accomplish His will on earth. The saved live their faith actively. Those who have placed saving faith in Christ alone for salvation receive protection from eternal condemnation (Rom. 8:1). Faith in Christ protects from the curse of the Law (Gal. 3:13). Faith in Christ shields believers from God's wrath that abides upon the unbelieving (Rom. 5:9). Faith in Christ is how temptation is overcome (1 Cor. 10:13). After Christ ascended (Acts 1:9-11), He took His rightful, exalted (Phil. 2:9-11) place at the **right hand** of God (Col. 3:1). As Christ **held up** the psalmist, Christ holds up believers. From God's right hand, Christ ever lives to intercede for the saints (Heb. 7:25). From God's right hand, Christ upholds all things by the Word of His power

(Heb. 1:3). From God's right hand, Christ's enemies are one by one being placed under His feet (1 Cor. 15:25). From God's right hand, Christ rules as Head of the church (Eph. 1:22). From God's right hand, Christ advocates for the saints (1 Jn 2:2). From God's right hand, Christ receives the cares that we cast upon Him (1 Peter 5:7). From God's right hand, Christ dispenses the peace that passes understanding (Phil. 4:7). From God's right hand, Christ mediates between God and Man (1 Tim. 2:5). From God's right hand, Christ aids believers in their trials of various kinds (Jas 1:2-8). From God's right hand, the saints receive fresh doses of the Father's new morning mercies (Lam. 3:22-23). From God's right hand, the Captain of our salvation (Heb. 2:10) gives us, His faithful soldiers (2 Tim. 2:4), their marching orders. From God's right hand, our Wonderful Counselor gives us His wonderful counsel (Isa. 9:6). From God's right hand, the One who began the good work in us continues to perform it until it is complete (Phil. 1:6). From God's right hand, Christ continues to receive glory from those who daily grow in grace (2 Pet. 3:18). From God's right hand, as the saints delight in Him, Christ gives them the desires of their hearts (Ps. 37:4). From God's right hand, Christ continues to cleanse the just from unrighteousness (1 Jn 1:9).

God exalted David, the psalmist, to his place of prominence as Israel's king. David, however, like the rest of us, was a sinner. David received his special position not because he was worthy but because God is merciful.

God's **gentleness made** David **great**. So, it is with all believers. There is nothing with which they can commend themselves to this holy and just God (Isa. 64:6, Rom. 3:9-23). Anything good that comes from us comes as a result of His goodness and grace towards us. Believers have an exalted state in which they currently dwell. They did nothing to earn that exalted position.

On the contrary, they are only seated there because God is rich in mercy (Eph. 2:4, 2:6). Christ's kenosis (emptying of Himself; Phil. 2:7) is the primary way He displayed His gentleness. That made Him great. The first time He came, He commended His love toward us (Rom. 5:8), His enemies (Col. 1:21). Because He is loving and merciful, He richly blesses all those who call on Him for salvation with every spiritual blessing (Eph. 1:3). When He returns, He will come as a righteous Judge on a warhorse with a sword in His mouth and a robe dipped in blood (Rev. 19:11-16).

To receive the gracious salvation offered by such a merciful God, sinners must humble themselves at the foot of the cross and place repentant faith in the Savior, the Lord Jesus Christ, who loved us and gave Himself for us (Ephesians 5:2). Because God is on their side, Christians have nothing to fear (Ps. 118:6). They can boldly come before the throne of grace (Heb. 4:16) with access to the Father that is theirs in Christ (Eph. 2:18). They can stand fast in the liberty that is theirs in Christ and keep from being entangled again with a yoke of bondage (Gal. 5:1). They can faithfully work out their salvation knowing God works in them (Phil. 2:12-13). They can walk in love when they meditate on the love that Christ has lavishly poured on them (Eph. 5:2). They can walk in the Spirit and not fulfill the lust of the flesh (Gal. 5:16). They can rejoice at all that is theirs in Christ; even if that includes suffering for the gospel (Matt. 5:11-12). When believers have trouble in the world, they can take heart knowing that their Forerunner prepared a place for them (Jn 14:2-3) in overcoming the world (Jn 16:33).

**Questions for self-reflection:**

(1) How does the shield of faith help you personally live the Christian life?
(2) What do you do to put on the rest of the Christian armor? How do you remind yourself to put it on and to keep wearing it?
(3) When you find weak spots in your armor, what do you do to strengthen it?
(4) How has Christ helped you to overcome temptation today? How has Christ held you up spiritually today?

**18:36. You enlarged my path under me, So my feet did not slip.**

---

This verse is almost a verbatim quote of 2 Samuel 22:37. The psalmist recognizes that the Lord sustained him in his battles against his enemies. Since the Lord does not change (Mal. 3:6), since Jesus Christ is the same yesterday, today, and forever (Heb. 13:8), the same sustenance that was available to the psalmist is likewise available to all who call upon the name of the Lord in every generation (Rom. 10:13). Believers in every age are hard-pressed on every side by various enemies (2 Cor. 4:8-12). The enemies may be physical people. The enemies may be spiritual forces employed by Satan that fight against the angels that God dispenses to aid believers (Dan. 6:22, Acts 27:23, Heb. 1:14). The enemies may even be circumstances that cause believers to choose to grumble against the providence of God in their lives. No matter who or what the enemy is, for all believers, they have unlimited spiritual resources at their disposal that they can tap into by entering into God's presence. They can remember things they already know from their time with Him in His Word. When temptation comes on every side, God provides the way of escape and, when they choose to take God's way of escape, enlarges the path for them to walk in obedience (1 Cor. 10:13).

When believers choose to build their lives on the firm foundation of God and His Word (Matt. 7:24-27), when the storms of life come crashing against them, they will stand because they trust in the Lord, who sustains them. By trusting in the Lord and leaning not on their own understanding, believers can trust that the Lord will direct their paths into His narrow way (Prov. 3:5-6, Matt. 7:13). By looking unto Jesus, the Author and Finisher of their faith (Heb. 12:2), believers can know that their feet will not slip when life gets dangerous because He will get them through their battle. The Captain of their salvation (Heb. 2:10), the Lord Jesus Christ, will lead His soldiers (2 Tim. 2:3-4) to safety.

Even when saints do slip and fall into sin from time to time, because Jesus is their perfect substitute (Jn 1:29), He will keep them in perfect peace (Isa. 26:3). Even when times of sin come, because those who He justified He will also glorify (Rom. 8:30), true believers will humble themselves when they have fallen so that God will lift them (Jas 4:10). Likewise, those who have not embraced the Savior can also humble themselves, receive God's gracious offer of salvation in Christ alone, and walk in an **enlarged path** as a believer.

As these words apply to believers, they can also apply to Christ Himself. God the Father enlarged the path under the Lord Jesus Christ such that Christ's feet did not slip and prevent Him from perfectly executing the Father's plan to provide salvation for sinners. Because Christ stayed on the enlarged path the Father made for Him and His **feet did not slip** from His Father's mission (Jn 8:29), He successfully and sufficiently made purification for our sins before He sat down at the right hand of the Majesty on high (Heb. 1:3). Because Jesus is the example that we should walk in His steps (1 Pet. 2:21), and since Father would do this for Him, believers can trust that God will likewise guide them in the enlarged path. Nothing can separate them from God's love (Rom. 8:38-39). Even though the feet of genuine believers are bound to slip from time to time, their Advocate continues to intercede for them (Heb. 7:25, 1 Jn 2:1-2). Since His feet did not slip when He was tempted, the saints can trust in His finished work on their behalf.

## Questions for self-reflection:

(1) What keeps you from tapping into the spiritual resources that are yours through Christ?
(2) Would you characterize your relationship with sin as more slipping into it or more jumping into it?
(3) If you look to Jesus and set your minds on things above rather than on things of the earth, would you be more successful or less successful at consistently living in Christlikeness?

**18:37. I have pursued my enemies and overtaken them; Neither did I turn back again till they were destroyed.**

---

This verse is almost a verbatim quote of 2 Samuel 22:38. David had **pursued and overtaken** his **enemies** by the Lord's strength. He won the battles he needed to win because the Lord fought for him (1 Sam. 17:47). The same is true of Moses when God employed him in the battle against the Egyptians. It was so apparent that even the pagan Egyptians recognized that God was on Moses' side (Exod. 14:25).

For the present-day believer, Jesus has already defeated the enemy through His death on the cross (Rev. 20:10, Rev. 20:13-14). Therefore, today's believer has nothing to fear (Ps. 118:6, 1 Jn 4:18). The worst that can happen to them is physical death. But that is not something to fear (Matt. 10:28) because when the soul departs from the body at the point of physical death, the believer's great hope is that they will be in heaven with their Lord for all eternity (2 Cor. 5:8) until they return with Him from heaven at the end (Zech. 14:5).

So, believers can face any adversity with confident trust that no matter what happens to them on this earth that causes them distress, they will surely be glorified if they have been justified (Rom. 8:30). Nothing can separate them from God's love (Rom. 8:38-39). Their destiny is fixed (Jn 10:27-28, Phil. 1:6). They are already seated in heavenly places (Eph. 2:6) while they await their permanent relocation to the Father's house. Christ has prepared the way to that place for us (Jn 14:2-3).

The believer's enemies of sin, death, and hell have been pursued and overtaken by the Captain of our salvation (Hebrews 2:10), the Author and Finisher of our faith (Heb. 12:2), the Alpha and Omega (Rev. 1:8), the Lamb of God (Jn 1:29), the Lord Jesus Christ (Phil. 2:11). Through faith in Him, we, His spiritual offspring, can enter any challenge with the confidence that, because of Christ, we are more than conquerors (Rom. 8:37). Since we have such a strong Advocate fighting for us (1 Jn 2:1), we should boldly enter into the throne of grace for mercy and help in time of need (Heb. 4:16).

**Questions for self-reflection:**

(1) Are you more likely to pursue and overtake your own enemies in your own strength or the Lord's strength?

(2) How would you know if you execute your pursuit of your enemies in your strength or the Lord's strength?

(3) Even though we remain in the struggle against sin and Satan's forces, what gives us the courage to go on? For what hope do we have to live?

**18:38. I have wounded them, So that they could not rise; They have fallen under my feet.**

---

This verse is almost a verbatim quote of 2 Samuel 22:39. God gave David victory over his physical enemies such as the Amalekites and Saul. It is likewise true that, for the Christian, because Christ has overcome death (Acts 2:24) and hell (Rev. 1:18) by His death on the cross, He has **wounded** the Christian's enemies **so that they could not rise**. When the Son of Man was lifted up (Jn 3:15), His enemies had fallen under His feet (1 Cor. 15:26-27). One by one, as the rejectors of the gospel breathe their last, they go to Sheol and are under the feet of the Lord, who is enthroned in heaven (Isa. 66:1). When Christ died on the cross for the sins of the world, He bruised the head of the serpent (Gen. 3:15), inflicting a blow that will ultimately be fatal. Satan is permitted for now to deceive people whose home is this world (2 Thess. 2:9-10, Rev. 12:9).

The Lord Jesus Christ has called His own out of the world (Jn 15:19) and procured for Himself a peculiar people (1 Peter 2:9), a special treasure (Exod. 19:5), that demonstrates His glory through all that they do (1 Cor. 10:31) to those that are on the outside. His people are more than conquerors (Rom. 8:37). His people have overcome the wicked one (1 Jn 2:14). His people are a city on a hill (Matt. 5:14). His people are like fruit-bearing trees (Matt. 7:15-20, Jn 15:1-8). His people await His glorious return when they will meet Him in the air and will be with Him forever (1 Thess. 4:17) and will be like Him and see Him as He is (1 Jn 3:2).

While they wait, their responsibility is not to join in the works of darkness produced by the world. Their responsibility is to reprove them (Eph. 5:11). Their responsibility is to work while it is daytime (John 9:4), while God has given them life, to bring others with them into the kingdom so they can tell their Lord that they did something with the talent that He gave them (Matt. 25:14-30). Their responsibility is to suffer with joy (Jas 1:2-8) so that the world will ask them for a reason for the hope within them (1 Pet. 3:15). While anguish in various forms fills their time on this earth, they must remember that this world is not their home (Phil. 3:20). They must bring to remembrance that a lasting city (Heb. 13:14) awaits them (Jn 14:2-3). In the end, at the consummation of all history, He will put all His enemies **under** His **feet.** He will cast the beast, the false prophet, and all those who follow that wicked duo into the lake of fire (Rev. 20:10, Rev. 21:8).

## Questions for self-reflection:

(1) What historical event forever wounded God's enemies so that they could not rise to a permanently victorious position again?

(2) Where will Christ's enemies ultimately end up?

(3) How does your life demonstrate that you are a called out peculiar person?

(4) If Christ had to prune you so that you would bear more fruit, is there anything that you would not want Him to prune?

(5) Would your family say that you join in the works of darkness or reprove them habitually?

(6) If someone were to ask you for a reason for the hope in you today, what would you tell them? Would your lifestyle make your response believable?

**18:39. For You have armed me with strength for the battle; You have subdued under me those who rose up against me.**

This verse is almost a verbatim quote of 2 Samuel 22:40. Believers, like David, are involved in a spiritual **battle** against the devil and his forces (Eph. 6:12). They need spiritual **strength** from the God of heaven if they will emerge from this battle victorious (Eph. 3:16). Because of their fallen natures, even believers who are overcomers because of Christ (1 Jn 2:14) will fall into sin from time to time (1 Jn 2:1). Because of this, they need to tap into the strength that Christ provides them through the Holy Spirit (2 Thess. 2:16-17, 1 Tim. 1:12). They have, through the Spirit, all they need to overcome any temptation that comes their way because God provides all they need (1 Cor. 10:13, Phil. 4:19).

Satan and God are involved in a battle that will not completely settle until Satan is cast forever into the lake of fire (Rev. 20:10). Between now and that day, Satan employs demonic means to undermine God's work that He is accomplishing in the world through His people (1 Pet. 5:8). Christ is always working behind the scenes to equip the sheep to be doers of the Word (Heb. 13:21, Jas 1:22). As believers abide in the Lord Jesus, Jesus abides in them, and they bear fruit (Jn 15:1-8). They work out their salvation as God works in them (Phil. 2:12-13). Sinful people and personal sins rise up and try to thwart believers from their goal of Christ-likeness. As believers abide in Christ, Christ empowers them, by the Spirit, to **subdue** their enemies.

An unbeliever may tempt the believer to sin with their mouth or with their actions. By the power of the Holy Spirit, the believer can tap into the spiritual treasure chest that is theirs because of Christ (2 Pet. 1:3). When they do so, in Christ, they can overcome any temptation that comes their way. When they overcome that temptation, they **have subdued under** themselves those **that rose up against** them. As they respond correctly to afflictions and temptations as they come against them, the power of Christ increases in them in sensitivity (Jas 1:2-8). His power is made great in their weakness (2 Cor. 12:9). When we are weak, we are strong because He is strong in us (2 Cor. 12:10).

**Questions for self-reflection:**

(1) What does it look like in your life to put on the Lord Jesus Christ?
(2) What provision are you making for the flesh that you need to cut off?
(3) Do you wish you could be in heaven out of the battle already, or do you enjoy earth that is not your home too much?
(4) What sins need addressing to improve your efforts at trending toward Christ-likeness?
(5) Are there any sins that you are better at subduing?

**18:40. You have also given me the necks of my enemies, So that I destroyed those who hated me.**

---

This verse is almost a verbatim quote of 2 Samuel 22:41. God had **given** David **the necks of** his **enemies** so that David could be victorious in battle against his enemies. His victory either involved death for his enemies (1 Sam. 17) or his enemies became his servants (2 Sam. 8:2). David killed those who fought against him in battle. In that way, God **destroyed** David's enemies.

For the present-day Christian, by His death on the cross and resurrection, the Lord Jesus Christ overcame the enemies of mankind: sin (2 Cor. 5:21), death (1 Cor. 15:26), and hell (Rev. 20:14). Jesus destroyed temptation when it came. One day, all God's enemies will be under His feet (1 Cor. 15:27). One by one, when the unregenerate sinner dies, that sinner has their divine appointment that awaits everyone after death (Heb. 9:27). That unregenerate sinner is an enemy of God (Col. 1:21). If they continue in their rejection of the Lord until their dying day, they will die as the enemy of God and will be under God's feet, awaiting their final destination: the lake of fire (Revelation 21:8).

By faith in the risen Lord, Jesus Christ, justified sinners are no longer enemies of God. The Lord is on their side (Ps. 118:6). They have access to every spiritual blessing (Eph. 1:3), including victory over temptation, a present-day enemy. By the power of the Holy Spirit, Christians can take the way of escape that God provides against temptation (1 Cor. 10:13). They can defeat individual temptations when they come, putting the personal temptations under them as the neck of an enemy under a foot. They can destroy the sin that hates them because Christ in them, the hope of glory (Col. 1:27), empowers them to overcome any temptation.

## Questions for self-reflection:

(1) What enemies can you subdue in your own strength?
(2) What enemies can you subdue in God's strength?
(3) How has your fear of events or people changed now that the Lord is on your side?

---

**18:41. They cried out, but there was none to save; Even to the Lord, but He did not answer them.**

---

This verse is almost a verbatim quote of 2 Samuel 22:42. The enemies of David **cried out** for deliverance. They looked all over for rescue. But all their crying and looking were futile as long as they chose to continue in their rebellion against David's God. Since David's God was not on their side, **there was none to save**. God fights for His people (Exod. 14:14). God fights against His enemies (Deut. 20:4).

The false gods that do not have the power to save like David's God does, like only the God of the Bible does, can do nothing to help because they are not even real, let alone helpful (Deut. 6:14, Isa. 45:5). Since the false gods are not real, they **did not answer** God's enemies, the people who called out to them. Since when all the other false gods failed to save David's enemies, David's enemies perhaps felt like they should give the God of David, the one true God, **the Lord**, a shot. Nobody else's God came through for them, so maybe David's God would.

The problem with such an attitude is that such insincere prayers will always be ineffective at reaching the God of the universe. God hears those with humble and contrite spirits (Ps. 51:17). God does not hear the prideful (Jas 4:6). At this point, the only way David's enemies could expect to hear from David's God in any beneficial way is if they humbled themselves and turned in repentant faith to Him, the one true God. Otherwise, they would hear from Him in judgment. Therefore, the only way to be spared the wrath that comes against the ungodly is to humble oneself under the mighty hand of God so that He can exalt you in due time (1 Pet. 5:6).

**Questions for self-reflection:**

(1) Have you ever cried to the Lord for help with something when He appeared not to answer you?

---

(2) When #1 above ever happened to you, did you examine your heart to see if there was something in you that prevented the receipt of your request?

(3) What things are unbelievers prone to trust that is not the one true God?

(4) What things are believers prone to trust that is not the one true God?

(5) How can we ensure we have the correct object of trust?

**18:42. Then I beat them as fine as the dust before the wind; I cast them out like dirt in the streets.**

---

This verse is almost a verbatim quote of 2 Samuel 22:43. After the enemies of the psalmist cried out for salvation and there was no salvation because they were at enmity with God, it became apparent that God gave these enemies of His over to their sins. They would reap what they had sown (Gal. 6:7-8). God's wrath abode upon them because of their unbelief (Jn 3:36). Their only hope was to humble themselves (1 Pet. 5:6), turn from their sin, and turn to the God whose hand was against them (Jas 4:7). If they did not, they would be subject to utter destruction and ruin at the hand of the One who created them (2 Thess. 1:9).

How insane it is for those God created in His image to rebel against their Maker (Gen. 1:27). Now, the God who sustains them (Col. 1:16-17), who loves them (Rom. 5:8), and who is kind to them (Ti 3:4) prepares to judge them (Ps. 7:11-17, Rom. 2:1-11)! God reasonably judges and punishes those who treat His goodness, which He designs to lead people to repentance, with such contempt (Rom. 2:1-4)! It is not that God forced this destruction upon them. They chose it themselves. They spurned the grace that appeared to them (Ti 2:11). They rejected to knowledge that God gave them. Since they rejected what God gave them, it was taken away from them and given to those who wanted it (Matt. 21:42-44, Acts 28:24-28). God did this to them because they did this to themselves. By the time they realize the foolishness of their choice, it will be too late. God's judgment will be so severe that those who reject will be beaten as **fine as dust** and scattered all over the place as if blown by **the wind**. They will be stomped upon **like dirt in the streets** and consumed in judgment.

### Questions for self-reflection:

(1) Who have you prayed for would come to know the Lord who has seemed to get worse in their rebellion?

---

(2) When you consider that the destruction that results from rejecting God's salvation rested upon you until you repented and believed, does it make you more grateful for God's work in your life?

(3) What have you done with the knowledge that God has given you? How have you used the knowledge God gave you to make a difference in the world - especially in the lives of those God has given you?

**18:43. You have delivered me from the strivings of the people; You have made me the head of the nations; A people I have not known shall serve me.**

---

This verse is almost a verbatim quote of 2 Samuel 22:44. Some people fought with David and tried to overthrow or kill him (2 Sam. 3:1). Some of those people included Saul. After Saul died, David's own people refused to recognize him as their rightful king (2 Sam. 2). However, they eventually did come to acknowledge his reign over them (2 Sam. 8:15).

In a Messianic application, the Lord Jesus Christ overcame **the strivings of the people**. David had become **head of the nations**. Christ became Head of the church (Col. 1:18). In one sense, it appeared that the people had succeeded in their plots against Him since they had Him crucified. But in an ultimate sense, their plan was unsuccessful since Christ rose from the grave. When Christ rose from the grave, that was how He was delivered (Acts 2:24).

Now, by the power of the Holy Spirit, believers in this risen Christ can experience deliverance from their enemies of temptation from personal sin (1 Cor. 10:13). Even if unbelievers strive with believers, believers can trust that, in an ultimate sense, that faith is their guaranteed victory that has overcome the world (1 Jn 5:4). Believers know that the Lord Jesus Christ is with them no matter what they face in this life (Matt. 28:20). They may have to travel into some fiery furnaces (Dan. 3), but Christ promises to be with them in the fire. He may not even allow them to be **delivered** from their trials in this life but may allow their trials to continue so that faith may have its perfect work (Jas 1:2-8).

Now, Christ is the head of the church. One day, Christ will put all His enemies under His feet (1 Cor. 15:26-27). The Father has given Christ all authority (Matt. 28:18). After Christ came the first time to the Jews, the Jews had an opportunity to embrace their Messiah and receive the promised blessings. The Jews, unfortunately, rejected their Messiah, and salvation went to the Gentiles (Matthew 21:43). Therefore, once Gentiles started coming in large amounts into the kingdom, these people that were previously not known to the Lord came to love and embrace the Savior. They began to serve Him, as all do who come to saving faith (Ti 2:14). Christ knew them as He knows everyone and everything. But the Jews did not know Him. The Jews had turned every one to their own way (Isa. 53:6). Their iniquities had taken them away (Isa. 64:6). Fortunately for them and all of us, the Lord laid on Christ the iniquity of us all (Isa. 53:6).

By faith in this risen Lord, people from every tribe, tongue, and nation who had previously **not known** Christ in a saving way came to embrace the Savior and receive the gracious gift of eternal life. The Father translated them from the kingdom of darkness into the kingdom of God's dear Son (Col. 1:13). They changed from children of wrath (Eph. 2:3) to children of the King. The Jews were mercifully given God's law and had prophets sent to them (Lk 24:27). They rejected all that. Gentiles did not receive those benefits. Yet God in His mercy has graciously saved those who call upon the name of the Lord (Rom. 10:13). Those who were previously not a people had become God's people (1 Pet. 2:10) because the Lord is rich in mercy (Eph. 2:4).

## Questions for self-reflection:

(1) Have you ever had to endure strivings with people for religious reasons?
(2) If you have not had to endure strivings with people because of religion, when you read the stories in Scripture of those who have, what have you noticed?
(3) Does it appear that God's enemies currently have the upper hand in the world in which we live?
(4) How can believers take comfort from knowing that God is sovereign even as the world lies under Satan's sway?

**18:44. As soon as they hear of me they obey me; The foreigners submit to me.**

This verse is almost a verbatim quote of 2 Samuel 22:45. **As soon as** the Lord's enemies **hear of** Him, if they have good-ground hearts that have been appropriately prepared to receive the gospel (Matt. 13:8, 23), **they** will **obey** the command to repent and believe the gospel (Acts 17:30, Acts 16:31). Faith will come by hearing the word about Christ. They will embrace the living Savior by faith when they hear the preached message (Rom. 10:17). They will willingly bow the knee to the One who translated them from the kingdom of darkness to the kingdom of His Son (Col. 1:13). They will live lives of faithfulness and confess sin when sin rears its ugly head (1 Jn 1:9). They will bear fruit, albeit in varying amounts (Matt. 7:15-20, Matt. 13:8).

All unbelievers are **foreigners** to the Lord until they hear and obey the gospel (Col. 1:21). Once the sinner receives the gospel, he **submit**s **to** God and flees from the devil (Jas 4:7) in the conversion experience where they receive Christ's imputed righteousness. Christ takes their sin upon Himself (1 Pet. 2:24), and they receive every spiritual blessing because of Christ (Eph. 1:3). He rules and reigns over the sheep now (Jn 10:11, 1 Pet. 5:4). He has the scepter as their King (Rev. 17:14). They gladly submit to Him as their Lord because He is rich in mercy (Eph.2:4), and He has given them everything they need for life and godliness (2 Pet. 1:3). In this specific context, since the gospel first went to the Jews (Rom. 1:16), the foreigners must be the Gentiles. When Gentiles responded to the gospel with saving faith, they became subjects in the kingdom belonging to the King of kings.

**Questions for self-reflection:**

(1) Is there anyone you know who has turned to the Lord that now hears of the Lord and obeys Him?

(2) Is there anyone you can think of who is a foreigner today who might have their heart prepared to receive the Lord through faith through the gospel?

(3) When you hear the Lord through His Word call you to make a change of some sort, how quick to respond to Him are you? Would those who know you best say that you obey Him as soon as you hear of Him?

**18:45. The foreigners fade away, And come frightened from their hideouts.**

---

This verse is almost a verbatim quote of 2 Samuel 22:46. As in Isaiah 64:6, **foreigners fade away** because their iniquities consume them. In contrast, the love of the Lord consumes the believer (2 Cor. 5:14). Foreigners fade away because their motivation for living is their own glory. The motivation for living for believers in the Lord Jesus Christ is living for God's glory (Col. 3:17). Foreigners to God's promises, those found only in the gospel, hide in **their hideouts** and stay insulated from their accountability to their Creator. Such unbelievers can hide behind false religion. They can worship any part of the creation. In doing so, they can successfully dull their consciences to the point that they successfully crowd out the truth of who God is and what God has done through Christ (Rom. 1:28). God, then, gives them what they want. He allows them to pursue what they want to pursue freely. The cares of the world can successfully choke out the Word so that it becomes unfruitful (Matt. 13:22).

**Questions for self-reflection:**

---

(1) Do you know someone who lives in such a manner that they appear to fade away in their sins?
(2) Are you controlled by the Spirit or the flesh?

**18:46. The Lord lives! Blessed be my Rock! Let the God of my salvation be exalted.**

---

This verse is almost a verbatim quote of 2 Samuel 22:47. Because the Lord intervened in the psalmist's life, because the Lord intervenes in all His people's lives in each generation (Ps. 77:14), believers from any time in redemptive history can rejoice with the psalmist at the greatness of **the Lord** that **lives** (Phil. 3:1). Believers know that the Lord's mercies are new every morning (Lamentations 3:22-23). Believers know that even when they are faithless, He remains faithful (2 Tim. 2:13). They know that when they lie, God can't lie (Heb. 6:18). Believers know that, even though sin separates them from His holiness, He is rich in mercy, He has made them alive, and He has seated them in heavenly places with Christ (Eph. 2:5-6).

The Lord is the only living God. All other gods of man's making cannot be said to be living. God's life never began like man's life began. God is eternal and infinite (Ps. 90:2). Man is temporal and finite (Jas 4:14). Man will reach a point where he will take a final earthly breath, and his life will cease (Heb. 9:27). God's life will never cease. It never began. God always has been. In addition to giving physical life to all of mankind and the animal kingdom, God also grants spiritual life and eternal life to those to come to Him in repentant faith (Jn 3:16). Even when people on earth cease to live, the Lord continues to live. He is busy sustaining everything that is (Heb. 1:3).

The Lord is the **Rock** of the psalmist. The Lord is the Rock of all who believe. When life creates trouble for man such that man needs Someone firm to rely on, God can be relied upon in times of distress (Ps. 118:5). In times of lack, His children can trust God to provide (Phil. 4:19). God provides all that His children need. Whether the needs are physical or spiritual, the sheep can trust God to provide. Israel received water from a Rock (Exod. 17). In the New Testament, that rock was identified as the Lord Jesus Christ Himself (1 Cor. 10:4). Christ called Himself the Living Water

(Jn 7:37-39). He provides all that His people need. His supply is sufficient to all those that avail themselves to it.

God was the temporal God of salvation to the psalmist because God saved the psalmist from temporary troubling circumstances. The psalmist had earthly enemies from which he needed deliverance. God was to be trusted to provide that deliverance in God's timing, not the psalmist's timing. God is the God of **salvation** to all the saved. God brings to pass every part of salvation. God the Father chose before the foundation of the world that all the saved would live a certain way (Eph. 1:4). God the Son lived a perfect life and died on the cross to save those that believe (Jn 3:16). God the Spirit leads believers into all truth (Jn 16:13). Such a God who can save such sinful humanity is worthy to be praised and exalted in men. The beauty of the gospel is that the redeemed get to convey God's power to the heathen. The work of salvation is how God gets **exalted** in the eyes of the heathen (Matt. 5:16).

**Questions for self-reflection:**

(1) Have you ever had a season of faithlessness in your walk with the Lord? In that season, how did the Lord remain faithful?
(2) How have you seen God provide for your needs?
(3) Are there any spiritual enemies from which the Lord has delivered you?
(4) Have you gotten any better at waiting for the Lord to work in a situation in your life?
(5) How does your life exalt the Lord?

**18:47. It is God who avenges me, And subdues the peoples under me;**

This verse is almost a verbatim quote of 2 Samuel 22:48. Vengeance belongs to the Lord (Rom. 12:19). The psalmist had to trust that **God** would **avenge** him in God's timing, which may not necessarily be as soon as the psalmist would have liked. God pays back sins committed against His people in His timing and His ways. His people are not to pay back the sins committed against them. The Lord Himself taught His people to turn the other cheek (Lk 6:29), to go the second mile, and to not repay evil with evil (Matt. 5:38-42), and to pray for those that persecute them (Matt. 5:43-48).

When enduring persecution, the psalmist likely could have felt discouraged at the lack of apparent success that living for the Lord led to. It can frequently appear that the unrighteous get their way while the righteous do not (Jer. 12:1). It can seem as if the God of the universe turns a blind eye to iniquity and the oppression of His people. As the righteous suffer for their faith or because the unrighteous prosper, these things become various trials to which James alludes (Jas 1:2-8). They feel like a momentary light affliction of which Paul speaks (2 Cor. 4:17).

Rather than respond with impatience and vengeance, the believer is to trust the Lord, not themselves (Prov. 3:5-6). They can know that, whether they see it or not, whether they experience it in their lifetime or not, a day is coming when the Lord will put all His enemies under His feet. All the enemies that afflict the lives of believers will be under the Lord's feet (1 Cor. 15:26-27). The Lord will deliver the godly out of temptation (2 Pet. 2:9). The godly will have their tears wiped away. Their sorrow will be gone (Rev. 21:4). Those things that in this life cause sorrow will be under the righteous and in subjection to God (1 Cor. 15:27-28).

God can use means to get vengeance. God instituted governments to bear the sword against evildoers on His behalf (Rom. 13:1-7). God's people should not enact what God has permitted the government to enact. The psalmist is by now in heaven with the Lord (2 Cor. 5:8). The people who afflicted the psalmist are **subdue**d **under** the psalmist's feet as the unrighteous did not join the psalmist in heaven.

## Questions for self-reflection:

(1) Have you ever grown impatient at waiting for the Lord to avenge you?
(2) How have you done lately at loving your enemies?
(3) As God's enemies rise up against God's people, what are some of your favorite promises of God's that you avail yourself of to help you to continue to trust Him?

**18:48. He delivers me from my enemies. You also lift me up above those who rise against me; You have delivered me from the violent man.**

---

This verse is almost a verbatim quote of 2 Samuel 22:49. The psalmist was privileged to be on the receiving end of God's deliverance on multiple occasions. He had past experience to which he could refer to undergird his praise of the Lord and to look forward to the next time that the Lord would intervene in his circumstances to provide deliverance once again. David experienced deliverance from dangerous enemies such as Goliath, Saul, and Absalom most prevalently. Present-day believers experience refreshing deliverance by the Lord from multiple **enemies**. Believers experience deliverance out of temptation (2 Pet. 2:9). The Lord delivers His people from sin's power and presence due to the finished work of Christ on their behalf (Rom. 8:2). Christ **delivers** sinners from the curse of the law by redeeming them (Gal. 3:13). Christ delivers His people from fear because Christians have nothing to fear since the worst thing that can happen to them is physical death. Death will usher them into the eternal presence of the Lord (Matt. 10:28, 2 Cor. 5:8). All the enemies of God's people will one day be under Christ's feet (1 Cor. 15:26-27).

David was exalted to rule over Israel. Present-day believers humble themselves before the mighty hand of God that He might exalt them in due time (1 Pet. 5:6). Believers access the grace that is theirs in Christ (Ti 2:11, Heb. 4:16). In this grace, they stand (Rom. 5:2). This grace helps them overcome spiritual enemies as they put on their spiritual armor (Eph. 6:12-18). As these enemies **rise up against** God's spiritual offspring, believers can rise up to the challenge and live righteously in a world of unrighteousness that surrounds them on every side.

The psalmist experienced the Lord's deliverance from a physical threat, possibly Saul. Likewise, believers, today can experience deliverance **from the violent man** when anyone oppresses or persecutes them for their faith (2 Tim. 3:12). They experience deliverance today when they successfully overcome temptation by responding to the temptation by accessing the grace in which they stand (Rom. 5:2). They experience this deliverance when they walk in the light and not in the darkness (1 Jn 1:6-7).

**Questions for self-reflection:**

(1) From what physical enemies has the Lord delivered you?
(2) From what spiritual enemies has the Lord delivered you?
(3) How can you be sure that you are adequately prepared for when the Lord lifts you above those who rise against you?

**18:49. Therefore I will give thanks to You, O Lord, among the Gentiles, And sing praises to Your name.**

This verse is almost a verbatim quote of 2 Samuel 22:50. The victories that the psalmist experienced, the successes that believers from every era experience over physical and spiritual enemies, are to be ascribed to the Lord. Any abilities man enjoys only result from the Lord's permitting the success of those abilities in an ultimate sense (Heb. 13:20-21). So, when a believer enjoys success in an environment of unbelief, the believer should ascribe the success to the mercy of the Lord and not their own knowledge or cleverness. The psalmist realized, and genuine believers realize, that anything good that comes from them comes from God's grace since nothing good dwells in us (Rom. 7:18, Jas 1:17). God's mercies are new every morning (Lam. 3:22-23). God's faithfulness is great. Believers come to appreciate that truth.

**The Gentiles** of that time were heathen because the promises funneled through the Jewish people. So, the psalmist declared that he would praise the Lord before the unbelievers in his circle of influence. Once the psalmist had conquered his enemies, survivors heard the psalmist praise and **give thanks** to the Lord. All those around the psalmist knew that the psalmist credited the Lord for anything good that came from him.

Believers in every generation **sing praises to** the Lord. Believers have great reason to sing praises to the Lord because of the great deliverance that the Lord has wrought on behalf of His people (Col. 1:13). Believers should sing praises to the Lord because He will one day glorify them (Rom. 8:30). Believers should sing praises to the Lord since, because of Christ, all believers have their sins forgiven and have access to every spiritual blessing meant for them in this temporal earth (Eph. 1:3-14). Once they finally get to leave, believers enjoy perfect fellowship with their Lord and can forever sing praises to the Lord for Who He is and for what He has done. In heaven, the departed saints sing praises to the Lord for all eternity. After all the time the saints spent here on earth enduring hardship as good soldiers of Christ (2 Tim. 2:3-4), it will pay off as they will be around the throne of the Lamb giving glory **and will sing praises to Him for all eternity.**

**Questions for self-reflection:**

(1) For what material things can you give thanks to the Lord?

(2) For what spiritual things can you give thanks to the Lord?

(3) How can you praise the Lord's work in your life in such a way that the unbelievers in your sphere of influence get a clearer picture of who He is and why He is worthy of their allegiance?

**18:50. Great deliverance He gives to His king, And shows mercy to His anointed, To David and his descendants forevermore.**

---

This verse is almost a verbatim quote of 2 Samuel 22:51. Since God is the King of Kings and Lord of Lords and since God is sovereign over the appointment of any earthly ruler (Dan. 2:21), divine permission allows any earthly king to experience any **great deliverance** (Eph. 1:11).

Christ, the Messiah, the Anointed One, will one day rule as **King** of Kings at His second coming. He is the rightful King of the Jews even though they did not receive Him during His first coming (Jn 1:11). Even as the heathen raged against Christ during His first coming (Ps. 2:1), He demonstrated His messianic credentials. He proved it by His earthly works and His resurrection and ascension (Rom. 1:4).

Christ experienced deliverance from the Father from death. Now, from heaven, He lives to intercede for the saints (Hebrews 7:25). He delivers the saints from their troubles. The Lord delivers the godly out of temptation while reserving the unjust for judgment (2 Pet. 2:9). The Father delivered Christ from the grave in His resurrection. Therefore, He is a sufficient Savior to all who trust in Him.

God showed **mercy to David** by establishing his kingdom (2 Sam.5:1-5). God showed mercy to David's **descendants forevermore** by sending Christ at the fulness of time (Gal. 4:4-5) as David's descendant (Matt. 1:1). That Christ would come from the line of David is merciful to David, especially in light of David's sin. Those who come to God by faith in Christ become the sheep (Jn 10:27-28), the descendants of Christ, who is the Good Shepherd. All the saved are given to Christ as His descendants (Jn 6:37).

Christ pleads to the Father to be merciful to them (Romans 8:34). Because God is rich in mercy (Eph. 2:4), when God looks at believers, He sees His Son's sacrifice on their behalf. Everyone deserves eternal judgment for their sins. Believers avoid that judgment because the Father can look on Christ and give them Christ's righteousness. Unbelievers reject the way of escape from God's judgment (Jn. 3:36, Rom. 5:9). Any good that comes to anyone is a result of God's mercy. This is true even of the unsaved. They oftentimes are recipients of the goodness of God because of God's desire that they repent and come to saving faith (Rom. 2:4).

**Questions for self-reflection:**

(1) How did the Lord specifically show mercy to David according to Scripture?
(2) How has the Lord shown you mercy throughout your life?
(3) How specifically has the Lord delivered you out of temptation recently?

# Psalm 19

**19:1. The heavens declare the glory of God; And the firmament shows His handiwork.**

---

In the beginning, God created **the heavens** (Gen. 1:1, Prov. 8:27). All God created **declare**s God's glory as the wisdom with which these were made points to the loving Creator (Prov. 3:19, Jer. 10:12). The heavens declare the reality that creation necessitates a Creator and the absurdity that everything came from nothing (Rom. 1:20, Ps. 14:1). The heavens are in the direction of where man looks to see the sun and moon and to show the changing seasons. The sun rises and sets, and the seasons change by God's power and permission (Gen. 1:14-15).

When a sinner humbly repents and believes the gospel, God reveals His glory in the transforming work that the gospel produces in the justified sinner (Rom. 1:16, Rom. 3:24). The plan of salvation originated in heaven with the Father choosing (Eph. 1:4), sending the Son to die (Galatians 4:4-5), and sending the Spirit to inhabit believers (Jn 16:13, 1 Cor. 6:19). Since heaven is God's throne (Isa. 66:1) and since God has been in heaven since eternity past before creation since at the beginning, **God** has displayed His **glory**. When God created what He created when He created it (Gen. 1), each detail of creation gives glory to God. All glory to God that redounds from creation originates in the heavens and declares that God is there. The creation account testifies to the infinite wisdom behind everything that we see in creation and the things that we cannot see that humanity discovers. The gospel originated in heaven.

The glory of God is magnificently declared when a repentant sinner humbly embraces their Savior, the Lord Jesus Christ. From that moment on, the justified sinner's life is a declaration of the glory of God (1 Cor. 10:31). Their life becomes a lamp (Matt. 5:14-15), a vessel of light that conveys the power of the gospel, which is the glory of God shone brightly in the heart (Rom. 13:12, 2 Cor. 4:6, Phil. 2:15). That God would plan from eternity past to send His Messiah to Israel declares His glory. Through these people came the prophets. Those very people would not receive Him who came to them (Jn 1:11). Their rejection declares His glory as that rejection opened wide the doors of the gospel to the Gentiles (Matt. 21:43, Acts 14:27). The church and its assembling and ordinances are a testimony to God's glory as each time they meet, they show the gospel's transforming power.

That God would ordain that there would be pastors to preach the Word declares the glory of God as this preached Word is a primary means which God uses to save sinners by His gracious gospel (Rom. 10:17). The doctrine taught in churches originated with God (Ti 2:5), in the heavens. When that doctrine, taught in the Word, goes forth, it brings with it the power of God unto salvation (Rom. 1:16). It transforms lives. The faithful saints prove its efficacy by their perseverance even in the most difficult of circumstances. A transformed life wrought in heaven by the Holy Trinity declares the glory of God.

God is in the heavens, and believers are extensions of Him, His **firmament**. Believers **show** forth God's **handiwork** when they live the way they should live (Eph. 2:10). They are the lights of the world. They are the city on a hill (Matt. 5:14). They are Christ's body, the church (1 Cor. 12:13, 1 Cor. 12:27, Eph.4:12, Eph. 5:15-16, Eph. 5:23, Col. 1:18, Col. 1:24, Col. 2:19), that goes into the world and preaches the gospel to every creature (Matt. 28:19-20). They are the objects of Christ's redemption, the vessels of mercy that have received mercy (Rom. 9:23). They are those in whom Christ has begun a good work. They are not passive as Christ performs it (Phil. 1:6, Phil. 2:12-13). They transform as they renew their minds (Rom. 12:2). The firmament that God created originally is so masterfully designed that it has to be the product of design rather than random processes.

## Questions for self-reflection:

(1) When was the last time that you actually thought about just how miraculous it is that we are here and how we got here?
(2) What was one of the first most dramatic changes that took place in you at the time of your justification?

(3) When was the last time you consciously thought about the Holy Spirit's work in your life?

(4) How does a blade of grass give God glory?

(5) How does a termite give God glory?

(6) If you have been saved for a long time, does your gospel lamp burn as brightly today as it once did? Why or why not?

(7) As a believer, how can you better show God's handiwork?

**19:2. Day unto day utters speech, And night unto night reveals knowledge.**

---

Night and day repeat showing that an orderly force, namely God, is behind their operation (Gen. 1:5). Only a Being with infinite wisdom could institute such an essential and repetitious process as the repetitive cycle of days and nights. It is the glory of God that causes night and day to continue. From Proverbs, wisdom and **knowledge** point to Christ (Prov. 1:20-33), point to God, so the fact that days and nights occur **utter speech** that unequivocally points to the existence of God. These expected events, day and night, point to a force working behind the scenes that stays constant, that is not always changing. The sun rises and sets. The moon comes and goes. The seasons arrive and flee away. Animals reproduce after their own kinds (Gen. 1).

The laws that science has discovered that operate in the world were not created by accident or by random chance. No. They began and continue by the One who upholds all things by the Word of His power (Heb. 1:3). Since Christ came to be the once for all sacrifice for sin (Heb. 10:10) and gave birth to the church (Eph. 5:23), until He comes again, the speech about Christ is uttered **day unto day** by His mouthpieces.

**Night unto night** gospel work continues in churches, families, and communities as the gospel goes into the world. As long as the world is allowed to exist, this gospel work will continue to go forth. Believers diffuse the knowledge of Christ into the world into which they have been planted (2 Cor. 2:14-15). They are a sweet aroma to a fallen world. The same gospel that saved sinners two thousand years ago still saves now as it still is the power of God unto salvation (Rom. 1:16). The more people get saved, the more Christ adds ambassadors (2 Cor. 5:20) to His team that can utter speech and can **reveal** the knowledge of Him to others who are ready and able to respond to God's gracious offer of salvation.

**Questions for self-reflection:**

(1) Do dependable, repetitive processes like night and day suggest that there is a dependable Creator that upholds the world and keeps it working?

(2) Are there any other things not mentioned above that occur consistently and repeatedly that point to a dependable Creator?

(3) As days and nights elapse and we get closer to the Lord's glorious return, how can you find creative ways to show others their need for the Savior?

**19:3. There is no speech nor language Where their voice is not heard.**

---

No matter the culture, **language**, or weather patterns that vary all across the globe, something points to a bigger force behind the weather that brings the seasons and keeps the world spinning. That force that brings the weather is the supernatural God. Conscience and creation point to the existence of God.

For the New Testament church, believers who have obeyed the Great Commission, starting with the original apostles and continuing with the present generation, the **voice** of God has been **heard** all over the globe when the Lord's servants brought the gospel to various people groups. Everyone is accountable to the revelation that they know (Rom. 1:20). Not everyone lives in the same culture. Not everyone speaks the same language. However, most everyone has an innate ability to deduce from what they know about the world in which they live that there must be a force higher than us that allows everything to be as it is. No matter the language or culture, the gospel can have an effect wherever it goes forth. As it happened at Pentecost (Acts 2), people from any background can hear the gospel and receive the transforming benefits of God's grace.

## Questions for self-reflection:

---

(1) What are you doing to demonstrate the glory of God to those with whom you interact?
(2) Are you being a good steward with the knowledge that God has entrusted to your care? Why or why not?
(3) Do you still have the same zeal that you first had when you initially believed? Why or why not? If not, what can you do to be more passionate about the things of the Lord?

**19:4. Their line has gone out through all the earth, And their words to the end of the world. In them He has set a tabernacle for the sun,**

---

The recurring, predictable patterns that exist with night and day and seasons exist all over the globe (Dan. 2:21). There is not a seeing person anywhere that cannot witness its effects. There is no living person anywhere that cannot feel its effects, even if born blind, as, even in that condition, they can typically still feel the effects of temperature. So, God screams silently through the world He created, telling us all that He is there and that we are responsible to Him (Rom. 14:12).

God had graciously given the law to the Jews (Exod. 20-21). The presence of the Jews throughout the whole earth was God's **line**, the line through which He would eventually bless the nations by bringing Messiah into the world through them. Noah and his family preserved the line of the Jewish people when they got the chance to restart the human race after the Flood not because of anything good in Noah but purely because Noah found grace in God's sight (Gen. 6:8).

Because God graciously preserved the Jews so that He could refill the world after the Flood, the Messiah graciously came as a far-off grandson of Noah and provided salvation to all who believe the gospel (Gal. 4:4-5). Christ's words inspired the apostles to be the church's foundation and to write Scripture that is still the inspired book for the church (Eph. 2:20). Their words have gone and will go to the end of the world as the gospel spreads and continues its advance throughout the earth.

As people come to saving faith in the Lord Jesus Christ, the line continues to go **out through all the earth** (Matt. 28:19-20). For Israel, the **tabernacle** was a portable worship center. It was always on the move because Israel was on the move. The sun gives light to everyone. Christ is He who tabernacled among men (Rev. 21:3-4). The Son of God gives light to everyone (Jn 1:4, Jn 8:12). Christ has reconciled the world to Himself and has left the ministry of reconciliation with His people (2 Co. 5:18-20). The

gospel is the mark by which all mankind will one day be judged
(Acts 17:30-31, Hebrews 9:27).

**Questions for self-reflection:**

(1) Have you recognized your responsibility to your Creator?
(2) If the gospel had not spread to you, what would you be doing right now?
(3) Who do you know who still needs to respond to the gospel of grace, and how can you show them their need today?

**19:5. Which is like a bridegroom coming out of his chamber, And rejoices like a strong man to run its race.**

Nature is such a powerful witness to God's existence, power, and glory that nature has recurring effects that are ready to burst onto the scene at the appropriate time. Many of the delights that winter snow brings, or the pleasures of sun, the joy of fall, or the benefits of rain, when the weather does the various things that it does, people often rejoice over what comes with the seasons. Others long for the changes that a season change brings. People eagerly wait with anticipation, as with the beginning of a wedding, at the changing of the seasons. God works behind the scenes to ensure that the seasons change (Dan. 2:21). Believers can look at the creation and know that it declares the glory of God (Romans 1:20). Each drop of rain points to the Creator. Each beam of sunlight points to the One who holds us accountable. Each fallen leaf reminds others of their weakness in comparison to their Creator. Each work of the seasons and the weather operates by the sovereign will of God.

By God's sovereign will, Christ came forth at the fulness of time to save those who believe the gospel. He is the **strong Man** that came before us and ran the **race** before us so that we could look to Him, the Author and Finisher of our faith (Heb. 12:2), and keep our focus on the race that we have before us to run.

### Questions for self-reflection:

(1) Does thinking about your accountability to God make you want to change anything about how you currently live? Why or why not?

(2) If you knew that there was something in your life that was a hindrance to others accepting the gospel, would you change whatever that was if you could?

(3) When you look to Jesus to lead you to glory, how can that help you live consistently, albeit imperfectly?

**19:6. Its rising is from one end of heaven, And its circuit to the other end; And there is nothing hidden from its heat.**

God's power put nature in place. The gospel is the power of God unto salvation (Rom. 1:16). The gospel brings the faith that comes by hearing the Word about Jesus Christ (Rom. 10:17). God influences the whole earth, **from one of heaven to the other end.** The eternal destiny of every human being that ever has lived and ever will live hinges on the historical event of Jesus sacrificial death. (Jn 12:32).

The gospel is a message that divides sheep from goats (Matt. 25:31-32). The gospel separates the wheat from the tares (Matt. 13:24-30). The gospel proclaims a message of human responsibility and accountability (2 Cor. 5:10) to a benevolent Creator who loves (Jn 3:16) those created in His image (Gen. 1:27) so much that He did everything possible to reconcile them to Himself so that they could enjoy eternity with Him forever (2 Cor. 5:18-19). **Nothing is hidden from its heat** in that God created the whole earth along with the unseen universe. Mankind has only begun to grasp God's somewhat hidden influence in the world in which we live. The nation Israel rose when God meant for it to emerge, and the gospel came to the world through Israel. The gospel is still affecting the globe and will continue to alter history forever until all Christ's enemies are under His feet (1 Cor. 15:26-27) and until the consummation of the eternal state.

Since God and His influence are such that it is always going to be impossible to escape it, mankind can save himself the trouble that comes upon those that ignore God's gracious warnings to repent and believe the gospel. Since nothing is hidden from God and the heat of His omniscient gaze (Heb. 4:13), it is better to submit to God and to resist the devil so that he will flee (Jas 4:7). Coming to God through faith in Christ is a better option than temporarily enjoying the pleasures of sin for a season (Heb. 11:25) only to have to endure eternal wrath afterward for willful unbelief (Jn 3:36). Failure to revere God while it is still day results in falling into His hands when one least expects it (Heb. 10:31).

**Questions for self-reflection:**

(1) Do you think it takes more faith to believe that God created everything and set everything in motion, or does it take more faith to believe that He did not do so?

(2) If you were an unbeliever living somewhere where the gospel had not previously reached, and someone came to you and told you about a Man named Jesus who came to an obscure village from an obscure background. If they told you that man, Jesus, claimed to be God and the Savior of the world, do you think you would believe the gospel the first time you heard it?

(3) Who do you know that currently abides under God's wrath that will have to endure the heat of His hell for all eternity if they do not believe the gospel? How can you share the gospel with them in the next week?

**19:7. The law of the Lord is perfect, converting the soul; The testimony of the Lord is sure, making wise the simple;**

---

The finished canon, the 66 books of Scripture, records every word of God. Taken together, it makes up God's **perfect law.** It tells us who He is and what He expects from us. There is no need to remove anything from it or add anything to it. God explicitly commands not to do so (e.g., Rev. 22:19). Since God is perfect (1 Jn 1:5), anything He gives us must be perfect (Jas 1:17), including His Word, His **Law.** All of it is profitable and serves the purpose of thoroughly furnishing man for every good work (2 Tim. 3:16). There is no issue in our frail human existence that God's Word fails to speak to in some way. It contains the full mind of God. It is how He has chosen to communicate to humanity, those created in His image (Gen. 1:27).

It teaches us that we need a Savior (Gal. 3:24). It shows us what sin is (Rom. 7:7, 1 Jn 3:4). It recounts our origins (Genesis). It predicts our end (Revelation). It tells us why we need to be saved, why our **soul** needs **converting.** It tells us that while the law can never save us, God is a great Savior who reconciles man to Himself through the death of the Great Mediator (1 Tim. 2:5), the Lord Jesus Christ (2 Cor. 5:19). It tells us that though we were alienated from God by our sins, He has reconciled us by Christ's death on our behalf (Col. 1:21). It reveals God's whole nature and character; everything man needs to know in this life about God to make an informed decision to submit to Him as Lord or flee from Him as a rebel (Jas 4:7). It tells us how our sin separates us from God and how God justifies us through the Lord Jesus Christ, how God can be just and the justifier of the ungodly (Rom. 3:26). It reveals God to those who search for Him (Heb. 11:6). Those who sincerely desire to know the God of the universe can learn all they need to know about Him in what He reveals on the pages of Holy Writ (2 Pet. 1:3).

It is what God meant for us to know. Scripture perfectly contains and reveals all that is necessary so that God can reward those who diligently seek Him. God's perfect law reveals God's perfect will. It does not have to contain all there is to know about God, but it does contain enough to make us, His creatures, accountable to Him (Acts 17:30-31, 2 Cor. 5:10). God's law perfectly reveals God to us in the way God wanted to reveal Himself to us. It is so perfect that when Jesus came, He did not add to or subtract from it but came to fulfill it (Matt. 5:17-18).

The law brings the knowledge of sin (Rom. 7:7). Such knowledge is essential in converting the soul. A sinner must realize they need saving before they will come to the Savior. They must realize they need to be saved from wrath through Him (Rom. 5:9). People must know that sin separates them from holy God (Isa. 59:2). The law makes room for the gospel so that it can convert the soul. It is the tutor that brings sinners to the Teacher, to the **Lord** Jesus Christ (Gal. 3:24). It is good if one uses it lawfully (1 Tim. 1:8).

The Word of God is also referred to as His **testimony**. It is God's testimony to humankind that He is there, we are accountable to Him, and He has made a way to reconcile us to Himself through the Lord Jesus Christ. As in a courtroom, the testimony helps or hurts a case. His testimony is always truthful and tells absolute truth about Himself and us. It makes plain the reality that we are hopeless and without recourse in our feeble attempts to earn His favor. It tells us that our righteous deeds are as filthy rags in His sight (Isa. 64:6). As such, if humanity stands a hope in heaven at seeing Him as He is (1 Jn 3:2), man must humble Himself before the mighty hand of God (1 Pet. 5:6). When man humbles himself, only then does God exalt him. The great oxymoron of the gospel is that God, the One to whom we must humble ourselves to be reconciled, took the initiative and humbled Himself so that we could be reconciled to Him (1 Tim. 3:16, Philippians 2:8). The worthy One who is perfectly just justifies unworthy sinners.

The testimony found in Scripture informs us that when we had separated ourselves and built a wall between ourselves and God, Christ came to tear down the wall and nailed what was against us to His cross (Eph. 2:14). This testimony is a **sure** testimony. We can trust it. It comes from the only source that is without sin. Sin stains mankind's works. Nothing God does is polluted by the Fall.

This is why His Word can be trusted not to return void, to accomplish what it went forth to accomplish (Isa. 55:11).

The **simple** is made wise by believing in the God of the Bible and believing the gospel. The Scriptures make the simple wise unto salvation (2 Tim. 3:15). This is not only a one-time belief. This is a continual belief. This is also a belief that produces results in the life of the believer. Before coming to saving faith, the lost are called fools (Rom. 1:22), dead (Eph. 2:1), alienated (Col. 1:21), and simple, among other things. God turns fools into wise people. God turns dead people into living people (Gal. 2:20). God turns alienated people into reconciled people (Col. 1:21). God turns simple people into able people (Phil. 4:13). God equips His offspring to be hearers and doers of the Word (Jas 1:22) and to be zealous for good works (Ti 2:14). They will not stay simple and immature forever. As they grow in grace and in the knowledge of the Lord and Savior Jesus Christ (2 Pet. 3:18), as they desire the pure milk of the Word that they may grow thereby (1 Pet. 2:2), as they seek the Lord, as they abide in the Lord, the Lord will reveal Himself to them (Jn 15:1-8). The Lord will reveal Himself to the babes while hiding Himself from the **wise** and prudent (Matt. 11:25). The wise realize that apart from Him, they can do nothing (John 15:5). They recognize that they are utterly dependent upon Him for their next breath, so they had better live carefully in His sight. The wise know that it is foolish for them to trust in themselves. As the wise get to know their Lord in His Word, they see more of who He is and more of who they are. When they begin to grasp the great chasm between them and how God took that away in Christ, worship should ensue in the hearts of the regenerate. As believers search the Scriptures, they realize that if they possess any wisdom, it is only the result of God working in them (Philippians 2:12-13). He has made them wise to salvation through the Scriptures (2 Tim. 3:15). He has saved them by grace through faith (Eph. 2:8). They have nothing they can boast about (Ephesians 2:9). The veil is removed (2 Cor. 3:16). Mysteries are revealed (Mk 4:11, Eph. 3:3, Col. 1:26). New life in Christ begins. All because of God's mercy.

## Questions for self-reflection:

(1) Why might God not want anyone to add to or take away from His law?

(2) If there was anything about God which was not perfect, how might that affect our ability to trust Him with our lives?

(3) Why might some people be willing to accept the gospel and others be unwilling to accept the gospel?

(4) What are some reasons why it is not unfair that humanity is accountable to God?

(5) Did Jesus come to correct God's law or to fulfill it?

(6) From what does a lost sinner need to be saved?

(7) What can humanity do to earn God's favor?

(8) How did God fix the separation that man created by his sin against God?

(9) What makes us wise unto salvation, according to what Paul told Timothy?

**19:8. The statutes of the Lord are right, rejoicing the heart; The commandment of the Lord is pure, enlightening the eyes;**

Statutes are authoritative statements to which the people under that authority are to be held accountable. The Word of God contains statutes by which His people are to conduct themselves. Those who obey the government's statutes get to live at peace with them in a civil setting. If the same citizens fail to observe the statutes that have been put in place by those whose job it is to punish evildoers, those citizens are to be held accountable for their failure to submit to the authority of the statutes. God employs governments as His agent by which His justice is carried out (Rom. 13:1-7).

**The statutes of the Lord** help the people of the Lord see how they should order their lives. There is nothing unjust in any of the laws of the Lord. They are there so that His people can show His glory to a watching world by their daily conduct. These statutes **are right** in that if they govern the people, there will be nothing crooked in their lifestyles. Since they are perfect, conduct ruled by these statutes will be perfect conduct. Since we are sinners by nature and by choice, we fail to conduct ourselves by these statutes perfectly. When God's Spirit enables God's people to follow God's statutes, the difference between God's people and Satan's people is made plain.

God's glory is demonstrated, and God's justice is illustrated as those who are vessels of wrath, Satan's people, are easily seen because they do not care to live by God's statutes. The sheep, on the other hand, those who know His voice (Jn 10:27-28), hear and obey His Word because it **rejoic**es **their heart.** God's Word leads the sheep into all truth and holy living as it is the agent the indwelling Holy Spirit uses to produce fruit in the good Christian trees that the heavenly Father plants (Matt. 7:15-20, Matt. 15:13). God's Word rejoices the heart because it contains the knowledge and information required to lead men to salvation (2 Tim. 3:15). The statutes of the Lord rejoice the heart because they teach about the Lord Jesus Christ, the spotless Lamb of God who came to take away the sins of the world (Jn 1:29) and be the Captain of salvation (Heb. 2:10) to all those who believe. Since the law of sin and death (Romans 8:2) entangles people in bondage (Gal. 5:1), this is not the law that rejoices the heart. The law that rejoices the heart must release men from the condemnation that their sin impresses upon them. In Christ, the condemnation goes away. The law of the Spirit of life in Christ Jesus sets men free from the law of sin and death (Rom. 8:1-2).

It is the job of faithful gospel ministers to preach the statutes of the Lord. It is right for the faithful ministers to preach the Word (2 Tim. 4:2). They thunder the law to bring the knowledge of sin (Rom. 7:7). They preach Christ and Him crucified (1 Cor. 2:2) because it is the power of God unto salvation (Rom. 1:16). The commandment of the Lord is any doctrine found in God's Word or any practical admonition based upon Scriptural principles.

Christians, those marked by walking out God's Word in their lives (Jas 2:19), know that God's commandments are pure and good for them like a refreshingly cool spring of water on a hot desert day. God's commandments **enlighten the eyes** of sinful man since they show man how lost and undone he is apart from the Lord Jesus Christ (Rom. 3:23). They show him his sin, how it qualifies him for death (Rom. 6:23). They show man how qualified a Savior the Lord Jesus Christ is in that He kept that law perfectly (2 Cor. 5:21). The commandments enlighten the eyes of the saved in that they are enabled to see how they have fallen off God's path. The commandments point them to the changes they need to make to get back onto God's way. The commandments magnify the glory of the Lord Jesus Christ in that He would condescend to save sinners as despicable as us, who deserve such wrath. Only because of such a good God's amazing love, grace, and mercy can this salvation be even possible and yet so accessible.

**Questions for self-reflection:**

(1) Have the Lord's statutes ever rejoiced your heart? Have you ever discovered something in God's Word that brought excitement to your soul?

(2) Have you ever seen a moral command in the Word of God that you were surprised to know that you knew you must commit to obey as best as you could because it was God's Word to you?

(3) Do you recognize the finished Canon as authoritative for your life?

(4) If you knew the laws of the government under which you lived, and you purposely disobeyed those laws, if the government found out about your disobedience, would you expect to continue to be able to live at peace under that government?

(5) Assuming you would not expect to live at peace under a government whose laws you flippantly broke, would you expect the God of the universe to wink at our sins against His governance?

(6) Who allows a justified Saint to obey the moral law of God, albeit imperfectly (Ezek. 36:26-27)?

(7) Even though the Law cannot condemn a justified sinner, is the justified sinner free to live however they want if they are under God's grace (Rom.6:1-2)?

(8) Would enlightened, previously blind eyes expect to see the world differently once they had become enlightened? Does a saved person see the world differently than a lost person?

**19:9. The fear of the Lord is clean, enduring forever; The judgments of the Lord are true and righteous altogether.**

There is no pollution in **the fear of the Lord**. It **is clean**. Sin pollutes and defiles. Following and fearing the Lord is the antithesis to following sin. The Lord cleanses from sin (1 Jn 1:9). The Lord **endur**es **forever** since He is eternal (Deut. 33:27, Ps. 48:14, Prov. 8:23, Isa. 40:28, Hab. 1:12, Rev. 1:8, Rev. 22:13). Likewise, those who fear Him endure forever in that they possess eternal life and will live forever with the Lord for eternity. In contrast, those without eternal life will perish (Jn 3:16). Those who have eternal life wear white and clean robes in the sense that God cleansed them of their sins not because of any righteousness of their own but because of the worthy Lord Jesus (Rev. 7:14).

The fear of the Lord endures forever because the Lord endures forever. He has made a way for humanity to be with Him forever by faith in the Lord Jesus Christ. By faith in the Lord Jesus Christ, the law's penalty is done away with, and the power and penalty of sin are overcome (Rom. 8:2). The sacrifices and ceremonies of the Mosaic economy are done away with and forever replaced with the once for all sacrifice of the Lord Jesus Christ (Heb. 10:10), which permanently endures (Rom. 10:4). Persecution and opposition will come against gospel adherents. But the Lord endures forever and will enable the sheep to overcome (1 Jn 5:4-5).

God has left His people with His Word. In His Word, His people learn to reverence Him and walk worthy of their callings (Eph. 4:1). A believer who walks worthy of the Lord with a proper fear (reverence) for the Lord sanctifies the Lord in their hearts (1 Pet. 3:15). He takes captive every thought to the obedience of Christ (2 Cor. 10:3-5) and considers that they do not want to be the stumbling block that prevents someone from coming to saving faith (Mark 9:42).

Unlike the ceremonial law, which Christ did away with, the moral law continues to be in place. The conscience is proof of this as God has written His law on the hearts of everyone (Rom. 2:15).

By it comes the knowledge of sin (Rom. 7:7). Breaking it (1 Jn 3:4) teaches sinners their need for a Savior (Gal. 3:24).

**The judgments of the Lord are** akin to the Word of God. The Word of God records how God has judged humanity generation after generation. Even though the canon was finished millennia ago, the principles contained therein are applicable today, so man can make applications to his life today based on the Word of God, which God finished inspiring thousands of years ago. God's Word, the finished canon, the 66 inspired books of holy writ contain God's **true and righteous** judgments. These show how God expects His people to govern themselves out of gratitude for all God has done for them in Christ. These show how Christ made atonement for sin and how God reconciles the world to Himself in Christ (2 Cor. 5:19).

### Questions for self-reflection:

(1) Is dishwater clean or dirty? Are you able to easily see through it to the bottom?

(2) Is sin more like dirty dishwater or clean, pure water?

(3) As you spend more time with the Lord, are you becoming more like Him? Is He cleaning up your life?

(4) Are you more like the world or more like the Lord as you acquire more of a fear of the Lord?

(5) As you walk in a sinful society that knows not the fear of the Lord, as the Spirit leads you to contradict immoral society, do you anticipate that your ability to live at peace with the community will be hampered or helped?

(6) As you renew your mind with God's truth, do you expect to have a greater understanding of the Lord's expectations on your life?

(7) If you had a fuller understanding of what the Lord expected from you if you intentionally dishonored that expectation, do you think that it would be more or less likely that the Lord might decide to bring retribution upon you for your disobedience?

**19:10. More to be desired are they than gold, Yea, than much fine gold; Sweeter also than honey and the honeycomb.**

The judgments of the Lord (Ps. 19:9), contained in the perfect Law of the Lord (Ps. 19:7), which is all of Scripture (2 Tim. 3:16), are **more to be desired than gold**. Gold is a precious, valuable commodity. Nobody or nothing is more valuable than knowing God through the Lord Jesus Christ. Christ Himself said that man should be willing to part with anything to obtain eternal life when he compared eternal life to selling everything to buy a field or a pearl (Matt. 13:44-46). As valuable as gold or diamonds or anything found on this earth may be, we cannot take any of the earthly wealth we amass with us into eternity (Mk 8:36). However, we can take the imputed righteousness of Christ with us as that is what we need to have the privilege of eternal life in heaven that the Trinity and the saints share.

**Honey** tastes delicious and desirable to most. It is a welcome addition to tea, coffee, and many other things. But, as pleasant as honey is to experience, nothing can compare to the sweetness of eternal life in Christ Jesus the Lord made available to all men. This grace of God has appeared and is readily accessible for sinners to seek it (Ti 2:11). As bitter as life and its adversity can be at times, the sweetness of the eternal life that comes with belief in the finished work of Christ on the cross on our behalf is sweet to the sheep. It is a savor of life unto life (2 Cor. 2:16). Christ sheds His love abroad in the hearts of believers (Rom. 5:5). They spend their lives getting to know Him. He reveals Himself to those who seek Him (Matt. 7:7).

### Questions for self-reflection:

(1) Generally speaking, would most people you know desire fine gold if they could get a lot of it?

(2) Generally speaking, do most people find honey pleasant to the taste?

(3) What should the desire of the law of the Lord be in proportion to desired commodities like gold and honey?

(4) If you surveyed most Christians that you know, out of one hundred, how many would you guess would say that they would desire knowing God more than a winning lottery ticket?

(5) If you could choose between a winning lottery ticket to go along with eternal hell and living in a cardboard box with eternal life in heaven, what would you pick?

**19:11. Moreover by them Your servant is warned, And in keeping them there is great reward.**

---

Saints serve the Lord. The psalmist is a **servant** of the Lord. Every believer in every generation is a servant to their Master, the Lord (1 Cor. 4:1). The psalmist received the wisdom to carry out his earthly offices from God's law, God's statutes, God's commandments, and God's judgments. As God revealed Himself to the psalmist and as the psalmist obeyed what he knew to obey, the more he knew God. The more he recognized God's will for his life, the more he recognized when God **warned** him.

Kings, such as the psalmist, especially needed to be held accountable. There is no better accountability than to be held to God's righteous standard since He is the One to whom all humanity will have to answer (2 Cor. 5:10). Kings had to avail themselves to God's law so they could adequately carry out God's will for the people over which they ruled (Deut. 17:18, 2 Kgs 22:11). The Lord's Word was sufficient for a king to execute his office then. The Lord's Word is sufficient for His people to perform the offices into which God has placed them today. The Scriptures are sufficient for every issue of life (2 Tim. 3:16). Even if the Scriptures do not speak as directly as one would like to a topic, the principles contained therein can be gleaned and applied to life by anyone possessing the Holy Spirit. God's Word provides ample instruction, sufficient warning, and suitable clarity to formulate an informed response to any issue.

When the Law of the Lord exposes sin in the reader (Rom. 7:7), the sinner does well to recognize that they have been warned. They do well to heed the warning and respond to it with humility. Responses of repentant faith by sinners to God's warnings provide opportunities for fruitfulness. As man diligently seeks God in God's Word, man will find God. If man responds to what he learns in the Word about how he is to conduct himself in this life, he will live at peace with God and with man more times than he will not (Rom. 12:18). God's Word illuminates the mind, fills the heart, and shows the glory of God to the heart that genuinely seeks Him diligently (Heb. 11:6).

---

A **great reward** that man experiences in this life is peace with God and man due to man's obedience to God. Even if man, by his obedience to God, is made an enemy with his fellow man, the obedient, persecuted man can still take solace in that it is better to obey God than man (Acts 5:29). He can still have comfort knowing that he, a servant, is destined to be like his Master, the Lord Jesus Christ, the Savior of his sins (Matt. 10:25). Jesus predicted that a servant should be like his master. As such, believers should not be surprised when they suffer for their association with the Lord Jesus Christ (2 Tim. 3:12).

Nevertheless, they can take comfort in knowing that God's grace is sufficient to any circumstance they face, even martyrdom (2 Cor. 12:9). There is no greater reward than knowing God through Christ as knowing Him and the power of His resurrection (Phil. 3:10) promotes peace, protects against sin, and is more precious than obtaining anything in this life. The Lord's disciples can discover these things by knowing God's will as God's Word reveals it. Knowing God's Word promotes peace between man and God and with man and man. Knowing God's Word keeps one on the way of truth and keeps one from the ways of error.

## Questions for self-reflection:

(1) Do you think the society in which you live would be better governed if society enforced God's moral law in its initially intended way? Why or why not?
(2) In most societies, why is adultery considered wrong? Why is murder mostly considered wrong?
(3) Is the Word of God sufficient for you to carry out your duties?
(4) If someone asked you for advice on an important decision they were wrestling with, would you now have enough cursory Bible knowledge to make a well-informed, biblically-based decision? If not, what would it take for you to reach that level of wisdom?
(5) What is the great reward of living a devoted life to God?

**19:12. Who can understand his errors? Cleanse me from secret faults.**

---

Man consistently underestimates how sinful he is. As a result, he does not correctly **understand his errors**. In every generation, believers such as the psalmist have a sinful disposition after their conversion to battle until their final breath (Rom. 7:19). His sins are the errors that separate him from his God (Isa. 64:6).

One of man's sad errors is thinking that his sins are not as bad as God says. Our iniquities take us away like the wind (Isa. 64:6). They earn us our physical death (Rom. 6:23). They hurt our relationship with God, even as believers (Ps. 66:18). They create contention with our fellow man. One sin is enough to separate man from God for all eternity (Jas 2:10). Even if man does not get caught in this life after every sin is committed, he still has to bear the consequence of a further dulled conscience (Rom. 1:24-28), one that is less receptive to the corrections given by God's Word.

Man consistently underestimates his sinfulness because man always fails to compare himself with a perfect and holy God (Rom. 7:13). Instead, man makes himself feel better than he should by comparing himself with his fellow sinful man. Man can always find someone who is more outwardly immoral than himself. He can always give himself the false sense of security that his neighbor is worse than he is. The problem is that man is looking to the wrong standard to make a judgment about himself in this instance. Instead of comparing himself to a fellow sinner, man should be comparing himself to the God who created him in His image (Gen. 1:27), to whom he is ultimately accountable (Acts 17:30-31). Each conscious choice to sin that man makes is a deliberate decision to make one's own desires superior to God's desires.

Man can get a more proper sense of who he is compared to a holy God by looking into the Word which God has left him with as a gracious gift. It shows how holy God is (1 Pet. 1:16), how sinful man is (Rom. 3:23), and how merciful God is to offer reconciliation to man after man spurned God (Eph. 2:4).

---

An honest man will admit that he has sinned in many public ways that he would not have a hard time admitting. The psalmist here is not asking about that. Here, the psalmist is asking God to reveal ways in which he has sinned that he, as yet, is not even aware of. Only God is aware of these sins. He is asking for God to show him a glimpse of how well God knows him. He wants to be so close to God that he can practically touch him, and he knows that his sins separate him from God. He wants nothing to separate him from access to the God who made him. If he has to make bare more things than even he knows about himself, he wants God to reveal those things to him so he can have an even richer relationship with God.

The good news for believers reading this is that Jesus Christ forever broke the sin barrier that separates sinners from God in His perfect life, sacrificial death, and resurrection from the dead (1 Cor. 15:3-4). If we humbly come to Him, we can receive His righteousness, and He can take our sin upon Himself and give us the righteousness that gets us to God (2 Cor. 5:21).

**Questions for self-reflection:**

(1) How do you think you would respond if God showed you a more complete picture of your sinfulness? Would it look more like Isaiah in Isaiah 6?

(2) According to Romans 6:23, what have we earned as wages because of our deliberate choice to sin?

(3) Why is it insufficient to compare our sinfulness with another person's sinfulness?

(4) Is God unfair to judge the world? Why or why not?

**19:13. Keep back Your servant also from presumptuous sins; Let them not have dominion over me. Then I shall be blameless, And I shall be innocent of great transgression.**

---

The psalmist here asks God to **keep** him **from** willful, **presumptuous sins** committed without considering God's thoughts on the matter. This is reminiscent of Paul's injunction to take every thought captive to the obedience of Christ (2 Cor. 10:5). The psalmist does not want to fall into the trap of living how the lost live, as if nothing in this life matters, that there is no God (Ps. 14:1), no afterlife. As a result of that destructive worldview, they often treat others poorly and live irresponsibly. The sins that the psalmist asks for help with avoiding are the sins that those without God commit without a second thought. People who commit such sins that the psalmist wants to avoid are prideful, self-sufficient people (Jas 4:6). He does not want to live like the rest who live as if this life is all there is. If the psalmist were to live in such a way, then God would resist him, which would be intolerable (Jas 4:6).

The psalmist wants to be subject to God's law because he knows that there is safety by remaining within its limits. The psalmist knows that he lacks sufficient resources to keep from hurting his relationship with God through sinning. While sin is inevitable, it is still incumbent upon the believer to choose each day who they will serve (Josh. 24:15) and to put on their armor (Eph. 6:10-20), so they will be able to wage successful war (Gal. 5:17). The psalmist knows that he knows better than committing the sins as recklessly as the lost, so he wants the Lord to help him refrain from such behavior.

Sin has dominion over lost people. Sin does **not have dominion over** the saved, as those not under the law but under grace have access to the Holy Spirit to help them overcome temptation when it comes (Rom. 6:14, 1 Cor. 10:13). Grace is the governing principle of the saved. In contrast, the lost person frequently runs headlong into sin without much restraint. The lost is more concerned with his own ease and not getting himself caught than he is with

---

living at peace with God and with his fellow man (Rom. 12:18). If it were not for the Spirit leading the believer and equipping them to handle anything that comes their way by the power of the Holy Spirit (Jn 16:13, 2 Tim. 3:17, Heb. 13:20-21), then they, too, would easily be led away from God's way and into the path of sin. The saved are kept from such a great transgression, such as would forfeit their eternal life (Rom. 8:30, 1 Pet. 1:5).

Nothing the saved do can lose their eternal life (Jn 10:28-29). They did not earn it. Christ earned it for them (Eph. 2:8-9). They cannot keep it. Christ keeps it for them. They cannot lose it. Their life is hidden with Christ in God (Col. 3:3). The Spirit will keep them from giving in to temptations when they listen to the Spirit and do not ignore its gracious warnings. When believers do sin, they are ultimately declared not guilty. They receive no condemnation (Rom. 8:1). Christ received the condemnation in their place. They will be acquitted as Christ, their advocate (1 Jn 2:1), intercedes for them (Heb. 7:25). Christ makes His followers **blameless** when He imputes His righteousness to their account. As they grow closer to Christ during the process of sanctification, cleansing from faults takes place, and their lifestyle, while never totally free from sin on this side of the grave, will resemble Christ more and more. They are deemed **innocent of great transgression** as their guilt is imputed to Christ, who can keep them from stumbling (Jude 1:24).

## Questions for self-reflection:

(1) How would our lives look different than they currently do if we actually did take every thought captive to the obedience of Christ? How would our marriages look? How would our families look? How would our societies look?

(2) Does it scare you when you see people who conduct themselves as if there is no God? If such people were to breathe their last today, what would be the result for them? Do you have enough compassion for them to try to reach them somehow?

(3) If you discovered that there was something about your lifestyle that caused God to resist you, what would you be willing to do to correct it?

(4) Even as a saved person, why is it important to you to live at peace with God and your neighbor?

(5) Do you think that you can grieve the Holy Spirit without a second thought because Christ has forgiven you? Why or why not?

(6) Does your life demonstrate that Christ has ahold of you such that He is keeping you from stumbling?

**19:14. Let the words of my mouth and the meditation of my heart Be acceptable in Your sight, O Lord, my strength and my Redeemer.**

---

The psalmist knew that God created mankind such that God closely connected his mouth and heart. In other words, what he said was a reflection of what was in his heart (Matt. 12:34). His words would either justify him or condemn him (Matt. 12:37). He wanted his **words** to **be acceptable** before God, and he knew that if they were acceptable before God, it would not matter if his words were not acceptable before his fellow man. The psalmist wanted to commend God's gracious love to his fellow man. Perhaps the best way for the psalmist to do that was with the words he uttered before them (Eph. 4:29), even if his fellow man wanted nothing to do with the psalmist's God. In addition to having godly words, the psalmist wanted to think godly thoughts. He wanted to have God always in his thoughts so that his life pleased God. He wanted his silent prayers that only he and God knew about to be acceptable to God. Even if his fellow man did not accept his God or did not accept him because of his God, the psalmist did not want there to be any overt sin in his life for which his enemies could reproach him. If the psalmist's thoughts, **meditation**s, and words were acceptable before God, chances are his actions would follow suit.

The psalmist knew that God was his rock, the source of his **strength**. God had redeemed him. In every generation, God is the **redeemer** of those who call out to Him for redemption. The saved were once slaves to sin (Rom. 6:20), but God bought them out of slavery to sin and redeemed them to Himself through the blood of the Lord Jesus Christ (Eph. 1:7). All believers are redeemed and rescued from the power and penalty of sin. They have the freedom to walk in the light instead of being confined to the darkness of sin. One day, God will completely remove them from this cursed world and free them from the presence of sin (Rom. 6:22).

**Questions for self-reflection:**

(1) How would we know if the words of our mouths and the meditations of our hearts were acceptable in God's sight?

(2) If you knew your words were not acceptable to your neighbor and might get you killed by your neighbor, but if those same words were pleasing to God, would you love your neighbor enough to put yourself at risk to share the truth with him?

(3) Can people with "right" actions trick people into believing they are right with God? Why or why not?

(4) Does God care if our actions are right if our thoughts and words are wrong?

# Psalm 20

**20:1. May the Lord answer you in the day of trouble; May the name of the God of Jacob defend you;**

---

David could have written this psalm when he was preparing to go to war. The days of Christ were **days of trouble**. As a babe, Christ had trouble that caused His family to have to flee from the clutches of Herod (Matt. 2:13-18). Christ had trouble after His baptism during His temptation in the wilderness (Matt. 4:1-11). Christ had trouble when His disciples failed to understand Him (Matt. 16:5-12). Christ had trouble when the multitudes failed to believe Him (Mk 6:1-6). Christ had trouble when the religious leaders of the day sought to have Him killed (Matt.12:14). Christ had trouble in the Garden of Gethsemane when He sweated drops of blood as He contemplated taking the wrath of His holy Father for the sins of the world (Lk 22:44). As he endured the mocking and beating during the whole event of His arrest, trials, and death, He had trouble.

When Christ hung on the cross when He cried out to His Father, as the wrath of God against sin came against Him, as His Father forsook Him, He had trouble (Matt. 27:46). Through it all, His God, **the God of Jacob**, did **defend Him. The Lord** Christ perfectly trusted in His Father to provide an example for all those sheep who walk in His steps (1 Pet. 2:23). Before then, Israel was troubled by various sources when they left Egypt (Exod. 16:1-36, Exod. 17:1-7). Unlike the Lord Jesus Christ, in whom there is no sin (2 Cor. 5:21), Israel sinfully murmured to Moses. Moses cried out in the day of trouble (Exod. 17:4). The Lord answered the people on behalf of Moses (Exod. 16:4).

Believers in every generation have trouble (Jn 16:33). Jesus said they should expect to have trouble. Jesus said that when believers have trouble in this world that they could be encouraged because He went before them and overcame the world. Since Jesus overcame sin, death, and hell, He is the perfect advocate (1 Jn 2:1), the all-sufficient High Priest (Heb. 4:14-15) that saves to the uttermost (Heb. 7:25). For the saint, there is no temptation for which God does not mercifully provide a way of escape (1 Cor.

---

10:13). For every trial, there is always a way in which persever-ance and patience can be enjoyed (Jas 1:2-8). Believers can enjoy perseverance and patience because as God the Father was there to defend His Son, the Lord Jesus Christ, so He remains there to defend all those whose faith is in His Son.

## Questions for self-reflection:

(1) What are some examples of things that showed that Christ's life contained days of trouble?

(2) How have you seen God come to your defense in your times of trouble?

(3) Can God's answers to our times of trouble take the form of godly thoughts? Oppressive situations coming to an end? Persecution situations coming to an end? Providing for a physical need? Providing for a spiritual need? Providing a way of escape from temptation? Can you think of examples from your own life where God provided in any of the above ways?

**20:2. May He send you help from the sanctuary, And strengthen you out of Zion;**

God dwelt in **the sanctuary**. God had a physical sanctuary, the tabernacle, built for Him under the authority of Moses, where sacrifices and offerings took place under the old economy (Exod. 26). After Moses, Solomon had a temple built where God's presence dwelt (1 Kgs 5-6). Now, in the church age, God dwells in all Christians via the Holy Spirit (1 Cor. 6:19). Human hearts are the sanctuary of God. God's presence, power, and promises are available to strengthen them all their days until they are with the Lord forever in heaven. God's presence dwells in Christians because of the finished work of Jesus Christ on the cross for them. Christ promised that He would return to heaven and send **help**, namely the Holy Spirit (Jn 14:16-18). After Christ died and rose again according to the Scriptures (1 Cor. 15:3-4), God sent forth the Spirit into the hearts of believers (Gal. 4:6).

The power of God is available to **strengthen** any believer in the face of anything the enemy may send their way. Believers bring good tidings of great joy to others when they share the gospel with them. They receive supernatural strength **out of Zion**, from God Himself, as they go into all the world and preach the gospel to every creature (Matt. 28:19), trusting God to bring fruit out of their efforts.

## Questions for self-reflection:

(1) How are Christians today like the Old Testament sanctuary?
(2) Since God is with them, what situations are believers not equipped to face?

**20:3. May He remember all your offerings, And accept your burnt sacrifice. Selah.**

When believers worship the Lord genuinely in spirit and in truth (Jn 4:24), God will **remember** the **offerings** they bring. Such worship reaches heaven as a sweet aroma before the Lord (Gen. 8:20-21, 2 Cor. 2:15). When believers sincerely praise the Lord for who He is, what He has done, and give thanks back to Him, He will **accept** their **burnt sacrifice**.

Under the old economy, literal sacrifices and offerings were mandated by God (See Leviticus). In the new economy, after the once for all sacrifice of the Lamb of God, the Lord Jesus Christ, the repetitious old covenant sacrifices are no longer required since Christ died once for all (Heb. 10:10). Now, believers can remember Christ, meditate on His person, and set their affections on Him (Col. 3:1-3). When they do that, they can be sure that when they come before His presence with sprinkled consciences (Heb. 10:22) that God will accept them.

Even after their conversion, believers still possess the sinful nature that wars with the flesh (Rom. 7:14-25, Gal. 5:17). If it were not for the fact of Christ's efficacious blood ever living to intercede for them (Heb. 7:25), they could not trust that their offerings and sacrifices of religiosity could ever be enough to procure recurring acceptance with the beloved. In Christ, however, since Christ was perfect for them since He intercedes for them, pleads for them, and fights for them, all the perfections of the Son of God smother the saints' imperfections. Christ is the One in whom the Father is well pleased (Matt. 3:17).

### Questions for self-reflection:

(1) What activities in your life prevent God from receiving your offerings and sacrifices of worship and devotion that you have directed to Him?

(2) Does the access Christ purchased for you that enables you to come into God's presence motivate you to enter into His presence more often? Do you ever take the access you have for granted?

**20:4. May He grant you according to your heart's desire, And fulfill all your purpose.**

---

When Christ called to His Father in His day of trouble, He needed His Father to sustain Him when His trouble confronted him in its myriad physical forms. His Father did perfectly help Him execute all His holy will during His earthly ministry (Jn 17:4). Christ perfectly **fulfill**ed **all** His Father's **purpose** for His life, which was primarily to be the propitiation for our sins (1 Jn 2:2). Christ desired to execute the mission His Father sent Him to earth to execute, namely, to secure the salvation of a people that the entire Trinity planned for before the foundation of the world (Eph. 1:4).

Christ is the worthy yet unattainable goal that all Christians should strive to imitate (Matt. 10:25, 1 Cor. 11:1, Eph. 4:13). The believer's **heart's desire** should be to be transformed by the renewing of their minds so that they will know God's perfect will for their lives (Rom. 12:2). They should desire, above all, to know Him and the power of His resurrection (Phil. 3:10). Should the believer ask God for this desire and should they seek it as they ask for it, they should expect to receive what they ask for, as such a desire is in line with God's will for every Christian (Matt. 7:7). The believer's heart's desire and purpose should not be to have as easy an earthly life as possible. Instead, believers should seek to be more like their Master, the Lord Jesus Christ, who did not seek to leave trouble as much as He overcame it. He did not shy away from responsibility. He embraced it. He did not succumb to temptation; He conquered it. He is the great High Priest (Heb. 4:14-15). His people can be more than conquerors (Rom. 8:37) as long as their hope is in Him and not themselves or some other part of this decaying world that is passing away (1 Jn 2:17).

## Questions for self-reflection:

(1) What was Christ's primary desire when He came to earth the first time?

---

(2) What is your primary desire with the time you have on this earth in this life?

(3) If becoming more like Christ is your primary desire, if God has appointed some challenging means for you to endure for that desire to be realized, would you be willing to endure whatever God appointed for you?

**20:5. We will rejoice in your salvation, And in the name of our God we will set up our banners! May the Lord fulfill all your petitions.**

---

The psalmist changes subjects from the procurer of salvation, the Lord Jesus Christ (Heb. 1:3), to the participants in salvation, the church (2 Pet. 1:4). The sheep can **rejoice in** the **salvation** which Christ purchased for them at Calvary (Phil. 3:1, Phil. 4:4). It is not owed to anything desirable in any of them. No. They are all unclean things, and all their iniquities take them away (Isa. 64:6). All the enemies that the sheep will ever face were forever defeated when Christ rose from the grave after His substitutionary death on the cross (Eph. 2:15, Col. 2:15). The sheep can rejoice in the salvation that Christ obtained for them since He ever lives to intercede for them (Heb. 7:25). While with every sin, they break His heart (Eph. 4:30), there is no final condemnation as the law of the Spirit of life has made them free from the law of sin and death (Rom. 8:1-2). Christ returned to the Father's right hand after His ascension (Acts 7:55-56) to the place of power (Mk 14:62). From there, He omnipotently exercises His power as intercessor (Rom. 8:34) and mediator (1 Tim. 2:5). As such, there is nothing that can separate the genuine believer from the love of God (Rom. 8:38-39). Since God is for them, none can be against them (Rom. 8:31). They are more than conquerors in Him (Rom. 8:37). They can go forth in His name and face anything, even death, because they know that, ultimately, even the gates of hell cannot prevail against them because Christ has already prevailed for them (Matt. 16:18).

They can go in God's name and set up their banners as they prepare to fight for Him. As they **set up** their **banners,** it will be a strong reminder for themselves that the Lord goes before them. It will be a reminder that is detectable by their enemies that they are not alone in this battle. With the banner of God in the corner of the believer, the saints can courageously wage war against Satan and the world. The armor which God supplies (Eph. 6:10-20) is an abundant source of protection and provision against any foe. Believers can go into any situation confidently because the Lord

Jesus Christ, the sufficient High Priest (Heb. 4:14-15), has already conquered death and will one day put all His enemies under His feet (1 Cor. 15:26-27). The church can trust the Lord will fulfill all their petitions according to His will. They can trust that anything that they ask in His name He hears them (1 Jn 5:14). Since He intercedes them, He will not withhold any good thing from them (Ps. 84:11). The problem for the church is that when they do not get what they ask for, they are prone to mistake their desire, which is affected by their indwelling sin, with God's will. It is not always God's will for Him to give His people precisely that for which they ask. He knows their motives and thoughts (Ps. 139:4, Matt. 9:4, Heb. 4:12, 1 Jn 3:20). He knows how they will respond to what He allows or does not allow them to have. Perhaps the petition is better fulfilled with the answer of "no," because a response of "yes" would be met with ingratitude or spending the received resources on our own lusts (Jas 4:3). The believer must respond to the seeming silence of God with patient trust that the Lord knows best even if it does not seem best to us in the moment of affliction. Whether the **Lord fulfills** our **petitions** in the ways we want Him to or not, we still have the privilege to rejoice in His salvation and set up our banner in His name.

## Questions for self-reflection:

(1) What made Christ want to die for you? Was it anything in you?
(2) Since you and I sin every day, how does knowing the fact that Christ continues to intercede and mediate for us affect you?
(3) If you could wear a banner out in public to show others that God is for you, so they better not be against you, what would your banner say, or what picture would it have on it?
(4) Of all the parts of the armor of God that work together to help us work out our salvation, do you have a favorite piece? Which one and why?

**20:6. Now I know that the Lord saves His anointed; He will answer him from His holy heaven With the saving strength of His right hand.**

---

David was temporarily the **anointed** king of Israel by Samuel (2 Sam. 5:4). The final anointed King over all, not only in Israel, is the Lord Jesus Christ. Christ, by His resurrection, emphatically declared Himself to be the Lord of everyone and everything to the glory of God the Father (Rom. 1:4, Phil. 2:11). Jesus was anointed from eternity past to be the long-awaited Messiah and declared Himself by word and deed to be just that. The throne of God and the current temple of God are in heaven. The earth is His footstool (Isa. 66:1). All His perfections are in His holy heaven. They are part of the daily experience of the saints and the angels. The prayers from the saints reach the throne of grace, located in the **holy heaven**. It is here that the cries of the saints are heard. Here, the Trinity works together, as three Persons in one God, to accomplish God's will on earth as it is in heaven (Matt. 6:10).

God's right hand strengthened Jesus, God the Son, to accomplish God's will when Jesus walked on the earth. **The saving strength of** God's **right hand**, Jesus' location (Heb. 1:3), answers the saints today as they make their requests known (Phil. 4:6-7, 1 Jn 5:14). Jesus was a man of sorrows and acquainted with grief (Isa. 53:3). As such, He became our sympathetic High Priest who experienced an even greater weight of sorrow than any of us will ever experience on this earth (Heb. 4:15). Because Jesus saves to the uttermost those who call upon Him for salvation, He is worthy to be trusted (Heb. 7:25).

## Questions for self-reflection:

(1) Can knowing that your prayers reach the holy heavens change your attitude toward prayer?
(2) How is Jesus the saving strength of God's right hand?

(3) Lookup other references in the Psalms to God's right hand. Are the things that are true of the right hand also true of the Lord Jesus Christ? If so, could the right hand references be veiled references to the Lord Jesus Christ?

**20:7. Some trust in chariots, and some in horses; But we will remember the name of the Lord our God.**

---

The Lord wants those created in His image (Gen. 1:27) to trust Him as Creator rather than in the things He has created. Chariots and horses were reliable means used when engaged with enemy forces in war in ancient times. War involves a battle. When God's people have battles to fight, God wants His people to trust in Him rather than their methods or knowledge (Prov. 3:5). Primarily, the conflicts that God's people wage daily are more of a spiritual nature than physical, though it is true that often Christians have physical enemies (Eph. 6:12).

God has equipped His people with everything they need to be successful (2 Pet. 1:3). He has furnished the required weapons to engage the enemy (2 Cor. 10:4). God's people should not place their hope in anything in this physical world, such as **chariots and horses**. Doing so is trusting in, in essence, worshiping, something created rather than worshiping and trusting in the Creator of all things (Rom. 1:25).

Misplaced affections characterize People who do not belong to God. They love and worship the creature rather than the Creator (Rom. 1:25, 1 Jn 2:15-17). In the contemporary church, a common temptation is to confuse trusting in Christ with trusting in the knowledge of Scripture, or baptism, or taking the Lord's supper, or leading a group. While these have their place and are helpful, we should not depend upon these things for salvation. Rather than trust in anything external, anything earthly, anything physical for deliverance from physical enemies, or spiritual enemies, such as Satan, his demonic forces, and sin, believers in Christ should trust in Him and Him alone to save them and to keep them saved (Heb. 12:18-24).

He calls us to **remember** His **name,** for there is no other name by which men can be saved than the name of the **Lord** Jesus Christ (Acts 4:12). His is the name above all names (Phil. 2:9). Only those who call upon His name will be saved (Rom. 10:13). The Lord Jesus Christ is the exact representation of God's nature (Heb. 1:3),

---

the fulness of the Godhead bodily (Col. 2:9), the one Mediator between **God** and man (1 Tim. 2:5). Before Abraham was, He is (Jn 8:58). Everything true about God is true about Christ because Christ is God incarnate.

The same power that raised Christ from the dead is available to Christians today so that they can walk in the newness of life (Rom. 6:4, Rom. 8:11). When the enemy comes after God's child with their proverbial chariots and horses, there is a whole army in the treasury of God, and God has equipped believers with armor to protect His people from enemy attacks (Eph. 6:10-20). The Lord wants His people to realize that their human strength is insufficient by itself to have success in this life in the spiritual battle that rages for the duration of our earthly pilgrimage. Once the people of God understand that, once they realize that they are woefully inadequate themselves to win the spiritual war that rages, they will have no recourse but to trust the One who is mighty to save. Because human strength is inadequate by itself to succeed, this is why without faith, it is impossible to please Him – because He wants us to trust Him (2 Cor. 12:10, Heb. 11:6).

All the sheep who avail themselves of His Word consistently get frequent reminders of how God came through for His people in various hostile environments against different physical enemies (Rom. 15:4). Believers who take God at His Word understand that the same God that came through back then for the people written about in that inspired book on those inspired pages (2 Tim. 3:16) is available to them. He does not change (Mal. 3:6). Jesus Christ is the same yesterday, today, and forever (Heb. 13:8) and is just as worthy of our trust today as He was for those people back then.

### Questions for self-reflection:

(1) Why are so many people more willing to trust in the creation before they will depend on the Creator?
(2) How does your trust in the Lord help you wage a successful war against your spiritual enemies?
(3) In what are you most prone to place misplaced trust?

(4) Have you considered how merciful it is of God to show you about your misplaced trust and allow you to make a spiritually beneficial change?

(5) How has God come through for you and aided you in overcoming specific trials and temptations?

**20:8. They have bowed down and fallen; But we have risen and stand upright.**

---

The enemies of God and God's people who have trusted in things rather than the Creator of all things **have bowed down and fallen** because they were unsuccessful in their feeble and futile attempts at supplanting the Lord. He sustains everything by the Word of His power (Heb. 1:3). The enemies failed to acknowledge that the very numbers of hairs on their heads were numbered by God and known to Him (Lk 12:7). Nothing they could do or dream of doing could thwart God's will or prevent God from doing whatever was necessary to accomplish His plans (Jb 42:2, Prov. 21:30, Isa. 14:27), which are always for the good of His people (Rom. 8:28). While the righteous suffer as they watch the wicked prosper (Jer. 12:1, see Job), they should take heart knowing that they know how to story ends. They have God's completed revelation to them in their hands in the completed canon of Scripture. They know that it is normal for the rain to fall on the just and the unjust (Matt. 5:45). It is normal for the saints to encounter various trials of diverse kinds (Jas 1:2-8). They should expect that the heathen will rage and plot vain things (Ps. 2:1). When these things happen, though, the righteous should remember that it is best to take God at His word.

The righteous should not necessarily react based on how things look. Instead, they should respond based on who God is, what He has done, what He is doing, and what we can trust him to do in the future. They should remember that, as temporal circumstances rage and cause inner turmoil in the lives of the saints, that there is nothing that can ultimately separate them from God's love (Romans 8:38-39). If He has justified them, they will be glorified (Romans 8:30). If God began the good work of salvation in them, He will perform it (Phil. 1:6).

The Lord Jesus Christ is the example in whose steps the saints should walk (1 Pet. 2:21). While He calls them to suffer with Him, they will also reign with Him (2 Tim. 2:12). They should live in great hope knowing that the worst that can happen to them in this life is physical death (Matt. 10:28). However, all that is is a new beginning, as physical death marks the beginning of eternal life in eternity in heaven with the Lord who brought us to Himself through His death on our behalf at Calvary (2 Cor. 5:8). The righteous can stand **risen and walk upright** because the God of the universe is their Advocate (1 Jn 2:1), not their enemy. If God is for them, none can be against them (Rom. 8:31).

## Questions for self-reflection:

(1) Sometimes, to the people of God, it can seem as if it is God's people rather than God's enemies that have bowed down and fallen. However, even if it appears that God's enemies are 'winning' for now, what hope does the believer have for the future?

(2) Why can it be so challenging to take God at His Word and trust Him even when we know how the story ends?

(3) What is the worst thing that can happen to a believer in a trial?

(4) Why is death not a big deal for a believer?

(5) If death is something to look forward to for a believer, why do so many believers try to delay it at all costs?

**20:9. Save, Lord! May the King answer us when we call.**

The psalmist knows that the only continually reliable One on whom one can safely depend to **save** him is the **Lord**. He is the only **King** whose kingdom has no successor (Lk 1:33). He is the One who ordains kings who have temporary kingdoms (Dan. 2:21, Dan. 2:37-28, Dan. 4:17, Jn 19:11, Rom. 13:1-2). The King of glory (Ps. 24:7-10) is the King of Kings (1 Tim. 6:15, Rev. 17:14, Rev. 19:16, Ezr 7:12, Ezek. 26:7, Dan. 2:37). He is the Lord of Lords (Deut. 10:17, Ps. 136:3). He exercises sovereign rule over His creatures. The supposed power finite man thinks he has is but for a moment.

When the saints **call** upon the Lord to save from their physical and spiritual enemies, the Lord is undoubtedly able to do so. He is rich in mercy (Eph. 2:4), and heaven rejoices when sinners repent (Lk 15:7, 10). Sin separates. The Lord saves. When a sinner calls upon the Lord, the **King** will **answer** them and usher them into His kingdom. Once they are subjects in His kingdom, they can continue to call upon Him. He continually helps them. He is the source of every good and perfect gift (Jas 1:17). His children recognize that about Him and thank Him for it. They become willing to risk all and even give up their own lives in service of Him who left heaven and gave up His life for them so that they all could be in heaven one day forever (Matt. 10:39).

The King of Kings, God eternal, answers us when we call, because of His Son, the Lord Jesus Christ, who gave us access by one Spirit to the Father (Eph 2:18), mediates (1 Tim. 2:5) and intercedes for us (Heb. 7:25). Because of Him, the Spirit is sent forth into our hearts so we can cry Abba Father (Gal. 4:6) when we are in desperate straits. Once the Spirit empowers us, one of the graces available to us is the ability to enter the Lord's presence and bring our burdens to Him (1 Pet. 5:7) even when we do not know what we should pray for or how we should pray for it. In those desperate times, the Spirit leads us to pray in accordance with His will (Rom. 8:26).

## Questions for self-reflection:

(1) Sometimes, as God's subjects, we find ourselves living in kingdoms that we feel are not supportive of believers and are not concerned with holy things. Since God is sovereign over the appointment of kings, godly or ungodly, what possible reasons could God have for putting godly people under the rule of ungodly kings?

(2) If we are in circumstances that we cannot change, can we go to God and ask God to help us endure the circumstances?

(3) Can God use the difficult circumstances of our trials to conform us into His image or give us a greater appreciation of some of the aspects of His suffering?

(4) Are you afraid to ask God to teach what you need to learn by whatever means necessary through a trial?

# Psalm 21

**21:1. The king shall have joy in Your strength, O Lord; And in Your salvation how greatly shall he rejoice!**

---

There is everlasting strength in the Lord (Isa. 26:4). The Lord provides unlimited strength to the king and all those that call upon Him. The strength is given to the children of God to be doers of God's will (Matt. 7:21-23, Jas 1:22). It is the power of God that fueled God's amazing miraculous works of the past, such as creation, such as the unveiling of human history. It takes incomprehensible strength for the Lord to govern the affairs of the world and work everything together for the good of those that love Him (Rom. 8:28, Eph. 1:11). God the Father gave God the Son, the Lord Jesus Christ, the strength to carry out God's will perfectly during His earthly life (Jn 17:4). It took God's power to raise Christ from the dead (Rom. 1:4). Every believer in the risen **Lord** receives the Holy Spirit who provides them with supernatural **strength** from on high (1 Jn 4:13). Believers have God's power in them by the power of the Holy Spirit. While they do not perform the same physical miracles that were common during the time of Jesus and the apostles, they can overcome temptation and practice righteousness in the world that makes them very uncomfortable since the world rejects the God of Christians so unashamedly (1 Cor. 10:13, Eph. 3:16, 1 Jn 2:29). When believers receive the Lord Jesus Christ, they are risen to walk in newness life (Rom. 6:4, Col. 2:6). This newness of life is a product of the strength of the Lord. Man needs power from the Lord to respond to the trials that God allows in his life (Jas 1:2-8).

Man possesses no innate goodness by which he can make himself more righteous before God (Rom. 3:9-23). His sins have taken him away from God, and he needs to return to God (Isa. 64:6). The only way anyone can be brought back to God is by repentant faith in the Lord Jesus Christ (Col. 1:19-21). Once saving faith in the Lord Jesus Christ is exercised, **joy** is a demonstrable byproduct (Gal. 5:22).

An earthly **king** or ruler will have those under his rule, some willingly, some unwillingly. He will also have enemies that threaten him and those under his rule. Anytime threats are removed so that peace can continue for the king and his subjects, the expected response is for the king to rejoice. **Salvation** from earthly danger is a cause for anyone to rejoice greatly. The Lord Jesus Christ has purchased salvation for the Christian (Acts 20:28, Gal. 3:13). For all that the Lord has done for them, the Christian should rejoice (Phil. 4:4). He has redeemed them (Eph. 1:7). He has justified them (Rom. 3:24). He has forgiven them (Col. 1:14). He has given them access to the Father (Eph. 2:18). He has adopted them into God's family (Eph. 1:5). He has declared the guilty to be not guilty (Rom. 3:19, Rom. 5:1). He has given them the Holy Spirit to lead them into all truth (Jn 16:13). He has given them an incorruptible inheritance (1 Pet. 1:4). He becomes for them a great High Priest (Heb. 4:14-15), an intercessor (Heb. 7:25), a mediator (1 Tim. 2:5), a sin offering (Heb. 10:14), and a substitute all because He loves them so much and wills for none to perish but for all to come to repentance (2 Pet. 3:9). He writes His law on the heart of His own that they might not sin against Him (Ps. 119:11).

**Questions for self-reflection:**

(1) The Lord sees when His people are so quick to run to the things of the world for refuge. How does it make you feel toward the Lord to know that He has been patient with you when you have done that?

(2) How does it make you feel to know that as a believer, you have been girded with strength like the Lord Jesus Christ so that you might live as a doer of God's will? Does the privilege of possessing this strength motivate you to live for God any more or less?

(3) If God has declared you righteous based on your faith in the finished work of the Lord Jesus Christ on the cross for you, you have everything you need to live for God for the rest of your life. Is there anything that keeps you from living for Him as you ought?

**21:2. You have given him his heart's desire, And have not withheld the request of his lips. Selah**

---

The heavenly Father gave the Lord Jesus Christ anything he **desire**d (Jn 12:28). Even when Christ prayed to let the cup of His suffering pass from Him, He prayed that the Father would allow that to happen only if it was the Father's will for that to happen (Matt. 26:39). God never **withheld the request of His lips**. Believers desire many things that God does not permit to pass because the Lord knows better than the people asking know what is best for them (Jas 4:3).

Christ asked for all that the Father had given Him to come to Him (Jn 6:37). They will. He asked to be glorified with His Father (Jn 17:5). He was. As He intercedes on behalf of His people from heaven now (Heb. 7:25), He receives that for which He asks. From His rightful place at the right hand of the Majesty on high (Heb. 1:3), He advocates for the pardon of the saints (1 Jn 2:2). He preserves them for all their earthly days. Since this God is so faithful, His people's response to such a gracious, kind offer of salvation and eternal life should be wonder, thanksgiving, and praise. God answers the prayers of believers according to His will (1 Jn 5:14).

Our human problem is that sometimes we mistake not getting the answer we want from God as God not answering our request. Just because we get an answer that differs from what we think it should be, does not mean that it is not a valid answer. Perhaps God's answer is "No," or "Not yet," or "My grace is sufficient for you (2 Cor. 12:9)." We should trust Him regardless of whether we get what we want because our wants are affected by the darkness of indwelling sin that pollutes, a darkness that does not exist in God (1 Jn 1:5).

**Questions for self-reflection:**

(1) Are you content with your circumstances even if God does not give you precisely what you ask for?

---

(2) Do you believe that God knows better than you do what you need?

(3) If God were to give you a choice to have anything on earth that you wanted only if you would have to miss out on heaven if God were to grant your request, would you take that trade?

(4) Does your answer to # 3 above affect how you pray?

**21:3. For You meet him with the blessings of goodness; You set a crown of pure gold upon his head.**

---

All those who have trusted in Christ for salvation can rejoice. God has chosen in His abundant mercy to **meet** the saved with the **blessings of** His **goodness**. God instigated the plan to meet them before the foundation of the world (Eph. 1:4) before the Word became flesh and dwelt among us (Jn 1:14) before humanity could behold His glory. The creation humankind enjoys in this life is good (Gen. 1:4, Gen. 1:10, Gen. 1:12, Gen. 1:18, Gen. 1:21, Gen. 1:25, Gen. 1:31). It is God's goodness that leads sinners to repentance (Rom. 2:4). All goodness comes from God since God is the only one who is perfectly good (Matt. 19:17). Man's supposed goodness is not actual goodness since everything man does, even the supposed good things, are tainted by man's sinfulness (Isa. 64:4-6, Rom. 3:9-23). Many of the blessings of God extended to and enjoyed by the saved are enumerated in Scripture (Eph. 1:3-14). Before God bestowed these blessings upon the righteous, the Lord Jesus Christ received the blessings so that He could receive the saved unto Himself and to His Father, so that the place that He prepared for them would be full (Jn 14:2-3).

The **crown of pure gold** was placed upon Christ's **head** as He is the King of kings and Lord of lords. The pure gold crown is perfectly pure, and it informs us that His kingdom will have no end (Lk 1:33). The crown given to Christ was given to Him by His Father (Ps. 2:6, Rev. 14:14). He reigns as King in His church now (Eph. 5:23) and will one day reign from the earth (Rev. 21:1-8). A crown could also be like a victor's wreath that is placed on the victor's head after a competition (1 Cor. 9:25-27). After Christ's sinless life (1 Pet. 2:22), substitutionary atonement for our sins (1 Pet. 2:24), and resurrection for our justification (Rom. 4:25) in which He conquered our enemies of sin, death, Satan, hell, and the grave (Col. 2:15, 1 Jn 2:14), He was given a crown of glory and honor (Heb. 2:9).

---

**Questions for self-reflection:**

(1)  In what ways can you think of that you have experienced the goodness of God?

(2)  Do you live as if Christ is your King? On what basis does He recognize you as one of His subjects?

**21:4. He asked life from You, and You gave it to him— Length of days forever and ever.**

---

The Lord Jesus Christ asked to have His **life** spared by His Father if it was the Father's will to spare it (Matt. 26:39). He would die for the sins of the world (Jn 3:16). He would shortly propitiate for everyone (1 John 2:2). In due time, He would die for the ungodly (Rom. 5:6). Imminently, He would commend His love toward us (Rom. 5:8). Very soon, He would bear our sins in His own body on the tree (1 Pet. 2:24).

But to prove Christ was who He said He was, He rose from the grave (1 Cor. 15:3-4). His life had been taken from Him by the foreknowledge of God and by the hands of wicked men. Then it returned to Him (Acts 2:23). The resurrection should not have been surprising to those who heard Him speak since He had said that He had the power to lay His life down and take it up again (Jn 10:18). Because Jesus rose from the grave, His people have the promise that they too will rise again (1 Thess. 4:16). **He asked** for **life**, and at the fulness of time, He came forth to live a perfect human life to be the once for all final sacrifice for humanity (Gal. 4:4-5, Heb. 10:10). He lived His life when it was the appropriate time for Him to live it. After Christ died, He rose again in a resurrection that was witnessed by many (1 Cor. 15:5-8). Now He intercedes for the saints (Heb. 7:25). Now he upholds all things by with Word of His power (Heb. 1:3). In response to that gracious, sinless life which the Lord Jesus Christ lived, He now gives eternal life to those who call upon His name in repentant faith (Rom. 10:13). When a sinner calls out to the Lord for the salvation that man could never earn for himself (Eph. 2:8-9), God graciously responds to penitent man by giving him the eternal life he so desperately needs. Even while dwelling on earth after their justification, the saved are already, in one sense, seated in heavenly places (Eph. 2:6). Their life is hidden with Christ in God (Col. 3:3). Their death does not mark the end; it marks a new beginning. The **days** of Christ last **forever and ever** in heaven. Because Christ rose, because Christ does and will live forever and ever in heaven, the days of the just also will last forever in heaven (Rev. 21-22). In heaven, there is no more death (Rev. 21:3-4).

## Questions for self-reflection:

(1) If the Lord Jesus Christ did not humble Himself, become a Man, and become obedient to the death of the cross, and then rise again, how would that affect our salvation?
(2) Does your life now indicate that the worship of God forever in eternal heaven is something in which you would want to participate? Do you worship God regularly now, even outside of church?

**21:5. His glory is great in Your salvation; Honor and majesty You have placed upon him.**

---

The **glory** of the Lord Jesus Christ **is great in** the **salvation** provided by the Godhead. When Christ successfully overcame temptation, God was glorified (Matt. 4:1-11). When Christ miraculously escaped from earthly enemies until the time of His appointment for death, God was glorified (Jn 8:59). When He took the punishment for humanity on the cross, God was glorified (1 Pet. 2:23-24). When He rose three days later, according to the Scriptures, God was glorified (1 Cor. 15:4). That He is qualified to be the provider of salvation to sinners such as us illustrates that He is a Man like no other Man. No other man was also fully God at the same time (1 Tim. 3:16).

God is glorified when Christ mediates on behalf of sinners (Heb. 7:25). They can cast their cares upon Him because He cares for them (1 Pet. 5:7). When they sin, He advocates for them (1 Jn 2:1). God gets glory in all of this. Sinners who come to Christ by faith, who have God's love shed abroad in their hearts (Rom. 5:5), begin to learn some of this glory as they become students of His Person and His Word.

After Christ suffered for sin and sinners, dying to save a people to Himself and rising again, He was given a place of **honor and majesty** on God's right hand (Col. 3:1, Heb. 1:3). God highly exalted Him and gave Him a name that is above every name (Phil. 2:9-11). God the Father is the One who has given God the Son, the Lord Jesus Christ, honor and majesty. God the Father has given all judgment to the Son, and the Son judges righteously (Jn 5:22-23, 1 Pet. 2:23). God the Father has given God the Son all authority (Matt. 28:18), and this is why everyone will bow the knee to Him at one time or another (Phil. 2:9-11).

## Questions for self-reflection:

(1) Is there anything that Christ did on earth that did not glorify His Father in heaven?

---

(2) Does the fact that Christ condescended to make your salvation possible make you want to give Him glory with your life? How can you do that today? How can you demonstrate His glory in you to someone who does not believe?

**21:6. For You have made him most blessed forever; You have made him exceedingly glad with Your presence.**

As fully God, the Lord Jesus Christ is already **blessed forever**. As God, Christ has always existed and was not made (Jn 8:58). By virtue of His incarnation, He was made a little lower than the angels (Heb. 2:9), He became sin for us (2 Cor. 5:21), He became the Captain of our salvation (Heb. 2:10). Because of who He is, He shares the blessings and inheritance with the sheep (Eph. 1:11, 1 Pet. 1:4). Every good thing about God and God's kingdom is shared with the saints because Christ has given them access to it all (Eph. 2:18, Jas 1:17). These blessings are what Paul refers to (Eph. 1:3-14).

For these reasons, since He is blessed forever, His children are also blessed forever. The blessings that Christ shares with all believers are forever theirs. Believers never have to be condemned again (Rom. 8:1). Believers are redeemed, never to return into slavery to sin (Ephesians 1:7). Believers are freely justified by His grace (Rom. 3:24). Believers are sanctified from the time of conversion throughout the duration of their earthly lives, becoming more like the Son (Romans 8:29) until they see Him as He is (1 Jn 3:2). Believers receive heavenly wisdom to know how to successfully navigate life in a world that is hostile to their God (1 Cor. 1:30, Col. 2:3, Jas 1:5-8). Once someone enters the family of believers, they are never kicked out of the family (Rom. 8:30).

After suffering and being the propitiation for sin (1 Jn 2:2), after saving us from wrath (Rom. 5:9), the Lord Jesus Christ was exalted back to the Father's right hand (Phil. 2:9). At the Father's right hand where Christ resides (Col. 3:1) are pleasures forevermore (Ps. 16:11). When Christ finished atoning for our sins, because He finished His work, He was able to sit at the Father's right hand, at the right hand of the Majesty on high (Heb. 1:3). When Christ had finished His suffering, on the other side of that, He was able to return in an **exceedingly glad** manner to His Father's **presence**, never to be forsaken again like He was on the cross. He had faithfully executed the tasks given to Him by His heavenly Father. He knew it. He returned to His heavenly abode exceedingly glad, knowing that He had finished the work of redemption. His suffering was over.

Believers can look at passages like this and know that, after the time of tribulation for their Savior, only pleasure and joy remained. For the child of God, this life frequently brings with it tribulation (Jn 16:33), but we can take great comfort in knowing that while in this world we will experience trouble, Christ has overcome the world. People change. Other circumstances change. But God never changes (Mal. 3:6). Jesus remains the same (Heb. 13:8). He will always be the faithful merciful High Priest who can sympathize with our weaknesses (Heb. 4:15).

## Questions for self-reflection:

(1) Is there anyone more blessed than the Lord Jesus Christ? Does He have an equal?
(2) Because Christ is blessed forever, what are some of the blessings that you enjoy now?
(3) Because Christ is blessed forever, what are some of the blessings that you will enjoy in eternity?
(4) What might be some of the reasons why Christ would be exceedingly glad in the Father's presence?
(5) Will you be exceedingly glad to be in God's presence in heaven? Are you exceedingly glad to come into God's presence now through prayer?

**21:7. For the king trusts in the Lord, And through the mercy of the Most High he shall not be moved.**

---

Jesus Christ is the **King** of kings and **Lord** of lords (Rev. 19:16). When he lived on the earth, He completely trusted in the Lord, His heavenly Father, for everything He needed to accomplish His earthly mission (1 Pet. 2:23). Christ trusted His Father to send Him to the earth at the appropriate time in history. Christ trusted His Father to deliver Him from His enemies until His time had come. Christ trusted His Father to raise Him from the dead when it was time for Him to do so.

As the example in whose steps the sheep follow (1 Pet. 2:21), we are to **trust** Christ as Lord (Prov. 3:5-8). We trust Him for salvation. During the rest of our earthly pilgrimage, we have the responsibility to continue to exercise trust in Him as we go through every circumstance. We can trust that His grace is sufficient to overcome any temptation as He provides the way of escape (2 Cor. 12:7-10, 1 Cor. 10:13). As Christ received everything that He needed to do His Father's will, believers have been given everything they need for life and godliness (2 Pet. 1:3), and can, by the power of the Holy Spirit, be doers of the will of God (Matt. 7:21-23) and will practice righteousness (1 Jn 2:29).

**Most High** refers to God the Father. Jesus Christ, God the Son, is the Son of the highest (Lk 1:32). The Holy Spirit is referred to as the power from on high (Lk 24:49). God is rich in **mercy** (Eph. 2:4) and pardons all who come to Him in repentant faith (Lk 13:3, Heb. 11:6). Christ faithfully executed His office as our Redeemer as King of Kings and was **not moved** from His position. He remains at His permanent position until it is time for Him to return in glory to receive His own and judge His enemies. He is still interceding for the saints as He has not moved from there (Heb. 1:3, Heb. 7:25). Therefore, the saints can trust in their High Priest (Heb. 4:15), the Lord Jesus, to keep them, sustain them, and glorify them (Rom. 8:30).

---

**Questions for self-reflection:**

(1) If God the Father is sufficient for God the Son to trust in, is He sufficient for the rest of us to trust in as well?
(2) How are you doing at consistently demonstrating that trust in the Lord?
(3) If you fail to continue to trust the Lord after sinning, does your lack of trust call into question His ability to do what He said He would do?

**21:8. Your hand will find all Your enemies; Your right hand will find those who hate You.**

---

The **hand** and the **right hand** both refer to the Lord Jesus Christ since Christ is seated at the Father's right hand (Col. 3:1-3, Heb. 1:2). The **enemies** and **those who hate you** both refer to God's enemies, Christ's enemies, the enemies of Christians. When Christ came the first time, the Jews were His primary earthly enemies. They expected a different type of Messiah than Jesus is. The Jews made it their mission to try to rid the world of Christ and His followers. Because God's will cannot be stopped ultimately (Isa. 46:9-11), they were unsuccessful in their plot.

In every generation, one can say that those who oppose God, those who do not know Christ, are enemies of God because of their sins (Col. 1:21). The devil, rather than God, leads all of these. They oppose God and His ways. God knows everything about everyone, including those who are His enemies. He knows the sins that have separated them from Him and that made them His enemies. Even professors of religion have fooled people they know on this earth and in the church. These pretenders have not fooled God. They remain God's enemies and, barring repentance, will face His judgment (Matt. 4:17, Lk 13:3). These enemies disguise themselves as believers. They pretend to belong to the Lord, but sin will eventually unmask them. If their unmasking does not occur during their time on earth, their unmasking will take place when they stand before the judgment seat of Christ. Christ knows who they are. His people may figure out who some are, but some may creep in unawares (2 Tim. 3:6, Jude 1:4). These have the potential to lead many who never truly belonged to the Lord to fall away permanently (2 Thess. 2:3, 2 Tim. 3:13, 2 Tim. 4:3-4).

The aforementioned enemies are marked as enemies by their doctrine. Other enemies are enemies because of their lifestyles. These may be harder to spot. They know the right things to believe. But their lifestyles are marked by fulfilling the flesh rather than by walking in the Spirit. God's genuine people are in a war with the flesh (Gal. 5:17). The enemies of God are not in such a war. They have no Holy Spirit that can wage war against their dominant flesh (Rom. 8:5-8). God's other enemies include Satan and his legion. When the Jews left Egypt and Egypt was drowned in the Red Sea (Exod. 14), God's hand was activated when Moses employed the rod. In that event, God found His enemies, in that case, the Egyptians, and they perished. The Egyptians hated Him. Their hatred was made plain by their treatment of Moses and the Israelites. Their treatment of Moses and the Israelites stemmed from their rejection of Israel's God, to whom they failed to acknowledge and submit. Christ, the **right hand** of God (Col. 3:1), will come in fire and judgment against all those who reject the Lord (2 Thess. 1:5-10) when it is finally time for Him to enact vengeance.

## Questions for self-reflection:

(1) Who leads the enemies of God and the enemies of Christians?
(2) What makes someone an enemy of God?
(3) Is there anyone you suspect is an enemy of God that attempts to disguise themself as a Christian? What are they doing or not doing that leads you to believe that they are not what they say? How are you able to recognize it?

**21:9. You shall make them as a fiery oven in the time of Your anger; The Lord shall swallow them up in His wrath, And the fire shall devour them.**

All those who oppose God receive differing amounts of grace, a time during which God allows them to live while they live in blatant opposition to Him (Ps. 90:12, Heb. 9:27). During this time, even while they may not even hear the message of the cross of Christ, there is still ample evidence around them to point them to the Creator to whom they are accountable.

If they have not worked too hard at silencing it, their conscience could still be screaming at them that their deeds are wicked (Rom. 2:15). With the light that they do have, enough is available to them that if they responded to it, God would make more light available to them until they hear the gospel to have the opportunity to turn from sin and come to saving faith.

Since most suppress the truth in an unrighteous manner (Rom. 1:18), God is angry at the wicked every day (Ps. 7:11). Even though they are wicked sinners, He still does love them. If He did not love them, He would not have sent Christ to die for them (Rom. 5:8). He would have left them alone to perish in their sins. Now that He has sent Christ to be the Savior for our sins, we have a way of rescue. Sinners who have God's wrath abiding on them can avoid that wrath by placing repentant faith in the Lord Jesus Christ (Rom. 5:9). Anyone who calls upon the name of Christ, the risen Lord, shall be saved (Rom. 10:13). Anyone who does not avail themselves to the One who is mighty to save (Zeph. 3:17), will be tossed into the **fiery oven** of God's righteous **anger** at sin. These reprobates will be those that **the Lord shall swallow up in His wrath**. The smoke of their torment will rise for all eternity as **the fire shall devour them** (Rev. 14:11).

## Questions for self-reflection:

(1) Is God merciful to give light to every man?

(2) Is God merciful to give more light to people who respond to the light that they recognize as light?

(3) Is God merciful to keep giving light to those who respond to the light they have received until they eventually hear the gospel?

(4) Is it merciful for God to forgive and pardon sinners who have traitorously sinned against Him, earning death and condemnation, when those sinners place repentant faith in the Lord Jesus Christ.

(5) The above questions have attempted to establish that God gives everyone the same merciful and gracious opportunity to repent and believe the gospel regardless of geographical location or other possible variables. Those who do not repent spurn His goodness, patience, and love. They were accountable to Him by their existence in His world. If they fail to acknowledge that accountability, does that make the judgment that this verse describes reasonable?

**21:10. Their offspring You shall destroy from the earth, And their descendants from among the sons of men.**

---

Those that oppose the one true God, the **offspring** of Satan, and those who have followed Satan instead of following the Lord, will be destroyed from the earth when, after they die, they meet God in judgment (Heb. 9:27, Acts 17:30-31). The offspring of the wicked often sadly follow in the footsteps of their ungodly parents. Disciples often become like their masters (Matt. 10:25), like those who teach them. If those who teach them live in such a way to give evidence that Satan is their spiritual father (Jn 8:44), then it is more likely, barring divine intervention, that their progeny will follow in the sinful footsteps of their parents.

The Jews were met by judgment for their rejection of the Lord when they wandered in the wilderness (Num. 33:1-49). So likewise, those who reject the Lord Jesus Christ, the only provision that a merciful God has made for sinful humanity, the Christ-rejectors can expect that God shall **destroy** them **from the earth and their descendants from among the sons of men** (Matt. 13:46, Jn 3:36, Rom. 5:9). For these reasons, godly parents need to raise up their children to know the one true God so that they can avoid such fate (Prov. 22:6, Eph. 6:1-4, Col. 3:20-21).

## Questions for self-reflection:

(1) The previous verse established that God is merciful to allow everyone to come to Him for salvation. Sadly, most will reject God's gracious offer. That is not God's fault. How did Adam and Eve reject God's request? Did Cain follow in his parent's footsteps?

(2) Is it surprising to see that idolatrous parents raise kids that turn out to be idolatrous?

(3) God gives us everything we enjoy. Is it too much for Him to ask us to worship Him for all He does for us and for who He is in return?

(4) For those who do not worship Him, does He have a right to be angry at them? Does He have a right to be angry at them for wasting the gifts and opportunities He gave them?

**21:11. For they intended evil against You; They devised a plot which they are not able to perform.**

---

When people **intend evil against** anyone, which is typical for the lost to do against the saved, the planned evil is ultimately against the people and the Lord Himself (Acts 9:4). The Lord gave mankind a law (Isa. 33:32), wrote that law on man's heart (Rom. 2:15), and man sins against God by ignoring his God-given conscience and breaking that law (Rom. 7:7, 1 Jn 3:4). The sin committed by man is evil at its core because it despises God's goodness, mercy, and patience (Rom. 2:4). This decision has eternal life implications. It exchanges the truth of God for the lie that this world is all there is and that we should live for the present rather than for eternity (Rom. 1:25). When someone chooses to abandon God and go his own way, he earns himself that just judgment.

The wicked have always tried to plot against God and His people by employing a variety of means. The Egyptians tried to plot against Israel. Since Moses led them, that did not work, but God's power was the ultimate source of Israel's exodus from Egypt. The Jews of Jesus' day devised a plot against Jesus to have Him killed and erase His influence. Still, they could not perform that in an ultimate sense because, while they did appear to succeed in having Him crucified, He rose from the grave, defeating death, proving that He was God manifested in the flesh (1 Tim. 3:16). So desperate were they to rid the world of His influence that they made up lies about what happened to Him after He rose (Matt. 28:11-15).

In every age since Christ's ascension, there have been people trying to undermine God's influence. They are not able to perform it either. The gates of hell will not prevail against the church of the Lord Jesus Christ. Though societies try to mute Christianity because they loathe the personal change it demands, the gospel goes forth strongly as ever, sometimes even spreading more rapidly where persecution is involved. Sometimes, persecution is the means to draw more people to Himself (e.g., Acts 11:19-24).

---

**Questions for self-reflection:**

(1) Do you know anyone who lives only for this life, refusing to consider there is a life to come after death and then the judgment?
(2) Why is it a bad thing to consistently ignore your conscience?
(3) What are some ways in Scripture that the wicked have plotted evil against the righteous?
(4) What ways in society today in which the wicked plot evil against the righteous?
(5) As the threats to gospel freedom pick up around the globe, how do Christians persevere? What are some Bible promises that speak to this issue and comfort those who wage war for human souls on the front lines?

**21:12. Therefore You will make them turn their back; You will make ready Your arrows on Your string toward their faces.**

When the wicked plan against the righteous (Ps. 2:1), God can work against the unrighteous such that the unrighteous know that something is against them even if they will not attribute that to God (e.g., Exod. 7:22). Maybe God abandons them and leaves them to themselves to pursue their ungodliness unchecked (Rom. 1:24, Rom. 1:26, Rom. 1:28). Perhaps God sets up obstacles in their way to prevent them from getting their way in an area (Gen. 20, 2 Sam.11). Then, when they cry out to God for deliverance, God does not deliver them because their sins have separated them from Him (1 Sam. 8:18, Jb 27:9, Jb 35:12, Ps. 18:41, Ps. 66:18, Prov. 1:28, Jas 4:3). God can make the ungodly turn their back to try to hide (unsuccessfully) from God who fights against them (Jb 34:22, Isa. 26:10, Jer. 23:24, Dan. 10:7, Amos 9:3, Rev. 6:15). They may not realize who or what is fighting against them. They may think they have offended a deity and will cry out for a reprieve. God judges the motives (Prov. 16:2, Prov. 21:27, Matt. 6:1, Eph. 6:5-8, Phil. 1:17, 1 Thess. 2:4, Jas 4:3) and can choose to deliver if He wills.

Even if the ungodly seem to prosper while the righteous seem to suffer (Ps. 73:3), the righteous can trust that God **will make ready His arrows on** His **string toward their faces**. God will make all wrongs right in His timing (Rom. 2:6-10). God's people need to trust that God is righteous (Exod. 9:27, Deut. 32:4, Judg. 5:11, 1 Sam. 12:7, 2 Sam. 23:3-4, 2 Chron. 12:6, Ezr 9:15, Neh. 9:8, Ps. 4:1, Ps. 7:9, Ps. 7:11, Ps. 9:4, Ps. 9:8, Ps. 11:7, Ps. 19:9, Ps. 35:24, Ps. 36:6, Ps. 40:10, Ps. 48:10, Ps. 50:6, Ps. 65:5, Ps. 96:13, Ps. 97:2, Ps. 97:6, Ps. 99:4, Ps. 103:6, Ps. 111:3, Ps. 116:5, Ps. 119:7, Ps. 119:137, Ps. 119:142, Ps. 129:4, Ps. 145:17, Prov. 21:12, Isa. 5:16, Isa. 41:10, Isa. 45:21, Isa. 46:13, Isa. 51:8, Jer. 9:24, Jer. 11:20, Jer. 12:1, Lam. 1:18, Dan.9:14, Dan. 9:16, Mic. 6:5, Mic. 7:9, Zeph. 3:5, Zech. 8:8, Jn 17:25, Acts 17:30-31, Rom. 3:5, 2 Tim. 4:8, Rev. 15:3). God always does what is right. If God is for them, God cannot be against them (Rom. 8:31). God will act on behalf of His people when God decides to act for His people. His people are not to get out in front of God.

Rather, God's people can be patient and trust God to make ready His arrows on His string toward the faces of His enemies. His enemies will all be under His feet one day (1 Cor. 15:27). God will be with His people for all eternity.

## Questions for self-reflection:

(1) What are some examples in Scripture when God worked against the enemies of His people?

(2) What difficult things have you had to accept while trusting that even in difficulty, that God is right?

(3) Why is it so difficult sometimes to wait for God to intervene in some of our trials? What bad things can happen to us if we are not patient and do not wait for God?

(4) Someone outside of Christ, in a sense, already has arrows pointed at their face. If they die in their sins, they miss out on heaven. So, what can you do as an act of kindness to someone you know outside of Christ?

**21:13. Be exalted, O Lord, in Your own strength! We will sing and praise Your power.**

When God displays His power through His works in the world and through His people living in the world by His strength, oftentimes, His people will **sing and praise** His **power**. His **strength** operating in His people allows the **Lord** to **be exalted** by the lives of His people. There will come a day when His power will vanquish all His enemies.

**Question for self-reflection:**

(1)  How does your life exalt the Lord and demonstrate His power?

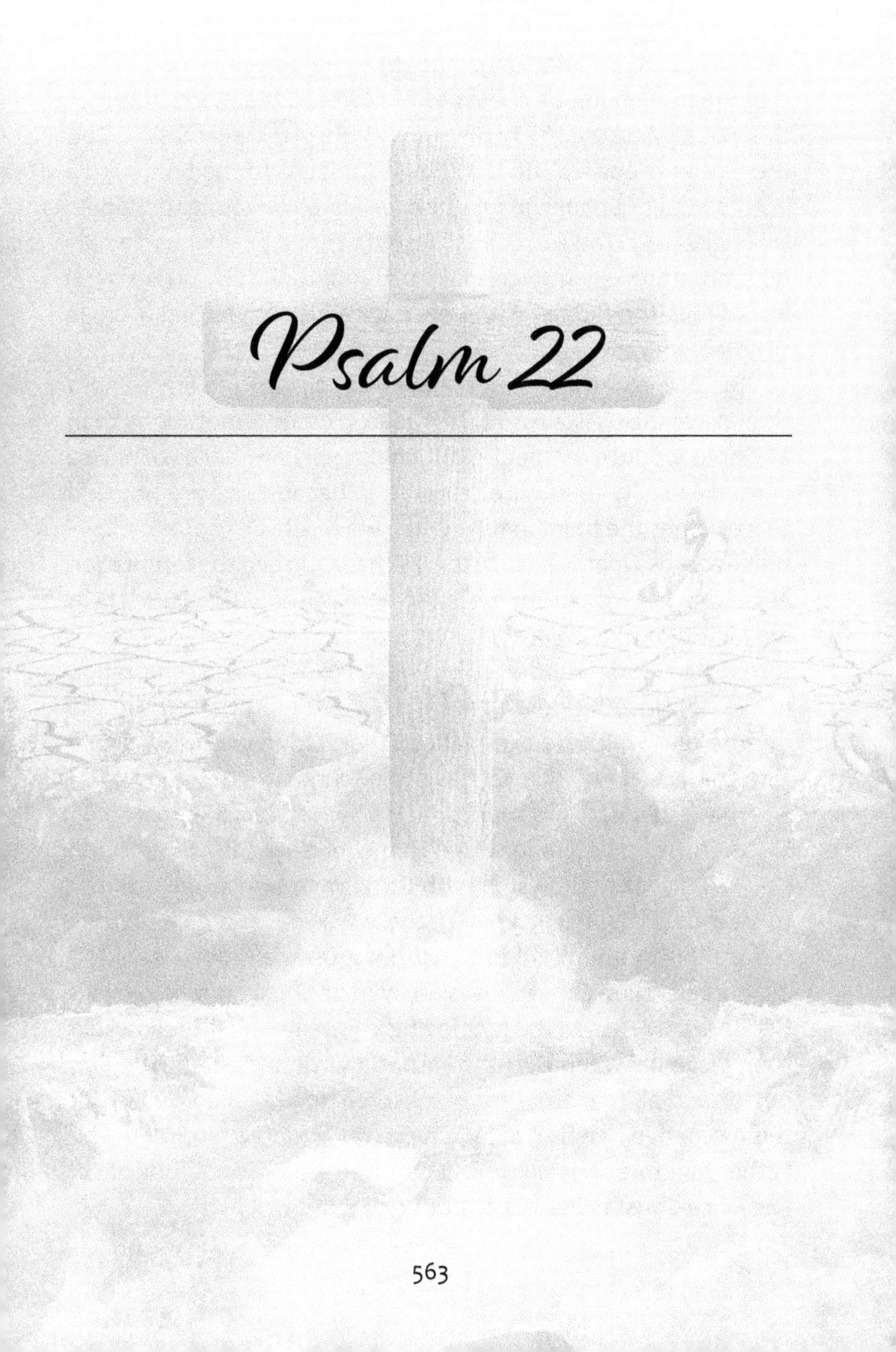

# Psalm 22

**22:1. My God, My God, why have You forsaken Me? Why are You so far from helping Me, And from the words of My groaning?**

This psalm is historically thought to be prophetic of Christ in that when He hung on the cross, He uttered the words found in this verse (Matt. 27:46). In His humiliation, in His incarnation, **God** the Father prepared the Lord Jesus Christ, God the Son, with a body so that He could be fully human and could atone for human sin (Heb. 10:5). The Man Christ Jesus (1 Tim. 2:5), who had a fully human nature, experienced pain, suffering, and sorrow (Isa. 53:3) included in the human experience without committing a single sin (Heb. 4:15).

His Divine nature did not allow Him to give in to any temptation as we face. As a result, He faced greater temptations than any of us would ever meet. With humans like us, since we have a limited capacity to endure temptation because we are not God, there comes the point in time when we reach a temptation level that exceeds what we can take (Jas 1:12-15). When the temptation exceeds what we can endure in the flesh, without the Spirit's help, we give in to the temptation, the temptation then ceases, and it turns into a committed sin. Since Jesus experienced temptation as we do, since He never gave in to the temptation to sin, the degree with which He experienced temptation was more significant than what we will ever have to endure.

The Father had fully supported His Son in everything He faced. Since Christ had a life in which He never gave into temptation, since sin breaks fellowship with God, since sin causes God not to hear us (Prov. 15:29, Jn 9:31), there was never a point in time before this moment when Christ hung on the cross when God did not hear Him. Christ always enjoyed perfect communion with His Heavenly Father. Perfect loving communion and fellowship took place between God the Father and God the Son. The Son performed all that the Father asked of Him (Jn 8:29). It was at this moment when that communion was temporarily cut off. The Father had **forsaken** His Son since a holy God cannot look at sin and since Christ became sin for us (2 Cor. 5:21).

After Christ completed His atoning work by voluntarily giving up His Spirit (Jn 19:30), three days later (1 Cor. 15:4), He rose triumphantly from the grave and was eventually exalted to the right hand of the Majesty on high (Heb. 1:3). But before Christ resumed His place next to the Father, God had forsaken Him. As God's wrath poured out on Him, God's Fatherly comfort was temporarily removed. When Fatherly comfort departed from Christ at this moment, the apex of sadness and sorrow, the sorrow of abandonment, the pain of wrath, the physical pain of the torture and crucifixion, came together as God's wrath against man's sin came upon His only sinless Son. The Father looked away. Even though the Father looked away for this time, the Father still loved His Son. The Son was still full deity.

Christ had temporarily lost the presence of His Father when the sins of humanity were imputed to the Son. Divine wrath abode upon the Son while He endured the punishment (1 Pet. 2:24). The Father was **so far from helping** Him. The Father was so far from hearing **the words of** His **groaning**. As God commended His love toward us sinners (Rom. 5:8), God simultaneously poured out His just anger. This anger toward the wicked is appropriately exercised every day because of the wickedness of the wicked. The sinful choices that the wicked make exposes the veracity of their sinful nature (Ps. 7:11-16). This just anger from a holy God emptied on the sinless Son of God. Christ had perfect trust in His Father. He knew that His Father would Help Him, but waiting for the help was not going to be easy, even for the perfect Son of God. Christ was groaning due to the extreme nature of His suffering. Not just the physical pain, which was torturous, but the emotional suffering He would endure to feel the deprivation of the Father's presence and the wrath of humanity's sin being emptied upon Him led to the groaning response.

Christ became the propitiation for our sins (1 Jn 2:2). Christ became the surety of a better covenant (Heb. 7:22). He is the example that we should walk in His steps (1 Pet. 2:21). As His people, we too can expect to experience something of God feeling as if He is far away from us as well. Christ knew that after

His passion, fulness of joy awaited Him in heaven (Heb. 12:2). There were pleasures forevermore at His Father's right hand (Ps. 16:11) awaiting Christ, His final location after His exaltation was His Father's right hand. The trial had to come before the triumph. He paid the penalty for which we lacked the resources to pay ourselves. He appeased the wrath that our sins deserved.

Those who have difficulty reconciling wrath coming from such a God of love consider that God is so holy so as not to be able to happily share the same room with sin (Hab. 1:13). Man as a sinner disqualifies himself from fellowship with God on that basis (Rom. 3:9-23). But the good news of the gospel is that God reconciled sinners to Himself (2 Cor. 5:18), He brought sinners back to God by humbling Himself, becoming Man, submitting to and perfectly obeying the Law that man breaks, and becoming obedient to the death of the cross (Phil. 2:5-11). There, on the cross, our sin was imputed to Christ while His perfect life was imputed to believers. By repentant (Matthew 4:17) faith (Heb. 11:6) in the finished work of Christ on our behalf, believers obtain an inheritance incorruptible (1 Pet. 1:4) and receive the spiritual blessings expounded upon in the New Testament (Eph. 1:3-14).

## Questions for self-reflection:

(1) When you think about your hardest temptation or trial, how does thinking about Jesus' temptation level exceeding your greatest temptation or trial put your temptation or trial into perspective?

(2) If a baby's mother always comes for them when they call to her, that one time when she does not come, is that baby likely to have anxiety? If that is the case with a solely human baby, could that also be the case with the God-Man? Could He have experienced non-sinful stress from being abandoned by His Father when He hung on the cross to atone for our sins?

(3) If we were to keep the sacrificial and mediatorial work of Christ on our behalf at the forefront of our minds, how might that change how we live in the present moment?

(4) How does reliving what Christ did for you on the cross lead you to think about your own sin? Do you think of your own sin the same as usual, or are you more broken over it?

(5) If we have received reconciliation to God through Christ, if we are ambivalent to sharing with others how they can also receive that reconciliation for themselves, does that show that we properly appreciate the reconciliation we say we have received? Why or why not?

**22:2. O My God, I cry in the daytime, but You do not hear; And in the night season, and am not silent.**

---

The Lord Jesus Christ, the sinless Son of God, cried out to God the Father, His Father, **in the daytime** all throughout His earthly ministry, well before He suffered on the cross for the sins of the world (1 Jn 2:2). In that moment, the Father did **not hear** the Son for reasons described in verse one above. When Judas Iscariot took the sop and left the disciples to betray Jesus, the Scriptures say it was night (Jn 13:30). That could refer to how demonic influences were having their way leading to the death of Christ. If that is so, the reference to the night season in this verse could refer to Christ calling out to His Father just before His arrest in Gethsemane.

**In the night season,** in the Garden of Gethsemane, just before His arrest, Christ was **not silent** as He asked His Father to let the cup pass from Him if that was His will (Matt. 26:39). In actuality, the Father did hear the Son, but when the Son asked the Father to remove the cup if it were possible, the Father did not remove the cup of suffering since Christ needed to consume it all. The Lamb of God had to take the stripes and the bloody death appointed for Him to be the perfect substitute for imperfect humanity. Christ couldn't pay for sin in any other way. Christ was more concerned with learning obedience through suffering than He was concerned with avoiding suffering (Heb. 5:8). One can imagine how Christ in His humanity would have had to be in constant prayer during the ordeal of suffering on the cross to fulfill it and submit to it as it transpired.

Christ crying out to His Father in prayer often, having constant communion with His Father, is another way in which He is an excellent example for the sheep (1 Pet. 2:21). Scripture calls the sheep to pray without ceasing (1 Thess. 5:16). They are wise to do so since by the death of Christ, free access (Rom. 5:2) to the throne of grace (Heb.4:16) is open so they can have mercy and help in their time of need. As saints cry out to the Father, mercy and help are at their disposal to overcome any temptation or trial

---

that awaits them. Christ made that possible. God's resources are available at any time, so as Christ was not silent about His needs, neither should believers in any generation be silent with their needs. Instead, they should fully trust and expect the Creator of all things to supply all their needs (Phi. 4:19).

**Questions for self-reflection:**

(1) If the Lord Jesus Christ availed Himself of His Father's resources by crying out to Him in the daytime, even if the Father did not hear at this time because Christ was dying for sin and sinners, what does it say about us if we are unwilling to go to God consistently? Are we too used to relying on ourselves that we forget that God permits us to be so self-reliant?
(2) Because the Father was not willing to let the cup pass from the Son, what are some of the benefits that you as an adopted son or daughter of God enjoy?
(3) If Christ was willing to learn obedience through suffering, what are we willing to endure to be conformed into His image?

## 22:3. But You are holy, Enthroned in the praises of Israel.

The psalmist, Christ on the cross, calls out to the Father, who has forsaken Him (Ps. 22:1), and importunately expects Him to answer Him and justifies the expectation that He would hear back from His Father in this verse. He expects God to answer Him because God is **holy**. He knows that while He became sin on our behalf (2 Cor. 5:21), He committed no actual sin (1 Pet. 2:22); therefore, inherent sinfulness is not an obstacle for Jesus' access to the Father. He knows that this was why He came to earth, to be a ransom for sinful humanity, and the time to pay the ransom to God had finally arrived (Ps. 49:15, Mk 10:45, Rom. 8:3-4, 1 Cor. 6:20, 1 Tim. 2:6, Heb. 9:12-15). Christ had perfect knowledge of God's revealed will, which, up to that point, included all of the Old Testament, to know that God did not separate Himself from those who had cleansed their ways before Him (Ps. 24:3-4). Christ also knew that there is no unrighteousness with God (Rom. 9:14). Since there is no unrighteousness with God, there must not have been anything wrong with God the Father abandoning God the Son as God the Son took the punishment for the sins of all humanity (1 Jn 2:2). He had submitted to the plan of the Father, knowing that this was the covenant they had made since eternity past (Heb. 9:15). He knew that this was necessary so that God could be both just and the justifier of the ungodly (Rom. 3:26). God is just to punish sinners for sin. Those whose faith is not in the Lord Jesus Christ must bear their own punishment. Those whose confidence is in the Lord Jesus Christ avoid taking their own penalty as Christ takes it for them.

In Israel, God's people built Him a temple where His presence would come and dwell among them. When it was finished and dedicated, God made an appearance (1 Kgs 9:1-9). For generations, people came and offered sacrifices because God told them that it was necessary, even though, in an ultimate sense, the blood of bulls and goats would never completely take away sins (Heb. 10:4). Only the shed blood of the Lord Jesus Christ, the Lamb of God, the final once for all sacrifice for sin (Heb. 10:10), completed that work that is only possible with God. Now, the believing community, the new **Israel** of God, lifts up **praises** to God's heavenly throne from the earth, God's footstool, for who He is and what He has done.

## Questions for self-reflection:

(1) If Christ expected the Father to answer Him and tells the sheep that they can ask and seek and knock, does Christ want the sheep to expect that the Father can do important things for them as well?

(2) Since Christ knew the Father was righteous and therefore did nothing wrong, what was wrong with the Father abandoning the Son during the Son's sacrifice for humanity?

(3) If Christ's death on the cross had happened any other way than how it did happen, how would that have affected our atonement?

**22:4. Our fathers trusted in You; They trusted, and You delivered them.**

---

The spiritual and physical ancestors of the psalmist, the psalmist's **fathers**, were people of faith. Some of them (Abraham in Heb. 11:8-10, Abraham in Heb. 11:17-19, Isaac in Heb. 11:20, Jacob in Heb. 11:21, Joseph in Hebrews 11:22, Moses in Hebrews 11:23-29) find themselves listed in the hall of faith in Hebrews 11. People like these listed in the passages in Hebrews whose stories fill out more completely elsewhere in the Old Testament were examples of faith that the New Testament believer is called to emulate (Heb. 11:6). As life got difficult, the faithful looked unto Jesus, the Author and Finisher of the faith and, with joy (Heb. 12:2), run their race (1 Cor. 9:24-27), knowing that as bad as the trials in this life can sometimes get, the worst that can happen is to be delivered by death (Matt. 10:28) and transported into the eternal presence of the loving Father who bought them (2 Cor. 5:8).

People who have come to God through Christ have the Holy Spirit in them (Rom. 8:11). Such people understand that anything earthly that will perish should not be **trusted** in like the eternal God and Christ, who made everything (Col. 1:16, Heb. 1:2) and sustains everything (Col. 1:17, Heb. 1:3) and will not cease to be (Rev. 1:8) should be trusted. God will not get weary or faint (Isa. 40:31). That is why believers can depend upon God the Father, God the Son, and God the Holy Spirit. The Trinity can help renew the strength of those who call upon and wait for the Lord (Isa. 40:31). The eternal God has left His completed Word to His people to encourage them and to be able to see life the way those that came before them saw life. The same word contains evidence of how God worked in people's lives in the past so they can know that the same God still works in the lives of people in every generation (Rom. 15:4, 1 Cor. 10:6).

In the Old Testament, God delivered His people even in times of sin (Judg. 2:11-23). When Israel complained about hunger, God sent manna and quail to deliver them (Exod. 16). When Israel complained about thirst, God quenched it with water from a rock to deliver them (Exod. 17). Before that, when they were in Egyptian bondage, God enlisted Moses to be the agent of God's deliverance in the lives of the people of Israel (Exod. 3:7-10). After that, in the book of Judges, Israel would get into trouble by their sin. They would respond by crying out to God for deliverance (Judg. 3, Judg. 4, Judg. 6, etc.). God, who is rich in mercy (Eph. 2:4), would send a deliverer to them repeatedly. While the earthly enemies and temptations might take on slightly different forms today than they did back then, the eternal truth that God is a deliverer to His people still rings true today and is an excellent source of inspiration to God's people.

### Questions for self-reflection:

(1) There are people written about in the Old Testament cited as New Testament examples of people whose models are worth following. Other than those listed in this paragraph, who else in Hebrews 11 is an example worth following?

(2) There are also examples of who not to follow. Who are some examples of those we should not emulate from the Old Testament or the New Testament?

(3) What are some reasons that no man is trustworthy? What does man have and do that God does not have and do?

(4) God the Son understandably expected that if it were possible, God could have spared him from the cross, but He was resigned to do His Father's will no matter the personal cost to Him. Can He say the same about you? Are you willing to follow God wherever He leads?

**22:5. They cried to You, and were delivered; They trusted in You, and were not ashamed.**

---

Israel **cried to** God, and God **delivered** Israel when Israel was freshly removed from bondage to Egypt (Exod. 16). The people were wayward and complained to Moses often about their adverse circumstances, yet Moses remained faithful. Sometimes the stress of the people's negativity that Moses led may have felt overwhelming to Moses to where it could have become too much for him to bear, but God always has proved Himself to His people then and continues to do so now. His grace is sufficient to meet all our needs (2 Cor. 12:7-10, Phil. 4:19). Now, God's people can cry out to Him much like the psalmist's cries are recorded, and God can deliver His people today (Heb. 4:16). Sometimes that deliverance could be a change in circumstances. Sometimes, after we have cried to God, we are delivered by God, not necessarily by a change in circumstances, but by grace to help respond in a God-honoring way to our circumstances. God's people know that God uses the prayers of His people to accomplish His purposes in their lives (Jas 5:16). This promise encourages them to cry out to Him. The resources that believers have at their disposal are unfathomable, so we would be wise to partake in the available resources whenever we can (Phil. 4:19).

Those who **trust in** the Lord will ultimately **not** be **ashamed** in an eternal sense (Matt. 11:6). However, to the lost, when the world of the redeemed seemingly comes crashing down around them, the lost see their own apparent success juxtaposed against the supposed lack of success of the saved, and they wrongly conclude that God is not worth trusting. No doubt, this is what the Pharisees of Jesus' day thought when their King hung on the cross. Since they were getting their way (so they thought – before He rose), whatever Jesus was trusting in must not have been good enough. However, when Jesus rose again, they were ashamed. When they faced God in judgment after they died, they were ashamed. Those who trusted in Christ, from then until now, however, are not ashamed because believers know that Christ saves to the uttermost (Heb. 7:25). Believers know that those that Christ calls, Christ justifies, and those that Christ justifies, Christ glorifies (Rom. 8:29-30). They know that since He has begun a good work in them that He will perform it (Phil. 1:6). They know that He loves them and that nothing can separate them from His love (Rom. 8:38-39).

In this verse, the Son could be reminding the Father that the pattern has always been God's people crying out to God for deliverance and God responding with the requested rescue. Christ here calls for His Father's deliverance to Him and refers back to the past where God delivered His people. History serves as a basis for which Christ could trust His Father in this most adverse of circumstances. No doubt that when He suffered the physical torture of the cross coupled with the abandonment of His Father, it must have seemed in His humanness to be discouraging. Deep down, the Son knew that He could trust the Father, and we can trust Him also today.

### Questions for self-reflection:

(1) Is there a story from your own life where you could show others that God still delivers His people similarly to how He delivered the Egyptians? You could start with your own salvation story in which you were delivered from Satan's kingdom and put into God's kingdom. There could be a specific story from your life where God removed you from a dangerous situation.

(2) Have you ever prayed about a difficult situation, and then after praying about it, even though the circumstances of the difficult situation did not change, your attitude about the difficult situation did change, and you were able to respond positively?

(3) How can the story of Jesus' humiliation and subsequent exaltation give you the courage to face your difficult situations even if you are not atoning for all of human sin?

**22:6. But I am a worm, and no man; A reproach of men, and despised by the people.**

---

As He was bleeding and His body was broken and torn, and His scourged flesh exposed His organs, Christ knew who He was and is. He knew He is eternal God hanging there between heaven and earth, bridging the gap between man and God. God had created man upright (Gen. 1-3). Man was deceived and had fallen into sin and had alienated himself from this God who loved him (Col. 1:21). God took the initiative in reconciling man to Himself by sending Christ at the fulness of time to redeem man (Gal. 4:4-5), to pardon man, to forgive man (Eph. 1:7), and to justify man (Rom. 3:24).

As Christ hung on the cross as is the scene in this passage, those around Him who mocked Him and wagged their tongues at Him and shook their heads at Him (Matt. 27:39-44) no doubt thought He was a **worm**, maybe only barely human. After all, when He came to His own, His own did not receive Him (Jn 1:11). He did not have the appearance physically of one who would be their Savior (Isa. 53:2). As strong as He is as omnipotent God, as fully human, He appeared to be physically weak like the rest of us and did evidence that in His humanity (Matt. 8:23-24, Mk 11:12, Jn 4:6-7). While Jesus is fully God (Col. 2:9), He is also fully human (Heb. 4:15). When He worked miracles, rather than elicit a response of repentant faith in the religious leaders of the day, it provoked hatred. The Jews surely treated Him as barely more than human. The God who loved them and made a way to forgive them by sending the God-Man into the world (Romans 5:8) was calling out to them to come to Him (Matt. 11:27-28). He was doing everything necessary to save them. But they did not recognize it. They thought this Jesus was an imposter. They thought He was a worm. If they could have, they would have squashed Him under their feet like a worm.

The prophet says that the Messiah would not appear as anything unique to those that beheld Him (Isa. 53:2). He would be remarkably unremarkable for all intents and purposes. There would be nothing about His person that anyone could observe as something worthy of worship. God and God alone is worthy of worship (Jn 4:21-24). Everyone knew that. The carpenter's Son from Nazareth was nothing special, was He? The Messiah was supposed to overthrow Rome. This Man just builds things. He is merely a carpenter's Son. Ah, but how outward appearances can deceive us! There is something called a crimson worm or a scarlet worm. Navigate to the link below to find more on this.

https://www.discovercreation.org/blog/2011/11/20/the-crimson-or-scarlet-worm/

When Christ referred to Himself as **"no man,"** rather than refer to only being divine and not being human, this must refer to the fact that, as crucified like a common thief, He was beaten and bloody beyond recognition as a man. The people there treated Him as if He was less than a man. He had no special status about which the people knew. He came from humble beginnings. He seemed like He was just like everyone else. It appeared as if nothing was different or unique about Him.

As a **"reproach of men,"** Christ was reproached by the multitudes then and is reproached by more than embrace Him today. The reproaches of men fell on Him when He was pierced for our transgressions (Isa. 53:5). Christ was despised by the people (Isa. 53:3) in that the people, rather than embrace Him as their long-awaited Messiah, rejected Him and had Him executed in fulfillment of prophecy. People were afraid to associate with Him because they feared what other people thought more than what God thinks. Today, people are reluctant to embrace Christ sometimes because of what other people would think about them if they did. Christ says people like these are not fit for the kingdom of heaven because His disciples care more about pleasing Him than they care about anything else. It is more likely that **the people** will **despise** Christ because Christ makes claims on people's lives that not everyone is willing to accommodate. Loving Him more than anyone or anything else is not for the faint of heart.

**Questions for self-reflection:**

(1) When you think about the humility with which Jesus handled His experience of His arrest, trials, and execution, why do we think we deserve so much better when God in the flesh received so much worse?

(2) In what ways does the scarlet worm remind you of Christ?

(3) What do you think causes people from our generation and those from previous generations (for those of us who have the completed Scripture) to reject Him? What are some of the most common reasons why someone would reject Christ?

**22:7. All those who see Me ridicule Me; They shoot out the lip, they shake the head, saying,**

As Christ hung on the cross to be the substitute for those who beat Him, pierced His hands and feet with nails, mocked Him, and ridiculed Him, someone there other than His mother, or John, or someone else at the foot of the cross could have at least acknowledged that the treatment He was receiving was uncalled for. Instead, **all those who** saw Him **ridicule**d Him. The people should have shown him compassion. As He died, Christ showed more compassion toward His executioners than most of those present at His execution. The Roman soldiers who whipped Him ridiculed Him. The Jews who did not want Him to be their Messiah ridiculed Him. The multitude that called for His death and had consciously decided to reject Him joined the Jews and Romans as they ridiculed Him.

Instead of **shoot**ing **out the lip** with praises to Him as is the duty of every person, they shoot out the lip with mocking and sarcasm. Instead of worshiping Him as their Savior, they insult Him. They treat Him like an animal. They think it is funny. They have no concern for human dignity. It does not cross their mind that they will face this Man in judgment after they die. When they see Him at the judgment seat of Christ (2 Cor. 5:10), when they realize who He is, what do they say then? Only heaven knows. By that point in time, the law will have done its work to stop the mouth (Rom. 3:19). But before the judgment seat of Christ, the seat before which we all must appear, it will be too late to change course. They will have made their bed. Their lives of derision and selfishness cannot be reclaimed for godliness now. It is too late. The day for salvation has passed. Abiding under God's unrelenting wrath will be their portion forever and ever.

## Questions for self-reflection:

(1) When Christ hung on the cross, who saw Him and ridiculed Him?

(2) It is easy for us on this side of the cross to criticize those who verbally rejected Christ. But, before your conversion, was that your practice? Did you verbally oppress the One you now call Savior? If you did verbally persecute Christ, do you think that you would have actively participated in His death if you were at the crucifixion scene?

(3) If you consider that you might have considered participating in His death, have you repented of your overt rebellion against Him?

(4) Have you thanked God for His patience and mercy toward you before your justification? Have you thanked Him for His continued patience with you since your justification?

**22:8. "He trusted in the Lord, let Him rescue Him; Let Him deliver Him, since He delights in Him!"**

Psalm 22:8 was quoted in Matthew 27:43 when the Jews mocked Christ as He was on the cross. Those that quoted this about Christ during that tragic scene at Calvary did not understand that the object of Christ's **trust** was really the **Lord** God, His Father, His **delight**. The Pharisees of the day thought that they belonged to the Lord. If they belonged to the Lord, Christ most certainly could not have belonged to the Lord since Christ taught against the Pharisees.

The Pharisees had misplaced affections. Everyone who has misplaced affections in every generation since theirs emphasizes the wrong object of worship. They do this to their peril. The Pharisees thought that fastidious law-keeping, festival, and observance were the way to enter the kingdom of heaven. They had their worlds turned upside down when Christ said the kingdom of God did not come with observation but was within its subjects (Lk 17:20-21). Their kingdom was not the kingdom of God. Their kingdom was the kingdom of Satan (Jn 8:44). God was not their Father. Satan was their father. Since Christ was not miraculously coming off the cross, whatever it was that He was trusting in must not have been the Lord. Or so the mistaken haters thought. They would not realize that His trust would be rewarded. The sarcasm with which they spoke would be rewarded with Christ stopping their mouth by His resurrection. His peril, though imminent, would give way to **rescue**. They would mock. But they would be proven wrong. Then they would be so embarrassed that they would make up a story about what really happened in order to save face (Matt. 28:11-15). His Father would rescue Him. He would be **deliver**ed. He would be vindicated. The mockers could not see that. Christ knew it because He knew it was impossible for God, His heavenly Father, the One that He was One with, to lie (Heb. 6:18).

**Questions for self-reflection:**

(1) Why did it appear that Christ would not be delivered from the cross?

(2) Despite Christ's horrific treatment, He resigned Himself to doing the Father's will. What can you learn from that commitment?

(3) If you consider that you might have contemplated participating in His death, have you repented of your overt rebellion against Him?

(4) In what/who are you trusting?

**22:9. But You are He who took Me out of the womb; You made Me trust while on My mother's breasts.**

God the Father was sovereign, in control, over when the Lord Jesus Christ would be born (Gal. 4:4-5, Eph. 1:11). God was sovereign over the miraculous circumstances that surrounded the birth of Christ. He had to be born of a virgin, which itself is a miracle (Isa. 7:14). God would have to be responsible for the virgin birth. The visits paid to Joseph (Matt. 1:18-25) and Mary (Lk 1:26-38) affirm this. The Holy Spirit, God the Spirit, conceived Christ in Mary's womb (Lk 1:35). Since the Holy Spirit conceived Jesus in Mary's womb, this is how Jesus could bypass the sin nature, and this is how the Scriptures can affirm that God the Father **took** God the Son **out of the womb**. It had to be this way. If Christ had a human father, He would have inherited Adam's pollution. Since Christ did not have a human Father, Christ did not inherit Adam's pollution, the sin nature. Therefore, He could not and did not sin, even though as fully human, He could be tempted like we are (Heb. 4:15).

Since it was typical for women to have assistance with births in biblical times (Exod. 1:15-22), and it was apparently impossible for Mary to have such assistance, God must have supernaturally protected and superintended the circumstances that culminated with Christ being born. Since this was the fulfillment of God's plan, it must be attributed to God's permission and power that Christ came forth into the world when He did, how He did, to whom He did. God worked behind the scenes in all the details bringing His will to pass providentially. Since God was at work in bringing Christ into the world when He did in fulfillment of various prophecies, it can be said that, while human instruments such as Mary and Joseph were employed, ultimately God took Him out of the womb.

In addition to being the fullness of deity (Col. 2:9), Christ is also fully human (Jn 1:14, 1 Tim. 2:5, Gal. 4:4, 1 Jn 4:2). As both fully God and fully Man, the Lord Jesus Christ is the only suitable substitute for humanity as the One who fulfilled the requirement of God for righteousness and who fulfilled the requirement for man to be perfect. As fully human, while **on** His **mother's breasts,** He was and had to be entirely dependent upon the Lord His Father to protect and preserve Him. He had to begin His earthly ministry and ultimately finish the work He had come to do (Jn 17:4) as the once for all sacrifice for our sins (Heb. 10:10). Jesus was dependent upon the Lord as He hid with Mary and Joseph in Egypt while wicked King Herod was on a mission to have Him destroyed (Matt. 2:7-21). When He was a babe, the Lord Jesus Christ was dependent on the Lord to provide milk from His mother's breast so that He could grow in wisdom and stature and favor with God and man (Lk 2:52). As believers in the Lord Jesus Christ, similarly, we are to desire the pure milk of the Word (1 Pet. 2:2) that we may grow into the measure of the stature of the fullness of Christ (Eph. 4:13).

## Questions for self-reflection:

(1) Who took Christ out of Mary's womb? Was Christ born on Mary's timetable or God's?
(2) How did Christ miss out on the sin nature that the rest of us inherit?
(3) If God can orchestrate the circumstances to bring about the birth of Christ in the manner that it transpired, is there anything that God cannot control if He chooses to do so as long as it is part of His plan?

**22:10. I was cast upon You from birth. From My mother's womb You have been My God.**

---

The Lord Jesus Christ had complete trust in His Father. His parents trusted in God as well, and they obeyed the revelation they received. Christ **was cast upon** God His Father, to do the Father's will, **from** His **birth** (Jn 4:34, Jn 5:30, Jn 6:38, Jn 8:26, Jn 12:49-50, Jn 14:31, Jn 15:10). Christ would not have been able to die until His appointed time for death (Jn 7:30). To be protected against death, He would have to be protected by His Father. There was the specific incident recorded in Scripture when King Herod tried to have Jesus killed with all the rest of the babies in the area (Matt. 2:1-18). God sovereignly intervened in that situation when Jesus was still in His **mother's womb** to ensure that the Savior would not be killed prematurely or in a manner other than on the cross as our substitute. The Holy Spirit would later inspire the apostle to write the sheep to cast their cares on the Lord because the Lord cares for them (1 Pet. 5:7). We know this because Jesus is our example, and we are to walk in His steps (1 Pet. 2:21). Paul admitted that Jesus was His example, and we should follow Jesus' example (1 Cor. 11:1).

During His whole life, from His birth until His sacrificial, substitutionary atoning death, the Lord Jesus Christ's cares were cast on His Father. His Father becomes our Father by faith in Christ (Rom. 5:1-2, Eph. 2:18). God the Father has **been** the **God** of everyone since eternity past (Deut. 6:4, Eph. 4:6). Before His incarnation, God the Son, Christ Jesus, is God from eternity (Jn 8:58). It was evident that Christ came from heaven once the very ones He came to save witnessed the powers of heaven in Him (John 8:23). He was supernaturally rescued and preserved from guaranteed death on more than one occasion because God, His God, our God, had made a plan to rescue a people from their sins (Lk 4:28-30, Jn 8:59). No wonder the cries from the cross asking the Father why He had forsaken Him were so desperate (Matt. 27:46)! He was used to uninterrupted sweet communion with His Father from all eternity, and then the wicked actions of others took it away from Him in a moment. In His humanness, that would have been awful, terrifying, and frightening to bear. From a divine standpoint, it would have been satisfying to know that this death was necessary to atone for the heinous crimes of humanity (Rom. 5:9).

**Questions for self-reflection:**

(1) How did Christ demonstrate by what He said that He was cast upon the Father from birth?
(2) How did Christ demonstrate by what He did that He was cast upon the Father from birth?
(3) This verse says that God the Father was God to God the Son in the Son's incarnation. If the Son could submit to the will of the Father, what keeps us from submitting to God's will for our lives when our lives get difficult?

**22:11. Be not far from Me, For trouble is near; For there is none to help.**

---

As Christ was paying the penalty for the sins of mankind (1 Jn 2:2), since God is holy (1 Pet. 1:16) and evil cannot be tolerated in His presence (Hab. 1:13), God could not have been close in proximity to Christ when Christ was taking our punishment upon Himself. As the Son became sin for us (2 Cor. 5:21), there is a sense in which God would have had to **be far from** Him. This, then, would be Christ's cry to the Father not to abandon Him. The Father had always been there for the Son. The Father was always a ready help to the Son. But as the Son became sin for the saints, the Father was no longer near in the same way. The Father had to look away. Before Christ's earthly ministry, when wicked King Herod attempted to have Christ killed when he had the babies of similar age killed (Matt. 2:1-21), trouble was near. During Christ's earthly ministry, **trouble** was **near** on more than one occasion when the wicked Jews tried to have their King crucified prematurely before His ordained time (e.g., Jn 10:39). Now, finally, when the appointed time for Christ to propitiate for our sins had arrived, trouble was near. The kingdom of darkness, comprised of Judas Iscariot, the chief priests, scribes, Pharisees, and the Romans, was finally having its way. Or so it thought. Satan led each of these in the attack at Gethsemane.

The weight of the sins of the whole world was about to come crashing down upon the sinless Son of God (Jn 3:16). The cup of God's wrath, which could not pass from Him, was about to be emptied on Him (Matt. 26:39). The chastisement of our peace was about to be on Him (Isa. 53:5). He was about to be pierced for our transgressions (Isa. 53:5). As His arrest took place, the disciples all fled (Matt. 26:56). There was **none to help.** As He had predicted, there would be none to support Him, despite their prior insistence (Matt. 26:35). It was the Son, the Father, the Spirit, the Three in One all alone. Then, on the cross, the presence of the Father had left the Son. As Christ told His disciples, He could have called a legion of angels to deliver Him from this divine appointment to bear the penalty we deserve for our sins (Matt. 26:50-53). But He knew that it had to be the way it was so that the Scriptures could be fulfilled (Matt. 26:56). He would have to be the One to atone for our sins because He had been ordained to do so (Acts 2:23, Acts 3:18, Acts 4:27-28). Thank God for fulfilling His Word in the salvation of sinners through the death of His Son, the Lord Jesus Christ!

**Questions for self-reflection:**

(1) Why would God the Father have seemed far from God the Son while Christ died on the cross for our sins?
(2) If God the Father can help God the Son in His trouble, can God help us in our trouble too?
(3) There was none to help the Son when He atoned for us. Now there is always One to help us at the time of our need. What can he help you with today?

**22:12. Many bulls have surrounded Me; Strong bulls of Bashan have encircled Me.**

---

The **bulls** that **surrounded** Christ in opposition to Him during His ministry up unto His death as our substitute included the religious leaders of the day, the Pharisees, the experts on the Law, the Scribes, the Jews who did not receive Him when He came to them (Jn 1:11). In addition, Pilate could have released Him since he recognized that He was guilty of nothing (Lk 23:4, Jn 19:4). Pilate can be included in the same group. Bulls rage when provoked to the point where they will try to kill those that provoke them. The aforementioned enemies of Christ had Him killed in fulfillment of prophecy.

A horn was a symbol for a king or for authority in the Old Testament (e.g., Dan. 7:24). The wicked rulers of Jesus' day used their power for evil in having the Messiah executed. Christ was surrounded by the corrupt rulers and those who worked for them when they were all party to His arrest, trials, and execution. The **strong bulls of Bashan** that encircled **Christ** could refer to the influential rulers of the day, such as Annas, Caiaphas, Herod, and Pilate, who each had a role to play in the crucifixion of the Lord. Like these leaders who surrounded and encircled the Lord playing their parts in His death, who were powerful like bulls, all these years later, we had a role to play in it as well as it was our sins for which Christ had to die. We are the reason God commended His love toward us. Our sins put Jesus on the cross.

## Questions for self-reflection:

(1) Who were the major parties that opposed Christ and were instrumental in leading to his death?
(2) When Christ was so vigorously persecuted, in whom did He place His perfect trust?
(3) Can Christ's example for us be applied to our lives? If God the Son needed to trust God the Father, how much more should we trust God in our dire straits?

---

**22:13. They gape at Me with their mouths, Like a raging and roaring lion.**

---

The people who were happy about Christ dying on the cross because they did not like Him or what He stood for are those that **gape at** Him **with their mouths.** Instead of worshiping Him as God and receiving Him as Messiah, they mock and insult Him (Matt.27:27-31, Matt. 27:39-44). To gape is to open the mouth wide. Therefore, the people gaping at the Lord must reference their insulting Him with their words. Since this psalm refers to Christ when He is already on the cross, the gaping must not be the call to crucify Him but must come after the crucifixion before He voluntarily gave up the ghost.

**A raging and roaring lion** celebrates when it has made its kill for its next meal. The people who so badly wanted Christ dead were like that lion because they finally had what they wanted (or so they thought). They had killed their King. A day is coming then they will look on Him who they have pierced and be sorry about what they have done (Zech. 12:10).

## Questions for self-reflection:

(1) Lookup in the gospel accounts at what some of the insults were that people shouted at Christ as He hung on the cross for everyone, including those that were busy insulting Him. Now think about the times in your own life when you have repaid evil with evil instead of repaying evil with good. What is your reaction to your own sinfulness in light of Christ's perfection?

(2) How do the sins you committed in the past affect you as you contemplate the price that Christ had to pay for them all?

(3) How do the sins you have not yet committed affect you as you contemplate the price that Christ had to pay for them? Do you mourn over your past and present sins?

(4) How do you balance the mourning over sin while rejoicing in what Christ had done to correct the sin problem?

---

(5) When you think about those who reject Christ now and those who make life difficult for those who embrace Christ now, are you angrier at the rejectors, or are you sadder that they reject. Why?

**22:14. I am poured out like water, And all My bones are out of joint; My heart is like wax; It has melted within Me.**

---

Christ sweat drops of blood when He contemplated being our sin-bearer (Lk 22:44). He perhaps knew the toll He would have to endure in His war against Satan and the enemy forces. Maybe He knew what the weight of all the world's sins would feel like (1 Jn 2:2). Perhaps the prospect of becoming sin for us became terrifying (2 Cor. 5:21). Perhaps He anticipated His Father abandoning Him and, despite the foreknowledge of it, the thought was sorrowful to meditate on (Ps. 22:1, Matt. 27:46). Perhaps the exhausting toll that His earthly ministry had taken on Him contributed to the exhaustion of this moment. Maybe the dullness of the disciples contributed to the understandable sinless frustration (Matt. 15:16). Perhaps He wept as He did at the death of Lazarus because the sinful state of humanity which led to this moment was depressing to think about (Jn 11:35). Perhaps He sweat blood in the garden of Gethsemane because of the intense stress of knowing what was going to happen to Him as the wrath of His Father would shortly be **poured out** upon Him for us (Lk 22:44). He had just lifted a prayer to the heavens asking the Father to glorify Him (Jn 17:1). He knew that He would be glorified but before His glorification could transpire, intense trial and suffering that, in His humanity, would be His lot that would have been difficult to bear. But what would have been difficult for Him would be impossible for us.

As His body stretched on the cross for hours, He would have been in such agony that it would have been as if all His **bones** were **out of joint**, at least figuratively, if not literally. The **heart** of Christ **melted like wax within** Him because God the Father's just and righteous wrath came upon Christ in our stead. It was poured out like fire in a furnace, and as the wax of a candle melts under exposure to heat, so did Christ's heart figuratively melt when the Father's wrath came upon Him. Sinners who refuse to embrace Christ should shudder at the fate that awaits them if Christ's heart became like wax when He faced the wrath of His Father.

---

## Questions for self-reflection:

(1) Have you ever been so stressed about a circumstance that it physically exhausted you? If so, how does your experience compare with Jesus' experience? Does your experience feel like it pales in comparison to Jesus' experience?

(2) Think about wax melting off a candle. It takes intense heat to cause the wax to melt. Think about your most intense trial. Now think about Christ's death for your sins on the cross. How can you praise the Savior for what He has done for you?

**22:15. My strength is dried up like a potsherd, And My tongue clings to My jaws; You have brought Me to the dust of death.**

As He was sleep-deprived, bound (Mk 14:53), scourged (John 19:1), and had to carry that heavy cross (with help) on the way to Golgotha (Mk 15:21-22), as He continued to lose blood and sweat, and deprived of replenishing liquid, Jesus' **strength dried up like a potsherd**. His organs were likely exposed. As He had dealt with the rebukes of the people and the abandonment of the apostles (Mk 14:50) and His Father (Mk 15:34), He likened Himself to a broken piece of pottery. The intense heat of the wrath of the Father emptying upon Him dried up His strength. Other than the cry that begins this psalm, and the willful giving up of His Spirit, there was not much to say on the cross (Lk 23:46). Before that, He had been accused, falsely, by the Jews (Matt. 26:65) and questioned by Herod (Lk 23:8-12) and Pilate (Jn 18:28-40). His **tongue** clung t**o His jaws**. He answered them with nothing. There was no point in saying anything because they would not believe even though one rose from the dead (Lk 16:31). Like a Lamb led to the slaughter, He fulfilled that prophecy the same way He did this one, by opening not His mouth (Isa. 53:7). When His enemies reviled him, He did not revile in return (1 Pet. 2:23).

When He was about to breathe His last, Jesus was **brought to** the precipice of **the dust of death**. Typically, when someone dies, they become dust in the ground over time. They get buried with dirt and dust. Not Christ. Three days later, He rose for our justification (Rom. 4:25). There was no time for dust or dirt to cover Him. God the Father had brought God the Son to the dust of death, but Christ would not stay there. No! He would rise triumphantly over death and be the first fruits of those who would rise from the dead (1 Cor. 15:20-28).

**Questions for self-reflection:**

(1) A potsherd is a broken piece of pottery. A potsherd is dried out and used up, unfit for any purpose other than to be discarded. How would this apply to Christ's atoning work?

(2) A tongue that clings to one's jaws does not make words. It describes someone who is remaining silent. Look in Isaiah 53 for a verse that may sound like this verse. Look in the crucifixion accounts to see where this Christ fulfilled this when He was before Herod and Pilate.

(3) Christ approached the dust of death as his physical death drew closer. Put yourself at Calvary as an eyewitness to the events. How would you have reacted to this? Would you have been outraged at what the Jews and Romans had conspired to do? Would you have supported them? Would you have had sympathy for the Lord Jesus?

**22:16. For dogs have surrounded Me; The congregation of the wicked has enclosed Me. They pierced My hands and My feet;**

---

The writer likened the people who opposed Christ to **dogs**. They had surrounded Him in their opposition which was truthfully opposition to God. All opposition to God is wicked. They thought they were God's allies when in reality, they were God's enemies. Dogs symbolized Gentiles in Scripture (Matt. 15:26-27). Roman Gentiles had united with the Jews in their opposition to Christ. The Jews would conspire to condemn Him and have Him executed (Matt. 26:3-4). Many of them gleefully watched as He hung on the cross (Matt. 27:39-40). The Romans participated in the plot also by guarding the tomb (Matt. 27:65-66). Dogs were scavenging animals that were not well-liked in the ancient world.

This could be the reason for the simile to compare those who had Christ crucified to dogs in that God the Father would not be pleased with those who executed His Son. Since dogs were unclean scavengers, perhaps those so intimately involved with and present at the crucifixion scene had made themselves so unclean that the reference to them being dogs would be fitting. Many who were present at the crucifixion scene were opposed to Christ and celebrated His execution.

Those who celebrated these tragic yet necessary events would make up **the congregation of the wicked** that **enclosed** Christ. The Jews who wanted Him killed make up the congregation of the wicked that enclosed Christ. They screamed for His blood when He was arrested and tried before Herod and Caiphas. They cried for His blood when He was delivered to Pilate. They had enclosed Him to the point where, one way or another, they would be rid of Him. But only because His time had finally come. He could have kept escaping if He wanted to. He had the power to lay His life down and take it up again (Jn. 10:18). It was time for Him to lay down His life willingly, become sin for us (2 Cor. 5:21), and propitiate for our sins (1 Jn 2:2). They **pierced** His **hands and feet** because that was the execution method that God ordained

---

for the day. It was a shameful, painful death, which was commonly employed in that day.

## Questions for self-reflection:

(1) In the ancient world, dogs were not the household pets that they are for many of us. Instead, they were scavengers. What does a scavenger eat? How would it have been fitting for dogs to surround the Lord Jesus?

(2) There were many present at the death of Christ that celebrated it. Are there people in the world today who celebrate the persecution and martyrdom of Christians?

(3) How could the psalmist be able to predict with such precision the details of Christ's death if God were not involved in supernaturally providing the psalmist with the information?

**22:17. I can count all My bones. They look and stare at Me.**

As the nails went through Christ's wrists and His Achilles, He could have looked emaciated. The agony only intensified as the nail went into the wooden cross beam for the wrists and the long vertical beam for His feet. As the post impacted the ground, the jarring that His body endured when the wood impacted the bottom of the hole could have caused the flesh to tear. The scourging would have so marred Him that some of His **bones** and organs could have been exposed and could have been visible to onlookers and to Himself.

His enemies could see Him as **they look and stare at** Him. He did not look like a King. He looked like a criminal. They ridiculed Him, supposing Him to be a lunatic rather than receiving Him as their Lord. They could have received Him and inaugurated their Kingdom. Instead, they had Him executed in the most humiliating of ways. They treated Him as less than human. He loved them regardless. Some who were there to witness the day's events would come to possess saving faith. One soldier testifies to His identity as the Son of God (Matt. 27:54). Instead of worshiping Him as God, the majority of those present treated Him with derision.

**Questions for self-reflection:**

(1) The wounds from Christ's scourging had perhaps left Him physically unrecognizable. Who would you guess is treated better, convicted American criminals today, or the sinless Savior at Calvary in that day?

(2) Looking back at your answer to the previous question, do you have a sense of outrage toward those who did that to Him? Describe your feelings.

(3) After thinking about the suffering of Christ and the outrage that you feel toward His executioners, how do you feel about your own sin that made this historical event necessary?

(4) What is your response now to the God who made way for your sins to be forgiven?

**22:18. They divide My garments among them, And for My clothing they cast lots.**

Roman soldiers gambled for the **garments** of Christ (Jn 19:23). Crucifixion victims were stripped naked to embarrass them further. Each soldier took a part of the criminal's clothes. Four soldiers were involved in this process with Christ, so they split his clothes four ways **among** the four soldiers. This God-Man died to save these wicked soldiers from their sins, died for Pilate's sins, died for the Pharisee's sins, and died for your and my sins. While the soldiers played games with His clothes, He upheld all things with the Word of His power (Heb. 1:3). He allowed them to take their next breath, while they derided Him, while His rich mercy dripped (Eph. 2:4) on them in crimson.

The **clothing they cast lots for** was a coat that did not have a seam. They did not want to tear it. So, they gambled it off to see who could take it in its fullness. When justified sinners see to what lengths their Savior went to save them, they should respond with overwhelming gratitude. There should be brokenness over indwelling sin in the saints that it is these continual sins, no matter how much we may try to trivialize them, that He ever lives to intercede for (Heb. 7:25). Believers should never think too lightly of their own sin. The price that Christ paid for their sins was far too high.

### Questions for self-reflection:

(1) How does the fulfillment of the specific details of the events of Christ's death increase your faith in God?
(2) How does the precision of the detail of the crucifixion account lend support to the sovereignty of God?

**22:19. But You, O Lord, do not be far from Me; O My Strength, hasten to help Me!**

A similar phrase to **"do not be far from Me"** was employed by our Lord in Psalm 22:11. See notes above. For the Son to mediate between God and man (1 Tim. 2:5), the Son would need to receive supernatural strength from His Father. In His humanness, He did suffer weakness (Hebrews 4:15). He slept in a boat (Matt. 8:23-27), He thirsted (Jn 19:28), and He hungered (Matt. 4:2).

The Lord Jesus Christ is the strength of those who call upon Him (Isa. 26:4). Christ received strength from His Father to execute His priestly office for us. When Christ hung on the cross, which is the backdrop of this psalm, He needed His Father's supernatural strength to enable Him to continue in His mediatorial work on our behalf until it was finished (Jn 19:30). There was nobody who had the supernatural strength required to bear God's wrath against the sins of all humanity. The weight of the sins of the whole world crushing Him, being consumed by the wrath of God, being forsaken, elicited a desperate cry for the Father to help Him. He knew that He was the Lamb of God to take away the sins of the world (Jn 1:29). Being able to endure such cosmic chastisement inflicted upon Him by sinful man, in which our peace was obtained (Isa. 53:5), would have required great **strength** to endure and would have been aided by the Father coming to **hasten to help**.

### Questions for self-reflection:

(1) Why was the Father 'far' from the Son at the crucifixion?
(2) How had the Father given strength to the Son during His ministry?
(3) How does the Trinity strengthen the believing community today?
(4) What happened after Christ's death to show that the Father did help the Son?
(5) How has God helped you in your trials?

**22:20. Deliver Me from the sword, My precious life from the power of the dog.**

---

When the Romans arrested Christ, the Romans who came with Judas to capture Him brought **sword**s and clubs (Matt. 26:47). These people joined with the murderous Pharisees, who intended to destroy Christ because He was a threat to their influence. They may have been mere foot soldiers. They may have only been carrying out orders and not even on board with the cause to destroy Christ. He was also their Savior. Blind hatred kept them from seeing Christ for who He is. Their blindness was both willful and judicial. Indifference also inhibited the entry of the truth.

In addition to employing a physical sword, the sword of their mouth also came against the Lord. False accusations (Matt. 5:11, Mk 14:55-56) and abusive language (Matt. 12:22-32) directed toward Christ were commonplace for His enemies. Their tongues were like swords in that their words were wounding and hurtful to their Creator. They ridiculed Him and mocked Him. He was repeatedly reproached and blasphemed. His sheep can expect similar treatment (2 Tim.3:12). He was sentenced and executed by a people fueled by jealous rage.

Christ's own **life** was **precious** to Himself and the Father. It was precious to Himself because, in it, He satisfied the just requirement that none of us could meet for moral perfection (Matt. 5:48, Rom. 3:25-26). His life was the only life that was not adversely affected by a sinful nature or sinful personal choices (1 Peter 2:22). It was precious because His life, perfect as it was, is the only one we can trust in for our justification (Eph. 1:12-14). The bloodthirsty Jews and Romans, typified by **the power of the dog,** took his precious life from Him on account of our own sin as well as on theirs.

## Questions for self-reflection:

---

(1) In what sense was Christ not delivered from the sword?
(2) In what sense was Christ delivered from the sword?

---

(3) How was the sword of the people's mouth used against Christ during His ministry?

(4) How is the sword of the mouth used against Christ and His people today?

(5) Can you think of any New Testament passages outside of the gospels that deal with the type of speech characteristic of saved people? Of lost people?

(6) Is your speech most often characteristic of saved people or lost people?

(7) What makes Christ's life so precious?

**22:21. Save Me from the lion's mouth And from the horns of the wild oxen! You have answered Me.**

---

Scripture refers to the devil as a roaring lion in the New Testament (1 Pet. 5:8). The devil, who is God's devil, has the whole world under his sway (1 Jn 5:19). He is the god of this age who blinds the minds of unbelievers and leads them away from the truth of who God is and what God has done (2 Cor. 4:4). Since he fell (Isa. 14:12-14, Ezek. 28:12-18), the devil has been at work trying to overthrow Christ and Christ's followers (e.g., Lk 22:31-32). Though he keeps trying, and some of his attempts might appear to be fruitful for a time, all his attempts will ultimately fail because Christ is sovereign over the whole world, including the devil (e.g., Jb 1:6-12). The gates of hell cannot prevail against the Lord Jesus Christ (Matt. 16:18). Christ rose from the dead and made a public spectacle of the demonic realm (Col. 2:14-15). Christ proved after His baptism that His power, God's power, triumphed over the power of the devil and his minions.

All through the ages, the devil has had the majority of the populace at his disposal. In every generation, those who are Christ's have in them He who is greater than he that is in the world (1 Jn 4:4). That is why those who are Christ's are more than conquerors (Rom. 8:37). The devil and all who opposed Christ at His arrest, beatings, trials, and crucifixion also make up those **from the lion's mouth and from the horns of wild oxen.**

As Christ was dying for the sins of the world, He knew that His Father would answer Him. The Father had answered Christ on other occasions (e.g., Jn 12:28). There was no besetting sin in Christ for Christ to lay aside that would hinder His Father from answering Him (Heb. 12:1). He knew His purpose was to defeat death on our behalf so that He would be the firstfruits of those who rose from the dead (1 Cor. 15:20). By rising from the dead, the Father **answered** Him resoundingly. Christ proved that He is God. He proved He had been given the keys to death and the grave (Rev. 1:18). He proved that He was our sufficient High Priest who endured greater temptation than any of us could ever endure, yet without sin (Heb. 4:15). Because the Father answered Him, we can trust that the Father will answer us with whatever we ask according to God's will (1 Jn 5:14). Therefore, it becomes incumbent on believers to renew their minds daily to know the good and perfect will of God for them (Rom. 12:2). Believers, like Christ, can expect to be subject to the forces of the spiritual enemy, headed up by Satan. Nevertheless, they can follow the Lord's example (1 Pet. 2:23) and overcome whatever comes against them by taking God's prescribed way of escape (1 Cor. 10:13).

## Questions for self-reflection:

(1) Who were those who made up the lion's mouth against Christ?
(2) At the time of Christ's death, why did it appear like the lion's mouth and the wild oxen were winning or getting their way?
(3) A short time later, how did Christ prove that they did not get their way?
(4) What happens to Christians in every generation since then that makes it appear like Christians are in the lion's mouth and are being impaled by the horns of wild oxen?
(5) How does God answer His people today? Even if Christians are imprisoned or martyred for their faith, how do they get the ultimate victory?

**22:22. I will declare Your name to My brethren; In the midst of the assembly I will praise You.**

---

The Lord Jesus Christ came to walk the earth at the fulness of time (Gal. 4:4-5). He came to declare the name of God to the people who were God's special treasure, the nation of Israel (Exod. 19:5), His brethren. The half-brothers with whom He undoubtedly grew up and spent much time around no doubt witnessed His perfect honoring of His parents (Exod. 20:12), His perfect honoring of the civil authorities under which His earthly family of origin lived (Rom. 13:1-7). Before His earthly ministry, one might imagine how Christ lived perfectly in every facet of life before all those He contacted. In doing this, He would have had to perfectly **declare** God's **name to** everyone He was around, including His **brethren** (Jn 1:18).

All who have received Him in every generation make up Christ's brethren (Mk 3:25). Those who receive Christ enter into God's adopted family and become doers of God's Word and will (Matt. 7:21-23, Rom. 2:13, Rom. 8:15, Gal. 4:4-5, Jas. 1:22). Christ reveals the Father to people who have responded to the gospel with genuine saving faith (Matt. 11:27). Unfortunately, many to whom Christ declared the name of God did not receive Him (Jn 1:11). Christ was Jewish in descent through Mary. So, any Jewish person to whom Christ revealed or declared Himself was His brother or sister in a national sense. He spent His earthly life ministering to mostly Jews, His brethren. There were some exceptions of Gentile ministry (e.g., Matt. 15:21-28). Christ declared God's name to the people He came to save by doing God's works (Jn 5:19, Jn 17:4) and speaking God's words (Jn 3:34, Jn 17:8).

**In the midst of the assembly** of the people He came to save, Jesus praised His Father by living perfectly unto the Father. All that the Father had given the Lord Jesus Christ to do, Christ perfectly executed. Christ perfectly fulfilled that last Passover with His disciples before converting it to the Lord's Supper (Matt. 26:17-30). Christ perfectly appeared to hundreds, including His disciples after His resurrection, proving who He said He is (1 Cor. 15:5-7).

Today, saints from every tribe, tongue, and nation praise the Lord Jesus Christ for His saving work in their lives (Rev. 5:9, Rev. 7:9). Today, the saints make up the assembly of the called-out ones that praise Father, Son, and Holy Spirit for the saving work they have wrought (Rom. 1:7, 1 Cor. 1:2). At the time that the psalm was written, it could have referred to God's disciples. It could also be a scene out of heaven where Christ praises the Father in front of the rest of the redeemed.

## Questions for self-reflection:

(1) How did Christ declare His name to those around Him, to His brethren, to His disciples?

(2) How did Christ declare His name to the rest of Israel?

(3) A short time later, how did Christ prove that they did not get their way?

(4) When Christ said everyone who does His will is His brother, sister, and mother, what did He mean?

(5) How did Christ praise the Father in the midst of the assembly?

**22:23. You who fear the Lord, praise Him! All you descendants of Jacob, glorify Him, And fear Him, all you offspring of Israel!**

---

All of God's redeemed people **fear the Lord**. This fear does not necessarily refer to being afraid of God, though it can. It has more to do with a reverence for, a respect for God. Jews are not the only people capable of having such a fear. Gentiles are not the only people capable of exhibiting such fear. Any person who has called upon the name of the Lord for salvation should fear the Lord. People pardoned because of the Lord Jesus Christ should not continue to live in unrepentant sin and expect grace to abound (Rom. 6:1-2). People who say they have fellowship with Him should not walk in constant darkness (1 Jn 1:6). People who name the name of the Lord should consistently, albeit imperfectly, depart from iniquity (2 Tim. 2:19).

People who fear the Lord are people who love the Lord because the Lord has translated them from the kingdom of darkness into the kingdom of His dear Son (Col. 1:13). People who fear the Lord were at one time dead in trespasses and sin, but God has made them alive and has seated them in heavenly places with Christ (Eph. 2:1-6). People who fear the Lord were alienated from God in their minds by wicked works, but the blood of Christ has reconciled them (Col. 1:21). People who fear the Lord can be afraid of living in such a way to elicit a response of divine chastisement from the Lord (Heb. 12:3-11). While no sin can separate a believer from the love of God to such a degree that they would ever lose their salvation (Rom. 8:38-39), sin in a believer can lead to a harsh yet loving response of discipline from a loving Father. Therefore, believers should have a healthy fear that seeks to avoid exposure to such disciplinary measures from a loving God.

Having a biblical fear of the Lord includes having a deep reverence and respect for God. Such saints should have some level of a growing appreciation of the extent to which their salvation is not something to take lightly. God did not spare His own Son, and, as a result, the saints enjoy this salvation (Rom. 8:32). **All descendants of Jacob** will not **glorify Him** because not all descendants of Jacob share in the saving faith that is common among all the saints, among all those that do glorify Him. Those who belong to the Lord will bear fruit, albeit in different amounts (Matt. 7:15-20, Jn 15:1-8). But true believers will without fail bear some level of fruit. Such fruit-bearing is what will glorify the Lord. The life of a saved person will take on the appearance of Christ-likeness, and such Christ-likeness is what brings glory to the Lord. Saints glorify their Savior by living in such a way that they look like Him. They walk as He walked (1 Jn 2:6). They do what He did. They give. They love. They display the fruits of the Spirit.

All the **offspring of Israel** make up the saved. They are referred to as Jacob. They make up the Israel of God (Gal. 6:16), God's special treasure (Exod. 19:5), and God's chosen race (1 Pet. 2:9). They have been born again (John 3:3). They have become partakers of the divine nature (2 Peter 1:4). They are children who all belong to the same Father through the Lord Jesus Christ. God has commended His love toward them in that while they were still sinners, Christ died for them (Romans 5:8). He has made them His spiritual seed by faith in Christ (Gal. 3:16). Because of their union with Christ, the **offspring of Israel are** blessed with every spiritual blessing (Eph. 1:3-14).

## Questions for self-reflection:

(1) How does the fear of the Lord look in your life?
(2) How has your relationship with sin changed since you began to fear the Lord?
(3) How has your love for the Lord changed since you began to fear the Lord?
(4) Do you think that you are above receiving chastisement from the Lord? Why or why not?
(5) How would you know if you ever took your salvation for granted?

**22:24. For He has not despised nor abhorred the affliction of the afflicted; Nor has He hidden His face from Him; But when He cried to Him, He heard.**

---

Affliction marked the ministry of the Lord Jesus Christ. Things that people said about Him and what people did to Him afflicted Christ. Direct temptations from Satan himself afflicted Christ (Matt. 4:1-11). The Father afflicted Christ when the Father laid on the Christ the iniquity of everyone (Isa. 53:6). Christ enduring the Father's sustained wrath because of the sins of humanity afflicted Him (Rom. 5:9). Humanity despised Christ so much that it brought mankind pleasure to cause Christ to suffer.

The Father and the saved take benefit from the **affliction**s of Christ as the afflictions led to Him being our sympathetic High Priest (Heb. 4:15). Christ's death atoned for man's sins (Jn 3:16). As the afflicted One on our behalf, the affliction that Christ suffered was the precursor that led to Christ being the Justifier of us, the ungodly (Rom. 3:26). The death of Christ, though not pleasing on the surface, was pleasing (in the sense of satisfactory) to the Father as it met the requirement of the Father for human perfection and divine substitution. On the cross, God the Son, the Lord Jesus Christ, became the substitute for mankind and appeased the wrath of God against man's sin. Christ enjoyed perfect fellowship with His heavenly Father until the Father forsook Him on the cross because He became sin for us (Matt. 27:46, 2 Cor. 5:21).

When Christ cried to the Father, the Father **heard** Christ in that He received Christ's spirit when Christ committed His spirit to the Father (Lk 23:46). When Christ asked the Father to forgive His murderers, the Father heard that (Lk 23:34). Christ asked that the Father be near to Him and to remember Him. Because Christ is a perfect doer of God's will, we know that no iniquity separated Christ from the Father, so there would be no reason for the Father to forever reject the Son after the Son finished with His atoning work. We know that the Father was pleased with the Son as He said so (Matt. 3:17) and since the Son rose from the dead (Rom. 1:4). Therefore, the answered prayers of the Son prove that the Father **heard** the Son when the Son **cried to** the Father. The Father had **not hidden His face** from the Son permanently once Christ had finished the atoning work. After Christ satisfied the Father's wrath and redeemed a people to Himself, their perfect fellowship resumed. Thank God that when the Son cried out to the Father that the Father heard the Son!

**Questions for self-reflection:**

(1) How have you benefited from the affliction that Christ endured?
(2) Who do you know that can benefit from Christ's death on their behalf?
(3) In what ways did the Father hear Christ when Christ called out to His Father?
(4) In what ways has the Father shown that He has heard you when you call out to Him?

**22:25. My praise shall be of You in the great assembly; I will pay My vows before those who fear Him.**

No doubt, when the Son returned to the right hand of the Majesty on High (Heb. 1:3) after accomplishing our redemption, **praise** was directed toward Him **in the great assembly** in heaven (Rev. 19:1). Also true is that God the Father had praise from God the Son throughout the earthly life and ministry of God the Son. Christ made it plain that He came at the direction and will of His Father (Gal. 4:4-5). Christ's life on earth was a mission to reveal the Father to the sinners who had separated themselves from Him (Jn 14:9). Christ gave praise to His Father in front of everyone He came in contact with when He repeatedly testified to the truth of His Father and when he did the works of His Father.

The Son knew that the Father would raise Him from the dead (Matt. 16:21). The resurrection was the Father validating Christ's praise of the Father (Rom. 1:4 Gal. 1:4, Eph. 1:19-23). This promise of resurrection would be cause for exuberant praise, even when going through intense suffering that the death for our sins was. The apostles made up the first great assembly. The apostles were eyewitnesses to this momentous event that is the resurrection. Because Christ rose, the church is built. The church built on the foundation of the apostles and prophets (Eph. 2:20) has become a great assembly located throughout the whole world.

Until Christ returns, the great assembly grows as more and more sinners hear the gospel and are converted. Now to the redeemed, Christ **will pay** His **vows** to **those who fear Him** by being their continual Advocate (1 Jn 2:1), their continual Intercessor (Heb. 7:25), and their continual propitiation (1 Jn 2:2). He does this to ensure that nothing separates them from God's love (Rom. 8:38-39).

### Questions for self-reflection:

(1) Using a little sanctified imagination, what might be some things that Scripture does not record that would have been

said to the Son when He returned to the great assembly in heaven after His ascension?

(2) Do you ever wish that you could have a communion with God that was so close like Christ had that you could quickly know and respond in ways that were always pleasing to Him? Do you desire to be so like Him as far as separated from sin that you can recite Romans 7:24-25 with Paul?

(3) How bad must the rebellion and rejection in the Pharisees have been for them to go to as great lengths as they did to cover up the resurrection?

**22:26. The poor shall eat and be satisfied; Those who seek Him will praise the Lord. Let your heart live forever!**

To be truly **satisfied** in an enduring way, one must cease striving for satisfaction in what this perishing world has to offer (1 Jn 2:15-17). Instead, the lost person that is alienated from God (Col. 1:21) has chosen to make themselves rich on the goods and philosophies that amount to wood, hay, and stubble and that do not bring lasting joy (1 Cor. 3:12). They become so fat on these deceitful riches that they do not realize that they are like animals being prepared for slaughter.

The poor in spirit realize that nothing about their sin can satisfy them in a permanent way (Matt. 5:3). They recognize that their sin most certainly will not please a holy God, regardless of how good they appear to be on the outside. They realize that even if they clean themselves up on the outside, inside, they are still corrupt and in desperate need of Christ to wash them (Matt. 15:18-20). The righteousness that the lost thought they had has turned out to be false and has come crashing down around them. They realize they have no recourse other than to flee to Christ. Only Christ's righteousness is suitable to cover their multitude of sins. Once their faith is in Christ, they realize that they never could put any confidence in the flesh (Phil. 3:3). They understand that any good that comes from them only comes as a result of the grace of God working in them as they work out their salvation (Phil. 2:12-13, Jas 1:17).

Because the **poor** disciple **eats** from the table of the Lord and is sustained by Him, they can experience affliction and persecution with joy because they know it makes them like their Master (Matt. 5:11-12, Jas 1:2-8). Believers can respond to persecutors who oppress them with grace and truth because their Example did so to His enemies when they were lost. The poor in spirit can eat the flesh and drink the blood of the Son (Jn 6:54-6:56) and know that meditating on His person and work and abiding in Him is the key to spiritual strength and fruitfulness (Jn 15:1-8). They will hunger and thirst for righteousness and be filled with it (Matt. 5:6). When people **seek** the Lord, **the Lord** will reveal Himself to them and satisfy them with His abiding presence. Those who abide in Christ will **live forever** with Christ in all eternity as their perseverance proves that Christ has begun a good work in them (Phil. 1:6). Their sustenance, as it was with Christ (Jn 4:34), is to do the will of God (Matt. 7:21-23, Jas 2:14-26), as it is the doers of the Word who are justified and who live forever.

## Questions for self-reflection:

(1) Are you truly satisfied with Christ such that you rarely struggle with contentment?

(2) Are you still trying to satisfy God with your insufficient external righteousness, or have you genuinely received Christ's imputed righteousness to your account such that your sins are forgiven?

(3) Is being poor in spirit only a requirement before salvation? Do the justified also exhibit poverty of spirit?

(4) Does the prospect of getting to live in heaven for eternity with the Trinity excite you and motivate you to holy living now? Why or why not?

**22:27. All the ends of the world Shall remember and turn to the Lord, And all the families of the nations Shall worship before You.**

When sinners on each **end of the world** see **the Lord** for who He is and what He has done, they will understand how their sins have created such a great chasm between themselves and God. These illuminated sinners will fall in love with Him and turn to Him not because they are afraid of Him but because He is so attractive to them because of who He is. They will see that He can spare them from eternal wrath by their humbling themselves, repenting of sin, and placing justifying faith in Christ alone for salvation (Matt. 23:12, Acts 20:21, Rom. 3:24-26). They will trust fully in Christ alone to deliver them from this present evil age (Gal. 1:4). Christ came to be the author of the salvation that humanity so desperately needs (Heb. 5:9).

When man recognizes his sin for what it is and sees Christ for who He is (Jn 19:37), He becomes not just Someone who takes the punishment they deserve. Christ becomes the One who is with them for everything they face (Heb. 4:15), someone Who intercedes on their behalf, (Heb. 7:25) Who is sufficient. Christ is the Person the saint will **turn to** out of love and **remember** Who He is. They will see God was good to lead them to repentance (Rom. 2:4). They will see God as rich in mercy to even offer salvation to such unworthy sinners (Eph. 2:4). They will stop trusting things that have no power to save and stop going to those things for temporal satisfaction. They will instead turn to the Lord for permanent satisfaction and repeated renewal (Rom. 12:2). They will respond to God's gracious offer to service based on gratitude and love, not based on fear. People who fall in love with God for Who He is will respond to His Word because they love it. After all, it came from Him, and His commands will not be burdensome (1 Jn 5:3).

Darkness will flee when the Light of the World exposes it (Jn 8:12, Jas 4:7). The Spirit of God using the Word of God will turn sinners to repentant faith in the loving Lord who died as a substitute for sinners (Rom. 10:17, 1 Pet. 2:24, 1 Jn 2:2). People from all types of **families**, from every tribe, tongue, and **nation** (Revelation 7:9-10), will worship the Lord because of who He is and what He has done. **Worship** will be done in spirit and truth by those with hearts of genuine faith (Jn 4:24). Devotion will be external and internal when the grace of God, which has appeared to everyone, affects hearts (Ti 2:11).

**Questions for self-reflection:**

(1) Did you have joy knowing that your sins were forgiven when you remembered God's mercy and turned to the Lord?

(2) Were you grateful when you understood that God's wrath was justly upon you but could be alleviated by your faith in the Lord?

(3) Do you feel awkward worshiping the Lord now after all that He has done for you, or does worship come naturally?

(4) How has God been good to you? Are any of these reasons worthy of worship?

**22:28. For the kingdom is the Lord's, And He rules over the nations.**

---

In context, the psalmist refers to **the kingdom** where Christ the King of kings and **Lord** of lords rules and reigns on the earth when He has put all His enemies under His feet (1 Cor. 15:26-27, Rev. 20:4-6). Christ was promoted to the kingdom's throne when God exalted him to His right hand (Col. 3:1) after His ascension (Acts 1:9-11). The resurrected Christ will deliver this kingdom to His Father (1 Cor. 15:24). The saints are the subjects that reign with Christ in the kingdom (2 Tim. 2:12, Rev. 20:4). The kingdom of God is now in the hearts of believers (Lk 17:20-21) as they abide in Him, and He abides in them (Jn 15:1-8). The gospel is the message of the Kingdom (Matt. 13:19). The message is what the King has conveyed to the world. This kingdom is not of this world (Jn 18:36). All of humanity, whether they acknowledge it or not, is under the authority of Christ the King (Prov. 8:15-16, Dan. 2:21). They will have to bow to Him one way or another, either in this life by turning in repentant faith to Him (Matt. 4:17, Lk 13:3, Heb. 11:6), or in the next life, as one of His enemies who has been put under His feet (Phil. 2:9-11). It is better to willingly submit to His Lordship now than to be forced into submission in the Lake of Fire (Rev. 21:8). Because He loves us, He gives us a choice. **He rules over the nations.** Now He rules over earthly authorities by upholding all things, including earthly rulers, by the Word of His power (Heb. 1:3). He rules His people by filling them (Acts 1:5, 1 Cor. 12:13, Ephesians 5:18) with and leading them by the Spirit (Rom. 8:14-15) and leading them into all truth (Jn 16:13). He rules over His enemies with a rod of iron (Isa. 11:4, Rev. 2:25-29, Rev. 19:11-15).

### Questions for self-reflection:

(1) Does the prospect of the Lord ruling over the whole earth excite you?
(2) Do you look forward to the day when the world will no longer be under the sway of the wicked one?

---

(3) Does the Lord rule your heart now? Would those who know you best agree?

(4) Is the message of the kingdom, the gospel message, important enough to you that you share it with your loved ones who need to respond to it?

(5) If you had to give up your most prized earthly possession to enter into the kingdom, would you be willing to do it?

**22:29. All the prosperous of the earth Shall eat and worship; All those who go down to the dust Shall bow before Him, Even he who cannot keep himself alive.**

---

Since **all the prosperous of the earth** in this verse **shall worship,** since only the redeemed worship God in Spirit and truth (Jn 4:24), the prosperous in this verse must refer to the redeemed. Among the redeemed include people from various social strata and socioeconomic statuses. The saved can either include people of low societal authority and others with high societal power.

While from an earthly standpoint, the degrees of material prosperity and societal clout will vary among believers, all believers share the same spiritual resources and spiritual prosperity (Eph. 1:3-14). All believers share faith in the same Savior (Eph. 4:5). All believers have the same capacity to comfort since Christ has comforted them (2 Cor. 1:3-4). All believers can project joy wherever they go because the names of all believers are written in heaven (Lk 10:20).

Not every believer understands things the same (Rom. 14). Not every believer is equally mature. Not every believer is equally victorious. The degrees of practical sanctification will not be identical in any two believers, and the reasons for that are too numerous to enumerate. But every believer, because of Christ, shares the same spiritual inheritance (Eph. 1:3) and the same access to the Father (Eph.5:2). For this, all believers have sufficient reason to worship.

Since the population of the saints will include some who had earthly wealth or who had earthly authority, which God in His sovereignty permitted them to accumulate (Deut. 8:18, Eccles. 5:19, Eccles. 6:2), they should use it for His glory and purposes (Matt. 6:33, 1 Tim. 6:10). The proper use of one's God-given resources can show a watching world that even though God allows some to prosper, a correct understanding of wealth includes that it comes from above (Jas 1:17), is a stewardship (1 Cor. 4:2), and is to be returned to the Lord in proportion (2 Cor. 8:11-12). What the servants of the Lord do with the resources entrusted to them by the Lord shows where their treasure is (Matt. 6:19-21).

Everyone who has ever lived or will ever live is included in **those who go down to the dust**. Man was created from the dust. Man will return to the dust (Gen. 3:19, Eccles. 3:20). These may or may not have been prosperous on the earth. Man may have gotten wealthy, or he may not have. In eternity, that will not matter. Those who humble themselves under the mighty hand of God will be exalted in due time by God (1 Pet. 5:6). God will exalt them, and they shall eat from His table and worship Him for all eternity (Rev. 19:6-9). In contrast to the saved, the lost will bow to God. God will crush them in the fierceness of the winepress of His wrath (Rev. 19:15). No man **can keep himself alive** apart from the influence of God. God permits man to take his next breath. God knows the extent of the amount of time for all of humanity (Ps. 139:16). He knows everything about what man understands to be the past, present, and future, as it is all as if it were the present to God as God does not dwell in the dimension of time since God is eternal (2 Tim. 1:9, Ti 1:2). If man avails himself to the living water (Jn 4:14) and the bread that came down from heaven (Jn 6:48-51), the Lord Jesus Christ, and lives this life by faith in the Son of God who loves him and gave Himself for him (Gal. 2:20), even if man cannot keep himself alive, he will fully entrust his life to the Lord. After all, it is the Lord who gave him life. Saved man will also be willing to lay down his life for his Lord since his Lord laid His life down already (Rom. 12:1, 1 Jn 3:16).

## Questions for self-reflection:

(1) When you think of the word "prosperous," what initially comes to mind?
(2) Is the type of prosperity this verse discusses the same type as first came to your mind with the answer to the previous question?
(3) Do you experience joy in your soul despite dire circumstances as a result of the saving work of Christ on your behalf?

(4) As the Lord has prospered you materially, have you held on to it tightly, or have you given some back to Him who first gave to you?

(5) How did the Lord make man from the dust? How does man return to dust?

(6) Either man will bow before God before he returns to the dust in death in saving faith, or man will bow before God and fearfully fall into His hands. Into which group do you fall? Is there anyone who you know that is not a believer? Is there anyone you know whom you fear may be self-deceived into thinking they are right with God that is not truly justified? How can you lovingly reach them?

**22:30. A posterity shall serve Him. It will be recounted of the Lord to the next generation,**

---

The saved, the elect, the sheep, the ransomed, the redeemed from every **generation** constitute the **posterity** that **shall serve** Christ for the duration of their earthly lives and for all eternity (Rom. 9:29). The saved are the spiritual offspring, Abraham's seed (Rom. 4:3, Rom. 4:23-25), that have been called, justified, sanctified, and have been or will be glorified (Rom. 8:29-30). They have been reckoned as righteous (Gen. 15:6, Rom. 4:5). The saved are not saved to sit. They are saved to serve. Christ is their example that they should walk in His steps (1 Pet. 2:21), and His steps were steps of service (Matt. 20:28). They have been saved unto good works that God has ordained for them to walk in (Eph. 2:10). God especially gifts and equips saints in a variety of ways to carry out the variety of tasks that the church has been ordained to do (1 Cor 12:1-31, Eph. 4:7-16, 1 Pet. 4:7-11). In every generation, the Lord has a posterity that He justifies to serve Him. They show that they belong to Him not merely by their verbal profession of belonging to Him but also by their life-styles of service dedicated to Him. When this posterity comes to grips with the understanding that the spiritual blessings are a gracious gift to receive rather than an entitlement owed, the natural response toward the benevolent Creator should be one of heartfelt gratitude and service.

## Questions for self-reflection:

(1) Did Christ come to serve or to be served?
(2) Did Christ leave us to walk after our own fleshly desires or to walk in His steps?
(3) What good works does your life consist of that God can use to bring others to saving faith?
(4) If God has ordained that His people live lives full of good works if our lives are devoid of such works, does that make it look like we love God and others more than ourselves?

---

(5) If God would be so benevolent toward us by giving us physical life and spiritual life through Christ, what would cause us not to want to give our lives to Him in humble, grateful service?

**22:31. They will come and declare His righteousness to a people who will be born, That He has done this.**

---

Saved people from every generation **will come** and **declare His righteousness**. Abel did what God asked (Gen. 4). Abraham (Gen. 15:6) believed in God, and his belief was counted to him for righteousness. People have always placed saving faith in the God revealed to them and have understood that God is a righteous Savior. Saved people from all walks of life understand to varying degrees that the gospel is a message of love (Rom. 5:8), grace (Eph. 2:8), and forgiveness (Col. 1:14). They also understand that the gospel is a message of justice (Rom. 3:26) and righteousness (Rom. 1:17). These saved people know that they have not qualified themselves for the salvation that they enjoy. Their sin had disqualified them (Rom. 3:23). Christ has qualified them (Col. 1:12).

**People will be born** in every generation who believe the gospel by faith (Rom. 1:16), by the power of God, have the **righteousness** of Christ imputed to their account. Their sin gets imputed to Christ (2 Cor. 5:21) so that Christ becomes the once for all (Heb. 10:10) final sin offering on their behalf. They receive the adoption of sons, redemption through His blood, and the forgiveness of sins (Eph. 1:7). They have been freely justified by faith (Rom. 5:1). To these people, faith has come by hearing the word about Christ (Rom. 10:17). They have believed the Scriptures, which have made them wise unto salvation (2 Tim. 3:15). They have humbled themselves like little children and have looked unto the Author and Finisher of the faith (Heb. 12:2), the Lord Jesus Christ, and have seen that **He has done this** marvelous thing and purified a people for Himself (Ti 2:14). He has obtained eternal redemption (Heb. 9:11-12). He has made a new and living way for us to draw near to God (Heb. 10:19-22). He has bought for Himself a peculiar people (1 Pet. 2:9). Those who believe the saving message of the gospel are born again (Jn 3:1-7, 1 Pet. 1:3).

**Questions for self-reflection:**

(1) Lots of people want to declare God's love. However, fewer people want to proclaim God's righteousness. Why is that?

(2) Saved people are declared righteous by God based on faith in Christ. Why are people unrighteous before that declaration is made?

(3) In the declaration of righteousness bestowed upon a repentant sinner, what exchange takes place between sin and righteousness?

(4) Why is it right that God should get the praise for your salvation even though you turned to Him in repentant faith?

# Psalm 23

## 23:1. The Lord is my shepherd; I shall not want.

David wrote this psalm perhaps when he needed divine comfort due to going through a trial such as persecution by Saul. However, David could have also written this psalm during his material prosperity, which he enjoyed when he was king of Israel. When in times of abundance or in times of want, the Lord is sufficient for His people.

**The Lord** Jesus Christ called Himself the Good Shepherd (Jn 10:11). In His humiliation, the Lord Jesus Christ was tempted in every way like we are yet without sin (Heb. 4:15). He humbled Himself (Phil. 2:8) by condescending from heaven to walk perfectly on the earth as fully God and fully Man (1 Tim. 2:5). In doing so, He became our faithful High Priest (Heb. 4:14), the propitiation for our sins (1 Jn 2:2), the Bishop of our souls (1 Pet. 2:25), our Head (Eph. 5:23), and the source of all wisdom and knowledge (Col. 2:3). The Father gave Him all authority so that He could be in that position (Matt. 28:18).

Christ's church members, like the psalmist, are His sheep. They are sheep by their faith in the **Shepherd** (Eph. 2:8, Heb. 11:6). It is the sheep who wander from the Shepherd. The Shepherd never strays from the sheep. When the sheep wander from the Shepherd, the Shepherd seeks them and brings them back to the fold. If they are sheep, they will remain sheep forever (Jn 10:28-29). Nobody can snatch them from the Shepherd's hand. The Shepherd knows all there is to know about the sheep and cares for them perfectly even though the sheep sometimes don't understand that what the Shepherd does in their life, though at times painful to endure, is for their ultimate good since the Shepherd does all He does for the ultimate good of the sheep (Rom. 8:28).

The Shepherd is a personal shepherd to each sheep. He meets the needs of each sheep individually. Because the Lord Jesus Christ is the Good Shepherd, and because He is God, the sheep can trust Him to supply all their needs (Phil. 4:19). As the sheep seek Him, they should trust Him to continue to provide for them (Matt. 6:33). They will **not** lack, or **want**, any good thing that the Father intends for them to experience. Everything good He intends for them to experience is a good gift from above (Jas 1:17). Some of it is for divine discipline as a result of sin (Heb. 12:3-11). Some of it is the reward of material prosperity (Gen. 13:1-3, Gen. 26:12-14, Gen. 30:43, Deut. 28:1-13). Nothing necessary for the sheep to experience will be withheld from the sheep. God knows what His people need before they even ask Him for anything (Matt. 6:8). So, it is not due to the Shepherd's deficiency when sheep, God's people, do not get what they think they need from the Shepherd, God, or the Lord Jesus Christ (who is also God in the flesh). Instead, it is due to an inadequate understanding on the part of the sheep. The Shepherd provides the sheep with sheep food and with quenching water (Jn 6:35).

## Questions for self-reflection:

(1) David had experienced the Lord's shepherding influence in his life. How have you experienced the Lord's shepherding impact in your life?

(2) Is it easier to recognize that the Lord shepherds us during times of ease and plenty, or is it easier to recognize that the Lord shepherds us during times of affliction and lack? Why?

(3) Does the Shepherd ever wander from the sheep, or is it always the sheep who stray from the Shepherd?

**23:2. He makes me to lie down in green pastures; He leads me beside the still waters.**

---

**Green pastures** are pastures that are not dried out. Green pastures depend upon water for hydration. Green pastures are healthy. They are not overgrown with weeds. The sheep fully trust the Shepherd to lead them to this green pasture because it is a place of safety for the sheep (Jn 10:9). The Lord Jesus Christ is the Good Shepherd that the sheep (Jn 10:11), the genuine believer, trusts for all their physical, emotional, and spiritual needs. A Christian, a sheep, remains healthy if they stay close to the Shepherd - if they stay close to Christ. The branches remain healthy if they abide in the vine. Christ's sheep stay healthy when they stay intimately connected to Christ (Jn 15:1-8). They know their life is hidden with Christ in God (Col. 3:3). Since they are secure in Christ, they have everlasting righteousness, which was accounted for when they believed the gospel (Rom. 4:5). They know that Christ has given them the pure milk of the Word for which they are to desire as newborn babes (1 Pet. 2:2). They mature into solid meat believers as they grow on the milk because they have matured spiritually as a baby grows on milk physically (Hebrews 5:12-14).

**To lie down** is to take the place of more permanence and safety instead of constantly wandering (Eph. 3:17-19) and escaping from danger. Pastors are to feed the flock of God as under-shepherds of the Good Shepherd. Christ raises up under-shepherds who care for the sheep, who are the flock of God (1 Pet. 5:1-4). As the pastors who are the under-shepherds preach the Word and teach the people what it means to follow the Good Shepherd, the Lord Jesus Christ (2 Tim. 4:1-5), the sheep lie down in restful paths along the narrow way that leads to eternal life that the minority finds (Matthew 7:13-14). The under-shepherds warn the sheep to avoid the broad paths that lead to destruction because most will be on the broad path, and the broad path will deceptively lead multitudes astray.

---

Still waters are calm waters. Still waters are not chaotic or frenzied waters. **Still waters** are comforting, soft streams. They are like the easy yoke and light burdens of the Lord Jesus Christ (Matt. 11:30). To be led by Christ is to be led into the green pastures and **beside** the still waters. To be led by Christ, to be led by the Spirit into all truth (Jn 16:13) is to walk into the storm knowing that when the waves crash against you that Christ keeps you from drowning as you follow Him on the narrow path (Matt. 7:13-14, Matt. 7:24-27). It recognizes that His grace sustains you and is sufficient for you (2 Cor. 12:7-10). God's love has been shed abroad in the hearts of the believers (Rom. 5:5). It enables the believers to live for the Lord even in the midst of the harshest of circumstances. The still waters of God's love are refreshing enough to quiet the most restless of hearts.

## Questions for self-reflection:

(1) What determines the level of one's physical health?
(2) What determines the level of one's spiritual health?
(3) If one is not physically healthy, what are the first two general recommendations?
(4) Referring to # 3, diet and exercise were the intended answers. How can diet and exercise improve one's overall physical health?
(5) If physical diet and physical exercise can improve one's overall physical health, how can spiritual diet and spiritual exercise improve one's overall spiritual health?
(6) Which pastures are healthier, green or brown?
(7) When the storms of life rage around you, is it evident that internally you are traversing by still waters gently being held by your Shepherd?

**23:3. He restores my soul; He leads me in the paths of righteousness For His name's sake.**

When the famished and parched soul hungers and thirsts (Matt. 5:6), He restores their soul. When the soul feels as if the enemy surrounds them on every side (2 Cor. 4:8), He restores their soul. When the circumstances of life beat the believer down to the point that they do not know how they will go on, He restores their soul. When the believer reaches the end of themselves in the issues of life, He restores their soul. When there is no place to look except up, He restores their soul. When the believer takes refuge in their present help in trouble (Psa. 46:1), He restores their soul.

The soul of the believer is restored because they waited upon the Lord (Isa. 40:31). **He restores** their **soul** and gives them the supernatural ability to face the most severe trials (Jas 1:2-8). They realize they cannot face these things in their own strength because their strength does not last. Their strength does not last because they are finite, created beings. They need strength from an eternal Being that does not faint or grow weary (Isa. 40:31).

When believers seek to endure the hardships of life in their own strength, once the believer reaches the end of their rope, when they turn to the Lord, they experience the soul restoration that only the Lord can provide. When their spirit is willing, but their flesh is weak (Matt. 26:41), when they find themselves doing the things that they know they should not do and not doing the things that they should be doing (Romans 7:15-20), this can make them feel discouraged that their efforts to live the Christian life are not as fruitful as they would like them to be. In these instances, when they go to Him, He restores their soul. When they feel so burdened by their own sin or by the sins of others perpetrated against them, they experience the restoration that can only come from the Lord by taking refuge in their Shepherd. When the sheep take every thought captive to the obedience of Christ (2 Cor. 10:5), the Holy Spirit comes to the rescue of the believer with the comfort of the truth of God's Word (2 Cor. 1:3-5). Such unchanging, enduring, and rock-solid truth can be a powerful means that God uses to restore the discouraged, weary, and burdened soul.

The Shepherd restores the souls of the sheep when they are weary and heavy-laden (Matt. 11:28). The Shepherd restores the souls of the sheep when they are without spiritual strength (Rom. 5:6). When the sheep feel as though they could die at any moment due to their current dire straits, He restores their souls (2 Cor. 1:9). The Shepherd refreshes the sheep by planting them as well-watered trees (Ps. 1:3). The Shepherd leads the sheep. The Shepherd knows the pastures better than the sheep because the Shepherd has gone before the sheep on the path (Jn 14:2-3). The Shepherd comforts the sheep (Jn 14:26-27) so that they can comfort others (2 Cor. 1:4).

So, the Shepherd is a worthy object of trust for the sheep. He is worthwhile to trust as the only One who is qualified to **lead** the sheep into **the paths of righteousness**. While less attractive than worldly paths, the paths of righteousness can be pretty easy to recognize for those who know God's Word, but the sheep have to know that trusting the Shepherd is always better for them in the long run. The paths of righteousness can be easy to recognize but difficult to follow. The paths of righteousness can be easy to discern but difficult to continue on.

Nevertheless, the paths of righteousness lead to eternal life. The Shepherd will lead the sheep on the paths of righteousness to become more like Him, conformed to His image over time (Rom. 8:29, Rom. 12:2). The more the sheep stay on the path of the Shepherd, the more they will remove themselves from the trinkets of the world (James 4:4). The sheep will live holy lives because, above all else, they want to be with their Shepherd, and they know that holiness is the requirement for that (Heb. 12:14). The sheep follow this Shepherd because they trust Him. They have entrusted their lives to Him. He has proven Himself to them to be worthy of their trust. They count the cost of following the Shepherd (Lk 14:28) because following the Shepherd can be difficult at times, primarily due to mistreatment by the world (Matt. 5:11-12). The sheep live lives for God's glory (1 Cor. 10:31). It is

Christ's name, the name of the Good Shepherd, that the sheep commend to the lost world that is without Christ (Matt. 5:16).

## Questions for self-reflection:

(1) When has the Lord come to your rescue after you spent some time waiting for Him to intervene in a circumstance and restored your soul?

(2) When have you felt spiritually weary and then felt your soul get restored after time in the Lord's presence before the throne of grace?

(3) When have you reached the end of your rope only to have the Lord hold you up so you could keep going?

(4) When have you felt the Lord strengthen your flesh so that it could follow the Spirit He put inside you?

(5) When have you felt the forgiving flow of Christ's intercessory sacrifice on your behalf after you have confessed your sins?

(6) When has the unbelieving world in which you find yourself burdened you so much that you wept only to have Him restore your soul and remind you that this world is not your home and the lasting city has been prepared for you?

(7) Have you improved at recognizing whether or not paths are righteous before you even travel down them? Are you better at discerning the Lord's will before you decide something so that you will not have to spend as much time making corrections caused by going down the wrong path?

**23:4. Yea, though I walk through the valley of the shadow of death, I will fear no evil; For You are with me; Your rod and Your staff, they comfort me.**

---

By this time in the psalm, the psalmist is in a circumstance that leaves him feeling that physical death is not far from him. Eternity, from the psalmist's perspective, feels like a breath or a heartbeat away. Perhaps he feels here closer to physical death than he has ever felt before. There will regularly be circumstances that make the believer feel like death could be perilously close. Perhaps, in a moment of desperation, they might think that physical death would be preferable to continuing to endure the momentary light affliction (Phil. 1:21-24).

Perhaps moments like those described are what the psalmist felt when the psalmist described this **valley of the shadow of death**. Despite **walking through** this most difficult of circumstances, the psalmist can boldly declare that he **will fear no evil**. This is not because there is no true evil around him. There is. The world in which redeemed sinners live is full of evil people doing evil things (Gen. 6:5, Gen. 8:21, Eccles. 8:11, Jer. 17:9, Ps. 2:1-3, Jas 4:4, 1 Jn 2:15-17, 1 Jn 5:19). The evil people of the world have the father of lies (Jn 8:44), the roaring lion (1 Pet. 5:8), the accuser of the brethren (Revelation 12:10), Satan, as the source of all evil. While the devil is powerful, the devil is still God's devil. From the book of Job, we learn that the devil can only do what God permits him to do (Jb 1:6-12, Jb 2:1-10). Knowing this fact helped the psalmist place absolute trust in the Lord his God.

Since a bird cannot fall to the ground apart from God's permission (Matt. 10:29), the psalmist could trust that nothing could happen to him without God's intervention or permission (Romans 8:28). And even these calamities that befell the psalmist would be for his good. As a child of the King of Kings, the psalmist knew that the worst that could happen was physical death. He knew that he need not fear the evil of wicked people who could only kill the body. There was no need to fear men since the psalmist already possessed a healthy fear of God, the One who can kill and cast body and soul into hell forever (Matt. 10:28). The psalmist knew, even though it had not been written for all posterity yet, that even if his soul became separated from his body in physical death, that nothing could separate him from God's love (Rom. 8:38-39, 2 Cor. 5:8).

One of the most glorious promises of the Word of God is that Christ dwells in the believer by faith (Eph. 3:17). Christ in believers is the hope of glory (Col. 1:27). Perhaps the psalmist gives a fore-taste of this when he says that God is **with** him. For the Christian, they know that their High Priest has gone before them (Jn 14:2-3). He was tempted like we are and endured it all perfectly (Heb. 4:15). They know that physical death is nothing to be afraid of (1 Cor. 15:55). They know that He ever lives to intercede for them (Heb. 7:25). He whispers into their ear in that gentle, still, small voice (1 Kgs 19:11-12) that reminds them of the truth that they already know because they have hidden His Word in their hearts that they might not sin against Him (Ps. 119:11).

He disciplines them when necessary (Heb. 12:3-11). The **rod** that goes out of God's mouth, God's Word, can be unpleasant to hear for the child of God that is in desperate need of correction. But if the believer heeds the warnings that God ordains as a mer-ciful means to bring the wayward sheep back to the path of righ-teousness, then repentance, restoration, and growth can take place and benefit all. The rod can **comfort** the wayward sheep if they understand its implementation to mean that He is there to lovingly warn them that if they do not return to Him, a much worse fate awaits them. The Word can steer the sheep onto the path of righteousness and keep them there. The rod of the Word of the Shepherd can give the sheep discernment against wolves, so they can recognize a wolf or a hireling who tries to lead the sheep away from the Shepherd (Jn 10:11-13). The sheep can do all of this because He, the Good Shepherd, the Lord Jesus Christ, is with them, enabling them to be doers of His will. They can do all things through Christ who strengthens them (Phil. 4:13). The **staff** directs the sheep into which way they should go. As the believer avails himself to the Lord's abiding presence, the staff is a ready instrument to lead the believer into the truth, into a life full of practical righteousness (1 Jn 2:29). God has given us His Word that informs the Holy Spirit to tell us which direction we should go (Jn 16:13). While the Bible does not answer every question anyone could ask, it is still sufficient because the principles contained therein are Holy Spirit inspired and entirely God's truth (2 Tim. 3:16). If believers esteem God's Word more than their necessary food (Jb 23:12) and faithfully apply it to their lives, which is the definition of biblical wisdom (Pro. 1:7), they will be like the blessed man in Psalm 1. They will be like the well-nourished tree that prospers (Ps. 1:3).

## Questions for self-reflection:

(1) What is the highest peak of life that you have experienced?
(2) What is the lowest valley of life that you have experienced?
(3) Have you ever felt like your physical death was imminent?
(4) Have you ever felt like you would rather die than endure what you had to endure?
(5) Does knowing that the devil can only do what God allows him to do help you trust God?
(6) Does knowing that whatever God permits to happen to you will happen help you to trust God?
(7) Do you think of God's correction as merciful and loving or overbearing and harsh? How do you mimic that for your children?
(8) How does the rod of God's Word comfort His people?

**23:5. You prepare a table before me in the presence of my enemies; You anoint my head with oil; My cup runs over.**

To have **a table prepare**d is language that is illustrative of provision. The psalmist here speaks of God providing what he needs in the presence of his enemies. When we face adverse circumstances, any of which could be analogous to being **in the presence of enemies**, God, in His benevolent Providence, welcomes His sheep to come to Him for mercy and help in time of need (Heb. 4:16).

The Christian has available to them an abundant feast as often as they care to partake in it. God invites them to eat the flesh and drink the blood of the Lord and Savior Jesus Christ (Jn 6:53). But, of course, Christ was not into cannibalism. He was calling His people to partake in His presence. He called His people to share intimate fellowship with Him through the Spirit. He called them to intimate union with Himself. He, in return, would fill them with the love of God shed abroad in their hearts (Rom. 5:5). He would lead them by the Spirit into all truth (Jn 16:13). The Son of God would equip them with grace to overcome temptation (1 Cor. 10:13). Their Advocate makes them part of a new family of other believers (Eph. 1:5). This new family provokes one another to love and good works (Heb. 10:24), and who would collectively proclaim the goodness (Rom. 2:4), grace (Ti 2:11), mercy (Eph. 2:4), and love of God (Romans 5:8) to a people, His enemies (Col. 1:21), in such desperate need of it.

This table includes the earnest of the inheritance of heaven (Eph. 1:11, 1 Pet. 1:4). Believers now get a small measure of what heaven is like in that they get to enjoy fellowship with their Lord and with one another (1 Jn 1:3). Believers should not fear because the enemies that are in their presence now will be under their feet, as they will be under Christ's feet once they have all had their coming day of judgment (1 Cor. 15:26-27). God's enemies, which are also enemies to God's people, the saints, see how God prospers some of His saints, adding to the discouragement of the lost. As the enemies of God see the church flourish because of God's magnificent work of grace in the lives of His people, the enemies strive to overthrow God and God's people (2 Tim. 3:12). But God from heaven laughs when the heathen rage and plot vain things (Ps. 2:1, Ps. 2:4). To **anoint** the **head with oil** is an illustration of benevolent, superfluous, abundant provision. God is the supplier of all the needs of His people (Phil. 4:19). He gives them everything they need for this life (2 Pet. 1:3). Those things might be material things. Those things might be spiritual resources to face any circumstances (Jas 1:2-8). It may include knowledge of who He is through his Word. With this knowledge, the believer can meditate on His person and work so that when situations arise in life that only Christ can help with, the knowledge of Him is the only sufficient resource to help overcome anxiety or difficulty (Phil. 4:6-8). It may be the Holy Spirit that leads believers in God's ways (Jn 16:13) that assures believers of the hope that is theirs, even in the presence of their enemies. God also provides gifts to each saint, especially equipping the saints to serve His church to demonstrate the grace of God to a watching world (Matt. 5:16, 1 Cor. 12:1-31, Eph. 4:7-16, 1 Pet. 4:7-11). Either way, the Holy Spirit is involved with the symbolism of the oil because it is the Holy Spirit in believers that energizes the functions described above.

The **cup runs over** for the believer who recognizes that God is the source of every good and perfect gift (Jas 1:17). The believer has joy inexpressible and full of glory, not because of their circumstances (1 Pet. 1:8). Their joy transcends their circumstances. Their joy comes to the surface many times despite their circumstances. A commonly referenced saying of this day is that "happiness depends on happenings." In other words, if moods ebb and flow based on what happens to someone, their joy is not the deep and abiding joy that is typical for a Christian. The Christian's joy does not go away when life gets hard. The Christian's joy remains no matter what happens in life. Endless joy happens because they know that no matter what happens to them in this life, that nothing can separate them from God's love (Romans 8:38-39) and that the sufferings in the life prepare them for the greater weight of glory that awaits them in eternity (2 Cor. 4:16-18).

## Questions for self-reflection:

(1) What enemies do you face?

(2) What has God provided you with to face those enemies?

(3) How can you demonstrate and proclaim the love of God to your enemies who do not know it?

(4) Where will your enemies, the enemies of Christ, end up one day if they do not repent and believe the gospel?

(5) When God's enemies try to undermine God's influence all over the world, do you get anxious, or do you understand this to be part of God's plan?

(6) What gifts has God provided you with so that you can be a means to lead others into the kingdom of God with you?

(7) What makes you the happiest?

(8) What brings you the most joy?

**23:6. Surely goodness and mercy shall follow me All the days of my life; And I will dwell in the house of the Lord Forever.**

Because the psalmist is in a right relationship with God, **goodness and mercy shall follow** the psalmist **all his days**. Because of the finished work of the Lord Jesus Christ on the cross in place of sinners, the benefits (Ps. 68:19) and blessings (Eph. 1:3-14) that are available to all the justified shall follow them all their days (Rom. 8:28-30). God cannot bestow the benefits upon the sinner because of any apparent goodness within the sinner (Romans 3:10-12). The sinner possesses no merit with which to lay claim to such blessings. God's mercy endures to generation after generation to those who fear Him (Lk 1:50). Those who have come to God by faith in Christ are saints. Saints receive mercy and help in time of need (Heb. 4:16) and receive goodness and mercy all their days and throughout eternity.

The goodness of God has led the saved to repentance (Rom. 2:4). Repentance and salvation have happened to the saved because the great God, our Savior (Ti 3:4), is rich in mercy (Eph. 2:4). The saved know that God will withhold no good thing from His own (Ps. 84:11). Though the sins of each person are as scarlet, because God is a God of mercy, He makes them as white as snow (Isa. 1:18). No sinner deserves any of the good that they receive. It all comes from God (Jas 1:17). They are gifts of His love that He reserves for His adopted children. His children do not deserve them, but He supplies them with these good gifts out of love for them.

Even the 'bad' things that God allows us to experience in our lives come our way by divine permission for the purpose that we might be more like Christ by sharing in His sufferings (Rom. 8:17, Phil. 3:10, 1 Pet. 4:13). So, when the loving Heavenly Father disciplines us His wayward children, the unpleasant discipline the Father does is for the goodness of the justified saint that the saint might be more like Christ afterward (Heb. 12:3-11).

Sometimes believers are most sensitive to God's goodness and mercy towards them when they find themselves in the crucible of suffering, which God allowed them to experience. Sorrow and sin happen as an overarching consequence of the sinful condition under which we all live. Since there will be no sin in heaven, there will be no more sorrow and suffering (Rev. 21:3-4). One of the means which God may employ to make His people long for heaven is to allow them to experience suffering in this life so they will seek to be more like their Savior. The saved may see these experiences as tools in a gracious Father's hand to remind the saint of the goodness and mercy shown them in that they are not going to get the sentence they deserve for their sins since Christ took their place (Rom. 6:23).

For all the days of the saint's life, there should be a growing awareness that God's mercies are new every morning (Lam. 3:22-23), that He is abundantly faithful, even if we cannot see it. That the sinner can draw their next breath is a testimony to God's faithfulness. The justified sinner receives every spiritual blessing in Christ because God is full of goodness and mercy toward them, and that goodness and mercy will follow them all the days of their life. The believer **will dwell in the Lord's house forever** when, after they take their dying breath, they will immediately be ushered into the Lord's presence (2 Cor. 5:8) and will worship around the throne continually (Rev. 4:10, Rev. 7:15). Since all believers are recipients of this grace and mercy, they will be followed by this grace and mercy all their days. Since believers will dwell in the house of the Lord forever, deep gratitude (Phil. 1:3), heartfelt worship (Jn 4:24), godly sorrow (2 Cor. 7:10), abundant joy (Phil. 4:4), dedicated service (Phil. 2:4), and abasing humility (1 Pet. 5:6) should flow naturally from a Spirit-led life.

## Questions for self-reflection:

(1) Why can the psalmist, and why can anyone who belongs to the Good Shepherd say goodness and mercy follow them everywhere?

(2) What prevents everyone else from receiving this goodness and mercy?

(3) What do we do to earn this mercy?

(4) As a recipient of God's goodness and mercy, what can separate you from His love?

(5) Are believers more prone to take notice of God's goodness and mercy in good times or in bad times?

(6) Can saints learn lessons about God's goodness and mercy from the suffering God allows them to endure in this life?

(7) To dwell in the house of the Lord forever is the end for each saint. Does that reality excite you? Do you want to see God's face?

# Psalm 24

**24:1. The earth is the Lord's, and all its fullness, The world and those who dwell therein.**

---

The Bible begins by establishing that God created everything (Gen. 1:1, Jn 1:3). God created the universe that exists and the planets about which we know. God created the planets that might exist that we may not have discovered yet. God created everything we know that has ever existed on earth or currently lives on earth. This includes plants, animals, and humans and the materials and the elements that make up the materials that compose everything. Therefore, by the right of creation, all of **the earth** belongs to Him. God is the rightful owner of everyone and everything because He created everything. For someone to not be willing to return worship to the One who owns them is the epitome of selfish rebellion.

Every non-human aspect of the creation declares God's glory without opposition (Isa. 6:3). Humanity, created in God's image (Gen. 1:27), when presented with the choice to glorify God by virtue of His creation of them, or to glorify self or some other aspect of God's creation, without fail, chooses to glorify something that was created (Rom. 1:25). Even when man chooses to sin against God, one of the parts of the human race that shows that man is superior to the rest of creation is that God created man with the ability to make choices. No other part of God's creation can make choices in the same way humans can. **The Lord** Jesus Christ is the Agent by which the earth **and all its fullness** came to be (Col. 1:16-17, Heb. 1:2). By virtue of Christ's creation of everything, including humanity, He can claim ownership of it all. Since Christians are heirs of everything Christ created and owns, God permits society to benefit from His creation, including the animal kingdom, whether for food or clothing. Everyone and everything that **dwell**s in **the world** God owns by the rite of creation. As a result of God's ownership, man owes God an unpayable debt. Man can begin to serve God. But because of man's sin, man has separated himself from God and incurred God's wrath (Jn 3:36). The Lord can only restore mankind back to a relationship Himself

---

through faith in the risen Savior, the Lord Jesus Christ. Christ made a covenant with His Father and, in the fullness of time (Gal. 4:4-5), condescended (Phil. 2:7, 1 Tim. 3:16) to live a perfect life (2 Cor. 5:21, 1 Pet.2:22), died a substitutionary death for sinners (Rom. 5:6), and rose again for our justification (Rom. 4:25).

## Questions for self-reflection:

(1) Of all that you enjoy on this earth, how much of it is yours in the truest sense?
(2) Why is it so evil to not return worship to God?
(3) Have you ever worshipped the creation more than the Creator?
(4) Why are humans able to make moral choices that animals are not able to make?
(5) Who is the Agent which God employed to create everything?

**24:2. For He has founded it upon the seas, And established it upon the waters.**

God created both the earth and the seas out of nothing by speaking it into existence. A postulate is that God created earth above water as if the earth was the outer crust of a piece of bread and the waters were the inside. Then the flood came. When the flood came, the crust broke, and the seas formed. This is how the earth could have been **founded upon the seas**. God **established** the earth **upon the waters**. He has ownership of it and has made Christ heir of all things (Heb. 1:2). Christ holds it all together (Col. 1:16-17).

**Questions for self-reflection:**

(1) If God can create everything by speaking it into existence, what can He do in your life?

**24:3. Who may ascend into the hill of the Lord? Or who may stand in His holy place?**

---

The hill of the Lord is analogous to entry into the church. Man enters the church upon being justified by exercising personal faith in Christ alone (Rom. 3:24-25). Today, none could **ascend into the hill of the Lord** had the Lord not first condescended to us. Man would not love God if God did not first love man (1 Jn 4:19). There is nothing lovely in man since man's sin has separated him from a holy God and left man without hope (Eph. 2:12). Man's sin has separated him from God like death separates the body and the spirit (Col. 2:13). In that state, man cannot ascend into the hill of the Lord. The Lord first had to come to man (Phil. 2:7). Man had made himself God's enemy through his sin (Col. 1:21). Christ reconciled man to God so man could ascend into the hill of the Lord through His shed blood on the cross as man's substitute.

To ascend into the hill of the Lord is also to **stand in His holy place.** These are two different ways to express the same thing. The Lord's presence is within believers (1 Cor. 6:19) and is where two or more believers gather in His name (Matt. 18:20). When a sinner humbles themselves in the sight of the Lord, then the Lord lifts them (Jas 4:10).

### Questions for self-reflection:

---

(1) Who is qualified in and of themselves to come to the Lord apart from the Lord's intervention?
(2) What or who qualifies someone to enter the church?

**24:4. He who has clean hands and a pure heart, Who has not lifted up his soul to an idol, Nor sworn deceitfully.**

Man cannot live with **clean hands** unless he first possesses **a pure heart**. Apart from God, man has an impure heart (Jer. 17:9). Man's heart, naturally speaking, is polluted by sin (Gal. 5:19-21, Eph. 4:22). Since man is a sinner by nature and choice, he will inevitably choose to sin since his sinful nature leads him to do so. Man's death proves that man sins since death is the wages of sin (Rom. 6:23). Other people cannot see a man's heart since the rest of his body hides it. The hands (and the rest of the extremities) will act based upon that which is within the heart (Matt. 15:19, Rom. 1:29-31). What enters the mind and then comes out of the mouth is first in the heart before it exits the mouth (Matt. 15:16-20). What man eats does not defile him but what comes out of his heart through his words and actions defiles him. What man does and says, after he thinks of it, is observed by others. It is the fruit that determines the nature of the tree (Matt. 7:15-20).

When a sinner receives justification as a free grace gift (Rom. 3:24), God cleans his hands and purifies his heart (Jas 4:8). God removes the stony, polluted heart and replaces it with a malleable, cleansed heart (Ezek. 36:25-27). The cleansed heart is the place from which cleansed hands operate. Clean hands demonstrate the works of the Spirit (Gal. 5:22-23). The condition of the heart is the precursor to the visible deeds produced by the hands. The cleansed heart produces the living faith that is illustrative of a genuine believer. Since the heart and hands are defiled apart from Christ, the convicted sinner needs to be washed by the cleansing blood of Christ (1 Cor. 6:11). They need to purify their hearts by faith. They need Christ's imputed righteousness (Rom. 4:5).

Once the sinner has been justified, because the remaining sinful flesh encapsulates the temple of God within the believer, there is an ongoing war between the flesh and Spirit that will not end until glory (Gal. 5:17). While in the struggle with sin and sometimes succumbing to it, the redeemed saint has a new holy disposition and strives, albeit imperfectly, in ways that the Lord prescribes as the Spirit leads him into all truth (Jn 16:13). The alienated soul **has lifted up his soul to an idol**. Mankind makes all sorts of things into idols when they replace the worship of the Creator who is blessed forever amen with that thing (Rom. 1:25). Man shows himself to be idolatrous and unfit for the kingdom of heaven from an early age. Instead of lifting up one's soul to an idol, the regenerate man lifts his soul up to the one true God (Col. 3:1-3). He is willing to sell all to buy the pearl of great price (Matt. 13:45-46) and field that contains the hidden treasure (Matt. 13:44). The saint has exchanged the idols of the world for the worship of the one true God. For this reason, the saint can ascend to the hill of the Lord and stand in His holy place (Ps. 24:3).

The saint no longer swears **deceitfully**. He makes it his habit to speak the truth to his neighbor and to love no false oath (Zech. 8:16-17). He knows that God desires truth in the inward parts (Ps. 51:6). He knows that His Savior, the Lord Jesus Christ called Himself 'the truth' (Jn 14:6). He knows that a disciple becomes like His master (Matthew 10:25, Luke 6:40). So, he should be truthful, even if the truth causes harm to himself.

## Questions for self-reflection:

(1) Based upon these two qualifications, who is ready to ascend into the hill of the Lord or stand in His holy place?
(2) Does having clean hands make the heart pure?
(3) Does having a pure heart cleanse the hands?
(4) Why is everyone polluted and in need of cleansed hands and purified hearts?
(5) Who can cleanse their own hearts? If we cannot purify our own hearts, who must cleanse our hearts?
(6) When does the war between the impure hands and hearts and the renewing hands and hearts wrought by the Holy Spirit in the justified saint end?

(7) What are the common idols in this society that we are so prone to lift up our souls to?

(8) Why does God want His people to be truthful? Does it have anything to do with His own nature?

**24:5. He shall receive blessing from the Lord, And righteousness from the God of his salvation.**

---

The one who may ascend into the hill of the Lord (Ps. 24:3), the one who may stand in His holy place (Ps. 24:3), the one who has clean hands and a pure heart (Ps. 24:4), the one who has not lifted up his soul to an idol (Ps. 24:4), and the one who has not sworn deceitfully (Ps. 24:4) **shall receive blessing from the Lord.** Believers in the Lord Jesus Christ meet each of these conditions. The forgiven sinner is a justified saint who has had Christ's **righteousness** imputed to their account. Their name is written in heaven (Lk 10:20). The one who has placed repentant saving faith in the Lord Jesus Christ shall receive every spiritual blessing (Eph. 1:3) when they come to God by faith in Christ for **salvation.**

When the saint renews their minds in God's Word (Rom. 12:2), they show they esteem it more than their necessary food (Jb 23:12). By esteeming it in this way, they become the blessed man who meditates on God's Law day and night (Ps. 1:2). They abide in Him, and He abides in them (Jn 15:4). They put on the armor of God (Eph. 6:11-20) and can experience spiritual victory over any spiritual foe because they know that Christ is the source of the faith that is the victory that has overcome the world (1 John 5:4). They know that, in Christ, they possess everything they need for life and godliness (2 Pet. 1:3). As members of God's family, they are loaded down with daily benefits (Ps. 68:19). They have received wisdom from above that helps them walk in the earth beneath (Jas 3:17).

## Questions for self-reflection:

(1) Based upon these two qualifications, who is ready to ascend into the hill of the Lord or stand in His holy place?
(2) Does having clean hands make the heart pure?
(3) Does having a pure heart cleanse the hands?
(4) Why is everyone polluted and in need of cleansed hands and purified hearts?

---

(5) Who can cleanse their own hearts? If we cannot cleanse our own hearts, who must purify our hearts?

(6) When does the war between the impure hands and hearts and the renewing hands and hearts wrought by the Holy Spirit in the justified saint end?

(7) What are the common idols in this society that we are so prone to lift up our souls to?

(8) Why does God want His people to be truthful? Does it have anything to do with His own nature?

**24:6. This is Jacob, the generation of those who seek Him, Who seek Your face. Selah**

---

**Jacob**, Israel, makes up the people of God (Rom. 9:6, Gal. 6:16). These are the people from every tribe, tongue, and nation (Rev. 7:9) who have been called, justified, sanctified, and will be glorified (Rom. 8:30). Christ dwells in the hearts of such people by faith (Rom. 3:17). These people **seek** the Lord and are found by the Lord (Jer. 29:13, Matt. 7:7). These are people who seek the abiding presence of the Lord, who seek the Lord's blessings, and who find them. They seek His **face**. These are people in whose hearts God has shed His love abroad (Rom. 5:5). These people, this ransomed group, ascends to the hill of the Lord (Ps. 24:3). Members from this ransomed group stand in the Lord's holy place (Ps. 24:3), with clean hands and pure hearts (Ps. 24:4), has not given into the temptation to forsake the Lord for the idols of this perishing world (Ps. 24:4), and has committed to the truth instead of deceitfully swearing to idols (Ps. 24:4).

Jacob, God's family of children, possesses a new nature (2 Cor. 5:17) and demonstrates characteristics, fruit (Gal. 5:22-23), that coveys that God has translated them out of the kingdom of darkness and has translated them into the kingdom of His Son, the Lord Jesus Christ (Col. 1:13). In every **generation**, there is a remnant, a people who rise up from the ashes of the world to seek Him, the Lord who has commended His love toward us in that while we were sinners, Christ died for us (Rom. 5:8). Man has separated himself from God by sinning away his blessing (Isa. 59:1-8). Man has alienated himself from God by His sinful thoughts, words, and actions (Col. 1:21). Man dies because the wages of man's sin is death (Rom. 6:23). In that separated state of spiritual death (Ephesians 2:1, 2:5), to end the separation, God came to man, (Gal. 4:4-5), lived a sinless life (1 Pet. 2:22), died on the cross for our sins (1 Pet. 2:24), and rose again for our justification (Rom. 4:25, 1 Tim. 3:16). Now all who seek His face in humble repentance will receive the free gift of eternal life. These make up the generation who seek Him. The seeking called for in this verse is not a one-time seeking. They can come whenever they have a need (Heb. 4:16). God provides for all the needs of the saints (Phil. 4:19).

**Questions for self-reflection:**

(1) If someone caught a snapshot of your life, would they conclude that you fear the Lord?
(2) Is your life one that makes those on the outside conclude that it is desirable to seek the Lord?

**24:7. Lift up your heads, O you gates! And be lifted up, you everlasting doors! And the King of glory shall come in.**

Jacob, the redeemed of the Lord, those who make up the church, which has its door open to hear, receive, and be changed by the gospel preached in its ears are the **gates**. Preachers, which get ordained according to Scriptural qualifications, are the mouthpieces (1 Tim. 3:1-7, Tit 1:6-9). God's grace changes believers. Such believers are on the path the sanctification and are the means that the world sees and God uses to add to His Kingdom (Matt. 5:16).

Christ is the **King of glory**. He only **comes in** to fellowship with or receive worship from His saints, from the sheep, those He has bought with a price (1 Cor. 6:20), those who glorify God in their bodies. The saints live to give Him glory (1 Cor. 10:31). Christ is the source of joy for the saints. They have gone into the Kingdom through the narrow gate (Matt. 7:13), or the door, of the sheep (Jn 10:7), Him being the Lord Jesus Christ. He has given them a reason to look up! Their redemption draws nigh (Lk 21:28)! The soil of their hearts has been prepared (Matt. 13:8, 23). They can receive the Word with joy and bear fruit because they are good trees and good trees bear good fruit (Matt. 7:15-20, Jn 15:1-8). They are sheep that hear the voice of the Good Shepherd (Jn 10:27-28).

The church is referred to here as being everlasting doors. They are the ambassadors of Christ that show Christ to those on the outside (2 Cor. 5:20). Those on the outside see believers' lives and testimonies which do commend or do not commend the gospel. In that way, the church members are like **everlasting doors** that commend the gracious gospel to a perishing world that is in such dire need of rescue that only the gospel can provide. Christ identified Himself as the door, or the gate, of the sheep. He being the Good Shepherd, and the church being the sheep, the sheep are those whose lives are the primary means by which the person and work of Christ are lifted up. Christ, Himself said that when He is lifted up, He will draw all men to Himself (Jn 12:32). The church draws the attention of the distracted world to this point. The church lives in such a way as to be a city on a hill or a lamp (Matt.

5:14-15). The love of God has been shed abroad in their hearts, and it constrains them to serve others with joy (Rom. 5:5).

The Lord Jesus Christ is the King of glory. As eternal God, He had glory in heaven with the Father even before creation (Jn 17:5). As a possessor of the Divine nature (Col. 2:9), Christ the Lord possesses glory that created beings do not. The fulness of the Godhead bodily dwells in Christ and not in the rest of the human race (Col. 2:9). He confirmed this by the miracles He performed (Jn 10:38). He proved this by the gracious words which He spoke (Lk 4:22). He demonstrated this by humbling Himself and becoming obedient to the death of the cross (Phil. 2:8). He proved this by His resurrection (Matt. 28). He continues to verify this by continuing to mediate for His people to bring many sons to glory (1 Tim. 2:5). When sinners embrace the Son by repentant faith, Christ dwells in their hearts by faith (Eph. 3:17), He abides in them, they abide in Him, they bear much fruit (Jn 15:1-8). God is glorified.

## Questions for self-reflection:

(1) How is your fellowship with the King of glory?
(2) Does your life promote the King's kingdom to those who are outside?

**24:8. Who is this King of glory? The Lord strong and mighty, The Lord mighty in battle.**

---

The psalmist's question at the beginning of this verse is not a question made out of ignorance or skepticism. The psalmist knows precisely who the **King of glory** is. The question at the outset of this psalm conveys a sense of awe or wonder that the psalmist has towards his Lord. His mission in life is to know the Lord, know the King of glory, and grow to be more like Him (Rom. 8:29). He has met the Lord through the Lord's faithful messengers.

**The Lord** has personally revealed Himself to the psalmist throughout his life. The psalmist is well aware that there is none like the Lord (1 Sam. 2:2-3). Therefore, the only One worthy of the psalmist's praise, of our praise, the One to whom every knee will bow, is the Lord (Phil. 2:10). He humbles Himself to behold the things in heaven and on earth (Ps. 113:6). There are no other Gods but Him (Exod. 20:3). He is the Lord that calls Israel to hear Him and only Him (Deut. 6:13). He is the One that laughs when the heathen rage (Ps. 2:1, 4). He is the One that spoke everything into existence (Heb. 11:3). He is the One who upholds all things by the Word of His power (Heb. 1:3). All things consist in Him (Col. 1:17). He intervenes on behalf of His people according to His purposes.

There are earthly rulers. The Lord appointed them (Dan. 2:21, Rom. 13:1). There are none higher than He. The Father, Son, and Spirit share in that strength and might. They collaborated on the plan to save mankind. The salvation of a lost sinner is the work of a **strong and mighty** God. The salvation of a lost sinner required the Father to choose them (Eph. 1:4), the Son to die for them (Gal. 4:4-5), and the Spirit to lead them (Jn 16:13) and keep them. The strong and mighty Lord created the church to be the home base for His redeemed people. His mighty working in the hearts of His people is what keeps the church going (Eph. 1:19). Yes, people work out their salvation with fear and trembling individually (Phil. 2:12), and the church works collectively to equip the saints and reach the lost (Eph. 4:12-13). Still, the Lord is behind all of it. The Lord works in His people (Phil. 2:13). He works all things together for the good of those that love Him (Rom. 8:28). He began a good work in the saved, and He will accomplish it (Phil. 1:6). He continues to work to meet the needs of His people (Phil. 4:19). He continues to receive the cares His people cast upon Him (1 Pet. 5:7).

The Lord has always been **mighty in battle**. He has always gone before the saints into their respective battles (Deut. 31:8). The battles belong to the Lord (1 Sam. 17:47). The Lord triumphed over His enemies (Col. 2:15, Rev. 20:7-10). The saints fight, but the Lord is the source of their strength. He gives them armor to take with them into the battle (Eph. 6:10-20). Any good that comes from His people ultimately is because of His provision. Even if the brain allows man to think of the right solution, so the right outcome is achieved, the Lord is still ultimately praised since the Lord created the brain. Even if the physical ability wins the battle, the Lord created the body and made it fit together like it should and enables it to work as He designed it to work. Man never has anything to boast about because anything good comes ultimately from God. Anything sinful comes from man because man took what God made and called good and twisted it sinfully in those instances. The army that fights battles needs a captain. The Lord Jesus Christ is the captain of our salvation (Heb. 2:10) who leads us by the Spirit into all truth (Jn 16:13).

## Questions for self-reflection:

(1) What has the Lord done in your life to prove that He is strong and mighty?
(2) How has each part of the Trinity worked to accomplish your salvation?
(3) Is it difficult to remember that God goes with you into your battles?

**24:9. Lift up your heads, O you gates! Lift up, you everlasting doors! And the King of glory shall come in.**

See note on Psalm 24:7. When the church is functioning as God designed it to function, the whole counsel of God (Acts 20:27) is taught from qualified leadership (1 Tim. 3:1-7, Ti 1:6-9). The layperson in the congregation obediently fulfills God's role for them in the exercise of their spiritual gifts (1 Cor. 12:1-31, Eph. 4:7-16). They are content with the gifts that God has blessed them with and are not covetous of gifts that God in His sovereignty bestowed upon others. Pulpits magnify the Lord Jesus Christ. Saints go into the world and preach the gospel with their mouths (2 Tim. 4:2) and with their quiet and peaceable lives (1 Ti. 2:2) that allow them to live at peace with the lost (Rom. 12:18). God intends for the church to be the means to bring the gospel to those missing out on its privileges. It is the **everlasting doors** that commend the gospel to the perishing world. When the church lives as it ought, the **King of glory** is pleased and will bless it and **come in** and encourage the saints so that they will not get weary in well-doing (Gal. 6:9).

**Questions for self-reflection:**

(1) What would the earth be like if everyone in the church exercised their spiritual gifts in the way God intended?
(2) What would the earth be like if everyone in the church actually lived consistently like God had called them to live.
(3) If the saints lived as they ought, and the Lord's presence came and dwelt among His people wherever they found themselves, would the whole earth break out into worship? Would all the rebels be overwhelmed by the power of God and bow before Him?

**24:10. Who is this King of glory? The Lord of hosts, He is the King of glory. Selah**

---

The question asked in verse eight of this chapter is repeated here. Once the **King of glory** comes in (24:9), all attention will be drawn to Him, making the question more understandable. This King of glory has magnificently made way for the human race, which has traitorously rebelled against Him, to be reconciled to Him (2 Cor. 5:18-20). When the greatness of who God is gets juxtaposed against the sinfulness of who mankind is, the only response that is fitting from the creature to the Creator is one of wonder and awe directed to God and shame over our own sinfulness (Isaiah 6:5). That the Infinite would be mindful of the finite is awe-inspiring. That the holy would be concerned with the affairs of the unholy is fortunate. That the God of light would give light to every man that frequently walks in darkness is gracious. That He humbles Himself to behold the things in heaven and on earth is wonderous (Psalm 113:6). That He cares enough about us sinful creatures to provide for our needs is merciful (Philippians 4:19, Ephesians 2:4). That He gives us second, and third, and fourth, and thousandth and infinite choices when we sin against Him and others daily conveys the vast richness of His mercy. That He gives us richly all things to enjoy shows that He is a God of abundant provision (1 Timothy 6:17). That He lets the rain fall on the just and the unjust (Matthew 5:45) for as long as He does shows that He desires all to come to repentance (2 Peter 3:9). No wonder He demands our allegiance!

## Questions for self-reflection:

(1) Do you ever get lost in the wonder of the salvation that Christ accomplished for you such that you ask, "Who is this King of glory?"

---

(2) Have you ever felt the presence of God so strongly that you reacted like Isaiah in Isaiah 6? What keeps us from being so convicted about our own sinfulness?

(3) For this great God to humble Himself and call you to be in a relationship with Him is an extraordinarily kind thing for Him to do? How can you demonstrate that kindness to others so others will want to come to Him as you have?

# Psalm 25

**25:1. To You, O Lord, I lift up my soul.**

The psalmist knows that he needs to put God first in everything (1 Pet. 3:15). He knows that he needs to go to God in prayer for his most basic needs (Matt. 6:33) and in times of desperation, such as the time about which he wrote in this psalm. Some assert that this psalm of David alludes to when Absalom rebelled against David (2 Sam. 15). He knows that he is in a relationship with the Lord by living a life of vibrant faith unto the **Lord**. He has not earned the right to have this relationship with God. Instead, God has been richly merciful to him to permit him to come into His presence despite his sin (Eph. 2:4). For sinners such as the psalmist and the rest of us, to even be able to **lift up** the **soul** to the Lord is an incredibly gracious privilege.

The psalmist did not lift up his soul to the Lord out of rote practice but rather out of heartfelt devotion. That is just the type of approach that God calls all the sheep to make towards Him. If we honor Him with our lips, but our hearts are far from Him, that will be ineffective (Isa. 29:13, Matt. 15:8). If we harbor iniquity in our hearts, He will not hear us (Ps. 66:18). He insists that we come before Him humbly, contrite, with clean hands and pure hearts (Ps. 51:17, Jas 4:8). If we draw near to God like this, God will draw near to us (Jas 4:8). If we seek Him like this, we will find Him (Jer. 4:29, Prov. 8:17, Jer. 29:13, Matt. 7:7, Lk 11:9). Being a hearer of the Word is not enough. The doers of the Word are justified (Rom. 2:13, Jas 1:22-25). The vain things of the world did not draw the soul of the psalmist. Instead, God drew the psalmist's soul to Himself and sustained him.

**Questions for self-reflection:**

(1) Why is the ability to lift up our souls to God even to be able to have a relationship with Him a privilege to be appreciated rather than a right to be demanded?

(2) Are you more drawn to the vain things of the world that have no power to save, or are you more drawn to the God who sustains you?

**25:2. O my God, I trust in You; Let me not be ashamed; Let not my enemies triumph over me.**

---

The psalmist knows that God has been with him and for him since their covenant relationship began by faith at a past point in time (Rom. 8:31). The psalmist knew that God expected him to **trust in** Him in the present and the future. The psalmist knew that **God** was worthy of such trust. God had proven this to the psalmist repeatedly in the past. For God to condescend and even offer to have a relationship with man is incredibly kind and gracious when considering how sinful man is (Ti 3:3-7). Man takes the goodness that God showers upon him (Matt. 5:45) and, instead of living for God, man lives for himself. When man sees the selfishness of his sinful ways, humbles himself, turns from his wicked ways, and seeks the Lord, the Lord finds him and justifies him (2 Chron. 7:14, Matt. 7:7-8, Lk 15:11-32). God does not hold justified, repentant man's sin against him (Ps. 103:12).

On the contrary, God abundantly pardons (Isa. 55:6-7). God begins a good work in the heart of justified man and performs that work until man meets God at the judgment, after death (Phil. 1:6, Heb. 9:27). Between the second birth (Jn 3:3-7) and the judgment (Heb. 9:27), God works His salvation in man while the man works out his salvation (Philippians 2:12-13).

The psalmist knew that based upon who God is and what God had done for him in the past, it was reasonable for God to expect the psalmist to trust Him. The psalmist was going to do that. The psalmist had resigned himself to the fact that His life was hidden with Christ (even though he did not know who Christ was yet) in God and, accordingly, his heavenly Father was to be trusted (Col. 3:3). The psalmist asked God to reward that trust with victory over his enemies. If the psalmist trusted in God and the psalmist's enemies triumphed over the psalmist, it would appear to the psalmist's enemies that the psalmist's God was not worth trusting. The psalmist did not want his enemies to get that message. The psalmist did **not** want to **be ashamed** for his conscious, deliberate decision to trust in God. The psalmist wanted his enemies to see the benefits that come to those who trust in God. Trust in God can help believers of any age to **triumph over** physical or spiritual **enemies.**

**Questions for self-reflection:**

(1) What has God done for you that you were at one time not even aware that He had done that makes God worthy of your trust?

(2) God works in ways for us to find Him throughout creation and within ourselves in our consciences. Yet, most of us go our own way because we want to reject His authority and be our own authority. If we willingly do this, why is God right, or why is God wrong to judge us due to our own choice to reject Him?

(3) How are you working out the salvation that God is working in you? How are you growing spiritually? Are you growing in conformity to Christ?

(4) How has God rewarded you for your trust in Him? What enemies have you overcome as a result of your faith in God? What victories have you experienced because you trust in God?

**25:3. Indeed, let no one who waits on You be ashamed; Let those be ashamed who deal treacherously without cause.**

For all saints of all ages, including for the psalmist and the reader and the writer, the people of the Lord can trust the Lord that anything that happens to them is for their good and for His purpose (Rom. 8:28). If they can keep that reality present in their minds, then there should be no reason to ever **be ashamed** about choosing the trust the Lord. Those who **wait** on the Lord experience the Lord's renewed strength (Isa. 40:31). It is this strength that equips the justified saint with the strength to face any obstacle. There is also the sense that the Lord's people expected that there would be a day in which the prophesied Messiah would come. His people back in that day had to wait for God's plan to unfold in God's time. They had to wait in expectant hope for the Messiah. He would not come in their lifetimes. They did not know that He would not. They still had the responsibility to wait on Him. Even though He was physically absent, He was spiritually present and could aid His people like He does today. Even if circumstances that have brought trouble on the saint never change on this side of the grave, saints can trust the Lord to provide grace, mercy, and help in the time of need (Heb. 4:16).

As sheep abide in Him, He abides in them (Jn 15:1-8). Their walk with the Lord gets more intimate and rewarding as His abiding presence rewards the believer who diligently seeks the Lord by faith (Heb. 11:6). **Those** who **dealt treacherously** with the psalmist and those who deal treacherously with the righteous in all ages will ultimately be ashamed. The wicked might appear to prosper for a time, perhaps even for a very long time (Jer. 12:1). But a day is coming when the Lord will put all His enemies under His feet (1 Cor. 15:26-27). David asked the Lord to intervene in the lives of his enemies since David did no evil against his enemies. It was going to take a work of the Lord for David's enemies to see the error of their way. The sovereign Lord could cause the plots of the wicked to fail so that David's enemies would have no place to look but up to the God who David served and who could save them. If their wicked plots failed, David wanted the Lord to help his enemies to see how evil their schemes were such that they would be ashamed for contriving of such designs.

**Questions for self-reflection:**

(1) What good has God brought out of the worst thing that has happened to you that shows you that God works all things together for your good?
(2) If your answer to the previous question is "nothing," could it be more about what God does within you and less about what God lets happen outside you?
(3) Take some time to make a list of as many biblical reasons you can think of for why it is good for you to trust the Lord.
(4) Have you prayed for your enemies today such that God would soften their hearts and they would believe the gospel? If you have prayed for your enemies, what effect does that have on your attitude toward your enemies?

## 25:4. Show me Your ways, O Lord; Teach me Your paths.

The **ways** and **paths** of the **Lord** are those that are visible with faith-filled eyes. The unregenerate man cannot see the Lord's ways no matter how evident they seem to the righteous. Not all the ways of the Lord are evident, even to the righteous. Personal sin and limited knowledge still inhibit the saints from seeing all of God's righteous ways. Creation intimates the necessity for a Creator (Heb. 11:3) and is one of the ways of the Lord (Gen. 1:1). To put the ability for reasoning in the human race is one of the ways of the Lord that shows that the Lord made man in God's image (Gen. 1:27). The Lord goes to great lengths to **teach** man His **paths** because the Lord wants man to come to Him (2 Pet. 3:9).

For the believer, God has given them His Spirit to comfort them, convict them, teach them, and keep them on the paths that lead to eternal life (Jn 16:7-11). God has given His completed Word for its Holy Spirit-led readers to see how He works by providence and by direct intervention in the lives of humanity (Rom. 15:4, 1 Cor. 10:1-11, 2 Tim. 3:16). Tragically, most of humanity will miss out on this knowledge because they will not pursue Him since they will be too content with the passing pleasures of sin for a season (Heb. 11:25).

The Lord shows His people His ways of mercy that He is rich in it (Eph. 2:4). The Lord reveals to His people that He is a God who is always working on behalf of His people (Rom. 8:28), and His people should be zealous for good works of their own (Ti 2:14). The Lord shows His people that He deserves their worship and that anything they make more important than Him is sin and inordinate affection (Exod. 20:5).

When God's people familiarize themselves with God through His Word and look for how He acts in His providence in their lives in the present day, that can be a tremendous encouragement for believers and an excellent means to strengthen faith. Strengthened faith will lead to faithful, obedient, disciplined lives, lives that reflect the attributes of our great God.

**Questions for self-reflection:**

(1) What are the people who cannot see the Lord's ways and the Lord's paths missing that the people who can see the Lord's ways and the Lord's pass possess?

(2) What prevents the righteous from seeing every single one of the Lord's ways and paths? Why does the Lord not reveal everything about His ways and paths to His people?

(3) How has God demonstrated His goodness to you?

(4) Why is God jealous such that we should not share the adoration that should be reserved solely for Him with anything created?

(5) How does God demonstrate that His ways include mercy, grace, compassion, forgiveness, love, and kindness?

**25:5. Lead me in Your truth and teach me, For You are the God of my salvation; On You I wait all the day.**

In the Old Testament, God revealed Himself by speaking directly to the fathers (Heb. 1:1). They directly spoke what God wanted them to say (if they were obedient). There was a four-hundred-year period of silence between the Old and New Testaments where there was no revelation. God did not come directly to anyone and reveal Himself as He had done up until that point in time. Leading up to Christ's birth, direct revelation given by an Angel of the Lord is seen (Lk 1:11-20). The Lord came directly to Paul (Acts 9). After Christ ascended, He sent the Spirit into the world in inhabit believers (Eph. 3:17) and to inspire apostles to write Scripture (2 Pet. 1:21).

God still uses His Spirit and the Scriptures to equip, **lead**, and **teach** believers His **truth**. It is the believer's responsibility to abide in Christ so that He will abide in them (Jn 15:1-8). God calls all believers to renew their minds in the Scriptures and good biblical resources so they will be thoroughly furnished for every good work (Rom. 12:2, 2 Tim. 3:16). As believers spend more time with their Lord in prayer and His Word, His truth leads them and teaches them. As believers let the Word of Christ dwell in them richly (Col. 3:16), they begin to practice it more consistently. The Spirit reminds them of God's expectations, and they can access the grace in which they stand (Rom. 5:1-2) to overcome temptation by taking heed to the Word (Ps. 119:9, 1 Cor. 10:13). They are not conformed to this world. Their minds are transformed (Rom. 12:1-2). They become imitators of Christ (1 Cor. 11:1).

God is the **God of salvation** for sinners (Ti 3:4). The Triune God planned for the salvation of the human race before the world was even created (Eph. 1:4, Rev. 13:8). The Father chose sinners for salvation (Ephesians 1:4). The Son died to save sinners (Rom. 5:8). The Spirit leads saved sinners into the truth (Jn 16:13). Only an only wise God (Rom. 16:27, Jude 1:25) could be capable of coming up with such a gracious, loving, yet just way to save sinners (Rom. 3:26). Since the Lord has bought sinners through the finished work of the Lord Jesus Christ, the redeemed sheep can **wait** on **God all the day** for the grace to be doers of God's Word (Jas 1:22) and will (Matt. 7:21-23). God's grace is necessary. He abundantly supplies it as a good and perfect gift from above. All those who have put their hope in the Lord receive God's grace. (Jas 1:17).

## Questions for self-reflection:

(1) What does God use today to equip, lead, and teach His people?
(2) If a believer is stagnant in their growth, what are some possible reasons for that?
(3) How did God plan for your salvation?

**25:6. Remember, O Lord, Your tender mercies and Your lovingkindnesses, For they are from of old.**

---

The psalmist was in a dangerous situation from which only the Lord could deliver him and in which only the Lord could protect him. The psalmist was in a covenant relationship with the Lord. In the past, the Lord had intervened in the psalmist's life. In such times, the Lord's **tender mercies and** His **lovingkindnesses** granted protection and provision when the psalmist needed it most. This time, the psalmist asked the Lord to do now what He had done in the past previously.

Sometimes when God permits saints to go through adversity, when God allows the lost to oppress the saints, when righteousness appears to be losing out to wickedness, saints can more easily be tempted to think that God is not there, that God has left, that He has no power to save. This could not be further from the truth. God has always been a God of mercy and a God of love. The fact that God saves anyone and permits even the lost, that He knows will never come to saving faith, to experience the blessings of common grace, shows that God loves even the reprobate. As the reprobates seem to have their way and prosper in the world (Matt. 5:45), the sheep seem to find more difficulty living in the world. Believers' afflictions, at least in part, have to do with the reality that the world continues to become increasingly hostile to Christ and the gospel (2 Tim. 3:12). It can be tempting for the saved to question God's reality or God's character.

The psalmist reminds us that God is merciful and kind to His people and everyone, even to His enemies, from eternity past, **from of old**. He gave the human race the privilege of being created in His image (Gen. 1:27). He gave lost sinners a chance to come to Him (Jn 3:16). Even to those who reject His provision, God demonstrates His mercy and kindness to the lost because they can choose to accept the provision.

To the saved, God is especially kind and rich in mercy (Eph. 2:4, Ti 3:4). Not only does God make the same provision available to them, but when they accept it, He showers them with grace and blesses them with every spiritual blessing (Eph. 1:3-14). Christ becomes their Mediator and ever lives to intercede for them (1 Tim. 2:5, Heb. 7:25). Nothing can separate them from God's love (Rom. 8:38-39). Since Jesus Christ is the same yesterday, today, and forever (Heb. 13:8), the benefits will belong to the saved permanently. As believers avail themselves to God's eternal, unchanging truth, they are reminded of how kind and loving He is, especially to those in a relationship with Him. His goodness has led them to repentance (Rom. 2:4). His love for humanity led to humanity receiving the gracious opportunity to avoid the wrath that is to come (Rom. 5:8-9). Humanity has always come to God by faith (Gen. 15:6, Rom. 4:5).

**Questions for self-reflection:**

(1) How has the Lord shown you His tender mercies and His lovingkindnesses?
(2) How does God show that He loves everyone, even the unsaved?

**25:7. Do not remember the sins of my youth, nor my transgressions; According to Your mercy remember me, For Your goodness' sake, O Lord.**

From the time that the psalmist was a **youth**, an infant, a toddler, a small child, a primary school-aged youth, the psalmist knew at varying levels a general sense of right and wrong because God has equipped humanity with a conscience to help them tell right from wrong (Rom. 2:15). This general sense of right and wrong would increasingly develop with time and age. This innate knowledge is true about the rest of humanity as well. The sinful nature with which the psalmist and the rest of all humanity were born rears its ugly head in various ways very early on. Youthful lusts lead to **sins** that would cling to the psalmist and the rest of humanity from which he would have to flee (2 Tim. 2:22). Worldliness takes on different forms at different ages. Regardless of the age, worldliness was nonetheless evident (Jas 4:4). If it is not dealt with aggressively, it can lead to a choking out of good spiritual fruit (Lk 8:14). Should this happen, the spiritual results can be devastating. God can still repay evil in more advanced stages of life.

The psalmist could now say, in his advanced maturity, that he had sinned at a very young age in various ways (Ti 3:3). God had been merciful to the psalmist to preserve him to this point. The psalmist had not been treated as his sins deserved. As he aged, the psalmist got more reckless with his sins, more blatant in his rebellion, and committed more pronounced transgressions. He grew more mentally and physically capable. He grew more sinfully capable. With an increase in sinful capability comes an increase in accountability (Lk 12:48). The psalmist knows there is no justifying himself in the sight of God for any of these sins (Rom. 3:19). It only takes one sin to condemn a sinner to death and hell (Rom. 3:23, Jas 2:10).

Praise the Lord that God is rich in mercy (Eph. 2:4). It only took one sacrifice, of the Son of God, once for all (Heb. 10:10), to bring many sons, like the psalmist, like the reader, like the writer, to glory (Heb. 2:10). God's mercy makes this forgiveness and redemption found only in the blood of Christ possible (Eph. 1:7). There is nothing with which the psalmist can glory about himself. His sins are too numerous. He can only stand before God because God has given him access (Rom. 5:2). What is true for the psalmist is true for all of humanity. Because of human sin, every person ever born is condemned already (Jn 3:18). If they will not suffer eternal wrath for their sins, the only way to avoid that wrath is to cast themselves on the **Lord** Jesus Christ, who loved them and died for them (Rom. 5:8-9). Because God is a God of **mercy and** has inherent **goodness** that man does not have, when humanity cries out to God for mercy, God hears, **remember**s, and restores.

## Questions for self-reflection:

(1) How do we know right from wrong?
(2) What do we possess that leads us to do wrong?
(3) How can we avoid letting the world choke out the spiritual progress we make?
(4) Why does our sinful potential get worse with age?
(5) How many sins does it take to condemn someone?
(6) How can anyone avoid that condemnation?

**25:8. Good and upright is the Lord; Therefore He teaches sinners in the way.**

---

God is **good and upright** by nature. Everything God does is good (Gen. 1:10, Gen. 1:31) because God is good (Matt. 19:17). There is no darkness in Him (1 Jn 1:5). There is extraordinary goodness that follows those in a covenant relationship with Him (Ps. 23:6). God is good to His people.

God is absolutely righteous in all that He does (Deut. 32:4, Ezra 9:15, Neh. 9:8, Ps. 7:9, Ps. 7:11, Ps. 11:7, Ps. 35:24, Ps. 36:6, Ps. 40:10, Ps. 48:10, Ps. 50:6, Ps. 57:10, Ps. 97:2, Ps. 97:6, Ps. 100:4-5, Ps. 111:3, Ps. 112:3, Ps. 119:89-90, Ps. 145:17, Isa. 5:16, Isa. 28:17, Isa. 45:21, Isa. 49:7, Isa. 51:8, Jer. 9:24, Jer. 12:1, Lam. 1:18, Dan. 9:14, Dan. 9:16, Mic. 6:5, Mic. 7:9, Zeph. 3:5, Zech. 8:8, Rom. 3:5). God is faithful (Exod. 34:6, Deut. 7:9, Deut. 32:4, Psa. 33:4, Ps. 36:5, Ps. 86:15, Ps. 89:1-2, Ps. 89:8, Ps. 89:33, Ps. 91:4, Ps. 92:2, Ps. 119:75, Ps. 119:90, Ps. 143:1, Ps. 145:13, Lam. 3:22-23, 1 Cor. 1:9, 1 Cor. 10:13, 1 Thess. 5:24, 2 Thess. 3:3, 2 Tim. 2:13, Heb. 10:23, Heb. 11:11, 1 Pet. 4:19, 1 Jn 1:9, Rev. 3:14, Rev. 19:11). Because God is good, righteous, and faithful, the Lord should be trusted by **sinners** as a sufficient teacher **in the way.**

The way of sinners is crooked and perverse. The way of the Lord straightens the twisted paths of sinners. The Lord sends His Spirit to indwell believers. The Holy Spirit leads believers into all truth (Jn 16:13). They renew their minds in His Word (Rom. 12:2), esteeming it more than their necessary food (Jb 23:12). As they meditate on God's Law (Ps. 1:2), they become more familiar with God's ways and God's will for their lives. They turn from their wicked ways (2 Chron. 7:14) at justification (Rom. 3:24) and continue to do so as part of the progressive process of sanctification (Rom. 6:11, Rom. 6:13, Rom. 8:13, 2 Cor. 3:18, 2 Cor. 7:1, Phil. 2:13, Phil. 3:12, Col. 3:10, 1 Thess. 4:3, 2 Pet. 1:5-11) until they reach glorification. The Lord enables justified saints to walk upright since He is **upright,** and they have become partakers of the divine nature (2 Pet. 1:4).

---

**Questions for self-reflection:**

(1) Since God's nature is perfectly good, is there anything God does that is not good?

(2) If there is something that God does that appears to us to be anything other than good, is it possible that we have a limited understanding and hold God to an unfair standard when we make Him conform to our definition of good?

(3) Since our way is crooked and perverse, can that cloud our judgment on what we perceive as good or bad?

(4) How can we better understand God's way of good and God's way of evil?

**25:9. The humble He guides in justice, And the humble He teaches His way.**

---

Those who are made to feel the weight of their sins are made **humble** (Lk 18:9-14 (tax collector)). They realize that their sins have separated them from a holy God (Isa. 59:2). They are without hope and without God in the world (Eph. 2:12). They are dead in trespasses and sins (Eph. 2:1, Eph. 2:5). They are alienated in their minds by wicked works (Col. 1:21). They are poor in spirit (Matt. 5:3). They mourn over sin (Matt. 5:4). They know they are miserable wretches that have no chance at being delivered from this body of death in their own strength (Rom. 7:24). They have been made humble and contrite (Isa. 66:2). As such, God will receive them. Because they have humbled themselves in the sight of the Lord, He has exalted them (Jas 4:10. 1 Pet. 5:6) to walk humbly before God (Mic. 6:8). God has taken their stony heart out and replaced it with a heart of flesh (Ezek. 36:26). The humble come to the Lord for rest because they are weary and heavy-laden from trying to live self-righteously (Matt. 11:28). They have grown weary of trying to appease God by trying to achieve righteousness on their own (Phil. 3:9). They have cast off pridefully trying to achieve their own righteousness and have, in humility, pursued Christ, the only source for true and lasting righteousness (Rom. 3:21-26).

Once the separated sinner realizes that salvation achieved by merit is an impossibility since all are sinners by nature and by choice (Eph. 2:9), that their righteousness is as filthy rags in His sight (Isa. 64:6), when they have no choice but to look up, then they will lift up their heads and see that their redemption is near (Lk 21:28). If they humble themselves, they will be exalted (Matt. 23:12). They will be on God's path, the path of justice. God will teach and **guide** them **in justice** by the Spirit into all truth (Jn 16:13). God can **teach** the humble **His way** because the humble are teachable because they realize they are woefully insufficient at life. They realize that they require God in order to be able to live, move, and have their being (Acts 17:28). The Holy Spirit will be the teacher of the humble as He will use the Word to bring conviction of sin, to pierce the heart, and to impress principles on the mind (Heb. 4:12).

## Questions for self-reflection:

(1) What keeps us from being properly humble? What is the opposite of humility?
(2) Can an acute awareness of our own sinfulness help or hurt us from practicing humility?
(3) Who can we compare ourselves to if we want to have a good sense of our need to remain humble?
(4) Who is God's way? Where do we learn God's way? How do we know whether we are following God's way?

**25:10. All the paths of the Lord are mercy and truth, To such as keep His covenant and His testimonies.**

---

The Lord's **paths** to reveal Himself to mankind for their salvation **are mercy and truth**. He has shown mankind who He is by revealing Himself to mankind in creation (Rom. 1:20). Creation proves that there must be a Creator. Nothing does not have the capacity to create anything. He has written His law on the hearts of everyone (Rom. 2:15), even the people who do not even acknowledge His existence (Ps. 14:1). For God to give man the opportunity to arrive at this conclusion, given the evidence around him, demonstrates that God is a God of mercy. The innate sense of right and wrong that humans acknowledge comes from a God extending mercy toward those who have chosen in arrogance to rebel against His kindness and reject the truth of who He is as He has revealed Himself to be via creation and conscience (Ti 3:4-5). For God to continue to allow man to exist after man chooses to rebel against God shows that God is a God of mercy. Once the separated sinner has come to God for mercy and experienced His gracious pardon, the newly justified sinner embarks on a lifelong journey of getting to know the God of truth.

For God to save anyone and reveal to mankind how they can experience such wonderful salvation shows that God is a God of mercy. Making it such that man does not have to work for his salvation (because man never could because man is too sinful) shows that God is a God of mercy. He is rich in mercy to send Christ to die on behalf of wicked rebels. He graciously rewards those who diligently seek Him (Heb. 11:6) when He reveals the truth of who He is and how the world works to those who pursue Him. God extends mercy by calling, justifying, adopting, sanctifying, and glorifying saints through faith in Christ (Romans 8:28-30). The paths of God are always the paths of truth. God has revealed the truth of who He is to man in proportion to what man is capable of comprehending. God shows mercy even to the lost in that they do not die the first time they sin against Him. Instead, he is gracious to them to give them opportunities to experience His grace and forgiveness and find the truth of who He is and what He has done for them in Christ. Those whose faith is in Christ have begun discovering these things and will give their lives to the pursuit of God and in living for Him. That Christ mediates on behalf of His people is merciful (1 Tim. 2:5).

The saved **keep His covenant and His testimonies.** Even though sinners are justified by faith in God (Rom. 5:1), saved people still cannot perfectly keep His covenant and testimonies (1 Jn 1:8). They still need an Advocate, Jesus Christ the righteous, to continue to propitiate for their sins and ever live to intercede for them (1 Jn 2:1). Even though they are saved and cannot be separated from God's love (Rom. 8:38-39), they still will sin every day and still will need the daily cleansing that Christ provides (1 Cor. 6:11, 1 Jn 1:9). Those who abide in Christ and in whom Christ abides are those who God has enabled to keep His covenant and testimonies. They are objects of God's love and can never be plucked from God's hand (Jn 10:27-28). That God will allow such rebels to partake in salvation and not revoke His calling from them shows that God is a God of mercy and truth.

### Questions for self-reflection:

(1) How has God shown us His mercy?
(2) How has God shown us His truth?
(3) Does keeping His covenant and testimonies save someone?
(4) Since God will not save one just for keeping his testimonies and covenant, what do people still need God to give them (from this verse)?

**25:11. For Your name's sake, O Lord, Pardon my iniquity, for it is great.**

---

Everyone ever born in every generation since Adam is born with a sinful nature (Rom. 3:9-23, Rom. 5:12-21) that will, without fail, at some point early on, lead them to choose to sin and transgress God's law continually (1 Jn 3:4). From this sinful nature, sins come to the surface that so easily beset us (Hebrews 12:1). This sin nature creates sinful choices in the lives of the unregenerate that separate the unregenerate from the **Lord** who made them (Isa. 59:2). Christ died for these sins (1 Cor. 15:3-4) to show us that God is rich in mercy (Ephesians 2:4) and desires that none should perish but that all should come to repentance (2 Pet. 3:9). The psalmist knows that the Lord is known for forgiving sins as much as the Lord is known for not clearing the guilty (Exod. 34:7).

God demonstrates His character in both forgiving and judging. In the New Covenant, when a sinner comes to God through faith in Christ, all of that sinner's iniquity receives a pardon. God is just to grant us pardon and impute our iniquity to Christ and to impute Christ's righteousness to us (2 Cor. 5:21). From that point forward, Christ continually propitiates (1 Jn 2:2) and cleanses (1 Jn 1:9) the justified saint and intercedes for them (Heb. 7:25). Pardon is received at justification and continually applied in sanctification. Despite this initial forgiveness, the Spirit will wage war with the flesh until the dying breath is taken (Gal. 5:17). The law in a sinner's members will continue to fight against the law in the sinner's mind (Rom. 7:21-23). Appreciation for that pardon results in the pursuit of Christlikeness and resultant holy living (Eph. 4:17-32, Col. 3:1-3). This holy living demonstrates God's work on the inside in a way that is visible on the outside (Phil. 2:12-13). Additionally, this holy living results in believers shining gospel lights that go before men who see the good works and glorify God in heaven (Matt. 5:16).

This pardon takes place for the sinner's benefit and the **sake** of the **name** of the Lord (1 Jn 2:12). The Lord's grace transforms sinner's lives. Sinners' transformed lives commend the gospel to the outside world that is perishing. **Iniquity** and sin separate the sinner from the God that created them and to whom they are accountable. It is the iniquity and sin, no matter how **great it is,** that the gracious God will **pardon** when we cry out to Him for that pardon (Isa. 55:7). God set forth Christ as a propitiation so that sinners could be pardoned (Rom. 3:25). It is great because we have taken the goodness that God has shown us and trampled it under our feet (Rom. 2:1-11). It is great because our choice to sin against His goodness (Rom. 2:4) was calculated and deliberate. We have taken the good and perfect gifts that God has showered us with to show us that He is there and that He loves us (Jas 1:17) and spat it in His face in a direct affront to His holy nature. For God to pardon sinners who respond to Him in such ways shows us incredible patience, love, and compassion on His part.

## Questions for self-reflection:

(1) Other than Christ, since Adam, who has missed out on inheriting the sinful nature?
(2) According to 1 John 3:4, what is sin?
(3) Do we need God only to pardon us once, or do we need God to keep pardoning us?
(4) How do we show that we appreciate the pardon that God has graciously given us?
(5) How do we commend the gospel to a perishing world? How do we show the lost that the pardon we have received is something the world should desire?

**25:12. Who is the man that fears the Lord? Him shall He teach in the way He chooses.**

---

The Lord Himself will **teach the man that fears Him in the way** that **the Lord chooses** for the man to take. The Lord has determined that there are two paths that man can take. Man can choose to take the broad way that leads to destruction that most sadly decide to take (Matt. 7:13-14). Those on this way have the Word snatched away from them so that it is not fruitful or is not even considered in their lives (Matt. 13:19). Some on this way can be self-deceived by religion. They can cross the religious T's and dot the spiritual I's. They can receive accolades from their fellow man, fool others, and even fool themselves into thinking that God is pleased with them. The sad reality for them, the motivation behind what they do is not God's glory (1 Cor. 10:31). Instead, it is for selfish ends. Despite all the spiritual energy they expend, such people will be unmasked as hypocrites and be excluded from heaven (Matt. 7:21-23). Some like the idea of missing out on eternal punishment, but they have no genuine concern to be more like the Lord. Because the Word has not taken root in them, they will not endure (Matt. 13:21). Others are too distracted by other things that prevent them from having any concern for fearing the Lord (Matt. 13:22).

The man that fears the Lord is happy. He has wisdom and understanding (Prov. 3:13). The Lord has applied the Word to his heart by the ministry of the Holy Spirit (Jn 14:26, Jn 16:13). Such a man is happy because he knows that the Lord is his Shepherd (Ps. 23:1). Since the Lord is this man's Shepherd, the sheep keeps the Shepherd close by so he knows what the Shepherd is like and what the Shepherd expects of him in each circumstance. As sheep of the Good Shepherd, believers in Christ bear much fruit if they abide in Him (Jn 15:1-8). He that fears the Lord loves the Lord and manifests that love through obedience to His commands (Jn 14:15). He that fears the Lord trusts the Lord more than he trusts himself (Proverbs 3:5-6). He that fears the Lord does not want to grieve the Holy Spirit (Ephesians 4:30).

---

As believers renew their minds on God's truth (Rom. 12:2, Ps. 1:2), the knowledge of His will fills them (Colossians 1:9). They become like their Master so they will willingly, out of love for their Master, take the way their Master wants them to take (Lk 6:40). The Lord will go before them as He did for Israel (Exod. 13:21) to give them light in the darkness and cool in the heat. Those that fear the Lord can know that as long as the Lord continues to guide them from His rightful place at the throne of their hearts, they have nothing to ultimately fear (Ps. 118:6, Matt. 10:28). The worst that can happen is physical death, at which time they will immediately be in the Lord's presence for all eternity (2 Cor. 5:8).

## Questions for self-reflection:

(1) What is your underlying motivation for why you do what you do?
(2) Do you see your need to fear the Lord?
(3) Why might one who has wisdom and understanding be happy?
(4) How can we keep the Shepherd close by our sides?
(5) How do we manifest our love for the Lord?
(6) Do you WANT to follow the Lord, or do you feel like you HAVE to?

**25:13. He himself shall dwell in prosperity, And his descendants shall inherit the earth.**

---

The man who fears the Lord **shall dwell in prosperity**. The man who fears the Lord will undoubtedly live in spiritual prosperity since those that fear the Lord have received every spiritual blessing in Christ (Eph. 1:3). The spiritually blessed possess these spiritual blessings because Christ has come to dwell in their hearts by faith (Eph. 3:17). The peace of the Lord that passes understanding guards their hearts and minds in Christ (Phil. 4:7). They can trust the Lord to be with them no matter what they face. The Lord has helped them see that they can be content in any circumstance (Phil. 4:11). The Lord has filled them with His Spirit, which leads them into all truth (Jn 16:13) and blesses them with everything they need for life and godliness (2 Pet. 1:3), including sufficient grace to handle the days' troubles (Matt. 6:34, Phil. 4:19). They have everything that they need physically to survive (Matt. 6:33). They possess everything they need spiritually to be successful in this life (2 Pet. 1:3). Even if hardship or trials of various kinds plague their physical life, they can rejoice because of the Lord who is at work behind the scenes in them to conform them into His image (2 Corinthians 4:16-18, Jas 1:2-8). When they are absent from the body, they will be present with the Lord and will at that time enjoy the ultimate prosperity (2 Cor. 5:8). In heaven, their spirit will joyfully wait for the time when their soul is reunited with their body (To dwell with the Lord in eternal bliss is to dwell in ultimate prosperity.

The Lord Jesus Christ said that the meek would inherit the earth in the Sermon on the Mount (Matt. 5:5). The saved will become joint-heirs with Christ and **inherit** heaven (Rom. 8:17, Eph. 1:11). Since this world is not home to the believer (1 Pet. 2:11) and since the believer has a greater home that is being prepared for them in heaven with the Lord (Jn 14:2-3), they are to look for the new home and long for the day when they are rid from their present sinful condition and clothed with immortality (1 Cor.

---

15:53-54). There could be no greater prosperity than to be with the Lord as at His right hand are pleasures forevermore (Ps. 16:11).

The man who fears the Lord will do what he can to pass his fear of the Lord on to his descendants (Prov. 22:6, Ephesians 6:4). Those descendants must not trust in their parent's faith. They must come to faith in the Lord Jesus Christ for themselves (Heb. 11:6). They must trust Him wholly with their whole lives and serve Him as Lord for themselves. There will be no progeny in heaven that arrives there based on the faith of their parents. But, when parents are faithful to train up a child in the way they should go, they will not depart from it when they are old. When the child appropriates living faith for themselves by coming to the Father through faith in the Son, they receive the imputed righteousness of the Lord Jesus Christ and become one of Abraham's descendants (Rom. 4:5). They inherit all the promises that all the faithful in Christ partake in (Heb. 6:12). One such promise is the new heavens and new earth in which there is no more sin, sorrow, or crying, where the former things have passed away (Rev. 21:4).

## Questions for self-reflection:

(1) In addition to or even instead of physical prosperity, in what other types of prosperity might the one that fears the Lord dwell?
(2) What are some ways that this spiritual prosperity manifests itself in the lives of the saints?
(3) What is the ultimate form of prosperity for the saints?
(4) The righteous inherit the earth. How can the righteous person help his descendants inherit the earth?

**25:14. The secret of the Lord is with those who fear Him, And He will show them His covenant.**

---

The ways the Lord reveals Himself in time and space to His people and how He effectually calls them is a secret. Exactly how the eternal counsel that planned for our redemption transpired when the Father and Son prepared with the Spirit to redeem a peculiar people unto themselves is a secret. Why the Lord has chosen to reveal some things to humanity and not reveal other things is a secret. The Lord instigated His relationship with believers. Both believers and the Lord enjoy this relationship, a secret relationship to the rebels on the outside.

Sometimes the ways **the Lord** works behind the scenes in the lives of His people, **those who fear Him,** is a **secret** to the watching world, to those whose faith is not in Him. Sometimes how God works in His people's lives is not revealed to those in a relationship with Him. Sometimes those who fear the Lord are allowed by the Lord to experience difficulty or adversity of some kind for reasons unknown to them, for reasons only known to the Lord (see Job). How the Lord knows what He knows and how the Lord does what He does is a secret.

Those who seek to know the Lord, how the Lord has revealed Himself to us, have some of the secrets of the Lord revealed to them since they are the ones who fear Him. Therefore, such people seek the Lord, and those who seek the Lord genuinely and diligently are found by the Lord as the Lord will not turn away those who come to Him genuinely and appropriately (Heb. 11:6).

Sometimes the Lord supernaturally let His servants know of some ways the Lord was going to work before He worked. For instance, the Lord let Noah know that He would flood the earth before He did it (Gen. 6:13). He let Abraham and Sarah know that they would have Isaac before they did (Gen. 17:14-21). He allowed Moses to know that Israel would be delivered from Egyptian bondage before they were (Exod. 3:10). Some people who have a fruitful walk with the Lord are able, by the Lord's grace upon them, to see the Lord working behind the scenes even in adverse circumstances. They see it as manifestations of God's grace at work in the lives of His people for His glory and their good (Rom. 8:28).

When sinners come to faith in God through the Lord Jesus Christ, the Lord begins to unlock some of the secrets of who He is, what He has done, how the world works, why people are the way they are, etc. Through the key of faith, the door to how the world works gets unlocked. Then the world is perceived through an entirely different lens. Since believers have begun to seek Him and will continue to seek Him throughout their lives, they will continue to find the Lord and learn more about Him and how the world that He created works.

The saints seek to know God's will through God's Word. In God's Word, the saints see God's covenant, for instance, His new covenant, where He takes out the sinful stony heart that is not responsive to God's Word and replaces it with a soft heart that is responsive to God's Word (Ezek. 36:26). They see where God writes His law on the heart and enables people to live for Him (Jer. 31:33, Ezek. 36:27). They see in God's Word the New Covenant promises fulfilled in the finished work of Christ on the cross on behalf of sinners and how that is a foretaste of the promises that God will still fulfill in the future. Thus, God is a **covenant**-keeping God.

## Questions for self-reflection:

(1) Does the lost watching world that does not fear the Lord understand the secret of the Lord that the sheep do understand?

(2) What prevents the lost from understanding the secret of the Lord?

(3) Does the Lord reveal all His secrets to the saved?

(4) Where do God's people find some of the Lord's secrets?

(5) For God's people, what is the key to unlocking the door to perceive the world differently?

**25:15. My eyes are ever toward the Lord, For He shall pluck my feet out of the net.**

---

In general, the psalmist knows that **the Lord** sustains Him. The Lord allows the psalmist to take his next breath (Isa. 42:5, Acts 17:25). The Lord that protects him from his physical enemies and his spiritual enemies (Ps. 91:1-3, Isa. 54:17, 1 Cor. 10:13, 2 Tim. 4:18). It is the Lord that has opened the eyes of the psalmist so that he could see the world in a whole new way (Eph. 1:18). It is the Lord who takes sinners who are dead in trespasses (Eph. 2:1), makes them alive (Eph. 2:5), regenerates them (Ti 3:5), makes them see where they once were blind (2 Cor. 4:4-6), gives them hearing where they were once deaf, and blesses them abundantly when they were accursed (Gal. 3:10).

When God sheds His love abroad in the heart of a previously alienated sinner (Rom. 5:5), no wonder they respond toward the Lord by willingly offering themselves as living sacrifices (Rom. 12:1). No wonder they realize that is their reasonable service. After all, the Lord has been beyond good to rescue us from the power for the grave (Ps. 49:15, Col. 1:13). The Lord has magnanimously and reasonably rescued us from the world that lies under the sway of the wicked one (1 Jn 5:19). Since the Lord did this for us, no wonder our eyes are ever toward the Lord if we have experienced such grace on such a personal level. Before God's amazing grace rescues us and points our eyes away from the earth and toward heaven (Col. 3:1-3), the only way we will look is horizontal. We get lost in a lifestyle of prodigality where we consume the blessings of God on our own selves (Jas 4:1-4). When God's magnanimous grace intervenes, we can take our eyes off the earthly and reset them to look heavenly. Sins prevent us from doing this. Sins separate us from God (Isa. 64:6). Scripture describes sins as besetting and ensnaring (Heb. 12:1), as a **net**.

Those who live after the flesh, entirely apart from the Holy Spirit, wage active war against God (Rom. 8:7-8, Gal. 5:17, Col. 1:21). Such separated sinners cannot avoid the net in a lasting sense. They are condemned already for their unbelief (Jn 3:17-19). They lack the spiritual resources of the genuinely converted to overcome temptation. The armor of God (Eph. 6:10-20) is not in the repertoire of the lost.

For the believer, however, the traps are still set. When they fall, the believer has an Advocate, Jesus Christ the righteous, the propitiation for their sins, interceding for them (1 Jn 2:1-2, Heb. 7:25). **He** is also there to **pluck** their **feet out of the net** when they do fall because they will fall (1 Jn 1:8, 1 Jn 2:1). The Lord has prepared the way for them. He can deliver them out of a multitude of temptations. Believers must submit to God, resist the devil, and the devil will flee from them. They must draw near to God and draw near to them (Jas 4:7-8). When believers do that, with their eyes toward the Lord, the Lord shall pluck their feet out of the net. When their eyes are on the Lord, the net will not go away. However, when their eyes are on the Lord, the Lord will help keep them from falling into the net. Christ will deliver them from the power of the grave and the power of sin.

### Questions for self-reflection:

(1) From the words in the verse alone, would you say that the psalmist HOPES that the Lord will deliver him, or would you say that the psalmist EXPECTS that the Lord will deliver him?

(2) Is it Scriptural to base our future trust in the Lord on the past deliverance from the Lord?

(3) What are some reasons to put your hope in the Lord?

(4) What prevents us from seeing reasons for putting our hope in the Lord?

(5) What are some ways that God delivers His people presently?

**25:16. Turn Yourself to me, and have mercy on me, For I am desolate and afflicted.**

Because of the negative, discouraging influence exerted upon the psalmist by the psalmist's enemies, the psalmist felt God fought for his enemies and against the psalmist. It appeared to the psalmist that the Lord turned away from the psalmist and turned toward his enemies. The psalmist could have felt that the Lord was hiding from him. When God's people feel this way, they can begin to become less sensitive to His gracious presence if they are not careful. Therefore, the psalmist had to ask the Lord in His abundant mercy to **turn** back **to** him.

The truth of God is that if God is for us, nobody can truly be against us (Rom. 8:31). The worst thing that can happen for the saint is physical death (Matt. 10:28). All that does is usher the believer into the presence of their loving Father for all eternity (2 Cor. 5:8). For the believer, death has lost its sting (1 Cor. 15:54-55).

For the psalmist to feel the **mercy** he asked for, it appears the severity of this trial would have to lighten. For the saint to experience hardship is not to say that the Lord has ceased to be merciful to that saint. However, the experiences of the trial can be so unpleasant and severe that, amid that unpleasant experience, it can be hard to see the Lord even though He really is there. For the psalmist to ask the Lord to turn to him suggests the psalmist once felt the blessings of what life was like when the Lord was on His side in more observable ways.

Like it is easy for many of us to do, the psalmist could have lost the sense of God's care for him the more the psalmist's life came to be marked by trials. Sometimes, though, the more severe the trial in the saint's life, the more apparent the presence of God in that saint's life (2 Cor. 12:9). The trial that the saint is permitted to endure conforms the saint into the image of the Lord, weans the saint from the world, and makes the saint feel more **desolate and afflicted**. While it is not pleasant for the saint to endure the trial, the benefits waiting on the other side of the trial can be very pleasing for the saint to experience (Jas 1:2-8). It is in the furnace of affliction where the refining process takes place. When darkness is all around, the light amid that darkness has the best opportunity to stand out (Phil. 2:15).

When God chooses to deliver one of His own, it is not because of any inherent goodness in the life of His child (2 Pet. 2:9). Anything good that comes from the child of God comes only as a result of God's grace. It is the grace the precedes the good works (Eph. 2:8-10). Even when man makes a choice that glorifies God, the Lord still gets the glory. If the hands and feet glorify the Lord, it is the Lord who made the hands and feet. If the mind contains thoughts that glorify the Lord, it is the Lord who made the mind. The Lord gave the Word to people who wrote it down for all posterity to provoke its readers to love and good works (Heb. 10:24) and fruit-bearing (Matt. 7:15-20, Jn 15:1-8).

## Questions for self-reflection:

(1) Have you ever felt as though God fought for those who fought against you?
(2) Have you ever felt like God hid Himself from you?
(3) Have you ever felt like you had less sensitivity to the Lord's presence?
(4) If the answers to 2 and 3 are 'Yes,' what happened when you asked the Lord to turn back to you?
(5) How have you been able to see the Lord even in the most challenging circumstances? What good has He accomplished for you in those trials?

**25:17. The troubles of my heart have enlarged; Bring me out of my distresses!**

---

Because physical and spiritual enemies surrounded the psalmist, he had many troubles. Ungodliness surrounded him from which he could not escape. Perhaps physical health had made life more difficult. All these troubles made it tempting for the psalmist to give up and to lose hope. However, he knew deep down that the Lord had brought Him so far to this point and that it was right for him to continue to trust the Lord despite how hopeless the **enlarged troubles of** his situation looked. He also knew that troubles or trials, such as this where the Lord forced him to trust instead of act, would be a vehicle by which spiritual growth could take place and where one could see the power of God (2 Cor. 12:9). If he abided in the Lord, the Lord would abide in him (Jn 15:4). He could sit back, live moment by moment in present obedience, and trust that God supplied all His needs (Phil. 4:19), including sufficient grace (Matt. 6:34) to handle the current present moment, followed by sufficient grace to handle the next present moment. And so on and so forth.

He knew that he lacked adequate resources with which to deliver himself. Because of that, he was entirely dependent upon the Lord. Living in the reality of this knowledge can give the saint a **heart** that becomes enlarged with the knowledge of God. This is where the Lord wants His children to be, entirely dependent upon Him. Paul said when he was weak, when we are weak, the Lord can show how strong He is by working His power in and through us (2 Cor. 12:10). The Lord could **bring** the psalmist **out of** his **distresses** in any way in which He saw fit. There was nothing that the enemies of the psalmist could do to prevent that from happening. The psalmist's future and the futures of those who trust the Lord, the Lord of the psalmist, is sure because the Lord fights for His people against their enemies (Deut. 20:4, Josh. 23:3).

**Questions for self-reflection:**

(1) Have you ever been surrounded by ungodliness from which you felt like there was no escape?

(2) How can you show the power of God on your life through your present trial?

(3) If you cannot change your circumstances by anything you do or not do, if the change you seek depends entirely on someone or something other than yourself, on whom must you entirely depend?

(4) How can filling your heart and mind with the knowledge of God aid you in responding to your trial appropriately?

**25:18. Look on my affliction and my pain, And forgive all my sins.**

The psalmist experienced **affliction and pain** as a result of others' actions or lack of actions. When David's son, Solomon, rebelled against him, that may have been the worst affliction and pain David ever had to endure. He asked God to **look on** this, see it, contemplate it, and ponder it. He knew God is a God of compassion (Ps. 103:8, Jas 5:11). He knew that God even allowed the wicked to prosper (Ps. 73:3, Jer. 12:1). If the wicked were allowed to prosper, then why not David, his humble servant? When David's enemies had success, David suffered perhaps physically and definitely emotionally.

When the actions of others leave us uneasy or in a place where we suffer emotionally and physically because of the choices of others, sometimes, we cannot do anything that would not be considered sinful to change our circumstances. When this is the case, the best course of action for us is to ask the Lord to look upon our affliction and pain. We can take God's promises to heart knowing that He cares for us (1 Pet. 5:7). Since He cares for us, we can be confident that casting our cares upon Him is always a better thing for us to do than acting with sinful impatience. We can ask God to remove the affliction and pain and trust that His choice is always best whether He does as we desire or not (2 Cor. 12:7-10).

When in the crucible of affliction, it can be common to think that some personal sins of our own have caused the pain we currently endure. Sometimes our suffering is a direct consequence of our own sinful choices. Sometimes we suffer not as a result of our own immoral decisions but rather the choices of others. Other times, bad decisions may not even be at play in the cause of our suffering. For David, some obvious sins needed addressing, such as the adultery with Bathsheba (2 Sam. 11) and numbering the people (1 Chr. 21). God would need to cleanse David if David would live by the Spirit and be pleasing to the Lord. David knew that he could not change his choices now. But the Lord could deliver him and bring him the peace that comes as the product of genuine repentance. David would have to place his whole trust in the Lord to cleanse him and deliver him (1 Jn 1:9).

Saints in every generation must go to the Lord for pardon, forgiveness, and daily cleansing. The blood of Christ pleads to the Father continually to **forgive** the saints (Heb. 7:25, 1 Jn 1:9). He removes our **sins** as far as the east is from the west (Ps. 103:12).

**Questions for self-reflection:**

(1) Have actions taken or not taken by others caused you to experience affliction and pain?
(2) What promises in God's Word can you look to that can remind you that the Lord is with you when you suffer?
(3) What changes might the Lord require of you if you have known sin in your life that you have successfully hidden from others that you cannot hide from God?

**25:19. Consider my enemies, for they are many; And they hate me with cruel hatred.**

The psalmist appears to be sure that if the Lord were to **consider** the psalmist's **enemies** like the psalmist asks the Lord to do, the Lord would vanquish them. The Lord has vanquished the enemies of His people in the past. The Lord vanquished the Egyptians from the presence of Israel by drowning them in the Red Sea (Exod. 14). Before that, the Lord vanquished all those who would not get into the Ark (Gen. 8). The psalmist, although knowing the sovereignty of God, attributes the lack of perceived action on the Lord's behalf to the inability or unwillingness of God to see the enemies and the affliction they cause the psalmist by their **cruel hatred.** The God of the psalmist, the only true God, sees everything (Prov. 15:3), is able and willing to act, and does when it is suitable for Him to do so.

The **many** enemies that plagued the psalmist were too numerous for the psalmist to conquer in his own strength. God would have to help the psalmist for the psalmist to experience victory. For David, the people who supported his primary enemy, perhaps Absalom, all became David's enemies. There were too many of them for David to be sufficient in himself to be victorious against them. For believers in every generation, the spiritual enemies that fight against God and His people are too many for us to be sufficient in ourselves for us to be victorious against them. Indwelling sin in the life of the believer is also an enemy that can be overwhelming at times. Believers can only overcome this enemy by the power of the Holy Spirit. Sinful people whose home is this world, people who lie under the sway of the wicked one (1 Jn 5:19), are also enemies of the godly. All of these collectively can make the righteous feel like they have many enemies that **hate** them **with** cruel hatred. These enemies can act harshly against the righteous. The righteous have the responsibility not to take vengeance into their own hands but to wait on the Lord. The righteous trust the Lord to act in His time in His way for His purpose (Rom. 12:17-21). The Lord will give His people grace to endure the trial against any enemy they face in this life (Phil. 4:19). The Lord will destroy all the enemies of He and His people and put them under His feet (1 Cor. 15:26-27). While the hatred of God's enemies towards God's people is at its strongest, the Lord's people must take refuge in God and trust Him to deliver them. Even if He does not remove them from the situation, they must trust the Lord to be with them in the situation to provide them with grace to stand (Deut. 31:6, Rom. 5:2).

**Questions for self-reflection:**

(1) What enemies do you have that are many and that hate you with a cruel hatred?

(2) What comfort can you glean from God's Word when you look at how God has dealt with the enemies of His people in the past?

(3) If people are causing you harm or distress because of your faith in the Lord, does God see that?

(4) Do you think that at times God intentionally gives us trials that we know that we lack the sufficient resources to solve on our own so that we will be forced to rely on Him to come through for us?

**25:20. Keep my soul, and deliver me; Let me not be ashamed, for I put my trust in You.**

---

The psalmist was in constant danger from physical enemies. Nevertheless, the psalmist knew that the Lord had appointed his days (Jb 14:5). He knew he had a divine appointment and that God would see him through to that appointment, but the psalmist also knew that he had to be vigilant and fulfill his responsibility to be as faithful as was possible (Heb. 9:27).

Trust in the sovereignty of God does not abdicate fulfilling one's responsibility to be obedient to God's revealed will. Walking in obedience to God leads to God's blessing on the believer's life even if that blessing looks different in different people's lives (Deut. 28:1-14). Sometimes blessing takes on the form of an inward invisible work of grace on the believer's heart that will not be visible to everyone. This work of grace can result in an increased faith that **keep**s the believer's **soul** and delivers them from temptations and sins.

Even if the believer is not in danger because of physical ene-mies, it will always be true that the spiritual enemy will always be out to keep the faithful believer from being as fruitful as possible (1 Pet. 5:8). The existence of spiritual enemies is an important reason why believers have armor to put on (Eph. 6:10-20). While Satan cannot ruin someone's justification or glorification, he can disrupt their sanctification and lead believers to become unfruitful or stagnant. The psalmist knew that God had given him life and that ultimately only God could take it away (Jb 14:5, Matt. 6:27). The psalmist was responsible for obeying God and not giving in to temptation when it came (1 Cor. 10:13). He knew that God had storehouses of grace with which he could supply saints like the psalmist so he would have everything he needed for life and god-liness (2 Pet. 1:3). The psalmist knew that it was God's power that kept him from stumbling (Jude 1:24). He knew it was his own fault if he did fall.

He wanted to be **deliver**ed from all his enemies. All evil is an enemy to the believer as it leads to sin, impedes growth, and hurts the relationship with God and with others. The psalmist had made the conscious choice to trust God with his life. His trust in God included the confidence that God would protect or keep him against his enemies. If God failed to preserve the psalmist as the psalmist had asked God to do, then the psalmist's enemies might wrongly conclude that the God of the psalmist was not worthy of anyone's trust, and the psalmist might feel **ashamed** for trusting in the Lord. That was not true and was not what the psalmist wanted to convey to his enemies. He was concerned that his suffering might convey the wrong message about God to his enemies. He knew that if his enemies got the message that God was not worth **trust**ing, that would not be good, nor would it be accurate.

## Questions for self-reflection:

(1) How has walking in obedience to God led to blessing in your life?
(2) Have you ever gone through a season where Satan has impeded your sanctification? What changed so that the season ended?
(3) Are you more concerned with your peace and ease or with God getting glorified through your life no matter the personal cost to you?

**25:21. Let integrity and uprightness preserve me, For I wait for You.**

It could be that the psalmist had a life that was outwardly moral for the most part, one of integrity, before the people over which he ruled. If this was the case, the personal **integrity and uprightness** of the psalmist should have been such that the enemies of the psalmist could find no legitimate reason to put the psalmist to death or in harm's way. The fact that they would do so indicates that they did so without a cause. If the people were going to rebel against the psalmist and endanger him, the psalmist wanted to be sure before God that his heart was pure and that he was not a stumbling block in any way to those that rebelled against Him. While he continued on the narrow road, he did not want Satan and the rebels to pull his supporters into their coup. Then again, Jesus lived a life of integrity and uprightness before everyone He lived among, and He was executed unjustly while still being according to God's predetermined plan (Acts 2:23). He was not preserved from the sinful mob that had decided to get rid of Him when it was time for Him to die for our sins.

For the most part, the psalmist was a man after God's own heart (Acts 13:22) and lived for the Lord with a couple of notable exceptions cited in Scripture. External integrity and uprightness before the people could be the object here. It could also be internal integrity and uprightness. It could be that the psalmist wanted to live in such a way that even his thoughts and motives were as pure as could be before the Lord so that there was nothing in his life that would be grievous to God. It could be both. The psalmist knew that God's character was utterly pure. It could be that he knew that Satan would tempt him, and he would need to call upon his spiritual resources to help him overcome the temptation (1 Cor. 10:13). It could be that Satan would employ evil forces to try to overthrow the psalmist as he did with Job. The psalmist wanted no such force to hamper his spiritual success. It could be that if the psalmist had a heightened awareness of his spiritual weakness and the enemies that surrounded him that he would realize his dependence upon the Lord and would take refuge in the Lord instead of in his own strength.

He could **wait for** the Lord to act in the way that the Lord saw fit to act to deliver the psalmist and deliver him. Even though the Lord preserves the way of His saints permanently (Prov. 2:8), having secured their eternal inheritance (Eph. 1:11), temporal preservation is also sometimes wanted and needed. The Lord can also provide that when it is in accordance with His will.

## Questions for self-reflection:

(1) Is it more important to you that those of the world approve of you or that God approves of you?

(2) Who is more likely to approve of your integrity and uprightness, God or the world?

(3) If people hated Jesus without a cause, and if a disciple is like his Master, is it surprising that unbelievers do not like many followers of Christ?

(4) Might anything in your life serve as a stumbling block to those who are outside of the faith? What can you do about that?

(5) Do you think that if your personal integrity and uprightness increased that your sense of proximity to the Lord would increase or decrease?

(6) If your personal integrity and uprightness decreased would your sense of proximity to the Lord increase or decrease?

(7) How has waiting for the Lord benefited you in the past?

(8) How is the Lord having you wait for Him now?

## 25:22. Redeem Israel, O God, Out of all their troubles!

If David, the king of **Israel**, could not trust the Lord **God** to **redeem** him out of his troubles, then the rest of Israel could not trust the Lord to redeem them **out of all their troubles.** David's son, Absalom, rebelled against his father, King David (2 Sam. 15). For the church, God redeems them out of their troubles. Sin troubles the world. God sent Christ in the fulness of time to redeem those who were under the law of sin and death and give them the adoption of sons. (Rom. 8:2, Gal. 4:4-5). Sin had separated the world from God, making everyone God's enemy (Col. 1:21). Christ came to reconcile God to the sinners who had sinned against Him (2 Cor. 5:17-21). God made believers alive who were all sons of disobedience, dead in trespasses and sins, and walked according to the prince of the power of the air (Eph. 2:1-2). He did this when they were at the height of all their troubles, children of wrath (Eph. 2:3).

God is a loving God (Rom. 5:8). God is a merciful God (Eph. 2:5). He imparts justifying grace to save (Eph. 2:5) to raise quickened sinners to life and seat them together in heavenly places with Christ (Eph. 2:6). To do this for anyone, since everyone is so rebellious against Him, shows that God is a God of kindness (Eph. 2:7). For God to bestow upon such wicked sinners such lavish grace and to bless with such magnanimous blessing (Eph. 1:3-14), to deliver them from the kingdom of darkness into the kingdom of Christ (Col. 1:13) is humbling for the sinner to experience and remarkable for God to do.

### Questions for self-reflection:

(1) Why is the redeemer of Israel also your redeemer?
(2) What is the greatest troubler of all people? From what do we need to be redeemed by God?
(3) What should be our response to God's gracious redemption?

# Psalm 26

**26:1. Vindicate me, O Lord, For I have walked in my integrity. I have also trusted in the Lord; I shall not slip.**

The psalmist wanted the **Lord** to **vindicate** him and show his oppressors that they were wrong to oppress him. Note that he does not take matters into his own hands to vindicate himself but trusts that the Lord will do so in the Lord's timing (Rom. 12:19). The psalmist indicated that others accused him of doing things that were not true. Only the Lord could indisputably clear his name. He did not want his fellow man to have a reason to have anything against him because his life was a life of integrity. The psalmist **trusted in the Lord**. The psalmist asked the Lord to reward him for that trust. The psalmist had to trust in the Lord since he did not possess any righteousness of his own that would be meritorious in his approach to God (Phil. 3:9).

He did **walk in integrity**. That is not to say that he walked in sinlessness, for no human can claim that (1 Kgs 8:46, Rom. 3:23). However, the psalmist had made the Lord the object of his trust. Although imperfect because of indwelling sin (Rom. 7:14-25), his faith in the Lord was genuine and sincere. He trusted that his adversaries would not ultimately condemn him because the Lord would not allow him to slip (Rom. 8:1, Jude 1:24).

Since the psalmist trusted in the Lord, the Lord was powerful to keep Him by the power of the Word (1 Pet. 1:5). Every believer, including the psalmist, struggles with sin that lasts until they take their final breath. Believers can trust the Lord to keep His Word and that they will persevere because as they work out their salvation, God is at work in them (Phil. 2:12-13). God begins and performs the work of salvation (Phil. 1:6). Sheep are not passive. He recognized that in his own strength, he was likely to **slip**. He would have to trust in the Lord to protect him from catastrophe.

## Questions for self-reflection:

(1) Have you ever had someone treat you poorly for no apparent reason?

(2) Have you ever had someone mistreat you because you are a Christian?

(3) If you answered "yes" to either of the two previous questions, then you are a victim of oppression. When you were oppressed, did you take revenge into your own hands, or, like the psalmist, did you ask God to deliver you?

(4) Has someone ever accused you of doing something that you did not do or of not doing something that you did do? If yes, you have been oppressed.

(5) If you had no way to prove to your accusers that you were right and they were wrong, how would you handle that? Would you ask the Lord to vindicate you?

(6) Would the people who know you best say that your common practice is to walk in integrity?

(7) Regardless of the treatment we receive by our oppressors, if we walk in our integrity, with hearts full of faith in the Lord who has redeemed us, are we more or less likely to slip if we trust in the Lord?

## 26:2. Examine me, O Lord, and prove me; Try my mind and my heart.

The psalmist wants the **Lord** to **examine and prove** him. He does not want there to be anything about his lifestyle that his enemies can use against him. He wants to be able to know that, before the Lord, even if not before his earthly enemies, he is blameless. He wants his faith to be proven to be genuine. If the psalmist compares his life to God's standard, he wants to be cleared from wrongdoing, even if that means that his enemies consider him to be in the wrong.

The psalmist undoubtedly grew up hearing about the story when God proved Abraham when God asked Abraham to sacrifice Isaac, his son. Abraham showed a willingness to obey God (Gen. 22). Scripture records no reluctance in Abraham to carrying out God's instruction (Gen. 22:3ff). Scripture does record God rewarding Abraham for his willingness to be obedient to what God had asked of him. The psalmist wanted to be known to have faith like that of Abraham.

Genuine believers in every generation want to be found faithful. When the furnace of affliction tries the faith of the righteous, they want to be able to prove themselves to be genuine (Jas 1:2-8). God knows the outcome before the trial commences, while the test lasts, and before the trial ends. But the believer can gain a great benefit from enduring trials. They can come out of the other side of the trial purified and stronger spiritually. Successfully enduring temptations can bolster the faith of the righteous.

Even when things get difficult, believers can have lasting assurance only by remaining faithful (1 Jn 5:13). Faithfulness is not the basis for salvation (Eph. 2:8-9). Faithfulness is the basis for assurance (Eph. 2:10), as the fruit is the basis for determining the type of tree (Matt. 7:15-20). The Lord often tests the **mind and heart** of His servants to prove to His servants that their faith in Him is genuine (1 Sam. 16:7, Jer. 11:20, Jer. 17:10, Jer. 20:12, Rev. 2:23). When saints come through these tests unscathed, it can go a long way in giving them boldness to stand in more severe trials that follow.

## Questions for self-reflection:

(1) Is there anything about your lifestyle that your enemies can use to discount your faith?

(2) Are you going through a prominent trial presently? During this experience, what good had the Lord brought out of it? What lessons are you learning?

(3) Is there a spiritual hero of the faith, either in Scripture or from church history, that motivates you to persevere in trials?

(4) How have you seen your walk with the Lord enhanced through the sanctifying work of trials?

**26:3. For Your lovingkindness is before my eyes, And I have walked in Your truth.**

---

The lovingkindness of God is for those who have come to God through faith in Christ. Before Christ came, the lovingkindness of God was for those who believed in God, like Abraham (Gen. 15:6). A list of several of those who believed in God before Christ came is found in Hebrews 11. Since Christ came, all those who are in Christ, those who have been justified by faith in Christ, who are now at peace with God (Rom. 5:1-2), who have God's love shed abroad in their hearts (Rom. 5:5), those who are growing in grace and in the knowledge of the Lord and Savior Jesus Christ (2 Pet. 3:18), can say that they have the **lovingkindness** of God **before** their **eyes**. Nobody can earn such lovingkindness. It is freely bestowed upon the objects of God's love (Rom. 3:24). Since they will be with God in eternal bliss in heaven, God's lovingkindness will always be upon the justified. God's lovingkindness is before the eyes of the psalmist because he recalls the truth that God's salvation is permanent on those who have received it (Jn 10:29, Rom. 8:30).

There is no longer condemnation once a sinner is justified, declared righteous, declared not guilty (Rom. 8:1). Once truly saved, there is no loss of salvation. If they fall away, they show they were merely enlightened and were never saved, to begin with (Heb. 6:4-6). The saved person knows that their future is secure in Christ. If that were not true, that would indicate that Christ was not a sufficient Savior. That is not something that even the most liberal theologian will admit. If a person claimed that Christ could save someone and then that someone can lose their salvation, they also would have to claim that the same God that is powerful enough to speak the world into existence is not powerful enough to complete the work that He began to save someone (Phil. 1:6). They would have to concede that the same power that upholds all things (Heb. 1:3) cannot truly uphold all things because it cannot uphold a sinner's salvation. They would have to concede that something can actually separate justified sinners from God's love (Rom. 8:38-39). To say that a justified sinner can lose their salvation would be to overthrow the character and promises of God. It would be tantamount to saying that a finite person's sin is stronger than the love of an infinite God. To meditate on these promises is to realize the security one has in Christ.

It is both loving and kind for the God of the universe, Whom we have offended so grievously with our sins, to send Christ to earth to substitute for man and to make way for mankind to be forgiven. When the justified sinner meditates on the person and work of the Lord Jesus Christ and lives in such a way as to bring honor and glory to Him, that justified sinner gives evidence to the fact that the lovingkindness of God is ever before their eyes. When they make it their aim in life to **walk in** the **truth** of God, their life will change for the better, and the lives of those around them can change for the better. The believer will walk as Christ Himself walked (1 Jn 2:6) since Christ is the Way, the Truth, and the Life (Jn 14:6). The Father will send the Spirit into the hearts of believers and will enable them to walk in the truth (Jn 14:26). As the believer gets to know God through the Word (Rom. 12:2), the Holy Spirit applies the truth of the Word to the heart and empowers the believer to live out the truth. The believer will walk in love as Christ also loved us and gave Himself for us as an offering and a sweet-smelling aroma (Eph 5:2). The believer will walk in the light rather than in the darkness (John 8:12). They will reprove the works of darkness rather than join in with them (Eph. 5:11). They will look unto Jesus, the Author and Finisher of the faith (Heb. 12:2), as the example that they should walk in His steps (1 Pet. 2:21). Because of His sacrifice on their behalf, they will be willing to offer themselves as living sacrifices (Rom. 12:1).

## Questions for self-reflection:

(1) How has God shown His lovingkindness to you when you go through times that are not hard?

(2) How has God shown His lovingkindness to you when you go through hard times?

(3) What did you do to earn the lovingkindness of God in your life?

(4) Do you believe that God is powerful enough to save you?

(5) Do you believe that God is powerful enough to keep you saved?

(6) Is it your aim to walk in the truth of God?

(7) When you fall short of your goal to walk in God's truth, what is your attitude about your sin? Do you treat your sin lightly and take God's forgiveness for granted? Or does the fact that Christ died for that sin break your heart? Do you have joy that despite your sins, He intercedes for you, and His blood continually cleanses you?

**26:4. I have not sat with idolatrous mortals, Nor will I go in with hypocrites.**

---

Believers constantly have to be in and around the **idolatrous mortals** of the world. We have to transact with them. We have to share many aspects of our lives with them. We will sit with them more than we would like to. We will wish we could insulate ourselves from the harmful worldly influences of idolatrous mortals. When we have such thoughts, we will do well to remember that the Lord did not save us to get fat with knowledge in pews while those on the outside of the kingdom perish. He gave us talents, expecting that we would use them (Matt. 25:14-30). We are to stay in the world. We are not to become like those of the world (Jn 17:16). Instead, He saved us so we could learn about Him (Phil. 3:10) and take His truth to a world that so badly needs it.

The Lord Jesus Christ brought the truth of who He is and what He has done to the world so that the world could be changed by Him and His truth (Eph. 5:11). So, this is not a command to avoid people as much as it is a command to avoid their sins. The people of the world have vain affections which are against God, God's people, and God's kingdom. The difference between the children of the wicked one and the children of the King of kings should be readily apparent and easily observable (Matt. 7:15-20). What the people of the world think, say, and do should be a stark contrast to what the justified think, say, and do. The light that comes out of the saved should expose the darkness that comes out of the lost (Jn 8:12). The Spirit fuels the saved (Rom. 8:13-14). The flesh (Rom. 8:5-8) fuels the lost. Humility marks the saved. Pride marks the lost (Jas 4:6). To the saved, Christ is a savor of life unto life while, to the lost, Christ is a savor of death unto death (2 Cor. 2:16). The righteous speak edifying psalms, hymns, and spiritual songs, whereas the reprobate speaks corruption (Eph. 5:19, Col. 3:16, Eph. 4:29). The redeemed exude wisdom while the outsiders erupt in folly. The forgiven follow the way of truth while the unforgiven follows the way of falsehood.

Saved people, like the psalmist, are to avoid the practices of lost people and not be carried away by their practices. The psalmist would not **go in with hypocrites** who make a show of religion on the outside but lack the reality of heartfelt worship on the inside. These hypocrites will do what they have to do and say what they have to say to make their own name. They will use others to achieve their own goals without taking into consideration the well-being of others. The saved consider others as more important than themselves, while the unsaved consider themselves as most important (Phil. 2:3). The hypocrites will make themselves out to be one way in public to win the approval of others, but in private will be the opposite, and their sin will run rampant. They are double-minded (Jas 1:8). They have a form of godliness but deny its power (2 Tim. 3:5).

**Questions for self-reflection:**

(1) In general, are people physically healthier if they do physically exercise or if they do not physically exercise?
(2) In general, are people spiritually healthier if they do spiritually exercise or if they do not spiritually exercise?
(3) Did God save you to get spiritually fat, die, and one day go to heaven, or did God save you to exercise your spiritual gifts and become spiritually healthy?
(4) If there should be a noticeable observable difference between a Christian and a non-Christian, what does that noticeable, observable difference, in general, look like?
(5) Does your life expose the darkness around you, or does it participate in the darkness around you?

**26:5. I have hated the assembly of evildoers, And will not sit with the wicked.**

---

The believer in God, the believer in the Lord Jesus Christ, lives a life of separation from the evil world system (Rom. 12:2, Jas 4:4, 1 Jn 2:15-17). They do not achieve perfect separation from the system in this life (Rom. 7:19), but, if the Holy Spirit has changed and is changing them, if a good work has begun (Phil. 1:6) and is being performed, there will be some level of observable change (Matt. 7:15-20). There will be a level of hating what was once loved and loving what was once hated. When the justified saint sees others, the lost, engaging in what God has saved them from, it makes the justified person uneasy. They do not want to join them in their sinful pursuits. Even if they do join them in their sinful pursuits, there comes a time where Holy Spirit conviction kicks in and makes them very uncomfortable with what they are doing because they can tell that the Lord would not be pleased with what they are doing.

While **evildoers** pursue their immoral lifestyles and try to undermine the righteous every step of the way, the righteous must not repay evil with evil but must repay evil with good (Matt. 5:38-48). Like those referenced here by the psalmist, Evildoers are an **assembly** of those who **hate** God's law (Rom. 8:6-8). The saint will not hate the sinner, but they will hate the sinner's sin so much that they will separate from it (Ps. 119:104, Ps. 119:163, Prov. 8:13, Prov. 13:5, Rom. 12:19, Col. 3:5). The wicked feel very uneasy unless they are doing wickedly. Maybe the wickedness they practice does not hurt anyone else. Perhaps it only hurts themselves. But they will not be satisfied unless they are filing themselves up on the trinkets of this world and its lusts.

The saved person still has to live in the world with the **wicked** (1 Cor. 5:9-11). The saved person should not join the lost in the activities that are illustrative of what lost people do (Eph. 5:8-14). Doing so will damage the testimony of the saved and will give the lost a false sense of comfort about staying in their sins. The lives of the unsaved should make the saved uncomfortable to the point where the saved will not want to run to the same excess of riot (1 Pet. 4:4). They will not want to join in on the works of darkness but should rather reprove them (Eph. 5:11). The lives of the saved should make the unsaved so uncomfortable that they want to leave their lives of sin and come to faith in the Lord Jesus Christ for pardon and forgiveness (Matt. 5:16).

**Questions for self-reflection:**

(1) Since your profession of faith in Christ, in what ways has your life changed? What do you now do that you did not formerly do? What do you now not do that you formerly did? What is your relationship with God's Word like? What is your relationship with other believers like?

(2) Who do you know that is outside of Christ that you can do good to today?

(3) What brings you the most joy? What do you enjoy doing the most? What does God say about that thing? Would He approve?

(4) Do you feel like you wish you could do some of the things that the unsaved do, but you cannot because you are a Christian?

**26:6. I will wash my hands in innocence; So I will go about Your altar, O Lord,**

When someone **wash**es their **hands,** water and soap surround their hands. The soap and water cover their hands thoroughly. Here, the psalmist spoke to being surrounded and covered thoroughly in a spiritual sense by people whose lives were marked by **innocence.** This innocence was a sharpening influence in the life of the psalmist. The psalmist's communication with others and the communication the psalmist received from others did not corrupt and was not evil. If sin went on around the psalmist, the psalmist did what he had to do to take a stand against evil. His actions would provoke others to do good and to love others. He did not even want to have the appearance of being in the flesh. He abstained from even the appearance of evil. (Prov. 27:17, Rom. 8:8, 1 Cor. 15:33, Eph. 5:11, 1 Thess. 5:22, Heb. 10:24, Jude 1:23).

There was no besetting sin that hampered the psalmist's life that made the psalmist unfruitful (Heb. 12:1). He had such an intimate relationship with his Lord that to surround himself with men of ill repute would not be fitting for him. Therefore, the psalmist kept his distance from wickedness and from those who practiced wickedness. If the psalmist were to **go about** the **altar** of the **Lord,** then the psalmist would be close in proximity to the place of worship, the location of the altar. The psalmist would not have been one who forsook the assembling (Heb. 10:25). If the psalmist knew of something that God expected of him, he would order his life such that he met God's expectations. In Hebrews in the New Testament, Christ is called our altar (Heb. 13:10). For the New Covenant believer, the expectation is that we will abide in Him, and He will abide in us (Jn 15:1-8). So, we will stay close in proximity to Him and be fruitful as a result.

**Questions for self-reflection:**

(1) What are some benefits of Christians surrounding themselves with a network of other Christians (those who have washed their hands in innocence)?

(2) Does it look to others like you are trying to live in enough sin to fit in with them, or are you trying to live separated from sin (albeit imperfectly)?

(3) Can you think of a few benefits of being a regular attendee of church services?

**26:7. That I may proclaim with the voice of thanksgiving, And tell of all Your wondrous works.**

---

The psalmist wanted the Lord to act on his behalf. He had lived in such a way not to dishonor God's name. His trust was entirely in the Lord. He wanted his life to be proven blameless before those in regular contact with him. He made it his practice to avoid the sin of others so that he could worship God with a pure heart. If he did so, God would receive his exuberant and free worship. If the psalmist knew that God accepted his worship, the worship offered up by the psalmist could be done with a **voice of thanksgiving**.

When saints worship God in spirit and truth (Jn 4:24), great joy can rise in the hearts of the saints (2 Sam.6). This is because all God has done previously, is doing presently, and will do in the future make up His **wondrous works**. These include but are not limited to the death of the Lord Jesus Christ on the cross to save sinners. That work is wonderous because, by it, people from every tongue, tribe, and nation will stand before the throne of God and worship the Lamb for all eternity and will miss out on having to suffer God's wrath for all eternity (Rev. 7:9). For who God is and what God has done in the world and in the lives of His people, the saints can praise the Lord with a voice of thanksgiving and **tell of all** the Lord's wondrous works.

### Questions for self-reflection:

(1) If you had five minutes with an unbeliever to share with them all the reasons why you are thankful to God, what would you tell them?
(2) What are some of the wonderful works that God has done in the world to people other than you that you could share with others to point them to Him?
(3) What are some of the wonderful works that God has done in you that you could share with others to point them to Him?

---

(4) If you share the good works that God has done for you personally with unbelievers, what is the worst that could happen to you personally? Is that worst thing terrible enough that it should prevent you from communicating the gospel to someone particular in your life that desperately needs to hear it?

**26:8. Lord, I have loved the habitation of Your house, And the place where Your glory dwells.**

At the time that this psalm was penned, the temple had not been built. The tabernacle was the meeting place. The Lord made His presence known in the tabernacle, His **house**. The glory of the Lord filled the tabernacle (Exod. 40:34-35). The psalmist **loved** the Lord's presence and wanted to be as close as possible to where the Lord's presence was while at the same time being as far away as possible from the assembly of evildoers. The Lord's people are glad when they go into the house of the Lord (Ps. 122:1). Their goal is to honor the Lord with everything they do (1 Cor. 10:31), and they know that one of the things that show honor to Him is participating in corporate worship with other saints who also gather to worship Him. They do not want to forsake the assembling (Heb. 10:25). They want to heed His Word when it is taught, especially in public worship services (Heb. 2:1). Where two or more gather in the Lord's name, the Lord is there with them in their midst (Matt. 18:20).

The fulness of God's glory resides in Christ (Col. 2:9). Anyone on earth in any generation can experience a taste of this fellowship with the Divine when they embrace the gospel and place personal repentant faith in the Lord Jesus Christ for salvation. God's glory dwells among the saints in services. God's glory lives via the Holy Spirit in the hearts of believers in every generation since Pentecost (Eph. 3:17). The Holy Spirit is Christ in us the hope of glory (Col. 1:27). If the hope of glory is in believers, then believers, the temple of God (1 Cor. 6:19), is **the place where** God's **glory dwells**. Because of Christ's finished work on the cross in which all believers participate, believers are recipients of the Holy Spirit, and they experience something of a foretaste of what the habitation of the house of the Lord in heaven will be like.

After believers die, their **habitation** will be in heaven, in the Father's house (Jn 14:2-3). God's glory will fill heaven (Ps. 19:1). It will completely surround and envelop believers. Believers are filled with a sense of God's glory now via the earnest of the inheritance (a.k.a. The Holy Spirit (Eph. 1:14)) and will experience God's glory as fully as they are enabled to in heaven when they are forever with the Lord (1 Thess. 4:17).

**Questions for self-reflection:**

(1) When it is time to worship the Lord publicly, do you look forward to that, or do you look to get it over with?
(2) What helps you sense the Lord's presence more closely outside of services?
(3) What keeps you from sensing the Lord's presence as closely outside of services?
(4) Would you rather be able to go to your heavenly habitation now, or are there things on this earth that you really want to do? If there are things that you want to do, do those things have any eternal significance?

**26:9. Do not gather my soul with sinners, Nor my life with bloodthirsty men,**

---

There was a stark contrast between the lifestyle of the psalmist and the lifestyle of the lost. The psalmist wanted it to stay that way. He knew it was his responsibility to maintain his testimony and to grow. The psalmist also knew that he needed help from the Lord to stand when the spiritual battle became severe (Eph. 6:11, Eph. 6:13). Herein lies the spiritual tension that the Apostle Paul identified for the Philippians when he commanded them with apostolic authority to work out their salvation with fear and trembling while also understanding that God worked in them both to will and to do for His good pleasure (Phil. 2:12-13). Since everyone is a sinner (Rom. 3:23), it is not realistic for anyone to avoid sinning perfectly.

For this reason, we need a Savior (1 Jn 2:1-2). The lives of righteous people will contain a noticeable separation from sin and unto the Lord. In contrast, the lives of the unrighteous will have no such separation. A distinguishing characteristic of the servants of the Lord is their conformity to the image of Christ (Eph. 5:8-14).

The psalmist does not want to be associated with what he is calling '**sinners**' or '**bloodthirsty men.**' Bloodthirsty men are ready to destroy others either literally or figuratively by harmful actions and words. Instead of tearing down with harmful actions by harming others, the righteous are do good to everyone, especially fellow believers (Gal. 6:10). The righteous are also to be doers of good to the lost (Matt. 5:16). Believers should not tear down others with their words but instead edify with their words (Eph. 4:29). Our words and bodies should be used as servants of righteousness rather than servants of unrighteousness (Rom. 6:12-14).

To **gather** the **soul** is to end the life. The psalmist asks the Lord not to take him to premature death on account of his sin. He would rather live a full life of service to the Lord if the Lord wills.

## Questions for self-reflection:

(1) Would it be easier or harder for redeemed saints to maintain their testimony if they always were very close to the same environment and engaging in the same activities as the unsaved sinners and bloodthirsty men?

(2) Is it better for winning the lost to join them in their ungodly activities to try to fit in with them and risk giving into temptation ourselves, or is it better to show them a godly lifestyle and share the gospel with them?

(3) Since God leaves us here after He saves us, it is evident that we will have to have contact with the lost world. What are some helpful ways to engage with the lost world while not compromising our testimonies personally?

(4) How can you avoid sinning yourself (trick question)?

(5) How can you edify rather than tear down with your words those who oppose the gospel while not compromising truth?

**26:10. In whose hands is a sinister scheme, And whose right hand is full of bribes.**

---

The **hands** of bloodthirsty men and the hands of sinners plot **sinister scheme**s **and bribes** against the psalmist and the rest of the righteous. The lost, represented by the bloodthirsty men and sinners in context, oppose the righteous because they oppose the God of the righteous. Lost people's lives consist of perpetually walking in darkness. Their darkness persists because they do not have the Light of the world (Jn 8:12) to be the lamp to their feet and the light to their path (Ps. 119:105). The schemes of the righteous plot to do good to everyone. Because the hearts of lost people lack the transformative power of the Holy Spirit, their lives lack practical righteousness. In contrast, believers possess the Holy Spirit that produces practical righteousness in believers' lives. The lost plot sinister schemes in which they plan to undermine anything good. – especially any good that comes from the righteous (like the psalmist).

This unrighteous behavior parallels the passages penned by the psalmist in Psalm 14 and Psalm 53 that the Apostle Paul quotes in Romans 3. They scheme to eat up God's people and neglect to call upon the Lord who can save them. They let their sinful desires take over as they ignore their conscience, which tells them the difference between right and wrong (Rom. 2:15). Man is born with an innate sense of right and wrong because man is born with God's law written on their hearts (Rom. 2:15). The more they listen to the conscience, the divine warning system, the more God will reveal Himself to them. The less they listen to the conscience, the less God will reveal Himself to them (Lk 12:48). If believers want a more potent dose of God's presence and reality in their lives, they must be faithful with what they do have, obey with what they know to obey with, and God will manifest more of Himself.

## Questions for self-reflection:

(1) If you were in a persecution or oppression situation, and people plotted sinister schemes and bribes to undermine any spiritual good you desired to accomplish, how do you think you would react?

(2) Is there some area in your life in which you are in blatant rebellion to God that would prevent Him from revealing Himself more to you? Is anything keeping you from a more prosperous relationship with God?

**26:11. But as for me, I will walk in my integrity; Redeem me and be merciful to me.**

---

Up until this point, the psalmist continued to **walk in integrity**. He did not intend to stop walking in integrity now. His fellowship with his Lord was so precious that he did not want any sin to interrupt that (1 Jn 1:7). He wanted the Lord to **redeem** him and reward him for his faithfulness by removing him from the sinful surroundings in which he found himself. Because such immoral influences surrounded the psalmist, he was in danger. Sinners and bloodthirsty men were taking bribes and plotting sinister schemes. Wicked evildoers surrounded the psalmist and no doubt caused the psalmist great fear. Idolatrous mortals and hypocrites threatened to steal his joy. As the psalmist continued to contemplate the lovingkindness of God, he was better prepared to walk in his integrity.

Integrity marks the righteous life, in contrast to the duplicity that characterizes the unrighteous life. By walking upright, in the light, and in integrity, the saved show the difference between them and the lost. They show that they are not being conformed to this world but are being transformed by renewing their minds (Rom. 12:1-2). Saved people are already redeemed (Eph. 1:7). They have redemption through the blood of Christ. Saved people who grow in grace and in the knowledge of the Lord and Savior Jesus Christ (2 Pet. 3:18) will desire to convey the mercy shown to them by walking in integrity before those who have not believed the gospel. The saved realize that God has been merciful to them. The saved recognize that God continues to **be merciful to** the lost even after they have chosen to live lives of rebellion to the God that made them in His image (Gen. 1:27).

**Questions for self-reflection:**

(1) If walking in integrity characterizes the lifestyle of the regenerate, what is an accurate description for the type of lifestyle that characterizes the unregenerate?

---

(2) Is there any hidden sin that might prevent you from experiencing fellowship with the Lord as richly as you could?
(3) Are there trials that you wish the Lord would mercifully bring to an end?
(4) If the Lord in His sovereignty would not bring those trials to an end, would you be able to learn from them any lessons He might want you to learn from them?

**26:12 My foot stands in an even place; In the congregations I will bless the Lord.**

---

When the **foot** of the psalmist **stands**, when our feet stand, **in an even place**, they stand in such a place that they will not slip. They will not get off balance and fall. The elements will not rock them. The place on which they stand is sure. When the sheep stand in the grace of Christ (Gal. 5:1, 1 Pet. 5:12), when they stand on the firm foundation (Matt. 7:24-27, 1 Cor. 3:9-12), when they stand on the Rock that is Christ (1 Cor. 10:4), when the sheep trust in the Lord (Prov. 3:5-6), they will not succumb when the storms of life crash against them. They will not fall even if they stumble. The storm that comes will not take their house away with it. Because of the Lord Jesus Christ, the footing of the saints stands in an even place. Christ has secured us such that we cannot lose our place in the Father's house with Him (Jn 14:2-3). Anyone who comes to Him will not be cast out (Jn 6:37).

Even when the sheep wander from the fold, the loving Shepherd seeks the sheep to return it to the fold (Lk 15:4-7). The Shepherd provides everything to protect the sheep against all predators adequately. The sheep's feet stand in an even place, not because of the sheep, but because of the great grace of the Lord Jesus Christ, which He lavishly poured out upon all the saints. Because the psalmist's foot stands in an even place, then the psalmist **will bless the Lord** whenever the psalmist is in the **congregation**. Whenever the saints congregate, because of the great grace of God seen in the Lord Jesus Christ that has bountifully blessed every believer with every spiritual blessing in the heavenly places (Eph. 1:3), all saints, including the psalmist, can bless the Lord. Everything good that comes to the saints comes from a loving God blessing His own with every good and perfect gift (Jas 1:17). When this life ends, and the next life begins, congregations of saints from all ages, from every tribe, tongue, and nation, will bless the Lord as they cast their crowns before Him and worship Him for the great salvation He provided for them (Rev. 4:10-11).

---

**Questions for self-reflection:**

(1) In whom must we be trusting if we want to ensure that our feet stand in an even place?
(2) Is there anyone you know whose life appears to be devoid of the fruit that is indicative of someone who has trusted Christ for salvation?
(3) Who do you know who would be willing to bless the Lord with you? Who could you mutually encourage in the Lord? Who would be willing to receive encouragement from you? Who would be willing to give encouragement to you?

# Psalm 27

**27:1. The Lord is my light and my salvation; Whom shall I fear? The Lord is the strength of my life; Of whom shall I be afraid?**

---

**The Lord** gives **light** to every man (Jn 1:9). Jesus Christ is the Light of the World (Jn 8:12) that lights the paths (Psalm 119:105) of those who have come to Him. He exposes the darkness of the sinful heart (Ps. 26:2, Rom. 1:21, 1 Cor. 4:5, 1 Thess. 2:4) so that sinners know that they need to come to Him for **salvation**. He also gives man a conscience, so the man knows the difference between right and wrong innately (Rom. 2:15). For example, man knows it is wrong to lie and steal because God gives light to understand a basic sense of morality.

When man was lost and dead in trespasses and sins (Col. 2:13), God shone the light of the glorious gospel in the heart of those who believed the gospel (2 Cor. 4:4). When those sinners came to repentant faith in the Lord Jesus Christ, Christ became salvation in those sinners (Heb. 5:9). As they live out the command to grow in grace and the knowledge of the Lord and Savior Jesus Christ (2 Pet. 3:18), they get more and more light from the Lord (Matt. 13:12). As they are faithful with the light that the Lord graciously reveals to them, the Lord responds to their faithfulness by lavishing more light upon them. Should they be unfaithful with the light they receive, the Lord will pull back. As believers respond to the grace supplied to them, God responds by giving more grace and strength to live faithfully (Phil. 4:19).

Believers understand that they shall fear nothing because the worst that can happen to them in this life is physical death (Matt. 10:28). In physical death, all the things from this earthly life that caused pain will cease causing pain. They will be forever with their Lord in heaven where there is no more sorrow, sickness, or death (Rev. 21:3-4). There is no need to fear death, then, for the believer. For the believer, Satan needs not be feared. He is the accuser of the brethren (Rev. 12:10), but he can only accuse as much as God allows him to accuse (Job 1:12). The stronger the believer's faith, the more the believer's mind is under the control of the Holy Spirit.

---

As God's Word controls the mind of the child of God, the less of a chance that the devil has to be influential.

The justified person does not need to **fear** when they look at the reprobation that is rampant all over the world. As the vast majority of humanity is on the broad road that leads to destruction (Matt. 7:13-14) and pursues their own lusts, God gives them what they want (Rom. 1:24, Rom. 1:26, Rom. 1:28). The ungodly have everything to fear because the Lake of Fire will be their portion (Rev. 21:8). For the believer, such a sure hope results in a lack of fear of death. As believers spend more time with the Light of the World, Jesus shines in their lives and reveals the truth of who He is and how to view this world. As the Word is confirmed and comes to pass in the lives of believers, greater boldness fills the believer and displaces fear (Eph. 3:11-12).

The justified person can fear the just discipline that the Lord inflicts upon the saved sinners for their unrepentant sin (Heb. 12:3-11). Believers have the Holy Spirit, and the Holy Spirit convicts them of sin (Jn 16:8) and leads them into all truth (Jn 16:13). Believers grieve the Holy Spirit by ignoring the warnings that come with sin (Eph. 4:30). The further believers push the Lord away in their relationship with Him, the harder it gets for believers to hear the Lord. It behooves the child of God to listen to the warnings that a gracious God puts on them since the way of the transgressor is hard (Prov. 13:15). The more the believer walks in the light as opposed to the darkness, the sweeter the fellowship with the Lord even during the most adverse circumstances (1 Jn 1:7).

**The Lord is the strength of life** for all believers. God gives life to every person (1 Tim. 6:13). Unfortunately, not every person reciprocates that mercy and grace with a life of service to the Giver of life in return. How tragic! God created man in His own image (Gen. 1:27). In Christ, believers live, and move, and have their being (Acts 17:28). Believers understand that every perfect gift, including life itself, comes from above (Jas 1:17). Christ supplies the spiritual strength into the lives of believers through the Holy Spirit (Phil. 4:19). It is the Spirit, who is Christ in us, the hope of glory (Col. 1:27) and that enables us to work out our salvation with fear and trembling God it is God that is at work in us both to will and to do for His good pleasure (Phil. 2:12-13). As believers live their lives by faith in the Son of God who loved them and gave Himself for them (Gal. 2:20), they are strengthened in the inner man (Ephesians 3:16) to be doers of the Word and not hearers only deceiving themselves (Jas 1:22-25). This strength helps them understand with the mind and live with the body in a way that is absent of fear. They can live in the absence of that fear because the perfect love of God has been shed abroad in their hearts (Rom. 5:5) and because perfect love casts out fear (1 Jn 4:18). Nothing will keep them from experiencing the eternal life that they already have received. Satan and the world may be strong adversaries, but Christ is stronger than all, and none can pluck any sheep out of His hand (Jn 10:27-28).

## Questions for self-reflection:

(1) In what ways has the Lord given you light?

(2) What ways have your perceptions of the people and the world around you changed since the Lord has given you light and has become your salvation?

(3) Has your faith largely stagnated, or have you consistently grown? If it is a mix, what could account for the difference? What could account for seasons of stagnation? What could account for seasons of growth?

(4) If your faith is in the Lord, what do you have to fear ultimately?

(5) How can we discover more light that we have at our disposal?

(6) Is there anything about your life that could invite unpleasant discipline from the Lord?

(7) Is there anything in the life of anyone you know that could invite the Lord's discipline to come down on them that you could help them avoid by aiding them to turn from their sinful ways?

(8) Why are believers able to live without fear in the world that is opposed to God?

**27:2. When the wicked came against me To eat up my flesh, My enemies and foes, They stumbled and fell.**

---

**The wicked** are all those who oppose the psalmist spiritually because all those who oppose the psalmist spiritually also oppose the God of the psalmist, who is the lone true God (Isa. 45:5). Those who are **against** God make their attacks in various ways, some more subtle than others. Some may physically attack the people of God by depriving them of something physical to get them to compromise. Some may attack the people of God spiritually by getting them to renounce the Lord by putting them through emotional suffering. The wicked hate the righteous because the righteous live lives that confront the sin of the wicked, sometimes in public ways (2 Tim. 3:12). These ways of public confrontation can leave the wicked looking embarrassed in public and lead to desires of revenge to be enacted by the wicked upon the righteous.

The wicked will respond to **eat up** the **flesh** of the righteous with their hostile attacks, some more overt than others. The wicked want to remove the righteous from their path so that the righteous will no longer be there to stop the wicked from freely practicing their wickedness. The wicked, any that make up the **enemies and foes** of the righteous, want to discourage the righteous to the point that the righteous will no longer see the benefit of living righteously. However, since the righteous renew their minds in God's true Word regularly (Rom. 12:2), they understand that these attacks and efforts to discourage employed by the wicked are normal. They know that the devil, the one for whom the wicked labor, is a relentless, roaring lion that will stop at nothing to exercise his sway over the world (1 Pet. 5:8). **They stumbled and fell** when the righteous stood their ground, continuing to firmly trust in the Lord who bought them (2 Pet. 2:1). When Satan tempted the Lord in the wilderness unsuccessfully multiple times, he stumbled and fell pathetically in the face of such perfect holiness (Matt. 4:1-11).

The Lord executes His avenging wrath against the enemies of the gospel (2 Thess. 1:8-10), His enemies and foes stumble and fall in their desperate attempts to stop the Lord's work (e.g., Acts 12). They may appear for a time to have the upper hand. However, they fail to realize while they are busy plotting their vain schemes that the Lord sits in heaven and laughs (Ps. 2:4) while waiting patiently for some of them to humble themselves and turn from their wicked ways (2 Chron. 7:14) and kiss the Son lest He be angry (Ps. 2:12). The wicked will ultimately stumble and fall. When they stand before the Great White Throne, they will be rejected and cast into the lake of fire forever (Rev. 20:11-15), weeping and gnashing with their teeth (Matthew 22:13), forever under the feet of the Lord (1 Cor. 15:27) who bought them (2 Pet. 2:1) who loved them (Jn 3:16) who they so callously rejected. God's goodness, which was designed to lead them to repentance, was spurned for a life of debauchery (Rom. 2:4).

**Questions for self-reflection:**

(1) In the terms of this verse, what makes someone wicked?
(2) Have you ever experienced the symbolic eating of the flesh by the wicked to which this verse alludes?
(3) What kind of reputation do you have amongst your enemies and foes? What type of reputation did Christ have around His enemies or foes?
(4) Is there any sin in your life that your enemies or foes could point to in order to use against you and undermine your testimony?
(5) How can understanding the persecution that believers endured in previous generations be an encouragement to those of us who suffer persecution in the present age?

**27:3. Though an army may encamp against me, My heart shall not fear; Though war may rise against me, In this I will be confident.**

As an army of ungodliness surrounds the psalmist, an army that stands against the righteous Lord to whom the psalmist belongs, fear would not overtake the psalmist's **heart**. As with all believers in the risen Lord Jesus Christ, who is the same yesterday, today, and forever (Heb. 13:8), the Lord was on the side of the psalmist (Ps. 118:6). There was nothing to fear. There was nothing that man could do to the psalmist apart from divine permission. As the psalmist entrusted himself to the Lord, everlasting strength was at his disposal. (Isa. 26:4). While the nations raged against the psalmist (Ps. 2:1), the psalmist knew that the Lord sat in heaven and laughed at them (Ps. 2:4).

The psalmist could stand back and see the salvation of the Lord (Exod. 14:13-14). The Lord had intervened on behalf of His people in mighty ways all through history. Nothing was going to stop that from happening now if it was the Lord's will. Legions of angels could be let loose on behalf of the psalmist at the behest of the Lord when the Lord chose to intervene (Matt. 26:53). The Lord could cause city walls to crumble at His Word (Josh. 6). The Lord could cause the earth to swallow the enemies of His people (Num. 16). The Lord could part the seas at His command (Exod. 14, Josh. 3). The psalmist held the shield of faith high as an able defense against his enemies (Eph. 6:16). With the omnipotent Lord on the side of the psalmist, there was no reason to fear.

Enemies of all forms rise against God's people in every generation. No matter the enemy, God's people can remain **confident**. The great High Priest, the Lord Jesus Christ (Heb. 4:14-15), has been tempted in every way like His disciples, and He did not sin. His people can trust in Him to provide a way of escape from any temptation (1 Cor. 10:13). When physical enemies try to destroy God's people, there is nothing to fear because God will provide the appropriate words in the proper time for His people (Matt. 10:19). The divine appointment for each person has been set so one will not die before the appointment comes up (Heb. 9:27).

**Though an army of ungodliness may encamp against** us, we can trust Lord with a confident trust to provide sufficient grace for the current moment, and then the next present moment, and so forth, and so on. Therefore, the believing **heart shall not fear**. The Lord's people can guarantee that the **war** will rise against them. Even if the war does not rage with their earthly enemies outside of themselves, it will **rise against** them internally. The devil, the roaring lion (1 Pet. 5:8), the accuser of the brethren (Rev. 12:10), is out to do damage to God's people.

Satan already knows that if anyone is in Christ, he is a new creation (2 Cor. 5:17). New creations cannot revert back to being old creations again. Believers are more than conquerors through Christ, the lover of their souls (Rom. 8:37). A sheep cannot become a goat once it is a sheep. None can pluck them out of God's hand once they come to the Father through faith in Christ (Jn 10:27-28). All that the Father has given Christ will come to Christ, and all those that come to Him will not be cast out (Jn 6:37). If God has begun the good work, He will perform it (Phil. 1:6). If someone is justified, they will be glorified (Rom. 8:29-30).

### Questions for self-reflection:

(1) Are there ways that you can relate to the statement that an army encamps around you? In what ways?
(2) Even if armies encamp around us, why do we not have to fear? Who is on our side that is stronger than our enemies?
(3) What ways can spiritual war arise against the godly in today's world?
(4) Why can the godly remain confident regardless of what happens to them in this life - even if that includes death?

**27:4. One thing I have desired of the Lord, That will I seek: That I may dwell in the house of the Lord All the days of my life, To behold the beauty of the Lord, And to inquire in His temple.**

---

The psalmist recognized that it was not necessarily best for him to have a life of ease and comfort. It was not necessarily best for him to always have his way. It was not necessarily best for all his earthly relationships to be perfect at all times. As sinful creatures, we tend to get attached to the things of this world (Eccles. 2:4-11, 1 Jn 2:15-17). We tend to acquire inordinate affections for things that we have seen. But God has put eternity in our hearts (Eccles. 3:11) so that we will pursue Him and find Him (Jer. 29:13). He has put eternity in our hearts so that we will realize that if we keep going to the well of being satisfied on the trinkets of this world, eventually, that well will dry up.

The Lord wants His people to realize that only He will satisfy them in an eternal sense (Matt. 11:28-30). The food that He provides to those who find Him will keep sustaining them (Jn 6:27). The things of this world will lose their attraction, and we will need to find something bigger, better, newer, or flashier to replace what once fit that bill in our lives (1 Tim. 6:6-10). Only when we keep returning to Him, who bought us for the satisfaction that only He can provide, will we realize that He is what we have been searching for all along. His people **desire** that He remove the affinity for the things of this world and replace that ungodly affinity with the godly affinity that is the hallmark of the regenerate. The psalmist knew he was responsible to **seek the Lord** while He may be found (Isa. 55:6-7). He knew that if His people diligently sought Him, they would be rewarded (Heb. 11:6). He knew from experience that as he besought the Lord by effectual and fervent prayer (Jas 5:16), the Lord would fill him with more of His presence and grace to persevere in the direst of straits. Once the psalmist took his last breath and gave up the ghost and fell asleep in a spiritual sense, he would awake in the Lord's presence and would **dwell in the** eternal **house** of the Lord **all the days of** all eternity (2 Cor. 5:8).

---

While the Lord kept him here, however, he could get a fore-taste of eternal glory by going to his local house of worship and fellowshipping with the brethren since where they gather, the Lord was in their midst (Matthew 18:20). The church, the pillar and ground of truth (1 Tim. 3:15), the called-out ones that the Lord Jesus Christ bought with His own blood (Acts 20:28), made of up those whose names are written in heaven (Luke 10:20), those in whom the light of the World (Jn 8:12) has made His home in their hearts by faith (Eph. 3:17), is where all the redeemed gather con-sistently to worship the One to whom all worship is due corpo-rately. It is here among the saints where those present can **behold the beauty of the Lord**. So, likewise, it is here where they witness the Lord's grace at work in the lives of the saints who are being transformed by the renewing of their minds (Rom. 12:2).

Their Mediator (1 Tim. 2:15), the Lord Jesus Christ, continues to exercise His High Priestly work (Heb. 4:14-16), ever-living to inter-cede for the saints (Heb. 7:25). Meanwhile, the saints continue to serve Him, who has blessed them with every spiritual blessing (Eph. 1:3) until they have their divine appointment (Heb. 9:27). Beholding this beauty here on earth is a preview of the beauty they will behold for all eternity as the elders will cast their crowns (Rev. 4:10) at the feet of the One who bought them. People from every tribe, tongue, and nation worship the Lord now here on earth in an imperfect sense and will one day do so from heaven completely free from the power and presence of sin (Rev. 5:9).

Now, the saints hear the Word and partake in the ordinances corporately. They do this to show what the Lord has done in their lives and to remember His death until He comes (1 Cor. 11:26). In addition, they do this to show how the Lord has called them out of darkness and into His marvelous light (1 Pet. 2:9). They one day will be with the Lord forever in heaven, in the New Jerusalem (Rev. 21:9-27). All the turmoil and toil that trials that marked this life will cease as they will be with the Lord in eternal bliss (Rev. 21:4). The saints will get to forever **inquire in** the Lord's **temple** and worship Him perfectly for who He is and what He has done to make these eternal moments possible. Now, before eternity, saints can have access by one Spirit to the Father (Eph. 2:18) because of the finished work of the Lord Jesus Christ who made a new and living way (Heb. 10:20) for us.

## Questions for self-reflection:

(1) Why might the Lord not desire that we have lives of ease and comfort all the time?

(2) What can happen if we try to satisfy our eternal longing with this temporal world?

(3) What would you do if you felt like you had been diligently seeking the Lord, but He had not rewarded you like you thought He should? How would you handle that?

(4) What are some ways in which corporate worship today will resemble eternal heaven?

(5) How has the Lord demonstrated the work of grace that only He performs in your heart?

**27:5. For in the time of trouble He shall hide me in His pavilion; In the secret place of His tabernacle He shall hide me; He shall set me high upon a rock.**

---

The psalmist knew that life contained a time of peace and a **time of trouble.** The Lord was his light and salvation (Ps. 27:1) in times of peace and crisis (Eccles. 3:1-8). He knew that because he trusted in the Lord, ultimately, he had nothing to fear (Ps. 112:7). The Lord was the strength of his life (Exod. 15:2, Neh. 8:10, Ps. 18:1, Ps. 28:7-8, Ps. 31:4, Ps. 37:39, Ps. 46:1, Ps. 73:46, Ps. 81:1, Ps. 84:5, Ps. 118:14, Isa. 12:12, Isa. 45:24, Isa. 49:5, Jer. 16:19, Hab. 3:19) There was nothing to fear. Even though the psalmist had many enemies that sought to destroy him literally, figuratively, or both, the Lord would enable the psalmist to overcome them all (Deut. 20:4, Deut. 30:7, 2 Sam. 22:18, Ps. 6:10, Ps. 9:3, Ps. 18:17, Ps. 31:15, Ps. 81:14, Ps. 118:6, Ps. 143:12, Mic. 7:10, Zeph. 3:15, Mk. 12:36, Lk 1:71, Lk 1:74). He had such strong faith because He knew what His God could do on his behalf. Because of all the Lord had done for him, the psalmist wanted to be where the Lord was and wherever the Lord's people were (Ps. 122:1). If the psalmist was close to the Lord, the Lord would be near to him, and nothing would be too difficult for him to face (Jn 15:1-8).

The **pavilion** was the place where the psalmist could go to **hide** from his enemies under the protection of the Lord (Ps. 17:8-9). For the believer in the Lord Jesus Christ, since He has taken their condemnation (Romans 8:1) since He has taken their wrath (Rom. 5:9) since He has taken their enmity, (Eph. 2:15-18) to be hidden from all that would be a great relief. The psalmist could go to the pavilion of the Lord to temporarily escape from the cares of this life that bog him down (Lk 8:7, Lk 8:14, 1 Cor. 7:32-33). The psalmist could go to the pavilion of the Lord to protect him from other harmful influences that the world contains.

All believers in the Lord Jesus Christ are believers in He who is called the **Tabernacle** of God (Rev. 21:3). The Tabernacle was the Old Testament building constructed under Moses' leadership (Exod. 26), in which God's presence went with Israel as they first became a nation. It was the place where worship took place, and Old Testament sacrifices occurred. Christians' lives are hidden with Christ in God (Col. 3:1-3). Christ hides believers from God's wrath that abides upon the unbelieving. (Jn 3:36, Rom. 5:9) Christ took the wrath that believers deserve and that unbelievers receive (1 Pet. 3:18).

The New Testament speaks about building believers' houses upon the rock (Matt. 7:24-27). Those houses built upon the rock of Christ and upon God's Word have a sure foundation that will stand when all soft foundations around it crumble (1 Cor. 10:4). The Corinthians passage refers to the Old Testament account of when Israel got water from a rock when they thirsted (Exod. 17:1-7). Christ the Rock protects believers from the storms of life that come against all people. For believers, they have a great hope that God works everything for the good of those who love Him when the storms come (Rom. 8:28, Rom. 15:4).

The unbeliever has no such hope. The unbeliever cannot say that God works everything together for their good. The unbeliever does not have the future hope that the believer has. The unbeliever is not hidden and protected like the believer is. Christ does not shield them because their faith is not in Him.

If earthly enemies attack God's people, the **rock**, the Lord Jesus Christ, is the hiding place that will ultimately protect them from everything, even death (Jn. 3:16, Rom. 8:1, 1 Cor. 15:50-58). Believers will never perish and cannot be plucked from God's hand (Jn 10:28). He is the refuge and strength (Ps. 46:1) of His people. The church is also a rock for God's people and is a corporate aid to believers (Matt. 16:18).

### Questions for self-reflection:

(1) How do you cope during times of trouble? Is going to God your first instinct?

(2) How has God protected you from physical enemies? How has God protected you from spiritual enemies?

(3) How has the local church been like a local rock for you?

**27:6. And now my head shall be lifted up above my enemies all around me; Therefore I will offer sacrifices of joy in His tabernacle; I will sing, yes, I will sing praises to the Lord.**

Because the Lord is the psalmist's light and salvation and the light for all those who belong to God through faith in the Lord Jesus Christ, believers have nothing to fear. When believers look at their enemies all around them, they can be prone to fear (Exod. 14:10). When believers keep their eyes on their Lord and not on their enemies, they are better equipped to rise above what causes them fear (Exod. 14:13-14). Believers can tap into the strength from on high with which God has blessed them. They can recall that they have nothing or nobody about which to be afraid (Ps. 118:6). When the circumstances of life come against them to do them harm to take their focus off of the Lord that had bought them and continually intercedes (Rom. 8:26-27, Rom. 8:34, Heb. 7:25, Heb. 9:24) for and sustains them (Neh. 9:6, 1 Cor. 8:6, Col. 1:17, Heb. 1:3), supernatural strength comes to the rescue. This supernatural strength enables the believer to victoriously overcome the temptation (Ps. 119:11, Matt. 6:13, Rom. 12:2, Rom. 12:21, Rom. 13:14, 1 Cor. 10:13, Gal. 5:16, Eph. 6:11, Heb 2:18, Jas 4:7-8).

While the believer experiences the victory of success in overcoming temptation, their enemies and foes stumbled and fell. No matter what they were up against, their heart would not fail. They would remain confident. They came to realize that at worst, they would lose their physical life (Matthew 10:28) and enter into immediate eternal life (2 Cor. 5:8). This is not a bad thing at all for the believer. In fact, it is the most blessed thing. It is the greatest gift that anyone could ever receive. Believers will be with the Lord in heaven forever, with their **head lifted up above** their **enemies,** beholding His beauty and inquiring in His temple.

While they await that glorious day, however, their job is to trust and obey in the next moment with the grace that is sufficient that the Lord provides to His people (Phil. 4:19). He has set His people high upon the rock that is Christ (1 Cor. 10:4). He is the firm foundation that will not wash away when the storms of life come crashing (Matt. 7:24-27). His people can inquire of Him and know the mystery of His will (Eph. 1:9). The Lord is on their side. They shall not fear. (Psalm 118:6) Man, even believers' surrounding **enemies**, can do nothing to them. They will one day be vanquished.

Because believers are so secure because of the finished work of the Lord Jesus Christ (Rom. 8:38-39, Phil. 1:6), no wonder they can **offer sacrifices of joy in His Tabernacle**. The object of joy should be the Lord Jesus Christ for believers. After all, He is the One who reconciled them to the God they most heinously offended (2 Cor. 5:18). He is the One that upholds all things by the Word of His power (Heb. 1:3). He is the One who enables us to bear much fruit as we abide in Him (Jn 15:1-8). The Lord Jesus Christ became the Tabernacle of God and dwelt with men (Rev. 21:3). If our joy is in Him, nothing can separate us from His love (Rom. 8:38-39). If he has begun the good work in us, He will perform it (Phil. 1:6).

We know that, because of Christ, the Father that had His arrows pointing at us because we sinned against Him (Ps. 7:11-13). Yet, because He is rich in mercy (Eph. 2:4), He made way for us not to have to be struck by the arrows. Instead of us receiving the just due for our sins (Rom. 5:9, Rom. 6:23), the beauty of the gospel is that Christ, the Lamb of God, became our substitute (1 Pet. 2:24), became sin for us (2 Cor. 5:21). He can take our sin, and we can have His righteousness when we come to the Father through faith in the Son. When believers realize that the punishment for their sins has been recompensed, that their fine has been paid, they can **sing praises to the Lord** because they now have an Advocate (1 Jn 2:1) that they did not previously have. They now have a High Priest that they did not previously have (Heb. 4:14-16).

## Questions for self-reflection:

(1) Because the Lord is your salvation, what are some of the things that you do not have to fear?
(2) Does the idea of being with the Lord in heaven one day please you?

(3) What caused God's arrows to point against us?

(4) What caused God's arrows to point away from us?

(5) Because God's arrows point away from us if we have believed the gospel, why does God deserve the praise for that and not us for us having the good sense to believe the gospel and flee from the wrath to come?

**27:7. Hear, O Lord, when I cry with my voice! Have mercy also upon me, and answer me.**

---

When the saints in all ages, from the time of creation to the time of the psalmist to the time of the first-century church to the present age, **cry with** the **voice** to the **Lord,** they do so in prayer. Prayer is how we communicate with God (Matt. 6:5-13, 1 Thess. 5:17). Believers have access by one Spirit to the Father (Eph. 2:18) because the Lord Jesus Christ has made a new and living way (Heb. 10:20). Though our sins were as scarlet, He has made them white as snow (Isa. 1:18). He has wiped away the ordinances of the law that we have violated and nailed them to the cross (Col. 2:14). In Christ, everyone who believes is a new creation that has passed from death unto life (Jn 5:24, 2 Cor. 5:17). Because of the forgiveness that is accessible because of Christ, people from every tribe, tongue, and nation (Rev. 5:9) can call upon the Lord and cry to Him with the voice. They can cast their cares upon Him because He cares for us (1 Pet 5:7). Sin separates believers from God (Isa. 59:2). If they harbor sin, God does not listen to their prayers (Ps. 66:18). Therefore, it is incumbent on the believer to deal with their sins and enter into God's presence, having come clean before God (Heb. 9:13-14, 1 Jn 1:9). It is not like believers can hide anything from God anyway (Hebrews 4:13).

Amid various trials (Jas 1:2), life can seem unduly hard. During the midst of the trial, if there is no end in sight to the trial, it can seem as if the Lord does not care. If all things are open and naked before Him with whom we have to do (Heb. 4:13), if they think they are fooling anyone, they are only fooling themselves. If believers are persistent in crying out to God, God will hear them (Lk 18:1-8). He will answer them from His holy habitation (Deut. 26:15). He is the rewarder of them who diligently seek Him (Heb. 11:6). God equips His people to face anything since He is in them (Rom. 8:31, Rom. 8:37, 1 Jn 2:13, 1 Jn 4:4, 1 Jn 5:4) and leads them by the way (Gen. 24:48, Ps. 25:8-10, Ps. 32:8, Ps. 143:8, Isa. 48:17). When we experience the deliverance that only the Lord can provide, we can be more prone to give God credit for our deliverance.

Other times, we can think of ourselves as better than we are and forget God (Prov. 16:18-19, Prov. 25:27, Eccles. 7:16, Rom. 11:20, Rom. 12:3, Rom. 12:16, 1 Cor. 4:7). If we become too self-sufficient, God might act to bring us back to a place of dependence upon Him. God wants His people to glorify Him. He wants His people to be lights in this dark world and to lead those on the outside into the kingdom of His dear Son (Matt. 5:16, 2 Cor. 4:4-6, Col. 1:13).

God is rich in **mercy** to make way for anyone to be forgiven (Eph. 2:4). Most people, unfortunately, don't realize precisely how merciful He is. By delaying punishment, the Lord shows mercy on all those who are created in His image. The Lord can **answer** His people by either giving His people the substance of their prayers (what they ask for) or by giving them the grace to endure whatever the circumstance is, even if God will not remove them from the events that cause heartache (2 Cor. 12:7-10). God will answer the prayers of the faithful. His people may not understand God's answer or may not realize that God's answer is best for them. But the finite understanding of the creation cannot surpass the infinite mind of the Creator. Therefore, God will and does hear the prayers of His own.

## Questions for self-reflection:

(1) What are some reasons why some believers do not pray as they should?
(2) What has made it possible for people even to be able to cast cares to heaven?
(3) What keeps God from receiving prayers?
(4) How has your own pride hampered you from receiving answers to your prayers?

**27:8. When You said, "Seek My face," My heart said to You, "Your face, Lord, I will seek."**

The Lord asks His people to **seek** His **face** (1 Chron. 16:11, 2 Chron. 7:14, Ps. 105:4, Hos 5:15). The **Lord** hides His face from His rebellious people (Isaiah 8:17, Isaiah 64:7). To be able to see someone's face is to be very close to them.

For the psalmist, to seek the Lord's face is to be very close to the Lord. It is to be in situations where one can draw near to Him. One such situation is in services on the Lord's Day (Heb. 10:25). One such situation is when remembering the two ordinances that the Lord has left for His church until He returns, the Lord's Supper (Matt. 26:26-28, 1 Cor. 10:16-17) and baptism (Ezek. 36:25, Matt. 28:19, Acts 2:37-41, Acts 22:16, Rom. 6:3-5, Gal. 3:26-28, 1 Pet. 3:20-21). Believers also seek the face of the Lord when they open His Word, which He has so graciously left us with so that we can know His will if we will expose ourselves to it (1 Pet. 2:1-3). If we treat His Word as if it is not mere words on a page but a letter written from the God of the universe who owns us by virtue of creation to His unworthy creature (1 Cor. 6:19-20), we will come to the Lord through His Word with more proper reverence.

We seek the Lord's face when we go before the Lord in prayer (Heb. 5:16). We can do this individually or corporately. We should appreciate the fact that we even can **seek** the **face** of the **Lord**. Our sins have separated us from Him (Isa. 59:2). If it were not for His rich mercy (Eph, 2:4), Christ would not have died to be our substitute (1 Pet. 2:24), and access to the Father would never have been opened to us (Eph. 2:18). If God were not gracious (Isa. 30:18), He would not have made way for us through creation (Rom. 1:20) and conscience (Rom. 2:15) to know that He is there so that we would seek Him while He may be found (Isa. 55:6).

The Lord Jesus Christ condescended, coming down to us from heaven so we could be exalted with Him back into heaven if we would humble ourselves (Phil. 2:5-10). It is only the humble that God receives (1 Pet. 5:6). The prideful are rejected (1 Pet. 5:5). The humble know that there is nothing good in them to commend themselves to a holy God (Matt. 5:3). That holy God humbled Himself in Christ's incarnation so He could bring that man to Himself (1 Pet. 3:18). God descended so that man could ascend. Now, when saints pray without ceasing to the Lord (1 Thess. 5:16), who enables them to do so, they can do so with uninhibited access to every spiritual blessing (Eph. 1:3-14). When believers seek the Lord with the whole **heart**, the Lord promises that they will find Him (Matt. 7:7-8). Who wouldn't want to seek for something that they wanted to find and were guaranteed to find? When believers seek the Lord, when they abide in Him, and He abides in them, they see and appreciate more and more His goodness and how He has sustained them to the present moment and will keep sustaining them for as long as they are appointed to live (Jn 15:1-8). His Spirit constantly renews them as they are with Him (Rom. 12:2). They stand in His grace (Rom. 5:2). He enables them to seek Him. They choose to seek Him (Phil. 2:12-13). The result is a relationship where believers seek the Lord because He commands them to and they want to. Also, the Lord delights in having relationships with His people and rejoices over them to do them good (Deut. 28:63).

## Questions for self-reflection:

(1) What does seeking the Lord's face look like for you?
(2) How can people who seek the Lord's face in different manners find the same Lord?
(3) What keeps people from finding the Lord's face even if they seek Him?
(4) How can you seek the Lord more reverently?
(5) How have you grown in sensitivity to the Lord's presence from the beginning of your Christian pilgrimage to now?

**27:9. Do not hide Your face from me; Do not turn Your servant away in anger; You have been my help; Do not leave me nor forsake me, O God of my salvation.**

---

Hardships affect everyone, including God's people (Jn 16:33, Rom. 8:19-23, 1 Pet. 1:6). Even though God sees everything that transpires on the earth (1 Chron. 28:9, Jb 28:24, Jb 34:21, Ps. 11:4, Ps. 33:13, Ps. 44:21, Ps. 14;2, Ps. 53:2, Ps. 139, Prov. 5:21, Prov. 15:3, Isa. 40:28, Jer. 16:17, Jer. 23:23-24, Heb. 4:13, 1 Jn 3:20) and is especially connected to the sheep (Jn 10:27) who have been bought with a price (1 Cor. 6:19-20), the sheep can lose the sense of intimacy with God as the cares of this life wrestle with God for first place in the life (Matt. 13:7, Matt. 13:22. Lk 21:34). They may feel like God has begun to **hide from** them.

In such times, while sin may grieve the Holy Spirit (Eph. 4:30), and may even drive God to inflict harsh discipline on His sinning son or daughter (Heb. 12:3-11), the unpleasant feelings and circumstances that result from such discipline are actually tokens of God's love for His own and not His abandonment (Jas 1:2-8). Such experiences are not enjoyable in and of themselves, but they have a glorious purpose of making the believer love the world less and long for heaven more (Heb. 13:14). They are good reminders that a disciple is supposed to be like His master (Luke 6:40), and our Master was a man of sorrows and acquainted with grief (Isa. 53:3). When the Lord's servant feels like God is not as near as once felt, it can seem as though God has turned away from His servant in anger. This loss of the sense of God's presence can happen when the servant is in a season of unrepentant sin since sin is known to separate us from God (Isa. 64:6). The psalmist knows that he is frail and sinful and for God to allow any frail and sinful creature of His into His presence is a strong testimony to the grace of a God who longs to have a relationship with us (Matt. 11:28-29, Rom. 5:8). God is right to **turn away** from all of us in righteous **anger** at our sin (Ps. 7:11). However, he is merciful not to do so (Eph. 2:4) and does not turn from us when we come humbly to Him for reconciliation (2 Cor. 5:20, 1 Pet. 5:6).

---

A saved person realizes their spiritual destitution and utter unworthiness before a holy God (Matt. 5:3) that stands with a whetted sword ready to strike (Ps. 7:12-13). Because He is full of compassion (2 Cor. 1:3) and loves us with an indescribable love, He does not treat us according to our sins (Ps. 103:10). He gives us chance after chance to be reconciled. When we do, when we once were servants of sin and unrighteousness, we become servants of righteousness, albeit unworthy (Rom. 6:12-19). Even when we are reconciled (2 Cor. 5:12-20) and justified (Rom. 3:24), He is still compassionate and merciful to keep receiving us and washing us from our daily defilements as we have to continue to own them and work on them with the help of His grace (1 Jn 1:9). He never leaves us or forsakes us when He could because of our constant weakness and failure (Heb. 13:5). When we go our own way (Isa. 53:6), away from Him, He draws us with bands of love (Hos 11:4) back to the narrow way of devotion to Him (Matthew 7:13). When Satan tempts us (1 Thess. 3:5), He gently reminds us that He overcame the world (Jn 16:33) and the power that raised Jesus from the dead is available and at work in the lives of all disciples (Rom. 8:9-11). The same power that split the Red Sea (Exod. 14) and the Jordan River (Joshua 3) is available to all who call upon the name of the Lord (Rom. 10:13, Phi. 4:13).

He is at work to **help** to drown our enemies, sin, death, and hell now. He did that in part at Calvary, where Christ took the punishment we deserve (1 Pet. 2:24). He continues to be at work in the lives of His people now as they grow in conformity to His image (Rom. 8:29 Phil. 2:13).

God is a saving God (Ti 2:13) and is the **God of salvation** to all who call upon His name (Ps. 86:5, Jl 2:23, Acts 2:21, Rom. 10:13). He demonstrated His saving work as early as the Garden of Eden when He covered Adam and Even when they sinned (Gen. 3). He showed that when He had Noah build an ark for his family to protect them from the floodwaters (Gen. 6-9). He demonstrated that when He raised up Joseph to deliver His brothers (Gen. 39-50). He demonstrated that when He used Moses and Aaron to bring Israel out of Egypt with a mighty and an outstretched arm (Exod.

3-12). He demonstrated that when Joshua valiantly led Israel into enemy territory. He demonstrated that when He kept providing for Israel as they kept sinning against Him in the wilderness. He demonstrated that when He kept sending judges to deliver them when they kept falling into sin and crying out for deliverance. He did **not leave or forsake** them.

Now, believers are tempted on every side. The world's allurements are perhaps more potent than ever before to lead any and all astray apart from divine intervention. But God sheds His love abroad in our hearts (Rom. 5:5) and helps us realize that the temporal satisfaction this world promises and fails to deliver will never satisfy us as only He can. When we stop pursuing contentment in things that perish and find the One who will never perish, not only do we find happiness and true contentment, we find salvation, righteousness, and rescue from certain doom.

**Questions for self-reflection:**

(1) What cares of this life seem to most strongly wrestle with God for first place in your life? How can you keep those cares at bay?

(2) Have you ever experienced what you now understand to be discipline from the Lord? Looking back on such discipline situations, have you had the privilege of seeing that, while it was unpleasant to endure, that it was beneficial and necessary that you do endure it?

(3) In what ways has your life shown that a disciple is like his Master?

(4) How has God shown you that He longs to have a relationship with you and the rest of those created in His image?

(5) In what ways have your trials shown you that God has had compassion on you?

(6) When has God drawn you with bands of love back to the narrow way of devotion to Him?

**27:10. When my father and my mother forsake me, Then the Lord will take care of me.**

---

When all sources of earthly help seem to fall by the wayside and cease to be a help to the psalmist here and to the believer in every generation by extension, the believer in every age has a recurring responsibility to remember that **the Lord** will continue to **take care of** them and provide for all their needs (Phil. 4:19). The difficulty for believers is distinguishing needs from wants. Many times, what we consider to be a need is merely a want. God promises to provide for our needs. God does not necessarily promise to provide for our wants, though God is very kind to provide for many of our wants (Ps. 68:19). God always knows better than us what is better for us and what we will be most responsible to receive by His permission. He knows if we will be good stewards of the gifts He bestows upon us (Matt. 6:8, Matt. 6:25-33).

We will always have people we depend on (Eccles. 4:9-12). Such people are imperfect sinners like us (Romans 3:9-23). If we put our total confidence in them, they will let us down (Ps. 146:3). God, on the other hand, is not imperfect. He knows no sin (1 Pet. 2:22). There is no darkness in Him (1 John 1:5). He is holy (Isaiah 6:3). We are unholy (1 Tim.1:9-10). He is loving (Rom. 5:8). We are unloving (1 Tim. 1:10). His justice is perfect (Rom. 2:2). Our justice is biased in our favor and against our neighbor (Rom. 2:3). Our love is imperfect, oftentimes based on partiality (Jas 2:1-13). His love is perfect (1 Jn 4:18). He will never let us down, even if we do not understand how He is working or what He is doing. When we feel forsaken, we can feel unprotected. Under God's care, we are always protected.

The Lord always will take care of His people. If He failed to do what is best for His people at any time, we could no longer say that He is good. But He is good (Rom. 2:4). Goodness is part of His very nature. It is His goodness that sets Him apart from us, His finite, sinful creatures. His goodness allows the rain to fall on the just and the unjust (Matt. 5:45) and take care of all. His goodness will enable Him to send food for the animal kingdom and then have the fields' herbs, and the animals provide for mankind. Mankind can look at the animal kingdom, see how God is at work behind the scenes to provide for and take care of them, and, from that, deduce that it is good for man to trust God to provide for us as well (Matt. 6:25-33). He knows what we need before we ask (Matt. 6:8). He can do above and beyond what we could ever ask or think about (Eph. 3:20-21).

We can see how the Lord has come through for us in times past while those close to us (father and mother) had not forsaken us. Surely it becomes easy to believe and understand that He will continue to come through and care for us into the present and future. He will continue to do so even when those we had previously relied upon do **forsake** us. Since the Lord does not change (Mal. 3:6), since He is the same yesterday, today, and forever (Heb. 13:8), nobody will be able to take care of us as well as the Lord can since nobody knows us as well as the Lord does (Jer. 1:5, Nah. 1:7).

#### Questions for self-reflection:

(1) Have you ever felt like you were the only one who cared about what the Lord thought on a matter?
(2) How do you distinguish needs from wants?
(3) Would you consider yourself to be a good steward of what God has entrusted to your care? Why or why not?
(4) Have you ever been let down by someone you had trusted?
(5) Have you ever let someone down who had placed trust in you?
(6) Even when we do not get what we ask for from God, why can we still say that God is good?

**27:11. Teach me Your way, O Lord, And lead me in a smooth path, because of my enemies.**

---

Because the **Lord** puts the Holy Spirit into His people, genuine believers (1 Cor. 6:19), He teaches them the **way** because the Holy Spirit leads believers into all truth (Jn 16:13). The believer who possesses the Holy Spirit, which is informed by the renewed mind (Rom. 12:2), becomes more acquainted with the way of the Lord as the Lord reveals Himself to the person that pursues the Lord (Jer. 29:13).

Scripture outlines the way of the Lord (2 Tim. 3:16). Scripture shows believers how the Lord reveals Himself, works on behalf of His people, and how He works against His enemies from every generation. They see that the way of the Lord is to follow Him in holy reverence (1 Pet. 3:15). It is to honor Him with the lips and the life. It is not to worship in vain (Matt. 15:8) but to worship in Spirit and truth (Jn 4:24). The way of the Lord is to have no other gods before Him (Exod. 20:3). The Lord's way is to entrust oneself to the Lord Jesus Christ completely. This type of trust includes persevering belief (Jn 3:16) that everything He has told us is true and worth following (Jn 8:31-32). The way of the Lord is the highway of holiness (Isaiah 35:8). The Lord's way is to abstain from fornication (1 Thess. 4:3). The Lord's way is to walk by the Spirit and not give in to the flesh (Gal. 5:16). The way of the Lord is the way of persecution (2 Tim. 3:12).

Enemies are all around the people of the Lord. The whole world lies under the sway of the wicked one (1 Jn 5:19) and, as such, the enemies of the Lord, the soldiers of Satan, often yell louder than do the righteous and often get their way in society at the expense of the righteous. Because the Lord's **enemies** surround and engulf the Lord's people in society, the people of the Lord need the Lord to **teach** them His **way** and to **lead** them in a **smooth path**. The smooth path is not necessarily the path of least conflict. On the contrary, the path of the Lord can be the path of the most conflict as the world and its philosophy is strongly opposed to God and His philosophy. The world is at enmity with

God (Jas 4:4). However, the path of the Lord is the smooth path because the Lord's path is perfect for believers to follow because the Lord has no darkness (1 Jn 1:5) and would create a path that was anything less than ideal. This path is the path of life (Ps. 16:11). This path is the path of righteousness (Rom. 4:5). This path is the path of forgiveness (Eph. 1:7). This path is the path of redemption (Eph. 1:7). This path is the path of freedom (Gal. 5:1). This path is needed to overcome the wicked one and not have fear in life or death. True believers find this path and ultimately stay on this path because the power of God in salvation is the same power that keeps them (1 Pet. 1:3-5).

## Questions for self-reflection:

(1) How does the Lord teach us His ways now?
(2) How has the Lord personally taught you His ways?
(3) How have some of your old ways had to be corrected by the Holy Spirit's new ways?
(4) How do the enemies of the Lord and the Lord's people make it harder for the Lord's people to learn the Lord's ways?
(5) How is the Lord's path smooth, even in the face of the Lord's enemies?

**27:12. Do not deliver me to the will of my adversaries; For false witnesses have risen against me, And such as breathe out violence.**

---

When Satan's army compasses about a believer (Ps. 17:9), it can make life for the believer treacherous. Satan is the roaring lion seeking to devour everyone (1 Pet. 5:8). Even though he cannot take away the salvation of the Lord in the life of a true believer (Rom. 8:38-39), the devil can potentially affect a believer and render them ineffective if they are not prepared (Gen. 3, Job 1-2, Eph. 6:10-18, Jas 4:7). While the Lord fights for His people (Deut. 1:30, Josh. 1:5), His people are not immune to ever being affected by Satan and the forces he employs. Since the enemies of God work for Satan (1 Jn 5:19), whether they realize it or not, they are a host of powerful **adversaries**. The Lord is more powerful than and is sovereign over them (Mk 1:27). He allows them to have as much influence as they do and permits them to live as long as they do. As strong as the Satanic influence in the world seems at times, the believer can trust that the Lord knows best and the Lord works everything according to the counsel of His own **will** (Eph. 1:11) and for the believer's good (Rom. 8:28).

Another unseen enemy of believers is their sinful flesh that wars against their Spirit (Galatians 5:17). They have to crucify the flesh (Gal. 5:24) and remember God's truth when temptation comes (1 Cor. 10:13) and tries to take them off the narrow way (Matt. 7:13), even if only for a moment. It is only with sanctified hearts (1 Pet. 3:15), renewed minds (Rom. 12:2), and proper motivation (1 Cor. 10:31) that the Lord's people, humanly speaking, can remain faithful. On the divine side of things, the Lord is at work mightily on behalf of His people to make them doers of His will (Matt. 7:21-23) and cause them to work and to will for His good pleasure (Phi. 2:12-13).

One of the ways the adversaries of the Lord and His people **have risen against** the work of the Lord is to **breathe out violence** and spread lies about the Lord or the Lord's people. This adversarial agenda should not surprise the student of Scripture since they would know that Jesus said that Satan is the Father of Lies (Jn 8:44). Since the beginning, Satan has been a liar (Gen. 3:4). Adam and Eve were the first to fall to his devices, and countless multitudes have followed in their steps ever since.

For the psalmist, perhaps the **false witnesses** lied and said that David was trying to harm the Lord's anointed, Saul. This was not true because there were times when David could have killed Saul, but David chose not to in an act of obedience to the Lord (1 Sam. 24-28). In the time of Jesus' first coming, people lied about what He had said and done in an effort to see their wicked goal carried out (e.g., Matt. 28:11-15). Since the world opposes God and His agenda (Rom. 8:7-8), since the world is not subject to God's Law because their minds are against God, it is not surprising that enemies' lies frequently encroach upon believers in the gospel.

The violence that comes from the enemies of God comes in words and actions, and it will continue and get worse until believers are in eternity (Matt. 24). The words that were spoken against the Lord during His earthly ministry during His first coming were words of violence. Those words expressed against His apostles were also words of violence. According to church history, as it was with the Lord, and each apostle, save John, who was exiled on Patmos, their lives each met a violent martyr's end. Church history is stained with the blood of martyrs. All over the world, those who oppose God breathe out violence to snuff out Christians. The efforts will ultimately fail because the gates of hell will not prevail against the Lord Jesus Christ (Matt. 16:18). God has ordained that His people stand out as lights in a dark world (Phil. 2:15). Likewise, God has ordained that He would use the foolishness of the message preached (1 Cor. 1:18) to save them that believe by the power of the gospel (Rom. 1:16).

**Questions for self-reflection:**

(1) How have you seen Satan render believers ineffective in their service to the Lord?

(2) How does knowing that the Lord allows Satan and his army to have the influence that they do encourage you?

(3) What disciplines and routines have you adopted or can you begin to adopt to help you crucify the flesh?

(4) How have the wicked one's forces risen against the Lord and His people and breathed out violence against the Lord and His people?

(5) How does your life stand out as one that has separated from the world?

**27:13. I would have lost heart, unless I had believed That I would see the goodness of the Lord In the land of the living.**

When the enemies of believers seem to have the upper hand in society as their voice seems the loudest and appears to successfully drown out that of the believers, it is understandable for the believer to focus on the present circumstances that elicit anxious responses. It is not difficult to see why even the most faithful believer can lose sight of the God that fights for them (Josh. 1:5) and is sovereign over their unpleasant circumstances (Rom. 8:28).

For the psalmist, false witnesses rose up against him. For present-day believers, at least in some parts of the world, it is more likely that there will be verbal opposition and less likely physical violence perpetrated against God's people (Matt. 5:11, 2 Tim. 3:12). That only speaks of persecutions from enemies. It says nothing of the hardships related to health, finances, or families. Even when viewing difficulties with eyes of faith and when taking every thought captive to the obedience of Christ, the believer can misunderstand the trials of life. Believers can misunderstand trials as being a punishment from the Lord (Heb. 12:3-11) rather than a test employed by the Lord as an instrument of growth in the lives of His children (Jas 1:2-8).

When the trials get so severe, it can feel to the redeemed that God has lost interest in them. No wonder some believers **have lost heart**. This losing of heart happens because we often give undue attention to our afflictions at the expense of the attention our Lord deserves. This happened to Peter when he looked down at the water. Instead, Peter should have continued to look at His Lord (Matt. 14:31). It is impossible to seek first His kingdom (Matt. 6:33) if we are too focused on making our own kingdoms more pleasant.

Believers can also be tempted to lose heart when it feels like their efforts at continuing the race (Heb. 12:1) and fighting the good fight of faith (1 Tim. 6:12) in their immediate circles is not reciprocated by those they are attempting to reach. Just because the believer lives the quiet and peaceable life God commands them to live in society (1 Tim. 2:2) does not mean that their neighbor will want to live at peace with them (Rom. 12:17-21). Just because they lay down their lives (Rom. 12:1) and pour out themselves like a drink offering (2 Tim. 4:6) for their unbelieving spouse or child does not mean that the loved one will come to saving faith (1 Pet. 3:1-7). That is up to the mystery of divine sovereignty and human responsibility. If the believer replaces feelings of godly contentment (1 Tim. 6:6) with fleshly entitlement (Rom. 8:8), bitterness can erupt and plague the saint and those they frequently contact (Eph. 4:31, Hebrews 12:15).

Believers can also faint when they get weighed down and overwhelmed by their own indwelling sin (Rom. 7:13-25, Heb. 12:1). They forget that there is no longer any condemnation for them (Rom. 8:1). They forget that even the beloved apostle Paul saw himself as a wretched man (Rom. 7:24) as he continually had to wage war in the Spirit against the flesh that fought with the Spirit for the place of preeminence in his life (Gal. 5:17). If that were true of arguably the most influential writer of Scripture, how much more should we expect it to be true of us!

Believers in these moments of weakness forget the precious promises handed down in the inspired Word include that when we sin, our glorious Advocate ever lives to intercede for us (1 Jn 1:6-2:2). His purification of our sins (Heb. 1:3) once for all (Hebrews 10:10) was a one-time act with lasting results. His performance of the saving work in our lives does not depend on our faithfulness, for when we are faithless, He remains faithful (2 Tim. 2:13). The blessings that the Lord showers believers with at justification remain theirs all through sanctification and into glorification (Rom. 8:28-31, Eph. 1:3-14). It is also possible for believers to pray for circumstances to change and for those circumstances not to change. If the believer fails to look at the undesired result from the eternal perspective, they can miss the lesson God has for them. Just because they did not get the answer they wanted does not mean that they did not get the best answer for them. No matter the answer, God's grace is sufficient, and His power is made great in our weakness (2 Cor. 12:7-10).

The believer must remember that they serve a good God, and nothing can change that. This means that nothing that happens to them, however unpleasant as it might seem, for the time being, does not change the fact that God remains good even as He allows us to experience circumstances that we would call anything other than good. This good God (Luke 18:19) hears our murmuring (Exod. 3:7, Exod. 16:12). Yet He still abundantly blesses us with all the necessities of life just like He did for Israel in the wilderness when He supplied them with water from a rock (Exod. 17:1-7, Num. 20:1-13), bread from heaven (Exod. 16:1-36), and quail (Exod. 16:11-13). This good God protects us from our enemies as long as it is His will to do so.

This good God planned from eternity past to send forth His Son made of a woman made under the law to give His people the adoption of children and make us heirs rather than enemies (Gal. 4:4-5). While believers remain in the land of the living, God makes known the mystery of His will (Eph. 1:9) to them that, as they renew their minds (Rom. 12:2) and come before the throne of grace (Heb. 4:16), as they do not forsake the assembling (Heb. 10:25), they are less conformed to the world and more conformed into His image (Rom. 12:2). This good God blesses us with every spiritual blessing (Eph. 1:3-14). This good God will never leave us or forsake us even when sin and trials heavily weigh us down (Heb. 13:5). When this truth, the truth of who God is, is constantly before us, it is harder for us to miss the reality **that the goodness of the Lord** is before us **in the land of the living.**

### Questions for self-reflection:

(1) As you look at the society in which you live, what do you see that could tempt people, even you, to lose heart?
(2) What are some good Bible promises to remember when we are tempted to lose heart?
(3) How can you tell the hardships in life are mere trials and not discipline for sin?

(4) How can you keep from putting too much undue influence on your adverse circumstances while keeping your eyes on the Lord?

(5) How can you keep from becoming embittered by circumstances that do not change to your preference?

(6) How have you seen God provide for you even in adversity?

**27:14. Wait on the Lord; Be of good courage, And He shall strengthen your heart; Wait, I say, on the Lord!**

The psalmist has seen the Lord's goodness in various settings (Ps. 27:13) in his own life and the lives of others. Consequently, the psalmist knew that it benefited him to **wait on the Lord** even though he felt tempted to lose heart because enemies that make life difficult surrounded him (Ps. 118:10-12, Rev. 20:9). The Lord lets the rain fall on the just and the unjust as part of the blessings of common grace (Matt. 5:45). So then, most assuredly, there is mercy for the saved that the psalmist can receive from the hand of the Lord. There have been times when the psalmist cried out to the Lord for mercy and help in time of need, and in those times, the Lord had shown Himself to be faithful (Heb. 4:15-16). The psalmist knew deep down that he could count on the Lord to come through for him once again. He knew that God was a promise-making God as well as a promise-keeping God (Num. 23:19). As such, the psalmist knew that God's character would require Him to keep His promises to His own. He knew that while He waited on the Lord, while that might tempt him to impatience from time to time as difficulty in his life persisted, he could not take matters into his own hands but had to wait on the Lord to provide in the Lord's own way of delivering (Jas 1:2-8).

Even if we don't feel like we get what we want from the Lord in a specific situation, we receive better than we deserve. That is grace. The Lord, who goes before His people and leads them in their battles, can help His people overcome any enemy (Exod. 13:21, Exod. 14:19, Num. 14:14, Deut. 1:30, Deut. 1:33, Deut. 31:8, 2 Sam. 5:24, Ps. 136:16, Is. 45:2, Is. 52:12. Jn 14:2-3). Therefore, saints in every generation can **be of good courage** and know that the God of the universe is on their side, so they have nothing to fear (Ps. 118:6). The saints have indwelling sin that causes issues in this life and a severe struggle between the Spirit and the flesh (Rom. 7:13-25, Gal. 5:17). While they are wretches who need deliverance from this body of death, they can trust that, one day, incorruption will replace corruption because of the salvation that is theirs in Jesus Christ (1 Cor. 15:50-58).

While Satan is alive and well now wreaking havoc in this world (1 Jn 5:19), believers can trust that the accuser of the brethren (Rev. 12:10), who has the whole world under his sway, is still only permitted to influence the world because God lets him do so (Jb 1-2). The devil always will be God's devil. God gives His children the resources to overcome temptation and resist the devil so that he will flee from them (1 Cor.10:13, Jas 4:6-8). He has given them faith which is the victory that overcomes the world (1 Jn 5:4). In Christ, they are more than conquerors (Rom. 8:37). God is at work in them to will and to do His good pleasure as they work out their own salvation (Phil. 2:12-13). The Lord has an entire army of angels at His disposal to work on behalf of His people. While the devil has a whole army of demonic forces at his disposal to do his bidding (Matt. 26:53, Eph. 6:12), God will ultimately cast the devil into the lake of fire (Rev. 20:10) and put all His enemies under His feet (1 Cor. 15:26-27).

He has given His people armor that they can successfully avail themselves of and wage the spiritual battle they were born into (Eph. 6:10-20). While God calls believers to be soldiers (2 Tim. 2:3-4), their Captain (Heb. 2:10) is the best leader they could ever have and will always lead them down the correct path (Ps. 23:2). Those that wait on the Lord can trust that the Lord will **strengthen** their **hearts** so that they can continue to serve Him all their days (Isa. 40:31).

## Questions for self-reflection:

(1) When have you been in situations when you could not change circumstances yourself but instead had to wait on the Lord?
(2) Do you implicitly trust the Lord to come through for you consistently?
(3) Have you ever not received the response that you had hoped for from the Lord but still felt content with that result?

(4) How does knowing that Satan is still submissive to God help you trust God better?
(5) How have you seen God work in you to will and to do His good pleasure?
(6) When in the furnace of affliction, how has God strengthened you to do His will?

# Psalm 28

**28:1. "To You I will cry, O Lord my Rock: Do not be silent to me, Lest, if You are silent to me, I become like those who go down to the pit."**

---

The psalmist lifts his **cry** to the **Lord**, the **Rock**, the redeemer of Israel, and people from every tribe, tongue, and nation (Rev. 7:9). Circumstances in the psalmist's life left the psalmist desperate for the Lord's help. When we find ourselves in distress from circumstances beyond our control, those that we cannot change by our own efforts, it becomes more natural for us to go to the Lord persistently, knowing that if He chooses to change our circumstances, it is in the best interest of His plan for our lives that that be done. If it is not in our best interests for His glory and kingdom that our circumstances change, but instead, if it is in our best spiritual interest for our own personal growth that our circumstances remain burdensome so that we will cling to the Rock that is higher than we (Ps. 61:2), trusting fully in Him, then we may stay in hardship. If we do so while allowing the Lord to have His way in us, then we will be weaned from the world and conformed to the image of the Lord (Rom. 12:2).

As our Rock, the Lord is our strong tower and defender. We have ultimate spiritual safety in Him. For this, we can count ourselves blessed to experience a taste of the sufferings that our Lord endured (Matt. 5:10-12, 2 Cor. 4:11, Phil. 1:29, Phil. 3:12, 2 Tim. 3:12, Heb. 11:25, Jas 5:10, 1 Pet. 3:14, 1 Pet. 4:16, 1 Pet. 5:10). If our Shepherd suffered, His sheep should expect to suffer. When we do face afflictions of various types, we can cry to Him and know that He hears us (2 Chr. 7:14, Ps. 4:3, Ps. 17:6, Ps. 18:6, Ps. 34:6, Ps. 34:15-17, Ps. 66:17-20, Ps. 145:18, Prov. 15:29, Isa. 65:24, Jer. 33:3, Matt. 7:7, Mk 11:24, Jn 9:31, Jn 16:24, Heb. 4:16, Jas 1:5-8, Jas 5:16-17, 1 Pet. 3:12, 1 Jn 1:9, 1 Jn 5:14-15). When we cry to Him, He will be strong for us when we are weak because when we are weak, He is strong (2 Cor. 12:10). While we change, he does not change (Malachi 3:6). We can trust him because we are like the waves going to and fro with the wind (John 3:8, Ephesians 4:14). He is the Rock that cannot be moved (Deut. 32:4, Ps. 62:6). In Him, we

---

are on the Rock and will not be moved. Our status before Him cannot change (Matt. 10:27-28). None can pluck us from His hands.

The psalmist had anxiety about his circumstances and asked the Lord to hear him when he cried to Him. When a saint cries to the Lord about adverse circumstances, they sometimes ask the Lord to change the events. For reasons known only to the Lord, those circumstances may not change. Despite the persistent hardship, believers understand that the Lord is there (2 Cor. 12:7-10). Those same believers expect the Lord to act in a certain way on their behalf. When He does not act in the way that they expect or desire, those believers can feel disillusioned by the apparent absence of the Lord. They interpret this lack of change to the present distress as the Lord having gone **silent**. They think He has forsaken them. In reality, the Lord truly has not gone silent to His people, even if it feels that way to His people at times.

A difference between the saved and the lost is that the saved have the Lord that they can go to in times of trouble, whereas the lost do not. The Lord is always silent to the lost (Prov. 15:29). They are **like those that go down to the pit**. There is no hope for them (Eph. 2:12). The saved can know that the Lord can pull them out of a pit if they fall into a pit. The lost have no such reason for optimism. In fact, the lost dig their own pits by their habitual choices to live for themselves rather than for the Lord and for others (Ps. 7:15). Should they go to the pit, the grave, there will be no rescue for them without taking refuge in the Lord Jesus Christ. There will be no salvation (Acts 4:12). There will only be the eternal wrath that they spent their lives storing up for themselves (Rom. 2:5). The preaching of the cross was foolishness to them (1 Cor. 1:18). Once they are in the Lake of Fire (Rev. 20:11-15, Revelation 21:8), it won't seem so foolish, but then it will be too late.

**Questions for self-reflection:**

(1) How has the Lord shown Himself to be a worthwhile rock for you to cling to?

(2) Have you ever experienced circumstances like the psalmist where you felt desperate for help from the Lord?

(3) If you have ever been in a circumstance that did not change for a long time, or perhaps never even did, as time went on, did it get any easier for you to trust in the Lord through the difficulty? Why or why not?

(4) Does knowing that the Lord knows your afflictions and hears you when you call to Him bring you comfort?

(5) Have you ever felt like the Lord was absent in your circumstances? What can you do to remind yourself that He is not absent?

**28:2. Hear the voice of my supplications When I cry to You, When I lift up my hands toward Your holy sanctuary.**

As the psalmist besought the Lord for the help that only the Lord could provide, the psalmist knew that he was utterly dependent upon the Lord to **hear** his **supplications** (Prov. 3:5-6). The psalmist knew that he was unworthy, and for the Lord to act on his behalf would be entirely a work of divine benevolence on the Lord's behalf. If the Lord was going to intervene on behalf of the psalmist, then the psalmist would have to entrust himself to the Lord fully. The psalmist would have to be willing to repeatedly avail Himself to the throne of grace (Heb. 4:16) and **cry to** the Lord as the Lord may not respond to the psalmist in the way that the psalmist preferred or as quickly as the psalmist might like.

The psalmist would lift his requests to the Lord in the physical location where God's presence came to dwell. New Testament believers are the temple of Christ (Rom. 8:6, 1 Cor. 3:16, 1 Cor. 6:19, 2 Cor. 6:16, Heb. 3:6). The fulness of God is at work in them (Ephesians 3:19). The power of God that raised Jesus Christ from the dead (Acts 2:24, Acts 2:32, Acts 3:15, Rom. 8:11, 1 Cor. 6:14, 2 Cor. 4:14, Eph. 1:20) works powerfully in believers as Christ dwells in them by faith (Eph. 3:17). When believers come before God humbly because they have been granted access by the finished work of the Lord Jesus Christ (Rom. 5:2, Eph. 2:18), the Lord answers and acts according to His will when believers ask according to God's will (1 Jn 5:14).

Believers may perceive that the Lord does not act (Ps. 10:1). That is not true. The perceived lack of an answer may be the Lord waiting or drawing out a response of perseverance from His child. The psalmist was one to **lift up** his **hands** in prayer. This was a common prayer custom in the Biblical era (Exod. 9:33, 1 Kgs 8:54, 2 Chron. 6:29-30, Neh. 8:6, Jb 11:13, Ps. 63:4, Lam. 3:41, 1 Tim. 2:8). When the believer lifts up the holy hands in prayer or in worship, it is as if they are reaching up to God, **toward** His **holy sanctuary,** and asking God to reach back out to them. It is a sign of longing for God's sustaining and strengthening presence in life. Here, the psalmist trusted that if he reached up, God would reach back. He had a strong trust in the Lord.

## Questions for self-reflection:

(1) What causes you to doubt that the Lord hears your supplications?

(2) How can you demonstrate complete trust in the Lord even if the Lord does not grant the request you ask for in the manner you ask for it?

(3) Does knowing that the fullness of God is at work in you help you to boldly, yet humbly, face your trials with faith-filled confidence?

(4) Do you long for God's sustaining and strengthening presence in your life?

**28:3. Do not take me away with the wicked And with the workers of iniquity, Who speak peace to their neighbors, But evil is in their hearts.**

---

Outwardly **wicked** people surrounded the psalmist. Such people opposed God because they were friends of the world and enemies of God (Jas 4:4). They had inwardly evil dispositions that produced outwardly wicked actions (Matt. 15:18-20). As they gave themselves over to a reprobate mind, God gave them up to a reprobate mind (Rom. 1:28). The psalmist asked God to keep him from following in their sinful footsteps. He asked God for grace to stay on the narrow road that leads to life that few find (Matt. 7:13-14).

The psalmist knew that temptation to follow his sinful flesh would come. He asked for wisdom and grace to overcome the temptation and maintain his fellowship with the Lord and his testimony (1 Cor. 10:13). He asked to be protected against the devices of the wicked so that the difference between him and them would be observable. He wanted his light to shine before the wicked so that they would see his good works, and it would lead to them glorifying God in heaven (Matt. 5:16). He knew that if God did not protect him, his enemies would have their way with him, possibly including his death.

If the psalmist could set his mind on things above, he could remain morally separated from his enemies and give His God glory by his different lifestyle (Colossians 3:1-3). He could point others to His God by His righteous conduct (1 Jn 2:29). He could prove that God had imputed righteousness to him (Rom. 4:5). Saving faith is demonstrated by righteous works.

The workers of iniquity were not affected by God's law like the psalmist was (Rom. 8:7). Even though God had written His law on their hearts as He does with everyone else (Rom. 2:15), they did not subject themselves to it. The God of the psalmist put too many limitations on their fun and freedom. They would rather not submit to God, resist the devil, and have the devil flee from them (Jas 4:7). Among these **workers of iniquity**, there may even be some who outwardly identified with religion but whose hearts lacked the reality of saving faith (2 Tim. 3:5). The Lord Jesus Christ spoke to this issue, as did the apostle Paul.

These workers of iniquity would **speak peace to their neighbors** or say the right things to get on the good side of the people over which they had influence. However, they had ulterior motives that were anything but pure. Their religion, or lack thereof, was anything but pure and undefiled (Jas 1:27). They proved they had **evil in their hearts**. They spoke lying, flattering words to the face of the hearers but secretly took advantage of them. In every era, God's people have had to be on high alert for savage wolves that would not spare the flock who make their way into churches and homes and destroy the faith of others (Acts 20:29). Therefore, they must renew their minds (Rom. 12:2), set their minds on things above (Col. 3:1-3), and seek first God's kingdom (Matt. 6:33), trusting that as they work out their salvation with fear and trembling that God is at work in them (Phil. 2:12-13).

## Questions for self-reflection:

(1) How can you protect yourself against being taken away with the wicked and with the workers of iniquity?

(2) If you work hard at hiding God's Word in your heart that you might not sin against Him, how might that help you recognize if someone has evil in their hearts and is trying to get you to stumble in your faith?

(3) How do you recognize the workers of iniquity in the sea of the outwardly religious? In other words, there are vast numbers of people who associate with Christ visibly, but their faith is not genuine. See Matthew 7:15-23. How can you recognize such people?

(4) As a believer, how would you respond if someone you thought you knew to be a believer turned out to undermine you and your faith behind your back? For example, if they spoke peace but had evil in their hearts, what would you do if you found out? How would you be able to maintain your testimony?

**28:4. Give them according to their deeds, And according to the wickedness of their endeavors; Give them according to the work of their hands; Render to them what they deserve.**

The psalmist asks the Lord to repay the wicked according to their works. Scripture promises that the Lord will repay people according to their works (Rom. 2:6-11). Reaping and sowing are guaranteed (Gal. 6:7-10). Everyone has sinned, and everyone has earned death (Rom. 3:23, Rom. 6:23). In that sense, everyone will be given wages according to their sinful deeds. However, in the immediate context, the psalmist asks the Lord to give the wicked an appropriate response for their wicked works. Even in the New Testament, it was not considered unacceptable for God to repay good with reward and evil with punishment (2 Tim. 2:14).

The **deeds and** the **hands** of the wicked are full of wickedness. It is reasonable for a just God to **render to them what they deserve**. The justified saint does not properly wish harm for harm's sake on his enemy. The justified saint knows that God will balance the scales in this life or the next life. He asks for God to accomplish His will in an adverse situation. Saints trust that God will do so. Even if the wicked are unsuccessful at accomplishing their wicked **endeavors**, God still holds them accountable for their intentions, and He will repay them **according to their wickedness** (Gen. 6:5, Gen. 8:2, 1 Sam. 16:7, Ps. 19:14, Ps. 26:2, Ps. 44:21, Ps. 139:4, Prov. 4:23, Prov. 16:2, Prov. 21:2, Prov. 27:19, Eccles.12:14, Jer. 12:3, Jer. 17:9-10, Matt. 5:8, Matt. 6:21, Matt. 12:34-37, Matt. 15:18-20, Mk 7:21, Acts 1:24, Acts 28:27, 1 Thess. 2:4, 1 Tim. 1:5, Heb. 4:12-13, Rev. 2:23).

## Questions for self-reflection:

(1) When you see wickedness running rampant around you, does your heart long for heaven where the evil will be no more, or would you rather stay here on this depraved earth so long as the wickedness affects you as little as possible? Why did you answer the way you did?

(2) Do you have a hard time reconciling how a good God can punish anyone regardless of how wicked they and their works are? Why or why not?

(3) How comforting is it to know that, even if the wicked are not seemingly held accountable in this life, they will be held responsible in the next life?

**28:5. Because they do not regard the works of the Lord, Nor the operation of His hands, He shall destroy them And not build them up.**

---

The psalmist asks the Lord to repay the wicked according to their evil deeds, which they commit **because they do not regard the works of the Lord**. Rather than submit to Him as Creator and Lord, they think that nothing created everything. They see no need to submit to God and resist the devil, so he will flee from them (Jas 4:7) because they do not understand that the Son was the agent of Creation (Hebrews 1:2). They think that random chaotic mutations created all this order. There must be a first cause to what we see. Not only does the wicked reject God's work of creation (Gen. 1:1, Col. 1:16, 2 Pet. 3:4), the wicked also does not regard the works of the Lord concerning His judgments against sin (2 Pet. 3:10-11). They perhaps think that there are two gods, one god is a 'God of the Old Testament' who is mean and vindictive, and all He does is punish. The other is this supposed 'God of the New Testament,' otherwise known as the 'God of Love,' who would never punish anyone because He is too loving. This 'New Testament God' has no holiness or righteousness. This God is more effeminate than He is God-like. They fail to acknowledge that the Lord says about Himself that He does not change (Mal. 3:6) and that Jesus Christ is always the same (Heb. 13:8). Ask Ananias and Sapphira if the God of the New Testament is all-loving and if He will not punish anyone (Acts 5). Ask the Romans if God who commends His love toward us (Rom. 5:8) is also a God who reveals His wrath (Rom. 1:18).

Sinners cannot pick which parts of God they like and reject the parts they do not like. Doing so would be to create a god in their own image and in their own likeness. This amounts to idolatry, and the idolatrous cannot inherit heaven (1 Cor. 6:9, Rev. 21:8). For the spiritually blind who exalt themselves against God's true knowledge, the preaching of the cross is foolishness to them because they are perishing (1 Cor. 1:18). God rejoices over His people to do them good (Deut. 28:63) while blessing them with every spiritual blessing (Eph. 1:3). God is angry with the wicked every day and whets His sword against them (Ps. 7:10-11). The same 'God of love' is also a 'God of justice.' Sinners must humble themselves before Him and take all of Him, or they will receive none of Him (1 Pet. 5:6).

The wicked do not regard as coming from God the things that God accomplishes hidden in His works of providence and the lives of His sheep (Rom. 8:28). Instead, they regard them as coming by mere chance. They do not attribute anything as being from **the operation of His hands.** Neither the good nor the bad that happen do they attribute to Him. Some would attribute the good that happens to God and the bad that happens to Satan, man, or something other than God. These reprobates attribute neither the good nor the bad to God. And, sadly, for those who choose this path, as they do not like to retain God as He has revealed Himself to us in Scripture and Creation in their knowledge, God gives them over to a reprobate mind (Rom. 1:28) and lets them freely pursue the path that they have chosen for themselves. Instead of seeking the Lord while He may be found (Isa. 55:6) because now is the accepted time and now is the day of salvation (2 Cor. 6:2), they are lulled to sleep by the intoxicating dainties that the world promises (Jas 4:4). They put their consciences to sleep and conduct themselves by man's law rather than God's law which, if they would let it, could be the schoolmaster that brings them to Christ (Gal. 3:24). They refuse to be subject to God's law (Rom. 8:7).

What they fail to acknowledge in this life, they will be forced to acknowledge in the next life. If they do not willingly bow to Him as Lord in this life, they will be forced to bow to Him in the next life. They will be one of the enemies that are under Christ's feet (1 Cor. 15:26-27) as His footstool (Ps. 110:1, Acts 2:35). If they do not acknowledge Him as Savior and Lord in this life, they will have to acknowledge Him as Lord and Judge in the next life. They will be weeping and gnashing their teeth (Matt. 8:12, Matt. 22:13, Matt. 25:30, Lk 13:28) in the lake that burns with fire and brimstone (Rev. 19:20, Rev. 20:10, Rev. 21:8). The smoke of their torment will rise before God's throne night and day, and they will never rest (Rev. 14:11). All this happens because they failed to submit to God (Jas 4:7) and love Him back after He first loved them (1 Jn 4:19). God is entirely fair and just to **destroy them and not build them up.** After all, He has provided them with everything they need to come to Him. He has given them a conscience so that they know the difference between right and wrong and has written His law on their hearts, so they are without excuse (Rom. 1:20, Rom. 2:15). He has created a world that has His fingerprints throughout it to show them that He is there. But they did not like to retain God in their knowledge (Rom. 1:28), and that to their own peril.

**Questions for self-reflection:**

(1) Is it easy or hard for you to wait for the Lord to repay iniquity? Why or why not?
(2) Do you have a hard time reconciling how a good God can punish anyone regardless of how wicked they and their works are? Why or why not?
(3) How comforting is it to know that, even if the wicked are not seemingly held accountable in this life, they will be held responsible in the next life?
(4) What keeps the wicked from regarding the works of the Lord?
(5) How can we protect ourselves from having idolatrous thoughts about the Lord?
(6) Do you have difficulty reconciling the truth that the same God that is all-loving will also judge the wicked?

## 28:6. Blessed be the Lord, Because He has heard the voice of my supplications!

The psalmist appears to recount some of what he has previously said in the Psalm. In verse one, he asks the Lord not to be silent, to answer when he cries. Then in verse six, the psalmist praises the Lord for the answer that He graciously gave. In verse two, the psalmist lifts his requests to God intensely, knowing his utter dependence upon God. The psalmist, in verse three, admits that God's enemies, who are the same as the psalmist's enemies, were becoming too much for the psalmist to bear. So, the psalmist asks the Lord to sustain Him, not to be taken away with the wicked. He asks the Lord to give his enemies what they have coming to them (Gal. 6:7-8) so people like the psalmist can continue to be doers of the Word (Jas 1:22). He asks the Lord to react against the wicked because the wicked have reacted against the Lord. He sees evidence of how the Lord has answered his prayers in that the wicked were not as prosperous as they once were. So, the Lord was working on behalf of His people and stopping the prosperity of the wicked.

The Lord answered the psalmist's request (Phil. 4:6). **The Lord had heard the voice of** the **supplications** of the psalmist. For that, the psalmist breaks out in a doxology of the Lord. The psalmist admits that the Lord is great and can do all He pleases according to His holy will (Gen. 18:14, Jb 42:2, Jer. 32:17, Matt. 19:26, Mk 10:27, Lk 1:37). One of the Lord's means to carry out His will upon the earth is the prayers of the saints (2 Sam. 22:4, 2 Chron. 7:14, Ps. 3:4, Ps. 4:3, Ps. 17:6, Ps. 18:3, Ps 34:15, Ps. 34:17, Ps. 55:17, Ps. 65:2, Ps. 91:15, Ps. 116:1, Prov.15:29, Isa. 65:24, Jer. 33:3, Matt. 7:7, Matt. 21:22, Mk 11:24, Jn 14:13-14, Jn 15:7, Jn 16:23, Phil 4:6-7, 1 Tim. 2:1, Jas 1:5-8, Jas 5:16, 1 Pet. 3:12, 1 Jn 3:22, 1 Jn 5:14-15, Rev. 5:8). The saints know that, as long as they do not harbor iniquity in their hearts, that their Lord hears them and answers them according to His will (Ps. 66:18). Having received answers in the past, they trust that they will continue to receive answers in the present and into the future. He has heard, He does hear, and He will continue to hear the supplications of His own people.

## Questions for self-reflection:

(1) In addition to hearing our prayers (the voice of our supplications), what are some other reasons why we should bless the Lord?

(2) How have you seen the Lord sustain you against your spiritual enemies?

(3) How have you seen the Lord use your prayers or the prayers of others lifted up on your behalf used by the Lord to accomplish His will?

**28:7. The Lord is my strength and my shield; My heart trusted in Him, and I am helped; Therefore my heart greatly rejoices, And with my song I will praise Him.**

---

**The Lord** gives His people physical and spiritual **strength** to accomplish His will. The Lord blesses those who do not even know Him with the strength to do their own wills. The lost live as though they are accountable to nobody but themselves. They do not acknowledge that a God upholds all things, including them, by the Word of His power (Heb. 1:3). The lost do not retain God in their knowledge (Rom. 1:28). God gives strength to the same profligate people who do not know Him and actively rebel against Him. The Lord created the mind and put it in those created in His image (Gen. 1:27) so that it functions on a plane above those creatures who have minds but are not created in His image, namely the animal kingdom. Whether the man or woman, boy or girl, follows God with their life or not, it is inescapable that God permits them to live and permits them to choose to serve this day whom they will serve (Josh. 24:15). In that way, whether they realize it or not, the Lord is their strength.

Since the psalmist belonged to the Lord by faith, and since all believers in the Lord Jesus Christ belong to God through faith in Christ (Rom. 5:1, Gal. 2:20, Eph. 2:8-9, Eph. 2:18), each believer can say 'the Lord is my strength.' In Him, they live and move and have their being (Acts 17:28). In Him, all things, including themselves, consist (Col. 1:17). He knows the number of hairs on their heads (Lk 12:7). He knows the afflictions of His people and promises to be with them in their afflictions even if He does not remove their afflictions from them (2 Cor. 12:7-10). When God is with us, and for us, none can be against us (Rom. 8:31). When the Lord is on our side, man can do nothing to harm us (Psalm 118:6). Nothing can separate us from God's love (Rom. 8:38-39). When we are in His hand in that love relationship, none can pluck us from His hand (Jn 10:28-29). Believers understand that the Lord is the source of their physical and spiritual strength.

---

On the other hand, the lost have no such security. It is a fearful thing for them to fall into God's living hand (He. 10:31). They abide under His wrath (Jn 3:36). His sword is whetted against them (Ps. 7:11-16). The only reason He does not strike as they continue to spit in His face and refuse to acknowledge Him as the Lord that He is rich in mercy (Eph. 2:4) and wishes that none perish, but all come to repentance (2 Pet. 3:9).

For the saved, God is also their shield because their heart trusted in Him. By faith in the Lord Jesus Christ, the saved, by their continual **trust** in Him, are equipped with the armor of God, including the **shield** of faith to protect them from the fiery darts of the Wicked One that come from every side (Eph. 6:10-20). He is their shield and defender (Ps. 84:9-11), the Ancient of Days (Dan. 7:13). The saints are **helped** by trusting in the Lord as He provides them with what they need to live for Him. The Lord Jesus Christ shields His own from the wrath of God that abides upon the unbelieving (Jn 3:36, Rom 5:9) as it was Christ, the Lamb who was slain before the foundation of the world (Rev. 13:8), who took the wrath that they deserve.

God's holiness and righteousness were offended by our sin. Every soul that has ever lived, that was created in God's image, by their own choice, sinned against God and placed themselves, willingly under His wrath, condemned already (John 3:18) and made themselves dead in trespasses and sins (Eph 2:1). They are made alive and seated in heavenly places with Christ by faith in Him (Eph 2:5). With the Lord Jesus Christ as their advocate (1 Jn 2:1), they are helped. He continues to intercede (Heb 7:25) and propitiate (1 Jn 2:2) for them. Because the Lord continues to work on behalf of His called ones (Romans 8:28), the saved can continually rejoice (1 Thess. 5:16-17). They can rejoice that even if their soul and body were separated, they would be forever with the Lord (2 Cor. 5:8). They can rejoice because the worst that can happen to them in this life is the end of this life (Matt. 10:28).

The sorrow and sadness that mark this life will go by the wayside and will be replaced with joy inexpressible and full of glory (1 Peter 1:8) as the saints will be before the throne of God, casting their crowns at the feet of the One who loved them and gave Himself for them (Rev. 4:10-11). When sinners come to the Savior by faith, He gives them a new song with which they can praise Him. Their words and actions are done to the glory of God rather than to the glory of self (1 Cor. 10:31). Instead of being a vessel of wrath fit for destruction, they are a vessel of mercy suitable for heaven (Rom. 9:22-23). The Trinity, who planned for the salvation of sinners from eternity past before creation, makes all this possible. God the Father chose a body of believers, the church, to be in Christ before the foundation of the world, that they would be holy and blameless before Him (Eph. 1:4). God the Son, the Lord Jesus Christ, in the fullness of time (Gal. 4:4-5), humbled Himself (Phil. 2:8), lived a perfect life (1 Pet. 2:22), and became obedient to the death of the cross. God sent the Holy Spirit forth into the hearts of all believers (Galatians 4:6) whereby they can cry 'Abba Father' (Rom. 8:15) and can know the will of God for themselves as they renew their minds (Rom. 12:2) and esteem His Word more than their necessary food (Jb 23:12). As they abide in Him, He abides in them. They bear much fruit (Jn 15:1-8). In this way, He is their **help.** In this way, as He reveals Himself to them, as they seek Him, they find Him, and He reveals Himself to those who diligently seek Him (Heb. 11:6). As their relationship grows more intimate, they **greatly rejoice** with the **heart,** and their life becomes a **song** of **praise** to Him.

## Questions for self-reflection:

(1) What are some examples of spiritual strength the Lord has provided to you?

(2) What are some examples of physical strength the Lord has provided to you?

(3) Are any of the Scriptural passages in this paragraph an encouragement to you? Are there others not in the commentary for this verse that reminds you of the strength of the Lord?

(4) Do you find it more often than not easy or difficult to trust in the Lord? Why or why not?

(5) When was the last time you spent time thinking about any of the reasons that you have to rejoice? How often should believers rehearse some of those reasons if they want to have a healthier relationship with the Lord?

**28:8. The Lord is their strength, And He is the saving refuge of His anointed.**

---

Because **the Lord** has not been silent to the psalmist, the Lord has proven Himself worthy to be trusted by the psalmist. Because the Lord has intervened on the psalmist's behalf and demonstrated to the psalmist that He hears the supplications of His people, the Lord has proven Himself to be worthy of trust. While evil influences surrounded the psalmist on every side, the psalmist has entrusted Himself to the Lord and has kept the faith.

Because the Lord is a God of patience, He is very patient with those who reject Him (2 Pet. 3:9). He is also a God of justice. The day of patience will run out (2 Pet. 3:10-13). They will have to give an account (Matt. 12:36, Rom. 2:6). The Lord will repay them for their deeds. Reaping will take place for the sowing that has been done (Gal. 6:7-10). People who live in opposition to the God of the universe will have a style of life that one can quickly identify as divergent from theism, most notably historic Christianity. As the psalmist faced and as believers in all generations face this opposition, it was as if they were on a small raft tossing about on the ocean waves of ungodliness. In such difficulty, they can cry out to the Lord, trust that He hears them, and that He will intervene on their behalf when the time is right for Him to do so (Ps. 34:4, Ps. 118:5, Ps. 120:1).

The Lord is the protector of those who fear Him (2 Thess. 3:3). He is the helper to those who go to Him for that help. The psalmist can rejoice because of the help that the Lord provides. The Lord continues to work on His people's behalf while His people live out the salvation that is theirs because of the finished work of Christ (Phil. 2:12-13). As they do so, His people prove that God invisibly yet visibly strengthens and equips them to do His will and let their lights shine before me that they may see good works and glorify God in heaven (Matt. 5:16). God protects His own when the attacks come, and He shows Himself worthy of worship and trust (Num. 14:9, Deut. 31:6, Ruth 2:12, Ps. 3:5, Ps. 27:1, Ps. 71:1-2, Ps. 143:9, Eph. 1:13-14, 1 Jn 5:18).

---

As believers walk in the Spirit and do not fulfill the flesh, believers show the power of God in their lives (Galatians 5:16-18). Believers show that God works in them to will and do His good pleasure (Phil. 2:12-13). Those that wait upon **the Lord** shall renew **their strength** because the Lord provides power to His people when they need it most at just the right time (Isa. 40:31).

The Lord **is the saving refuge of His anointed**. God anoints people to unique callings in every age. Perhaps the Lord has raised up the reader for such a time as this (Est 4:14). If the reader entrusts themselves to the Lord, they can know that God can work on their behalf to accomplish anything He wills to accomplish for His glory and the good of His people (Rom. 8:28). God the Father saved Christ from premature death (Lk 4:30). God saved David from death when Saul pursued David (1 Sam. 19). God saved the apostle Paul while it was time for Paul to accomplish God's call for His life as a missionary (Acts 23). His people should trust Him to be with them as long as He keeps them on this earth. Entrusting themselves to Him allows Him to work mightily in them and accomplish great things through them. The Lord Jesus Christ is the anointed One in that He is the One that was anointed to the special calling to be the special sin-bearer for God's people. God delivered Christ from the power of sin, death, and hell when He rose Him from the grave such that He defeated death. Then Christ was exalted to the right hand of the Majesty on High and given the name that is above all names, a name that all are accountable to (Phil. 2:9-11).

## Questions for self-reflection:

(1) How has the Lord shown Himself to be your strength and saving refuge?
(2) Have you gone to the Lord recently for refuge with your troubles, and how has He responded?
(3) How have you noticed that the Lord has equipped you to live for Him?

(4) Do you know anyone who has faithfully fulfilled a special calling on their lives, perhaps to serve someone or to bring the gospel elsewhere?

(5) How would you know it if the Lord were to call you in such a manner?

**28:9. Save Your people, And bless Your inheritance; Shepherd them also, And bear them up forever.**

The psalmist began this psalm with a cry unto the Lord for the Lord to hear him. He knew that if the Lord did not listen to him and did not act on his behalf to **save** himself and others who have called upon the Lord (Rom. 10:13) that there would be no hope for any of the Lord's **people**, His **inheritance** (Eph. 1:3-11). Believers make up the Lord's inheritance as they are all in Christ and are joint-heirs with Christ (Rom. 8:17). Fortunately, for those whose hope is in the Lord, since His Word is settled in heaven (Ps. 119:89), and since He will do what He says (Num. 23:19), His people can trust Him to act according to His nature and for their good (Rom. 8:28). The difficulty of the psalmist's circumstances made the psalmist feel as if the Lord had gone silent. The psalmist knew that the Lord was strong and worthy of his trust, but he had lost the sense of the Lord's presence and nearness for protection. He knew that his enemies, who were also the enemies of the Lord, had no lasting hope. If they did not humble themselves and turn in repentant faith unto the Lord, then they would perish (Lk 13:3, Jas 4:6-10, 1 Pet. 5:6). There would be no hope beyond the grave for such people. All there was for them was this life. So, this life became a prideful pursuit of power and control while the psalmist spent the time of his pilgrimage growing to be more like his Lord (2 Pet. 3:18). That pursuit on this side of the grave for the psalmist would never attain perfection, but it would be a life of growth and progress until he would take the final breath and he would see the Lord and be like Him (1 Jn 3:2).

The psalmist knew that the Lord, in His sovereignty, heard His people when they cried to Him. He knew that it was his responsibility to cry to the Lord and trust that the Lord would provide him with everything he needed to live the life the Lord had called him to live (Phil. 4:19). The psalmist knew that he had been given access to God by faith (Rom. 5:1-2, Eph. 2:18). He knew that the end for the duplicitous wicked and the workers of iniquity would be a hopeless one (Matt 7:21-23, Revelation 21:8). He knew his end was eternal and hopeful (Ti 1:2, 1 Pet. 1:6). He knew it was not his job to take vengeance into his own hands but to trust the Lord to repay every man according to his deeds and in His time (Deut. 32:35, Rom. 12:19, Rom. 2:6).

The reason the Lord would have to save His people and judge His enemies had to do with who did and who did not acknowledge the Lord for who He is. Those who did not give Him their lives even after all He had done for them to provide for them physically and spiritually would miss out on heaven. The psalmist knew that the Lord was worthy of his trust. He had example after example that he could point to where the Lord had come through for him. The Lord asked for the psalmist's faith (Heb. 11:6). The psalmist put his faith in the Lord. The psalmist diligently sought the Lord. The Lord rewarded the psalmist for diligently seeking Him. The Lord allowed trials into the life of the psalmist (Jas 1:2-8). The psalmist trusted the Lord to be with him to **shepherd** and support him in his trials and came out of them on the other side with his faith strengthened (Ps. 23). The supernatural strength from on high coming upon the psalmist helped the psalmist know that the Lord was his strength and shield beyond a shadow of a doubt. The Lord protected the psalmist from all that tried to separate him from God's love (Rom. 8:38-39).

Having seen the Lord come through for Him over and over again helped the psalmist have a heart that continually repeatedly trusted in Him and was frequently often aided by Him. Because the Lord worked mightily in the psalmist's life by the power that rose Jesus from the dead (Eph. 1:19-20), the heart of the psalmist, just like the hearts of every believer in every generation, greatly rejoices. The lives of the people of the Lord become lives in which they offer themselves as living sacrifices (Rom. 12:2). They do not do this begrudgingly but willingly. They do this willingly because of the great love wherewith He loved us (Eph. 2:4). They praise Him in song all their days. Their changed life becomes, as it were, a new song (Ps. 40:3), a sacrifice of praise on their lips (Heb. 13:15). They cannot wait to give an answer for the hope that lies in them (1 Pet. 3:15), even in the face of hostile enemy opposition. He is their strength, their everlasting strength (Isa. 26:4). He upholds them by the Word of His power (Hebrews 1:3). He knows what they need before they ask Him (Matt. 6:8). As their refuge and strength, the very present help in trouble (Ps. 46:1), He meets them where they need it most.

The psalmist knows that as hard as this life can be from time to time, one day, he will put off corruption and put on incorruption. He will put off immorality and put on immortality (1 Cor. 15:53-54). He will be like His Lord and see Him as He is (1 John 3:2). Every blessing that the Lord has bestowed upon Him will be his in actuality. The promises will all see their fulfillment. The race that he runs for the glory of God will finally be complete, and he will forever be with the Lord with no sorrow or crying (2 Tim. 4:7-8, Heb. 12:1, Rev. 21:3-4). The former things will have passed away. In the meantime, the Lord continues to bless His inheritance as they serve Him. He continues to **bear them up** now as He will **forever** as they confront the lost world that so desperately tries unsuccessfully to bring them down with it. Their efforts will fail because greater is He that is in us than He that is in the world (1 Jn 4:4).

## Questions for self-reflection:

(1) How have you seen evidence that the Lord has heard you when you call to Him?
(2) Read Ephesians 1:1-14. How are those who are the Lord's inheritance blessed?
(3) If the Lord has allowed something difficult to come and go in your life, looking back on that adversity, how can you see that the adverse circumstance was actually for your good? How did the Lord support you in it?
(4) Since your justification, looking at various snapshots of your sanctification journey, are there seeds of growth? Is there evidence of growing in conformity to the image of Christ?

# Psalm 29

**29:1. Give unto the Lord, O you mighty ones, Give unto the Lord glory and strength.**

---

This psalm is thought to have been written by David when he finished the tabernacle made for the ark. Those who may be considered **mighty ones** have obtained a position of rank, authority, influence, or power. They can tell others what to do, and those others must follow. Such mighty ones who have been blessed with authority must realize that such privilege comes with serious responsibility. Such rule is ultimately stewardship that God grants as part of His ultimate plan (Dan. 2:21, 1 Cor. 4:2). These rulers ultimately have the responsibility to honor the Lord in their time in charge. Sadly, many earthly rulers, perhaps the vast majority of earthly rulers, instead heap up glory and honor unto themselves. Rulers who give themselves the honor and glory meant for God only need to be called to repentance. They should give unto the Lord the glory and strength that are ultimately meant for Him alone.

Any Christian has been given a sphere of influence. God has entrusted something or someone to their care. The Christian is responsible for giving **unto the Lord glory and strength** in every facet of their lives (Col. 3:17), so they will be a fragrance of life unto life to fellow believers and a fragrance of death unto death to unbelievers (2 Cor. 2:16). When the Holy Spirit-led Christian walks in the light (Eph. 5:8), they will emit such a fragrance (Rom. 8:14). A Christian who abides in Christ (Jn 15:1-8), who is walking in the Spirit, will affect those with whom they interact. Their lives should produce overwhelming evidence that God is light and in Him is no darkness at all (1 Jn 1:5). Their conduct should display that the God of the universe has made them partakers of the divine nature (2 Pet. 1:4) and that divine nature should flow out of the believer's transformed life (Matt. 5:16, Eph. 2:10). The believer's works should give the Lord glory, and it should be evident that the strength to accomplish these deeds comes from the Lord. When we were without strength, Christ died for the ungodly to give the ungodly strength to commend God's love to a dark world that so desperately needs it (Rom. 5:6-8).

Believers show the strength of the Lord when they live according to the precepts that He has laid out for them in His Word. The Holy Spirit empowers believers to live out the Word and be doers of the Word and not hearers only deceiving themselves (Jas 1:22). Some of the communicable attributes of God are made visible to a lost world when the believer lives out God's ways before them.

## Questions for self-reflection:

(1) Is there a public figure that you can think of (a "mighty one") who publicly gives God glory in word and deed?
(2) How can your life be more of a fragrance of life unto life? How can you live in such a way to others that it will be evident that you strive to give unto the Lord glory and strength?
(3) Does your life help others see the truth of the gospel, or does your life keep others from seeing the truth of the gospel? What changes can you make so that others can see that truth more clearly?

**29:2. Give unto the Lord the glory due to His name; Worship the Lord in the beauty of holiness.**

---

Because of who the Lord is and what the Lord has done in the earth and in the lives of His people, it is reasonable for the people who belong to the Lord to **give the Lord the glory due to His name.** He has given them life and breath (Acts 17:25). He has loaded them down with benefits (Ps. 68:19). He has given them everything they need for life and godliness (2 Pet. 1:3). He has blessed them with every spiritual blessing in the heavenly places (Eph. 1:3). When we were dead in trespasses and sins, He made us alive together in Christ (Eph. 2:1-5). Even when we sin, Jesus advocates for us (1 Jn 2:1), ever-living to intercede for us (Heb. 7:25). Now, we have no reason to fear because His perfect love casts out fear (1 Jn 4:18).

Because, as a result of HIs rich mercy (Eph. 2:4), God does not treat us the way our sins deserve to be treated (Lam. 3:22), it is reasonable for God to ask us to **worship** Him **in the beauty of holiness.** That worship is to be carried out in spirit and in truth (Jn 4:24). It is to be accompanied by reverence. This worship and reverence are suitable for God the Father, God the Son, and God the Holy Spirit to receive. It is not appropriate to worship anyone or anything else. This worship and reverence are unsuitable to be received by anything that is or ever was created, including angels (Rev. 22:8-9). The created angelic host is beautiful as God created them. Even they bow and worship around the throne as they wait for the Lord to command them to do His bidding (Rev. 11:16). Believers in every generation who consecrate their lives unto Him live lives that are a fragrant offering of worship unto the One who loved them and gave Himself for them (Rom. 12:1, Eph. 5:1-2).

## Questions for self-reflection:

(1) What are some things that the Lord has done for you that make it reasonable for you to give Him the glory due to His name?

(2) Outside of services on the Lord's Day, how can you worship the Lord in the beauty of holiness?

(3) How can you cultivate an attitude of worship such that worship is the natural outflow of your daily life?

**29:3. The voice of the Lord is over the waters; The God of glory thunders; The Lord is over many waters.**

---

**The voice of the Lord is over the many waters** in that He commands them to advance and recede. So many people today are guilty of worshiping the creation. Such people have misplaced worship. God is the Creator of the heavens and the earth (Ps. 146:6). God commands and demands that we, His creatures, worship Him, not what He has created (Rom. 1:25). God uses the things He has created as an apt testimony to show us that He, by virtue of creation, is superior to the earth and superior over everything that is in the earth, including all people, who He created in His image (Gen. 1:27). Since He created us, He owns us. Since He owns us, He is right to command us to worship Him (Matt. 4:10). Since the Lord rules as sovereign authority over the waters and thunder, water and thunder are right to do as He commands them to do.

He has not created waters and thunders with wills of their own, however. He has created mankind with wills of their own. With their wills, God commands man to honor Him, who has given them everything they need and everything they enjoy. **God thunders** in judgment against those who rebel against His will. Thunder pictures judgment in God's Word. When God speaks, it thunders in the Bible. By thundering, God makes His presence known. When His Spirit-filled people bring His powerful truth to bear on the lives of those accountable to Him, it is as if God thunders down. The works of God are as thunder, majestic in power, and illustrative of God's incomparable strength.

## Questions for self-reflection:

(1) Do a Bible search for how God is in control of nature. How do seasons change? How does the rain come? If we can trust God to bring the weather upon us by His sovereign power, can He control our circumstances?

---

(2) Why do some people exchange the true worship of God for the worship of something created? What is so alluring about that?

(3) How do you feel knowing that you have avoided that judgment that God thunders against the ungodly? What did you do to avoid the judgment? What did God do so you could avoid the judgment?

(4) Because of the saving work of the Trinity on your behalf, you will avoid judgment. How does that make you want to respond to God's work of grace in your life? How can you show Him and others your devotion to Him?

**29:4. The voice of the Lord is powerful; The voice of the Lord is full of majesty.**

---

**The voice of the Lord** commands the elements of creation to do His bidding, and they follow Him with no questions asked (Ps. 33:6, Ps. 104:4, Ps. 135:7, Ps. 147:18, Ps. 148:5, Jer. 10:13, Jer. 51:6, Ezek. 13:13, Amos 4:13). None of those elements were created in His image, however. The voice of the Lord commands the winds to blow where they will (Jn 3:8). The voice of the Lord commands the storms to come, and they come (Zech. 10:1). The voice of the Lord commands the seasons to change (Dan. 2:21). The voice of the Lord commands the angels to minister (Heb. 1:14). The voice of the Lord goes forth when the Word is preached, and the gospel powerfully converts separated souls (Isa. 55:11, Rom. 1:16). Sadly, the pinnacle of His creation, man, that was created in His image (Gen. 1:27), has used the free will that he received as a gracious gift from a gracious Father as a tool to precipitate sin (Isa. 14, Ezek. 28, Gen. 3).

When God's truth is taught, the Holy Spirit mixes it with faith in the soil of the prepared human heart (Matt. 13:23, Heb. 4:2). It becomes powerful fruit in the lives of the good trees that bear much fruit (Matt. 7:15-20, Jn 15:1-8, Gal. 5:22-25). It results in light that shines (Matt. 5:16) in this dark world that the light of the glorious gospel would overpower the blindness caused by the god of this age, and lives would be transformed (2 Cor. 4:4).

When Christ came to earth, His voice was the voice of the Lord live and in living color in the lives of the people to whom He ministered (Jn 5:19, Jn 10:30, Jn 12:49). Those who witnessed the works that He did witnessed first-hand that the Lord **is powerful.** The Lord is powerful to give the blind sight (Matt. 11:5), let the lame walk (Matt. 11:5), unstop deaf ears (Matt. 11:5), calm seas (Matt. 8:23-27), create food (Matt. 14:13-21), and raise the dead (Jn 11) (to name a few things). The Lord Jesus Christ did all these things to show that He and the Father are one (Jn 10:30). God used His power to raise Christ from the dead three days after He was crucified for the sins of the world (Acts 2:24). After Christ breathed

His last (Matt. 27:50, Mk 15:37, Lk 23:46), the powerful voice of the Lord came forth and caused a great earthquake that ended with the dead coming out of graves and the ground splitting (Matt. 27:51-53, Lk 23:45). The Lord is so powerful that He caused the earth to crack open and swallow up three rebels (Num. 16).

**The Lord is full of majesty** now. Christ, after His humiliation, has been exalted (Phil. 2:9) and sits at the right hand of that majesty (Heb. 1:3), now interceding for the saints (Heb. 7:25) and authoritatively upholding things by the Word of His power (Heb. 1:3).

## Questions for self-reflection:

(1) Think of the Lord next time it thunderstorms, or when a hurricane strikes, or when a tornado touches down, or when a predator kills its prey. All these elements of the created order give glory to God. Now think about how your thoughts and actions today have failed to give glory to God at one point or another. Does that humble you? Can you ask God to help you be humbler so that you will be in awe of His power and majesty?

(2) Would the people who know you best say that you are a tree that bears Christian fruit? Why or why not?

(3) Does your life commend to a watching world that the Lord is full of majesty?

**29:5. The voice of the Lord breaks the cedars, Yes, the Lord splinters the cedars of Lebanon.**

A cedar tree produces durable and strong wood. Cedar trees are found all over the globe. The deodar cedar can grow to 40-50 feet tall. The atlas cedar can grow to be 40-60 feet tall and have a trunk that is 5 to 6 feet in diameter. The Cyprus cedar can grow to be 50-80 feet tall. More cedar tree varieties are unique to different geographic regions across the globe. The aforementioned varieties would take something exceedingly mighty to break them. **The voice of the Lord** is that exceedingly mighty thing that can **break the cedars** all by itself. The Lord can splinter the cedars of Lebanon, which are an actual cedar tree variety, by an act of His power, such as a thunderstorm, a tornado, an earthquake, or a hurricane. This verse is a powerful testimony to the strength of the Lord, the power of His Word, and should instill awe in His hearers (Gen. 18:14, 1 Chron. 29:11-12, Jb 9:4, Jb 42:2, Ps. 73:26, Ps. 147:5, Isa. 40:28-29, Isa. 43:13, Matt. 19:26, Mk 10:27, Rom. 8:37-39, 1 Cor. 4:20, 1 Cor. 6:14, Eph. 3:20-21, Phil. 4:13, Jude 1:24-25).

When God's people consider how mighty the Lord is, they should respond in careful reverence. In addition, they should rejoice that this powerful God that could consume them in their sins (Lam. 3:22) chose instead to shed His love abroad in their hearts when He commended His love toward us in that while we were sinners, Christ died for us (Rom. 5:5-8).

The lost sinner is something like the cedar of Lebanon. As the wood of the tree hardens the tree, sin hardens the lost sinner (Heb. 3:13). Sin separates them from the God that created them (Isaiah 64:6). Nevertheless, the voice of the Lord can come to them in that proud, hardened state, while they are dead in trespasses and sins, and make them alive (Eph. 2:1-5). Their hard heart can be broken into **splinters,** like **the cedars of Lebanon**, and can be made to be responsive to spiritual things by God's grace (Ezek. 11:19-20, Ezek. 36:26-27). They can be born again and receive a new heart and a new nature (Jn 3:1-8). They can be given a new song (Ps. 40:3). They can be transformed by the renewing of their minds (Rom. 12:2) and be led by the Spirit into all truth (Jn 16:13, Rom. 8:14) because God is rich in mercy (Eph. 2:4) and does not want anyone to perish by wants all to come to repentance (2 Pet. 3:9).

## Questions for self-reflection:

(1) Do testimonies to the strength of the Lord like this one do anything to help your faith?
(2) Is there any seemingly insurmountable obstacle that is like a strong cedar tree that you can trust the Lord to break and splinter for you?
(3) Do you know anyone who does not know the Lord whose heart is like the cedar that needs to be broken so that it can reach a place of humble repentance?
(4) Do you have any unresolved sin issues that keep you from being as fruitful as you could be?

**29:6. He makes them also skip like a calf, Lebanon and Sirion like a young wild ox.**

---

This verse refers back to the previous verse. The Lord brings winds (Gen. 8:1, Exod. 15:10, Num. 11:31, Ps. 104:4, Ps. 107:25, Ps. 135:7, Ps. 147:18, Ps. 148:8, Prov. 30:4, Jer. 10:13, Jer. 51:16, Ezek. 13:13, Hos 13:15, Jon. 1:4, Jon. 4:8) and rains (Lev. 26:4, Deut. 11:14, Deut. 28:12, Judg. 5:4, 1 Kgs 8:36, 1 Kgs 18:1, Jb 5:10, Jb 26:8, Jb 28:26, Jb 37:6, Jb 38:28, Jb 38:37, Ps. 68:9, Ps. 147:8, Isa. 30:23, Jer. 5:24, Jer. 10:13, Jer. 14:22, Ezek. 13:13, Joel 2:23, Zech. 10:1, Matt. 5:45, Acts 14:17, Jas 5:18) that make trees move, break, and splinter. Branches break off. Hurricanes and tornadoes come and rip trees up by roots and cause extensive damage. **Lebanon and Sirion** are thought to be names of mountains. **A young wild ox** can move out of control and cause damage. Mountains can shift in violent weather, such as earthquakes or tornadoes. They can erode in torrential hurricane rains. Trees that have taken hundreds of years to grow on mountains that have been in place for millennia can be made to snap like toothpicks. Winds can also uproot trees from the ground, and the uprooted trees can crush dwelling places, vehicles, and people in their paths. It appears that there is no control over these events. But since God is sovereign even in bringing such conditions, one must return to the overarching truth that God is allowing storms such as these. He promises to be with His people when they endure physical storms like these. He promises to be with His people when they endure spiritual storms as well (Jb 23:10, Jn 16:33, Rom. 8:28, 2 Cor. 1:4-5, 2 Cor. 4:16-18, 2 Cor. 12:7-10, Jas 1:2-8, 1 Pet. 4:12-13).

If the world that He allows to be ravaged like this to illustrate His power can be so affected by His permission and will, mankind should be very careful to trifle at His grace. Humanity should be wary at scoffing at His goodness which is there to lead them to repentance (Rom. 2:4). Mankind should respond to the grace of God, which brings salvation that has appeared in the person of the Lord Jesus Christ (Ti 2:11), as well as His kindness (Ne. 9:17, Ps.17:7, Ps. 31:21, Ps. 36:7, Ps. 63:3, Ps. 69:16, Ps. 117:2, Isa. 54:8, Isa. 63:7,

Eph. 2:7, Ti 3:4-6). Such a response should be made with humility (Eph. 4:2), brokenness (Ps. 34:18), repentance (Matt. 4:17, Lk 13:3, Acts 2:38) and gratitude (1 Chron. 16:34, 1 Chron. 23:30, Ps. 92:1, Ps. 106:1, Ps. 107:1, Acts 24:3, Col. 2:7, Col. 3:17, 1 Thess. 5:18). If people come to God through faith in the Lord Jesus Christ, they will avoid the wrath of God that abides upon the unbelieving (Jn 3:36, Rom. 1:18-32, Rom. 5:9). They will not have to wish they could have rocks fall on them (Lk 23:30). They will not have to worry about being fearful of falling into the hands of the living God (Hebrews 10:31). Instead, they will have great hope that their names are written in heaven (Lk 10:20). They will have great peace knowing that if God is for them, none can be against them (Rom. 8:31).

## Questions for self-reflection:

(1) What force is there on earth from nature or the human race that is more powerful than God or that is not subject to His sovereignty?

(2) If humanity that is separated from God by their sin is not consumed in their sins but instead is allowed to live and continue in their overt rebellion, what does that say about God's grace? Is human sin more powerful than God's grace? Is God merely a little merciful?

(3) When you think about the worst spiritual storm in life you have ever endured or perhaps presently do endure, how does the awareness of God's promise to be with you in it comfort you? What do you do when you need to be reminded of that promise?

(4) When you see the world full of scoffers ridiculing God and believers, do you get angry? Does your heart break for them? A little bit of both? Do you even care about them, or are you just relieved that God's wrath against you has been satisfied?

## 29:7. The voice of the Lord divides the flames of fire.

In this psalm, **the voice of the Lord** is demonstrated as being powerful enough to employ the forces of nature. These forces were put in place by God for His purposes. Thunderstorms bring thunder and lightning, rain, and sometimes hail to bear on communities (Jb 36:32). Fire can result from that. The Lord descended in a fire when He gave the Law to Moses on Mount Sinai (Exod. 19:18). At Pentecost, tongues of fire moved through the people (Acts. 2:1-4). The voice of the Lord, the preached cross of Christ and Him crucified, also has an effect that divides (1 Cor. 1:18). On one half of the division, believers are filled with the Holy Spirit. The Holy Spirit controls believers and overtakes them as a fire engulfs a building in its flames (Rom. 8:8-14).

**The fire** that belongs to the sheep, the fire that the Lord puts in them that results in zeal, is very different from the fire that awaits the goats, those on the other half of the previously mentioned division. God, the consuming fire (Heb. 12:29), consumes the wicked in the lake that burns with fire and brimstone (Rev. 21:8). The Lord **divides** the sheep from the goats (Matt. 25:31-46). They will not be together in eternity. The sheep hear the voice of the Lord (Jn 10:27-28). Goats do not listen to the voice of the Lord. Therefore, the Lord is right to divide them. The wicked want nothing to do with the Lord anyway. He is not unloving to let them be where they want to be. He would be unloving to force them against their will to be with Him when they do not want to be with Him.

Fire provides both light and heat. When the light of the gospel shines on hearts, either the heart will prove itself to be changed by the Lord or the heart will run away from the light because it loves the darkness too much (Jn 1:5, Jn 7:7, 2 Cor. 4:3-6). That change that is characteristic of a saved person will manifest itself in deeds of light that commend the gospel to an unbelieving world (Matt. 5:16, Eph. 2:10, Ti 2:14). In contrast to the holy deeds done by the regenerate, the lost walk in darkness (Jn 8:12, 1 Jn 1:6). They do not see where they are going. The fire of the Lord repulses them. They run from it instead of to it. The lost are the oil that does not mix with the living water that is in true Christians (Jn 4:10). It is an unmistakable fact that the gospel divides (Matt. 10:34-39). To those that are being saved, the gospel is a savor of life unto life. The gospel is the power of God unto salvation for those that believe (Rom. 1:16). The gospel opens the eyes of some to see their greatest need and see how Christ meets that need for them. In contrast, for those who do not believe and those who are perishing, the gospel is foolish. To such people, the gospel is a savor of death unto death (2 Cor. 2:16).

God will be glorified in the justification of sinners to humble themselves in repentant faith and believe the gospel. God will also be glorified in the damnation of saints who spend eternity in hell (Ezek. 39, Matt. 25:31-46). Both ends glorify God. Christ is the dividing line of the two groups. What one does with Christ determines how eternity will play out.

**Questions for self-reflection:**

(1) The next time you see a thunderstorm or hear of terrible weather, in light of verses like this one, how does that affect your thinking about that weather event?

(2) When you think about the giving of the Law being compared to a frightening weather event, what sorts of imagery come to mind? What do you picture God being like in that environment?

(3) Who do you know who has the zealous fire that burns with passion for God? How can you be more like that person or people?

(4) Who do you know who has yet to believe the gospel to whom God is a consuming fire that could devour them in judgment if they do not humble themselves and repent and believe the gospel? How can you pray for them or otherwise meet their needs to help them see the love of God through Christ?

(5) When you think about God being glorified in salvation and in judgment, does that bother you? Why or why not?

**29:8. The voice of the Lord shakes the wilderness; The Lord shakes the Wilderness of Kadesh.**

---

The sovereignty of the Lord continues to come forth mightily in this psalm. In **the wilderness**, the terrain will be canvassed. Trees will reach up to the sky, and beasts will roam the landscape. As the elements and seasons come and go in that literal wilderness, the underlying principle that the Lord brings those effects will be unmistakable to those with the ability to make spiritual perceptions.

Spiritually speaking, those outside of the covenant of mercy, those who have not exercised saving faith in the Lord Jesus Christ, are in a spiritual wilderness. Their lives are barren. There is no good fruit-bearing in them (Matt. 3:10, Matt. 7:15-20, Jn 15:1-8). They are spiritually dry because they have not come to the Living Water for refreshment (John 4). Though they may not feel the flames that await them should they stay in their sins, it is nonetheless true that God's wrath does abide upon them (John 3:36) and is revealed against them (Rom. 1:18). They may not realize it due to being 'past feeling' (Eph. 4:19).

Because the Lord is rich in mercy (Eph. 2:4) and rich to those who call upon Him (Rom. 10:12), the Lord makes overtures. He woos and beckons while the objects of His wooing continue in sin despite His efforts at reconciling them for various reasons (Matt. 13:18-23). He forestalls judgment while He wills that none should perish and that all should come to repentance (2 Pet. 3:9).

When the saints go into all the world to preach the gospel to every creature (Mk 16:15) as ambassadors of Christ (2 Cor. 5:20), as the gospel goes forth, the wilderness that is the unbeliever's heart **shakes** by the gospel, which is **the voice of the Lord**. As the separated sinner hears its demands, perhaps now will be the accepted time, and now will be the day of salvation (2 Cor. 6:2). Once they realize they are condemned already for their failure to believe in the only Son of God (Jn 3:18), perhaps they will flee to the Savior for refuge, receive His pardoning grace, and experience the peace that passes understanding (Phil. 4:7). This peace

---

only comes when the war between man and God ends. The war only ends when man repents and believes the gospel (Rom. 5:1). Once they realize that their iniquities like the wind have taken them away (Isa. 64:6), while they are in that barren **Wilderness of Kadesh** that is their alienated heart (Col. 1:21), perhaps they will repent and believe the gospel. God is certainly not at fault if they do not.

**Questions for self-reflection:**

(1) Think back to the time before your conversion. How does the description of a wilderness in this verse apply to you in your lost condition?

(2) Who do you know that is lost today? They are in this wilderness condition as well. What can you do to bring them to the lush green pastures of faith?

(3) As an ambassador of Christ, do you represent Him well? In what ways is your representation lacking?

(4) What can you do to make sure that nothing in your life is a stumbling block for someone?

**29:9. The voice of the Lord makes the deer give birth, And strips the forests bare; And in His temple everyone says, "Glory!"**

**The voice of the Lord makes the deer give birth.** The voice of the Lord makes every species give birth (Isa. 66:9). The Lord is the giver of life to every species (Gen. 2:7, 1 Sam. 2:6, Jb 33:4, Isa. 42:5). When those created in His image (Jn 1:27) kick against the pricks (Acts 26:14) that He brings to bear upon them, it is the height of foolishness. It is He that has given us life. Who are we to rebel against Him? Is there anything more foolish than for the thing made to say to his Maker, "Why have You made me like this? (Rom. 9:20)"

Birth for any creature is a scary proposition. For a mother and her offspring to even survive the birth takes a divine miracle every time. To know that the voice of the Lord elicits the events that precipitate labor should make any pregnant female tremble in wonder to see that they are utterly dependent upon the Lord's mercy to make it out of the agony of the throws of labor alive. As a result of sin in the Garden of Eden, human birth is a painful, trying experience (Gen. 3:16). It is a necessary affliction. By it, the species continues. Its bitter properties remind us that, as God informed Eve, sin has its consequences. Thankfully, due to the privilege of getting to hold and care for the newborn, it also reminds us that sometimes on the other side of the bitter trial is a blissful reward. Life is full of painful trials. Heaven is the reward for believers.

Thunder, a topic previously discussed in this very chapter, evidently makes the birthing process easier for some. This can be likened to the gospel. When the gospel thunders from pulpits and streets, some respond with saving faith. Faith comes by hearing the word about Christ (Rom. 10:17). When saving faith fills the heart, sinners are birthed into God's kingdom (Jn 3:3-7). As physical birth makes its recipient an earthly citizen, so the new birth makes its recipient a heavenly citizen (Phil. 3:20). The heavenly citizen has their name etched in heaven (Lk 10:20) and on their Savior's hands (Isa. 49:16). They are blessed with every spiritual blessing (Eph. 1:3). A new song comes from their lips (Ps. 40:3). Their works testify to the glory of God (Col. 3:17).

A deer is quick to run from location to location. A servant of the Lord is quick to hear and slow to speak (Jas 1:19). A servant of the Lord is quick to take inventory of their lives to see how they can better fulfill the Lord's will for them. A servant of the Lord that has free access to the throne of grace can quickly avail themselves to the Lord's presence at a moment's notice whenever they need to do so (Heb. 4:16).

Forests are covered by leaves and branches and things that obscure a clear view of predators or other things that need to be seen. Alienated sinners take significant measures to protect themselves from the convicting influence that God's Word brings upon their lives. It is the great divider of the thoughts and intents of the heart (Heb. 4:12). Alienated sinners may build themselves a forest of distraction and sin to hide within. Eventually, the voice of the Lord will expose the truth, and they will have to come out of hiding (Eccles. 12:14). That may happen in this life. It may not occur until the next life when it would be too late (2 Cor. 5:10). Eventually, sin will find them out (Num. 32:23).

The Lord **strips the forest** that is the human heart **bare**. All things lay open and bare before Him with whom we have to do (Heb. 4:13). The gospel shows the prepared heart that it is utterly destitute of the righteousness required to enter heaven. The gospel then becomes necessary to birth sinners into God's kingdom. The gospel lays bare the heart.

In heaven, angels and redeemed saints will give glory to the Lord forever in a way that is not hindered due to the lingering effects of sin that plague this earth. Now on earth, the church, local and universal, is where saints speak and serve to the glory of God. The Christian's body is the **temple** of the Holy Spirit (1 Cor. 6:19). That temple is filled with the Lord's glory now in all believers as believers work out their salvation with fear and trembling (Phil. 2:12) and proclaim the **glory** of the Lord.

## Questions for self-reflection:

(1) Think about your own physical birth into the world when your mother went into labor. Your physical birth involved the voice of the Lord in that. His incredible power allowed you to develop in the womb, and He created you with senses to be able to hold this book and read it. Do these facts cause you to wonder at the tremendous power of the Creator who also makes the deer give birth?

(2) If you are a mother reading this book who has survived the miracle of childbirth at least once when did you last praise God for His miraculous intervention on your behalf on that momentous occasion and life-altering event?

(3) When you think about how sin's entry into the world resulted in the consequence of painful human childbirth, do you also praise God for heaven where there will be no more sorrow and pain?

(4) As a professing Christian, how has your attitude toward the gospel changed? Do you look forward to others getting the opportunity to hear the gospel so they, too, can humbly repent and avoid God's eternal wrath? Or are you too busy enjoying this life even to be concerned about the eternal fate of the lost?

**29:10. The Lord sat enthroned at the Flood, And the Lord sits as King forever.**

The Flood has reference to Noah's Flood. This verse speaks to the Lord's kingship from all eternity, from the beginning, then to the present, and finally to the eternal state. He has always been the King of kings (1 Tim. 6:15). When humankind got more and more wicked (Gen. 6:5), the time for patience ran out, and God judged the whole world with a global flood that killed every human and land animal that was not in the Ark (Gen. 7). God caused the forty-day and forty-night rain shower, the first and last of its kind. After the forty days ended (Gen. 7:17), God caused the rain to stop (Gen. 8:1). He was sovereign over it all. He was merciful to give everyone who heard Noah's warnings a chance to enter the Ark and avoid judgment (1 Pet. 3:20). But all refused. It was the fault of the sinner, not the fault of God. When they refused, and God shut the Ark door (Gen. 7:16), the opportunity for mercy had passed, and the time for judgment had arrived. After the storm had run for as long as it was ordained to run (Gen. 7:4, Gen. 7:12, Gen. 7:24), the rains stopped by the Lord's command (Genesis 8:1). The Lord showed Noah how to know when to disembark from the Ark (Gen. 8:1-19). Noah followed God's instructions for Ark construction and reentry into society to a T. **The Lord sat enthroned** over the most minute details of **the Flood.**

Today, **the Lord sits as King forever**, as He always has been, enthroned at the most minute details of our lives, including the flood-like afflictions that we endure as a natural consequence of living on a cursed earth (Matt. 10:30, Rom. 8:28, Eph. 1:11). He is also enthroned even as we sin against Him and trample the grace that the blood of Christ purchased for us. We had better not count that blood and that grace a common thing (Heb. 10:29). We had better not live lukewarm lives and therefore cause Him to spit us out of His mouth (Rev. 3:16). Today, the Lord still works everything after the counsel of His own will.

The Lord still knows everything about everyone, down to the number of hairs on their heads (Lk 12:7). Each of us goes through 'floods of our own.' He calls us to trust Him in the midst of what He allows us to experience (Jas 1:2-8). The trials are a means by which growth in the grace and knowledge of the Lord Jesus Christ takes place (2 Pet. 3:18). As wickedness seems to have too much freedom to traverse the earth (1 Jn 5:19), saints can take comfort to know that the Lord is still in charge. He continues to be patient with His enemies as He always has been, giving them gracious opportunities for repentance (2 Pet. 3:9). He is King in the hearts of His saints. These have humbled themselves and come to the Savior in repentant faith. They walk by faith in Him (2 Cor. 5:7). One day, all the Lord's enemies will be under His feet (1 Cor. 15:26-27). He will sit on His throne as King forever. The saints will reign with Him. The kingdom will have no end (Rev. 22:1-5).

## Questions for self-reflection:

(1) Was there ever a time, or was there ever a circumstance when the Lord was not King over everything and everyone?

(2) What does it say about the nature of man to continually reject God's gracious offers for reconciliation?

(3) What does it say about the nature of God to continue to be gracious to give man opportunities to repent and come to Him for forgiveness despite man's wickedness and rebellion to God and God's authority?

(4) How have you wittingly treated the blood of Christ as a common thing this week in your spiritual apathy?

(5) Since the Lord knows everything about you, including how many hairs you have on your head, how does God's infinite knowledge help you to trust Him in your most difficult trial?

(6) What is your attitude toward the day when all the Lord's enemies will be under His feet when you are in heaven with Him forever, and all those things that caused you pain, sorrow, and sadness will have gone away?

**29:11. The Lord will give strength to His people; The Lord will bless His people with peace.**

The people that belong to **the Lord**, those that are **His people**, belong to Him by faith (Eph. 2:8, Heb. 11:6). They are His special treasure (Exod. 19:5) and are adopted kingdom citizens of His family (Rom. 8:14-15, Phil. 3:20). He has given them citizenship in His habitation, heaven (Ps. 115:3, Eph. 2:6). By the Holy Spirit, the free gift to those who believe the gospel by faith (Gal. 4:6), the Lord consistently fuels **His people** with the **strength** to be hearers and doers of His Word and will (Eph. 3:16, 2 Tim. 1:7, Jas 1:22). The grace and faith that the saved have is a free gift with which God blesses His people (Eph.2:9). That grace and faith provide the strength that believers need to keep the faith to continue to trust in the Lord and continue to remain faithful on the narrow way. In contrast, most of those around them continue blindly to go down the broad road that leads to destruction (Matt. 7:13-14). The same power that raised Jesus from the dead is available to all who trust in the Lord today and every day (Rom. 8:11).

Many believers do not realize the vast amounts of grace and strength that are available to them today. They settle for being less than they could be because they fail to understand who they are. They have vast seas of grace made available to them by the finished work of the Lord Jesus Christ on their behalf. They are weak in and of themselves. However, in Christ, when they are weak, He is strong (2 Cor. 12:10).

The Lord does and **will bless His people with peace**. Christ first made peace on the cross for them when He broke down the wall that separated us from the Father (Eph. 2:14-18). We made this separation ourselves when we, in our pride and selfishness, spurned the goodness of God that He meant to lead us to repentance (Rom. 2:4) and took the blessings of common grace that He lavished upon us and spent them on ourselves. Christ's reconciling work was there while we lived in prodigality (Eph. 2:2-3, Ti 3:3). He had finished the work and made the payment. We didn't want it because it demanded change which we did not want to make. One day something changed. The change happened to us as a result of His working. When we saw Him as He is, we became broken over our sins and realized our need for the grace and forgiveness we had previously mocked (Matt. 5:3-4, Lk 15:11-31). When we humbled ourselves and turned in faith to the Savior, the Lord Jesus Christ, who is God blessed forever amen (Rom. 9:5), the Lord was able to bless us with every spiritual blessing that awaited us as it was then that we became one of His people (Eph. 1:3). It was then that the enmity that we had created could finally be replaced with peace (Rom. 5:1). Instead of being God's enemy, we became His friend (Col. 1:21). Instead of hatred for God, love for God was shed abroad in our hearts (Rom. 5:5). Instead of lovers of sin and self, we became lovers of righteousness and others (1 Jn 2:29, 1 Jn 4:7-11).

When grace changes the hard heart and makes it into a soft heart and gives the anxious heart peace, the justification that belongs only to the sheep gives them confident assurance that since Christ is for them, none can be against them (Rom. 8:31). None can pluck them out of His omnipotent hand (Jn 10:29).

## Questions for self-reflection:

(1) What has the strength that the Lord has provided you with enabled you to do that you could not do before belonging to the Lord?

(2) Have you grown at all in overcoming temptations since you first named the name of the Lord?

(3) How has the bounty of grace that the Lord has laid upon you helped you in difficult situations and with difficult people?

(4) How have your relationships with people, both Christians and non-Christians, changed since you became a Christian? Are the relationships characterized by more peace, less peace, or the same amount of peace?

(5) How do you think obedience is related to assurance?

# Psalm 30

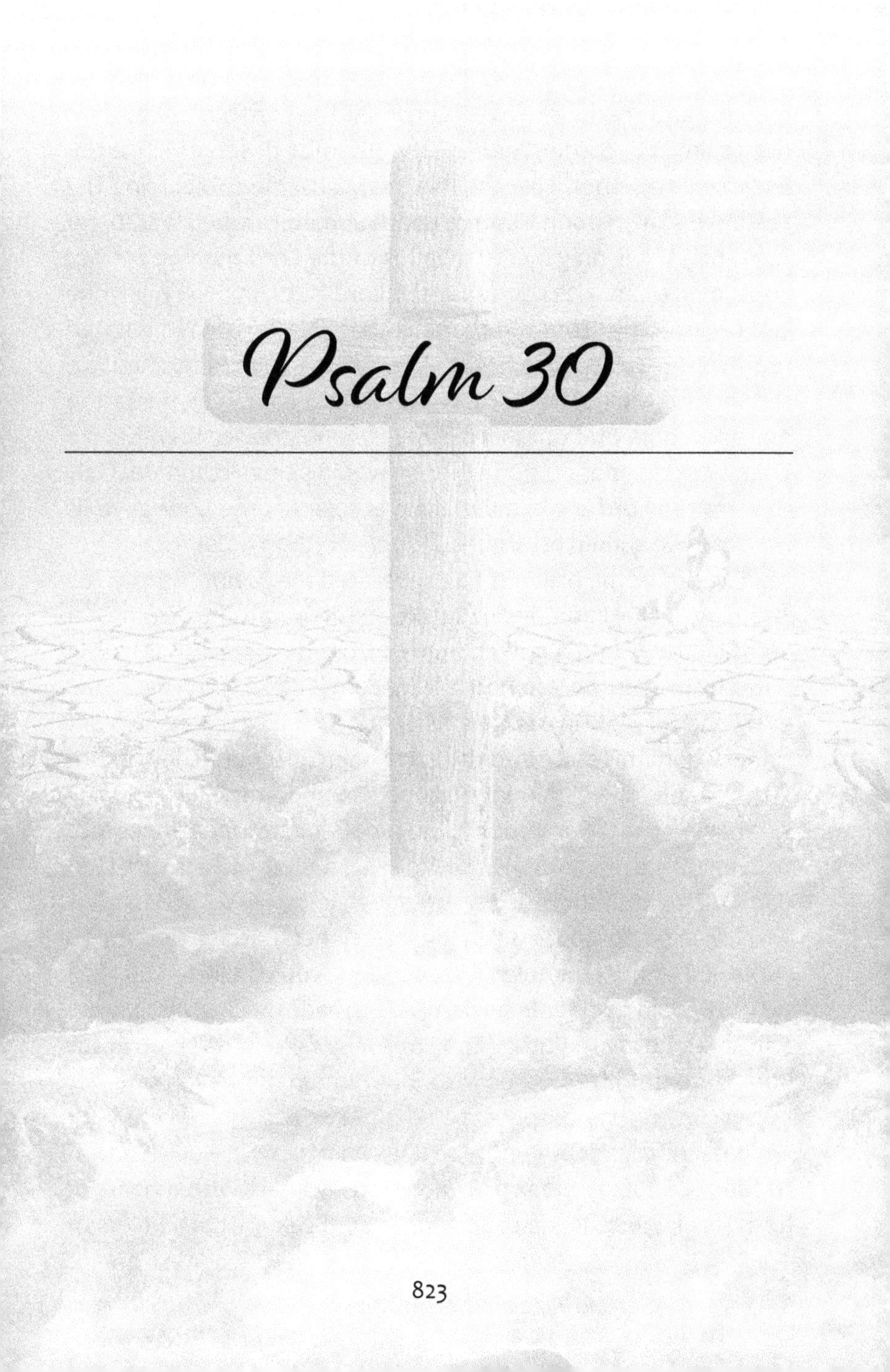

**30:1. I will extol You, O Lord, for You have lifted me up, And have not let my foes rejoice over me.**

---

The psalmist, by grace, has realized that the Lord has been merciful and gracious to him. Mercifully, the Lord has not treated the psalmist according to how the psalmist deserves since the psalmist is a sinner. Like the psalmist, all sinners, including the writer and the reader, deserve death and eternal hell (Ps. 103:10, Rom. 6:23). It is only by the mercies of the Lord that we are not consumed (Lam. 3:22). Because the Lord is rich in mercy, anyone can be lifted up from the dunghill that their sins have created (Eph. 2:4-6). In response to such lavish grace, the psalmist and we should readily **extol** the **Lord.** He deserves our wonder, our praise, our adoration, and our love. There is none greater than He. No created gods or angels or other heavenly beings compare. Only this exalted Lord is worthy of such accolades. The Lord gave us His best. We should return the favor (1 Cor. 10:13, Col. 3:17).

The sins of the psalmist had separated the psalmist from God (Isa. 64:6). Our iniquities have likewise separated us from God. Spiritual decay and death emanated from the psalmist as it emanates from every person born after Adam (Col. 2:13). Sin has made everyone very low in a state of alienation (Col. 1:21). God must lift sinners from this state into the state of justification. They cannot lift themselves. No amount of good can undo the bad that their sins have caused. Perfection is the requirement for entrance into heaven (Matthew 5:48). Unfortunately, nobody meets that standard. All fall well short (Rom. 3:9-23).

Praise be to God, while we were sinners, Christ died for us (Rom. 5:8). Christ humbled Himself so we could be **lifted up** (Phil. 2:8). We could not lift ourselves up. God made us alive, lifted us up, and seated us with Christ (Eph. 2:1-6). By faith in the Lord Jesus Christ, we get lifted up now to join Him up in heaven one day forever. When the gospel entered our ears and mixed with faith, we passed from death unto life (Jn 5:24). He wrote our name in heaven (Lk 10:20). He replaced the stony heart with a heart of flesh (Ezek. 36:26). The dry bones lived (Ezek. 37:1-14). Rivers of living water came out of us (Jn 7:38). We were born again (John 3:3-7). He put into us a new song (Ps. 33:3, Ps. 40:3, Ps. 96:1, Ps. 98:1, Ps. 144:9, Ps. 149:1, Isa. 42:10).

Satan rejoices over God's enemies because God's enemies do not belong to God. Since God's enemies do not belong to God, God's enemies belong to Satan (1 Jn 5:19). While they belong to Satan, in constant rebellion to God, they do Satan's work and try to hinder God's work. Therefore, they are foes of God and God's people. The psalmist asks the Lord to let him prosper to the extent that Satan and his minions do not have a reason to rejoice that their efforts to overthrow the Lord and His people are becoming successful. He asks the Lord to show Himself to be powerful in his life so that it will be unmistakable that the Lord is more powerful than Satan. Since the Lord is all-powerful, He is more powerful than Satan. The people who belong to the Lord have access to God's power, which is more influential than Satan's power. So far, the psalmist has experienced this victory over his enemies and asks that it be allowed to continue so that his enemies, God's enemies, will get discouraged and perhaps humble themselves and turn to the Lord in repentant faith themselves.

### Questions for self-reflection:

(1) What are some of the reasons which the Lord has given you to extol Him?

(2) What do you think the Lord's reaction is when He looks on the earth and sees those created in His image who should be extolling Him instead of spurning His influence?

(3) How do you view life differently since the Lord has lifted you up?

(4) When you fall into sin and your foes have an opportunity to rejoice over you, how do you react?

(5) As you see the foes to you and to the Lord appearing to win in the world in that they seem more influential than do believers, are you still able to trust that the Lord will have His way in judgment in the end? Why or why not?

**30:2. O Lord my God, I cried out to You, And You healed me.**

---

The psalmist had a need that he was unable to meet by himself. As was discussed in the previous verse, the mercy and grace of the Lord poured out upon the psalmist gave the psalmist reason to praise the Lord who met him right where he was in his time of need (Heb. 4:16). As the Lord met the psalmist in his area of need, the same God who does not change (Mal. 3:6) meets all His people in their place of need. He promises to be with them (Deut. 31:6, Josh. 1:9, Isa. 41:10, Zeph. 3:17, Matt. 28:20, Heb. 13:5) and uphold them (Deut. 28:1, 1 Sam. 2:8, 2 Sam. 22:49, Jb 5:11, Ps 27:5, Ps 30:1, Ps 30:3, Ps 71:20, Ps 113:7, Ps 145:14, Ps. 146:8, Ezek. 2:2, Ezek. 3:12, Ezek. 3:14, Ezek. 8:3, Ezek. 11:1, Jon. 2:6). He does not promise to remove them from the situations that they find themselves in. However, he does promise to supply them with the grace that they need to endure whatever the Lord has ordained or permitted them to endure (2 Cor. 12:7-10, Phil. 4:19).

The Lord will save those who call upon Him (Jl 2:32, Acts 2:21, Rom. 10:13). This is true of those who come to the **Lord** for eternal life. Their sins had separated them from **God**, leaving them in desperate spiritual need (Isa. 64:6). The Lord met and healed that need in the life of the psalmist and in the lives of all the justified (Rom. 3:24-25, Eph. 2:1-10).

The Lord, the Great Physician (Matt. 9:12), is merciful also to heal physical maladies in His people (Ps. 103:2-3). The Lord does not always physically heal people who need physical healing in this life. He is capable of such healing, but He does not always promise to heal in such manners. Some physical afflictions are means which God permits in saints' lives to elicit spiritual growth and trust (2 Cor. 12:7-10, Jas 1:2-8). Sometimes the healing comes in the form of spiritual maturity or overcoming affliction and temptation with faith instead of discouragement or sin (1 Cor. 10:13). To heal from the doldrums of discouragement into a response of faith is a legitimate consideration for the healing referred to in a passage like this (Ps. 34:17-18, Ps. 37:7, Ps. 103:13-14, Ps. 126:5-6, Is. 43:18-19, Rom. 8:28, Rom. 15:4, Gal. 6:9, Phil. 3:13-14, 1 Pet. 5:7).

---

This is especially a possibility for the psalmist who frequently **cried out to** the Lord and wrote of discouragement and fear caused by the enemies around him (Ps. 3:7, Ps. 7:6, Ps. 10:15, Ps. 17:13, Ps. 139:21). When saints realize all that is theirs in the grace of God supplied through the finished work of the Lord Jesus Christ (Eph. 1:3-14), they regularly can experience the type of spiritual healing that can fix the brokenness that sin causes. Even if sin's effects are not removed, attitudes and responses toward sin in ourselves and others can change in the life of the redeemed saint. These types of changes bring healing to the saint and result, at times, in healed relationships with those around them.

Perhaps the psalmist endured spiritual hardship caused by his own sin or by the sin of others. Perhaps the Lord healed the psalmist by supplying the psalmist with a fresh dose of grace to see his affliction as God sees it. Maybe the psalmist was encouraged to know that the momentary light affliction God had appointed for Him better prepared him for eternity (2 Cor. 4:17). Perhaps the affliction was to cure the psalmist of something in this world that robbed the psalmist of devotion to his Lord (Jas 4:4, 1 Jn 2:15-17). Perhaps the earthly relationship that the psalmist had enjoyed at one point had been brought to an end by reasons known only to the Lord. While the initial shock of the end of that relationship would cause sadness to the psalmist, perhaps the psalmist has seen over time that it has been replaced by love and devotion to the Father and godly service to others. The spiritual good that results from such circumstances far outweighs the sadness brought on by the end of the relationship. This could be a form of healing that the psalmist needed to experience. Perhaps the Lord appointed the psalmist for affliction so that the Lord could have **healed** the psalmist by bringing comfort to the psalmist so that the psalmist could later comfort others (2 Cor. 1:3-7). Regardless the world was a better place because of the Lord's work in the life of the psalmist. For any believer reading this, substitute yourself in the place of the psalmist, and see what the Lord might be teaching you as you navigate through your afflictions.

**Questions for self-reflection:**

(1) When has the Lord met you at a time of intense spiritual need in your life and met you to help you in ways in which you could not do for yourself? How has He helped you when you were unable to help yourself?

(2) Have you ever asked for a physical need to be met, not had that need met, but instead were blessed with a unique mental and spiritual capacity to endure the affliction?

(3) How might your outlook on your afflictions change if you were to write out your prayers in times of adversity as the psalmist did for us?

(4) How have you seen the Lord use your afflictions in such a way that because of what you learned during the afflictions, you were able to comfort others?

**30:3. O Lord, You brought my soul up from the grave; You have kept me alive, that I should not go down to the pit.**

---

The psalmist had been close to death due to conflicting with his enemies. The Lord had protected him and preserved him such that the Lord preserved him from death because it was not yet time for his divine appointment (Heb. 9:27). It is reasonable to expect that the psalmist could have been fearful for his life at times as he fled from his enemies. It could be that at times that the psalmist had expected that death was near. If he expected to die and avoided death, it is as if that the Lord brought up his soul from the grave. Instead of dying and taking up his place in **the grave**, he got to continue to live because God is merciful. The wages of his sin deserved death, but the Lord was not ready for him to have to pay those wages just yet (Rom. 6:23).

Scripture describes lost sinners as "dead in trespasses and sins" (Eph. 2:1, Eph. 2:5, Col. 2:13). They walk in a perpetual state of spiritual death, though they possess physical life. When the psalmist exercised personal faith in the plan of salvation, and when sinners today exercise personal faith in the Lord Jesus Christ, they raise from, their **soul** is **brought up** from spiritual death and into spiritual life (Rom. 6:4-14). They pass from death to life (Jn 5:24, 1 Jn 3:14). They are seated in heavenly places with Christ (Eph. 2:6). All of this is possible, not because of any works of righteousness done by them, but because of God's grace and mercy (Ti 3:5-7). The psalmist experienced personal rescue from the Lord in that the Lord **kept** the psalmist **alive** in perilous physical circumstances in which his enemies could have killed him if they had found him if it were not for God's protection. Spiritually speaking, the Lord upholds everything, including all people, including His own, by the Word of His power (Heb. 1:3). Believers' faith in the Lord, who causes or allows all things to work together for the good of His own (Romans 8:28), is the vehicle that God uses to enable them to grow in grace (2 Pet. 3:18). As we trust in Him, He reveals Himself to us. As we seek Him, we find Him (Deut. 4:29, Prov. 8:17, Jer. 29:13, Matt. 7:7). As we abide in Him, He abides in us (Jn 15:1-8).

---

As believers spend time with the Lord in the Word and in prayer, their faith increases. The Lord sovereignly protects His own from death according to His will.

The psalmist knew he was on a divine timetable. The enemies of the psalmist could not trust in the same protection. They were under His wrath (Jn 3:36). The **pit**, the grave or hell, awaited them. The psalmist, however, had eternal life to look forward to, while the Lord's enemies did not. The psalmist, by faith, had eternal life, whereas the enemies of the Lord would perish if they did not repent (Lk 13:3).

**Questions for self-reflection:**

(1) Have you ever suffered from a trial to the extent that you thought your own death was imminent? If you had not, imagine someone like the apostles who were punished severely for their belief in the risen Lord. Imagine after they had been sentenced to a martyr's death, as they awaited the execution of their sentence in their dungeon cell. If you were in that situation, would you be thinking more about your impending death, or would you be thinking more about getting to see the face of your Lord for the first time? Why?

(2) Who do you know who is outside of Christ, who is walking in spiritual death, that you can show the gospel to such that they would be able to see the life of Christ emanating from you? Then, once you determine who needs to see your new life in Christ, what would be some of the things you would do to most strongly demonstrate the same new life?

**30:4. Sing praise to the Lord, you saints of His, And give thanks at the remembrance of His holy name.**

---

The psalmist has already spent some time making a case for why the Lord's people should extol Him in 30:1. He praises the Lord for the work that the Lord has done in his life. Everyone who has a testimony of salvation from sin, death, and hell can tell a version of such a story. There was a time in the life of each sheep where they sensed their poverty of spirit (Matt. 5:3). There was a time in which their sin burdened them (Matt. 5:4). There was a time when they hungered and thirsted for a righteousness that they could not achieve based on their own efforts (Matt. 5:6). This was when they humbled themselves in the sight of the Lord so that He could exalt them in due time (1 Pet. 5:6). This was when they wept and lamented and submitted to God so that the devil would flee from them (Jas 4:6-7). This was when they drew near to God and when God drew near to them in response. This was when they sensed, although they were dead in trespasses and sins, God was rich in mercy to still condescend and save them through the sacrifice of Christ (Eph. 2:1-10).

God did not have to provide a rescue for anyone to take. God could have justly let humanity receive the wages that their sins deserve (Rom. 6:23) without giving them a chance for rescue. That He would provide a rescue is merciful and loving in and of itself. Those saints who have come to God through faith in the Lord Jesus Christ see many reasons why they can **sing praise to the Lord.** He has set them apart to serve Him and be a light in the dark world (Matt. 5:16). All that God does testifies to His character. He never acts inconsistently with His nature. He never acts in a way that is inconsistent with any of His attributes. If the way He works on the earth seems unfair or unjust or otherwise does not make sense to us, since God is light and in Him is no darkness at all (1 Jn 1:5), the problem must be with us and our understanding and not with Him. The problem must not be with His character.

When sinners get reconciled to God through faith in the Lord Jesus Christ (2 Cor. 5:20), the holiness that belongs to God is imputed to people such that they begin the sanctification process whereby they are conformed to the image of Christ (Rom. 8:39) until they take their final breath when they will be like Him and will see Him as He is (1 Jn 3:2). As believers seek the Lord, they find the Lord (Deut. 4:29; Prov. 8:17; Jer. 29:13; Matt. 7:7), and the Lord reveals Himself to them. Believers **give thanks at the remembrance of His holy name** when they consider how God operates in the world. In the things that God causes or permits to happen, all those things are good. His saving, sanctifying, and glorifying work in the lives of the saints is good work. His judgment of the wicked is good. His providence is good.

### Questions for self-reflection:

(1) When was the last time you rehearsed the story of how God changed your life?
(2) God could have justly let humanity perish because of their sins, but He did not. Why not?
(3) Does God ever act inconsistently with His nature (character)? Since He does not ever act inconsistently with His character, if something seems wrong or unfair about what He does in the world or on the pages of Scripture, does the problem lie with Him or with us?

**30:5. For His anger is but for a moment, His favor is for life; Weeping may endure for a night, But joy comes in the morning.**

---

Since God is light and in Him is no darkness at all (1 Jn 1:5), any **anger** that God exercises towards anyone **for a moment** must be proper for Him to exercise. We, sinful humans, provoke God's anger because of our sins (Deut. 9:7). God is slow to anger (Ps. 103:8). We are not always slow to anger. If we always were appropriately slow to anger, we would not need Scriptural commands to be slow to anger (Jas 1:19-20). We do not have to completely understand why God's anger must be proper for Him to exercise. We can try to understand such things. It will not always be possible for us, His finite creatures, to fully understand everything there is to know about Him. While we are finite, He is infinite. While our knowledge has limits, He is omniscient (1 Chron. 28:9). Our power dwarfs His omnipotence (Jer. 32:17). He is omnipresent (Heb. 13:5), and timeless (Rev. 4:8). We are temporal (2 Cor. 4:18, Jas 4:14). He is eternal (Deut. 33:27, Isa. 40:28, 2 Cor. 4:18). We are sinful (Rom. 3:9-23). He is holy (Lev. 19:2, Isa. 6:3). He formed us. We did not form Him (Rom. 9:20). We, His sinful creatures, are free to express multiple emotions, including anger. The anger we typically express is not ordinarily the type of anger that is not sinful to express. No. We usually practice the sinful outbursts of wrath that the New Testament condemns (Gal. 5:20).

God's anger is entirely consistent with His love. We can understand that. If we have children, we can comprehend that it would be possible for us to love them while at the same time being angry at them for something that they have done. It is possible that what they have done may compel us to react with the discipline that we do not enjoy to exact but that we understand at times can be necessary (Heb. 12:3-11). While our lives are not right before Him, our sense of the anger He feels toward us may be more acute. Then when we return to the path of obedience, our sensitivity to His anger dissipates, as if it lasted **but for a moment,** while the sense of His pardon is more abundant. Those who have come to God through faith in Christ are objects of God's favor. They have received the free gift of eternal life (Rom. 6:23). They cannot lose the eternal life they have received (Rom. 8:28-30, Rom. 8:38-39). Those who are called are justified and will be glorified. Those who are the objects of God's **favor** receive all the spiritual blessings reserved for the saved (Eph. 1:3-14) and are bestowed upon them as part of the favor that is theirs by virtue of their covenant relationship with God through Christ. Those blessings cannot be revoked (Rom. 11:29) but will last **for life**. God calls His people to a living faith in which they grow in the grace and knowledge of Christ (2 Pet. 3:18) while being conformed to His image (Rom. 12:2). They come to appreciate that, as much as this life includes troubles, these troubles prepare them for a greater weight of glory (2 Cor. 4:17). This is one of the ways that the true believer, the servant, becomes like their Lord.

The Lord had many things in His life that caused Him trouble. In this life, we will have trouble (Jn 16:33). But believers take solace in that since Christ overcame the world, they will one day overcome the world and be in heaven with Him forever. They come to realize that this world is not their home (Jn 15:19, Jn 17:16, Phil. 3:20, Heb. 13:14, 1 Pe. 2:11). Trials and afflictions wean us from the love of this world, this temporal home, and help us to long for our better home, heaven above (Jas 1:2-8, 1 Pet. 1:6-9).

**Weeping may endure for a night** in the life of saints. They may feel the weight of the chastising of their own sin. But even that is done because a loving Father disciplines His children (Heb. 12:3-11). Because of the condition of sin under which this world operates (Rom. 3:9-23, 1 Jn 5:19), sad events will occur that precipitate weeping. Saved and unsaved people alike should expect as much. Any sorrowful circumstance that befalls a child of the King only lasts during part of the saint's earthly pilgrimage. Suppose the saint is called to endure a trial that lasts the entire duration of their earthly life, compared to eternity when they will be absent from the body and present with the Lord (2 Cor. 5:8), where they will be in their Father's house where a place has been prepared for them (Jn 14:2-3). In that case, there will be no more sorrow

(Rev. 21:3-4). Weeping will have endured for a night, the length of time on this earth.

**Joy comes in the morning**. When they take their final breath, the justified saint enters immediately into the presence of the Lord who bought them. There they worship around the throne day and night (Rev. 4:6-11). The Light of the World (John 8:12) is the light of heaven (Rev. 21:23). They have complete joy because their sins were paid for by the Lamb of God, who took away their sins (Jn 1:29), who loved them and gave Himself for them (Eph. 5:2). It was their privilege to offer their bodies as a living sacrifice to Him. It was their reasonable service (Rom. 12:1). They have fulness of joy because all that caused them sorrow on earth will be no more. Perfect peace replaces sorrow in heaven. Their minds can be kept in perfect peace now as nothing from the world will compete for affection (Isa. 26:3). The mind will be perfected in that it will perfectly meditate on things above now, and the things of the earth will pass away (Col. 3:1-3). This, our final heavenly state will be the fulness of joy morning after morning for all eternity.

## Questions for self-reflection:

(1) What was it like before you became a Christian when you sensed God's anger against you because of your sin? Since you have been justified and while you become progressively sanctified, do you sense His anger against you at all for your indwelling sin?

(2) Even though you have sensed His anger against you, how does the joy that you now know as His redeemed child compare? Is the joy greater in weight to experience than the anger?

(3) What causes you to weep more now - your own sin or the sin of others?

(4) Does joy come before or after repentance? Why do you think that is?

**30:6. Now in my prosperity I said, "I shall never be moved."**

When the righteous feel like the effects of adversity have reduced or disappeared, this can feel like a time of spiritual **prosperity**. God's mercies are more likely to be taken for granted by some. This could be because when our trials barrage us, we are more prone to cry out to God for deliverance. We are more likely to see and acknowledge our need for God's sustaining presence when things do not go our way. But, as Israel did, like many of today's professors of religion, when prosperity comes, a common tendency is to forget about the Lord and to trust in oneself instead of Him. Sometimes it takes tragedy or trial or difficulty of some kind to bring us back to our godly roots.

The psalmist was saying that this would not be true of him. He would **never be moved**. He would stay committed to the Lord in times of adversity and in times of prosperity. This continual reliance upon the Lord is the heartbeat of the true child of God. Before the tornado comes that destroys everything, God is their source of strength and blessing. After the tornado comes that takes away everything dear to them in this life, they still trust that God's ways are not their ways (Isa. 55:8). They still trust that the Lord is good no matter what happens to them in this life (Prov. 3:5-7). They remember that the Lord gives and the Lord takes away. Whether He gives or takes away does not depend on the true child of God's determination to bless the name of the Lord (Jb 1:21).

There is also a sense that we can experience seasons of spiritual prosperity where we are more sensitive to God's Spirit. During these times, we grow in Him as His Word opens up to us in our private study of it. The preaching of it in these seasons seems to have a more personal impact on our life. It is as if the preacher is speaking directly to us. We are spiritually prosperous in this season because, as we abide in Him, He abides in us. His forgiveness is more precious to us. We are more apt to notice the grace and peace that is ours because of Christ. We are less spiritually dull and more spiritually acute to our surroundings.

However, if we are not careful in those seasons of spiritual well-being, we can be tempted to think that those seasons will never change, that nothing will ever move us from such a prosperous estate. This is not true. God has ordained the joyous times and the negative times (Eccles. 3:4). As quickly as the rain of spiritual blessings can overtake us, just as quickly can the desert of spiritual dearth overcome us. Therefore, we should be wary (1 Cor. 10:12). Our times of blessings should elicit humility and gratitude rather than entitlement.

## Questions for self-reflection:

(1) In times of physical prosperity, are you more prone to recognize your abilities and wisdom, or are you more prone to acknowledge the God who blessed you with those abilities and that wisdom?

(2) Is it easier for you to remain committed to the Lord in times of adversity or ease?

**30:7. Lord, by Your favor You have made my mountain stand strong; You hid Your face, and I was troubled.**

---

Sometimes when things go as we wish they would go, we tend to take credit for that without giving God the credit that He should receive. We have a selfish, sinful tendency to only go to God when things don't go our way, or when we need something, or when we need Him to fix something that our sin has broken. We have a selfish tendency to praise God for the times which we perceive to be 'good' and a tendency to blame God for the times which we perceive to be 'bad.' We see from people like Job that trials and hardship are normal parts of life – even for the righteous (Jb 1, Jb 2).

According to James (Jas 1:2-8) and Peter (1 Pet. 1:6), trials are to be expected by any true child of God. Trials are not evidence that God's favor is not upon us. Many times, the very opposite of that is actually true. Often, the trials that come into the lives of believers by Divine permission are a means by which the light shone into their hearts can radiate out into a lost world that would otherwise have no contact with the gospel. They can be a means by which patience has its perfect work (Jas 1:2-8). While trials can come in the form of discipline as a consequence of sin in the believer's life (Heb. 12:3-11), trials do not always have to be viewed as an indication that God's **favor** is lacking from the life of the believer.

Because of the **Lord** Jesus Christ, all those whose faith is in Him alone for justification can trust that, since the good work has begun in them (Phil. 1:6), He will perform and complete that good work. They will be glorified (Rom. 8:28-30). The favor of God is upon them. Since nothing can pluck a sheep from the Father's hand (Jn 10:28-29), the Father's eternal blessing will always be upon the sheep in that sense. We tend to want to take credit for it when things go well for us.

At times we are allowed to suffer as a loving reminder that God ordains what we endure in this life. God allows suffering in part to remind us that He is to be praised in the good times and

---

in the bad times (Jb 1:21). Suffering can be an unpleasant yet necessary reminder that God, not we ourselves, needs to be trusted. In the good times, it feels like our **mountain stands strong**. We must not be so foolish as to think that the times of prosperity result from our inherent worth or goodness (1 Cor. 10:12). God's free grace is the reason for such benevolence. In the bad times, despite how it feels, God is still there. He is before us, even when He is **hid**den from us, and we are **troubled**. When we feel like God hides Himself from us, we remain permanently secure by virtue of the finished work of Christ on our behalf. Our security must be based upon the unchangeable God and not finite humanity.

God leads us into and through our trials. As we depend on Him to carry us through our trials, He will get us out on the other side of our trials. His grace is sufficient. One day, the suffering will end, even if that is not until we take our final breath and open our eyes in eternity and in Abraham's bosom (Lk 16:22). Until then, we can rejoice because of all we have (spiritually speaking) in Christ. Nobody on earth can take that away from us (Rom. 8:38-39).

It is better to be troubled by a lack of sense of God's presence than a lack of ease and comfort. The reason for this is because if we sense our discomfort because we perceive a lack of proximity to God, we will do what we can to correct that, and we will draw near to God so God will draw near to us (Jas 4:8). We will seek Him, and we will find Him (Matt. 7:7-8). We will abide in Him when we did not before. He will abide in us when He did not before (Jn 15:1-8). The result will be an incalculable spiritual benefit in the life of the believer. As the world crashes and implodes around us, inside us, we will have a settled confidence. We will be the reason that others ask us for the reason of the hope that is within us (1 Pet. 3:15).

## Questions for self-reflection:

(1) During a time of spiritual or physical prosperity, have you ever forgotten that God was looking out for you allowed you to experience the blessing you enjoyed? When you came to that

realization, did it break your heart that you could be so selfish and nearsighted?

(2) Have you ever experienced a trial that helped you live as a stronger Christian as a result? Have you ever experienced hostile opposition to the gospel that caused you to react to opposition with humility?

(3) When you suffer, are you more concerned with having the suffering on earth end so that you can continue to enjoy this earth, or are you more concerned with having the suffering end differently so that you can be with your Lord forever? Why?

**30:8. I cried out to You, O Lord; And to the Lord I made supplication:**

There was a time during which the psalmist started to lose hope. He could not see the end of his suffering. He believed God was there because that was all he knew. He had past experience he could point to for God coming through in his life. These more positive times seemed like a thing of the distant past. God felt far off. God, it appeared, had hidden Himself. God felt as if, perhaps, He did not even exist at all.

The psalmist knew better than that. We should not always trust feelings because feelings can change like the weather. The Lord, however, does not change (Mal. 3:6). In reality, the Lord is always there. Maybe our sin separates us from His presence (Ps. 66:18). It could be there is some lesson the Lord sees fit to have us learn that requires a time of silence on His part (Ps. 10:1). We may not know the entire purpose behind what we endure in this life. We may only know that God calls us to endure whatever it is. Maybe we need to learn contentment in any circumstance (Phil. 4:11-13, 1 Tim. 6:6). Our perseverance and proper responses in the crucible of affliction may be the only godliness some in our sphere of influence ever see (Matt. 5:16). We want to make sure that we commend the gospel to the people around us. Rather than be the millstone that leads someone to everlasting destruction (Matt. 18:6), let us be the city on a hill that points others to the all-powerful Savior (Matt. 5:14).

When we feel as if we are in a spiritual desert, it is appropriate to remember that the Lord has told us that if we seek Him, we will find Him (Matt. 7:7-12). He rewards those who diligently seek Him (Heb. 11:6). To **cry** to the **Lord** in hardship shows love for and faith in God. God rewards even mustard seed faith. Even mustard seed faith can accomplish great things (Matt. 17:20). The psalmist knew, despite the perceived lack of presence of God in his life, the only worthwhile answer to his dilemma was to continue to seek the Lord and to continue to trust that the Lord would keep His promises to reveal Himself to those who seek Him. Such promises made by God to His people can be the fuel that continues to inspire believers to make **supplication** (Phil. 4:6-7) and continue to seek to receive fresh supplies of mercy and help in time of need from the throne of grace (Heb. 4:16).

## Questions for self-reflection:

(1) Have you ever endured a trial, or are you currently enduring a trial that appears will never end, or that did seem as though it would never end?

(2) If you are enduring such a trial currently, even if the trial were not to end, is there an alternative outcome that would indicate to you that the Lord had heard you when you cried out to Him?

(3) Would you be willing to consider the possibility that an alternative response from God to our request to have Him bring a trial to an end could be to have God provide us with the grace to endure and respond appropriately to the trial?

(4) Who do you know who especially needs to see your godly responses to the adversity that God has allowed into your life?

(5) How have you seen God reward you for diligently seeking Him through supplication?

**30:9. "What profit is there in my blood, When I go down to the pit? Will the dust praise You? Will it declare Your truth?**

If the psalmist were to die, the psalmist would cease to have the opportunity to be a vessel of mercy (Rom. 9:23) in the lives of those who sought his destruction (2 Tim. 3:12). The psalmist knew that his primary responsibility was to the Lord for as long as his life continued. Whether he lived or died, he was the Lord's (Rom. 14:8). If he did die and **go down to the pit**, the psalmist knew that His hope was secure. He would be in the presence of the Lord immediately after he took his final breath (2 Cor. 5:8). He did not have to take vengeance against those who had harmed him but could instead trust the Lord to repay (Rom. 12:19). He knew that the Lord knew the end from the beginning (Isa. 46:1) and that the Lord had already appointed his death (Heb. 9:27). He wanted others to know the Lord as he did. He had devoted his life to that pursuit. He had Paul's heartbeat in that he wanted others to know the Lord (Rom. 10:1).

The psalmist knew that one of the most excellent tools that God can use to change the lives of the lost is to have the lost see the changed lives of the saved (1 Pet. 3:1). The grace of God poured out upon the life changes a person from a sinner to a saint (Ti 2:11). It changes a goat to a sheep (Jn 10:27). It gives life to the spiritually dead (Eph. 2:1-5). Apart from divine intervention, we are without hope and without God in the world (Eph. 2:12). Praise the Lord that in that sad, desperately wicked state (Jer. 17:9), the Father condescended, sending Christ at the fulness of time, to redeem those who were under the Law, to adopt them into His family, to give them life when they had no life (Gal. 4:4-5).

Those who are Christ's learn that it is not through their own filthy-rag-righteousness that they commend themselves to the God they had sinned against (Isa. 64:6). It is only by God's mercy that they are not consumed (Lam. 3:22). Only because He is faithful to His promises will they live to see another day (Ps. 71:22, 1 Thess. 5:24). Only because He is rich in mercy do the unmerciful get to see mercy (Eph. 2:4). It is because He is kind that His love appeared to the unkind (Ti 3:4). This love changed the psalmist and continues to change people worldwide in every generation (Rom. 5:5).

But if the psalmist died, he wondered how others would see the grace of God if he were no longer be there to convey it. He knew God gave no extra merit to martyrs. He wondered if **there** would be a **profit** if he shed his blood, if he died, and if his witness ceased. He trusted that God could do anything, that nothing was impossible with God (Matt. 19:26). Humanly speaking, however, he felt as if he had to keep going, to keep serving the Lord. If he were to die, if his blood was to spill, he could not atone for the sins of anyone. God is the justifier (Rom. 3:25-26). He could not bring peace between God and the world. God made peace through the sacrifice of Christ that we look back on today and that people like the psalmist looked forward to in his day (Eph. 2:14-18).

As a righteous person, the psalmist, like Paul, knew that it was better for him to depart and be with the Lord, but it was also needful that he continued to live because there were people he presently influenced (Phil. 1:22-25). As long as God permits any of us to live, He has a purpose for us. Nobody is purposeless. The death of the psalmist, when he would enter the pit, would not merit salvation for himself or anyone else. The death of Christ is the only means by which people can have access to the Father and entrance into heaven (Rom. 5:1-2, Rom. 5:6-8). But if the psalmist died, he would no longer be able to testify to God's working in the lives of His people. He did not want to lose that opportunity.

When the psalmist did die, he would return to the dust (Gen. 3:19). The **dust** would not be able to **praise** the Lord. It would stay silent. It would not and could not on earth **declare** the **truth** of who God is, what God has done, and what God will one day do for His own glory and in the lives of His people.

## Questions for self-reflection:

(1) Giving glory to God through a righteous life for others to see the glory of God and for them to want to glory God themselves motivated the psalmist to righteous living. How does your life demonstrate such motivation?

(2) How have you successfully overcome the temptation to repay vengeance yourself and instead waited upon the Lord to act in His timing?

(3) How can you show others that you are grateful for the mercy that has been shown to you?

(4) If you knew that you would be the only righteous influence someone would ever see, that you were the only person they would have a chance to hear the gospel from, how would that change how you live and interact with people?

The **Lord** had lifted up the psalmist. The Lord had healed the psalmist. The psalmist was near death, and the Lord delivered him from that desperate state. This deliverance was a reason for the psalmist to sing praise to the Lord.

While sin had led to God's pouring out His anger and difficulty resulting from that, the Lord had been merciful and restored the psalmist. He had shown mercy to the psalmist after a time of showing His anger. The Lord had hidden from the psalmist causing the psalmist to experience trouble. He had been a **helper** to the psalmist in the past. The psalmist asked the Lord to do so again in the present and the future. The psalmist trusted that the Lord would **hear** him if he separated himself from any known sin in his life. As long as he continued to live, the Lord must have a plan. The Lord was merciful to allow the psalmist to live. The psalmist had experienced the Lord's deliverance from the penalty and power of sin. Such results from justification and the lasting results of progressive sanctification were pieces of evidence for the work of God in the life of the psalmist. One day, in glorification, the Lord would deliver the psalmist from the presence of sin (Rom. 8:28-30, Col. 1:13). The psalmist wanted to feel the Lord's mercy by avoiding some of the trials from his life. He wanted his burdened eased.

It is not necessarily true that the absence of conflict is proof of God's presence or existence. Sometimes it is the trouble that produces the response to the trouble that is evidence for the power of God on the saint's life (1 Pet. 1:6-9). Sometimes it is the negative experience of difficulty in life that enables the power of God to be seen in the life of the believer. Sometimes that power is the only witness for God that the lost may see. This is a display of the **mercy** of God. It is merciful for the Lord to allow the sufferer to live as even saints sin every day, and the wages of sin is death, for both the just and the unjust (Rom. 6:23). It is merciful for the Lord to allow the sufferer to live. The righteous lifestyle of the saint could be a means graciously given to the unsaved. It could be that the gracious perseverance of the righteous, when it is witnessed by the unsaved, is a further opportunity from witnessing the life of the sufferer, that the saved sufferer has access to a power to which lost people do not have access. By a divine, gracious work, perhaps someone in the camp of the lost will see that in the life of the saved sufferer, the power is of God and not of them (2 Cor. 4:7). Perhaps the good works and responses could be a vehicle to elicit saving faith in the faithless.

## Questions for self-reflection:

(1) In what ways has the Lord demonstrated that He is your helper?

(2) What was your response when the Lord proved to be a helper to you?

(3) The longer you follow the Lord, do you find it to get any easier to continue to trust in Him to provide?

(4) How have you seen the Lord deliver you from the power and penalty of sin? Since your justification, are there things that you thought or did without second thought before your justification that now, after you have been declared righteous, that you would think differently about?

(5) Have you been able to see that trials that the Lord allows you to experience can be an effective means to demonstrate the power of the Lord upon your life?

**30:11. You have turned for me my mourning into dancing; You have put off my sackcloth and clothed me with gladness,**

---

The psalmist, David, praises the Lord in this psalm because the Lord did not permit those who opposed David to be successful. When their success or lack of success was still in question, David called to the Lord, and the Lord answered him. The Lord proved Himself faithful to David. He gave David more evidence for His faithfulness and trustworthiness.

David was near death, but the Lord prevented the death that seemed sure to David from happening. This seemingly inevitable appointment with death had led to David **mourning** over his sad state of affairs. But once the Lord intervened on David's behalf and rescued David from His affliction, David's mourning had **turned into dancing**. He could then celebrate God's work in his life. David pled for his life. On the one hand, for David to be free from earthly trouble and be with his Lord in his death would be a relief. On the other hand, however, David felt as though he had not completed what he had been left on earth to complete (Phil. 1:23). When David cast his cares upon the Lord because He cares for His people (1 Pet. 5:7), David had his mourning turned into dancing. He had called upon the Lord in distress, and the Lord answered David and put David in a high place (Ps. 18:6). This reassured David that the Lord was indeed on David's side and that there was nothing that man could do to prevent the Lord from fighting for His people (Deut. 3:22, Deut. 20:4, Josh. 23:10, Ps. 118:6).

God's people can mourn over adversity from trials (2 Sam. 12:16-22, 1 Pet. 1:6). This sounds like something of what David refers to in part of this psalm. When God's people mourn over adversity from trials that are not necessarily directly connected with some sin in the life, God can turn the mourning from that into dancing when He gives relief from the anxiety that the trial causes and turns the anxiety into peace (Phil. 4:6-7).

God's people can mourn over personal sin. Jesus, in the Beatitudes, said that those who mourn over sin and go to God over their sin could expect to receive supernatural comfort. This is because the Holy Spirit can comfort the heart that is broken over sin with a revelation of the peace with God that Christ obtained through His sacrifice on our behalf (Matt. 5:4). Peter wrote to believers grieved by various trials, no doubt mourning over those. The apostle reminded them that they could turn their mourning into dancing if they remembered that the calling into the gospel that they responded to included suffering for their faith (1 Pet. 1:6-9). James wrote to believers who faced various severe trials, and James reminded his audience that they could count the trials that they faced as pure joy because of what God would accomplish in them through their trials (Jas 1:2-8).

Sometimes the temptation to sin can be so strong that when believers cave into the temptation, lust turns into enticement, and they commit sinful acts, they can mourn over their sinful choices (Jas 1:12-15). They mourn because they knew better. They mourn because the Lord, the Holy Spirit, God the Holy Spirit, is grieved by their deliberate choice to reject God's revealed will for their selfish desires (Eph. 4:30). These choices are constant reminders that we cannot live the Christian life alone and in our own strength (Rom. 8:8). While we are responsible for choosing who we will serve (Josh. 24:15), the flesh that wars against the Spirit (Gal. 5:17) is often strong and harder to overcome. While we possess the capacity to do so, we will not always be successful at doing so (Rom. 7:13-24). Thank God that we have an Advocate (1 Jn 2:1) to intercede for us (Heb. 7:25) when that happens. When we mourn over that sin, He can turn that mourning into dancing when we go to Him. He can remind us that He paid not only for our past sins but also for our present and future sins as well (1 Jn 1:9).

So that we do not get calloused to our own sinfulness, we should be willing to take regular inventory of our lives to see if any sins, public or private, need to be confessed (1 Cor. 11:27-32). When the Holy Spirit reminds us of the forgiveness that is ours because of Christ, that can turn our mourning into dancing.

Sometimes God hides Himself from His people. This can be from sin in His people, or this can be not from sin in His people.

When the believer perseveres from this perception of God hiding Himself, when they diligently seek Him and find Him (Heb. 11:6), this can turn mourning into dancing. Strength can replace the weariness that accrued during spiritual drought by those that wait upon the Lord (Isa. 40:31). He is the Living Water that quenches the drought of those who hunger and thirst for righteousness (Matt. 5:6, Jn 4:10). When in the throes of affliction, the psalmist could and many other believers can feel like they are wearing **sackcloth,** common garments for mourning in the first century. However, when the Lord works on behalf of His people in unmistakable ways, He can help them **put off** the sackcloth and **clothe with gladness** all who go to Him. Sometimes this involves a change in circumstances. Sometimes this consists of a shift in attitude in unchanging circumstances. Either way, in the life of the believer the sadness is replaced with Holy Spirit-induced joy.

**Questions for self-reflection:**

(1) When did the Lord turn sadness into joy by His power in your life?
(2) How can mourning be an effective tool in helping us long for our reunion in heaven with the Lord?
(3) How has the Lord turned anxiety into peace for you at various times?
(4) Which person from the Bible or church history can you identify with who turned mourning into dancing and sorrow into gladness?
(5) What are some spiritual reasons that believers, regardless of their external circumstances, can dance rather than mourn and be glad rather than sad?

**30:12. To the end that my glory may sing praise to You and not be silent. O Lord my God, I will give thanks to You forever.**

The psalmist and all the people of God **may glory** in **God** and may **sing praise** to God **and not be silent** in doing so as they recount the marvelous works that God has done in all the earth and the lives of all His people. God's people can praise Him for saving them from physical death. Everyone is a sinner by nature and by choice. For each person, the wages of that sin are the same: death (Rom. 6:23). Every sinner, every human born since Adam, deserves death. Everyone will suffer that penalty (except Enoch – Gen. 5:21-24). They have nobody to blame for that but themselves.

God is rich in mercy to everyone (Eph. 2:4), even those not in a relationship with Him through the Lord Jesus Christ. He mercifully lets the rain fall on the just and the unjust (Matthew 5:45). He allows the lost and the saved alike to enjoy certain things in common. Letting such unworthy sinners enjoy these things illustrates God's goodness, which is meant to lead people to repentance (Rom. 2:4). More times than not, however, people are not led to repentance by God's goodness. As God does not confront some about their sin, they mistake that patience and grace as a license to sin (Rom. 6:1). This fatal error can lead to further hardening, culminating in death without the Lord and eternal judgment if they do not repent (Rom. 2:5).

However, the righteous, those like the psalmist, realize that God is the source of life (Deut. 32:39, Acts 17:25, Acts 17:28). Therefore, he permits them to take their next breath (Jb 14:5, Ps. 39:4, Ps. 90:2, Ps. 139:16). They determine that because this life is such a gracious gift, they will do what they can to serve the Lord and make a difference for Him as much as possible with the time that God allows them to remain on this earth. After believers' time on earth is over, they **will forever give thanks** to the Lord in heaven.

## Questions for self-reflection:

(1) Besides eternal life in Christ, what are some reasons for the psalmist and, by extension, all believers to sing praise to the Lord and not be silent?

(2) What would you say to someone who claims to be a Christian who would rather fool around with worldly pleasures? If they do not spend much observable time praising the Lord on earth now, what reason do you have, or do they have to think that they suddenly would be interested in doing so in heaven? Is this sort of attitude more illustrative of a saved person or a lost person?

(3) How often do you think of life in terms of life being a gracious gift? If you were to consider life to be a gracious gift more regularly, do you think you would spend more time in your life doing things for yourself, or do you think you would spend more time doing things for others?

# Conclusion

Thank you for taking the time to read from this work. It has been a pleasure to create as it is the fruit of hours of study. Through hours of meditation on the Word, God has internalized His truth to this hungry heart. Hopefully, this undertaking has revealed the glory of the Lord, and hopefully, some of His truth blesses you, the reader.

This journey through the first fifth of the book of Psalms has resulted in spiritual growth and enhanced faith in this writer's life. For all the world's arguments as to the archaic nature of God's Word, the beginning of this journey through the Psalms has revealed that, despite the objections to the contrary, our world shares a lot in common with the world in which the inspired Psalms were penned.

The God who was there for the beginning and for the present will also be there for the end as all of human history works towards its apex. He is not only concerned about significant matters such as creation and judgment. He is also concerned about you and me as well. He knows the number of hairs on our heads and asks us to bring our requests to Him. He does not necessarily promise that He will remove us from the fires, but He does promise to be with us in the fire.

The Psalms are a great testimony to the Divine nature of Scripture. If one reads the Psalms looking for Christ, one can find the Lord all over. One can discover fulfilled prophecy in the life of the Lord Jesus Christ. One can find direct quotations of the Psalms from the New Testament. One can find commentary on the Old Testament. Calls to salvation resonate with the reader.

May God bless and keep you, and may the Good Shepherd be your intimate friend as you make your earthly pilgrimage. May His Spirit and His Word sustain you as you face your trials. May His kindness cause you to rejoice in all seasons of life.

Blessings in Christ,
Andy

CPSIA information can be obtained
at www.ICGtesting.com
Printed in the USA
BVHW041815120322
630948BV00007B/10

9 781662 839696